The Fundamentals of C/C++
Game Programming

The Fundamentals of C/C++ Game Programming
Using Target-Based Development on SBC's

Brian Beuken

CRC Press
Taylor & Francis Group
Boca Raton London New York

CRC Press is an imprint of the
Taylor & Francis Group, an **informa** business

AN A K PETERS BOOK

CRC Press
Taylor & Francis Group
6000 Broken Sound Parkway NW, Suite 300
Boca Raton, FL 33487-2742

Printed on acid-free paper

International Standard Book Number-13: 978-1-4987-8874-8 (Paperback)
978-0-8153-5527-4 (Hardback)

Library of Congress Cataloging-in-Publication Data

Names: Beuken, Brian, author.
Title: The Fundamentals of C/C++ Game Development : using Target-based
Development on SBC's / Brian Beuken.
Description: First edition. | Boca Raton, FL : CRC Press, Taylor & Francis
Group, 2018. | "A CRC title, part of the Taylor & Francis imprint, a
member of the Taylor & Francis Group, the academic division of T&F Informa
plc."
Identifiers: LCCN 2017048100 | ISBN 9781498788748 (pbk. : acid-free paper) |
ISBN 9780815355274 (hardback : acid-free paper)
Subjects: LCSH: Computer games--Programming. | C (Computer program language)
| C++ (Computer program language)
Classification: LCC QA76.76.C672 B49 2018 | DDC 005.13/3--dc23
LC record available at https://lccn.loc.gov/2017048100

Visit the Taylor & Francis Web site at
http://www.taylorandfrancis.com

and the CRC Press Web site at
http://www.crcpress.com

Printed and bound in the United States of America by Sheridan

Contents

"From Hello World to Halo—It's Just Code!" xv

Thanks xxvii

Brian Beuken: Who Is He? xxix

1. Getting Started 1

 Mine Looks Different?..1
 First Steps 2
 Setting Things Up 2
 Introducing Visual Studio 2
 Hello World..10
 Hello Place of My Choosing...11

2. Getting Our Target Ready 13

 Setting Up the Target...13
 Oh Wait...Did We Plug-In? 15
 Starting Up VisualGDB for the First Time 16

Getting the Machines to Talk 17
Sending Our First Program 18
Debugger Hangs Too Much? 28

3. Using the Target   31

Ready to Rock and Ermm Indeed Roll! 31
Graphics Explained! 32
So It Be OpenGL ES Ye Be Wanting Arrgghhh! 33
Where Is OpenGLES2.0 on My Target? 33
A Nice New Project with Graphics 35
   So Much Typing? 35
Our First Graphics Project! 36
Are We There Yet? 41
Houston We Have a Triangle 41
Behold the Triangle Code! 44
Why Are We Working in a Window? 50
2D 51

4. Putting It All Together   53

Expanding Our First Graphics Program 53
Loading Graphics or Other Assets 53
Adding Assets to the Build Chain 57
Keeping Things Tidy 58
Add Some Code 59
Displaying More Images 64
But I Didn't Do Anything Wrong? 65
But I Fixed It? 66
Making a Dynamic Playfield 68
Old School Frame Buffers 68
Setting Up the Frame Buffer and Switch System 74

5. Finally Our First Games   77

5.1   Invaders from Space 77
      Using the OS 78
      Start as We Mean to Go on 85
We're Here Now 87
      Inheritance 88
      Every Story Needs a Villan 91
      Arrays or Vectors 93
      Move Em Out! 96
      Animation 101 98
      Hand Me a Bag of Bullets 100

Did We Hit It?. 101

    Box Checks. 102

    Circle Checks. 102

    Give Me Shelter 104

    So Which Is Better?. 110

    Final Details. 110

    Simple Text Display. 111

    A Simple Font 113

    How Did We Do? The Infamous Postmortem .118

Fix Question 4. 119

A Pat on the Back 122

Kamikazi Invaders 123

    The Ship 128

    Da Baddies! 130

    Now We're Talking 132

        Make Them Move 135

        Get Them Flying 136

        A Nice Arc 137

        Step by Step. 141

        Dive Dive Dive. 142

        Bombs Away. 144

        Get Back to Where You Once Belonged. .145

        Home Again! 145

    Vectors, Our Flexible Friends 146

        Lets Get Lethal. 151

        Bombs Away for Real Now. 154

        Danger UXB. 161

        Stepping Back, Deciding When to Go 162

        Breaker Breaker Rubber Duck. 167

    Fred Reacts! 169

        Tidy Up the Logic 173

        Twiddles and Tweaks 173

    Postmortem 173

        Jumping around a Bit Though? 174

    Crawling Over, Time for Baby Steps 175

    Object-Oriented Programming Is Not an Error. 175

        Encapsulation. 176

        Abstraction. 176

        Inheritance 176

        Polymorphism 176

    Start the Music. 176

        Welcome to OpenAL. 177

        Installing OpenAL. 177

        Getting OpenAL Working 179

Dealing with Sound as Data 182
    How Does OpenAL Work? 183
    How Does Alut Work? 184
Horrible Earworms. 190
    Streaming 191
The War against Sloppy Code Storage! 192
Our Own Library 193
Using This New Library 196
Lets Get a Bit More Compiler Speed 198

5.2   Tiles and Backgrounds 198
What Do We Mean by Tiles? 199
Working with Tiles 199
What a Wonderful World. 199
    Homing in 208
    Wrapping It Up 211
    Is This All We Need? 211

5.3   Single-Screen Platforms. 214
A World with Gravity. 214
Routine Bad Guys 221
Point-to-Point 221
Patrolling Enemy. 224
Homing Enemy 226
Ladders and Effects. 229
    Data, Our Flexible Friend. 234
    Loading Our Maps (and Other Resources) 235

5.4   Lets Scroll This 239
Simple Scrolling Shooter 244
Let Them Eat Lead 248
Bring on the Bad Guys! 249
Process Everything? 251
No More Mr Nice Guy 252
What Will Make It Better? 254
There's No Wrong Way…But There Are Always Better Ways. 255
For a FireWork, Life Is Short But Sweet! 255
    A New Dawn for Particle Kind!. 261
    There's Always a Price to Pay 270
    Handling Large Numbers of Objects 271
Locking the Frame Rate 271
Recapping the 2D Experience. 272

6. A New Third Dimension   275

A Short Explanation of 3D 276
MATHS!! Don't Be Scared (Much) 280
How Does This Witchcraft Work? 281
This Is All a Bit Much? 288

Installing a Maths Library 288
    Danger, Will Robinson! 289
    Normal Programming Resumes 290
Three Types of Matrix 291
    Model Matrix. 291
    View Matrix 291
    Projection Matrix 292
    The Relationship of These Three Matrices 294
    Other Matrix Functions. 295
    Moving Around 296
Revisiting Hello Triangle 296
    Let's Try a Cube. 300
    Mistakes Waiting to Happen 302
A Quick Word about Using Quaternions. 303
HelloCubes 304
    I Thought We Could Move 100's of Thousands of Them? 306
    How the GPU Gets Data 307
    Buffers, Buffers Everywhere 308
    Vertex Buffers 309
    Attribute Pointers 311
    Texture Buffer 312
    Frame Buffer 312
    Render Buffer. 313
    Buffers Are Not Free. 313
Let's Get Back to It 314
    Time to Texture Our Cube 315
        The Fixed Pipeline Isn't Quite Dead. 318
        Mapping a Texture to Our Faces. 319
        Choose the Size to Suit 320
        Limited Numbers of Textures? 320
    Everyone Loves a Triangle But! 322
3D Lets Get into the Heart of Our GPU. 325
    What Else You Got? 325
    Loading Models (OBJ) 327
    Locate and Install an OBJ Model Loader 327
    Installing and Using TinyObjLoader 329
    Do We Care about the Data?. 330
Lights Camera Action 332
    The Return of the Vector 335
    Dot Product 335
    Another Fun Vector Fact-Cross Product 336
    Who's to Say Whats Normal? 336
    Types of Light 338
    Light Sources 339
    Shadows, a Place Where Danger Hides. 339
    Shaders 340
    So What Is a Shader? 341

Keeping Track of Them 344
Introducing the Shader Language 344
Let's Light It Up! 346
The Camera Never Lies 350
But What Does It All Do? 351
In Space, No One Can Hear You Smashing Your Keyboard As You Scream
Why "Don't You Work!!!" 353

7. Space the Final Frontier   355

Space, Why All the Asteroids? 360
Skyboxes 361
The Game's Afoot Which Way to Turn? 363
We're Going to Need Some Game Mechanics 365
    HUD and Cockpits 365
    GUI 365
    Screen or Render 366
    3Dfont 366
    Hit Em Where It Shows 366
    3D Collision 368
    Primitive Collision Types 368
    Culling Concepts 369
    Grids, Quad Trees, and OctTrees 369
    Possible Collision Systems 372
    Sphere-to-Sphere 373
3D Particles 374
    The Wrap Up 375

8. Recognizable Environments   377

Let's Talk about Time! 378
    Animating Models 379
    Limitations of OBJ 380
    The MD(x) Systems 381
Controlling the Animation of Our MD2 Model 385
Explaining Environments 389
    The Ground, the Place Where You Will Fall to! 390
A Simple Ground Plane 390
    Level of Detail 391
    Mipmapping 393
    Filtering 394
We Don't All Live in the Netherlands 395
    Using an OBJ File—The Simple Solution 396
    How Far above Sea Level Are We? 396
Interacting with Our World 397
    Collision Maps 397

Render Culling!..398
    Adding the Functionality 400
Physics, More Scary Maths Stuff? 401
    Subtitle...More Long Winded Explanations!...................401
    Introducing Bullet Physics 402
    How It Works, and Finally Quaternions........................ 403
    Let's Get to It, at Last 404
    Setting Things Up... 406
    Stepping Through 407
    Visualizing Things 407
    Force, Torque, and Impulse..................................410
    Collisions 412
    The Downside 415
Basic Racing Game 416
    Getting and Making the Car Controllable......................417
    I Like to Move It, Move It 418
    Staying on Track 421
    Using Bullet to Collide with the Terrain...................... 423
    Can't Find My Way Home? 427
Other Optimizations... 430
    Other Performance Options 431

9. Let's Go Indoors   **433**

The Beginnings, Doom, and Beyond 433
Occlusion, a Discussion to Have for a Problem to Solve Later 434
Exploring the Maze 436
    Moving the Baddies Around, Things! 438
    What Do We Draw? 441
    Whats the Point?... 442
    Ray Cast and Picking....................................... 443
    Are We Going to Do Any AI?................................. 444

10. Graphics Need a Boost   **447**

That Cat's Been in the Bag Long Enough........................ 447
Shadow Mapping 448
Recap the Processes 452

11. Populating the World   **455**

Keeping Track of the Assets 455
Scene Management 456
Wrangling All That Data 459
    Asset Management 459
    Fragmentation, a Problem That's Hard to Solve 460

Expanding to an SDK? 461
The Last Project 462
Ready-Made or Roll Your Own 462
　　　　Limitations of Hardware 463
Cross-Platform Compilation 464

12. Some Advanced Stuff　　　　　　　　　　　　　　　　　　　　467

Multicore Fun. 467
What Is Threading? 468
Threads and Pthreads 471
Job Managing, Also Kinda Simple 471
With Great Power Comes Great Heat. 473
The End Is Near!. 474

Appendix I　　　　　　　　　　　　　　　　　　　　　　　　　　　477

Where Files Live on Non-Raspberry Machines 477

Appendix II　　　　　　　　　　　　　　　　　　　　　　　　　　479

Updating versus New SD 479

Appendix III　　　　　　　　　　　　　　　　　　　　　　　　　481

A Word or Two about Source Control 481

Appendix IV　　　　　　　　　　　　　　　　　　　　　　　　　483

Bits Bytes and Nibbles Make You Hungry! 483

Appendix V　　　　　　　　　　　　　　　　　　　　　　　　　485

OpenGLES3.0+ 485

Appendix VI　　　　　　　　　　　　　　　　　　　　　　　　　487

The Libs We Used. 487
On the PC End 488

Appendix VII　　　　　　　　　　　　　　　　　　　　　　　　489

Writing My Own Games?. 489

Appendix VIII　　　　　　　　　　　　　　　　　　　　　　　　491

Visual Studio 2017 491

Index　　　　　　　　　　　　　　　　　　　　　　　　　　　　493

"From Hello World to Halo—It's Just Code!"

Who Is This Book for?

The Fundamentals of C/C++ Game Programming: Using Target-Based SBC's, is quite a mouthful, isn't it, as a title, it's also making a few promises that it probably can't keep, because there are so many definitions of what are the fundamental skills a game programmer needs to have. But it's my view that there are a few things that can get people up and running and develop their hunger for learning, and it's those things I want to bring to you here. This is for people who want to be game programmers, but probably don't quite know how to do it or feel a little daunted that their coding skills don't really let them explore their game-creation skills. Although this is *very much a beginner's* book, it is not really aimed at a total novice who has never programmed before; you should be able to understand at least the basic concepts and syntax of C/C++ programming.

There are some excellent beginner's books that I recommend to all my students, such as Michael Dawson's excellent *Beginning C++ Through Game Programming* (2014; Cengage Learning; Australia), which though it throws little light on actual graphic gaming, is a superb foundation for C++. I will give some very simple getting-started examples and build on those, so even the most code wary the beginner, should pick things up as they go.

None of the code in this book is complex, indeed it can be comfortably argued that it's oversimplified, it's designed as a jumping-off point for a novice to expand their knowledge and most of the initial explanations are going to be understandable even for a total beginner. I'll start slowly and explain much at first, but the pace will pick up as we get going and I'll let the online source code go into more detail as I explain the overall intent of what we are doing rather than the specific functions. If you still don't understand the syntax of the code, you should undertake a beginners' coding course, there are several online.

In addition, despite the title, this isn't a book solely about programming Single Board Computers (SBCs). The use of a cheap target system is a means to an end to encourage the reader to limit expectations and work within tight constraints, which game programmers, especially console programmers have to work with. I want primarily to focus on gameplay concepts and game structures, which will let us get games up and running really quickly. However, we do have to introduce some technical concepts later, when we're a bit more comfortable, because most of these technical concepts will have a direct impact on the performance of your games. You will need to know just enough to avoid some pitfalls and get things up and running correctly.

SBCs are usually quite simple systems, so building a working knowledge of the fairly generic hardware to produce graphics, sound, and data storage is generally easier to learn on them, than it would be on your up to the minute PC, which will shield you from errors by virtue of massive processing performance and near unlimited memory.

Once understood, all of the concepts and projects in this book are easily transferrable to any development target where the reader can stretch their growing skills on more powerful systems while still being mindful of the need to work within constraints of hardware, which are hard to push, and personal limits, which should always be pushed.

But SBCs are really fun to work with, cheap to acquire, and present a real sense of achievement when you make them to do more than just act as media servers or control units.

Most important, this is not a how to do x, with y kind of book. I want to take you through a journey of discovery, mine as well as yours, and provide suggestions and working examples on how to do things that games need, and let you decide if the approach I've taken is valid. I want to make you question things and hopefully come to different conclusions, using what I supply as a base for debate and expansion rather than a gospel to be followed. When working with beginners, I don't believe in imposing *the right way*, I prefer to have faith in, "this works for me, can I make it better?" The *right way*, for you at least, will come with practice and the joy of achievement.

What Are We Gonna Do?

For the last 9 years, I've been teaching beginner-level game programmers how to write computer games. Not so much the actual languages used in programming, but the principles of actually creating games. Starting with simple space shooter games, scrolling platformers, maze games, character animation games, and so on!

Eventually, at some point in their development when they start to move beyond such simple themes, and their confidence is high enough, I then encourage them to take their first steps in writing more complex 3D immersive games on consoles, such as the Nintendo Wii U, Microsoft Xbox One, and Sony PlayStation 4.

It sounds like a massive leap, to teach beginners how to make a simple space shooter game in 2D to then write games on the most powerful consoles on the market, but in fact the progression is really quite simple. Coding is coding…once you have the basics in your head, the rest of it is down to understanding how to get your code to work on different machines and with increasingly larger projects, only the levels of complexity change.

Internally, you could not find more different machines than a PC, a Nintendo Wii U, and a PlayStation 4. However, the basic ideas of getting something to appear on screen, move around under some kind of control, and process some form of logic are what the games programmers are really trying to do. That is independent of any machine architecture!

Through various concepts such as APIs, Libraries, and Engines, a lot of the complexity of how the screen objects appear is hidden from the programmer and is accessed via simpler means, though there is always a chance to unhide it, usually causing untold damage as a result. We generally leave the technical side of the machines to tools and graphics coders who make those APIs, Libraries, and Engines available to us, so we can focus on the simpler concepts of getting our chomping pizza to move around the maze collecting his trademarked pills.

When you move away from the worry of the technical issues of how to draw things and start to abstract your thinking toward making, a *thing*, do a *thing* you want that *thing* to do, you find yourself to be able to explain and understand your game concept far easier. What you understand, you can code!

For some time, I wanted to write a tutorial that could take some of my methods of learning as you go/do, taking beginners from their first simple projects to producing fully working games on consoles. But there are some roadblocks I have to overcome. Not least of which is while PC coding is easy enough to enter into, and I would have no problem converting my first-year courses into a simple tutorial. Console coding, which I also teach, is essentially a closed shop, open only to industry and a few elite educational institutions.

So I thought it might be an interesting journey to take a machine I'd never worked on before and document my way through it, simulating the out of my depth feel many new programmers have when confronted by a blank screen, while at the same time giving the reader a chance to understand the basic concepts of game programming I've been involved with for more than 30 years.

First things first, I need a target machine….In my normal game dev career; I've worked mostly with consoles from Nintendo and more recently Sony. So my basic techniques of coding are firmly entrenched in the idea of writing games on an editing system that you don't actually run the code on.

For the vast majority of my career, I've used what we call a development machine, more often than not a PC, to write the code, which in turn is transmitted via some kind of network link to the actual target machine the games will be played on, usually some form of specialist development kit that allows communications and debugging to take place. All the main console systems use Dev Kits, and I'm incredibly lucky to have access to all of them.

That creates something of a problem. The general public are not actually allowed to purchase these dev kits, also I'm not allowed to talk about them, having Non-Disclosure Agreements (NDAs) all properly signed up, so even if I wanted to, I can't tell you how to write games on a PS4 or Nintendo Wii, but I do very much want to give you a flavor of it.

Looking around at the kind of equipment most beginner programmers have, there are however a few choices. The most obvious are Apple devices and Android phones. These days almost everyone has one of these, to take selfies or spend a few minutes playing games, so it seems like an ideal choice.

But there are issues with them. Apple devices really work best when using Mac's and their own idiosyncratic (but by no means bad) Objective C-based development tools. These are great tools, but I find them a little too specific for my liking, and since one of the objectives in writing this is to get you, the reader, to be able to work on standard types of machines, I feel I should rule them out, perhaps that's another book.

Android uses Java......I suppose now it is a good time to admit I don't like Java...but the reasons for that will take too long to go into, but I'm certain that in at least one chapter of this book or forum post, I'll explain and you may feel I'm overreacting...I am of course, but allow me a little bias. I believe Java is a fine language for some things, just not console games. Again that may be another book.

That said, it's quite possible to code at a low level on an Android system using the Native Development Kit (NDK) essentially working on the hardware level; however, that then raises another issue with Android machines, at the hardware level there is a massive amount of difference from one maker to another, resulting in what are called abstraction layers between the hardware and Android to maintain compatibility for the Android OS, but less consistency in access methods, if you want to deal with hardware direct. Since I want you the reader to have as few issues with the hardware as possible, and not be wrestling with it, it means we cannot be 100% certain that the code is going to work on every Android system. That, more than the Java, rules out Android for us.

So common devices exist, there are ways to hook them up to the PC but do they provide a good experience that simulates development for consoles?

I don't think so, Apple comes close and indeed for all basic definitions most Apple devices are small consoles but the Objective C issue and confusing tools make it a bit too specialized, If you want to do apps for Apple devices, I think there are more than enough excellent tutorials out there.

Most industry programming is done in C/C++ so that's what I want to work with. Yes...before someone pipes up, you CAN do C/C++ on Apple and Android devices....it's just not as easy as I want it to be, and while I don't anticipate this journey to be without incident, I prefer to keep to paths I know I can travel.

This book is intended to be a tutorial...So I wanted to find a simple and easy system to work with.

I didn't find one!

And there's a good reason for that, pretty much any computer system has its own drawbacks when it comes to getting it set up, often this is software based and that in turn led me to another decision I needed to make before starting. What kind of standard development Integrated Development Environment (IDE) was I going to use...I wanted to use Visual Studio.

Why? Well because I like it! I'm used to it, almost every other game developer not doing Apple or Android product uses it, and moreover...it's now free! Free is good. Especially since I am going to encourage you to spend a little bit of money to fund your journey into the joys of game programming.

It's not everyone's favorite IDE; in fact, I know Pros who will spend hours explaining to you just how bad it is, but truthfully if you're a beginner and all you want is a simple system to write code, press a deploy button and watch the fireworks...It does just that. If you're a Pro, you want to totally investigate the code, be able to search for sections that contain information, and so on...Visual Studio does that too, it won't stop me cursing it from time to time, but I never met a programmer who was 100% happy with his tools.

As with most things in life, once you get used to something, you don't like to change. Mac users love X-code (mostly) and PC users love Visual Studio (mostly). We'll just use what works.

So, our development system is chosen, we are going to use a PC or a Mac, running Windows and Visual Studio. But we don't really need to worry about what kind of

Windows; I'm still using 8.1 on my main system, as I write this and occasionally on my laptop running Windows 10. At the time of writing, I've just upgraded to Visual Studio 2015 and I'm sure it's going to annoy the hell out of me for all the things it does different from Visual Studio 2013. That anger will pass but for this book, I mostly used my trusty Visual Studio 2013. I'm not planning to do anything Visual Studio specific, so all should be good whichever version you are using.

Now for the tricky bit, what's the target system going to be…As I said before I wanted to use a machine I'd never used before so that I could also experience some of the things a new coder will come across. It also needed to be able to hook up to the PC somehow and it needed to be available to the general public.

$2\pi \mid !2\pi$

Ok, let's stop beating about the bush, after all the section heading gives it away. I chose the Raspberry Pi, because it's cheap, it's freely available all over the world, it connects to a PC via network cables or wirelessly, it has consistent hardware, so what works on one is sure to work on another even if a few differences in speed happen, and in my opinion, it's a machine that has largely been ignored by the games development community. So you're going to be treading in largely virgin sand, that's quite exciting.

I need a consistent, fun bit of hardware, with sufficient power, reasonable graphic abilities, and onboard memory to create a range of decent little games to learn with. The Raspberry Pi gives me all that, and most of its clones are close enough to also give us some insight into the fragmentation issues in a small enough scale to cope!

Now it also has to be said, once I settled on the Raspberry machine I had my eyes opened up to the fact that there are several Raspberry Pi-type machines out there; in fact, there is a thriving community of similar small board System on Chip (SoC) machine's with their own communities. So I expanded my remit a little to include as many of the main ones as I could find with a simple limit of cost. I only looked at units I could buy for under U.S.$100.

So if you have one of these other systems then it's only fair that I make sure what we do here are going to work on them too, so long as they run some form of Linux and have OpenGLES2.0 for their Graphics systems. We *should* be able to get our games to work on them too. I'll try to give a summary of machines I've tried, and maintain an update on the support site.

Of course, technology never stands still, and as I was a quarter of the way in writing this book, the Raspberry Pi foundation announced a new model, the Raspberry Pi 3, and as usual it sold out within hours of its announcement. Not quite as big a leap in performance as the 2 was over the 1, but still another boost in performance for the same price is much appreciated.

So I guess most of you will now be on model 4 by the time this comes out. But the nice thing about the Raspberry range is that aside from memory and speed, they all are based on the same hardware principles and they have maintained the mantra of compatibility. So even though I'm going to continue with my Raspberry Pi Model 2B for now, swapping over to the Model 3B quite soon I am sure, everything in this book will be checked on the latest models before it goes to the printers.

I should say to owners of earlier Raspberry Pi models, all the things in this book will work for you, but the later explanations on multicore processing will be useless as earlier models had single core processors. You may find speed is an issue on the later 3D projects, but given the cost of a Raspberry Pi 2(3/4/5), why not upgrade? The extra power is well worth it. I do have a small collection of the earlier machines and will be trying the code out on them as we go to give you notice of any issue I find.

Also, since part of the thinking behind writing this book is to introduce some of the concepts and limitations of working on consoles, I have set myself some limitations. As *far as possible*, I plan not to use any external third-party libraries, though consoles do sometimes use external libs (audio for example, commonly uses third-party libs even though SDKs usually provide some support). Wherever possible, the only libraries I will try to add will be on the Raspberry Pi already. This will create some difficulties for us and require a bit of imagination to overcome them, but will hopefully create a more rewarding experience and producing more compact code on machines with limited memory. I will, of course, break this rule, it's impossible to keep really, but I will not do so lightly, if we do have to use an external lib I will ensure it is free and easily available. You will also have to take care if you distribute your projects, that the end user also has access to those libraries, either supplied by you, or with a helpful test and request to install if missing.

You Call This Code?

A word about my coding style in this book….Aside from some quite deliberately poor design choices, I fully intend to make to show you how to improve, the style is, ermm, my own!

I tend to write in a mixture of C and C++, partly because many consoles and embedded toolchains I use still use C, and partly because it's a style I have found my students pick up quite well before fully adopting C++. I find full Object-Oriented Programming (OOP) C++ to be a little unreadable, and confusing, especially for beginners. I also don't want to have to spend two or three pages to explain why C++ wants you to do things a certain way, before we can move forward. So I'll continue with my C with classes approach until we find that it does not fit our needs. But I will be introducing more structured C++ as this book goes on.

The thing about a computer language is this: it is there to make your life easier. If you find it easier to write in mostly C...do so! Never let anyone stop you unless you are in a team doing OOP. But on your own at this stage, I encourage you to simply write code that works, something that makes sense to you, at least until you are 100% sure you know what you are doing, then you can explore the majesty, or lunacy, of coding standards. With practice you will naturally start to see patterns in your code that will lead to improvement and understanding of the more advanced quirks of any language, once you start to see faults in your own code and that becomes the second nature to you, you're a coder.

But my C with classes style, is functional, my aim here is to make things clear, to give you room to expand and improve on the basic systems. I'm also not a hardware expert, so much of the information I am going to pass on is taken from a basic users' view point, based on what I have found the machine can do within the project I am producing. I am quite sure a technical graphic coder could get and give a lot more info on the tech side of things but that's not really what I want to focus on here.

That's not to say we should not learn new things, I always aim to improve, but I'm usually just too busy making games! It's supposed to be fun! This means a lot of the early samples in this book will be mostly C based to tie in with the traditional starter projects found in most textbooks. I'll introduce some classes and then hopefully some more recognizable standard C++ as we progress. I don't use a lot of C++11 usually, but I will introduce some more useful and up-to-date C++11 concepts when we need them, as we go through the projects. I hear that there is now a C++17....meh, mañana!

If you want to write tidy sharable code for the team, I suggest a Computer Science (CS) course somewhere. If you just want to gain confidence in coding, make something work and improve your understanding of how to make games. Read on, and feel free to rework my code when you are confident enough to do it. Also take note, most of the technical stuff we have to deal with, in the 3D sections in particular, *can ALL be done better*! I'm giving you functional, but deliberately not optimal systems, it leaves you open to play with and improve things, and I will suggest some ways for you to explore and research, so you get a bigger confidence boost from doing it yourself.

Uggh It's All So Old

One other thing you need to also consider is that many of the libraries, file, and data formats used in this book are older concepts that don't have too much traction any more in modern game dev. So why present them here? Simple, we are using target machines that do not have the horsepower of a modern computer system; in fact, they are about 10–15 years behind the current power level of even a modest PC. A great many cutting-edge concepts need a lot of horsepower or large data stores to function; we just don't have those resources available to us.

So it's quite appropriate that we are going to use some techniques from the good old days, which are still perfectly functional and once grasped will make updating these methods a journey you will want to take with foundation knowledge to help you.

Coding and using, things that work, will give you a sense of achievement and quick visible results, rather than a sense of frustration that tends to cause new coders to give up. We will enhance some of the older ideas with our more modern systems and methods where viable, so you are always free and encouraged to try to use more modern concepts as soon as you feel you are capable of writing them. If your target can handle them! But I am deliberately presenting relatively simple methods, which are compact, fast, and effective even on the lowliest of target system.

Finally, though most of the current range of SBCs are multicore and get a significant boost when using parallel processing, I'm not going to explore that in the projects presented here, though I will explain the concepts and some of the projects should be suitable for parallel processing if the reader feels they want to tinker. I do this because parallel coding works best if the projects are built with this in mind, but as this book is targeting beginners I want to avoid potentially confusing technical concepts until such time as the beginner starts to understand what they are doing. There's no rush, when you *get it*, you're free to do anything you want to the code and enjoy the achievement of improvement for yourself.

What Do We Need to Get Started?

As with every new technical challenge the first thing you need is some cash, you're going to have to spend a bit of money. Not much, trust me, as a Scot, with Dutch ancestry, spending money is as painful to me as it is to you, so we'll limit it to what we need.

Throughout this book I am going to refer to our target machine as the Target or Raspberry Pi, which due purely to its massive market lead, I am going to assume you will be using. But with very few exceptions any SBC with onboard/integrated Graphics Processing Unit (GPU), keyboard and mouse connections, and a display output can be used. So long as it's running some form of Linux, which we only need for file and I/O handling, and most important is using and has drivers for OpenGLES 2.0 or higher as a graphic Application Programming Interface (API). This will all be explained in more detail later.

I don't have the foggiest idea how Linux itself works, so I'm only going to use what I need to use to make the code work. I tend to use Rasbian or Debian, because that's what the Raspberry Pi uses, but a few machines prefer Ubuntu. As I say, once we are running our code we don't care about the OS. I'll limit my usage to getting the IP address, installing some libraries, and making sure it has a compiler and required drivers on it, some things may need to be downloaded, but are all available for free!

Those of you with Android installed on your (non-Raspberry) machines will need to change, Android is something else entirely though and not supported in this book but it is supported by some of the tools we use. It's not impossible to convert the projects to work with an Android-based machine; however, you do risk incompatibility because of significant differences in machines, which again is a chief reason this is not a book about Android programming. That may come later. It might be a fun project for you when you're done with this book to try using any new skills you develop to get the projects running on Android, it can be done, I've got them all running on a couple of brand name tablets with little real effort but can't get anything to work on another leading brand phone.

There are some issues with the different SBCs and Linux methods of setting up rendering windows, but for the most part all these machines provide drivers that make that possible, usually in some sample OpenGLES2.0 code you can find in the makers downloads.

Some of the most popular SBCs are detailed on the support site and I will have personally tried all the samples on them so can give good feedback on any set up and execution issues you might come across. I'm picking up as many as I can over the next months to make sure I can give you a chance to use your SBC of choice.

Once individual drivers are set up and installed, after any specific initializing systems are called the code samples in here should work on any valid target with few issues. However, computers are interesting things and even two machines of the same model from the same maker but with different production runs, may display differences, or have different user set ups, so it would be naive of me to suggest everything is going to work on every machine on a first attempt, but as far as possible, it should. Any significant differences in machine setup or installation will be covered as much as I am able to on the support site.

The Target

We need an SBC of course; for the most part I will assume Raspberry Pi, 12 million+ users would indicate that most of you are using that. So that's your first purchase, if you haven't done so already, you need to do this now. At the time of writing, I'm using the current model, a Raspberry Pi 2 Model B, but am soon going to plug-in my new Raspberry Pi 3 Model B. I will do the odd sanity check with older Raspberry Pi Model A+/B+/Zeroes I have to hand. I also have picked up quite a few of the so-called Raspberry Pi *beaters* that are on the market, such as, Nano Pi, Banana Pi, Orange Pi, Pine A64, and so on, which also use a Linux OS. One awesome thing about these little SBCs is most are pocket money cheap, so adding to my collection is proving to be a fun hobby. I'll document any issues I find in the support site. I do know that some of the others are faster or have more impressive graphic systems and a few have SATA and USB3 to make disk access a factor, but I strongly suggest we all stay with the Raspberry Pi's for learning and then transition to others if that's what you want to use.

I hope the later versions of the Raspberry Pi that are sure to come, will be as compatible. I'm sure they'll be even more powerful allowing you to fully explore that power with this book.

Buying an SBC on its own is a bit useless though, it usually needs an SD card, to act as its boot drive and storage medium, ideally preformatted with some form of Linux, which on the Raspberry Pi is called Rasbian, (there are other options but Rasbian is easy to use). It also needs some means to power it, ideally a 5 V, 2–3 A, wall wart.

Internet access for your target is needed to install libraries and updates. A wifi dongle is a wise extra purchase if your target does not have it onboard, and is especially useful on boards with no wired network connection, though aftermarket USB-based network systems are available. Wired network connection to your PC is preferred for faster communication between the target and dev system.

I'd recommend a case to keep the Raspberry Pi safe and tidy. These are minor extra costs and usually most sellers will offer you a bundle. I got my new Model 3 for under €60euros.

Remember that the Raspberry Pi is a computer…therefore, it will also need a display, a keyboard and a mouse to get the most out of it, I tend to have a few broken and bashed keyboards lying around, which met their fate during some horror bug hunting session, but any simple cheap keyboard and mouse will work. We will be doing our coding on our own PCs, so the Raspberry Pi's keyboard and mouse only needs to be functional and you can pick up really cheap combination keyboard/mousepads.

As noted, your target also needs to have a display, it may be you have a monitor on your PC that has dual HDMI inputs or you want to use a KVM system, this will work, but will not be effective when you want to debug on one screen and see the project running on another. Display switching between the two images will not be a satisfactory experience. A small monitor with your Raspberry Pi hooked up, beside your main monitor is ideal. There are also some very serviceable low-cost LCD panels you can hook up to the boards directly but don't get less than 7″, our early games are mostly going to run in 1024×640 pixel resolution, which we'll scale to the screen's resolution most of the time and the small sub 7″ screens can't really handle even that low res making scaling look odd. If you are using a really low-power machine like a CHIP or Pi Model A, you can always drop the resolution down to 640×480, or even worst case 320×200. It will provide a speed increase, especially on the 2D projects.

If you plan to use a target system you already had for a while, and it currently is set up with lots of apps, which are set to run in the background, it would be wise to create another project-based SD to boot clean, so that we make sure our target machine is not using resources on other applications when we are developing. Throughout this book, I am assuming a total clean fresh install of Rasbian or your usual flavor of Linux, with all default settings.

People have many reasons for buying SBCs and game programming is rarely one of them, so there are many keen users out there who have expectations that focus on their particular needs. When researching a board to buy, you may see a lot of comments on what the best board and passionate explanations of why a particular board is bad, very bad, a total con, and so on!

It's quite true that some of the boards out there are, shall we say, less than optimal for use as so-called maker boards. They may have badly implemented certain important features, have a chronic lack of support, or any number of an absolute plethora of quite genuine issues that will get people raging on their keyboards.

But very few of these genuine issues have a direct impact on us using our boards as programming tools for the game development. We don't care about the OS; we don't care about the I/O Pins or the hardware's layout. So long as it runs some form of Linux, has OpenGLES2.0 with drivers, and can display an image. We should not have too many problems…famous last words there!

The Development Machine

Any desktop or laptop style PC can be used, we are really only interested in its performance as an editor, so a decent keyboard, mouse, and display are all you really need. The only hardware consideration is that it needs to be able to network in some way, via standard cables or wirelessly.

Next, you'll need a copy of Visual Studio. This presupposes you are running on a computer with a Windows OS. Later, models of Mac's can run Windows, so pop-off to Microsoft's site and see if you can download a version, it can sometimes be obtained for free or on discount for students. Visual Studio itself is free in its rich featured Community version from https://www.visualstudio.com.

I must take a moment to thank Microsoft for this; it really is a great gesture to make such professional tools free to everyone.

Next you need some software to allow you an easy connection from your PC to the Raspberry Pi. Whether you do this via a network cable direct to your PC, or via a router, or even wirelessly. A network connection needs to be made. Wired connections are much faster, but wireless can be tidier if you don't mind the speed lag.

If you are of a technical mind you can probably work out how to get two machines with different operating systems to work together, maybe even get them to communicate via Visual Studio. But that takes time and effort, and if you're reading this you're probably a beginner, so why go to so much effort? I am of a technical mind, but I'm also quite lazy when it comes to doing things when I know there are easier solutions, so I decided to have a serious hunt around for a solution to this, and I found it.

There is a wonderful piece of software called VisualGDB, which allows you to get your version of Visual Studio to talk to a whole range of different machines, send them code, run it, and debug it on your development machine.

I therefore give you a choice:

1. Write your own interface between Visual Studio and a Linux-based Raspberry Pi

2. Download and install the 30-day free trial of VisualGDB

I'm pretty sure you will opt for option 2. If you went for option 1. Close the book now, go write your interface, and be sure to write to me in a few months' time when you're ready to start again.

VisualGDB is available from Sysprogs website at https://www.visualGDB.com.

It's free for 30 days, which if you spend a few hours a day, should be more than enough time for you to work your way through this book and decide if it's worth investing around U.S.$100 (50% Student discounts are available) for something that will make your programming life so much easier. Take note though, the trial starts when you first run it, so if you're waiting for your Raspberry Pi to arrive, don't run it till it's purring away and we are ready to start working on our target.

That's it…a total outlay of around €60 for a target (excluding keyboard/mouse/monitor) should see you with a tasty little machine you can target and software you can use to write to that target for the next 30 days.

We're ready to get started.

Why Can't I Use Linux for Everything?

You can, be my guest I don't mind at all, the problem is I don't have a clue about Linux, I don't really want to have a clue about Linux, and you will discover as you read this that I'm never going to have a clue about Linux. So I'm totally not qualified to give you any real insight into or advice on using Linux. Which means you're on your own? Which is kind of the way most Linux coders seem to work!

We use Linux in some form on our target machines, simply because it provides an easy use of Secure Shell connections (SSH) via a network, and a means to create a graphical interface to let our projects run and access to some input and output functions.

I'm not anti-Linux in any way; it's a fine OS, especially as it's basically free. It's just not one I personally have ever really wanted to use or found easy to keep up-to-date with. I know only a few basic features, which are used in this book, anything I don't know I'm going to Google for, just like everyone else.

One thing I do have a problem with though, is the massive variety and quality of the distributions of Linux, which are available on SBCs, even of the same types of Linux. My recent tests into running Linux on many different target machines has demonstrated that it's rare to find a fully featured version of any brand of Linux, which is the same from one machine to another, even from the same makers.

But the core versions at least should contain the ability to access, send, compile, run, and debug, which is all I will focus on.

Support Website

Almost all the code in this book, and some other things that didn't make it in the final edit will be available online at my website (https://www.scratchpadgames.net). Most of the *missing* parts are things I want you to enter yourself for the practice. I'll also maintain an errata and update on systems or tools I use, color versions of all screenshots, and final and much more complete versions of all the demos in this book for you to download, review, and try out.

For brevity, the listings in this book are sometimes incomplete or have had formatting altered to fit on a page. Later in this book, when you should be more proficient, I'm not even going to provide the code as a listing, you can review the downloaded source code itself, which will be commented and tied in with the text. I'll provide suggestions on how to deal with a problem and some outlines, confident that you already have the requirements from previous examples. Downloading the demo base code will allow you to get your systems' setup ready to add your own additions as this book outlines.

But there will be *final* versions of the demos available, so you can compare your efforts with mine. I only ask that you please please please, don't just look at the final versions and cut and paste the code, you really will not benefit from doing that. Work with the support site, in conjunction with this book.

It's quite probable that I will cleanup, tinker with, or fix bugs in the source code after this book goes to print. But don't worry, I will make as few changes to the base online code as possible, and the source code will have descriptive comments, especially if it varies from the printed versions.

Thanks

There are a lot of people to thank for this book, but at the top of the list as always for me is my daughter, Danielle, who has somewhat reluctantly featured in the credit list of every game I've written since she was born. Giving her the dubious distinction of numerous mentions, on several game credit sites, without ever having any interest in playing or making computer games.

The addition in December 2015 of her son Harvey, my first grandchild, gives me even more cause to consider her the greatest achievement of my life, games being a very distant second, or probably third as I am quite proud of my guitar collection, though not my actual playing!

Thanks to my friend Professor Penny De Byl for helping me to find a means to publish this nonsense, and her help with checking my concept and invaluable advice and encouragement on what to add and take away from the original concept to keep it fun and interesting.

Thanks also to friend and now former colleague, Jamie Stewart for taking the time to go through this book at different times and comment on any mistakes I made, deliberate or otherwise.

Thanks to Grumpy old Git developers (Facebook group, not an insult) Gareth Lewis, Rob Wilmot, and Paul Carter; Paul for helping me find and convert some low poly car models for producing some nice LOD versions of the cars. Gareth, for his timely help with a Rasbian compatible key reading routine when I was on the point of throwing the Raspberry Pi out the window, and also to my student Petar Dimitrov, who came up with a neat keyboard scan system to determine which keyboard event was actually active, which was much tidier than the one I had, so I shamelessly stole it, with his consent ☺

Thanks also to old friends Shaun McClure and Ocean Legend Simon Butler for their pixel-pushing prowess on the 2D art you can find on the site and use, and Colin Morrison for his 3D race track tiles and a few other models I wasn't able to fit in but you can find on the site.

I have to give a huge shout out to the incredibly talented Pim Bos, one of our family of NHTV students studying Visual Arts, who did the cartoons that illustrate this book. His fun take on complex concepts is inspiring and made me chuckle every time he sent one in.

A special shout out to the small band unsuspecting volunteers who ran through this book for me, finding multiple spelling errors, and more than a few issues with my coding, especially to colleague David Jones who I now owe free drinks for life for his proofreading and eye for detail.

Finally, my thanks to the management, staff, and all students past and present at the International Games Architecture and Design (IGAD) programme of NHTV University of Applied Sciences* in Breda, The Netherlands, which has been my home for the last 9 years. I've learned much from them and I hope I've given a little bit back at times.

---

* Soon to be renamed Breda University of Applied Science.

Brian Beuken: Who Is He?

Brian Beuken is a veteran games developer, having started in the early 1980s writing his first games on the venerable Sinclair ZX81. Self-taught as many were at the time, Brian wrote games in Basic and Assembler, selling them via mail order before branching out to form his own small company specializing in conversion of projects from one popular machine to another. A chance to work for Ocean Software in Manchester, England, then one of the largest games companies around, saw Brian leave his native Scotland and become a full-time game programmer, staying in the center of the tech bubble that was Manchester and working for several companies producing a host of projects in quick succession.

Eventually, the Manchester bubble burst as companies began to merge and moved away. Brian became a well-established freelance coder specializing in Z80 systems and handheld devices from Nintendo and Sega, before again taking a leap into entrepreneurship and forming his own company, Virtucraft. Virtucraft grew from 3 to 30+ people in the space of 4 years, until once again the bubble burst and the company was forced to close. Brian went on to become Head of Development at an emerging mobile games company, which was later sold and became part of the mighty Square Enix. But Brian had left before that happened, unhappy with the distance from development in the management role, he returned to coding, and once again entered the freelance market for several years again specializing in handheld consoles.

A chance encounter with a tutor at NHTV in Breda, The Netherlands, resulted in Brian being offered a teaching position at the still new IGAD program they had established to bring game development skills that the industry needed, to education. Finding the program offered far more than he'd seen in any comparable education, Brian signed up thinking he'd try it for a year. Nine years later, he's still there, still coding, and adding to his 75+ published titles and enjoying watching his students find the joy of game development, which they can take with them to an industry that sorely needs more programmers.

1 Getting Started

Mine Looks Different?

It's in the nature of commercial software to update from time to time, and even as I write this I will have to deal with software updates of at least three of my key tools, which are known to update regularly. When I finish writing this, I will go back through it and change as many old images as I can to be as up-to-date as possible, but even then, by the time you read it there are likely to be many subtle differences in the layout and format, even sequences of some of the tools, especially visually. I also use at least two development machines: (1) home and (2) office with different versions of the main tools and multiple targets, so I fully expect a lot of images to be different to your basic first time setup.

However, don't panic! We can do that later when we get into the tricky stuff!

It's unlikely that any of the functionality will change in successive updates, so if the screenshots presented in this book don't look exactly the same, consider the images as guides only, and take note of what that image and the text around it is telling you to add/ change/remove and don't panic if it looks different, be adaptable. Any updates/changes that have real functional issues for the book code, I will document and maintain fixes on the support site.

■ First Steps

It's a common rule that programmers must never assume anything, so I'm immediately going to break that rule and assume you to know how to install Visual Studio, VisualGDB, and get your Target; in this case, a Raspberry Pi, set up to go. No? Ok well let's do the simple things first.

Set up the Raspberry Pi: This is relatively easy, especially if you opted for a preformatted SD card when you purchased. If so, insert the card into the Pi, hook up your *power, keyboard, mouse, wifi (if you bought one), and display and fire it up.*

If you didn't opt for the preformatted card, you have a bit more work to do, but it's always best to go to the Raspberry Pi website and follow the latest instructions. https://www.raspberrypi.org/help/quick-start-guide/.

Install Visual Studio: This also should be pretty simple, Microsoft downloads tend to be painless, if a little slow because of their size. Installation can take a little while but there's not a lot of input required from you, so once you've started it and ticked all the right boxes, you can go and make a few cups of your favorite beverage and come back when it's done.

Install VisualGDB: One thing you should do before you install this, is make sure you have run Visual Studio at least once, and closed it down. On its first run, Visual Studio sets up a lot of things, and that can interfere with the settings of some plug-ins, which is what VisualGDB is, a plug-in, a piece of software which extends Visual Studio's features.

Once you've run it, the installation of VisualGDB is totally painless, but *do not activate it* yet!

■ Setting Things Up

Sadly, we still have a few confusing steps to go through to write our first Raspberry Pi program, so let's start by introducing ourselves to Visual Studio. If you've already used it and know some C/C++, you can skip to the section titled, setting up the Raspberry Pi and other targets.

■ Introducing Visual Studio

Those of you still with me, prepare to be amazed and scared, mostly scared, because Visual Studio is indeed an incredibly scary thing when you first fire it up but we're only going to use some of the most basic features to start, so let's just play with those first before we even think about the scary topic of connecting to the target machine.

Depending on your version of Windows, you should have a link somewhere on your start menu or taskbar for the version of Visual Studio that you just installed. I prefer to keep it on my taskbar at the bottom, so it's always accessible.

Fire it up and if you have already sneaked ahead and installed VisualGDB, it will immediately ask you if you want to start the VisualGDB trial…answer no at this point, we have things to set up and we're going to do one or two little PC programs to get ourselves comfortable with the Visual Studio.

You're going to get something like this, a start screen. It won't look exactly the same as my screen, I've got a lot of different plug-ins on my version, also I've used it for several projects already but the main areas should be similar.

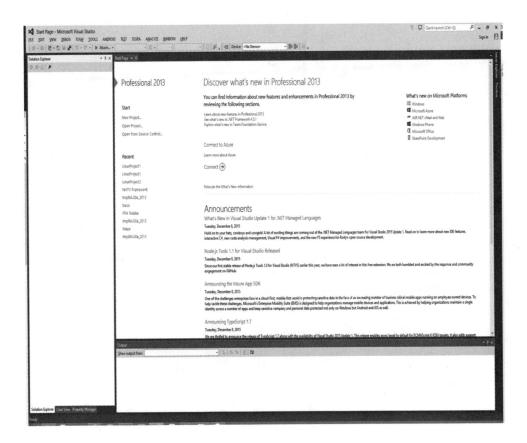

For now, ignore the Start options in the main window, and look at the top left corner, can you see the FILE tab? Click on it and select New, then Project.

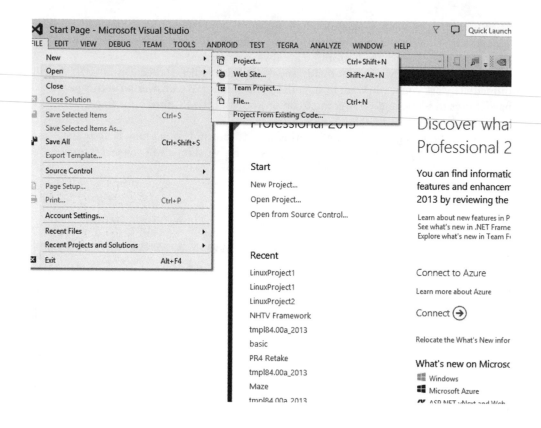

This will give us something like this, I say like this, because it's quite possible that the later version of Visual Studio you may be using will have some variation on this, but we should still have some of the basics in place to do this.

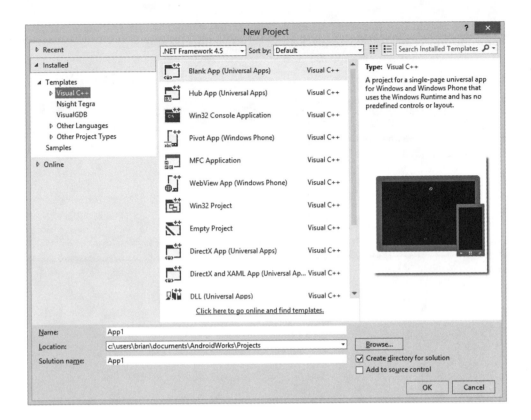

Notice we have a group of templates, I've selected the Visual C++ group, which we'll quickly use to get started, but there is also an option for Visual GBD...we'll click that soon.

For now, click on the Win32 Console Application, Visual Studio will automatically name the project and locate it somewhere on your machine for you.

You'll see a box like this appear.

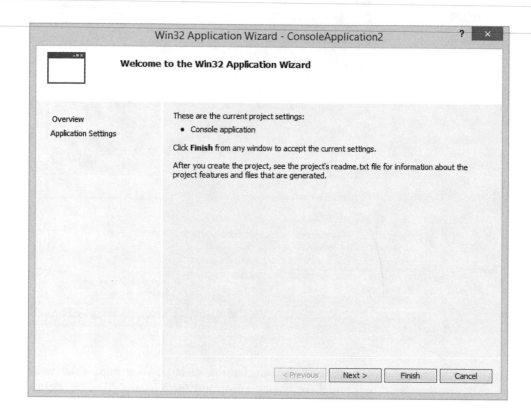

Go ahead and click Finish.

And like Magic (that's why it's called a Wizard), you will now have a small project in your Visual Studio.

Now this is a very, very simple project, it actually doesn't do much, but you can run it..... press F5.

Wait for it.

Wait for it.

Wait for it.

Yup that's it, that's all that's going to happen, you will have seen a small output window at the bottom saying something like this.

```
1>------ Build started: Project: ConsoleApplication2, Configuration: Debug
Win32 ------
1> stdafx.cpp
1> ConsoleApplication2.cpp
1> ConsoleApplication2.vcxproj -> c:\users\brian\documents\AndroidWorks\
Projects\ConsoleApplication2\Debug\ConsoleApplication2.exe
========== Build: 1 succeeded, 0 failed, 0 up-to-date, 0 skipped ==========
```

And then a black box appears and then disappears on your screen. Well done, you just ran your first ever Visual Studio-built program. Of course, it really didn't do too much but if you look carefully at the code in the large window, you'll see there's very little code to run.

```
// ConsoleApplication2.cpp : Defines the entry point for the console
application.
#include "stdafx.h"
int _tmain(int argc, _TCHAR* argv[])
{
 return 0;
}
```

There's only one function, called _tmain and it has one instruction to return, that's exactly what it did. But how did it do it?

Running a program consists of at least three main stages: (1) compiling, (2) linking, and (3) then running.

If you look at the Build output, you can see that two cpp files were compiled; they were then linked together, though it does not explicitly tell you, it then made the resulting EXE file, the actual program was stored in a directory, called, on my machine; c:\users\brian\documents\AndroidWorks\Projects\ConsoleApplication2\Debug\ConsoleApplication2.exe.

Visual Studio then automatically ran the program in something called Debug Mode and executed the first instruction it saw…which was to return.

Now we don't really need to know much about how the black box gets created and the program starts up, but let's try to slow things down.

Visual Studio is an Editor, but it is also a very powerful debugger. That allows us to examine code while its running and also to stop code at certain points, hover your cursor over the gray bar next to the return 0; instruction. Press the right mouse button and a gray dot will appear.

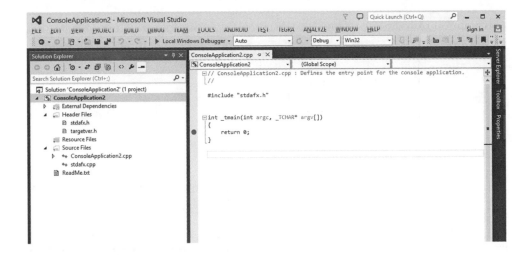

This is a breakpoint. Hit F5 again.

Now what do we see?

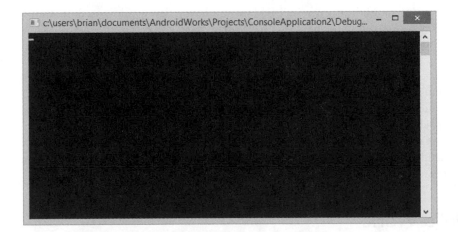

We should see an Empty window, this was the black box that popped up and disappeared before we could see it. This is called a console window; it's basically a small user output box that we will often display some text in, usually to tell us something important about our programs.

But why can we see it now?

Look at the Visual Studio again…it seems to be doing something interesting.

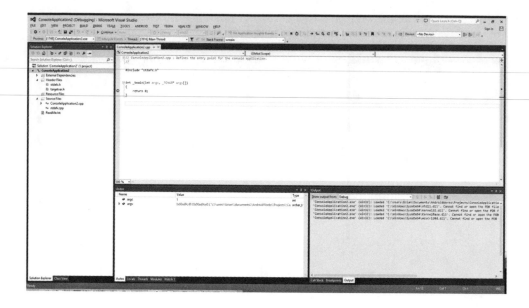

Our gray dot, now has an arrow in it, and we now have a new window on show, though this may vary on your machine because I have some presets that show me autos and arrange my windows the way I like them, but, we will share the same experience of how our code runs.

The program has stopped, dead in its tracks and is waiting for you to allow it to continue or to step through its instructions. Press F5 again…or press the green Arrow Continue box…the window now vanishes again. The program continued and did its return, closing the program and closing the console window.

So far so good, but it's not exactly the cutting edge, let's make it do something.

Traditionally, the first program that any new coder writes is a *hello world* program, so let's try to do that now.

▋ Hello World

In this very simple console application, we really only can do one or two things, we can print some text, and input some text. So let's start with printing some text.

The simplest way to print text in a C++ program is to use a function called cout, its part of a family of routines from what's called the STL, or Standard Template Library. All C++ programs have access to these functions, and there are a lot of them. However, we're only interested for now in cout, which a quick check of my favorite C++ reference site www.cplusplus.com tells me is part of the <iostream> class.

Now, if I want to use things in a class I need to make sure my program includes the class definitions, I also need to check the format for the function, again check my favorite site.

For speed, I've added them here.

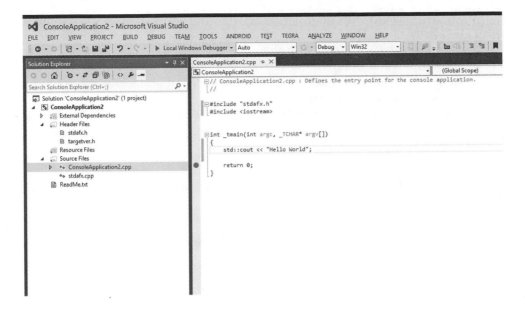

Add the lines.

```
#include <iostream>
```

and

```
std::cout << "Hello World";
```

As I have in the screenshot. Notice the breakpoint is still there, hit F5 again and you should see Hello World at the top of the console window. If you get a build error, carefully check the typing, at this point, the only thing that can really go wrong is a typo.

Congratulations! You have your first Hello World, or whatever childish expletives you decided to use. There's nothing funnier for beginners than to make a computer swear.

▮ Hello Place of My Choosing

Let's expand on things a bit, and try to change the output depending on an input.

This means using cout 's partner in crime cin.

Did you notice the format of cout?

```
std::cout << "Hello World";
```

The std:: part indicates that the cout belongs to the namespace of the Standard Template Library, namespace is a concept in C++ that allows us to group things together, and reuse common names, a bit like a family name. There are many people called Brian in the world, but not so many in the Beuken family, I think I'm the only one, Brian is a common name, Brian Beuken is specific to me. So, I'm Brian from the Beuken namespace.

The << part indicates that the text is going out to the console, it wouldn't be of much use if it was going in…in fact it would not compile if we used >>.

So, cin will also need that std identification and some indication of the direction of flow of the data.

If text goes << (out) then input must come (in) >> but it also means it needs to be stored somewhere, usually in a variable of our choice.

We want to enter some text, which is best stored in what's called a string. Now string is also a std class and so we need to also include the <string> class header, like we did with <iostream>.

Add the new lines like this;

```
// ConsoleApplication2.cpp : Defines the entry point for the console
application.

#include "stdafx.h"
#include <iostream>
#include <string>
int _tmain(int argc, _TCHAR* argv[])

{
  std::string mystring;
  std::cin >> mystring;
  std::cout << "Hello "<< mystring;
  return 0;
}
```

You should still have a gray dot on your return 0; line to indicate a break point, if not, add one, so your program will stop long enough for you to read your efforts. Press F5… the screen will be blank, but you can enter some location, or friends name, when you press Enter, you will display Hello…then whatever you typed.

Not bad…we've done our first input and output and compiled and ran our first two Visual Studio programs, only a few million more to go till you master it. As an exercise, see if you can remove the breakpoint, and add another instance of cin to let it create a pause for you…hint, cin will finish and move to the next instruction when you press Enter.

Now it's time to focus on the target system we are using, we'll come back to the Visual Studio soon.

2 Getting Our Target Ready

Now before we get into the setting up, it might be wise at this point for you to skip ahead to the Appendix section of this book and quickly read Appendix III, which covers the importance of using source control? You don't *need* to use source control, especially if you are finding it a bit confusing at this point, but after a while source control is going to be something you really will *need* to start using. It's ok, there are many free options, but you can make up your own mind whether now is the time to start using it. I want you to be comfortable in what you are doing first before adding new tools you may find confusing.

▐ Setting Up the Target

If you bought a preformatted SD card or managed to install it from the website, our target should be quite happily running its OS now, but ironically we're not going to spend a massive amount of time using it.

It really is wise though, to spend just a little bit of time reading the manuals, or wiki sites that your maker recommends just to familiarize yourself with your target machine. As I write here, I'm using a Raspberry Pi, but I am aware that how this works now, is quite different to how it worked 6 months ago, so minor variations will have to be expected and dealt with by you using a tiny bit of imagination.

We're not really here to talk about the joys of navigation on a Linux-based system, and I have never touched Linux before I got my first Raspberry Pi, so I've been on my search engines to find out the key things I need to know. It turned out that I needed to know a lot!

But probably the first and most important thing you need to know is how to make sure your version of Rasbian (or other Linux) is up-to-date.

I wish I could spend some time explaining to anyone not using a Raspberry machine, how to get it set up and running it but in truth there are just too many of them out there, and I really don't want this to be a book about single board computers (SBCs) and their idiosyncrasies, it's meant to be about programming. So I will apologize straight away if I miss out some small detail that your particular SBC has or does not have that will prevent you from moving forward. I am trusting that you know just enough about your unit to get it set up and working. In nearly every unit I've looked at, SBC makers maintain forums/ wikis or other means of keeping their communities updated. That's where you need to look for specific information on your system. I will post some info on the support site, but I can't really guarantee to cover all the possible systems.

Throughout this book I am only going to show code for the Raspberry range, but fear not, the only significant* differences relate to the graphic setup and whether it works in a window or full screen. So you will find that on the non-Raspberry machines everything should work if you use the standard Linux version downloads from the support site, and do NOT set up a Raspberry value in the Preprocessor Macros (explained later). Later I will provide a Graphics Class that allows you a duel option of Linux X11 and Raspberry, which should cover pretty much any standard Linux display. In addition, take care to note some of your include and library directories will be different. Most versions of Linux keep the files we need in the same places, but reality can bite sometimes, and the fact is that a few systems will have different locations of those files. I will record as many as I can on the support site but really it's up to you to find them as I won't have every single machine available to test and check.

That said, I've collected quite a few of the little beasties, so I'll try to maintain a running list of issues on the support site.

Generally, the version of the OS you get from the target maker is going to be the most up-to-date, and you will use that to burn your first SD card, you'll find instructions on how to do that with your documentation or makers website, so I won't repeat that there. If you find, however, that your makers OS is not up to scratch and a lot of them are quite poor, Armbian from Armbian.com is a very good alternative, often providing a more stable and driver-equipped OS on a very wide range of chipsets.

However, it is wise to know the OS's update from time to time as do several standard apps that come with your OS and these are not all updated at the same time. Makers will post new builds for you to create new SDs. However, be aware that every time you make a new fresh SD you lose any package libraries or projects that you installed on the previous version. So rather than continually burning SDs every time a new build comes, and potentially losing your useful tools and libs, use the update/upgrade routine described in Appendix II. It's not a bad idea to make a backup ISO file of your SD card from time to time, in case you need to reburn it for some reason.

From our view point as programmers, it's a just a target to run code, whether it runs in its console text mode or a Graphic User Interface (GUI), we're going to make it do other things and the only thing we want most in the world right now is the IP address of the target machine.

Personally I prefer to have the GUI running while developing keyboard-based games, and console for mouse games, for reasons that will become clear later, but it should be

---

* There is one other significant difference, which relates to Shaders, but so far I only find this to be a problem on intel-based machines, full info is on the support site.

noted that the GUI is eating up some of the CPU and GPU bandwidth, actually quite a lot, so it's your call at this point if you want to allow it to run. If you booted up as a console text system, enter `startx` to go to the GUI. Nothing we're going to do so far is going to really stress the target, so keep it in whatever mode works for you. Of course, if your system defaults to a graphic interface, you can ignore this.

First thing we must do, once we're all connected up correctly, is to ID our target on our network. If you don't have the graphical interface and have a console screen, then we can simply type `ifconfig` and press enter, we'll get a slightly confusing set of numbers, I'll explain them in a moment.

If we have the GUI on screen click on the terminal button to open a window that allows us to enter `ifconfig` to get the IP address. You can also hover your mouse pointer over the wifi/network icon usually on the top right of the screen.

▮▌ Oh Wait…Did We Plug-In?

Of course, we have to assume that it is either hooked to the Dev PC via a cable, or it plugs into a router on the Dev PC's network, or that it is connected up to the same wifi network as the DevPC with a USB→Network dongle. The key point is that your target and your development PC/Mac need to be on the same network and they need to be connected. This needs to be a network connection, not USB.

Let's get back to those numbers, whether you entered `ifconfig` in the console mode or in the terminal window, you should get something like this.

A lot of confusing numbers. But we're looking for the wired and wifi Ethernet connection. Either will do, but ideally the wired one, which is described as eth0.

If you don't have a wired connection but you do have a wifi dongle plugged into your Raspberry Pi, you should then have a wlan0 connection. We can use that too, it's going to be a lot slower but we're not trying to shift gigabytes of data, so we can use it.

We're looking for the IP address, here called the inet addr. This is a number that identifies your computer on your network, each computer on your network will have a different IP number, and when connecting to the Internet, this is like your computer's name or phone number to the network.

The default IP number for any unassigned computer connection is usually 127.0.0.0 or 127.0.0.1, and you will probably see that on the second set of numbers, if your Raspberry Pi is still all fresh and new with nothing else added.

If you see 127.0.0.0/1 on both the first and third set of numbers it means there may be a connection issue with your Raspberry Pi and you'll have to try to resolve that...I can't offer a lot of help beyond, try turning it on and off again, check the dongle, change the cable, and review the Raspberry Pi forums for help.

The number on my machine is currently 192.168.178.13, a pretty common standard internal IP address for a home network. If you're connected directly to your target, or using a network system in an office or school you may have a completely different set of numbers decided on by your ICT dept... But the key is, it's not 127.0.0.0/1.

So find the wired IP address, and if not wired, find the wifi IP address.

Take a note of the number; we'll need that to set up VisualGDB, so it knows what target machine to talk to.

You *probably* will have to do this again from time to time, especially if you are responsible and switch all your equipment off when done. The IP address is assigned by the system when it starts up and connects, and though, if all things are equal it will provide the same number, you can't be 100% certain. The order things power up, or adding new computers onto your network may change the assigned IP address. But it's simple enough to reset, now that you know how to get the IP address.

You can also hover your mouse cursor over your network signal indicator, this works on the Raspberry range and most others, ignore the /24 part at the end.

▮ Starting Up VisualGDB for the First Time

Getting back to your development PC, it's now time to make sure it's all ready to be your main tool for programming. Setting up VisualGDB is really simple, but do make sure you have run Visual Studio at least once and shut it down before you try.

The installation process is really painless, if you have not done so already, download and install from this webpage following the simple instructions:

http://visualgdb.com/download/.

And then next time you fire up visual studio and agree to the activation of VisualGDB, you won't see anything new, until you select.

File→New→Project.

And you will discover this in your Installed→Templates→VisualGDB section.

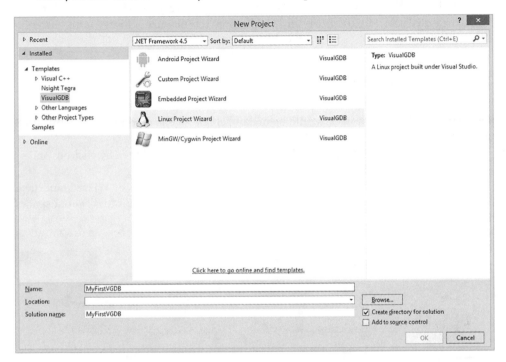

We are going to be always using the Linux Project Wizard option; we'll discuss this more when we start our first project. Before that, let's get a connection sorted.

▐ Getting the Machines to Talk

There are two basic ways that our PC can talk to our Raspberry Pi via a hardware cable, which is generally going to be the fastest, or via a wifi, which assumes that both machines are on the same network.

Though you can hook the PC up directly to the Raspberry Pi, most people with multiple computers use some form of router, it doesn't make a lot of difference, so long as both machines are on the same internal/home/office network and therefore can *ping* each other to create a network communication. I suppose it's possible to even connect to them over the Internet…but I can't see the point really.

Wifi basically works the same way as a cable, but is a lot slower. Basic wired net speeds are rated around 100Mb/s, which is the max our Raspberry Pi can handle, despite some PCs and SBCs having 1000Mb/s systems. Although wifi tends to be under 10Mb/s, though as with all techs, they are getting faster, and 10Mb/s is just fast enough to work with, but more speed is always better, so try to use a wire. I find mine tends to hover around 30Mb/s on a supposedly stated 100Mb/s capability. Don't be too alarmed if you find that actual performance of your equipment does not match the stated performance on the box.

I actually have a small technical issue on my main home dev PC, which prevents it from hooking up directly with a wired connection, (i.e., it's borked and I never managed to fix it) so I only use it with wifi or a network switch attached to a router. How you hook it up is not as important as the fact it is actually hooked up.

All this technical talk makes it sound like we have to perform some kind of black magic rituals, but in reality hooking our machines up is pretty automated by VisualGDB.

▌ Sending Our First Program

We've already seen that convention dictates our first program on a new machine should be hello world, so let's repeat what we did before and create a hello world program, this time on the target system.

Let's start a new fresh project, by firing up Visual Studio, and then by clicking on. FILE→New→Project.

To bring up the New Project Dialog Boxes, choose Linux Project Wizard, and take care to name it HelloWorld with no spaces. Rasbian/Linux can be a bit fussy about spaces in filenames.

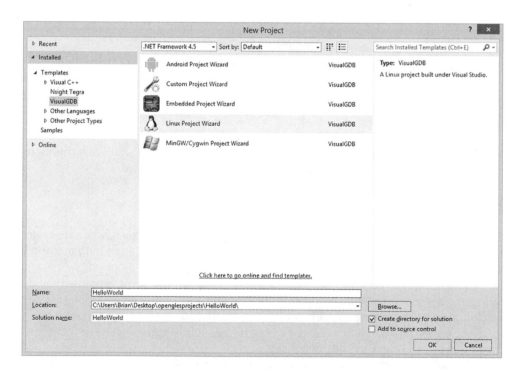

Take note that the Location here does not exist on your machine; it exists on mine! You can use the Browse button on the right to find a suitable location on your hard drive to place this project. Ideally, somewhere from your root Directory in a folder called OpenGLESProjects or simply SBCProjects. Avoid branching off from directories that may have spaces. This directory structure will be copied on your target machine, and spaces can cause problems for Linux-based compilers. In fact as a general rule of thumb, always create dev directories off a main drive location. The confusion with spaces in Directory naming is a long established conflict between Windows and Linux; let's not allow it to get in our way.

Once you are happy with your project name and location, press the OK button and this will appear.

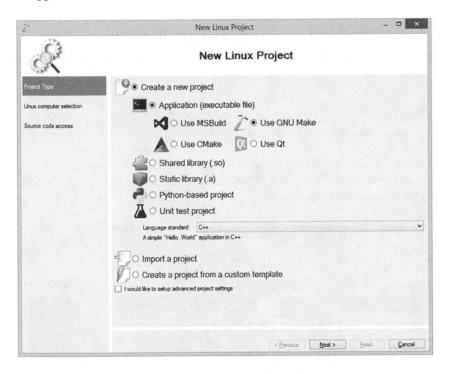

You can choose one of four build systems, I want you to use GNU Make, as you are a beginner, it exposes more of the values we need to see directly inside the VisualGDB, select that and hit next. MSBuild is a generally nicer system to use when you are a little more experienced, but it does hide some things from the VisualGDB, which we don't want you to be hunting for. CMake is an awesome system if you have a more advanced understanding of how make files work. I've never used QT, so won't make any comment on that. However, GNU is the system we need to use for now, so hitting next will bring up this next popup which is a nice and important dialog as this is where we tell our PC, where our target system is by entering the IP address and name.

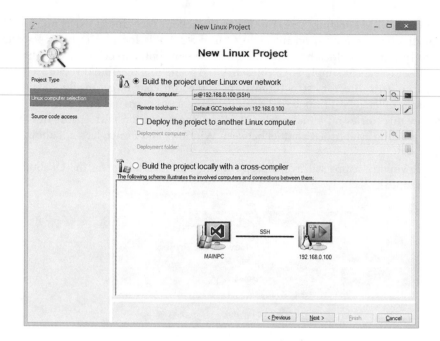

As you can see, I already have a Raspberry Pi, listed as the remote computer, this time on 192.168.0.100, but chances are you will not, so click on the down arrow at the end of the info box to get something like this.

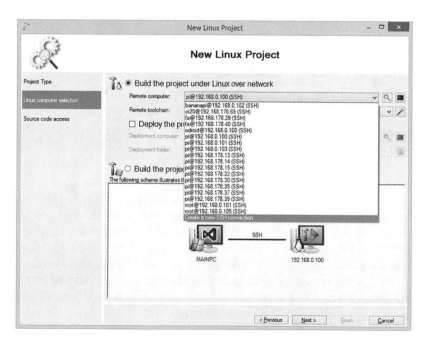

Again, as I have had a lot of machines attached, many of which have altered their IP as I was using them, it is showing all the machines it knows, on your first setup you won't get this. What we really want is the Create a new SSH connection option.

Click on that to open up the setup box that is where most of the good stuff happens.

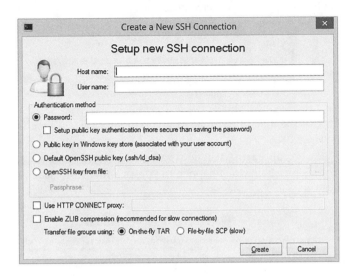

Here you can see a blank box, you have to give it the IP address as the Host name, the user name (pi) and the password, (raspberry), and also tick the box for setting up the public key authentication. That by the way is why I have so many options on my computer for target machines, they all are getting saved.

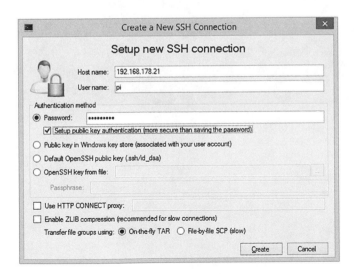

If all has been entered correctly, a short handshaking dialog box will pop up then you will see this.

Hit save and now that the machine will be locked into your system's memory saving you have a lot of time later.

You'll then see a box appearing as it does various tests and checks, which will vanish if all is ok. Again this probably won't happen to you as a first time user, but you may get this box appearing.

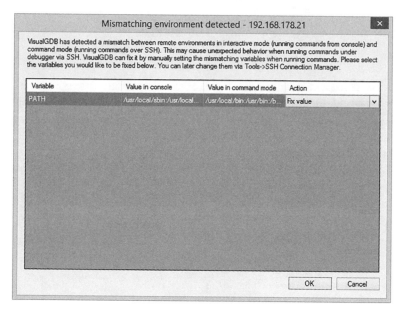

Just press ok.

Your dialog box will now come up with this.

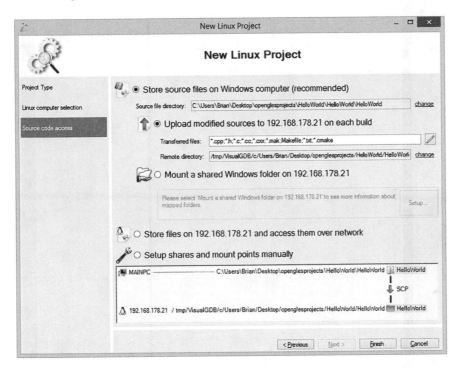

Take note of the transferred files section. This lets the system know what kind of files we have to send down to the target to compile. Again you may not see this on your first try, but as I have been using the system for some time, it has remembered some of the file types I want to send…You probably only have a few and at this point that's ok, we'll add to them as we go, and this can be edited later if we need to.

That's it, hit Finish, the system will do some testing, a few boxes will pop and progress bars will seem to do their thing. They are indicating the testing of compiles and sending of data to the target machine, including setting up some annoyingly complex directories. But when you check things out on your Visual studio it should seem remarkably familiar.

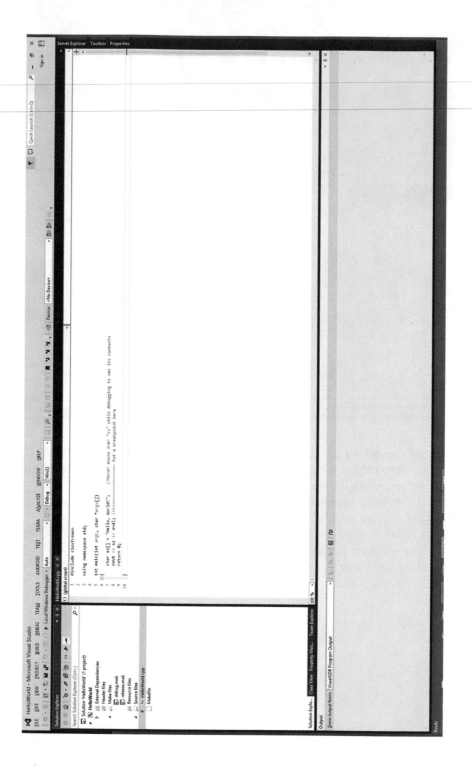

Go on run it. Click on the green arrow.

As before, the project compiled in the background switched its display to a debug display for a moment then something different happened.

Instead of a black console window appearing and disappearing, we got this apparent error, with a big scary! in a triangle.

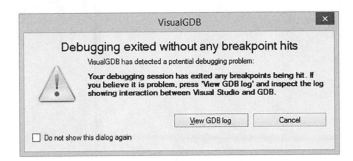

It's not actually an error, it is simply telling us that the program has stopped suddenly... and it found that a bit odd!

But also look closely at your output window (if you have one open, I hope you do).

Can you see it says Hello World?

Instead of opening up a console window on our Target, VisualGDB has intercepted that output and sent it to an output window.

Now do what we did before and put a breakpoint at the return instruction. Hit the run button and look for what we get. It should all be very familiar to us now.

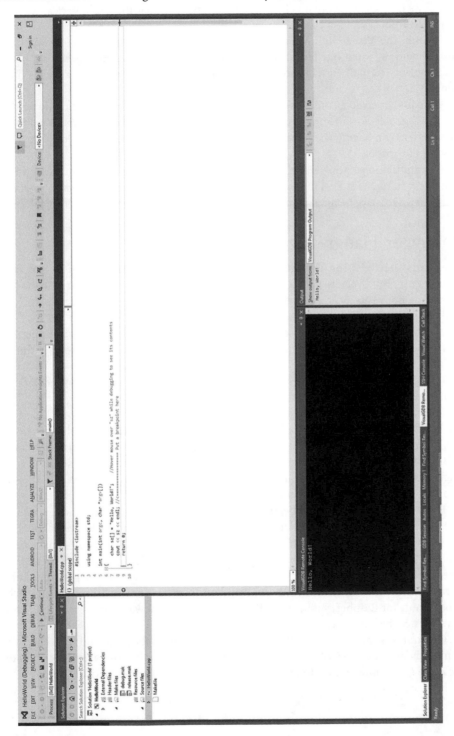

There are only two things we need to know here... first and most important, our code is not running on our PC, its running on our target. Our PC is talking to it, and getting info that allows it to know where it is in the program cycle so that the debugger can correctly display the info.

Second, the VisualGDB console on our PC is actually pretending to be our targets console window, when our target sends to its console it will appear there. It's a process called routing (Actually it will cause a couple of minor issues later but for now we'll leave it alone).

We could open up a console window on the machine if we wanted, but really we don't, consoles are really for information only, and having them on our development machine is much better than having them on the target, which we want to be a graphic display when we write our games.

Congratulations! You've just had your first project run on your target. And it really wasn't very hard at all. Feel free to change it, add silly names and extra output, get comfortable with this, we have taken an important first step in a target-based development.

▉ Debugger Hangs Too Much?

When I first started using VisualGDB, I had no issues with it at all; it was, in fact, seamless in its use. But over the past 3 or 4 months, I've had some serious frustrations with it hanging on my Visual Studio, targeting any Raspberry Pi, when trying to single step or set break points in the debugger.

A debugger that crashes constantly isn't a very good debugger, and I was rather irked by this and contacted Sysprogs who make VisualGDB. Their advice was to replace the copy of GDB on the Pi itself.

GDB is the program that does most of the debugging work on the Pi to send data back for display. Without it we can't access data on the Pi.

It seems that at some point during its updates, the Rasbian version of GDB version 7.7.1 has fallen behind the update loop, and it's not actually VisualGDB that is crashing but GDB on the Pi, because VisualGDB is expecting a later version. Updating Rasbian, or GDB itself will not help, as it considers the current version to be the latest, for Rasbian, which it is! However, GNU who make it do have a most up-to-date versions and it would seem that VisualGDB much prefers these.

Replacing GDB on the Raspberry Pi is a bit of a task, especially for a Linux noob like me. However, I had to bite the bullet and use what little understanding I have of how Linux installs things, to replace GDB. Here are the steps I worked out, but only consider these if you are getting unacceptable hangs in your debugger. This may happen later as your projects get more complex, so you can come back to this then. Other targets should have the most up-to-date version of GDB unaltered on their versions of Linux, so should be a problem only for Raspberry machines. But I did notice that it was also present in the Nano Pi systems. So best to check.

On your Raspberry Pi connected to the Internet, open a terminal and then enter these commands one at a time, some take a lot longer than others but the overall process does take quite some time, so best to do it over lunch or some other noncritical time.

```
wget https:/ftp.gnu.org/gnu/gdb/gdb-7.12.tar.gz -P ~/Downloads/
tar vxzf ~/Downloads/gdb-7.12.tar.gz -C ~/Downloads/
sudo apt-get update
sudo apt-get upgrade -y
sudo apt-get install libreadline-dev
sudo apt-get install texinfo
sudo apt-get autoclean
cd ~/Downloads/gdb-7.12
these last two take the most time
./configure --prefix=/usr --with-system-readline && make -j4
sudo make -j4 -C gdb/ install
```

The update and upgrade commands are just to make sure you have the latest version, if you are sure you already have that you can skip those two lines, but it's usually better to be safe than sorry (also if using a single core Pi, you can leave out the −j4 arguments, which are really for multicore compiling). After doing all this, we should be good to go, reset your Raspberry Pi, when it comes back, you can open a terminal and type gdb –version and it should now report a new generic version 7.12.1 (or later) of GDB, which is not the Rasbian specific version. I can't say if this will have an impact on any programs or projects that are relying on the Rasbian specific version, so you install this *fix* at your own risk.

What I can say with some happy certainty is that it cured my constant and very random hang-up issues, and saved a few keyboards from coder rage smashes. I hope that the Rasbian version gets an update soon, so this fix will no longer be needed.

All this only impacts us if we are using default toolchain settings when we start a project up to build on a remote target, if, when starting, you choose the option available, to try loading the GDB installed on your target, it may be happy enough to use it. As I recommend all beginners should start with default settings, there's a pretty fair chance that you will have this issue on systems which have earlier than 7.12.1 GDB.

3 Using the Target

■ Ready to Rock and Ermm Indeed Roll!

So far so good, we have a dev system on our PC, which gives us a professional Integrated Development Environment (IDE) and a means to send code and other data to the Raspberry Pi for compiling, then running, and debugging.

At the moment we are using a remote-based compiling system, this is effective and simple to set up, but has some drawbacks, mainly on the compilation speed. Our target machine has only a fraction of the power of our PC, so it is going to compile our code much slower than our PC could do it, so it makes more sense to do the compilation on our PC.

That's something we'll discuss later, as this kind of cross platform Dev has one or two minor pitfalls I want all of us to avoid till we're more comfortable with our set up. If we just use the compiler on the target, which was already there or we installed it, there is basically no doubt that it works on that target. Running a compiler to output code on our PC is 99.9% of the time going to be fine, but I want you to continue doing what you're doing now. I want you to get a sense for how long compilation can take so that when we do switch you will know the benefits.

For now though we've achieved something, getting code from our keyboard onto the target screen, that's worth a pat on the back and celebratory swig of strong programmer coffee.

But in the next chapter, it's time to get serious after a bit of explanation and some proper setting up!

◼ Graphics Explained!

So far we've managed to get a bit of code going and print some text; however, to write games we need nice pretty graphics in glorious color with lovely animations. But to do that we need to ask the video system in our target to draw our graphics. And there lies a problem for us as novice coders. Asking a very complex hardware chip to do even the simplest things is really a hard work, and we generally don't have access to all the relevant registers and access protocols the chip wants…How then do we do graphics?

Back in the (good) old days, screen displays were generally memory mapped in some way, so if you wrote a byte to the memory area representing the screen then a pixel would appear.

Sadly those days are gone, with the advent of ever more powerful graphic chips whose sole purpose was to produce 3D objects in virtual space on a flat panel, actually drawing flat-panel graphics directly has fallen out of favor (though it can still be done on some machines).

The preferred method these days is to ask our Graphics Processing Unit (GPU) to draw things for us, usually triangles. Those are the most beloved of all coder graphic primitives.

But getting our GPU chip to draw even simple triangles means a lot of very low-level requests for hardware to set up registers, send data, confirm data, attach data, and so on… it's a pain.

To relieve that pain, hardware manufacturers make their systems compliant with graphic Application Programming Interface (APIs), or more accurately graphic API's are produced for hardware systems, but given that there is no sense in limiting your market, hardware makers generally introduces new features to their hardware slowly, to allow the API's a chance to incorporate new features.

There are two dominating APIs in the games field. Direct X from Microsoft, which is used by PCs and most other Windows-based systems, and Microsoft's Xbox consoles. It's a vast, frequently updated, and powerful API, which on recent versions of Windows has been rolled into the OS itself, so is no longer an additional download.

This is very much a workhorse API for any PC, and its constant development over the years has created a standard where its market dominance was so powerful that hardware was forced to comply with it allowing for widespread standardization of desktop GPUs, which, in turn, allowed the hardware makers to focus more on performance ahead of fancy new graphic gimmicks that most users could not access. This also had the benefit of allowing coders to specialize and drive the graphics tech forward to the levels that we see today.

New hardware features do come along but under controlled release conditions and almost always with the APIs updated and ready to use them when they come to market.

The other giant is OpenGL, which is available for almost every computer-based system imaginable, it is a more open and community friendly API than DirectX, but it does have a standards body, The Khronos group who maintain and update it when needed, and enhances performance, maintaining the reference materials that users and hardware makers can use to develop new software and hardware.

It also has a very popular subbranch called OpenGL ES, the ES stands for embedded systems, and is considered a low overhead high-performance version for use in machines that need low power consumption and do not have massively powerful chips or memory. It does have some limitations and a lot of previously deprecated but still usable features of full OpenGL that have been removed to keep it slim. But it is a popular API because of its use in the vast majority of mobile phones and other small devices, including our Raspberry Pi and almost all other SingleBoard Computers on the market.

There are also proprietary APIs from Nintendo and Sony, which are unique but familiar in their approach to things, taking the best of OpenGL and Direct X and adapting them for their specific needs. As they are only available on the makers own machines, these APIs are highly specialized and optimized for known hardware configurations and are generally very high performance.

In addition, sadly they are 100% confidential and not to be discussed in this book. However, it's fair to say once you understand how to use one API you should be able to adapt to the others because they all generally try to do the same things in similar ways at least from the users point of view. What happens under the hood should probably stay under the hood unless or until you are an expert in 3D maths and hardware coding.

So It Be OpenGL ES Ye Be Wanting Arrgghhh!

Is it Talk like a Pirate day (September 19)? No, oh well every book should have at least one talk like a pirate comment, that's mine…it if is Talk like a Pirate day, add an arghhh at the end of every sentence in this section, maybe an occasional, me hearty, too.

We're almost ready to start some proper tech coding; we are going to enter the world of graphics by doing some 2D games, let's stick to a few very simple concepts and add to our knowledge of how to use OpenGL ES as we go.

This is one point where our SBC target as a console concept lets us down a little. Consoles, of course, have those very powerful graphic hardware features we all love, and also have those specialized APIs I mentioned before. What these do is allow for a more high level of manipulation of all the machines graphic systems, which, in turn, forms the basis of their SDKs, which is a collection of enhancements to the Software Development Kit (API), and various software packages to control graphics, assets, memory, sound, and so on.

We don't have an SDK…and writing a fully functioning SDK is a way beyond the scope of this book. But we can identify the key components we will need to write basic game concepts and put together our own very basic project layout as we go. We'll talk about that more after we've done our project work. To begin with, the collection of routines and functions we will put together throughout this book, is more of a framework than a fully formed SDK; but we will add to it as we need to, until we have something we can be happy to share with others. When you do eventually manage to get your hands on a proper console, this experience of what goes into the framework will be a massive boost to you. Programmers never like to reinvent the wheel but they do like to know how to make them should they ever find themselves having to work with square ones.

As we go along with each game, we'll try to add various components to our framework and make things easier for the games that follow. To start with we need to use the most basic graphic functions we have available, which in our case is…drumroll, OpenGLES 2.0…arrghh me hearty!

Where Is OpenGLES2.0 on My Target?

It's interesting that the Raspberry Pi, having by far the largest market share of all SBCs is actually the one machine out of dozens, which is the exception to the rule when it comes to OpenGLES libraries. It was always designed to be a machine that users could write anything on, so it's OpenGLES2.0 was part of the OS distribution from day one, even better; the Raspberry Pi foundation somehow convinced Broadcom to provide extra functions to make using the GPU even easier, which basically means that the Raspberry range does its graphics setup one way, and all the others do it....well the correct, but slightly trickier way? So the set up and location of libraries for OpenGLES2.0 will vary on any non-Raspberry machine.

Now if you are using a sensible target, you will have your OpenGLES2.0 fully integrated into your hardware, you will have KHR, EGL and GLES2 folders somewhere on your machine, and your system is capable of completely accessing the GPU. Most of the main targets do that. Sadly a few of them don't and it could be a real chore to locate and install the correct libraries. The reality is if you want your particular machine to have its GPU fully functioning where the makers have not provided software to do that, that's a task you need to take on yourself. I have spent hours on forums and google, hunting down libraries only to find that they don't work on a particular target even though it has the same GPU.

In addition, there are legal aspects that limit where you can access the particular library you need for your particular brand, that would take way too long to debate and discuss. So your main recourse if you do not have default Open GLES installed, is consult your maker, the user community, and the hardware manufacturers. The answers should be there somewhere.

However, if you find that you can't locate them there is a reasonable catch (almost) all solution, which works for most machines, which is the Mesa 3D Graphics library, which will make use of any exposed GPU features you have on your system where it can detect them, and where not, the software emulate them as best as possible.

What that gives us is a pretty reliable way of having the OpenGLES2.0 functions available to us, even if not all the hardware is otherwise available. So if you are using a machine where you have to install OpenGLES2.0 libs, and you cannot get them from the maker's site for your specific GPU....do this in a terminal in your target.

```
sudo apt-get install libgles2-mesa-dev
```

(You don't need the sudo if you are using a machine that gives you a root terminal).

Now you should find the EGL and GLES2 folders in your /usr/include folders, which is where most normal forms of Linux seem to install the files. You'll also almost certainly get at least one binary lib, libGLESv2.so, which is compatible with your hardware or provides the same functions in emulation. It will be in your /usr/lib/*name_depends_on_cpu* folder.

I have to make clear though, on SBCs, these are not always optimal, they will let you create and build graphic games but the performance is going to be variable if your hardware has not made direct access available. As soon as possible you need to replace them with proper drivers for your machine, if they are not available, hassle the makers on their forums. A board without proper graphic drivers is simply not going to perform at optimal levels and that does not help their cause of selling a board for multiple uses. This is in my view one reason why the Raspberry range is such a success, everything you need is there ready and waiting, even if it's in odd directories.

I've noted that all this works for most machines, sadly there are a few that just don't have their GPUs open to our code and nothing we do is going to get them working. Chase the makers, that's all you can do, or buy a cheap simple unit with OpenGLES2.0, such as the Raspberry Pi Zero, or NanoPi M1. Before buying any SBC for this kind of work, make sure that the OpenGLES2.0 drivers are available and working. I will post some updates on the support site of systems that I've tried.

▌ A Nice New Project with Graphics

Our old console program has served its purpose, it's time for us to produce a proper game project, so let's start a new one and go through the process of setting up an OpenGLES2.0 graphics system, which will let us produce our first couple of very simple games.

This is the point in most books where you are told to go and download a project from a website and work on it, and this book is no exception, you'll find the project GameProject1 on the support website, but if you are new to coding, it is really a good idea to get some practice of just entering code into your IDE, and if you are a beginner, I strongly suggest you to enter the next program in by hand as I go through it. You'll make a ton of typing errors, but that's all a good practice for finding real bugs later. We're going to go through the whole process of starting a project and building up the small arsenal of files we're going to use throughout this book to create a framework for writing all manner of simple games.

At this point, it might be wise to locate some good online resources for OpenGLES2.0. Googling for OpenGL will bring up a plethora of main OpenGL sites and some of those are really good until they get deeper into full OpenGL which we can't really do, or are too focused on the older OpenGL1.x, which is no longer in general use.

The Khronos Groups' page's main focus is on documenting the feature set of OpenGLES2.0, so there's not a lot of easy to use tutorials but it is the goto place for information on how to gain access to all the features of OpenGLES2.0 (and other versions).

The main documentation can be found here:

https://www.khronos.org/opengles/sdk/docs/man/

Bookmark this into your browser; you will need it at different points.

For a quick reference check, The Khronos Group also supplies a handy reference card at:

https://www.khronos.org/opengles/sdk/docs/reference_cards/OpenGL-ES-2_0-Reference-card.pdf

Again bookmark this on your browser bar or better yet, print it out and put it on the wall next to where you work.

In addition, I hope my publisher does not object, but the primary reference book for OpenGLES2.0 is the so-called Gold Book, endorsed by the Khronos Group: *OpenGLES 2.0 Programming Guide* by Aaftab Munshi, Dan Ginsburg, Dave Shreiner (2008; Addison-Wesley Professional; Upper Saddle River, NJ). A copy of this book is considered to be essential to keep by your side when working on OpenGLES2.0. It's not as easy to find as it once was, but the updated version for OpenGLES3.0 is almost as usable.

So Much Typing?

One of the *problems* with OpenGLES 2.0, is that, unlike its predecessor OpenGLES1.1 it needs a lot of setting up, specifically it needs fancy bits of code called *Shaders*, because OpenGL 2.0 onward uses them, and OpenGLES1.1 doesn't. Coding ES1.1 was, therefore, sometimes a lot easier and setting it up didn't need as much effort.

So why not take the easy route and start with OpenGLES 1.1, after all Shaders are also a little bit complex for a beginner, and in some ways are a special kind of new code mystery we could do without as we have to learn a ton of new things, but though almost all SBC targets support OpenGLES1.1, it's pretty obsolete now and we should try to make use of the best API we have.

We're not really going to do any Shader work till much later, so we can content ourselves with some very simple *get things running*, type Shaders. But we still have to type them in and at this point we have no idea what they are doing…so it's a potential minefield of confusion I want to avoid. But it's a minefield we'll get to grips with later when we are more comfortable with what we are doing.

For now, we need to create a project, set it up to initialize OpenGLES2.0 and then get it to set a screen up for us to draw to. That's the most fundamental basics we have to do first, the rest will fall into that. So if you want to start fresh rather than load the GameProject1 files, let's get started.

▮ Our First Graphics Project!

Let's start a new project as we did before, by clicking on FILE→New then Project to bring up the New Project Dialog Boxes.

Just like before we are going to select the VisualGDB template, choose a Linux Project Wizard, and enter our project as GameProject1. This is the last time I'm going to explain this process, so make sure you totally understand it, from now on I'll just tell you to set up a project, you can refer back to this or the previous example if you really need to. But it's pretty intuitive, so I'm sure you'll know what you're doing now.

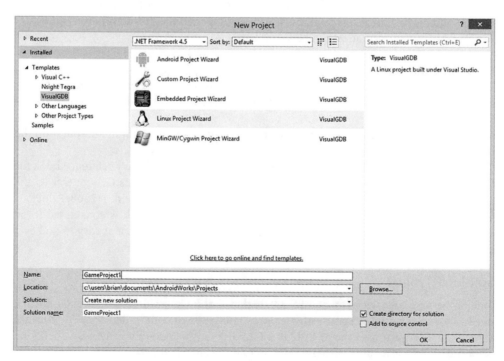

Make sure you name it and put it in a suitable file path. This example is not suitable, because it is using *previous use*; default path to the Android projects I had been working on before I did this example. Take note to check the directory before you click OK. I'll enter a path to my SBC projects instead. Once done, pressing ok, takes us to the type of project we want to build.

We are now once again at the New Linux Project Dialog box, which should be set to use your choice of make; as I've said before I tend to prefer GNU make, especially for target-based building. For Language standard, Choose C++ for a simple Hello world start project.

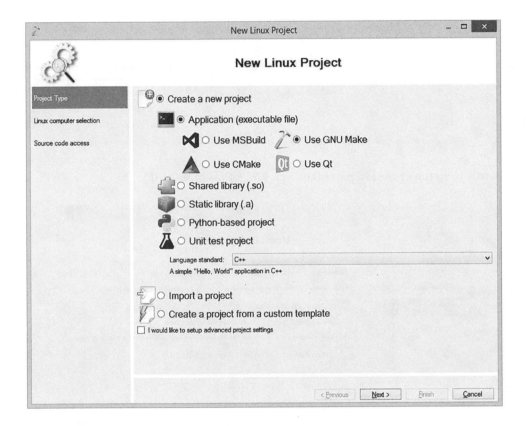

If you have this, just hit next and then repeat the earlier process for connecting your machine, though if the IP address has not changed you no longer need to set up a new SSH connection.

Click Next, let the wizard do its thing to take you to the second page of New Linux Project where you can enter your targets detail. Then once more click on Next, it will do a bunch of checks to make sure that the connection is good.

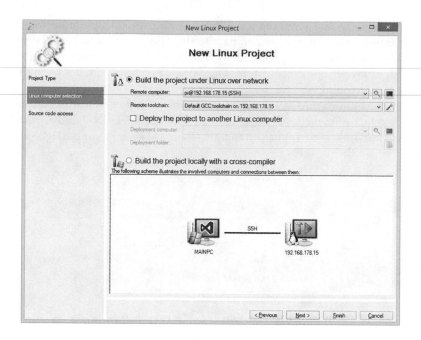

Finally bringing up the last part of the New Linux Project Wizard.

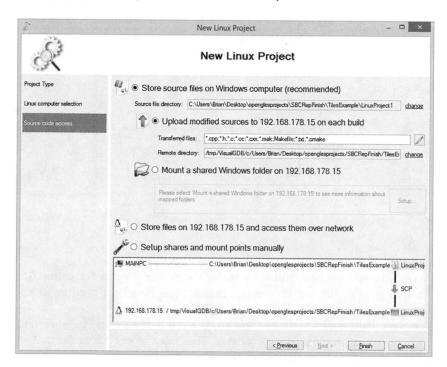

Where you now get the chance to add the list of transferred files and make changes to the way files are accessed. You don't usually need to alter anything from the defaults, and if you know all the file types you are going to add, you can list them in the Transferred files. But if you don't it's ok, it's possible to add them later.

At this point, you think we'd be ready to go, but no, all we've done is set up a standard C++ project, not a graphic project. We're going to use OpenGLES2.0 and perhaps a few other things that use header files that related to prebuild libraries...so we have to add those to our project.

Click on the VS Project tab and at the bottom you will see VisualGDB Project properties.

This brings up this the Project properties, select Makefile Settings, and you should get a pretty empty list of Configuration settings.

Add this line to include directories.

/opt/vc/include/opt/vc/include/interface/vcos/pthreads/opt/vc/include/interface/opt/vc/include/interface/vmcs_host/linux

And this line to Library directories.

/opt/vc/lib

And finally these *names to* Library names

GLESv2 EGL bcm_host

(*Take note, if not using a Raspberry Pi, you'll need different directories and libs, see Appendix 1*) As this book was going to press, The Raspberry Foundation, released an updated version of Rasbian, which annoyingly uses different and new library names which you may need to use if you have downloaded a fresh version of Rasbian. Please add/replace these library names to your VisualGDB properties>Makefile settings>Library names, section. This is a great example of having to be flexible and adapt as systems change and evolve over time. Check the support site for any other updates that might be needed

GLESv2_static (name change)

EGL_static (name change)

vchiq_arm (new library)

vcos (new library)

khrn_static (new library)

So you have a properties sheet like this;

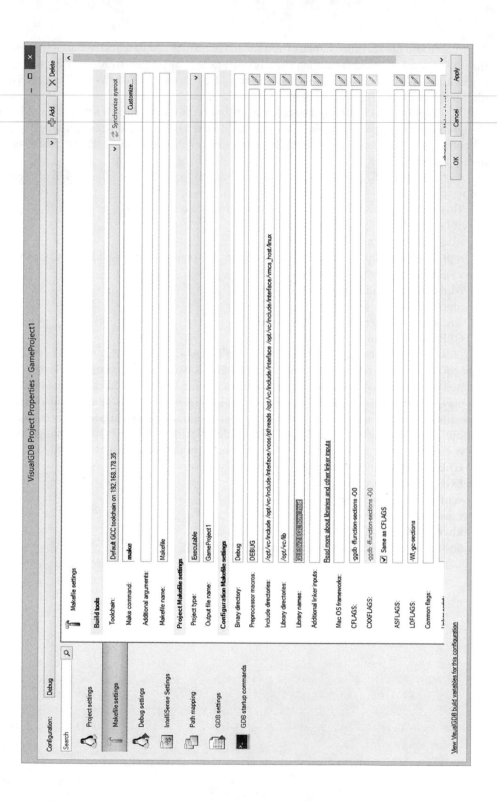

What we have done is tell the compiler (on the Raspberry Pi) to look inside three important directories on the Pi itself, which contain the Raspberry Pi's very own versions of OpenGLES2.0 and a special exclusive library called bcm_host to allow graphic coding on the Broadcom GPU. It's not needed with other GPUs and I'll explain later how to prevent it from being compiled when it's not needed.

There are actually a whole bundle of different libraries on your Raspberry Pi that will probably get used at some point in later projects. Other SBCs may require you to download and install these libraries and locate them yourself.

For the next couple of projects, this is all we will need, but later we will add more system libs, as we need extra features that we know are available in the libraries that come supplied with the Raspberry Pi, or are supplied by third parties.

When we click Apply or Ok, we may have to wait just a little while as the directories we listed will now be transferred and cached to our PC, because I'm on a wifi network, this takes a minute or two, but once done we are ready to go.

Good now we're finally ready to go with our standard boring blank graphic project, I won't repeat this process too often in future setups, except when explaining something that will be markedly different.

▮ Are We There Yet?

No, not quite. That was just us loading the car; we still have a journey to make.

Hello World is the first thing we traditionally do when writing a text program, when writing a graphics project, traditionally the first thing we do is draw a triangle, so let's not alter the tradition. The OpenGLES2.0 Programming guide, informally known as the Gold Book describes this as the Hello Triangle, so let's do our own twist on Hello Triangle.

▮ Houston We Have a Triangle

It seems like eons ago I suggested we do something really simple to start with and put a triangle on screen, but now we can make a start on it.

We have a lot of things we need to set up, until that's done, we can't get anything on screen, so we need to first of all create what's called a render surface, which is basically the image we want to display on our screen, using something called EGL, which is a low-level API that sits above the core OpenGLES2.0 code, and acts as a collection of helper routines to get things going and provides the direct link to your video hardware.

We also have to do something about our Shaders, even though we have no idea at the moment what they actually do, OpenGLES2.0 insist we have some. Talk about carts before horses?

Then we have to actually do the creation and drawing (rendering) of our triangle.

Then make it visible!

These steps all need to be set up before we can even begin to see something. That is just so much work! But that's just how it is, once we've got these ideas worked out and coded, we don't really have to think about them again, so let's bite the bullet and make a start.

The first thing we have to do (after setting up our project of course) is remove the contents of that example's main function; we need something a bit more substantial.

We also need to deal with the fact that not everyone reading this is using a Raspberry Pi, even though most of you are using a target that accepts our C/C++ code, will compile to our target machine's CPU code, we may find that we have different GPUs. And that creates a few minor differences in how we can set up and initialize our code.

Broadcom GPUs on Raspberry, Mali, on most others, but also Power VR on some, need slightly different libs, and slightly different setups. So we should be aware of that and later we will keep our OpenGLES2.0 setup code in a separate file, which will make it easier for us to track that, for now though let's have it as a simple single file project.

Also some of us might want to try and run our projects on PC and our targets. Now the level of variety in our GPU has scaled up quite a bit, but this is quite a handy thing to be able to do, especially if you want to work away from your target machine.

Ok let's first do our project on our target, then talk about setting up different systems, this is a variation on the *standard* OpenGLES2.0 project modified to run on a Raspberry Pi, a Raspberry, and non-Raspberry version can be found on the support site, but please try to type this in and get some practice handling some strange looking code to let you get used to Visual Studio and understand the compile process.

You're almost certain to make typos and omissions, so this small program is a good start to help you learn where to find the errors and fix them.

Before you enter the code though, make sure you go into you VGDB proper and add the correct library paths and names to the Makefile settings. If you don't then the standard OpenGL libraries present on your Raspberry Pi (I'll explain other targets later) will not be located and you cannot compile.

So be sure to add the following include and library directories and names as seen in this screen pic;

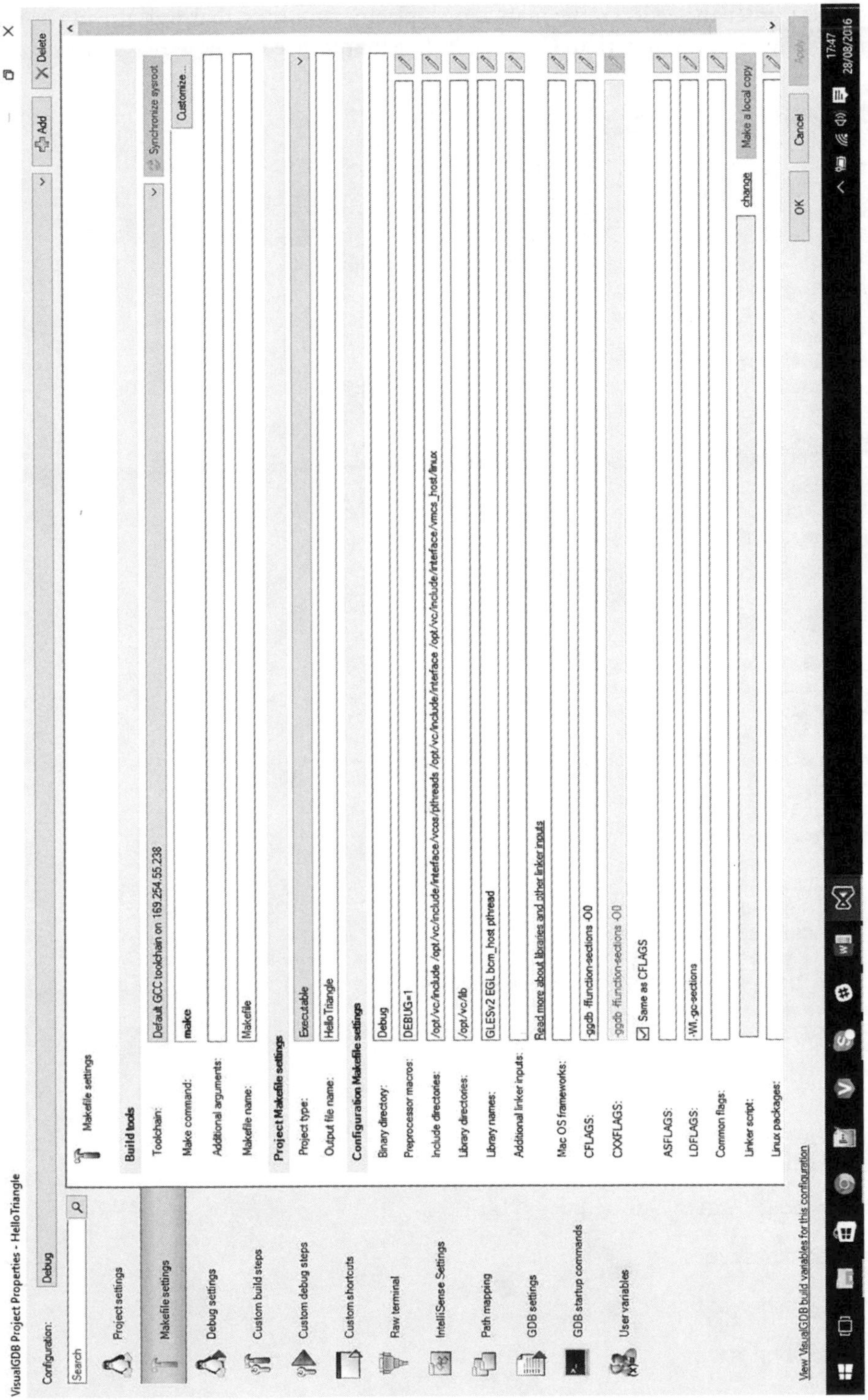

VisualGDB Project Properties - Hello Triangle

Configuration: Debug

Search

- Project settings
- Makefile settings
- Debug settings
- Custom build steps
- Custom debug steps
- Custom shortcuts
- Raw terminal
- IntelliSense Settings
- Path mapping
- GDB settings
- GDB startup commands
- User variables

Makefile settings

Build tools

Toolchain:	Default GCC toolchain on 169.254.55.238
Make command:	make
Additional arguments:	
Makefile name:	Makefile

Project Makefile settings

Project type:	Executable
Output file name:	Hello Triangle

Configuration Makefile settings

Binary directory:	Debug
Preprocessor macros:	DEBUG=1
Include directories:	/opt/vc/include /opt/vc/include/interface/vcos/pthreads /opt/vc/include/interface /opt/vc/include/interface/vmcs_host/linux
Library directories:	/opt/vc/lib
Library names:	GLESv2 EGL bcm_host pthread
Additional linker inputs:	Read more about libraries and other linker inputs
Mac OS frameworks:	
CFLAGS:	-ggdb -ffunction-sections -O0
CXXFLAGS:	-ggdb -ffunction-sections -O0
	☑ Same as CFLAGS
ASFLAGS:	
LDFLAGS:	-Wl,-gc-sections
Common flags:	
Linker script:	change
Linux packages:	

Make a local copy

Synchronize sysroot
Customize ...

Add   Delete

OK   Cancel   Apply

View VisualGDB build variables for this configuration

Now, let's enter the code, in the main.cpp, replacing anything that was already in there. This is written in C rather than C++ but its fine for our needs.

▐ Behold the Triangle Code!

```c
/* Hello Triangle
code adapted from OpenGL® ES 2.0 Programming Guide
and code snippets from RPI Forum to set up Dispmanx
*/

#include <stdio.h>
#include <assert.h>
#include <math.h>
#include <sys/time.h>
#include "bcm_host.h"
#include <EGL/egl.h>
#include <EGL/eglext.h>
#include <GLES2/gl2.h>

#define TRUE 1
#define FALSE 0

typedef struct
{
 //save a Handle to a program object
   GLuint programObject;
} UserData;

typedef struct Target_State
{
    uint32_t width;
    uint32_t height;

    EGLDisplay display;
    EGLSurface surface;
    EGLContext context;

    EGL_DISPMANX_WINDOW_T nativewindow;
     UserData *user_data;
    void(*draw_func)(struct Target_State*);

} Target_State;

Target_State state;
Target_State* p_state = &state;

static const EGLint attribute_list[] =
{
   EGL_RED_SIZE,
   8,
   EGL_GREEN_SIZE,
   8,
   EGL_BLUE_SIZE,
   8,
```

```
      EGL_ALPHA_SIZE,
      8,
      EGL_SURFACE_TYPE,
      EGL_WINDOW_BIT,
      EGL_NONE
};

static const EGLint context_attributes[] =
{
      EGL_CONTEXT_CLIENT_VERSION,
      2,
      EGL_NONE
};

/*
 Now we have be able to create a shader object, pass the shader source
 and then compile the shader.
*/
GLuint LoadShader(GLenum type, const char *shaderSrc)
{
// 1st create the shader object
      GLuint TheShader = glCreateShader(type);

      if (TheShader == 0) return 0; // can't allocate so stop.
      / pass the shader source
      glShaderSource(TheShader, 1, &shaderSrc, NULL);
// Compile the shader
      glCompileShader(TheShader);

      GLint  IsItCompiled;

// After the compile we need to check the status and report any errors
      glGetShaderiv(TheShader, GL_COMPILE_STATUS, &IsItCompiled);
      if (!IsItCompiled)
      {
        GLint RetinfoLen = 0;
        glGetShaderiv(TheShader, GL_INFO_LOG_LENGTH, &RetinfoLen);
        if (RetinfoLen > 1)
        { // standard output for errors
            char* infoLog = (char*) malloc(sizeof(char) * RetinfoLen);
            glGetShaderInfoLog(TheShader, RetinfoLen, NULL, infoLog);
            fprintf(stderr, "Error compiling this shader:\n%s\n", infoLog);
            free(infoLog);
        }
      glDeleteShader(TheShader);
      return 0;
 }
 return TheShader;
}

// Initialize the shader and program object
int Init(Target_State *p_state)
{
    p_state->user_data = (UserData*)malloc(sizeof(UserData));
```

```
        GLbyte vShaderStr[] =
             "attribute vec4 a_position;\n"
             "attribute vec2 a_texCoord;\n"
             "varying vec2 v_texCoord;\n"
             "void main()\n"
             "{gl_Position=a_position;\n"
             " v_texCoord=a_texCoord;}\n";


        GLbyte fShaderStr[] =
             "precision mediump float;\n"
             "varying vec2 v_texCoord;\n"
             "uniform sampler2D s_texture;\n"
             "void main()\n"
             "{gl_FragColor=vec4 (1.0,0.0,0.0,1.0);}\n";

      GLuint programObject,vertexShader, fragmentShader; // we need some
      variables

// Load and compile the vertex/fragment shaders
        vertexShader = LoadShader(GL_VERTEX_SHADER, (char*)vShaderStr);
        fragmentShader = LoadShader(GL_FRAGMENT_SHADER, (char*)fShaderStr);

// Create the program object
        programObject = glCreateProgram();
        if (programObject == 0)  return 0;

// now we have the V and F shaders  attach them to the program object
        glAttachShader(programObject, vertexShader);
        glAttachShader(programObject, fragmentShader);

// Link the program
        glLinkProgram(programObject);
// Check the link status
        GLint AreTheylinked;
        glGetProgramiv(programObject, GL_LINK_STATUS, &AreTheylinked);
        if (!AreTheylinked)
        {
          GLint RetinfoLen = 0;
// check and report any errors
          glGetProgramiv(programObject, GL_INFO_LOG_LENGTH, &RetinfoLen);
          if (RetinfoLen > 1)
          {
            GLchar* infoLog = (GLchar*)malloc(sizeof(char) * RetinfoLen);
            glGetProgramInfoLog(programObject, RetinfoLen, NULL, infoLog);
            fprintf(stderr, "Error linking program:\n%s\n", infoLog);
            free(infoLog);
          }
          glDeleteProgram(programObject);
          return FALSE;
        }

        // Store the program object
        p_state->user_data->programObject = programObject;
        glClearColor(0.0f, 0.0f, 0.0f, 1.0f);
        return TRUE;
}
```

```
void init_ogl(Target_State *state, int width, int height)
{
            int32_t success = 0;
            EGLBoolean result;
            EGLint num_config;
//RPI setup is a little different to normal EGL
            DISPMANX_ELEMENT_HANDLE_T DispmanElementH;
            DISPMANX_DISPLAY_HANDLE_T DispmanDisplayH;
            DISPMANX_UPDATE_HANDLE_T DispmanUpdateH;
            VC_RECT_T dest_rect;
            VC_RECT_T src_rect;
            EGLConfig config;
// get an EGL display connection
            state->display = eglGetDisplay(EGL_DEFAULT_DISPLAY);
// initialize the EGL display connection
            result = eglInitialize(state->display, NULL, NULL);
// get an appropriate EGL frame buffer configuration
            result = eglChooseConfig(state->display, attribute_list,
            &config, 1, &num_config);
            assert(EGL_FALSE != result);

// get an appropriate EGL frame buffer configuration
            result = eglBindAPI(EGL_OPENGL_ES_API);
            assert(EGL_FALSE != result);
// create an EGL rendering context
            state->context = eglCreateContext(state->display, config, EGL_
            NO_CONTEXT, context_attributes);
            assert(state->context != EGL_NO_CONTEXT);
// create an EGL window surface
            state->width = width;
            state->height = height;

            dest_rect.x = 0;
            dest_rect.y = 0;
            dest_rect.width = state->width; // it needs to know our window
            size
            dest_rect.height = state->height;

            src_rect.x = 0;
            src_rect.y = 0;

            DispmanDisplayH = vc_dispmanx_display_open(0);
            DispmanUpdateH = vc_dispmanx_update_start(0);

            DispmanElementH =  vc_dispmanx_element_add(
                DispmanUpdateH,
                DispmanDisplayH,
                0/*layer*/,
                &dest_rect,
                0/*source*/,
                &src_rect,
                DISPMANX_PROTECTION_NONE,
                0 /*alpha value*/,
                0/*clamp*/,
                (DISPMANX_TRANSFORM_T) 0/*transform*/);
        state->nativewindow.element = DispmanElementH;
        state->nativewindow.width = state->width;
        state->nativewindow.height = state->height;
        vc_dispmanx_update_submit_sync(DispmanUpdateH);
```

```
        state->surface = eglCreateWindowSurface(state->display, config,
        &(state->nativewindow), NULL);
        assert(state->surface != EGL_NO_SURFACE);
        // connect the context to the surface
        result = eglMakeCurrent(state->display, state->surface, state-
        >surface, state->context);
        assert(EGL_FALSE != result);
}

/********************************************
Draw a triangle this is a hard coded
draw which is only good for the triangle
*********************************************/
void Draw(Target_State *p_state)
{
        UserData *userData = p_state->user_data;
        GLfloat TriVertices[] =
        {
                0.0f ,   0.5f, 0.0f,
                -0.5f, -0.5f, 0.0f,
                0.5f ,  -0.5f, 0.0f
        };

// Setup the viewport
        glViewport(0, 0, p_state->width, p_state->height);
// Clear the color buffer
        glClear(GL_COLOR_BUFFER_BIT);
// Use the program object
        glUseProgram(userData->programObject);
// Load the vertex data
        glVertexAttribPointer(0, 3, GL_FLOAT, GL_FALSE, 0, TriVertices);
        glEnableVertexAttribArray(0);
        glDrawArrays(GL_TRIANGLES, 0, 3);
        if (glGetError() != GL_NO_ERROR) printf("Oh bugger");
}

void esInitContext(Target_State *p_state)
{
        if (p_state != NULL)
        {
            memset(p_state, 0, sizeof(Target_State));
        }
}

void esRegisterDrawFunc(Target_State *p_state, void(*draw_func)
(Target_State*))
{
        p_state->draw_func = draw_func;
}

void  esMainLoop(Target_State *esContext)
{
        int Counter = 0; / keep a counter
        while (Counter++ <200)
        {
            if (esContext->draw_func != NULL)
              esContext->draw_func(esContext);
// after our draw we need to swap buffers to display
          eglSwapBuffers(esContext->display, esContext->surface);
```

```
        }
}
int main(int argc, char *argv[])
{
        UserData user_data;
        bcm_host_init(); //RPI needs this
        esInitContext(p_state);
        init_ogl(p_state, 1024, 720);
        p_state->user_data = &user_data;

        if (!Init(p_state))
            return 0;
        esRegisterDrawFunc(p_state, Draw);
// now go do the graphic loop
        esMainLoop(p_state);
}
```

Sorry for making you type all that, but you'll thank me one day. You will probably make a few errors, and it won't work for the first time. Even if it seems to compile and run, but not do what you expect, it will have errors. That's normal, you need to develop some practice in finding mistakes, usually small ones, such as a missing line, or a mistyped symbol, but whatever you do, do not cling to the dogma, that you typed it in exactly...because if it does not work, you didn't! Be cool with that. Learning to accept you will make errors, often, oh so often, and taking responsibility for those errors so you can find and fix them, is vitally important to being a responsible programmer.

There's not really a lot to this code, but it is confusing that you have to do so much to do so little. At this point, I'm not going to explain everything in here; the comments can do that for you. But this will serve the purpose of making sure you can compile and run an OpenGLES 2.0 project.

Compile and run, and, all being well, lo and behold, we have a triangle.

Now all this is fine and dandy and you can take some pride in getting this up and running if you typed it in yourself. But I find most entry-level programmers who are trying to write games, come across this or similar small start-up programs, and then realize there is a massive disconnection between putting a triangle or square on screen and their latest, poly laden 60GB game on the consoles. Sadly this often stops them in their tracks because it's just too big a disconnection for them to see a way forward.

And they are right, there is a massive disconnect, it's totally confusing. But it's mostly a case of scale. That 60GB game is simply moving a lot of triangles around, and it's using the code that allows the programmer to manage how many of these triangles are drawn at any given time and in any given way, in any given color. The problem we have is that we now know how to draw a triangle, but we don't really have any idea how to create games with it. That management of the way we draw things is much more important to us than the actual mechanisms that draw all the pixels on screen.

There are not many games that you can do with one static, colored but rather uninteresting triangle, but this is mainly a test, we know it compiles, transfers, and runs on our target, so we should be confident that everything works, the key point here is we have four basic game program features in place that we coded ourselves, and can now expand on.

- An initialization system.

- A processing system, which will/can include user input or counters and will later include enemies/AI.

- A display system—which loops back to the processing until we decide to end creating a main loop.

- An exit.

These four things are vital to almost any game program, the concept of a main loop is especially important, and though there are variations on how it's done, almost all games have these. But it's time now, to make something cool happens.

▮ Why Are We Working in a Window?

One thing we might have noticed is that our triangle display isn't filling the screen, it's living in a small window…that's ok, we can work with that, and there will certainly be situations when it is desirable but for games, really it's better to get the system to fill the screen, I could just change the line.

```
init_ogl(p_state, 1024, 720);
```

To 1920 and 1080, and I'd get it filling up the screen but if I did I be making a big mistake, which some, but not all of you reading will have issues with. Let me explain:

On most HDMI-displayed targets the physical pixel size of our screen is fixed, that's probably going to be 1920 × 1080 but notice I said probably. We really cannot always assume that our potential end user has the same screen setup as us. There are some who are using 320 × 200 pixel LCD panels, some on 800 × 600 panels, some on 720p HDMI, and so on.

Common sense allows us to discount anything that is way too small to use, or way too big for our limited target to handle, we can put minimum and maximum limits on our project, so let's assume a smallest screen size of 320 × 200 and a max up to…well 2560 × 1920 isn't impossible, but 1920 × 1080 is more common.

There are a whole range of *standard* screen sizes between targets. That lack of consistency is an annoyance but one we have to deal with, so we need to think of our size values as variables so that we can easily change them and avoid the so-called, Hard-coded or Magic, numbers, which can never be changed in a running project.

We will try to get information from our target system values or in a worst case from our users, that we can store and use when needed. On Raspberry Pi, the Broadcom libs provide a useful little routine to return the physical pixel size of our display screen, other targets may have a similar system. Unfortunately, standard Linux machines don't usually have this trick, they may have others. But the ability to work to a full screen directly with no apparent window is one of the Raspberry Pi's rather cute specific tricks. But in all targets we need to use something called an EGL window, on a screen size dictated by you or your OS. If I find a way to get a standard Linux to do full screen (it is always possible) I'll update this. For now then full screen display is a Raspberry Pi thing only.

Once we have our screen's physical size, we can then make a decision on how big our working size or window, should be, then let our GPU scale our working size to fit our physical size.

So if we want full screen, we do this;

```
uint width, height;
graphics_get_display_size(0, &width, &height);
```

This simple little routine, does exactly what it says it does, it gets the size of the current display, and stores the result in the variable's width and height.

After that we can then use the values in the init_ogl routine to create a full size screen.

```
init_ogl(p_state, width, height);
```

Now that the little trick, will for now, on a Raspberry Pi,* allow our projects to run on pretty much any screen size and be visible, regardless of the actual pixel resolution we set. Let's get on with making a project that puts this to use.

▎ 2D

We are going to start our game-programming journey with some 2D games; I know some of you want to leap right into your grand, photo quality Hi Def, 3D, Massively MultiUser Online Cloud processing realistic AI with real lasers, game. But trust me, getting the basics right is very important and also a load of fun!

Many if not all the concepts used in 2D games are directly transferred to 3D games and allow you the chance to properly visualize what you are doing, and measure it against what you were expecting.

I often try to explain to my students with my tongue loosely in my cheek, how Space Invaders and Halo are basically the same game. You control a character; you can move around and shoot things, while at the same time trying to avoid being shot by those same things.

---

* Other systems use slightly different means to determine the screen size; this is noted on the support site.

They are essentially the same game, only the visualization, level of complexity, and amounts of data being shoved onto our screen are variable.

It's quite possible to break any shooting style game down to the basics of moving around, shooting while avoiding being shot. If we simply consider that as being what we have to code, we can add the complexity and additional eye candy as we go.

Of course, there are many other types of 2D game, Puzzle games, platform games, and racing games, the list is probably endless, and trying to cover them all, even in a book as big as this, is going to extremes, but you will be able to employ the concepts explained here in any kind of game, and more importantly you'll be able to expand and develop the concepts to suit any new game genre you are lucky enough to think of.

4 Putting It All Together

Expanding Our First Graphics Program

So far we've not done anything that has needed actual *graphics*, our triangle and possibly other shapes you might have dabbled with are mathematical concepts rather than images as we recognize images, we can alter their color and size but there's no actual image or texture yet and that will severely limit the games we can produce.

This is mainly because displaying actual graphics that look like chomping a yellow pizza, or avenging hammer-wielding plumbers, is a whole new set of problems we have to introduce and get over. But if we want to be game programmers we need to have the ability to display images, which are either created by the program (procedural graphics) or produced by someone or something else (assets) for incorporation into our program.

Loading Graphics or Other Assets

It's not impossible to enter graphics into our project as typed data, but it's extremely impractical for anything more than a small monochrome image. Modern games have gigabytes of graphic images, and converting them into source data would be a monumental and unwelcome task. So instead, our assets are usually stored in a usable file format on our storage system for loading into the program and set up to use in the game.

So now we've reached the point we need to load something from the computer's storage system, which ideally we have made or downloaded from our PC. Since we are doing remote building, we are going to take advantage of the transfer of data that VisualGDB handles for us more or less automatically.

Anything that is not actually compiled but is instead used by your program is called a resource or an Asset, the terms are often interchangeable, but I prefer *Assets* when talking about graphics, or sound data. I use the term *Resources* to describe other files that may provide information to or be used in our project, such as a script or list file of some kind. I may be wrong with this terminology, but no CS graduate has ever told me different.

But assets are what we need to get access to, at this point we need to load some simple images, and then find a way to display them.

Loading files is a pretty simple thing, C/C++ STL gives us loading and saving abilities, but graphics are not just files, they are *data* files, data which are actually encrypted into a particular format, and there are many formats.

We simply don't have the time (our 30 days of free VisualGDB will fade away in no time) to write decryption system to turn graphic files into simple pixel data that we can actually draw on screen, so we need some way to do that.

Lucky for us the world is full of programming geeks, who like to write graphic systems that we can use freely.

As I write this after a short session of getting things set up, I have come up against a few issues. My intention was to use a simple standard library called Simple OpenGL Image Library (SOIL), because it is free, available for Linux-based systems, and quite easy to get hold of. But as I tried to install it I had nothing but hassle, because of my Raspberry Pi being unable to install the libs. Now it may just be that the mirror site is down today, or that since I'm not that up-to-date with Linux, I was doing something wrong, but I didn't want to spend days waiting for it, so I decided to try another approach.

SOIL itself is a wrapper program for collection of image-manipulation programs, including an Image Loader called stb_image, which is a widely supported and reasonably easy to use, set of routines to load various common formats. It's actually all we really want from SOIL, it also works just fine for Linux…so let's work just with that. It's simple enough to get hold of. If you have a Git client on your PC it's available from GitHub, if not, go to…

https:/github.com/nothings/stb

And download the Zip file (Button on the top right).

This will give you a whole load of files contained in the zip, but for now, we only want stb_image.h, but you will probably use a few of the others later as we get more up to speed with the process, and maybe I'll get SOIL to actually install properly one day!

Let's set about adding stb_image to our project.

I won't ask you to type in another long initialization system, we can use the Hello Triangle for now; we're just experimenting with a file loader.

Look inside the SOIL zip for stb_image.h and copy it into your projects source directory; in this case, it's just going to be in the root directory of our project. If you are unsure where your root directory is, just right click on your HelloTriangle.cpp file and select Open Containing Folder, which will open it up for you allowing you to copy things into it with ease. Go ahead and copy stb_image.h from the zip into your project directory.

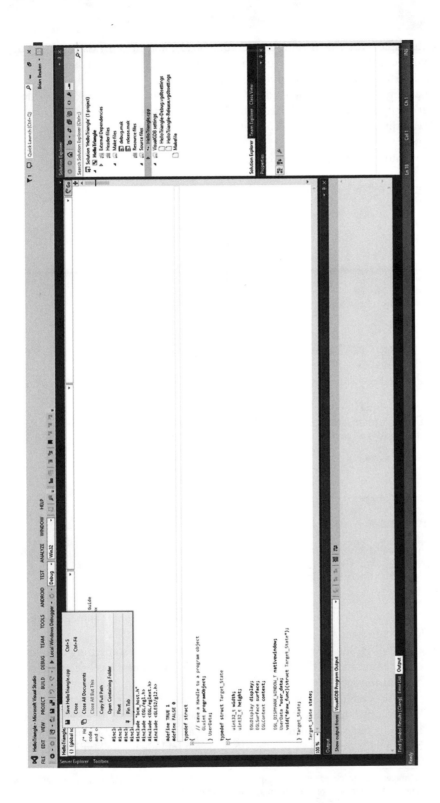

Once its copied you can then add it to your header files as an existing file, but that's optional, we're hopefully never going to edit it, so its existence in an accessible folder is more important than its inclusion in the solution.

That done, I also need you to add two new files to this: a header and a cpp file.

Let's call the header as MyFiles.h and the cpp as MyFiles.cpp.

Try adding them to the correct solution *filter*, which looks like a folder on your solution view.

Now into MyFiles.h, add this code;

```
#pragma once
class MyFiles
{
public:
  MyFiles();
  ~MyFiles();
  int height;
  int width;
  int comp;
  char* Load(char const *filename,int*,int*);
};
```

That's, it's pretty easy, we're creating a small wrapper class that will allow us to load a graphic file and convert it into normal raw memory.

The actual code for this now goes into the MyFiles.cpp file and looks like this:

```
#include "MyFiles.h"
#define STB_IMAGE_IMPLEMENTATION
#include "stb_image.h"

MyFiles::MyFiles()
{}

MyFiles::~MyFiles()
{}
  char* MyFiles::Load(char const *filename,int* width, int* height)
{
      unsigned char *data = stbi_load(filename, width, height, &comp, 4);
      // we are always going to ask for 4 components for RGBA
      return (char*) data;
}
```

Now we have two very useful files...which will allow any program that includes them to be able to load some standard image* formats.

Try compiling this, it won't do much but there should be something to take note of! Did you notice that adding that file means that our build process has become a lot slower?

Try compiling again? It was very fast that time.

The first slow build is because this header stb_image.h header file is actually quite large and includes many other files. Also because it's a header file, if we included it in our main project it's going to get compiled EVERY time we alter the file that includes the header... that's a bit of a pain. Because we put the stb_image.h include in the Myfiles.cpp that's only

---

* Standard images usually include png, bmp, tga, and jpg, but do be aware that there are some variations in the formats and you need to be sure that stb_image can handle your image.

likely to ever get built one time, and then the resulting code that's made from that is reused over and over again. As long as we know how to create and load our files, which we do by including the MyFiles.h we won't need to compile the header file on every build.

We can use that for all subsequent 2D graphic loading needs in our games. Just make sure we have an instance of a MyFiles object somewhere and include the MyFiles file in the other classes that want to use it.

For now, we should have managed to get our project to build and run, but of course we don't have any graphics to actually load, and because we are remote compiling, we need to get them onto the Pi at the compile time…

▐ Adding Assets to the Build Chain

VisualGDB uses a feature called file synchronization when using remote compiling, which essentially means that any files we tell it are important, are checked with the copy files on the Raspberry Pi, and if we've changed them on the PC they will be updated on the Raspberry Pi.

This is, of course, essential for the compiler to be able to compile all our cool CPP and H files, but it has the extra benefit of automatically sending over any assets we define as needed and creates copies on the target automatically. This is why we're sticking with remote compiling for the moment rather than the much faster Cross-Compiling system we could have!

That's something we've already done, when we set up the VisualGDB link, the most important thing is to tell it about the types of files we are interested in. As we are going to use graphics, I'm going to use a .jpg image; it's a common compressed image. And as you can see in the files to transfer I've added;*.jpg

Be very careful not to have any spaces in your files to transfer list. I accidently added;<space> *.jpg when I was setting this up, which led to much confusion when my jpg files were not sent across.

Of course, there are many other formats, feel free to add ;*.png;*.bmp;*.GIF, and so on. Make sure you have the *include all subdirectories* option ticked as that will also force the target to create these important subdirectories when things synchronize.

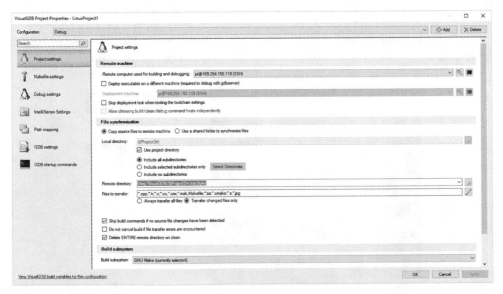

▮ Keeping Things Tidy

Now that means we will send over any jpg files we happen to add to the project folder, but it's not a good idea to just dump all your graphics into the project folder, we really need a proper folder structure, so I'm going to add an Assets folder.

I think it's also a good point now to add header and source folders and from now on add our header files to the header folder and our cpp files to the source folder, later when we do some assembly coding, we will also have an assembler folder.

Folder management is one of those never-ending debates about how your project should be arranged and there are good arguments for having different file types in different folders, but really just try to keep code and data and other resources clean and separate and it'll all look good.

For now, let's add the assets folder, and also add a filter in our Visual Studio Solution to keep it looking tidy.

Visual Studio allows you to add new filters to the solution view frame, but even though it uses the tradition folder style Icon, it is not actually creating new folders in your projects directory of your PC. This is both a blessing and a curse, because it allows us to keep all the files with .h or .cpp endings in one view on the solution view, but it does mean that we may have added those files from any number of different folders in our directory.

That's the curse part, our system of transferring data down to the target really relies on us having a root folder, where our project is stored and then transferring all the files we need from that root and its subfolders to the target. So to allow our assets to be accessible, which are not actually compiled, our assets folder needs to live on the root. When we compile our games, the systems on both machines will create extra folders for debug and release builds. And we can step back one folder then into our assets folder with simple filenames that have the following format:

```
"../Assets/filename.ext"
```

If we don't keep our folders and files under control, it can get quite messy quite quickly, it's very tempting to put all our files in the same root folder and just use filters. I've seen this done often but it's not a good practice, even though we're doing it now we are going to change it later, it will all depend mostly on where we decide to put files when we add them to the project. But folders containing assets are best located on the root directory.

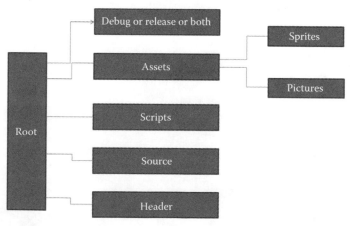

You should see now that if our executable is in a Debug folder then *../Assets/Sprites/fname* takes us down one level *../* to root, then switches to Assets then Sprites, so we can get our file from that folder.

Then when the time comes to send files over, the system checks the headers in the root, and all its subfolders, sending the required files to the target and making new subdirectories on the target when needed.

▍ Add Some Code

Let's try to load and display an image, nothing fancy, just find a decent-sized image, smaller than your screen size, but big enough to be seen, something from 512 × 512 up to 1024 × 1024, that will fit on screen and be visible. When you have one save it to your assets folder.

Ok we now have an image, let's make a small program to display it.

If you don't have any suitable images on your PC, have a hunt on the old interwebaroonies for an image that you would like to use, ideally png, jpg, or tga, for this. Copy/download it into your Assets folder and be sure to add the file extension into your Project settings *files to transfer* list.

You can add any number of images, and alter the file name to load them.

So far so good, we have been able to load an image, store it in its raw data format in memory somewhere, and it's now ready for display.

Our loading and graphic conversion systems are now in place, but currently we are still only able to draw a triangle, which isn't ideal; images are usually rectangular, so we should alter the draw routine to draw two triangle and make a square, that's ok, but we are also going to turn whatever we load into data that can be displayed on the square in the form of a texture.

Two things now are needed: (1) the ability to create a texture and (2) the ability to display that texture using a different form of draw.

Add this code to your project, near the top, just before LoadShader, it's self-contained, though at the moment pretty nonfunctional as it needs data to work with. Data we have to load in. Even then though it can create a texture at the moment there's no way to draw it.

```
/* Create a texture with width and height */
GLuint CreateTexture2D(int width, int height, char* TheData)
{
 // Texture handle
 GLuint textureId;
 // Set the alignment
 glPixelStorei(GL_UNPACK_ALIGNMENT, 1);
 // Generate a texture object
 glGenTextures(1, &textureId);
 // Bind the texture object
 glBindTexture(GL_TEXTURE_2D, textureId);
 // set it up
 glTexImage2D(GL_TEXTURE_2D,
   0,
   GL_RGBA,
   width,
   height,
   0,
   GL_RGBA,
```

```
    GL_UNSIGNED_BYTE,
    TheData);

if (glGetError() != GL_NO_ERROR) printf("Oh bugger");
// Set the filtering mode
glTexParameteri(GL_TEXTURE_2D, GL_TEXTURE_MIN_FILTER, GL_NEAREST);
glTexParameteri(GL_TEXTURE_2D, GL_TEXTURE_MAG_FILTER, GL_NEAREST);
glTexParameteri(GL_TEXTURE_2D, GL_TEXTURE_WRAP_S, GL_CLAMP_TO_EDGE);
glTexParameteri(GL_TEXTURE_2D, GL_TEXTURE_WRAP_T, GL_CLAMP_TO_EDGE);
if (glGetError() == GL_NO_ERROR) return textureId;
printf("Oh bugger");
return textureId;
}
```

We need some data; I've added a few nice pics from my photo album in the assets listed on the support site. But for this first attempt at doing graphics, let's use the most famous public domain graphic test image there is. Lenna.png.

Our task now is to load this in, convert it to a texture, and then display it. We have the load part, though we must first make sure that the image is located on our source directory for now. Later we'll tidy up the directories, and more important we have to ensure that we add the *.png to the type of files that are transferred to our target.

I like to add the image to the solution too, for now add it to your resources filter. Let's load it up and convert it. After the FileHandler add this code;

```
    MyFiles FileHandler;
/ now go do the graphic loop
    int Width, Height;
    char* OurRawData = FileHandler.Load((char*)"../Lenna.png", &Width,
&Height);
    if (OurRawData == NULL) printf("We failed to load\n");
```

Note that I have purposefully put a small test to report a failed load. Because at the moment we're not actually able to display this, so we'll never know if it loaded. Error traps like this are invaluable to make sure you don't write buggy code while blind, and assume later that it's the draw routines that have failed. Try mistyping Lenna and compile and run to make sure you get a notice telling you that it failed.

Loading, is done, we're also pretty sure that converting to texture code is done, so time to worry about drawing.

Remember I told you OpenGLES2.0 used Shaders? Well there's a first clue as to what will need changing, our current; triangle shader does very little, it simply draws a red pixel, we now need a shader that will take a pixel from a texture and draw it.

Look at the shader code in Init again. Check out this line

```
"{gl_FragColor=vec4 (1.0,0.0,0.0,1.0);}\n";
```

This is the main line that needs to be changed so that it can do more than just write a red pixel.

You may have noticed the shader code itself, references other variables: a_position, a_texCoord, v_texcoord, and so on.

We never actually did anything to set up those variables, because for the most part they were ignored as we are just dumping a hard pixel to screen.

They need to come into play now, and be part of our program somewhere as these provide a means to access particular pixels for any modifications we need. I don't want to get into this too much as I am going to assume that you're still finding your feet with coding, so explaining how this shader works could be confusing, so for the moment all I'm going to do is set it. Explanations will come later when we really need them.

Here's what your Shaders should now look like. The gl_FragColour is now going to take a value from a texture coordinate.

```
GLbyte vShaderStr[] =
  "attribute vec4 a_position;\n"
  "attribute vec2 a_texCoord;\n"
  "varying vec2 v_texCoord;\n"
  "void main()\n"
  "{gl_Position=a_position;\n"
  " v_texCoord = a_texCoord;}\n";

GLbyte fShaderStr[] =
  "precision mediump float;\n"
  "varying vec2 v_texCoord;\n"
  "uniform sampler2D s_texture;\n"
  "void main()\n"
  "{\n"
  "gl_FragColor = texture2D( s_texture, v_texCoord );\n"
  "}\n";
```

Without going into massive confusing detail, we can see that we are now using a few extra values in this shader, and our code needs somehow to know about this, which needs some additions, we have to tell our code about a_position, a_texCoord, and s_texture, and store handles to them in our structure so that we can set them up for our shader to work correctly.

Now go back to the top of your code, alter the UserData Structure so that it looks like this:

```
typedef struct
{
 // save a Handle to a program object
  GLuint programObject;
   // Attribute locations
  GLint positionLoc;
  GLint texCoordLoc;

   // Sampler location
  GLint samplerLoc;

   // Texture handle
  GLuint textureId;
}UserData;
```

Our structure now has values we can use to store the shader's attribute and sampler locations, so let's add some code to our Init routine to do that; at the end of Init, you can see we are loading a ProgramObject value (which is actually a duplication of a redundant ProgramObject variable you can remove) ...continue with the next three lines with save our location information so that we can set up the shader.

```
 // Store the program object
 p_state->user_data->programObject = programObject;

  // Get the attribute locations
 p_state->user_data->positionLoc = glGetAttribLocation(p_state->user_data-
>programObject, "a_position");
 p_state->user_data->texCoordLoc = glGetAttribLocation(p_state->user_data-
>programObject, "a_texCoord");

 // Get the sampler location
 p_state->user_data->samplerLoc = glGetUniformLocation(p_state->user_data-
>programObject, "s_texture");
```

Now that they exist they can be used, our draw routine needs quite a bit of modification, so rather than talk through it, replace it all with this.

```
/******************************************
Draw a Rectangle with texture this is a hard coded
draw which is only good for the Rectangle
******************************************/

void Draw(Target_State *p_state)
{

 GLfloat RectVertices[] = {
  -0.5f, 0.5f,
  0.0f, // Position 0
```

```
 0.0f, 0.0f, // TexCoord 0
-0.5f,
-0.5f,
 0.0f, // Position 1
 0.0f,
 1.0f, // TexCoord 1
 0.5f,
-0.5f,
 0.0f, // Position 2
 1.0f, 1.0f, // TexCoord 2
 0.5f, 0.5f,
 0.0f, // Position 3
 1.0f, 0.0f // TexCoord 3
};

GLushort indices[] = { 0, 1, 2, 0, 2, 3 };

// Setup the viewport
glViewport(0, 0, p_state->width, p_state->height);
// Clear the color buffer
glClear(GL_COLOR_BUFFER_BIT);
// setup the program object
glUseProgram(p_state->user_data->programObject);
// Load the vertex position
glVertexAttribPointer( p_state->user_data->positionLoc,
 3,
 GL_FLOAT,
 GL_FALSE, 5 * sizeof(GLfloat), RectVertices );
// Load the texture coordinate
glVertexAttribPointer( p_state->user_data->texCoordLoc,
 2,
 GL_FLOAT,
 GL_FALSE,
 5 * sizeof(GLfloat),
 &RectVertices[3]);

 glEnableVertexAttribArray(p_state->user_data->positionLoc);
 glEnableVertexAttribArray(p_state->user_data->texCoordLoc);
 // Bind the texture
 glActiveTexture ( GL_TEXTURE0 );
 glBindTexture(GL_TEXTURE_2D, p_state->user_data->textureId);
//actually draw the rect as 2 sets of 3 vertices (2 tris make a rect)
 glDrawElements ( GL_TRIANGLES, 6, GL_UNSIGNED_SHORT, indices );

 if (glGetError() != GL_NO_ERROR) printf("Oh bugger");
}
```

It's not too different, but you can see now that there's a bit more to it, we're setting up more vertices, because a rectangle has six being made from two triangles, and it's also having to deal with the textures points and setting up the Attribute Pointers so that the data in our p_state is used by the shader.

Compile and run, and you will still get a blank rectangle window on screen. There's one last important part to add to this.

Go back to the main loop, which in this case, is the while (TRUE) loop. After we check if our data are valid with this;

```
if (OurRawData == NULL) printf("We failed to load\n");
```

add this line;

```
p_state->user_data->textureId = CreateTexture2D(Width, Height, OurRawData);
```

This final bit of the puzzle will tell our p_state structure, that it has to use the texture ID supplied by the CreateTexture2D routine.

Compile and run, and we should see this lovely screen.

Well done, we can now display images. That's a very important step. Of course, this code is just horrible; it's a mashup of HelloTriangle and a few bits of things we added. It's very rigid and is only really good for one rectangle on screen at a time. It's been hacked together to do one particular thing. But it works; now we have to make it into something more usable and a lot tidier. It also helps to demonstrate that the shader code we need to use is a little confusing; that can sometimes be the second hurdle after the triangle disconnection that holds new programmers up and scares them off.

But not to worry, we're going to try to get past that confusion, trust me for a while so that I can set some code up that will allow us to largely ignore the hardware and get some actual game coding done.

▋ Displaying More Images

Now that we have our first images up and running, let's try expanding our simple load/display system to do a bit more work and in the process get some code working to control the display a bit more.

Get hold of a few more images, at least five and put them into your assets folder, if they have different file types to what we have already, remember to add the file extension to the files to transfer list in your VisualGDB Project Settings.

We're going to create a small array of filenames, and load the files, one at a time, display it, count to 100 and then load and display the next one.

Easy....what can possibly go wrong.... Oh...you'll see

I'm not going to be cruel to you anymore and make you type in the whole project from scratch, we saw how messy that got. There's a nice little project on the support site called PhotoFrame. Download it and put it in to a folder called PhotoFrame, preferably on your root directory, or close to it.

It's not a complete project, I do want you to do some work ☺ but code wise it is all there, what you need to do is go and add those nice pictures of your own, you put in the assets folder then include them as existing items in the Assets filter so that you can visualize them in the editor. Try to make sure the images are png, jpg, or tga, as they tend to be the easiest to use. Remember to add the file format to your VisualGDB Project Settings/Files to Transfer list. (Oh! you could add the actual names to ensure that only those images are sent...your call!)

You should recognize the code, it's our HelloTriangle/Rectangle code, but cleaned up and much tidier with folders and filters set up, so you can easily locate things. It's still not perfect but this is a small project and it's manageable.

Now depending on how many images you add we have to type in a small array with the names of those files. In the PhotoFrame.cpp file where I've indicated at the top, notice you have to type in the full path name "..\\Assets\\filename.ext" I've given you Lenna and another image to start you off.

Now make sure you set the NUMBEROFPICS to the actual number you have included and compile and run. You should now have your first image up on screen, and then after a few seconds, the next one.

Let it run for a few more cycles....what happens?

▮ But I Didn't Do Anything Wrong?

Well yes you did, I allowed you to experience something every programmer dreads. A memory leak, in this case a pretty quick one only after four or five images the program reports errors and stops working. That initial flush of excitement when the code did what you wanted it to do, suddenly becomes a real downbeat bit of head scratching? But just ask yourself why did we have a memory leak?

The golden rule is, if you allocate memory, you need to be sure you release it when it's done with; in this case, the error we get is actually because of the GPU running out of memory.

When we make a texture, which we did when we used CreateTexture2D, we are allocating some space in our GPU memory. Unless you've set the size of your GPU memory, we don't really have a good indicator of how much memory we have but on SBCs it's not all that much, often as little as 64MB. So, two or three 1024×1024 images that take up 4MB each, with some other overheads in the GPU memory, 64MB will vanish pretty quickly, even 256MB will vanish fast on an app that is gobbling 4MB's every frame.

So we have to make sure that when we've done with our image, we remove it. Fortunately, we have the means with this standard OpenGL function glDeleteTextures, which we can use like this;

```
glDeleteTextures(1, &p_state->user_data->textureId);
```

Just before we increase `WhichImage`. Now run it again....we should be comfortably getting past the four or five images now, we can really start to feel confident, we've resolved the GPU memory leak. Why not add a few more images and then let it run for a while and check it out, how stable is it?

▌ But I Fixed It?

Did you now? Well, it runs longer but it still seems to crash, probably in an unpredictable way, in fact my demo just seems to exit normally, but I know that's wrong because I have not allowed it to exit normally. If I observe the Visual Studio output window it also shows that a while before it stops running, it certainly stops loading images. How can that be when we freed the GPU memory?

The clue is in the fact we freed the memory on our GPU, but we never freed the memory our CPU used to hold the image that became the texture. It's not obvious because we didn't actually write the code that allocates the memory but if you load something into memory, it stands to reason it's going to occupy memory somewhere!

Every time we loaded an image for display, the stbi_load function allocated some memory, we were not totally aware of this because we have only focused on the ability to load an image, we've not considered how to remove it. Code wise, this could be considered a perfectly *acceptable* way to do things. I mean the code does exactly what it's supposed to do, right? But clearly after a while it stops doing what it's supposed to do, as the load systems cannot get new memory from the system to load up, and it all starts to go wrong.

When we allocate some data space for our image, we store the start of that data in our OurRawData variable, but when we load another one, we use the same variables to point it, effectively the new address of the image overwrites the pointer that points to the old image and is lost forever, because a pointer can only hold one value at any given time.

But that the old image is still very much there in memory and your new image will simply get allocated to another chunk of memory from the system and load its graphics in there.

By constantly creating new images, we are constantly allocating more new memory, but we have a finite amount of memory available, which quickly fills up with these old unused instances of a surface with graphics.

It's important for us as programmers to remember that we have full control over our targets, and we have to be sure that we exercise that control with care. There is nothing technically wrong with the code we wrote here, but there is a massive problem with the use of the target resources. There's no point being able to code a cool photo frame program if it stops working after a few minutes. Likewise, a game that constantly loads graphics at inappropriate times and with no regard to memory usage will quickly fail.

The lesson to be learned here is that coding isn't just about mastering the languages, it's also very much about using the equipment we have in a sensible way. We have the ability to write perfectly correct code that because of poor management can stop working owing to very small errors, such as forgetting to deallocate some memory. So, let's make sure that every time we want to disregard something which lives in our memory we must first make sure it is properly discarded, a bit like putting things in the bin when you're done, and recycling. If you just keep allocating new resources, and don't clear up when finished, you eventually end up with your memory in a terrible mess and no more unused resources for you.

But, by recycling the memory and putting it back into circulation you can, more or less, use it over and over again, with almost no limits.

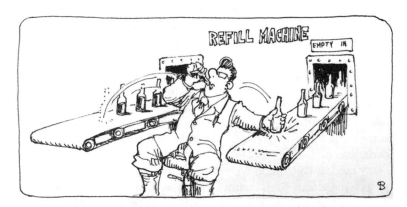

So how do we recycle the memory? Our load routine in the stb_image.h files uses a method of allocation called a malloc(). This returns an address, called a pointer, which points to where the data are, our load routines then filled that up with our image. To free up that memory, the corresponding function is called `free()`.

By passing the pointer to the data, we want to release or free within the free() function, the memory goes back in to general use. So just after you delete the texture add this line:

```
free(OurRawData);
```

Now, run our program, in fact run it, go make a nice hot beverage, mix some pizza dough, let it rise, knock it back, let it rise again…and you get the idea. This program can now be left on its own forever, because memory will now be allocated and deallocated correctly.

This is our first most important lesson in memory management; never allow an allocated pointer to be lost without clearing up the memory it's pointing to. There are a couple of different methods of allocating memory as standard, `malloc()` and `free()` are legacy systems from the old days of C, but as C is a full subset of C++, you will still find it used often, especially when the intent is to just allocate a big chunk of empty memory for something. C++ also has the `new` and corresponding `delete` commands, which create and destroy instances of classes or objects. All we have to remember is that every `malloc()` or `new` must have a corresponding `free()` or `delete`.

If we can keep that in mind we should manage to avoid the dreaded memory leak, at least in our own code!

▮ Making a Dynamic Playfield

So we know how to make an image-sized texture and display it, is there a way we can also change that texture, allowing us to draw objects into it, or text, or change colors or…basically have the visual image on our screen behave similar to screens in the good old days and have pixels mapped to (texture) memory?

Well the answer, of course, is yes, but with some pretty major qualification. We know we have an image somewhere in memory, and that image is effectively a big chunk of RAM, which then gets sent to the texture memory for display, what we want to do though is alter it, and resend it to the texture memory to be redrawn with changes. We effectively want to turn our image in memory into a pixel buffer, which we alter in code and then have displayed.

This is the basic principles of a back or frame buffer. RAM-based frame buffers are a pretty old concept these days, with graphic cards to do all our work, we don't really need the idea of a RAM double buffer where we write to one buffer while displaying another, then swap. But for our initial projects they work very well, it will give us our sense of dynamic playfields and perhaps more importantly force us to use our coding skills to get the graphics on screen.

This is very much a CPU-intensive process; our GPU is going to be used for nothing more than displaying screen-sized textures. Better state-up front, this is a pretty primitive way to do a 2D game on any machine with hardware graphic systems, and it is NOT the way OpenGLES2.0 likes to work, but it is a quick and dirty way to get set up, very effective and pretty much certain to work on any machine. We will almost certainly find a use for this kind of pixel buffer manipulation in some kind of game.

There are, as I must stress, much better ways to do this, which we'll touch on later.

For now like you, I really want to get a game written and not worry about the specifics of the machine, we need to get a framework together so that I can teach you some code and not have you stressing out about accessing the mysterious GPUs before we are ready. We will have plenty of time to do that when we get some things working and feel comfortable with our code.

▮ Old School Frame Buffers

A back or frame buffer works on the simple principle that while one buffer is being displayed, we are working on the next one to be ready for display when all our graphics are drawn.

So the principle is simple enough, write to a clean area of memory, which is not being displayed and is set up to be drawn to, then when finished make it into a texture, and send it to a currently undisplayed screen-sized Quad (2 triangles), and then tell our system to swap textures while we draw the next one. Rinse and repeat over and over again.

Well that's the principle, but doing it on a system with no direct memory to display correlation, it's actually pretty horrible, once a texture is created its image is then located in the GPU memory and the CPU cannot access it. So every time we create a texture with this idea, the target needs to first delete an old currently undisplayed texture, then internally copy the modified memory up to the GPU's texture memory. That deleting and shifting takes time. For now, though we have more than enough bandwidth to get away with it.

In addition, OpenGLES2.0 actually already has a double buffer concept, where we get the GPU to draw everything to somewhere not being displayed then swap it with the screen display, that's the main purpose of this line of code

```
eglSwapBuffers(esContext->display, esContext->surface);
```

….Adding even more kind of buffers makes my eyes bleed when I see them. But there is a method in this madness!

This is one of those deliberately bad (very bad) design choices I mentioned at the beginning of this book, so it's a fair question to ask why are we doing this?

It's to do with the history and the fact that a lot of old online tutorials you may find, used systems like this, you may come across them and will want to implement them on your chosen target. In addition, I want to remove the use of the GPU from your mind for the moment so that we can focus on developing some coding concepts and not worry too much about how to display things. A straight display to screen relationship is simple to visualize and code for. An abstract, point in space, drawing machine, that works in a virtual space if you feed it just with the right data, is a slightly scarier concept for you to digest right at this moment.

It was much easier to do this on older systems where you could actually gain access to, and manipulate the memory that was your display/texture, but now with the way OpenGLES2.0 and other modern Shader-based systems work, it becomes an ungainly method.

So let me again be quite clear...before the real coders start tearing out their hair in frustration. This is only to demonstrate a simple means of displaying our own 2D display buffer using CPU manipulated graphics, so we can focus on what we are doing rather than how it is doing it. We'll upgrade to a *proper* way of rendering as soon as their basics are understood. This is also going to stand as a good example of why a system that works is actually not a good system.

We need to first set up the buffers, and I have found the best way to do that is to use a variation of a system my old colleague Dr. Jacco Bikker produced in our old OpenGL1.1 coding template for the first years at NHTV, it was made available online for several tutorials and a lot of games were written using it. I've modified it a lot to work with our OpenGLES2.0 targets but the principle is based on a class type we call a Surface, java coders might be more familiar with the term canvas, but it is effectively the same thing.

A Surface Class is a pretty simple concept, it's a buffer of memory, with some functions that allow us to make/fill/change/copy that buffer and interact with other Surfaces. For now, we're not even too worried about how it gets displayed; it's simply a means to write screen style pixels that we *later* plan to display. That's it! Let's get started.

We won't need to type all this in this time, I think you've cut your teeth on typing now, so from now on you can download the base code from the support site. For any historians reading this in the next century, here's the basic Surface Class that we'll add to as we build up a need to do more.

Ok, once you've downloaded the `Surface.h` and `Surface.cpp` files, you can move them to your source folder (on the Dev machine, remember VisualGDB will send them to the target when it syncs before it starts compiling), then use the *add existing files*, options to add our friends here.

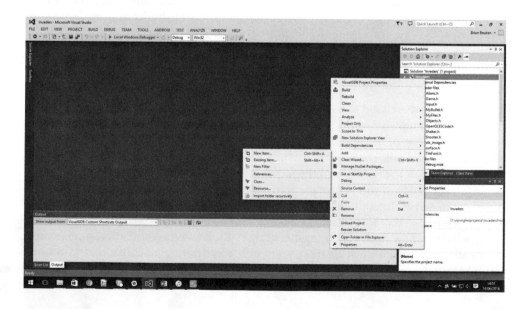

Let's have a quick look at this header file. Headers are way more important to us than the .cpp files because they tell us at a glance what our class can do; it's not cluttered up with masses of code and formatting info. It's normally just the declarations of functions (called methods in pure C++ geek speak) that the class can do, a few defines and the variables a class contains when you make an *instance* of that class.

They also let other parts of our program know what a class can do. This can be very useful as we'll discover. A header file acts similar to an instruction manual for you and the code you create, which will give information on what the names of the methods are, what passed values you need to give these methods, and the variables the class has access to.

```
#pragma once
#include "MyFiles.h"

#define REDMASK (0xff0000)
#define GREENMASK (0x00ff00)
#define BLUEMASK (0x0000ff)

 typedef unsigned long Pixel;

inline Pixel AddBlend(Pixel a_Color1, Pixel a_Color2)
{
const unsigned int r = (a_Color1 & REDMASK) + (a_Color2 & REDMASK);
const unsigned int g = (a_Color1 & GREENMASK) + (a_Color2 & GREENMASK);
const unsigned int b = (a_Color1 & BLUEMASK) + (a_Color2 & BLUEMASK);
const unsigned r1 = (r & REDMASK) | (REDMASK * (r >> 24));
const unsigned g1 = (g & GREENMASK) | (GREENMASK * (g >> 16));
const unsigned b1 = (b & BLUEMASK) | (BLUEMASK * (b >> 8));
return (r1 + g1 + b1);
}

   // subtractive blending
   inline Pixel SubBlend(Pixel a_Color1, Pixel a_Color2)
   {
        int red = (a_Color1 & REDMASK) - (a_Color2 & REDMASK);
        int green = (a_Color1 & GREENMASK) - (a_Color2 & GREENMASK);
        int blue = (a_Color1 & BLUEMASK) - (a_Color2 & BLUEMASK);
        if (red < 0) red = 0;
        if (green < 0) green = 0;
        if (blue < 0) blue = 0;
        return (Pixel)(red + green + blue);
   }
}
class Surface
{
public:
 // constructor / destructor
 Surface(int a_Width, int a_Height, Pixel* a_Buffer, int a_Pitch);
 Surface(int a_Width, int a_Height);
 Surface(char* a_File,MyFiles* FileHandler);
 ~Surface();
 // member data access
 Pixel* GetBuffer() { return m_Buffer; }
 void SetBuffer(Pixel* a_Buffer) { m_Buffer = a_Buffer; }
 int GetWidth() { return m_Width; }
 int GetHeight() { return m_Height; }
```

```
int GetPitch() { return m_Pitch; }
void SetPitch(int a_Pitch) { m_Pitch = a_Pitch; }
void Clear(Pixel a_Color);
void Line(float x1, float y1, float x2, float y2, Pixel color);
void Plot(int x, int y, Pixel c);
void CopyTo(Surface* a_Dst, int a_X, int a_Y);
void BlendCopyTo(Surface* a_Dst, int a_X, int a_Y);
void ScaleColor(unsigned int a_Scale);
void Box(int x1, int y1, int x2, int y2, Pixel color);
void Bar(int x1, int y1, int x2, int y2, Pixel color);
void Resize(int a_Width, int a_Height, Surface* a_Orig);
private:
// Attributes
Pixel* m_Buffer;
int m_Width, m_Height, m_Pitch;
   };
```

You can see that the class actually only contains four variables, m_buffer being the most important, because it contains our data, width and height are obvious, Pitch, however, will become apparent later.

As C++ variables in a class are known as members, the prefix m_ is commonly used to indicate that the variable is a member of a class.

The Pixel stuff at the top is to allow us to grab the data in a recognizable pixel format, which will be much easier later. It's using the Inline directive because this isn't something we want in a routine, if it is used it needs to be pretty quick and this is the best way to do it.

Also notice this section here:

```
Surface(int a_Width, int a_Height, Pixel* a_Buffer, int a_Pitch);
Surface(int a_Width, int a_Height);
Surface(char* a_File, MyFiles* FileHandler);
```

We have three different declarations of constructors for our Surface Class, each of which contains different variables, which identify them as specific *overloads*, this will allow us to create a surface, from a filename, or a width and a height, or with width and height and the address of another buffer.

You'll also notice that all the variable names start with a_; this is another common way to indicate that a parameter is a variable that is given to the method. It's not a hard and fast rule, and indeed in the header you don't even need to name the variables, you could just as easily write declarations like this;

```
Surface(int, int, Pixel*, int);
Surface(int, int);
Surface(char*, MyFiles*);
```

The only thing the compiler actually wants to know in the method declaration is what kind of values are the methods going to use. How many parameters, what type they are, and the order are very important, because it defines which particular version of the constructor we are going to use when we call it.

Even though it's valid, we don't need to use logical variable names, but adding a variable name, which is also descriptive, makes for easier to read code; for example, look at the following:

```
Surface(int a, int b, Pixel* c, int d);
Surface(int a, int b);
Surface(char* a, MyFiles* b);
```

You can see the problem! Nondescriptive variable names, in a header, might be valid code, it will compile, but for the poor human trying to read it, it's not much fun and gives little away. Always try to use descriptive variable names, even in the header declarations.

```
Surface(int a_Width, int a_Height, Pixel* a_Buffer, int a_Pitch);
Surface(int a_Width, int a_Height);
Surface(char* a_File, MyFiles* FileHandler);
```

Much nicer to read, and easier to understand what we are passing, or trying to return.

We'll start to write the constructors first as they are the most important.

It's a rather nice feature of C++ that, when we define a class, we can add the concept of methods we want to have in our class, but don't actually have to write them yet. It lets us think about it first. That's basically all a declaration is, a concept of what we plan to write. We only actually have to write it if we try to call it.

The accessor functions are usually nice short Get and Set routines whose job is to access and perhaps consistently modify a value before returning it. Since these are nearly often very small, they are often best done in the header, so the Get and Set functions are basically commands that will let us keep our variables private and allows flexibility later if we perhaps have to modify our values in some way, before we return them to a calling routine. If they need more than a couple of commands to return their values, then move them into the .cpp files because they have become proper code methods rather than simple accessors.

Private members are variables that are usually only accessible by the class methods themselves. I'm not a massive fan of private members as you will discover, as an old school assembler coder I like to have all variables open and available to me and not worry about additional calls using up CPU time. But they are a C++ convention and if you are working with code that's likely to evolve and change or you work with other programmers, keeping variables safe from interaction with other classes can have great benefits, and accessors do allow you to make controlled consistent alterations to data you want to give to other classes.

Ok, let's look at the constructors, which will let us create these lovely little pixel buffers! Of course, you've downloaded it, put it in your source folder, and added the existing file, but here's the code anyway, so I can explain it.

```
Surface::Surface(int a_Width, int a_Height, Pixel* a_Buffer, int a_Pitch)
  : m_Width(a_Width)
  , m_Height(a_Height)
  , m_Buffer(a_Buffer)
  , m_Pitch(a_Pitch)
{}

Surface::Surface(int a_Width, int a_Height)
  : m_Width(a_Width)
  , m_Height(a_Height)
  , m_Pitch(a_Width)
```

```
  {
   m_Buffer = (Pixel*)malloc(a_Width * a_Height * sizeof(Pixel));
  }

Surface::Surface(char* a_File,MyFiles* FileHandler)
  : m_Buffer(NULL)
  , m_Width(0)
  , m_Height(0)
{

   m_Buffer = (Pixel*)FileHandler->Load(a_File, &m_Width, &m_Height);
   if (m_Buffer == NULL)
   {
    printf("File %s cannot be loaded, check name and dir \n", a_File);
   }
   else
   {
    printf("Buffer loaded with %s image, size is %i,%i\n", a_File, m_Width,
m_Height);
   }
  }
```

Our first one assumes a pixel buffer has been set up and simply passes it to our m_Buffer pointer along with size and pitch. So our class is complete.

The second is a meatier one it actually makes some space in memory that's big enough to accommodate our buffer. I am using malloc instruction here for the moment, which is a standard way to allocate some memory, but it does not guarantee that the start of that memory is on what we call an alignment, usually for 32bit machines that will be at every fourth byte, which is far easier for the CPU to access when grabbing a memory. For now, we'll work with it and check later if it is aligned and see what we need to do to fix it, there are work arounds.

The third actually loads up an image, in the same way our picture displays program and uses its data in memory as our m_buffer. Notice, we are passing it a file handler to use, because I don't really like to create two of them, any classes that need to use a file handler should be given the address of the one we created at the start. Later though we'll close the one in the Main argument and explore other options.

You may notice I also like to inform my user of the files being loaded, or when they failed to load. This is me being a bit overcareful with my errors, but it would be wiser to use a function of my own, something like notify_user(char* msg); which can actually be stopped from outputting when running in a release mode. But I've not written it yet, so we'll do it later when we refactor the code and we're sure it's all doing what it should do.

▮ Setting Up the Frame Buffer and Switch System

So this is where it gets messy, because OpenGLES2.0 does not provide a simple means to get CPU access to the pixels that make up a texture, once it actually becomes a texture! So we can't do anything with a currently active texture, only with the memory buffer full of pixels we plan to make a texture.

It's logical when you think about it. When a texture is created, the raw image of the data as pixels is copied and stored in the GPU's own memory, we can delete the file data we loaded, the texture is still there, somewhere! But now the GPU owns it and it does not want to share with the CPU. This is why a GPU has its own memory, having two processes trying to access the same memory at the same time is not usually possible, causing one to stop and wait for the other. Hardware makers don't like that, so generally it's not allowed.

But back to our dynamic playfield; let's layout what we need to create a double buffer?

First, pretty obviously we need two buffers: one to work on and one to display.

Second, we need some way to keep track of which one we are drawing to.

Third, we need a means to do the swapping and put our texture on screen.

Part 1: This is the easy bit; let's make two buffers that are big enough to hold our screens data.

```
Pixel* Locations[2];

bool createFBtexture()
{

  int Red = 0xff0000ff;
  int Green = 0x00ff00ff;

  Locations[0] = (Pixel*)malloc(SCRWIDTH * SCRHEIGHT * 4);
  Locations[1] = (Pixel*)malloc(SCRWIDTH * SCRHEIGHT * 4);
  //set it all to black
  memset(Locations[0], 255, SCRWIDTH * SCRHEIGHT * 4);
  memset(Locations[1], 255, SCRWIDTH * SCRHEIGHT * 4);

  m_Screen = new Surface(SCRWIDTH, SCRHEIGHT, Locations[0]);
  m_Screen->SetPitch(SCRWIDTH);
}
```

`malloc` and `memset` are those old throwback systems from the days of C, which allow us to allocate an area of memory of a specific size. It returns the start of that area as a pointer and we store it in our Locations array. `memset`, lets us quickly set that buffer to a value, I don't really need to do that here but it can be useful when debugging to see if the memory has been cleared/written to have it all set to a simple to view value.

Part 2: Let's create a few simple variables and a Surface Class, which we are going to work with as our *screen* surface. But whose m_buffer value will point to the buffer we are currently drawing to.

```
Surface* m_Screen;

GLuint framebufferTexID[2];
```

Part 3: The messy bit, promise me you will never show this to a real OpenGL/ES coder…ever. The death and rebirth of the textures to create the display.

```
bool swap()
{
 bufferIndex++;
 bufferIndex = bufferIndex % 2;
 glDeleteTextures(1, &framebufferTexID[bufferIndex]); //delete the old
texture (displayed 1 frame ago)
 framebufferTexID[bufferIndex] = CreateSimpleTexture2D(SCRWIDTH, SCRHEIGHT,
(char*)m_Screen->GetBuffer());
}
```

Finally, let's set the screen size to work on any size of screen. For Raspberry Pi, we have a nice little function called

```
graphics_get_display_size(0,&scr_width, &scr_height);
```

which gives us the physical pixel size of the screen we have. Sadly, we don't have that on our other possible targets, but I've added a best guess system that will work on most on the downloaded versions. We can use the display size to set up our EGL window, and then the screen will fill up. But...if we use the full HD 1080 size, it gives us a screen size of 1920 × 1080, that's rather large, and our textures allocate internally as a closest power of two (POT), so it will actually create two 2048 × 2048 textures, our max size. Testing shows this to be a bit too much effort for our humble targets, so I've set the maximum buffer sizes to 1024 × 800, a decent-sized screen, which the display system will scale to fit on whatever size screen we are using, even those little 3.2″ LCD. Internally, the texture generated is 1024 × 1024 so that means we're not wasting too much actual space.

So there you have it, a working double buffer system, and a Surface Class we draw that effectively becomes a screen to see the results...

We've done rather a lot so far without blowing anything up, but we now have a viable system, albeit clunky, that will let us write our first basic games.

Yes, we're ready to make a game now. Save our project somewhere safe, this is going to be our starting block for the next couple of projects.

5 Finally Our First Games

5.1 Invaders from Space

Let's begin our first proper graphic game with homage to a classic, which has almost no graphics, which for copyright reasons I probably can't name, but you should all be familiar with.

Looks familiar?

Using the OS

I said right at the start that I didn't want to add any third party libraries and to stay away from the OS as much as possible, BUT this is one of the places where that is going to create some issues for us.

Our projects need to have some kind of input, keys/mouse/joystick to be usable. This is exactly the thing our OS is designed to do for us, handle I/O. We've already used it for our loading files, though C/C++ abstracted that away from us and we didn't need to see the underlying code that actually switched on the drives, moved the heads, and pulled in the data, now we have to use the OS, for our key handling. But it's not quite as simple as entering and printing text was, which was also our higher level C++ code talking to the OS, which controls the console.

We only really want to detect key/button presses and in the case of the mouse, position changes. The STL does not provide for that, it really only provides for character-based concepts; it supplies the character *A* not the fact that the A key was pressed. Testing individual keys or device positions is problematic.

Normally, we'd probably have a consoles SDK, or in a PC, another library in place like SDL/SDL2 to take care of things like that for us, we have no SDK and SDL/SDL2 is rather a big clunky library, which though available and does a lot, I want to maintain my promise of no third party libs, especially big ones.

So we have to write some code that asks the OS for some info on what keys are pressed, which can then be used in our games.

So...let's be honest... This turned out to be hard to do. I scanned the Raspberry Pi forums, and Linux sites, and could not find a simple direct method to get key scans. I was starting to feel I was going to have to dig up a load of Linux source code and decipher it myself, when a friendly colleague on an old developers Facebook page came to my rescue.

My thanks to Gareth Lewis, who provided me with a basic method for handling the key input events that the OS generates and storing the results. As an added bonus, it is also a very useful introduction into Thread/multi core management, but more on that later.

It's not a massively complex bit of code, though some of the ways to access data are odd, but I took what Gareth gave me and wrote up a simple Input Class, which you can find listed here or download from the support site.

In the Makefile settings of your VisualGDB Properties you have to add `pthread` to the list of library names. Like this:

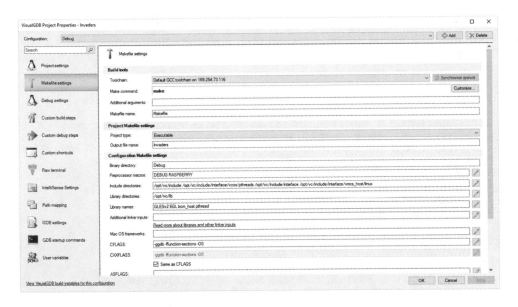

Now I really would like you to type this in again, because the practice you get typing in code is far more valuable than just blindly adding a file. But if you really don't want to type this in, the input.h/cpp files are on the download site. But please. Type it in!

If you are adding the files, then copy them into your folders and add an existing file to include them; otherwise, if you are taking the sensible approach and practicing your code entry skills, go back to the Visual Studio Solution explorer and right click on the filter for Header Files, and add a new file called Input.h, and start typing this in.

```cpp
#pragma once
#include <stdio.h>
#include <cstdio>
#include <iostream>
#include <pthread.h>
#include <linux/input.h>
//*************************************************************************
Mega thanks to Grumpy old Git Developer Gareth Lewis for his help with this
Keys[] sets the relevant index to TRUE when pressed and FALSE when
released, index names can be found in <linux/input.h> and follow the usual
KEY_A...KEY_Z format mouse keeps track of the motion of the mouse not the
absolute position, which needs to be known beforehand if you plan to use
the mouse for direct control. Wherever the GUI mouse is at startup is
considered 0,0 and all movement is offset from there. If no GUI it assumes
0,0 is start. User must draw their own mouse! */


#define SCRWIDTH 1920
#define SCRHEIGHT 1080 // at some point we will need variable access


class Input
{
#define TRUE  1
#define FALSE 0


public:
 typedef struct // A very simple structure to hold the mouse info
  {
   int PositionX; // contains the relative position from the start
point (take care to not confuse it with the GUI mouse position)
   int PositionY;
   float RelY;
   float RelX;
   unsigned char LeftButton;  // TRUE when pressed FALSE otherwise
   unsigned char MidButton;
   unsigned char RightButton;

  } MouseData;


 char Keys[512]; // maximum possible keys is a little less than this, but
best to be careful in case of future expansion
 MouseData TheMouse;

 pthread_t threadKeyboard;
 pthread_t threadMouse; // handles for the threads

 bool mQuit;  // set true to kill the mouse thread
 bool kQuit;  // set true to kill the key thread

  int iterations;
  bool KeyPressed;
```

```
/****************************************************************************
Intended to be a thread which processes the mouse events and stores  Mouse
info in TheMouse struct.
****************************************************************************/

  static void*  ProcessMouseThread(void* arg);

/****************************************************************************
This thread processes the keys, and stores TRUE/FALSE values in the Keys[]
array.
****************************************************************************/

  static void* ProcessKeyboardThread(void* arg);


  //small accessor function to test a specific key
  bool TestKey(unsigned char WhatKey);
  bool SimpleTest();
  /***********************
  must call init before use
  ***********************/
  bool Init();
/****************************************************************************
this will test for our keyboards
****************************************************************************/
 int AreYouMyKeyboard();
 std::string kbd; // this will be the event filename for the keyboard
discovered in the init/AreYouMyKeyboard test

}; // end of class
```

Now with that done we need an Input.cpp file to go with it.

```
#include "Input.h"
#include <dirent.h>
void*  Input::ProcessMouseThread(void* arg)
{
 FILE *fmouse;
 fmouse = fopen("/dev/input/mice", "r");
 if (fmouse != NULL)
 {
  while (((Input*)arg)->mQuit == false) // so as long as mQuit is FALSE,
this will endlessly loop
  {
   signed char b[3];
   fread(b, sizeof(char), 3, fmouse);
// if we do plan to scale, best make these into floats for greater
precision before they are cast down to ints.
   float mousex = (float)b[1];
   float mousey =  -(float)b[2];

   ((Input*)arg)->TheMouse.RelX = mousex;
   ((Input*)arg)->TheMouse.RelY = -mousey;
   ((Input*)arg)->TheMouse.PositionX += (mousex / 1.0f); // 1.0 can be
replaced by a scale factor (entierly optional)
```

```cpp
    if (((Input*)arg)->TheMouse.PositionX > SCRWIDTH) ((Input*)arg)->
TheMouse.PositionX = SCRWIDTH;
    if (((Input*)arg)->TheMouse.PositionX < 0) ((Input*)arg)->TheMouse.
PositionX = 0;

    ((Input*)arg)->TheMouse.PositionY += (mousey / 1.0f);

    if (((Input*)arg)->TheMouse.PositionY > SCRHEIGHT) ((Input*)arg)->
TheMouse.PositionY = SCRHEIGHT;
    if (((Input*)arg)->TheMouse.PositionY < 0) ((Input*)arg)->TheMouse.
PositionY = 0;
    ((Input*)arg)->TheMouse.LeftButton = (b[0] & 1) > 0; // using a
test(x>0) allows it to return and store a bool
    ((Input*)arg)->TheMouse.MidButton = (b[0] & 4) > 0;
    ((Input*)arg)->TheMouse.RightButton = (b[0] & 2) > 0;
  }
  fclose(fmouse);
 }
 printf("Mouse Thread closing \n");
 pthread_exit(NULL);
}

void* Input::ProcessKeyboardThread(void* arg)
{
 FILE *fp;
 fp = fopen(((Input *)arg)->kbd.c_str(), "r");
 struct input_event ev;
 if (fp != NULL)
 {
 while (((Input*)arg)->kQuit == false) // kQuit is set to false by the init
  {
    fread(&ev, sizeof(struct input_event), 1, fp);
    if (ev.type == (__u16)EV_KEY)
    {
    ((Input*)arg)->Keys[ev.code] = ev.value>0 ? TRUE : FALSE; // never gets
here to give me key values
     ((Input*)arg)->KeyPressed = true;
    }
    else ((Input*)arg)->KeyPressed = false;
  }
  printf("quit responded too\n");
  fclose(fp);
 }
 printf("Key Thread closing\n");
 printf("  err %d \n", errno); // we closed so let's see the error
 pthread_exit(NULL);
}

bool Input::TestKey(unsigned char WhatKey)
{
 return Keys[WhatKey] == TRUE; // simply return binary true or false
}

bool Input::SimpleTest()
{
 return KeyPressed ;
}
```

```cpp
bool Input::Init()
{
 kQuit = false;
 mQuit = false;
 iterations = 0;
 int result;
//mice don't usually provide any issues
 result = pthread_create(&threadMouse, NULL, &ProcessMouseThread, this);
// we send the Input class (this) as an argument to allow for easy cast
((Input*)arg)-> type access to the classes data.
 if (result != 0) printf("got an error\n");
 else printf("mouse thread started\n");

 if (AreYouMyKeyboard() == false) printf("Oh Bugger, we can't seen to find
the keyboard\n"); // go find an active keyboard

 result = pthread_create(&threadKeyboard, NULL, &ProcessKeyboardThread,
this);
 if (result != 0) printf("got an error\n");
 else printf("Key thread started\n");
 return true;
}

// tests for the keyboard, which can be on different events in Linux
// thanks to my student Petar Dimitrov for this improvement to the keyboard
search systems
int Input::AreYouMyKeyboard()
{
/*  **Note** linux machines may have their key and mouse event files access
protected, in which case open a command line terminal, and enter
 sudo chmod  a+r /dev/input/* (assuming your input event files are there)
 this is kinda frowned on by linux users, but I don't know a way to
overcome this in code yet.  It may also be possible to get VisualGDB to
execute the build as sudo for root access but I find that flakey */

 // Some bluetooth keyboards are registered as "event-mouse".
 // If this is your case, then just change this variable to event-mouse.
 std::string pattern = "event-kbd"; //<-change to event-mouse if your BT
keyboard is a "mouse" or test for a failure to find a kbd, then try as a
mouse.
 std::string file = "";

 DIR *dir;
 struct dirent *ent;

 printf("Checking for active keyboard\n");

 if ((dir = opendir("/dev/input/by-path/")) != nullptr)
 {
  while ((ent = readdir(dir)) != nullptr)
  {
   fprintf(stdout, "%s\n", ent->d_name);
   file = std::string(ent->d_name);
   if (!file.compare(".") || !file.compare("..")) continue;
```

```
    if (file.substr(file.length() - pattern.length()) == pattern)
    {
     kbd = "/dev/input/by-path/" + file;
     fprintf(stdout, "%s\n", kbd.c_str());
     return true;
    }
   }
  }
  return false;
}
```

Do take notice of the small comment in the code regarding Linux machines, you may have to manually change permissions to access the key event handlers, which are basically files in a particular directory.

Regardless of how you entered it, it's time to make use of it, to use this we just need to add a #include *Input.h* to our list of header files.

In our main program loop, we will need to have an instance of an Input Class like this:

```
Input Input;
```

And thereafter in our initialization system we can switch on keyboard and mouse scans by using

```
Input.Init();
```

We can then access keys using

```
if (Input.Keys[KEY_A] == TRUE) Do_something
```

Or use a test that provides a binary true/false

```
if (Input.TestKey(KEY_ESC)) Do_something
```

You can find a complete list of all the KEY_XXX codes in the linux/input.h header, we'll talk about the mouse later, for now we don't need to use it, but we now have some very useful access to our keys!

There is a downside to this code though! When our project is running, our background system, Linux, is running its own version of this key scan, so it still has its keys working. That means we will provide input to our terminal/Graphic User Interface (GUI) and our project when we press keys, this is not desirable. We need to stop that happening. But for now, if you run in GUI mode, the GUI will ignore all the key inputs. GUI takes up some memory though, so it's important we come back to this issue and find a way to either switch off the key input or ensure key input is transferred only to our project.

We'll do this later, for two reasons;

1. I don't want to complicate things at this point.

2. It's actually a bit of a bug. VisualGDB uses a bit of a hacky means to send info back to our development PC, and that basically stops any normal attempts we have to redirect the native OS's outputs…so for now, we need to live with it, it will only be

a problem on our debugging station, and there are ways to avoid it. If we run our projects directly from our targets, this problem vanishes. I will post updates on the support site when I or Sysprogs provide a solution to this.

So taking stock, now we can load graphics, display screen graphics, read keys and even have a pretty good handle on how our four main game states work. But we do need a few more things in our arsenal before we can make an actual interactive game. We need to have an ability to create and display some form of graphic object. In this case, sprites.

Sprites are a pretty old fashioned name for a graphical object that is displayed on screen and moves over/in/out of the screen area under programmed control. So far we have screens, now we need things that move within the screens.

This is where it starts to get complex, but fun...Let's start coding up some means to display sprites and then use them to make our first game.

Start as We Mean to Go on

Yup you guessed it, we have to do some setting up before we can actually write the game, which means a new tidy project and perhaps more important a simple way to keep track of the initializing and setting up of our OpenGL 2.0 graphic setups, as well as things that will be used a lot and can be expanded on as we go forward.

I'm not going to be cruel again and make you type in everything...there are a couple of setup files you need to have which probably could need some explaining but that will stop us getting to the good stuff.

So on the Support site, you'll find a project called InvaderStart, download it and fire it up.

It clearly doesn't do much yet but the basic structure of our 2D games is there and we'll improve on it as we go.

For now, let's ignore the OpenGLES code files, they are tech files doing what we need to do to get our game image on screen. We'll make more sense of that later.

The most important thing is that our project fires up into an application entry point, which is used to set everything up. On this project it's called Invaders, we'll rename it in different projects and expand it a bit but really it has one purpose, to get our game up and running.

Let's look at the main function, which is where everything starts:

```
int main(int argc, char *argv[])
{
 ProgramData user_data;
// this is a little trick for the Raspberry
 bcm_host_init();
 graphics_get_display_size(0,&scr_width, &scr_height);
 TheInput.Init();

 FileHandler = new MyFiles();
 printf("filehandler set up\n");
 esInitContext(p_state);
 init_ogl(p_state, scr_width, scr_height);

 createFBtexture();
 p_state->user_data = &user_data;
```

```
if (!Init(p_state)) return 0;
esRegisterDrawFunc(p_state, Draw);
eglSwapBuffers(p_state->display, p_state->surface);
esMainLoop(p_state);

}
```

You can see it starts off making a small structure for some Program data that will be used to draw. It then does a little bit of machine specific magic to get the width and height of our screen stored in variables. Note, graphics_get_display is a Raspberry function, I'll find something equivalent for non-Raspberry machines.

Then two cool things happen. We initialize our Input and File handlers. And notice we do them a different way? Input is declared as an instance at run time with this simple line near the top of the file

```
Input TheInput;
```

So it's created and constructed when the project fires up, so that when we use TheInput, we are actually always talking about the instance of the class we created there.

FileHandler though is declared like this;

```
MyFiles* FileHandler;
```

The * or dereferencing symbol means that FileHandler is actually a pointer to somewhere in memory that holds the instance of MyFiles. This is an example of a pointer, and it's an important concept to get used to. We read that as a Pointer to an instance of MyFiles Class.

When we create a pointer like

```
MyFiles* FileHandler;
```

There is NO value in there, or to be more exact, there is an unpredictable value. But.

```
Input TheInput;
```

Creates and instantiates that at the location where the value is declared, it might seem like it's the same thing but there are subtle differences.

We have to create an instance of MyFiles and store it in FileHandler to use it. That's done with

```
FileHandler = new MyFiles();
```

This is referred to as a Dynamic allocation, in other words, we create it when we need it, and also we can remove it when we don't.

Addressing variables or functions inside the classes will also depend on how they are created. We'll talk more on this as it comes up.

Compile and run your project, it won't do very much but you should get something simple on screen.

So we now have a very straight forward system. That initializes our machine, jumps to a Game Class and goes about its business. Initializing on the first pass, creating our instances, and then returning to a main loop, which checks for an esc key press to allow a clean exit.

This is a good framework to build on.

We're Here Now

Let's get this game written, if you're not familiar with Space Invaders, you're missing out on one of the greatest games ever made, though I have my rose tinted glasses on, it is the perfect first game to try to code, let's get on with it.

So what do we need to do?

- We have 5 rows of 11 baddies, which change frames and slight differences in graphics.

- We have bullets our shooter can fire.

- We have missiles raining down on us in an apparently random way.

- We have a saucer that pops out from time to time.

- We can hit the invaders with our bullets—they blow up.

- And we can be hit by our bullets—we blow up, and we lose a life.

- We also have some score system.

- We can hide behind shelters, which get destroyed.

- And we move our shooter left and right, and fire.

- The invaders move left or right then move down at the edge.

- If they get to the bottom we are dead.

- If we kill them all, they come even faster.

It's important to think about what we are going to display, this little list and a rough screen drawing give us a lot of information. We need the game to able to draw different images, respond to key presses, move objects semi-intelligently, create new objects when needed, bullets and missiles, and somehow do it all at the same time. Take some time before ever putting fingers to keyboard, to think about what kind of code we need.

Seems simple enough, Ok, so we've described the main features, these are things we need to code and the order we do seems fairly simple, we'll start by putting a shooter on screen.

On the support site, you will find two projects InvadersStart and InvadersFin. I really want you to use the InvadersStart, which is the basic framework and assets we are going to use, I'll put down the code in here that you need to enter in to get it all working, and let you try out things as you go. The InvadersFin project is just so you can see the finished work, but only use it if you really mess up. You should get as much practice as you can entering code and trying out things before moving the next steps.

Our first task is to put a player on screen, let's call him Bob, cos I like the name Bob.. BOB, it has a nice ring to it. But before we do that we need to think a bit more about what other kinds of things are going on screen.

Inheritance

As coders, we need to notice patterns in the way things behave…looking at our outline we have a few *types* of *thing* we are going to put on screen, but we should consider that these visually and functionally different objects share certain concepts between them.

They have position variables, they have a graphic and they have some kind of repeating function to make them do stuff.

At the moment that's really all they have but if we were to treat the variables as being pretty consistent for anything, which needs to be drawn on screen, we can also be sure that we are going to need some kind of code to update them, then also some code to draw them.

So let's make things tidy, and create a class to keep track of our objects common values. We'll call it, naturally enough, an Objects Class

```
enum Types { Bullet,Missile1,Missile2, Alien, AShooter,AShelter };
class Objects
{
public:
 Objects();
 ~Objects();
 Types Type;
 float Xpos, Ypos;
 bool Update(Surface* s,Input* InputHandler);
 Surface* Image;
};
```

Now that isn't too bad, but that type variable in the members list is a bit clunky, every time we do the update, we have to use a switch system or condition test, to get to the bit of code we want that relates to the type of thing we are updating, and we are now going to fill our Object Class with update code for all the different types of *thing* we have, even if the instance of *thing* does not need them. We really only want the type to be used for ID purposes, not for decisions on which update routine to use.

There has to be a better way? Of course, there is, it's called inheritance! Inheritance is a key part of C++'s makeup, which allows it to do a range of nice things, if we consider that Objects is a Base Class that contains all the prime concepts of an *object*, such as its position and its image, and an update routine, then that's all we need. But we want to create different types of objects we should be able to create a new class that has access to all the base values.

Think of it like this, you, me, and everyone we know, are humans, (I hope?). We all derive from a basic concept of what a human is. Bipedal, four-limbed mammals with big brains and stereo vision. But if we are all built from the same base model. Why are we all different, and how do we even begin to explain males and females?

A male human is derived from the basic concept of a human template, but has a few extra bits. A female human is also derived from the basic concept of a human template, and has a few different extra bits.

The human genome, defines a whole range of different variables and values, they alter our looks, build, skin color, eye color, hair, and so on. The vast range of these variations are common variables to both and our genes switch different things off and on. But some genes are only found in our Y Chromosomes, meaning only Males can have them or set things to on/off in our base variables. Making Males and Females quite different (as if we didn't know that already).

But, both derive from a human template, so both are human. If we wrote that in code we could use this

```
class Female :public Human
{
 Female();
 ~Female();
};
class Male :public Human
{
 Male();
 ~Male();
};
```

What this basically means is that we have two types of Human, each has their own constructor and can be identified as being of a class Female, or Male. They are unique, but share the fact they are Human, and their differences can be listed in the class definitions, or used to set up the values contained in variables in the base human class.

So how does this amazingly over simplistic explanation of the battle of the sexes help us draw and update things? We have a base class, called Objects, it's going to grow a little as we go, but basically even now it tells us all we need to know about things that are going to be drawn on screen. But the behavior is going to be different. Say however we write a Bullet Class, which inherits from Objects we can put the behavior of our bullet in its very own class definition and not clutter up the Objects Class.

The definition of our bullets can then look like this.

```
class MyBullet : public Objects
{
public:
 MyBullet();
 ~MyBullet();
}
```

So now, we have a Bullet Class, (actually I called it MyBullet), which derives from Objects, so it has all the Objects traits and variables. It even still has a variable called type though we may not need it any more.

What is different though and now neatly contained in its own class definition and has the code that is unique to it and its update function are now cleanly held in a simple class and readable file.

Now let's get back to Bob, Bob, is a shooter, so we need to create a class for him, so to your project add a Shooter.h file, which contains this class definition code

```
#pragma once
#include "MyFiles.h"
#include "surface.h"
#include "Objects.h"
#include "Input.h"
class Shooter :public Objects
{
public:
 Shooter();
 Shooter(char* f, MyFiles* fh);
 ~Shooter();
 bool Update(Surface*,Input*);
};
```

That's not too complex, we're simply defining a shooter as a type of Objects, which has a constructor without a file name, a constructor with a file name, a destructor, and the important one an Update routine, which passes a pointer to a surface and a pointer to an input system. Oh it also returns a bool. I'm thinking ahead here, that bool might prove to be useful to indicate something that the calling routine might want to know.

Remember, because this is derived from the Objects Class, all the attributes of an Objects are automatically attached to our Shooter Class.

Ok so that's simple enough, let's look at the actual code that we need to write. Add a Shooter.cpp file to your source folders.

And start off by adding the two constructors.

```
#include "Shooter.h"
#include "Game.h"
Shooter::Shooter(){} // empty
Shooter::Shooter(char* f, MyFiles* fh) :Objects(f, fh)
{
 MarkForRemoval = false;
 Type = AShooter;
}
```

We could also add the destructor here, but if we don't enter anything, it will simply use the Base Class destructor, which for our likely needs is all we need. It's up to you. You can add a destructor of your own if you want?

The Constructor is only setting up a few variables. MarkForRemoval will become apparent later.

Now the meat of this class is the update routine, which is actually going to move old Bob around, so add your movement routines now

```
bool Shooter::Update(Surface* a_Screen, Input* a_Input)
{
 bool fire = false;
 if (a_Input->TestKey(KEY_LEFT))
 {
  Xpos--;
  if (Xpos < 0) Xpos = 0;
 }
if (a_Input->TestKey(KEY_RIGHT))
{
Xpos++;
if (Xpos > SCRWIDTH - Image->GetWidth()) Xpos = SCRWIDTH
- Image->GetWidth();
}
Image->CopyAlphaPlot(a_Screen, (int)Xpos, (int)Ypos);
 return fire;
}
```

Ok, so Bob is now happily moving left and right and being drawn. We're done with him for a few minutes.

Now we can see clearer that MyBullet, and Shooter have a lot in common. They both need coordinates to tell us where on the screen they are, they both have surfaces, which need to be copied onto the active screen buffer before they can be seen. These are now nicely contained in our Objects Class. The only real difference between Bob and our nameless bullet is that Bob responds to key controls, and bullets just fly up until they go offscreen.

But we need to be aware of something, Bob and MyBullet both use an update routine, and each update routine is specific. If I want to call the update routine for Bob. Then I must specifically call the update routine for Bob, and also for the Bullet I must specifically call the routine for the Bullet. That's a bit of an annoyance.

But inheritance comes to our rescue again in the form of virtual functions. Our Objects Class also has an Update routine even though it does nothing, which Shooter and MyBullet both can access. But what we really want is for Shooter and MyBullet to use their own Updates but have a single call. We want to be able to call the *Objects* update function and have it use the correct update function for the type of class that the object ultimately is, a Shooter or a Bullet, or even as we will add, the enemies.

This is easily done, we are going to refer to all of our objects regardless of their types as Objects and we're going to call their *Objects Class* update routines. If we make the base objects Update function a virtual function, it means then any class that inherits from Objects and also has an Update function, with the same arguments, will replace or override the Base Class.

This has tremendous benefits for us because we can now keep a list of all the different types of Objects and only ever call one function to update them. If this was not possible, we'd have to do separate calls to each types update function.

Let's examine that more by putting some enemies on screen. We need to add a class, derived, as with MyBullet and Shooter, from our Objects Class. But we are going to make a modification to the Objects Class and add the virtual keyword,

```
class Objects
{
public:
 Objects();
 ~Objects();
 Types Type;
 float Xpos, Ypos;
 virtual bool Update(Surface* s,Input* InputHandler);
 Surface* Image;
};
```

Now any class that derives from this, which has an Update function with the same return value and argument list, will replace this call.

We could also do this;

```
virtual bool Update(Surface* s,Input* InputHandler) = 0;
```

That would indicate this function is a pure virtual, in other words the Base Class has no update routine at all, and therefore any derived classes are forced to provide it. But for now we'll stick with an overridden Update to give us a bit of flexibility.

Every Story Needs a Villan

Ok make an Enemy Class, as before derive from Objects, and it really does not need too much additional content. We don't even really need an update at this point, we'll add that once we've got them set up and displaying.

Now we've got to put 55 enemies on screen here, and each has to somehow be addressed so we can call their update functions, how can we name them in such a way that we know who they all are? We could name them all as postfixes to a name, Galroth the Destroyer and his offspring. So Galroth1, Galroth2, Galroth3, and so on, hmmm 55 of these could get a bit heavy, and besides do we really want to get to know their names before we unthinkingly blast them into atoms?

No, not really, but we do need some way of addressing them, something a bit more usable than third Guy that looks a bit like Galroth to the left, isn't the most effective coding directive!

We know they are all based on an Objects Class. So let's just create some means of storing 55 of them that lets us address them by a single name. There are two traditional ways. Arrays and Vectors.

If we create an array for our 55 guys called Galroth, C++, let's use that name to access them.

```
Objects* Galroth[55];
```

What this code does is create space for 55 pointers to Objects, and we can reference them by using Array indexing, so Galroth1, who sadly will never live long enough to attend a naming ceremony on his victorious return to his home planet, can simply be addressed as Galroth[0]...ermm wait he's Galroth1 not Galroth0.

Well that's to do with a little quirk of array-based indexing, we need to start with 0 as our first index, so our index range for our 55 Galroths is Galroth[0].....Galroth[54], and besides we really don't care what he's called. From now on he's an index, and the cool thing about indexes is we can use variables to get to them.

If we define a variable with a number, we can access the objects update function like this:

```
int I = 25;
Galroth[I]->Update();
```

Is the same as

```
Galroth[25]->Update();
```

Or, had we actually bothered to name him.

```
Galroth26->Update();
```

But to update or otherwise do anything with 55 Galroths, we would have needed 55 individual calls to their proper names. That's not practical, so an array is best because we can loop through it with ease.

Of course so far all we have, is just an array full of empty spaces or random rubbish, there no actual values in there at the moment, so our Game initialize routine must now create our Galroths, line them all up and put them on screen, a bit of work, but it does not now have to create and keep track of 55 individually named objects.

We can still keep Bob as Bob, because there's only one and he's a fairly important object, but these invader scum don't deserve our time to name them all.

Arrays or Vectors

Vectors work a little like Arrays in the way we use them, but the way we create and load them is different, and the reason is really simple. Arrays are absolutely the best thing ever, when you know exactly how many things you are going to create and manipulate at the time of compiling, and don't have any plans to alter that number.

But what if you are not 100% sure how many things you are going to generate…how many missiles can the invaders fire for example? We could limit the amount, but it's more fun if we let them create as many as they want, so that means at compile time we have no real idea how many missiles will be made. We could make an array big enough to cope with the maximum we think we will use, but that's quite wasteful.

Vectors allow us to create dynamic arrays, we can add to it whenever we find we need a new element, we can even remove things if we want, as we shall see soon.

The choice of arrays versus vectors is always an important one. Vectors are functionally a little slower to use, and require more space to set up, but their flexibility is amazing.

Let's try out both systems. We know we have 55 invaders, but we don't know how many missiles/bullets we have so let's use arrays for the invader and vectors for the missiles/bullets.

If we're going to create Aliens though, we will need an Alien Class, so start off making that. All it needs is this for the Aliens.h file

```
#pragma once
#include "MyFiles.h"
#include "surface.h"
#include "Objects.h"

class Aliens :public Objects
{
public:
 Aliens();
 Aliens(char* fName, MyFiles* fh);
 ~Aliens();
 bool Update(Surface*, Input*); // the update we override needs both params
even if we don't use Input
};
```

We'll talk about update in a few moments, but for now this is enough. You can work out the default constructor and destructors, which are not going to do much, so let's look at the main constructor for this.

```
Aliens::Aliens(char* fName, MyFiles* fh)
{
 Image = new Surface(fName, fh);
 MarkForRemoval = false;
 this->Type = Alien;
}
```

And the update function, which for now can be a simple call to the base functions update to provide a draw to the screen.

```
bool Aliens::Update(Surface* S, Input* In)
{
 Objects::Update(S, In);
 bool ReturnValue = false;
 return ReturnValue;
}
```

That will give us now a simple basic ability to create and *update* an alien. Now go inside the Game.cpp file at the init, and let's set about creating 55 invaders, which might seem a simple task, it is slightly complicated by having different graphics on different lines, so we'll create a small array of filenames for the graphics for each line first.

```
char* Names[] =
  {
   (char*)"../Assets/invaders8x8/InvaderA-1.png",
   (char*)"../Assets/invaders8x8/InvaderB-1.png",
   (char*)"../Assets/invaders8x8/InvaderB-1.png",
   (char*)"../Assets/invaders8x8/InvaderC-1.png",
   (char*)"../Assets/invaders8x8/InvaderC-1.png",
  };
AlienCount = 0;
for (int i = 0; i < 5; i++)
  {
   for (int x = 0; x < 11; x++)
   {
    Aliens* T = new Aliens(Names[i],a_FileHandler);
    T->Xpos = (x * 11) + 5;
    T->Ypos = (i * 11) + 40;
    AlienList[AlienCount] = T;
    AlienCount++;
   }
  }
```

Now there was a perfect example of how to use an array when defining a set of objects at compile time, I could have used a hard number 5 like this:

```
char* Names[5] =
```

But as I was defining them as I created them, the compiler was happy to count how many strings I entered. So the number of entries was clearly known at compile time.

AlienList on the other hand, had to be defined in our Game.h file as an array of pointers to Alien instances with 55 entries. As there is no way for the compiler to know how many things were going to be entered into it, compilers have no way to look through your code and understand what you mean by a pair of nested loops creating 55 aliens. So you have to explicitly tell them.

```
Aliens* AlienList[55];
```

All we need now is a small update loop in the Game Update,

```
for (int i = 0; i < 55; i++)
{
 AlienList[i]->Update(a_Screen, a_InputHandler)
}
```

And we're ready to feast our eyes running our project now, we should get our aliens on screen, looking scary and menacing, in a 1978 kind of way. So now we've got our 55 invaders, all lined up and ready to go, but how do we get 55 individual objects to move, bearing in mind that if we shoot some of them the group still exhibits individual movement and any one of them can tell the others to change direction.

Now, that's a perfectly fine example of using an array, but I don't like it, if you look at our Game update function its updating first our player, then 55 objects in an array, and then, though we've not added them yet, we also have to handle bullets and missiles. So that will add an update via a vector (a kind of dynamic array). Giving us, three different updates inside one function. It's not wrong, but for me a golden rule I try to stick to, even though I often fail, is to keep the main update loop as simple as possible. There will always be exceptions to that rule, but the simpler I can keep things the less impact those exceptions with have. So I'll change things now and use a vector for ALL our objects, Player, Aliens, bullets, and missiles.

The change isn't massive but we do have to go back and make a few dirty edits, sorry, I just wanted to you see an array working even if you don't use it this way ever again. Oh and for the more savvy C++ coders, yes, this is terrible code, please wait, I will explain soon.

In the Invaders.cpp add this line to your code outside of any function, this will put it in what is known as global or unreserved space. Here's an especially bad way to define our vector.

```
std::vector<Objects*> MyObjects;
```

As it's in the Invaders.cpp file, only that file will know about it and we really want the Game Class methods to see it, so we need to tell the Game Class, which wants to use that vector that it actually exists, we can do that with this line of code, at the top after the headers

```
extern std::vector<Objects*> MyObjects;
```

So now the Game Class can use the MyObjects vector. Its nasty, but it works.

If we now ensure that our init system in Game loads up the MyObjects list to a vector, although we're not doing it yet, it means we can also load and process other objects in that list, exactly the same way we would with an `Aliens* AlienList[55];`

```
char* Names[] =
{
 (char*)"../Assets/invaders8x8/InvaderA-1.png",
 (char*)"../Assets/invaders8x8/InvaderB-1.png",
 (char*)"../Assets/invaders8x8/InvaderB-1.png",
 (char*)"../Assets/invaders8x8/InvaderC-1.png",
 (char*)"../Assets/invaders8x8/InvaderC-1.png",
};

for (int i = 0; i < 5; i++)
  {
   for (int x = 0; x < 11; x++)
   {
    Aliens* T = new Aliens(i,a_FileHandler);
    T->Xpos = (x * 11) + 5;
    T->Ypos = (i * 11) + 40;
```

```
      MyObjects.push_back(T);
      AlienCount++; // keep track of how many we create so we can tell when
they are all dead
    }
```

And the principle is now exactly the same. But I know that no matter how many other objects I put on this list, or even perhaps remove from it, they will update.

Move Em Out!

Let's get them moving, they move left and right and sometimes down…which means we need a value for them… Since they all move in the same direction at the same time, we can keep that direction as a game variable. Let's use an enumeration to specify the directions and give them easy to remember names. But one thing to remember is they all move as a group, so we need to work out a way to do that, moving them individually isn't going to work.

Add this to the Game.h file before the class is described because this will be used in other places not just in the class

```
enum Directions {Left, Right, Down };
```

And also in the class itself, let's keep a variable, which is going to be one of those directions

```
Directions Direction;
```

Now back to our Game.cpp file. Our update routine only draws our guys at the moment, and it would be nice if we could get them to move but we don't have that. Yet!

So we need our Game loop to do the movements, even though it's against our golden rule to have too much code in there. But at the moment, we don't seem to have a choice, if we want them all to move, we need to do that at the point of access. Let's make it simple… Add this code to your Game loop just before the update loop.

```
for (int i = 0; i < 55; i++)
  {
   float Xstep = 0;
   float Ystep = 0;
   switch (Direction)
   {
   case Left:
    Xstep = -1;
    if (MyObjects[i]->Xpos < 1) Direction = Right;
    break;
   case Right:
    Xstep = 1;
    if (MyObjects[i]->Xpos > SCRWIDTH - MyObjects[i]->Image->GetWidth() - 1)
Direction = Left;
    break;
   case Down:
    Ystep = 1;
    break;
   default:
    printf("Huston, we have a problem");
    break;
   }
```

```
  MyObjects[i]->Xpos += Xstep;
  MyObjects[i]->Ypos += Ystep;
 }
```

Now at first glance this looks ok, we're moving all the 55 aliens depending on the direction they travel, when it gets to the edge, the direction changes…easy huh?

Ok run it and see…

Kinda cool to see the aliens bouncing left and right, but it's not right is it? We've somehow got one guy sticking out and creating a gap.

Why?

Well there's a simple flaw in our system, yes we are moving a group in the same direction, but we also need every single one to check if they are at an edge. That means that five guys at different times in the update cycle are going to change the direction and the guys in front of them, will get the message, the guys behind won't, so there's going to a gradual change in their motion. Not good.

So rather than let them cause the change direction when they detect the edge, we must let them signal that a direction change is needed, and only after all the aliens have moved can we then set a change in direction.

The code for that now looks like this:

```
Directions ShallWeChange = Direction; // keep track of the current Direction
for (int i = 0; i < 55; i++)
{
 float Xstep = 0;
 float Ystep = 0;
 switch (Direction)
 {
 case Left:
  Xstep = -1;
  if (MyObjects[i]->Xpos < 1) ShallWeChange = Right;
  break;
 case Right:
  Xstep = 1;
  if (MyObjects[i]->Xpos > SCRWIDTH - MyObjects[i]->Image->GetWidth() - 1)
ShallWeChange = Left;
  break;
 case Down:
  Ystep = 1;
  break;
 default:
  printf("Huston, we have a problem");
  break;
 }
 MyObjects[i]->Xpos += Xstep;
 MyObjects[i]->Ypos += Ystep;
}

 if (ShallWeChange != Direction) Direction = ShallWeChange;
```

Run that, and check out our cool new left <> right aliens.

Nice, but there's another issue, it's far too smooth, we don't want our aliens to glide like that, we want them to step, and soon to animate. So let's make them move in slightly bigger steps, and also add a timer variable to our Game.h file after direction.

```
int StepTime;
```

Now we need to make sure it's initialized and also we need to create a value that we can easily alter. Let's set a #define TIMEPERSTEP 50 in our game cpp at the top.

Also let's set another #define for SIZEOFSTEP 2

The reasons for this are really simple, we may not be happy with the step size and speed of our movement, but to make adjustments in the code we have to change values like

```
Xstep = -1;
```

Every time we want to make a change, that's two sets and two checks…four times, but by using a defined value we only have to change the defined value once. And there's no danger of us forgetting to change a value somewhere in the code.

Now go ahead play with the TIMEPERSTEP and SIZEOFSTEP values, until you get a nice jerky movement in your aliens. I'm going to stick with 50 and 2 for now.

All pretty neat so far, we've got nice jerky moving aliens, but it's still not right, we need to go down. And Down is a direction all on its own, we also need to change direction after we've gone down… So a bit more logic is needed, we want to go down, then change to a new direction.

Our `Directions ShallWeChange` variable is a local variable, which means it's going to be lost once this routine is finished, so we need a more permanent variable

```
Directions SavedDirectionToChangeTo;
```

So there we have it, aliens moving left to right and dropping as they go. We have our baddies. This is an example of the game loop doing the logic for our enemies, which is not very Object-Oriented Programming (OOP), and also not very flexible. Though for these particular very basic baddies we can live with it for now.

But do you see how cluttered our main loop and Game.cpp file has become…Its really only supposed to process our baddies and check if we're done with our slaughter of invading hordes, but now it's handling the main logic of our aliens. We'll look at this later, for now, let's pat ourselves on the back.

So we've got baddies, we've got Bob, the last savior of the human race, we're almost ready to start killing baddies. But there is something missing before we start on the shooting and the killing and the maiming and the ewuugh. We want to put a bit of animation in here….

Animation 101

Animation at this level really is nothing more than changing our displayed image every so often so that we can create some semblance of motion. It's very much the same concept as flicker books; as you flick through the book, each image is seen by the eye, and for a moment that image is retained, so that when you see another image, slightly different it appears to be a transition.

Cartoons have relied on this concept since the dawn of the film. And computers pretty much are like a bank of Disney animators at a giant desk drawing 50 or 60 frames of screens every second so your eye thinks that things are moving smooth, it's not, it's just images that one after another combine to give the appearance of a smooth moving image.

But all this talk of 50 or 60 frames per second is not relevant to our invaders…who have two frames, and we only really need to change them every couple of seconds.

To make animation work we need to get the right kind of frame in place so let's make a small change to our projects organization.

Our Aliens, are all basically doing the same thing, even though they have three different styles of graphics, they don't do anything different, so we can group them all into one class, which we'll call Aliens. We *could* do three different classes for Aliens, if you plan to make your Aliens do slightly different things that's a good plan, but here, they all just move left/right and down…with different animations, so one class is enough to keep them tidy.

Let's make an Alien Class, also, let's remove the responsibility from the Game Class for initializing the graphics. We do need to know what kind of aliens we're making, but we can define that using a Row value during our set up loop.

As the group movement, is still best controlled by the game loop, which is able to *see* all 55 aliens at once, we won't give our alien any responsibility for movement, we will just allow it to control its animation and keep track of its graphics, so we can remove some of that from the Game Class initialization.

Small point…and this is me being lazy as well as trying to avoid confusion, did you see all those warnings that came up on compile? Now a warning is not an error, but it is a warning that you might have made an error. In this case the warning is

```
warning : deprecated conversion from string constant to 'char*'
[-Wwrite-strings]
```

It's not the worst warning ever, it just means that because we are using char* to track our file names, it's asking us to use the more up-to-date C++ string type. So we can do that… or…we can tell it, no, I really want to use chars please…and that's done by explicitly casting to char*.

Adding a (char*) cast to the start of the strings ensures that our compiler will know that these are char*, you are telling the compiler, "it's what I expect them to be compiled as, now stop complaining and do as I ask" (Use appropriate power crazed internal voice for that statement). It might seem a bit of a chore but it's very good practice to be clear to the compiler!

The key point you must keep in mind, don't let warnings pile up, they are there for a reason, and while most of the time you *can* ignore what they are telling you, sometimes, often in fact, there are good reasons for the compiler to warn you that you might be making a mistake, and those good times, can be obscured by the thousands of simple situations when being clear and explicit costs you nothing. Treat warnings as errors, and make sure your code tells your compiler exactly what you want it to do at all times.

So now our Aliens Class is the type of object we want to create, we can make a few simple changes to our Game::Init so it now looks like this. Much tidier…We moved all the main init code into the Aliens constructor, which you'll find in your folder, but not added to the project.

```cpp
bool Game::Init(MyFiles* a_FileHandler)
{
  int imageWidth, imageHeight;
  StepTime = TIMEPERSTEP;
  for (int i = 0; i < 5; i++)
    {
    for (int x = 0; x < 11; x++)
      {
      Aliens* T = new Aliens(i,a_FileHandler);
      T->Xpos = (x * 11) + 5;
      T->Ypos = (i * 11) + 40;
      MyObjects.push_back(T);
      }
    }
  Bob = new Shooter((char*)"../Assets/invaders8x8/shooter.png",
a_FileHandler);
  Bob->Xpos = SCRWIDTH / 2 + 16;
  Bob->Ypos = SCRHEIGHT- 48;
  MyObjects.push_back(Bob);
  InitDone = true;
  return true;
}
```

Add a #include *Aliens.h* to your Game.h file under the current list of #includes, then alter Game.cpp's init to the new version. Now you can add the new Aliens files into your project. They are very simple, so have a quick look at them. By adding the Aliens.cpp and Aliens.h code to your project, and compiling we will see our baddies are animating and moving... we're nearly there.

Did you notice though that in Game::Update() we didn't do anything to the update loop itself

```cpp
for (int i = 0; i < MyObjects.size(); i++)
{
 MyObjects[i]->Update(a_Screen,a_InputHandler);
}
```

It's still happily processing all the objects in the vector, by calling their update (Surface*,Input*) functions, Aliens, are all Objects Class things, in the same way that Bob, our Shooter, is an Objects Class thing!

Now this still isn't ideal, and the shortcomings, might become apparent soon, but for now we've got movement and animation and we're ready to do the next cool bit. Shooting!.

Hand Me a Bag of Bullets

We put all our input handling code, quite sensibly in the class that actually needs to act on it, our Shooter Class. We can move it left and right simply by testing for key presses. We can also decide when to shoot if the space bar is pressed.

Go ahead and add this code to our Shooter Update code after the left and right Tests and before Image-CopyAlphaPlot.

```cpp
if (a_Input->TestKey(KEY_SPACE))
  {
  fire = true; // fire
  }
```

So, we're just setting a flag, not actually creating any bullets. That's because as it stands this class isn't really able to do that, we can certainly detect our users desire to shoot, but we need a way to create a bullet and put it on our list of things that have to be updated. The problem is our Shooter Class has no access to the main list. That is indeed a problem.

So we're going to have to consider what the best option is. The Game Class is our root for all the game play code, and the list is held in there, which means I have no way in my Shooter Class to add a bullet, only the Game Class can currently do that.

Now there's a few ways around this, and really at this point recognizing the fact our code does not provide the flexibility we need, we should really rewrite it. But as this is a quick and dirty bit of code, let's instead try something else.

By returning a bool value from the update we can leave the code that controls Bobs update to check for that bool value, and if true, get the Game Class to create a nice new Bullet and put it in the update lists. Like this

```
>>>in the Game.cpp file Update function
bool WantToFire = Bob->Update(a_Screen, a_InputHandler);
if (WantToFire)
{
 // do we have a bullet in flight?
  if (Bullet == NULL)
  {// ok let's make a new bullet
   printf("We fired a bullet/n");
   Bullet = new MyBullet("../Assets/invaders8x8/bullet.png", a_FileHandler);
   Bullet->Yspeed = -4; // give it a speed
   MyObjects.push_back(Bullet);
   Bullet->Xpos = Bob->Xpos+4;
   Bullet->Ypos = Bob->Ypos - 12;
  }
}
```

So now the bool that Bob returns, which indicates a desire to Fire, true or false, is stored in another bool, and then tested. We only allow Bob one bullet at a time so a check to see if a Bullet currently exists, is needed, and if we do not currently have a bullet in place, we can now create one, set its values to be starting just at Bob's nose, and then leave it to do its thing. Now we have firing! There's no end to the damage we can do!

▌ Did We Hit It?

Something very important for our bullets is next, knowing whether we hit something, which is harder to do than you might think? It's easy for us to see our bullets travelling up or down screen, and then coming into contact with the enemies or our shooter. But the CPU does not have the benefit of a pair of eyes watching the screen. It knows only a few bits of data that relate to the Objects positions and in fact it actually does not even know that unless we bring it into focus.

That is almost enough, but we also need to know a bit about the size of the sprites we are testing to see if they *collided* on screen with each other.

There are many forms of collision detection used in game programming, but for 2D games using sprites, which are basically squares, one of the most reliable is a box check, which relies on knowing the position of the objects we are testing, and then their height and width. These data are available to us based on a very simple check.

Box Checks

This is the very common box check, or more accurately an axis aligned box check or AABB. It's an algorithm, which is easy to implement, reasonably fast and pretty accurate for objects that are made up of square/rectangles. It does have a few limits though, as you can see in the diagram, it only detects the fact the squares have overlapped, it does nothing to test if the overlap area actually contains any part of the graphic. Testing for that needs a bit more work. But usually it's not needed if our game is moving reasonably fast.

The basic code format for the box check is something like this;

```
if (
 (rect1.x < rect2.x + rect2.width) &&
 (rect2.x < rect1.x + rect1.width) &&
 (rect1.y > rect2.y + rect2.height) &&
 (rect2.y > rect1.y + rect1.height)
 )
{ printf("overlap detected"); }
```

Not too shabby, though even when laid out in one line you can see there are a number of compares, tests and && checks going on so it's got to check quite a few things, you can speed it up a little by breaking the test down into pass/fail tests and returning as soon as a fail is encountered but generally we leave it like this for speed and ease of use.

Circle Checks

Another very popular 2D collision system, is the circle to circle test. It works in a very similar way to the box check but is a little bit faster. It works using our old friend Pythagoras' theorem, to test if the distance between two circles, which encapsulate the main part of our sprite, is less than the combined two radius of the circles.

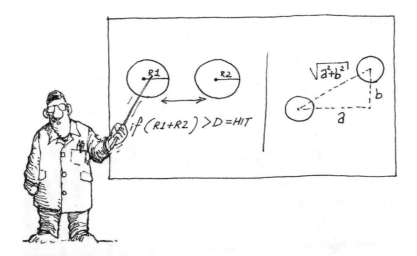

For a simple and quick test, either of these methods are good for us to use. I tend to use the circle to circle test.

```
float R1 = sqrtf((My_Height*My_Height) + (My_Width*My_Width));
float R2 = sqrtf((Ob_Height*Ob_Height) + (Ob_Width*Ob_Width));
// assuming sprite ref is top left, move to the centre
int diffx = ((Xpos + My_Width) - (TheObject->Xpos + Ob_Width));
int diffy = ((Ypos + My_Height) - (TheObject->Ypos + Ob_Height));
float Dist = sqrtf((diffx*diffx) + (diffy*diffy));
if (Dist < (R1 + R2)) return true;
return false;
```

This can be optimized a little by not actually caring about the square root and keeping track of the squared Radius values in the object somewhere because it's unlikely to change. This is my personal preference for a quick fast, reasonably accurate obj<>obj collision test.

```
// do a simple circle/circle test
 float R1 = TheObject->RadSq;
 float R2 = this->RadSq;
 // assuming sprite ref is top left, move to the centre
 int diffx = ((Xpos + My_Width) - (TheObject->Xpos + Ob_Width));
 int diffy = ((Ypos + My_Height) - (TheObject->Ypos + Ob_Height));

 float Dist = ((diffx*diffx) + (diffy*diffy));
 if (Dist < (R1 + R2)) return true;
 return false;
```

Collision checks are one of the most intensive things we can do on a game, because we have 55 invaders, all of them need to check with our shooters bullet to see if they have been hit. That's a lot of tests. And in other games where objects may collide with other objects, each of those objects will have to test with every other object as it tests with you. The number of tests in most games can become very large very quick. So an effective fast test is essential.

Give Me Shelter

The last thing we need now is a series of bunkers or shields to hide behind that provide us with some kind of ablative protection from bullets.

I don't want to spend too long on this, as we need to crack on with other things, but we should certainly put something in here, and you can make it more complex later if you want, but for now let's make this a very simple system of four shield areas each made of four simple squares…

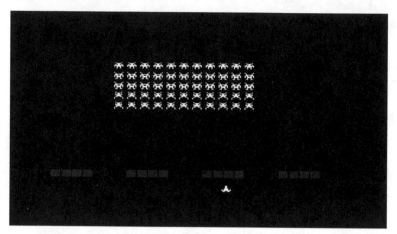

Now you may think that these are totally passive and uninteresting things. They don't move, they don't shoot, they simply stay on screen and degenerate/vanish with hits, it's the bullets and missiles that can do all the work? But they are still objects, so they need to exist as a class.

Create and add Shelter.h and Shelter.cpp files to our projects.

The header is going to look very familiar.

```
#pragma once
#include "Objects.h"
using namespace std;
class Shelter :
 public Objects
{
public:
 Shelter();
 ~Shelter();
 bool Update(Surface*, Input*);
 bool TestForHit(Objects*);
};
```

It's not dissimilar to a Bullet Class, but we're not going to need any graphics for it, so it does not need a file-based constructor. It needs an update, and a hit test, but unlike the bullets, it has to check for hits from both the player and enemies bullets. So it's going to need its own hit routine.

And that presents a problem.

Neither the bullets nor the Invaders have any idea what the shelters are, they have no access to the Shelter instances, which are going to be contained, most likely in the Game Classes MyObjects list.

This is a problem, not insurmountable, but one we need to keep in mind later, because this is an issue of design. We're starting to find the limits of this dirty code. Our classes can't really talk to each other, only through the Game Class. Our own bullet, is a named object we're quite happy to have a bit of code in the update loop as each object is being processed to see if it gets hit by the bullet.

```
if (Bullet) // if we have a bullet check if it hit anything
  {
   if (MyObjects[i] != Bullet)
   {
    if (Bullet->TestForHit(MyObjects[i]))
    {
     MyObjects[i]->MarkForRemoval = true;
     Bullet->MarkForRemoval = true;
    }
   } // if !Bullet
  } // if Bullet
```

Look at that, isn't it horrible? Right in a the end of an already cluttered loop, after we update an object, we then have to make sure we're not the actual Bullet, then test if our current test object is hit. Fair enough, that works we can use that. But that game update loop is starting to look more than a little untidy.

#side note- One thing you might notice is the way my brackets line up. And I also have a couple of comments to show which bracket is associated with which condition. This is a format I like to use, when loops or conditions start to get intense. Having the brackets line up like this, and the code within indented, gives an immediate visual clue as to the way the code works, at least as long as it stays on screen. Massive global wars have been fought and many kittens killed over the correct way to use brackets like this. I try to stay 100% neutral, and use the correct, proper, and only sensible way. But it's up to you! Just make your code as readable as possible, especially when you are going to be prone to errors at this stage of your development.

Right, let's get back to it, we've got maybe 10–12 invader bullets, and 16 shelter blocks to test, to make it even worse our own player bullets can hit the shelters and kill them. Things are starting to get a bit strange. It's no longer a simple case of 1 object testing 1 object, its 10 or more, each testing 16. And to make it even more fun, we don't really know how many bullets are in play, or how many shelters are still standing.

Now you should start to realize why collision tests need to be fast, there's a lot of them likely to happen and for the most part 99% of them are going to result in a negative test.

With the system we have at the moment, there's no real way round this, but, we do have a pretty simple and fast test and a reasonably small number of objects, so let's allow it to do its thing, because trying to test if a collision is needed is probably not going to give us a great advantage.

The first problem though is identifying our interested parties. We know where in the vector things started, but things might move around, that's the nature of dynamic arrays.

As our bullets are more variable in their numbers, we'll let the bullets test for the shelters. But for that to happen we must know where all the remaining (active) shelters are.

This is where we have to hold our hand up and admit, that we can't keep that game loop nice and simple, if we put our Shelters into the normal MyObjects list we will just lose track of them.

So for collision purposes we need to allow the bullets, both types, to be able to test a shelter list, which means another array or vector. Our update loop can update the MyObject list and any bullets in there can access the shelters. But it will also need to update the Shelters so they can be drawn.

Since we do know exactly how many shelter sections there are, 16, we will use an array to store pointers to the shelters, and this has the added bonus of letting us see how both systems work.

Our Game update loop has sadly started to fill up with a lot more code, but we'll learn in time how to improve on that.

Let's make some shelters first, we've got the header, and for now still the code can be empty. But we need to make a few changes to the way we initialize our game.

Go to the Game.h file, and add Shelter.h to the headers and in your Game Class definition add this line

```
Objects* Shelters[16];
```

Now in the Game.cpp file, let's create the shelters in the init function, and also use a generated array to work out where to place them, to make our lives a bit easier when using a loop.

```
// because these are not at equidistant points let's keep a simple table of
x locations to place them
#define BARRIER1 32
#define BARRIER2 BARRIER1+64
#define BARRIER3 BARRIER2+64
#define BARRIER4 BARRIER3+64
 int BarrierPositions[] = {
  BARRIER1, BARRIER1 + 9, BARRIER1 + 18, BARRIER1 + 27,
  BARRIER2, BARRIER2 + 9, BARRIER2 + 18, BARRIER2 + 27,
  BARRIER3, BARRIER3 + 9, BARRIER3 + 18, BARRIER3 + 27,
  BARRIER4, BARRIER4 + 9, BARRIER4 + 18, BARRIER4 + 27
 };
 for (int i = 0; i < 16; i++)
 {
  Shelter* s = new Shelter();
  s->Xpos = BarrierPositions[i]; // use the counter as an index
  s->Ypos = SCRHEIGHT - 48 - 16;
  s->Type = AShelter;
  s->MarkForRemoval = false;
  Shelters[i] = s;
 }
```

Pretty simple, not really much different from the way we created enemies, but rather than using a push.back() function, we just load the empty array position with the pointer to the shelter we just made.

And now the game update needs to also loop through the shelters to draw them. After the main MyObjects loop, add this very simple loop.

```
// Update the Shelters looping 16 times
  for (int i = 0; i < 16; i++)
  {
    Shelters[i]->Update(a_Screen, a_InputHandler);
  }
```

Even though the Update routine for a shelter does return a bool, it is after all an overridden update function; we don't use it, so there's no need to collect it. It's simply going to go to the update and inside that go to the Draw, because the shelters have zero logic to process.

You can compile this and you should now see 16 nicely positioned but currently inactive shelters.

Ok that's drawing and logic where needed, done. Time to do the collision.

We already have the bullet test but it's currently just testing the invaders, we now need to do a second test just after that, to test for the shelters and now the reason for a pair of data lists become clearer.

And now to wrap it up, we need to add some code, so that the bullet objects in our MyObjects list can check this array and see if there is a hit.

Hmmm how do we know which of our MyObjects are Bullets?

Well this is a point where the type variable we included in our Objects Class now actually comes in handy. Though we do now have to make sure that we have the types we have been given during construction, go back and check that when you made an Alien, in the constructor(s) you did set the type to Alien, same for Bullets and shooter. Remember this list?

```
enum Types { Bullet,Missile1,Missile2,Alien,AShooter,AShelter };
```

First let's add to the Bullets test so it can shoot shelters, currently we should have this

```
// if we have a bullet check if it hit anything
 if (Bullet)
   {
    if (MyObjects[i] != Bullet)
    {
     if (Bullet->TestForHit(MyObjects[i]))
     {
      MyObjects[i]->MarkForRemoval = true;
      Bullet->MarkForRemoval = true;
     }
    } // if !Bullet
   } // if Bullet
```

Let's add to that.

```
// if we have a bullet check if it hit anything
  if (Bullet)
   {
    if (MyObjects[i] != Bullet)
    {
     if (Bullet->TestForHit(MyObjects[i]))
     {
       MyObjects[i]->MarkForRemoval = true;
       Bullet->MarkForRemoval = true;
     }
    } // if !Bullet
  // did we hit a shelter
    for (int i = 0; i < 16; i++)
    {
     if (Bullet->TestForHit(Shelters[i]))
```

```
        {
          Shelters[i]->MarkForRemoval = true;
          Bullet->MarkForRemoval = true;
        }
      }
    }
  } // if Bullet
} // update loop
```

So after our own Bullet tests it exists, and makes sure it isn't trying to test on itself, it tests for any Object in the MyObjects list, which contains Aliens and their missiles. AFTER which it then test for all 16 shelters.

Yeah, it's starting to hurt a bit now, our lovely clean Game Update is far from clean with loops inside of loops. But it works. Though the Shelters don't yet remove themselves when hit, in fact nothing does.

This is where that MarkForRemoval comes in, it's been there from the beginning, but now its purpose can be coded.

When we hit something with a bullet, we want it to blow up and vanish, blowing up, we'll get to another time, but certainly we need it to vanish because a dead character that does not go offscreen and out of the MyObjects list is just going to create zombie objects that will never die. We could remove them from the list as we do the update but to be honest that creates a few problems, since objects just killed might have info that objects not killed need. Not that that is the case here but we need to think about it. Removing them should really be done after the update loop has completed, in a clear-up operation. Getting rid of any dead objects and removing them totally from the processing lists so they are no longer actually updated.

As we have two lists of objects we need to clean up loops. MyObjects is the easiest to do first and view.

Remember to add this AFTER the update loop has closed.

```
// scan for a clear up
for (int i = MyObjects.size()-1; i >= 0; i--)
{
  if (MyObjects[i]->MarkForRemoval)
  {
  if (MyObjects[i] == Bullet) Bullet = NULL;
  if (MyObjects[i]->Type == Alien)
    {
    AlienCount--;
    if (AlienCount == 0)
      {
      InitDone = false; // force a new level
      }
    }
  delete(MyObjects[i]);
  MyObjects.erase(MyObjects.begin() + i);
  i--;
  }
}
```

Notice, that the loop runs backward, because if you remove things from the list the number of items in the list is reduced, which can cause a loop counter moving forward to lose track of the number it's testing, but running backward and decrementing the counter when you remove an object gets over that problem. Run your project now, and try shooting a few aliens through the gaps in the shelters. You can see we are actually removing aliens when they are shot. Nice, we're beginning to get some gameplay. But now we have a snag, we have to do the shelters. And we chose to use an array to store those so we need to do things a little differently. In principle, we need to do this;

```
// scan for a shelter clean up
for (int i = 0; i < 16; i++)
{ if (Shelters[i]->MarkForRemoval)
  {delete Shelters[i]; // delete the instance of object
   Shelters[i] = NULL;
  }
} /#note*
```

It does not have to run backward because our Array size is fixed and never changes, so we're not going to have to worry about resizing the array and losing track of how big it is. Enter this, just after the MyObjects clean-up, compile and run, and shoot a shelter, and… we get this

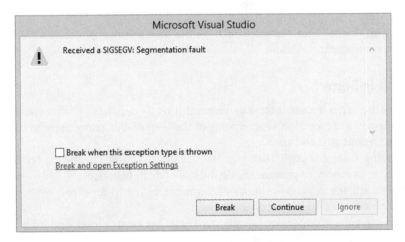

Uggh that's not good. Pressing break will give us a yellow arrow at this line:

```
Shelters[i]->Update(a_Screen, a_InputHandler);
```

which might seem odd, as that's not the code we just entered? But the code we just entered did something very simple to a hit shelter.

```
Shelters[i] = NULL;
```

It caused it to have a NULL or 0 value… the update routine could not call from 0. And created a break.

---

* Please note, I cleared the Shelters[i] value with NULL after the delete, to not do so would leave a dangling pointer, that is, a pointer to an instance of something, which is no longer in use. It might keep working, but the reality is that memory has now gone back into general usage and the next new command that is used could re-use that memory. This is a time bomb of a bug, and often not immediately obvious. Always, NULL or nullptr any pointer immediately after you delete it.

Obviously, this is a bug, but it's an easy one to find and fix, in fact it's one of the very reasons we NULL our dead pointers so that we can get this error coming up if we accidently try to use an invalid pointer. We need to recognize the fact that when we kill an object, we don't want it to be updated. So the fix for this is simple, we might not be able to call a NULL pointer, but we can test if we have a NULL pointer and not try to use it.

Like this;

```
// Update the Shelters looping 16 times
for (int i = 0; i < 16; i++)
 {
 if (Shelters[i] != NULL) Shelters[i]->Update(a_Screen, a_InputHandler);
 }
```

There are two other cases where we are potentially going to use a NULL Shelter, one is in the Bullet test for collision with the Shelters, so you can do a double test on that;

```
if (Shelters[i] != NULL && Bullet->TestForHit(Shelters[i]))
```

I'll leave you to find the other yourself, it's quite simple, Visual Studio will give you a break when you hit it.

Once you've done that, we will now have the basics of our game, go ahead, unleash hell on the alien scum.

So Which Is Better?

So which is the better option, Arrays or Vectors? It really depends on what you need them for and how you use them. We've seen some of the issues when using them to store pointers. Both have and pros and cons.

Removing from an Array isn't possible, leading to extra checks for NULL values, assuming you use them, to prevent accidental use of dead instances.

Once we hit the assigned number of items we define in an array, we can't (easily) create any new entries, so the fixed size limits us.

Removing from a Vector needs a slightly tricky backwards loop, and it's a lot slower, but we can track and alter its size as we please.

But ultimately, you choose what works for you. In an ideal world, we could have all the objects including shelters in one single list, but keeping track of where the shelters are as the vector alters size becomes a challenge, but hardly a difficult one.

Final Details

There are still a last few details we really should add; we need to actually include some game rules, allow ourselves to actually be killed and detect game over when all our lives are gone.

Also the enemies can win, when the invaders get to the bottom of the screen, it's game over.

These game rules should really have been applied right away, but we were having too much fun so now we have to somehow squeeze them in.

These last few things are tasks hopefully kept on our mental to-do list, and are important to making the game fun, but not actually a major part of the game mechanics. These kinds of eye candy features though can make or break the game.

We should have a random mothership popping out from time to time...giving us a chance to do some decisions and divert the players focus for a few moments. It's also possible we can make it do something cool when it comes on or dies...you decide?

Also there's a life counter, which needs to be displayed and updated when we die, or perhaps give ourselves extra lives?

What's left is to indicate an end of game, which, of course, is going to happen when our lives get to 0? But also we have to indicate the end of a level and then reset it to play again, hopefully with some increased level of difficulty.

These are things you should return to later when you are more confident in your coding.

We should have kept a record of the score in a Score variable, which incremented with each kill, but we don't have any way to display it. We know about cout and printf as a means to send info to our console. But that's not going to be much use to a player, who wants to see the score of the game on screen as they progress.

So we need to take our first steps into the world of fonts. This will get a bit more complex later, but for now, on a very simple 320 × 200 size screen, all we need is a some images that look like letters and numbers and come up with a way to display them.

Simple Text Display

Invaders doesn't need any text, but it could make use of a score, which is basically a short string of numerical characters. Since we know how to use surfaces to draw graphics, it should be possible to create Alphanumeric characters as graphics? Let's do that here, by including in our game a screen containing the images for the letters of the alphabet, in an ASCII order so that we can mathematically index to the right character in our set so that we can draw it using our simple square draw system. Oh ASCII, stands for, American Standard Code for Information Interchange, it's the way we arrange our various characters in the English and most other western alphabets so that we know a certain character is attributed to a specific number. It is very useful to keep a copy of the ASCII table to hand. Sadly it's not so useful for eastern and pictorial languages but there are other systems you can research for those. Here's the ASCII table (image from public domain) for the first 127 chars in the western alphabet. The second 129 usually contains the accents and diphthongs of non-English languages.

ASCII TABLE

Decimal	Hex	Char	Decimal	Hex	Char	Decimal	Hex	Char	Decimal	Hex	Char
0	0	[NULL]	32	20	[SPACE]	64	40	@	96	60	`
1	1	[START OF HEADING]	33	21	!	65	41	A	97	61	a
2	2	[START OF TEXT]	34	22	"	66	42	B	98	62	b
3	3	[END OF TEXT]	35	23	#	67	43	C	99	63	c
4	4	[END OF TRANSMISSION]	36	24	$	68	44	D	100	64	d
5	5	[ENQUIRY]	37	25	%	69	45	E	101	65	e
6	6	[ACKNOWLEDGE]	38	26	&	70	46	F	102	66	f
7	7	[BELL]	39	27	'	71	47	G	103	67	g
8	8	[BACKSPACE]	40	28	(	72	48	H	104	68	h
9	9	[HORIZONTAL TAB]	41	29	)	73	49	I	105	69	i
10	A	[LINE FEED]	42	2A	*	74	4A	J	106	6A	j
11	B	[VERTICAL TAB]	43	2B	+	75	4B	K	107	6B	k
12	C	[FORM FEED]	44	2C	,	76	4C	L	108	6C	l
13	D	[CARRIAGE RETURN]	45	2D	-	77	4D	M	109	6D	m
14	E	[SHIFT OUT]	46	2E	.	78	4E	N	110	6E	n
15	F	[SHIFT IN]	47	2F	/	79	4F	O	111	6F	o
16	10	[DATA LINK ESCAPE]	48	30	0	80	50	P	112	70	p
17	11	[DEVICE CONTROL 1]	49	31	1	81	51	Q	113	71	q
18	12	[DEVICE CONTROL 2]	50	32	2	82	52	R	114	72	r
19	13	[DEVICE CONTROL 3]	51	33	3	83	53	S	115	73	s
20	14	[DEVICE CONTROL 4]	52	34	4	84	54	T	116	74	t
21	15	[NEGATIVE ACKNOWLEDGE]	53	35	5	85	55	U	117	75	u
22	16	[SYNCHRONOUS IDLE]	54	36	6	86	56	V	118	76	v
23	17	[ENG OF TRANS. BLOCK]	55	37	7	87	57	W	119	77	w
24	18	[CANCEL]	56	38	8	88	58	X	120	78	x
25	19	[END OF MEDIUM]	57	39	9	89	59	Y	121	79	y
26	1A	[SUBSTITUTE]	58	3A	:	90	5A	Z	122	7A	z
27	1B	[ESCAPE]	59	3B	;	91	5B	[	123	7B	{
28	1C	[FILE SEPARATOR]	60	3C	<	92	5C	\	124	7C		
29	1D	[GROUP SEPARATOR]	61	3D	=	93	5D	]	125	7D	}
30	1E	[RECORD SEPARATOR]	62	3E	>	94	5E	^	126	7E	~
31	1F	[UNIT SEPARATOR]	63	3F	?	95	5F	_	127	7F	[DEL]

So if we lay out our graphic representations of our characters in the same order as the ASCII values, we can do a simple look up system to draw the characters in a string and visualize them on screen. The letter *A* is 65; *X* is 88 and so on. We generally don't store any graphics for the first 32 characters, though as they are actually rather old representations of teletype and printer control codes, but still used in some circumstances. That's ok; as long as we have graphics for space to *z* we just subtract 32 from our alpha numeric char to get the right index. So we can easily represent the text we print or type with numbers that give us indexes into an array of graphics. Simple, though it has limits, we can't scale, for example, whatever size our images are, is the size we will display, but until we need that, this is fine. Once we have some proper access to hardware scaling and some proper fonts, we can expand things.

A Simple Font

Here's our Font

As you can see it goes from a blank space, through punctuation, then numbers, upper case letters, then lower case, up to a few characters beyond a lower case. It's also laid out in a grid, eight characters per line. So we should be able to load it into a Surface, and work out how to copy the right tile into a nice receptive surface that will then contain the new graphic.

There are several ways we can work with this, some more efficient on memory or speed than others. But let's focus on a simple system to get it working. First thing to do is create a new font class and load this image up so we can use it.

Now one thing about our font image is, it's not actually an RGBA image, it has no alpha value and we basically have an image that has 0's for transparent and 1's for any black pixels in it. That presents us with some interesting opportunity to manipulate the data to produce different colors. We could for example decide to create a Red character, which is simply done by taking the 0 or 1 value of the pixel and multiplying by our desired color value, making sure to add an Alpha value so it can be visible.

I'd suggest a fairly simple method we can use, first of all load this into a surface which will act as our store for the font. Then we need a new method in our Surface Class that will draw a selected character using simple x y offsets to locate the 32 × 32 pixels that relate to our character and draw the pixels.

That will give us a very effective font drawing system, our new method can be set up to provide useful features such as color, alpha values, and perhaps even scale. But we do have to write it ourselves.

It's not going to be the most efficient or fastest system but hey we already know that our double buffer system is an insult to the gods of programming so let's keep insulting them. At least it gives us a chance to play with fonts, so let's write a font display system.

The principle is simple, make a surface from that image, and draw the relevant character as from the Font Surface to the game surface. We can enhance it with color and maybe even scaling, but to be honest that will look pretty nasty, this kind of system is best thought of as a straight draw to the screen, if you want bigger text we will need bigger characters. But later we can find ways to scale up.

As with most things, we are going to think of the font as an object to be manipulated, but it's not a game object, so it does not need to inherit from that. So create a new class. I'm calling it TileFont. And this is your header.

```
#pragma once
#include "MyFiles.h"
#include "surface.h"
#define PRINT_AT 1
#define NEWLINE 13
class TileFont
{
public:
 TileFont();
 ~TileFont();
 void FontPrint(char*, Surface* mScreen);
 void SetScreenSizes(int height, int width);
 void SetPrintPosition(int PrintX,int PrintY);
 void SetColour(Pixel Col);
private:
 Surface* TheImage;
 int Xpos, Ypos;
 int CharWidth, CharHeight;
 Pixel TextColour;
};
```

So we can see a familiar looking class formation, a constructor and destructor, and some useful methods, which should be fairly obvious.

Notice this time I made the variables or members as they should be called, for the class private. That forces me to use get and set routines to make changes to them, in this case three set routines, I don't need any get systems just yet so I've not added them.

I've done that because despite my normal preference to make everything public, it's not considered good coding practice, and this class needs to be totally portable, and independent, so ensuring that its members are private, and that it will use its own routines to set them keeps it cleaner for later insertion into a routine.

The cpp file will look like this:

```
// very basic tile font display system
#include "TileFont.h"
TileFont::TileFont()
{
 MyFiles* FileHandler = new MyFiles();
 this->TheImage = new Surface((char*)"../Assets/fontwhite.png",
FileHandler);
 delete FileHandler; // we opened some memory, make sure it is reclaimed
}
```

```
TileFont::~TileFont()
{
 delete this->TheImage; / we don't need this now
}

void TileFont::SetPrintPosition(int PrintX, int PrintY)
{
 this->Xpos = PrintX;
 this->Ypos = PrintY;
}

void TileFont::SetColour(Pixel Col)
{
 TextColour = Col;
}

void TileFont::FontPrint(char* Text, Surface* mScreen)
{
// parse the string till you find the terminating 0
 char* TheString = Text;
 while (*Text != 0)
 {
  char Ch = *Text;
  int index = (Ch - 32);
// now convert index to an offset
  int X = index % 8;
  int Y = index / 8;
  TheImage->CopyBox(mScreen, X,Y, 8, 8, mScreen->GetPitch(), Xpos * 8,
Ypos * 8, TextColour);
  Xpos++;
  Text++;
 }
 return;
}
void TileFont::SetScreenSizes(int height, int width)
{
 this->CharHeight = height;
 this->CharWidth = width;
}
```

There's a new loop system, and a new way to access data.

```
while (*Text != 0)
```

Although for and while loops test for conditions, for is usually associated with an iteration, while however, is looking to see if a particular test condition is done with no regard to how often the loop repeats. We're also using an interesting way to access memory using *Text, which is checking for the value contained in the address Text holds. Since I used a "set of characters contained in quotes" the internal method C++ has for storing such strings adds a 0 to the end to terminate it. My while loop is then searching to see if we've reached the 0 yet, and if not it prints the character and then increments the pointer in Text to look at the next character.

The parsing through the characters is fairly mundane, but the drawing of the characters is a bit more fun, and relies on the idea that we have eight characters in a line, starting with the space character. We then take the ASCII value of the letter we want to print, use modulus to work out which column we want, and a simple divide to an int to get the row.

That will then get us to the character we want to print, which I'll explain in a minute.

Now back to the TileFont Class, notice that I quite deliberately let the constructor create its own file handler, which once used, it deleted. This might seem a bad idea, and indeed it probably is. We know that our Game Class has access to the original apps file handler. But remember I said I wanted this to be an independent plug-in class. So having this temporary filehandler allows me to plug it into any project so long as it also has the MyFiles header available.

You can if you choose to, optimize this and you should later. Since creating a class that you don't really need is quite wasteful. You might also consider not limiting the constructor to loading only one font. I'll let you think about things like that.

There's just one more thing, the actual drawing, from one surface to another, isn't quite covered in the current Surface Class. I need to add a new method to the Surface Class, as the existing copy systems don't work for me. So add this definition into your Surface.h

```
 void CopyBox(Surface* Dst, int X, int Y, int Width, int Height, int
srcPitch, int DestX, int DestY, Pixel Colour);
And the corresponding routine in Surface.h
 void Surface::CopyBox(Surface* Dest, int SourceX, int SourceY,int Width,
int Height, int dstPitch, int DestX, int DestY, Pixel colour)
 {
  Pixel* dst = Dest->GetBuffer();
  Pixel* src = GetBuffer();
  src += SourceY*(this->GetPitch()*Height);
  src += SourceX*(Width);
  if ((src) && (dst))
  {
   dst += DestX + (dstPitch * DestY);
    for (int y = 0; y < Height; y++)
    {
     for (int x = 0; x < Width; x++)
     {
      if (src[x] & ALPHAMASK) dst[x] = colour;
     }
     dst += dstPitch;
     src += GetPitch();
    }
  }
 }
```

We can now print any color of text by setting the color and we can choose the location where it starts and write the text, each frame (remember our screen is cleared every cycle).

Of course, we need to have an instance of a font, so let's get the Game Class to make it like this in the Game.h Class

```
TileFont Font;
```

Not a pointer this time but an example of an automatic instance, which is constructed when the instance of Game is created so there is no pointer. We don't use the "->" operator to access its methods, we use the "." operator as you can see here.

```
// draw the text to screen
 this->Font.SetPrintPosition(10, 14);
 this->Font.SetColour(GREENMASK+REDMASK + ALPHAMASK);
 this->Font.FontPrint((char*)"This is my test text", a_Screen);
```

Print systems usually print text at character positions, within the size of the character itself, so 8 × 8 in this case, rather than pixel positions, but it's a simple thing to change this from character to pixel if you want to add that ability.

So now we can display text. It's not very advanced at the moment, and needs a little help to be able to print a variable since this will only print ASCII chars, but we have STD functions to do that.

If you are wondering about these lines;

```
#define PRINT_AT 1
#define NEWLINE 13
```

They are a maybe, for later. I nearly always use a Print At style text draw when I print text to allow me to, well, print at, any point on the screen and have the locations built into the string I send. But for simplicity and demonstration I used a separate set function. Newline should be obvious too, for the moment we can only print along one line, and this will allow us later to add the concept of a print at newline. If you decided to code it up.

This line below is fine if we want to just print a text line, but it does not really work if we want to print a mix of text and numbers, or indeed even numbers since a variable like score is not stored as a set of characters.

```
this->Font.FontPrint((char*)"This is my test text", a_Screen);
```

So we need to do a bit of formatting, or rather we don't, because C/C++ kindly provides a nice routine for us that prints and formats in to a character buffer, which we can then print with our simple text printer.

So if we want to print our score, we can do something like this:

```
char buffer[50];
 int n, a = 5;
 n = sprintf(buffer, "this is my test buffer %04d", a);
 buffer[n] = 0; //ensure we have a 0 in there
```

This is a cool, old, but clearly still useful, C system that lets us print a formatted string into a buffer, and can also convert numbers into strings even giving them leading 0's (%04d), that buffer is then passed to our text print, which can remove that horrible cast to char* like this

```
this->Font.FontPrint(buffer, a_Screen);
```

Aside from the fact we to have a buffer somewhere accessible, and that has to be big enough to cope with our largest possible string+1, this is a very easy and simple system, which will let us print scores, lives, and hello world on screen.

And now we can print some text and numerical data, it's a little primitive but it will serve our purpose of displaying the score and number of lives we have.

I want to move on now, I know it's far from a finished product, but we have learned all we can from this project for now, it's time to move forward. If you can think of any other features, eye candy or new game mechanics to add, feel free, though as we will discuss in the postmortem, the way this game is put together has some issue that might make it harder than it needs to be, all will become clearer.

How Did We Do? The Infamous Postmortem

So now we're done, we have our game and we can be rightly pleased, or can we? It's rare that any coder should feel 100% happy with their efforts at the end of the project. There are several issues I have with this code that I want us to think about carefully.

1. Why did we have the ugly extern in the code?

2. Why were we not able to get the invaders themselves to fire their missiles?

3. Why is the Game Class still handling all the logic?

4. Why are we loading graphics during actual gameplay?

5. Are we leaking memory?

6. Why didn't I do it right from the offset?

7. That game update loop…ugggh.

8. How can we make it better?

These and a few others you can think about for yourself, are extremely important questions. As our games become more complex we may find ourselves becoming more limited in our ability to do things, so we need to review this. We really need to ask is this the best way to do this project, even though it works, and works very nicely, it's a very poor example of a C++ program.

We had the extern because our vector of objects was based in free memory, in other words it was not held in a class. That made it very hard for us to pass the address of the vector to any routine, which might have wanted to manipulate it. It was convenient to use an extern, but not at all elegant!

This also answers our second question, we could have passed the vector address, and a load of other addresses to the Game Class, and it, in turn, could have passed the address to the update routines, had the update routines themselves been passed a vector address. It would have been far easier though to simply pass the address of a Startup Class, which held these main game variables, if you have the class address, you can access all the values in that class, meaning instead of passing 2, 3, 4 or more different important addresses or variables, we just pass the address of the *Master* Class. We'll do that next project.

Question 3 is a good one, because in some ways we certainly needed the Game Class to control the directional aspects of our alien's movement, but we let it do movement as well, and our animation of our aliens. We're also passing flags back from objects, which are telling our game loop to make new things such as bullets and bombs. That's messy. Ideally, we want this class to simply provide a means to service the objects, not do their actual logic for them.

Question 4 is another good one, and one we need to address right after this so we're ready for the next time. Loading graphics, especially from an SD card, is painfully slow, and here we are every time a bullet or missile gets fired, we are using up several thousand cycles loading the same graphics over and over and over again. We're not really noticing it, because we don't do it more than a few times per frame, but it's still a bottle neck. We don't need to do that. It's important to keep track of things like this. It can lead to memory leaks and massive performance issues.

Question 5…hell yes, we're leaking like a sieve, if you don't know where it will be a very good exercise to look. The problem is we probably will never notice, you might have to play the game 1000 times before you suddenly get an unexpected out of memory error, but it's there…oh it's there. Don't worry you'll realize later, much later on. But I'll give you a clue, every new, should have a corresponding delete. There are a couple of *new*s, which don't!

Question 6, is simple I wanted you to appreciate that even though our game works perfectly, plays well, and does everything we wanted it to do, it's not very well written, you should have felt a little twinge of inefficiency in the way we did it, that twinge is what is going to make you a better coder in the years to come. If you don't like something you really should try to avoid doing it!

So these issues need to be addressed. This will be a good exercise for you later.

Question 7, that update loop, oh that loop, it's painful to look at isn't it? A game loop really should consist of just an input, and update and a draw, in an ideal world! It's not always possible though, but we certainly should not pollute our game loop with movement logic, collision logic, and so on. We'll improve on this as we get better at designing our framework and encapsulating some of the tasks into objects so that their functions become part of the update cycle and we can keep it as clean as possible.

Question 8, leaves the best to last…we need to take note of what we learn; every project is a learning process. We're going to do a lot wrong, there's no need to get upset about it, but the trick is to do less wrong each time and review what we did. If you're really serious, you can go back and rework past projects to avoid the mistakes you made. Let's start by dealing with something that really made my skin crawl.

▌ Fix Question 4

So yes, this one bothers me so much, and it's hopefully bothering you to want to fix it now before we move on. Let's consider this, we've got 55 invaders, all loading 2 images for their animation, but there are only actually 6 images….our game is loading and storing space for 110 images. But we only display 6, 6 is all we display, not 110, 6. There are only 6 images!

You get the idea. This is kind of wrong. Surely there is some way to re-use the images?

'Course there is…let's consider what our surface class calls an Image, it's just a pointer to a pixel buffer. So if we create six pixel buffers containing our images. Then can tell the Objects to simply point at the right image.

Let's make a new constructor, which does not create a new pixel buffer, but uses an existing image. Like this

```
Objects::Objects(Surface* a_Image)
{
  Image = a_Image;
  MarkForRemoval = false;
}
```

So rather than passing a file name and making a brand new image every time, we can pass it an image, perhaps already loaded in the Game Class during its initialization, and it will create that image.

Another option is to use a list of images and pass that to a constructor, there really are no limits on how many constructors we make; the only constraint is they must pass different types or quantities of parameters or a different order. Since C++ differentiates a constructor by the fingerprint of the type of parameters it needs to send and return.

Our Aliens need two images, to be stored in Image1 and Image2, which during the course of animation are loaded to the Objects main display Image. So we need a constructor for the Aliens that can take two images.

Now by choosing to load the actual images in the Game Class at the start of initialization, we're only loading six images, which can be stored somewhere to be given to the Alien Class. So the start of our Game Init can now look like this:

```cpp
bool Game::Init(MyFiles* a_FileHandler)
{
 int imageWidth, imageHeight;
 StepTime = TIMEPERSTEP;
 AlienCount = 0;
#define PRELOAD
#ifdef PRELOAD
 char* Names1[] =
 {
  (char*)"../Assets/invaders8x8/InvaderA-1.png",
  (char*)"../Assets/invaders8x8/InvaderB-1.png",
  (char*)"../Assets/invaders8x8/InvaderC-1.png",
 };
 char* Names2[] =
 {
  (char*)"../Assets/invaders8x8/InvaderA-2.png",
  (char*)"../Assets/invaders8x8/InvaderB-2.png",
  (char*)"../Assets/invaders8x8/InvaderC-2.png"
 };
 Surface* Images1[5];
 Surface* Images2[5];
 for (int i = 0; i < 3; i++)
 {
  Surface* s = new Surface(Names1[i], a_FileHandler);
  Images1[i] = s;
  / reload s
  s = new Surface(Names2[i], a_FileHandler);
  Images2[i] = s;
 }
/ rearrange things because we have 3 images to fill 5 rows.
 Images1[4] = Images1[2];
 Images1[3] = Images1[2];
 Images1[2] = Images1[1];

 Images2[4] = Images2[2];
 Images2[3] = Images2[2];
 Images2[2] = Images2[1];
 for (int i = 0; i < 5; i++)
 {
  for (int x = 0; x < 11; x++)
  {
```

```
    Aliens* T = new Aliens(Images1[1], Images2[1]);
    T->Xpos = (x * 11) + 5;
    T->Ypos = (i * 11) + 40;
    MyObjects.push_back(T);
    AlienCount++; // keep track of how many we create so we can tell when
they are all dead
   }
 }

#else
 for (int i = 0; i < 5; i++)
 {
  for (int x = 0; x < 11; x++)
  {
   Aliens* T = new Aliens(i, a_FileHandler);
   T->Xpos = (x * 11) + 5;
   T->Ypos = (i * 11) + 40;
   MyObjects.push_back(T);
   AlienCount++; // keep track of how many we create so we can tell when
they are all dead
  }
 }
#endif
>>>cont
```

I used a nice preprocessor feature here too, with the #ifdef, #else and #endif. These are compiler directives that ask if the label I am testing exists, not that it has a value, but has it been defined, and if yes, it will compile the snazzy new code. And if not it will compile the old and wasteful code. If I want to use the old code, just comment out the #define PRELOAD.

The snazzy code needs a different constructor in Alien Class, which can use the two Surfaces; can you work out how to add that yourself?

The Aliens will still work exactly the same way. Using them exactly the same way, and we saved 104 * 32 * 32 * 4 bytes that's 416 k ...Also, though it might not be so noticeable, we're not loading 106 extra images, which takes up a fair chunk of time saved on our initialization, that's nothing to sniff at.

There are reasons of course why we might want to have 110 separate images but not today! It's generally better to ensure images are not duplicated and loaded at times when speed is not important.

We may not really have noticed this though, because we only did these loads when we set up the aliens for the first time, so it was our initialization system that was a little bit slow, however that was largely done in under a second just before the game started. Chances are we simply never thought about how long it was taking, and never gave much thought to the waste of memory.

It's MUCH more worrying to think that every time we fire a bullet or missile and create a new instance of one of those things, this loading process is happening for every single thing, so we must resolve that.

So as with the aliens, make sure you load the graphics in the Game Class initialization and make sure the update routine passes the location of the Game Class to the actual invaders update, that will then ensure that the Aliens can get access to the bullet graphics, to make a new instance of a bullet and are able to look at the list of currently active objects for any other tests we may want them to do.

Now that, is a far better and more effective system and clearly one we should have done right away. But let's not wallow too much in doubt and self-loathing, we have our whole careers ahead of us to indulge in that, for now we've written our first actual game, albeit with a few concepts altered from what you may remember from the original game. Keep this game safe for now, as we learn new things, I want you to come back to this and add new features so that you can customize and enhance this game to make it your own special personal version.

▌ A Pat on the Back

Let's examine what you did, not the code, that's pretty simple stuff with lots of errors, what have you achieved in making this game, what are the component parts of the game you just made?

You learned how to draw things, and create things that can actually respond to key presses and shoot more things that have a form of movement logic. You can see the process in terms of bullets and missiles flying and causing things to die, you tracked the score, you can avoid being shot and see these events take place on screen. You even started to gain some insight into why code that seems to work does not really perform the way you need it to.

It's all a bit rough and ready, and has quite some number of little bugs that you can try to find, but as our first attempt to write an arcade game it's pretty neat.

What you did, is really quite amazing, you have created a virtual world where you are the person controlling Planet Earth's last defence against a band of marauding arm waving pixel monsters…but really you've done so much more.

It is vital that you realize, ALL the concepts presented here are observable in any modern First Person Shooter (FPS*) you will see on the latest PCs and consoles. Time now to put my tongue in my cheek and do my Halo is Space Invaders, pitch….But really think it over, the only real differences between our invaders game and the year 2045s Halo 26, The Return of Master Chiefs Grandson on Xbox 19, is complexity. In Halo, you move around under user control, you shoot baddies, and they in turn shoot at you, you accumulate a score, you hide behind things and you see it all rendered on a screen, the power of your imagination and the computers response to your input, makes it as real as you need it to be.

Your first proper game project has all the same basic qualities as the most advanced FPS games you can buy……the only difference is complexity! Even the story boarded, cut scene, dialog-driven immersive 3D aspect of modern games is rather irrelevant to the fact that you are still moving around in an area, shooting projectiles at things and avoiding being shot. Games really have not changed that much. We've added to them for sure, in spades, and there's no real way we can individually hope to put in the man hours needed to make a modern FPS from scratch, but you must take notice of the fact that almost every shooting game you can think of, owes its basic DNA to your first proper game project!

Let's take our invaders game and add a little more complexity as well as a touch more refinement, to change it into another classic homage to a retro game from the 1980s, which I'll also avoid naming but I hope you will seek it out.

---

* FPS also stands for Frames Per Second in relation to programming, I will probably use this term a few times but you should get the meaning from the context.

⬛ Kamikazi Invaders

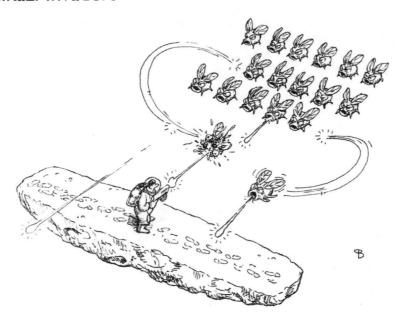

This game involves some nice new graphics, this time in color. The original was one of the first games to use color sprites, which really made it stand out and become a classic.

Rather than just simply moving left and right, sometimes we're going to let a few of our invaders fly and drop a hail of bombs on your poor shooter, which operates pretty much the same way as before but without any shelters to hide behind.

We're also going to tart it up a bit, the plain black background of our invaders game needs a bit of pizazz to make it more fun.

Download the Kamikazi base project from the support site, you will see its essentially still the InvaderStart project we achieved before adding gameplay, but I've renamed a few things, this is going to be our baseline project for the next few games.

We're going to keep our original Game Objects Classes, Collision Classes, and input systems from Invaders, so I've copied them from the Invaders Project directory into the Kamikazi directory and added them to the new project, but the graphics and Game Class are not going to be usable for this, so we'll need new ones for this.

Also it's time for us to increase our screen resolution to 1024 × 720, still an older resolution but will give us a better level of detail. We'll use some much bigger sprites though still quite simple.

Finally we're going to organize our classes a little better so we can do away with those nasty extern commands and get better access for all our objects to info held in the main Game Class.

Good, we're ready.

Let's do what we did before and list the games basic features and mock up a screenshot:

- We have five rows of baddies, slightly different numbers in each row, which change frames and slight differences in graphics.

- We have bullets our shooter can fire.

- We have missiles raining down on us in an apparently random way.

- We have aliens, which seem to fly down intent on crashing into us.

- Aliens return to their formation position if they make it offscreen.

- We can hit the aliens with our bullets—they blow up.

- Our bullet sits on our ships nose when available, only one at a time.

- And we can be hit by their bullets—we blow up. And we lose a life.

- We also have some score system.

- We move our shooter left and right, and fire.

- The invaders move left or right then back.

- If we kill them all, they come even faster.

- We have a moving star field in the back.

So a lot of similarities, and a few interesting differences. We know how to create things that move left and right. We know how to make bullets fly, we know how to do the collisions.

The unknowns are the dive-bombing aliens and the star field.

We also have the advantage of experience now; we know we did some things badly last time, so let's work to avoid that this time.

- Let's do the Star field first.

- Create and control our shooter.

- Give the shooter bullets and test for hits.

- Set up the enemies moving left and right.

- Then work on the dive bombing.

Star fields are pretty easy, as you can see the stars are all moving in one direction, they are randomly placed, and for fun we'll make them twinkle a bit. The StarField Class is all set up for you but has no actual code yet. First up, decide on a number and add this in StarField.h

```
#define NUMBEROFSTARS 50
```

Anything between 50 and 100 should be ok!

There is a keyword in our description of star fields, they need to be *Randomly* placed. So we are going to need our random functions again. This time though instead of using them to make decisions, we will use them to actually generate positions.

Like everything else we can use Stars as derivations from Objects with a surface to hold their graphics, so let's make them up, and put them into an Objects list, which can easily be an array this time as we are fixing the amount of them.

So first things first, let's define a new class for stars in Star.h

```
#pragma once

#include "simplebob.h"
#include "surface.h"
#include "Game.h"

class Star : public SimpleBob
{
public:
 Star();
 ~Star();

 bool Update(Surface*, Input*);
 bool Update(Game* G);
 void Draw(Surface*);
private:
 Pixel Colour1;
};
```

It's a very small class because it really does not need much, it derives from SimpleBob, an equally simple class that essentially is empty at the moment but may be useful as a graphic object that by definition is going to be simple, at this point I am thinking it might end up being removed, but for now I'll allow it to stay in case I think of something else I want to create that derives from it.

We could even make our stars purely as SimpleBobs, but as I want to do a few different things I prefer to keep the SimpleBob Class as separate as possible. As often, this is a choice you need to make, create a Star Class on top of the SimpleBob, or replace SimpleBob with a Star Class?

SimpleBob though does itself derive from our Standard GameObject so all the usual game object values we might need are there for us, also since SimpleBob supplied versions of the GameObjects virtual functions I only need to supply one Update routine and one draw routine for Star.

The actual star code in Star.cpp looks like this

```
#include "Star.h"

Star::Star()
{
 this->Xpos = Rand(SCRWIDTH);
 this->Ypos = Rand(SCRHEIGHT);
```

```
  Colour1 = REDMASK+BLUEMASK+GREENMASK+ALPHAMASK;
}
Star::~Star()
{
}
bool Star::Update(Game* G)
{
  this->Ypos++;
  if (this->Ypos > SCRHEIGHT - 2)
  {
    this->Ypos = 0;
    this->Xpos = Rand(SCRWIDTH);
  }
}
void Star::Draw(Surface* TheScreen)
{
  Pixel* dst = TheScreen->GetBuffer();
  dst[TheScreen->GetPitch()*(int)Ypos + (int)Xpos] = this->Colour1;
}
```

This is really nice simple code, a constructor, to place it randomly within the top of the screen and give it a color, which for the moment is fixed, an update routine to move it down, and reposition it when it gets to the end, and lastly a draw routine to display it.

Notice, there is no Surface or Image to draw here, it's just a pixel. If we used a surface we could have used a simple copy-to function but here we can see the idea of using a single-dimensional array, in this case our screen, being accessed by the X and Y values. This is a nice feature of C/C++ using a base pointer address as the start of an array; it allows us to directly access memory using index values from that base. Though, a small caution is needed. It does not ever check if your index is outside the range you allocate to the array space/buffer allocated. So an incorrect address will still be written to, often with unpredictable results.

Run your new code with stars and see what happens?

Cool, we have stars; they are currently a bit dull, though let's work on that twinkle idea.

Our update routine needs to move them, down at a steady place.

Our Update can do more things though, let's add a little animation counter and other things, and we can if we want to use an image rather than a pixel. The choice is entirely ours.

Let's try drawing a couple of very small images and creating some effect.

Now if you look in the Star Class header file, you will see we only have 1 Pixel, called Color1

Add three more, called Color2, Color3, and Color4.

```
Pixel Colour1;
Pixel Colour2;
Pixel Colour3;
Pixel Colour4;
```

Run your code... fixing any typo's you might encounter, there shouldn't be much too worry about here as we only added some Pixels into the mix, we're not using them yet.

So, now we have colors, all currently defined but empty, let's load them up with nice values. Our Pixels are made up of different intensities, or levels, of Red, Blue, and Green, and what's called an Alpha value, to decide how transparent it is on screen.

In our Star constructor method, we have this line of code.

```
Colour1 = REDMASK+BLUEMASK+GREENMASK+ALPHAMASK;
```

This effectively sets the Colour1 to white, because these Mask values have all the binary digits set for those colours. We'll discuss masks and binary a bit more later.

We could make Colour2–4 variations after you set the value for Colour1

```
Colour2 = BLUEMASK + GREENMASK + ALPHAMASK;
Colour3 = REDMASK + GREENMASK + ALPHAMASK;
Colour4 = REDMASK + BLUEMASK + ALPHAMASK;
```

Now hopefully you've been paying attention, and you remember that having to reference individual variables by their specific name is a bit of a pain, especially when we want to reference them using a variable… So we're not going to change the code a bit here and get rid of Colour1 and replace it with a nice array called Colours.

```
Pixel Colours[4];
```

All we have to do now is alter the code in our Star constructor to create four colours, which live in this array, like this.

```
Colours[0] = REDMASK+BLUEMASK+GREENMASK+ALPHAMASK;
Colours[1] = BLUEMASK + GREENMASK + ALPHAMASK;
Colours[2] = REDMASK + GREENMASK + ALPHAMASK;
Colours[3] = REDMASK + BLUEMASK + ALPHAMASK;
```

Notice I made sure that was always there ALPHAMASK, this will make sure that we can see it but we can still play with it later. Now in the Star::Draw method, let's add a line and alter one.

```
Pixel Col = Colours[Counter];
dst[TheScreen->GetPitch()*(int)Ypos + (int)Xpos] = Col;
```

I have a Counter variable, be sure to add that as an int into your Class definition, and in the update method, we'll add this

```
Counter++;
if (Counter > 3 ) Counter = 0;
```

Ok, so we're good to go? Compile, and run, if you've made any typos, or forgotten to add the Counter in the Class definition then go do your fixes and try again.

Not bad eh, but you can barely see the blinking, it is happening, but the update rate is so fast, probably well over 30 fps, that it just makes it seem a bit blurry. It's up to you if you want to keep this, but for me, it's not quite having the impact I wanted, how can we slow the animation down?

Simply using numbers 0–3 creates too fast an animation so let's try something else, use a much bigger number and scale it down, let's allow the counter to go up to a large multiple of 4, try this;

```
Counter++;
if (Counter >= 4 * 32 ) Counter = 0;
```

Why are we using 4 * 32 and not 3 * 32? Well it's due to the fact we are going to divide it down, and we want to have; 32 uses of 0, 32 uses of 1, 32 uses of 2 and 32 uses of 3, so there are actually 4 numbers we want, 0,1,2,3. We want to display each color for an equal amount of time. We basically are allowing it to go over 3..so that 3 gets used, but never over 4.

So now we have the counter working, change Draw, to use this line instead.

```
Pixel Col = Colours[Counter/32 ];
```

And there you can see the /32, which makes sure we never have a value bigger than 3, since the index is an int, the floating point part will always round down so we'll get 0,1,2 and 3 as possible index values. There is however a better way to do this, I won't say what just now, but if you know a bit of maths and C++. Feel free to change it. Run that and you should see them all changing color.

Ok but they are a bit uniform…let's give them different numbers, and keep a copy of it, (in the Star's specific member list). Let's make sure that the counter is slightly different for each one when we start them, using our friend Rand(32), add this after your array setup in the Star Constructor;

```
Counter = Rand(32);
```

Much better, 50–100 little stars moving down screen at a nice steady pace twinkling… hmmm should we try changing the speeds? It might add a little more variation? Add more color, change the Alpha values? Feel free, it won't do any harm and it's a good little enhancement you can work out yourself.

That's our stars done; we can be comfortable with that. Or can we? The Pixels work very well, but you could just as easily do the same effect with small images, four small representations of stars, why not try that for yourself. Try adding a few surfaces in your Star Class, and draw those rather than pixels, change the image to create animation and watch it do its thing autonomously!

So…Stars, not quite the dumb things we thought, they move, they *animate* and they reposition themselves when they go offscreen. It's not complex logic, but it is logic. You can add to that any way you want, make them move diagonally for example?

All the code is neatly contained in the update method of the Star Class so to make changes we just alter the update routine, we can even have variations of type, as we'll see a little later.

The Ship

Our shooter is a little better defined in this game, so let's call it a ship this time. It's not really very different from the Invaders ship, we still create a class, load a graphic, and control it left and right with firing, there is a slight difference, though it keeps its bullet at its nose ready to fire.

So let's write our Ship Class:

```
#pragma once
#include "GameObject.h"

class Shooter :
  public GameObject
```

```
{
public:
 Shooter();
 ~Shooter();
 Shooter(char* filename, MyFiles* filehander)
  : GameObject(filename, filehander) {}; // creates an image from the file
// these replace the pure virtuals
 bool Update(Surface* s, Input* InputHandler);
 bool Update(Game* g);
 void Draw(Surface* TheScreen);
};
```

No real difference here is there? Everything should be pretty familiar with the original invaders shooter.

The class itself is supplied to you as an empty class, all we really have at the moment is the draw routine. I'll let you add the update function, which uses the InputHandler to make your ship move left and right.

```
#include "Shooter.h"
Shooter::Shooter(){}
Shooter::~Shooter(){}
bool Shooter::Update(Surface* s, Input* InputHandler){}
bool Shooter::Update(Game* g){}
void Shooter::Draw(Surface* TheScreen)
{
  Image->CopyAlphaPlot(TheScreen, Xpos, Ypos);
}
```

The bullet presents a minor problem, when it is available to fire; it needs to be on the nose of the ship. But for that to happen, we need to know where the bullet is, or the bullet needs to know where the ship is, the choice is up to us.

I prefer to have the ship know where the bullet is, because the ship is going to be a fairly constant object in our world, though in truth so is our bullet as it never actually gets deleted. But the Ship is where most of our control goes and we want the bullets to be as autonomous as possible, so let's make sure the Ship knows, by adding a value into the Shooter Class, which can point to where the bullet is (once it's created).

```
GameObject* TheBullet;  /Bullet location
```

Ok, so make a little note somewhere that when you initialize the bullet you must make sure you tell the Ship where the bullet is, we're going to come back to this later. For now, just make sure that value has a null in it, when you create the shooter, so we don't accidently end up pointing at mad memory, we do that with this bit of code at the Shooter constructor

```
Shooter::Shooter()
{
  TheBullet = NULL;
}
```

This seems fine so far, let's get our init systems to create our ship and try moving him around a bit.

Da Baddies!

Now the baddies this time are arranged a little differently, but essentially do the same left<>right thing, but no down movement... So that's easy.

However, we don't have a nice even 5 × 11 grid like Invaders had, so we can't use a simple mathematical method to position our aliens.

But we can take a note of x and y positions we want them to be when they start, but like any other list we can write it down, but to avoid having a massive list of *hard* numbers that can't be changed without having to edit every number we'll define them from previous values.

```
#define Row1 48
#define Row2 (Row1 + 32 + 8)
#define Row3 (Row2 + 32 + 8)
#define Row4 (Row3 + 32 + 8)
#define Row5 (Row4 + 32 + 8)
#define Row6 (Row5 + 32 + 8)
```

By defining our Row1 as 48, we can accumulate previous defined rows to give us a fairly easy set up for the y positions of our aliens. Also we are going to keep our aliens at a specific distance away from each of them, so we can define that distance as a variable... And then lay out our new aliens.

```
#define DIST 40
 int AlienCoords[46 * 3] = // we could use a [46][3] but it's not so hard
to use a single
 {
   // top row ALIENS we use X,Y,Type
   (SCRWIDTH / 2) - 100,Row1, 0,
   (SCRWIDTH / 2) + 100 - 32,  Row1,  0,
 //2nd row 6 aliens
   (SCRWIDTH / 2) - (3 * DIST), Row2, 1,
   (SCRWIDTH / 2) - (2 * DIST), Row2, 1,
   (SCRWIDTH / 2) - (1 * DIST), Row2, 1,
   (SCRWIDTH / 2) + (0 * DIST), Row2, 1,
   (SCRWIDTH / 2) + (1 * DIST), Row2, 1,
   (SCRWIDTH / 2) + (2 * DIST), Row2, 1,
   // 3rd row 8
   (SCRWIDTH / 2) - (4 * DIST), Row3, 2,
   (SCRWIDTH / 2) - (3 * DIST), Row3, 2,
   (SCRWIDTH / 2) - (2 * DIST), Row3, 2,
   (SCRWIDTH / 2) - (1 * DIST), Row3, 2,
   (SCRWIDTH / 2) + (0 * DIST), Row3, 2,
   (SCRWIDTH / 2) + (1 * DIST), Row3, 2,
   (SCRWIDTH / 2) + (2 * DIST), Row3, 2,
   (SCRWIDTH / 2) + (3 * DIST), Row3, 2,
...continues (see source)
```

Notice that we are also using SCRWIDTH, because it's a predefined value that we can be confident of using that will allow us to center these aliens in the middle of the screen. Though we are still using a few hard numbers but we can make simple adjustments by altering the value in Row1 and DIST rather than altering 46 entries we only need to make a few small changes.

Now in code, we can represent lists like this, which have a set number of entries as a 2D array:

```
int AlienCoords[46][3]
{
  { 300, 100, 0},
  { 320, 100, 0},
  { 320, 100, 0},
  ...
```

So this is an Array just like we had with our invaders that has 46 entries, with 3 values in each entry. You look down to find the relevant alien you want using a variable or a hard number to pick.

Like this:

```
XCoord = AlienCoords[23][0]; // get the first value, which is where we have
our x's
```

And this:

```
YCoord = AlienCoords[23][1]; // get the second value, which is where we have
our y's
```

Two-dimensional arrays are very important as we'll discover later, but it's not always necessary to set them up, where we have an equal number of elements per entry, it's simple enough for us to know that can do a simple calculation of the Y index * the number of elements and add an x offset/index to get the value we want.

Two-dimensional arrays need a bit more typing and can also present a few minor issues when passing a 2D array as a parameter, though none of this is an issue in this project. I'm just being a bit lazy and making sure you are fully comfortable with single-dimensional arrays before we move on.

Now that we have the positions, and types of aliens we can go right ahead and create our aliens and put them on screen.

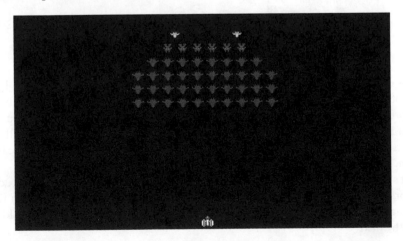

So we have our ship and baddies, we might as well get the bullet and collision done, exactly the same as we did before. I'll leave you to add that?

Now We're Talking

Ok, so here we go, time for the major difference in this game, we have to make these baddies fly toward us, but we're going to do it in a particular way. Only the top two aliens should dive bomb at us first, before we let the others have a go.

But how do they dive-bomb…we can break it down into steps

1. Doing an Arc

2. Flying down toward the ship on a death dive

3. Dropping bombs on the way

4. Going offscreen if they don't crash

5. Returning to their position

There is one other feature that would be nice to have, it would be very cool to have the aliens rotate around their center in order to make the arc and dive more impressive create the impression that they are banking as they change direction. However, we don't have a rotation method in our Object Class or draw system. Hmmm well for now we'll have to leave it…but how cool would it be? Why not try to create a new draw system that can allow rotation. Put it on a to-do list.

Let's consider the steps, or as coders like to call them the states. We have six distinct behaviors that our individual alien needs to do…and lucky for us they can do them in order, that lets us track certain conditions that will indicate when one state should transition to the next.

1. Moving left and right, this seems like a no brainer but we have a small complication that will be more obvious in Step 6.

2. Arcing, well arcing needs a bit of maths, if you remember your high-school maths you will know you can draw a circle using sin or cos of an incrementing angle to plot points, we can use that here, so long as we keep an incrementing angle, this can also indicate to use when our arc is finished since if it goes over 180°, we are done with arcing and ready to fly.

3. Diving, so this state is easy, we want to dive bomb our ship, so we are going to aim our alien just to the left or the right of the ship depending on our direction and set up something called a vector, which will be explained in a bit.

4. Dropping bombs. While diving, at a certain point we are going to open the bomb bay and let a load of bombs drop, hopefully catching the ship at its current position.

5. Going offscreen, again continuing to Dive but now checking to see if we have gone offscreen.

6. This is a slightly tricky move because they need to come back in from the top of the screen and home into the position they were in before their dive, so we need to know where our position is to return to, and as the aliens will have moved while we are diving that position is changing every single frame... So in Step 1 we need to keep track of their left<>right positions and whatever position they have when they are flying.

So again by laying out the features we have identified some new variables we are going to need to keep track of and a problem in that we need to keep track of our normal left/right moment position. We also need to give the top aliens a priority for when to start a dive, and decide when to dive. Perhaps we can even let them take a few of their chums with them.

In code, we can define these different states using an enum command, because it's easier to add to the states and change values when we don't have to look for hard numbers.

This means a command like:

```
if (State == Moving) DoMove();
```

is a lot easier to alter than:

```
if (State == 0) DoMove();
```

Why? I hope you're asking yourselves. Well if you remember that moving is 0, then that's good, but suppose you decide to add another state, or you end up with 20 different states and then need to add one in the middle, it can get a bit hard to keep track of which number means what? Confusion is the enemy of all coders, so it's good that our C++ and other languages provide options to keep things in order for us.

We could #define multiple values, but since we might add things in the middle, it might mean hunting down and changing multiple #defines.

A much simpler trick is to use an enum, with an extra twist of a typedef like this

```
typedef enum Status
{
 Moving = 100,  Arcing,Diving,Bombing,FlyOff,FlyBack
} Status;
```

So what this means is that Moving has the value 100, and Arcing 101, Diving 102, and so on. But more importantly typedef creates a new type of variable, which in this case can consist only of these listed values, Moving, Arcing, and Diving. We can insert or remove values into this list quite easily and the numbers assigned will change but the code does not need to. So we can now define our variable State as a type Status like this;

```
Status State;
```

Finally, why did I start with 100? Well when all said and done, the Status type is still basically an int, and it's not impossible for us to accidently test for something using another typedef'd int that has the same value, so it's wise to make each enum start at a different base. It's not essential, but it is wise. The compiler will take care of the numeric for us, we just have to use the names we've assigned to the numbers, the numbers can change each compile but the code will always look the same and be understandable to us.

Now we can put a simple switch/case combo into our Alien::Update methods like this:

```
switch (this->State)
{
case Moving:
 break;
case Arcing:
 break;
case Diving:
 break;
case Bombing:
 break;
case FlyOff:
 break;
case FlyBack:
 break;
default:
 printf("Something undefined happened in Alien Update!\n");
 break;
}
```

We now have to fill in the code for each step, notice the default state, which is there to catch anything we forget to write code for. If you see that text in your console, fix it right away! It's also another reason why I set up the Moving value as 100, because if you don't initialize it, it will most likely be set to 0, causing this to immediately trigger. And making sure you check your initialization/constructor settings.

Make Them Move

Ok, so first on our list of steps is to make them move. We did this in the Invaders game but here it's actually a lot simpler, there's no down step but we do want them to switch direction when they get to the edge.

Notice that in the `Alien::Update` definition, I return a `bool`, we'll use that to tell the group manager, which controls the aliens, that the direction has changed. But as with invaders we won't let the aliens themselves change the direction.

Ok, the code for the movement is pretty simple, note that we are going to add a

```
bool ReturnState = false;
```

Just before the switch statement, this will provide a value to return, so our first task now looks like this in Alien.cpp.

```
case Moving:
 if (TheGame->AlienGroup->Direction == true)
 {
  this->MovingX++;
  if (this->MovingX > (SCRWIDTH - 64))
   ReturnState = true;
 }
 else
 {
  this->MovingX--;
  if (this->MovingX < 64)
   ReturnState = true;
 }
 this->Xpos = MovingX;
 break;
```

We also need to add

```
return ReturnState;
```

At the end of the update routine, but that's it for moving. I trust none of this needs much explaining now?

In the GroupManager.cpp code, we just have to make sure we check for this return value, add this to the GroupManager::Update

```
// this only needs to update the aliens left and right
 bool Changed = false;
 for (int i = 1; i < 47; i++) // 0 is the ship
 {
  if (Game::MyObjects[i]->Update(G) == true)
      Changed = true; // we could get a few things returning true, so be
sure to change here
 }
 if (Changed == true)
  Direction = !Direction; // then check if Changed was set which indicates
a direction change
```

And that's that for movement, compile and run, watch them go left and right forever and ever assuming they are in the `Moving` state

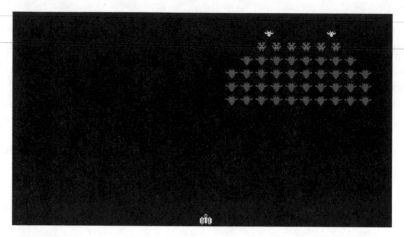

Now did you notice, that my Alien code did not actually update the `Xpos`, it updated the `MovingX` then moved that value into the `Xpos` to create the movement, the reasons for this were briefly discussed, I hope you were paying attention, but I'll let it become more apparent later.

Get Them Flying

This is an interesting point, we need to get the Aliens to do their thing, but at the moment we don't have all their logic coded. We want these Aliens to start their attacks in a semi-logical and calculated way. But that means we need to have the game actually playing to decide if our approach is working. Talk about the cart before the horse?

If you are really confident about what you are doing, you could indeed write a whole set of routines that would carefully trigger the right Aliens to fly at the right time, perhaps even taking an escort or two with them, but most of us are not that confident at this point. So here's a suggestion.

Write something that will work for now, and allow us to move forward. Something we know is not actually good enough for the finished game but which will give us a quick and dirty way to get what we need to happen, in this case to trigger an Alien to fly. And that we can come back to later and either enhance or scrap.

We call routines like this *Holding Routines*, things we allow to function in a non-final way, that we fully intend to remove later. Artists also do something similar with artwork that is put in place as a temporary measure so the project can continue, coders often work in advance of artists, but need something in place to get their code working, so they use holding art, and naturally we also use holding code to let things move forward. But be sure to mark down that this is holding code that must be updated, though sometimes, very occasionally we might keep it, with a few tweaks to make it up to final standards.

We could trigger a move based on a special key press, that's actually a very cool and popular way to do things but I want to trigger a number of aliens to run, so I think a simple random trigger might be best here.

So in the Moving step add this code:

```
case Moving:
 this->Xpos = MovingX;
 this->Ypos = MovingY;
 if (Rand(1000000.0f) < 1100.0f && TheGame->Fred->State == Shooter::Normal)
 {
  State = Arcing;
  ArcInit = false;
 }
 break;
```

There, couldn't be simpler could it? Though why am I using such a big number 1,000,000 and testing for 1100, which is about 1.1%? Why not test for 100 and <1 Not great odds is it, if you were only throwing the dice once?

We're throwing the dice 30 times a second or more and you really will throw up a lot of 0's and 1's triggering a near constant stream of Aliens, because even low odds will eventually hit if you try often enough. Having a larger number as the seed, when you are repeatedly calling a random system, reduces those chances quite a bit. But when all said and done it's a case of try it and see, I found 1100 out of 1,000,000 to be a good result, increase or decrease as you need.

A Nice Arc

Ok, so we are ready for Step 2 of our Kamikazi's attack, the Arc, which if you remember your high school trig is a semicircle, and that's neat because we can draw semicircles using very simple Pythagoras calculation. Ah! Reasons to love tringles, are never far away when you are doing programming.

So let's think about how to plot a circle, If we were to assume a radius of r' and assume we have 360°, we can make a circle using two simple formulas to calculate the x and y points.

```
xPoint = cos(angle)*r'
yPoint = sin(angle)*r'
```

Really simple, and if you do a `for` loop, of 0–360 as the angle value, you will get 360 dots that will more or less form a circle...we can actually plot that... try entering this code?

```
for (int angle = 0; angle < 360; angle++)
{
 float Xpos = cos(angle) * 30;
 float Ypos = sin(angle) * 30;
 TheScreen->Plot(Xpos + 100, Ypos + 100, REDMASK + ALPHAMASK);
}
```

Put it in the Game::Update method, just after the check for init, it's not going to stay around long, it's just so we can see what's happening.

Now we added an offset to our point to move it away from the 0,0 origin point of the screen, and in fact we can use any value as that offset, which means we can replace that offset and use it to plot a circle from any specific start point.

What we get then is this. A nice gray circle.

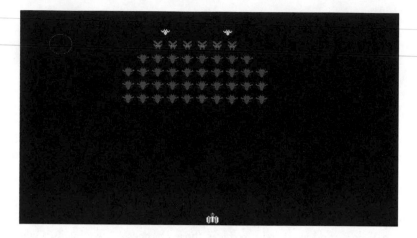

In fact that could be a nice way to create a shield of some kind around our ship, suppose we move the offset to Fred's position with this code.

```
for (int angle = 0; angle < 360; angle++)
{
 float Xpos = cos(angle) * 30;
 float Ypos = sin(angle) * 30;
 TheScreen->Plot(Xpos + Fred->Xpos, Ypos + Fred->Ypos, REDMASK +
ALPHAMASK);

}
```

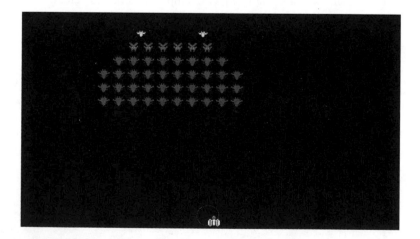

Hmmm something went a bit wrong? No not really, you see our circles center point is based on Fred's top left corner, because that's how we decide the x and y start points of our sprites. To balance it out we would need to add half the height and half the width to get to the center of the sprite image.

Assuming a radius of 30 pixels, we can do that like this:

```
for (int angle = 0; angle < 360; angle++)
{
  float Xpos = cos(angle) * 30;
  float Ypos = sin(angle) * 30;
  TheScreen->Plot(Xpos + Fred->Xpos + (Fred->Image->GetWidth()/2), Ypos +
Fred->Ypos+(Fred->Image->GetWidth()/2), REDMASK + ALPHAMASK);
}
```

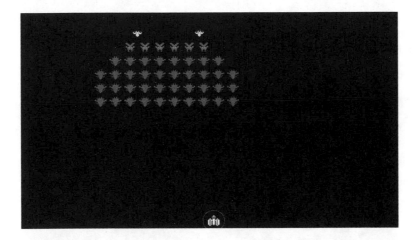

Ok, that actually looks quite nice; it's not really part of the game though, unless you feel like adding a shield or some kind of impact marker, I'll leave it up to you.

But I do want you to look at this image carefully....and then ask yourself, how this line;

```
if ((xpos >= 0) && (ypos >= 0) && (xpos < m_Width) && (ypos < m_Height))
```

Hidden away in the plot routine in your Surface Class, has prevented you from doing some massive damage? Any ideas?

Of course a semicircle only needs 180 steps so try running the code with 180 steps instead of 360. What happened? Not quite what you thought? You were maybe expecting a nice arc pointing up, but we ended up with a circle again, but with holes in it? That's ok, I was expecting it. There are two minor things wrong with what we are doing, even though it seemed at first to be doing what we wanted.

First is our use of degrees. Degrees are easy things for humans to understand but not so easy for computers, they tend to use things called Radians, which are essentially proportions of the circumference of a circle. Radians go from 0 to 2PI (6.2831...) And the way the cos and sin functions work, is to use a modulus value of 2PI so whatever number you put in, it will range between 0 and 2PI. So let's fix that first and make sure we send Radians to our sin and cos routine.

It's still ok for us to use Degrees, as I say, humans understand them better than Radians, but we do need to convert, this is done with a simple formula;

```
Radians = (Degrees*Pi)/180
```

And for completeness the formula for Radians to Degrees is;

```
Degrees = Radians x (180/Pi)
```

As I'm a bit old fashioned and like to use Degrees when possible, I swap back and forward as I need to, so I define a couple of simple macros to do this for me;

```
#define DEG2RAD(x) (x*PI)/180
#define RAD2DEG(x) x*(180/PI)
```

These usually live in a common file, such as a Defines.h file, but here for now I will use the Surface.h file, immediately after the PI define that it relies on. Now, let's try again this time sending Radians to our sin and cos functions, like this:

```
for (int angle = 0; angle < 180; angle++)
 {
  float Xpos = cos(DEG2RAD(angle)) * 30;
  float Ypos = sin(DEG2RAD(angle)) * 30;
  TheScreen->Plot(Xpos + Fred->Xpos + (Fred->Image->GetWidth()/2), Ypos
+ Fred->Ypos+(Fred->Image->GetWidth()/2), REDMASK + ALPHAMASK);
 }
```

That should do it…but not quite.

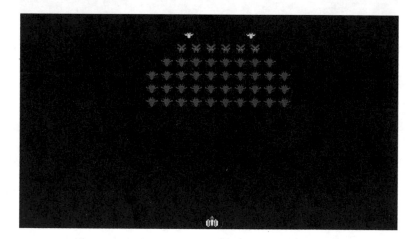

We got a semicircle ok, but it's the wrong way up; 0° to 180° should have drawn half a circle from the top to the bottom, has the world and the laws of maths gone mad?

No not really, it's because we tend to think of 0° as being straight up, but our C/C++ maths systems prefer to think of it as pointing to the right at 90°, there's a couple of ways round this, we could add/subtract an offset to the angle, but that's not ideal, as we already have a lot of calculations going on in the loop. Or, we simply accept that the start point we want at 270° as we see it, is 90° less at 180°, and change the step values.

Now our code looks like this,

```
for (int angle = 180; angle < 360; angle++)
{
 float Xpos = cos(DEG2RAD(angle)) * 30;
 float Ypos = sin(DEG2RAD(angle)) * 30;
 TheScreen->Plot(Xpos + Fred->Xpos + (Fred->Image->GetWidth() / 2), Ypos
+ Fred->Ypos+(Fred->Image->GetWidth() / 2), REDMASK + ALPHAMASK);
}
```

And the image like this; Success!

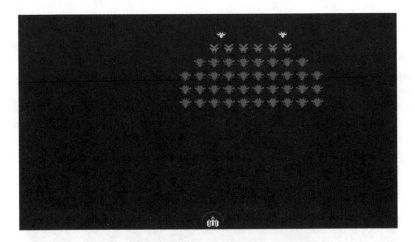

Good, that was a nice and interesting bit of simple maths wasn't it? Let's try to use it to get our aliens to move in an arc. We know the formula; we just have to work out how to do them in steps so that our movement is visible over a period of time.

Step by Step

We already understand the basic idea of steps, because we are doing our state processing. We know that if we are in a certain mode our switch statement is going to take us to the right case to process that particular movement. In the case of arcing though, we only really need to be sure of one thing… That we have set up the step value and that we don't keep resetting it. So we need a variable to indicate that Arc initialization has been taken care of.

```
case Arcing:
  if (ArcInit == false)
  {// so now we set up the variables
   ArcInit = true;
   ArcStep = 180;
  }
```

So add this, and remember to make sure you have declared `ArcInit` and `ArcStep` as a `bool` and an `int` in your class definition.

Once the arc has been set up, all that remains is for us to actually do it…using the arc step as the Angle, which allows us to add this

```
else
  {
    Xpos = MovingX + ARCRADIUS + (float)(cos((ArcStep)* PI / 180)*ARCRADIUS);
    Ypos = MovingY + (float)(sin((ArcStep)* PI / 180)*ARCRADIUS);
    ArcStep += 3;
    if (ArcStep >360 ) State = Diving;
  }
  break
```

Yes, that really is all that's needed. Define ARCRADIUS as some reasonable value, I have 44, and your Aliens will now do a semicircle centered on their MovingX, MovingY position, until they have completed it. Before we did our circle in a loop, this time we do it in a step each time the method is called, the only variable changing is ArcStep, which like the angle in our circle drawing for-loop, dictates the new placement of our alien.

Try it, you have a very simple trigger routine ready, which we're going to refine shortly but let's see if you can get your Aliens to arc. Notice I added three to the step rather than one. Well it's all a matter of balance; I want them to move fairly smoothly and quick, one step at a time is too slow, three is nearly right, play with the value and see what works best for you.

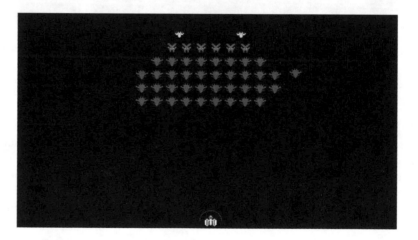

Ok good, that should not be too hard. When the Arc is complete it changes into the Diving sate, which we can now cover. I personally find the Arc to be a little too regular; I'd like a more oval shape, any thoughts on how that could be achieved?

Dive Dive Dive

Diving, like Arcing, also needs to be initialized…because we have to work out where we are diving to. We have established we want our aliens to aim for the ship. So we have to work out the direction of travel we need to move our alien to intercept the ship, like this;

5. Finally Our First Games

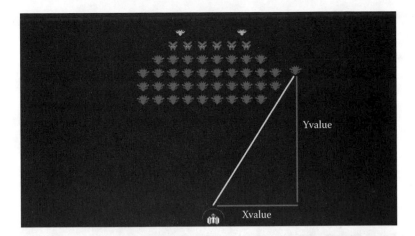

Clearly we need to move along the hypotenuse of a triangle to get to our man in the shortest possible time. If only there was some way to work out what those Xvalues and Yvalues were, I hear you cry?

Please tell me you have worked this out? Remember triangles are a programmers best friend because it allows us to get so much information, angles, distance, how much to move along the X coordinate to be at a point, how much to move along the y coordinate, to be at a point.

And that's what we want here…how much to move? But we can't just move Xvalue and Yvalue. We need to move them in steps. Ideally converting the amount to move in the X direction and Y direction in to small useful chunks.

First thing, first calculate those X and Y values, by subtracting the X position of the alien form the X position of the Ship, and same for the Y positions.

As we are going to do this one time, it becomes part of the initialization process, we can make a choice here to do it at the point where the state changes, or use a flag to indicate that an initialization is needed the first time we do the Diving code.

On the off chance that you might want to go into a dive without first doing an Arc, let's give the Diving system its own init flag, but do remember to set it to false when you set the State to Diving, we should also have done the same with Arcing, since we may have a ship arc more than once.

Diving now looks like this, a simple case of working out the X and Y Values and reducing their scale to provide a value that should mean in 32 frames it will hit our man.

```
case Diving:
  if (DiveInit == false)
  {
   float Xvalue = TheGame->Fred->Xpos - this->Xpos;
   float YValue = TheGame->Fred->Ypos - this->Ypos;
   this->StepX = Xvalue/32 ;
   this->StepY = YValue/32 ;
   DiveInit = true;
  } else
  {
   Xpos = Xpos + StepX;
   Ypos = Ypos + StepY;
```

```
    if (Ypos > SCRHEIGHT / 2) State = Bombing;
  }
  break;
```

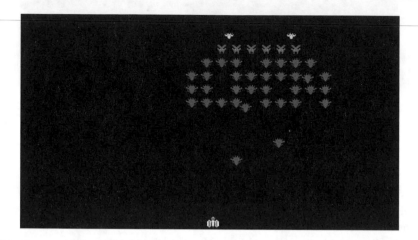

Bombs Away

This looks like it works wonderfully, if we actually leave out the check for change state, our aliens will come heading toward us at the end of every arc. We can choose when to decide to start Bombing at around the midpoint of the screen. Bombing will basically repeat the dive code, but also add some random factor to decide if we should drop some bombs.

```
case Bombing:
  // now we must decide if we are going to drop bombs
  if (Rand(100) < 5)
  { //drop a bomb once you create the class;
  printf("bombs away\n");
  }
  Xpos = Xpos + StepX;
  Ypos = Ypos + StepY;
  if (Ypos > SCRHEIGHT * 2) / let them get off screen before changing
  {
  State = Moving; / temp normally change to FlyBack
  }
```

We don't yet have a Bomb Class, so consider the printf to be a temp thing that will show us the code is working, and let us continue.

Starting to look like a game now, you can alter your random timers to increase the incidence of dives just so we can continue the tests, but for now all we really want to do is step through the different states and make sure our aliens do what they are supposed to. Without actually causing any virtual loss of life. You can change the State to Moving if you want them to just reappear at the end of their dives, while we work on the tricky Fly back to the top, and the return to formation.

Get Back to Where You Once Belonged

So we are now in the Flyoff stage where we want the alien to get back to the top of the screen, while staying offscreen. We can do this in two ways. These are as follows:

1. The easy way... Actually place them back at the top of the screen.

2. Let them move up to the top of the screen, usually off the side but just enough to see them heading back.

On face value the easy way is clearly the best, and simplest. But a small part of me would love to have them on the edge of the screen being seen to be moving back up.

I'll tell you what, for brevity, I'll do the easy way. You do the cool way, you already know how to make a step system work for a target point, so you have all the tools needed.

But both systems need a target point. I'm going to pick a point above and outside the screen, on the left and another on the right, depending on what side of the screen the alien is when we trigger the state.

Since I'm doing a single step I don't need to use a target variable, I'm just going to set Xpos and Ypos like this.

```
 case FlyOff: // here we must return to a point top left or top right,
depending on where we are.
  Ypos = -64;
  if (Xpos > SCRWIDTH/2) Xpos = SCRWIDTH+64;
  else
   Xpos = -64;
  State = FlyBack;
  break;
```

Cool, so now when the FlyOff is called it will set itself to the top left or right of the screen ready to start homing to its correct position.

Home Again!

So now what we want to do is get our alien to slowly move back into its position where it should be in the ranks of Aliens back where we first flew off. Now you see why we kept that MovingX and MovingY variables. But we have to home in.... hmmm basically this means we need to check where we want to go to, and move in that direction, can we use triangles again?

Yes, of course, we can, it's exactly the same process as the target we chose for the dive, but this time we have a moving target, as the MovingX and Y values are, ermm moving.

So that means we have to recalculate the target every time and add our step value. When both our X and Y positions are the close to being the same as our MovingX and Y, we're done. Let's try that out.

```
case FlyBack:
  {
  float Xvalue = MovingX- this->Xpos;
  float YValue = MovingY - this->Ypos;
```

```
this->Xpos+= (Xvalue / 32);
this->Ypos+= (YValue / 32);
 if (fabs(Xpos-MovingX) <4 && fabs(Ypos-MovingY) <4) State = Moving;
}
break;
```

Ok looks simple enough, if we're about 4 pixels away on the x and y, we'll change into moving mode, which will snap them back to the moving mode and moving positions, try it out, what happens?

So, it kinda works, but can you see sometimes the aliens are struggling to home to that final point before they can be allowed to reset back into moving mode. They get there, but it's clearly a bit of a struggle often playing slow motion chase until the pack changes direction. Why?

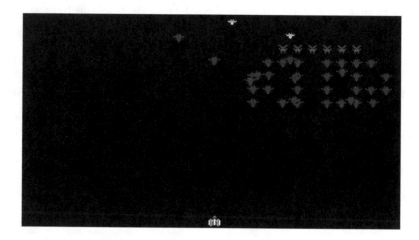

Well, the closer they get to their target point, the smaller the step value we calculate, and we even scale it down by dividing it by 32. So the closer they are the smaller the step value causing them to need the target to slow down or move toward it before it catches up. It does work, sort of, and the speedup then slowdown effect we get is actually quite nice, but are we happy with it? I'm not!

We need to talk about a different way of creating those step values.

Vectors, Our Flexible Friends

Now when they are in full motion, we are moving our aliens in a simultaneous X and Y direction to create the directional movement we want. The two values are linked and create an X step and a Y step, which results in the alien moving in a certain direction. That's basically what vectors are; they are directions, represented by step numbers. Not to be confused with the dynamic data store system, or indeed even the data type, which also share the name vector.

A mathematical vector is a numerical quantity having direction and length/magnitude. They are incredibly useful concepts and can represent a lot of different things, but for now we're going to restrict it to the idea we currently need, which is direction. It's probably easiest to visualize vectors as the Hypotenuse of a right angled triangle. With an added arrow to represent that it has direction. It's the Hypotenuse itself, here with a magnitude of five units, which is the vector, and vec2(4,3) is how we represent it.

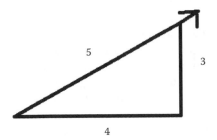

For this representation to work we need to consider the start of the triangle as being at a 0, 0 origin, and a lot of maths assumes that, but no matter where a (4,3) vector starts, it's going to point the same relative direction from its own origin.

We can have any numbers, that can therefore represent any direction we want, but generally if using vectors only to indicate direction, we keep them as numbers less than one. The reason is really simple an X of 2 and a Y of 2 mean you will always move in a diagonal from a start point, but an X of 0.5 and a Y of 0.5 will ALSO go in exactly the same diagonal just in a smaller step within a square unit, so lots of numbers can represent the exact same direction, though having different magnitude, or length of movement.

If we keep them all under 1 or −1 for opposite directions, using a process called normalizing to create a unit vector, we can be sure our object is going to move within a given 1 × 1 square in the direction we want. And here's a bonus, by multiplying that unit vector by a scale value we can change the effective amount of the movement keeping the same direction.

That scale can be a number from 0 to 1 for even slower movement, to, well, anything that the game needs. We can consider that scale value Speed and alter that to create variable speed in our object, in the direction we set the vector at, and if we set it to negative values, Speed will move the object backwards. Win!

Normalizing isn't as mad as it sounds, it's simply a standard equation that considers the X and Y values of a vector to be the height and width of our visualization triangle, which as your old high-school teacher tried to tell you, in those boring trigonometry classes, if you know those two, you can work out the hypotenuse of that triangle (and quite a few other things we will discover later). As we now know, the Length/Magnitude of the vector...dividing the X and Y by that Length will always result in a numbers between −1 and 1. Perfect for movement.

A small confusing point, vector2D types are not a standard part of C++ they are part of a maths library, and C++ provides only basic functions for numbers, so if you don't use a maths library, you have to code them up yourself. They are, however, pretty much standard.

Although it does seem a little odd, a neat thing about vector2D as a code type, is that they can represent different things, like points in a grid and a direction, which means we can add one set of vectors to another, so you can add a Vector2D of a movement vector to a vector2D of coordinates to create new coordinates.

So if we store our X and Y Screen positions in a vector type we can move our object by adding any other vector type. This makes things quite simple and we can still access x and y individually if we want.

Later we will discover we can actually use vectors for all sorts of different things, not just coordinates, we can also different types of vectors, which could have three and four dimensions, but for now, we're going to think of them as convenient storages for coordinates and as a direction for movement!

I hope you can see that vectors are really useful things they have a lot of different uses in games, for now using them to create movement is an ideal introduction, as this is the fact they can be considered as kinds of incomplete triangles, so some understanding of the maths behind triangles is going to be a great thing for us. For 2D maths we don't need too much more than trigonometry, so the sooner we learn to love the triangle the better. We've already used it in a few things, did you notice?

We used Sine in our arcing function to create semicircles, and it's not the first time we will come across Sine, Cosine, and the mysterious and occasionally frustrating Tangent, but we'll bring them in when we need them so as not to bring up those bad memories of trigonometry classes you slept through because you could not ever see a situation where you would ever need them. Yup! I was wrong too! Boy, was I so so sooo wrong.

Remember though this is important, sin, cos, and tan all use radian values, so we need to choose if we're going to use radians or degrees and stick with it. As noted I tend to use degrees, but translate them to Radians at the point of use. It's probably more than a little wasteful but when debugging it's far easier to read a number as a degree from 0 to 360 and relate that to a direction even if a little twisted, than a radian from 0 to 6.28318530717958 6476925286766559

If you are comfortable using Radians all the time, feel free to do so. If not, remember those macros to convert between them will make life a lot easier.

Sadly, our current standard maths library does not include any maths vector classes. So we are going to have to write our own. For now! Later as we get a little more complex we'll consider an open source library to save time. So for now we'll just include a simple Vector2D Class in our project and put this into a new .h file called Vector2D.

```
#pragma once
#include <math.h>
class Vector2D
{
public:
 float x, y; //everything we do with 2D vectors revolves around these 2
numbers
 Vector2D(float X = 0, float Y = 0) // allows us to create an empty vector
 { x = X;
  y = Y;
 }
 ~Vector2D() {};
// we need a few standard arithmetic functions
 Vector2D operator*(float scalarValue) const
 { return Vector2D(x * scalarValue, y * scalarValue); }
 Vector2D operator+(const Vector2D &vect2d) const
 { return Vector2D(x + vect2d.x, y + vect2d.y); }
 Vector2D operator-(const Vector2D &vect2d) const
 { return Vector2D(x - vect2d.x, y - vect2d.y); }
 // magnitude (length) of the vector
 float mag() const {return sqrtf(x * x + y * y);}
```

```
  // return cross product
  float cross(const Vector2D &vect2d) const
  { return (this->x * vect2d.y) - (this->y * vect2d.x);}
// normalise
  void normalise()
  { float mag = sqrtf(x* x + y * y);
   this->x = x / mag;
   this->y = y / mag; }
  // dot product
  float dot(const Vector2D &vect2d) const
  {return (x * vect2d.x) + (y * vect2d.y);}
};
```

This little class throws up a couple of interesting points, which you may not have encountered yet in your C/C++ journey. Most interesting is the use of operator, which is a cool but dangerous C++ feature. We are essentially telling C++ that when it sees a *(multiply) operator in code, that it needs to look at the kinds of objects it is acting on, if it is acting on a Vector2D and a float value, it uses the routine here, which is actually doing two multiply commands.

Also for + and −, if it sees they are acting on two Vector2D's it uses the code listed. + and − will still work perfectly on every other kind of number, but when it is used on Vector2D's from now on, it does a different kind of addition/subtraction that creates new vector values.

Cool eh? But also as I say, very dangerous, this is a concept known as overloading, allowing a command or operator to do more than one thing under specific circumstances. Don't overload an operator unless you really need to, it might seem fun, but it can lead to a world of pain for you later, when you forget you overloaded the + function on two floats to return an int for one particular circumstance, where it seemed to make sense, but if you actually needed a float returned, you did a bad thing.

Here though it's pretty safe, there are no current concepts of how to multiply Vector2D's by scalers, or add or subtract 2 Vectors2D, so this is a clear case of need.

We're also adding a few functions to our class, such as Dot Product, Magnitude (which I hope you recognize from school Trig Class), and the important one, Normalize. What are the others for? Well you will need them later, and they are very trivial to code, so doing them now is going to be useful. I will explain later. There are many other functions that we can add to this as we get more into our maths journey, but for now these will do what we need and allow us to expand a little later.

Another thing was the use of const, in some of those functions; this is just a way of making sure we don't let the function change anything it's not supposed to. In such small functions, it's a bit moot, but it's a good habit to get into, since accidently altering the x and y values in more complex functions could have a disastrous impact. If we added some code that did make changes the compiler would then complain and force us to think about what we are doing.

Ok, time to convert our project to use vectors and normalized step values, which we hope will give us a more accurate stepping and allow for fluid movement.

The actual Dive and bombing systems are not really badly impacted by the bad maths, so let's focus on the step where it was most apparent, the FlyBack step. Feel free to *fix* the Dive and bombing later.

To make that more effective we need to know the normalized vector, between where we are and where we want to be, remembering that it's a moving target so it needs to be updated every cycle. This gives us something like this:

```
Vector2D Vec(MovingX - this->Xpos, MovingY - this->Ypos);
float Speed = Vec.mag();
Speed /= 32;
if (Speed < 3) Speed = 3; // we need a decent speed to nail the position
as its moving
Vec.normalise();
Vec = Vec * Speed;
this->Xpos += Vec.x;
this->Ypos += Vec.y;
if (fabs(Xpos - MovingX) < 2 && fabs(Ypos - MovingY) < 2) State = Moving;
```

Replace the code in the current FlyBack step with this. Notice, I've reduced the approximate point of impact check from 4 to 2, as it's a lot more accurate now. Also to maintain the idea of speeding in, then slowing up as it gets to its target, I've used the distance/length/magnitude whatever you wish to call it, as a factor, but ensuring it never gets too slow. Since a normalized number is always less than one, so we need to be sure we can at least move at the speed of the MovingX motion in order to catch it up. This is the big advantage of a normalized vector; we can alter the scale of it very easily by multiplying by a float value, it's still going to point the same way. In fact aside from a means to indicate direction, a vector is very important for having a magnitude. To be mathematically correct for a moment, it has both direction and magnitude. That will become much more important later when we use Vectors for things other than simple 2D motion.

How much more visually neater is that? We see our Aliens flying in and smoothly taking their place, no chasing and neatly slotting in place.

Ok, time for me to confess, we could have put a small minimum value on the scale system too, and yes I must be honest it would have given more or less the same result, but this was meant to be a painless introduction to Vectors, did you feel any pain? No? That's ok, it'll come later!

Of course we're still using a mix of separate X and Y values and Vector2D in this project but now that we have a Vector2D Class, let's use it for all future situations where we have an object that has X and Y motion.

Oh one final thing on this, we are calculating the magnitude of the vector when we calculate speed. But later, we're doing a rather clumsy calculation with this line here.

```
if (fabs(Xpos - MovingX) < 2 && fabs(Ypos - MovingY) < 2) State = Moving;
```

Can you think of a really simple way to remove this line and change the code to achieve the same result? I'll give you a clue, we're effectively trying to work out if we're within a certain distance of our goal, and we should not really need to calculate that *twice*!

There are a couple of other fantastic and very useful things that vectors can do for us, but we don't quite need them yet, so we'll not clutter your head at this point. But rest assured we're a long way from being done with vectors.

Lets Get Lethal

Now that we know our aliens are all working fine, it's time to give them some weapons, and also get our ship moving and firing, and making sure we collide and blow things up, to complete the gameplay and yes, we must make sure our bombs use vectors as that the way we want to do things now. Let's start with the ship as that's the easiest to do.

We left our Shooter Class with only the basics to create it and draw it, it's update routine currently does nothing, but it's not dissimilar to our Invader Class, so let's put that same code in here:

```
bool Shooter::Update(Game* g)
{
 bool fire = false;
 if (g->InputHandle->TestKey(KEY_LEFT))
 {
  Xpos-= 1;
  if (Xpos < 0) Xpos = 0;
 }
 if (g->InputHandle->TestKey(KEY_RIGHT))
 {
 Xpos+= 1;
  if (Xpos > SCRWIDTH - Image->GetWidth()) Xpos = SCRWIDTH
- Image->GetWidth();
 }
 if (g->InputHandle->TestKey(KEY_SPACE))
 {
  fire = true; / fire
 }
}
```

Only a minor modification from the methods we used for Invaders from Space. Do make sure you add

```
#include "Game.h"
```

To the top of the Shooter.cpp file or it won't know that the Game Class has an InputHandle to get info from.

So it's all working, but it's a bit slow, try changing the increments to values you find give you more smooth movement, I'll let you pick the numbers, try a few, and see what works best for you. Hopefully, you've left your aliens in working order, so you will see that as you move around they still attempt to crash into you, or at least the point where you were when they started their dive. This adds some gameplay as you now really have to keep moving to avoid the diving aliens. Later we should increase the frequency of these dives to make the game a lot more intense, and avoid bullets too.

Now, you are asking yourself, why do I still have an empty Update function? Well that's a fair question, and the answer is, because when I laid it out I felt I might need a routine that only passed a surface and a handler, but since I've moved more to using an update that passes the Game Class address, and with that everything that the routine will need accessed via that instance of game, it has become redundant. But since I made the original Abstract Class have those updates, I have to at least provide the empty version.

I should go back to the original Base Abstract Class and remove it. But I'll let you do it, it's good practice for you. Note that the Aliens are using the Update with Surface and

Input, even though they don't actually care about the input. So you may choose instead to leave that alone (it ain't exactly broke, so does not need fixing) or make sure that both the Aliens and the shooter use one type of update, then remove the other. It's entirely your call! Let's see how OCD you are? (hint…leave it for now, OCD be dammed!)

Now unlike the Invaders from Space shooter, Fred, our shooter here, can access the Game Class, and maybe that is where our bullet should live, because it, like Fred here, is going to be always on screen. Either moving to shoot, or stuck on the end of Fred's nose. So our concept of fire is a little different from Invaders, but I have a reason for not including Bullet in the Game Class, which will make sense in a bit.

We're not going to create a new bullet; we're simply going to check if the current bullet is ready for firing. But we do need a Bullet Class, so let's add that.

Create a new header file called Bullet.h

```
#pragma once
#include "GameObject.h"

class Bullet : public GameObject
{
public:
 Bullet();
 ~Bullet();
 Bullet(char* filename, MyFiles* filehandler)
  : GameObject(filename, filehandler) {};
// these replace the pure virtuals
 bool Update(Surface* s, Input* InputHandler);
 bool Update(Game* g);
 void Draw(Surface* TheScreen);
 bool ReadyToFire;
 Surface* Frame1;
};
```

Nothing too strange there, I'm maintaining the two types of update for now but I am only going to use the version that passes Game, as I want the shooter to make decisions on when to fly. I also have a bool in there called ReadyToFire, because the bullet has only two states, flying, or on the ships nose. I can use a bool to inform me.

Then we must create our Bullet.cpp file, so add that into your source lists.

```
#include "Bullet.h"
#include "Game.h"
Bullet::Bullet() { this->ReadyToFire = true;} // we can't do this here
Bullet::~Bullet() { }
bool Bullet::Update(Surface* s, Input* a_Input){ }
bool Bullet::Update(Game* g) { }
void Bullet::Draw(Surface* TheScreen){Image->CopyAlphaPlot(TheScreen,Xpos,
Ypos);}
```

Ok, we're almost ready. Let's try to create a bullet in the Game class, we can create it just after we make Fred, but do not add it to our vector of game objects until AFTER we make all the aliens, because we are doing some stuff that relies on the aliens starting at a set value in the list, and we don't want to hunt through the code to find it, let's just make sure our bullet is the last thing added for the moment until we add bombs at least.

We should also remember we actually told Fred where our Bullet was going to be in the Shooter.h Class with this line;

```
GameObject* TheBullet; /Bullet location
```

This was ok as a holding value, because when we wrote this, we didn't actually know what a bullet was. But now we do, and we want to make a new bullet and modify the flag it has which a `GameObject` does not have, so we must change this now to

```
Bullet* TheBullet; /Bullet location
```

And remember to include the Bullet.h file at the top of the file.

Now, back to why the Bullet is in Fred, there probably is no need to keep Fred's bullets address in Fred. We could just as easily put it in the Game.h file as we did Fred himself. But Fred and the bullet are linked, so it's slightly more sensible to let Fred reset the `ReadyToFly` flag at the appropriate times by accessing his own variables rather than dipping back into the Game's variables. But that really is a choice you can make for yourself, keep the Bullet separate from Fred in Game, or keep in in Shooter.h. I going to leave him for now inside Fred, but it does mean we should be careful to delete Fred's bullet when Fred's destructor is called.

But now, let's now get the bullet to stick to the nose of Fred. Change the Bullet update routine to this;

```
bool Bullet::Update(Game* g)
{
 if (this->ReadyToFire == true)
 { / it's on the nose of Fred
  Xpos = g->Fred->Xpos + g->Fred->Image->GetWidth() / 2 - 4;
  Ypos = g->Fred->Ypos - 12;
 }
}
```

We're using the Game* g update because our main loop in Game calls that update pattern for all non-Alien objects (unless you fixed that?).

Annoyingly I had to subtract a tiny offset of 4 to get the line in the middle, can you guess why? Now it's not good to use hard numbers in code, so I really would like to fix this. Perhaps then you can work out a way to alter this line so that if we change the bullet graphic to something thicker it will still center. For this it's a trivial problem, so if you don't know why it's doing this, just leave the −4 in place.

Ok compile and move Fred around and you see the bullet stays on his nose. Time now to get him to fly.

The bullet actual movement is going to be achieved by simply moving up whenever the `ReadyToFire` flag is false, so we can add this to our update

```
else
{
 Ypos -= 10;
 if (Ypos < 0) ReadyToFire = true;
}
```

Just after the code to fix the bullet. Now all that remains is for Fred to test if the bullet is ready to fire, and if so, has the fire button been pressed. In the shooter.cpp file, we can change the fire code to this

```
if (g->InputHandle->TestKey(KEY_SPACE) && TheBullet->ReadyToFire == true)
{
  fire = true; // fire
  this->TheBullet->ReadyToFire = false;
}
```

Now run that, you should now get a nice bullet firing, and returning to your nose tip when it gets to the top. Notice I am checking that the bullet is in ready to fire mode, we don't want to fire it when it has already been fired.

Notice also that the shooter's fire code contains a redundant fire variable, we really don't need it in this game, so unless you feel there is some need to keep it, it can be removed.

Our shooter can now shoot. Its bullet is smart enough to test for the end of the screen and reset itself, all done by simply setting a flag. There is one other condition, which would reset the flag. If it actually hit an alien!

So why don't we get the bullet to test for Alien hits? Well it's the same issue we had with the Invaders from Space, we don't actually always know how many aliens there are at any given time and we'd waste processing cycles if we blindly tested every single one dead or alive, worse, we may be reducing our vector list of objects as they die, so we could end up testing something else.

No, far better to let the Aliens test if they've hit our bullet, and also for the Bombs to test if they've hit our Shooter.

But we'll do collision in a bit, first let's give our Aliens the chance to drop some bombs on us, and make our bombs a tiny bit more interesting.

Bombs Away for Real Now

Bombs, like Bullets also need their own class, because they do something different from everything else. So create a Bomb Class. And presto:

```
#pragma once
#include "GameObject.h"
#include "Shooter.h"
#include "Vector2D.h"
class Bomb : public GameObject
{
public:
 Bomb();
 ~Bomb();
 Bomb(char* filename, MyFiles* filehander)
 : GameObject(filename, filehander) {};
// these replace the pure virtuals
 bool Update(Surface* s, Input* InputHandler);
 bool Update(Game* g);
 void Draw(Surface* TheScreen);
 bool DidWeHitFred(Shooter* Fred);

 Vector2D BombMotion;
 float BombSpeed;
 Surface* Frame1;
};
```

Yes, you guessed it, it's pretty much the Bullet code with a different name and no need for the ready to fire flag. It does add a few things though, it's got a collision test and a vector for its motion, and a speed value; this will make their movement much more interesting.

So with the Bomb code looking pretty similar to the Bullet code it's going to be no surprise to see that the base Bomb.cpp looks like this:

```
#include "Bomb.h"
#include "Game.h"
Bomb::Bomb(){ }
Bomb::~Bomb(){ }
bool Bomb::Update(Surface* s, Input* a_Input){ }
bool Bomb::Update(Game* g){ }
bool Bomb::DidWeHitFred(Shooter* Fred){ return false;}
void Bomb::Draw(Surface* TheScreen)
{
  Image->CopyAlphaPlot(TheScreen, Xpos, Ypos);
}
```

I've left the Updates empty, and for now, made sure that `DidWeHitFred` always returns false. There is one condition I want the Update routine to test for, Bombs going offscreen. But what exactly do we do when bombs go offscreen or hit? Unlike our bullet, which always exists, bombs are dynamically created, so we need to remove them from the object list which means our old friend `MarkForRemoval` comes back into play.

One more thing though, when we work out the `BombMotion` we are going to target a fixed point, probably where Fred is at that point. So we need to know the normalized vector. It's a calculation that needs to be done every time a bomb is set off so to keep our trigger routines clean, we should do that calculation and the subsequent setup of `BombMotion` in this class, so add one more method definition in `Bomb.h`

```
void SetBombMotion(Shooter* Fred, Alien* Host);
```

Remember to add Shooter.h and Alien.h so that the Bomb knows what they are.

The code for this is simply:

```
void Bomb::SetBombMotion(Shooter* Fred, Alien* Host)
{
  Vector2D Vec(Fred->Xpos - Host->Xpos, Fred->Ypos - Host->Ypos);
  Vec.normalise();
  this->BombMotion = Vec;
}
```

And the update routine can now be altered to this:

```
bool Bomb::Update(Game* g)
{
  Vector2D Step = BombMotion*10;
  Xpos += Step.x;
  Ypos += Step.y;
  if (Ypos > SCRHEIGHT + 10) this->MarkForRemoval = true;
}
```

There's that `MarkForRemoval` flag, if our bomb gets too near the bottom, we set it to indicate to our game loop that we want it to be removed.

In our game update loop we now need to add a small check for our `MarkForRemoval` Flag. Like this:

```
// we don't need to update the 1st 46 because those are the ship and aliens
handled by AlienGroup->Update(this)
  for (int i = 48; i < Game::MyObjects.size(); i++)
  {
   Game::MyObjects[i]->Update(this);
   if (Game::MyObjects[i]->MarkForRemoval == true)
   {
    delete Game::MyObjects[i]; / delete the object in memory
    Game::MyObjects.erase(Game::MyObjects.begin() + i); / remove from the
vector
    i--;
   }
  }
```

What this is doing is interesting and needs to be looked at carefully, we're updating all the nontrivial enemies such as Fred and the Aliens, before this loop, then the stars and now the Bombs that may have been added. To remove an object from play we have to delete it, because it was new'd, then erase it from the list. The reasons for the `i--` should be apparent but are often forgotten. When we start this loop we may have 150 objects to parse, suppose we are looking at the 100th. And we remove it. The vectors erase function will remove it, then shift everything down 1 step, entry 101 now goes into entry 100's space after the erase. If we don't decrement the counter, which currently stands at 100 the next loop it will be 101, and the new occupant of space 100 will get ignored.

We also need to go back into our code, and check all the object constructors take care to set MarkForRemoval to false when instantiated, or we may delete things we don't want to delete because of a assumed false setting on creation.

So we're looking pretty good so far, lots of bombs trying to hit Fred and Kamikazi aliens trying to smash into him. We're close to our conclusion for this game, but let's add the all-important collision, and with it we need to add some gameplay rules, for lives, and so on.

Like our previous game we really don't need anything too fancy on this collision, a simple circle to circle check will do fine. Start by getting the Aliens to test if they hit the bullet. Or if they hit Fred. Both of these conditions end our Aliens life, either in Glory or in misery!

Add a definition for a new method in your Alien.h file

```
bool DidWeGetHit(Shooter* Fred);
```

And then in your Alien.cpp file add this

```
bool Alien::DidWeGetHit(Shooter* Fred)
{
return false;
}
```

Now this is interesting because this actually helps us to justify the decision to keep Fred's Bullet inside Freds Class, as we only need to pass this function Freds address to get access to both Fred, for a suicide collision, and Fred's bullet for an ignominious defeat.

Let's fill in the code, both conditions do, in fact, result in a death, so the bool returning true should be a hit condition. We'll write the hit a bullet condition first as it's the easiest.

This should be very familiar to you now?

```
bool Alien::DidWeGetHit(Shooter* Fred)
{
 int My_Height = this->Image->GetHeight()/2;
 int My_Width = this->Image->GetWidth()/2;
 int Ob_Height = Fred->TheBullet->Image->GetHeight()/2;
 int Ob_Width = Fred->TheBullet->Image->GetWidth()/2;
 // do a simple circle/circle test
 float R1 = sqrtf((My_Height*My_Height) + (My_Width*My_Width));
 float R2 = sqrtf((Ob_Height*Ob_Height) + (Ob_Width*Ob_Width));
 // move to the centre
 int diffx = ((Xpos + My_Width) - (Fred->TheBullet->Xpos + Ob_Width));
 int diffy = ((Ypos + My_Height) - (Fred->TheBullet->Ypos + Ob_Height));

 float Dist = sqrtf((diffx*diffx) + (diffy*diffy));
 if (Dist < (R1 + R2)) return true;
 return false;
}
```

Ok add some code in the update, to run this test and if true, for now set the MarkForRemoval flag.

Compile and run, and then try shooting an alien, what happens? Not what you were expecting? Any ideas why? Let me give you a clue, in our Game.cpp file we have this update sequence going on:

```
// lets move our ship and shoot things
 Fred->Update(this);
// now do the normal update code?
 AlienGroup->Update(this);
// we don't need to update the 1st 48 because those are the ship and aliens
handled by AlienGroup->Update(this)
 for (int i = 48; i < Game::MyObjects.size(); i++)
 {
  Game::MyObjects[i]->Update(this);
  if (Game::MyObjects[i]->MarkForRemoval == true)
  {
   delete Game::MyObjects[i]; // delete the object in memory
   Game::MyObjects.erase(Game::MyObjects.begin() + i); // remove from the
vector
   i--;
  }
 }
```

Can you see it? I put a comment in there for you to take note.

We update our Aliens in the AlienGroup->Update(this); which is great as it keeps them all nicely grouped together so we can keep the moving status updated regardless, but it does mean those first 47 objects, Fred, and the 46 Aliens we created, do not respond to the Update loop that follows, which starts from Object 48, which is the first star.

Well, that's a good thing? Or a bad thing?

It's kind of both. Bad, because hard numbers really suck, but the fact is the group manager really needs to work on the Aliens and only aliens, it could have scanned the vector to ID the Aliens but that adds cycles, so in this case, it's a slightly better idea that it moves those objects in isolation of the other updates and for that it has to know exactly when they start and end. Hard numbers being one of the easiest ways, despite our well intentioned reservations.

So we keep our Aliens at 1–47 to allow them to move and be treated as a group. But it does mean we can't ever really delete the Aliens when they are hit, so we need to find another way to remove them from the game.

What I suggest, is to create another state for them, maybe even two states. Dead and Dying. Dying being a good state to perform some explosion animation and take care of housekeeping, like adding to a score. And Dead to allow it to be processed but not actually do anything.

These two extra states should be very easy to add, as we've already done a great job of producing the current set of states. So let's start with adding them to the enum list and producing some code for it. Our enum in Alien.h now looks like this

```
typedef enum Status
{
Moving = 100, Arcing,Diving,Bombing,FlyOff,FlyBack,Dying,Dead
} Status;
```

Just a simple addition of two new states, which is why enums are very cool, we can add things to them with ease.

In the Alien.cpp file, where we process the states, add two empty states handlers, just before the default, they can go anywhere in any order between the switch brackets but convention is to do them in order.

```
case Dying:
 break;
case Dead:
 break;
 default:
 printf("Something undefined happened in Alien Update!\n");
 break;
```

Ok, now that's added, rework the collision system, not to change the MarkForRemoval flag, but to set the State of the Alien to Dying. Now we just need to write some code to handle these states and we're good to go.

```
if (this->DidWeGetHit(TheGame->Fred))
{
 printf("He done got me in my killin' parts\n");
 this->State = Dying;
}
```

If you run this now, and shoot, you'll see that when they are hit, they freeze, because they now no longer have a state that currently functions, so they are stuck. That shows the code is working but needs more.

We also should have noticed our bullet didn't stop and went on to disable many more aliens. That's something we also have to fix. Do that first by simply setting the Bullets ReadyToFire flag, which will, of course, return it back to Fred's nose.

```
if (this->DidWeGetHit(TheGame->Fred))
{
 printf("He done got me in my killin' parts\n");
 this->State = Dying;
 TheGame->Fred->TheBullet->ReadyToFire = true;
}
```

But be careful, it's still considered to be active, so let's also use that flag to actually decide if the bullet is currently lethal by wrapping the collision check for the bullet in a test like this:

```
if (Fred->TheBullet->ReadyToFire == false)
{
 int My_Height = this->Image->GetHeight()/2;
 int My_Width = this->Image->GetWidth()/2;
 int Ob_Height = Fred->TheBullet->Image->GetHeight()/2;
 int Ob_Width = Fred->TheBullet->Image->GetWidth()/2;
 // do a simple circle/circle test
 float R1 = sqrtf((My_Height*My_Height) + (My_Width*My_Width));
 float R2 = sqrtf((Ob_Height*Ob_Height) + (Ob_Width*Ob_Width));
 // move to the centre
 int diffx = ((Xpos + My_Width) - (Fred->TheBullet->Xpos + Ob_Width));
 int diffy = ((Ypos + My_Height) - (Fred->TheBullet->Ypos + Ob_Height));
 float Dist = sqrtf((diffx*diffx) + (diffy*diffy));
 if (Dist < (R1 + R2)) return true;
}
```

Now, when we compile and run, we should be able to shoot the aliens, and have them freeze, and our bullet returns back to our nose where it does no harm to any suicide attacks.

Perfect, we're almost done with this part now, just need to make some decisions on how we plan to show them dying and how we plan to remove them from play.

Dying is an important state, because it provides a means for us to check on how we have done in the level, perhaps alter some factors as more aliens get killed and to check if we're at the end of the sequence. So Dying needs a bit more work.

Dead though, is really easy. Just position them offscreen. There's still a little processing going on, and the draw routines later will try to draw them, but that's ok, we don't mind that on this game as we're not really taxing our CPU……..Wait…did you really think that was ok?

Hell no! We have to make sure they are not drawn at all; even a draw that does not show them is a draw that's wasting CPU cycles deciding not to draw them. We need to stop that. But how?

Well we have a flag in GameObject Class that has been there for a long time but has not been tested

```
bool onscreen; // we might mark an object as on/off screen to avoid
processing
```

It's been there all this time quietly being ignored, but now its time has come. We should now use this flag, so that the part of our update in Game.cpp, which does the drawing can test this to see if some objects have been switched off or not. Of course though since it was never initialized, its state at the moment on each of our drawable objects, including stars and missiles, it's currently undefined, so we have to take a few steps back to make sure when we create any Objects that we set it to a known value, in this case true.

Since all our graphic objects are based on the concept of a GameObject, all we need to do is make sure each of the three current constructors in the GameObject has the following line added to it.

```
onscreen = true;
```

Now every Bullet, Bomb, Alien, and even Fred who is created, will use one of those base constructors and will therefore have its onscreen flag set to true. All that remains is to alter the draw loop to take that into account.

```
// having updated lets draw them all
for (int i = 0; i < Game::MyObjects.size(); i++)
{
if (Game::MyObjects[i]->onscreen == true)
Game::MyObjects[i]->Draw(TheScreen);
}
```

And we should find on a test run, that nothing will be different until we set that flag to false in an object. Let's make that happen in Dying for now;

```
case Dying:
 onscreen = false;
 break;
```

Compile and run, not too shabby is it?

But…again, something isn't quite right, there appear to be invisible ships, which the bullet is hitting? Making it really hard to kill the ships above it.

Yes. Even though the Alien is *dead* or rather Dying, and not being drawn, it's still there in the spot where it was hit, and it's still processing collision tests. We need to stop that.

Two ideas come to mind…put the Alien WAAAY offscreen so it could never be hit, or have the DidWeGetHit routine, take account of the fact a dead or dying ship is no longer able to be hit.

I think we should do both, start with putting it offscreen.

```
 case Dying:
  Ypos = 2000;
  onscreen = false;
  State = Dead;
  break;
 case Dead: // I really don't need to do anything here just acknowledge
that I am dead
  break;
```

And then deal with the collision system:

```
bool Alien::DidWeGetHit(Shooter* Fred)
{
 if (Fred->TheBullet->ReadyToFire == false && State != Dead && State !=
Dying)
 {
..etc.
```

Now we're talking… We have a bullet that works, we have Aliens that check for collision with it when it's lethal, and that die and vanish to clear the play field. Though it would be nice if you could add some explosions to it? You could create a very nice set of explosions from this site http://www.explosiongenerator.com/, which allows you to fiddle about with lots of settings and create nice sequences of explosions. Perfect for sprite-based explosions, we will certainly use these at some point in upcoming demos. We can work around the fact that they bleed over the size of the sprite boxes we use with an art package.

Danger UXB

Next up is the bombs we have to make lethal to Fred, and also we need to consider what happens to Fred when he is hit. We know there are two circumstances where Fred can be killed, a Kamikazi hit, and a bomb hit.

Dealing with the Kamikazi hit first should be trivial, as it's really just extending the concept of the `DidWeGetHit` routine because it relates directly to the Alien, who sadly dies in a blaze of green slime glory if he manages to collide with our heroic Fred. So that's the first thing to do. Add the following after the bullet test. It's still the same circle to circle code but with different targets:

```
// now check for a Kamikazi test
 if (State == Diving || State == Bombing)
 {
  int My_Height = this->Image->GetHeight() / 2;
  int My_Width = this->Image->GetWidth() / 2;
  int Ob_Height = Fred->Image->GetHeight() / 2;
  int Ob_Width = Fred->Image->GetWidth() / 2;
  // do a simple circle/circle test
  float R1 = sqrtf((My_Height*My_Height) + (My_Width*My_Width));
  float R2 = sqrtf((Ob_Height*Ob_Height) + (Ob_Width*Ob_Width));
  // move to the centre
  int diffx = ((Xpos + My_Width) - (Fred->Xpos + Ob_Width));
  int diffy = ((Ypos + My_Height) - (Fred->Ypos + Ob_Height));
  float Dist = sqrtf((diffx*diffx) + (diffy*diffy));
  if (Dist < (R1 + R2)) return true;
 }
```

Notice, I have a different condition wrap around the code this time, I'm testing if the Alien state is currently set to Diving or Bombing. I don't really need to, I could just test regardless, but I know that most of the time the Aliens are not actually in a place where they are likely to ever collide with Fred. This test therefore is what we call a cull.

We use culls in collision a lot, especially in 3D because a collision check is a fairly decent amount of calculation. Here, for example, we have three square roots, a notoriously slow function, and several multiply and divide functions. If we have 46 Aliens, and only 2 of them are Diving, it's far more effective for me to only test the ones who are diving. I will save 44 totally useless and processor expensive, collision tests, which I know will not produce a result.

We basically also culled the Bullet collision when `ReadyToFire` was not set; avoiding any collision call when you know it's not needed is a good practice to maintain.

Compile and run, with this new addition to the collision and hold off firing at things, as you want to see the result of when they collide. You should see them acting in exactly the same way as if they were shot, crashing into you, entering their Dying state and leaving the game.

But what of Fred, who has had this confirmed collision. We have to do something about that?

Stepping Back, Deciding When to Go

So, we've got all the Alien code working, and we know it's working fine, but remember that routine we put in place was always intended to be a holding routine. This is where we have to make a choice, is it working well enough as it stands to leave it? Will it allow us to alter the difficulty as the level progresses or changes? I think not, though as a random trigger it works just fine and let us test things, it really does not provide any flow or uniqueness to the game, we have to scrap it and do something else.

Our problem has not changed, we simply want to provide a more refined and interesting way to trigger our Aliens. Let's consider what we are going to need?

- We want to have some code to decide when someone is going to fly, generally this is done on either a timer or as we did, random coin toss system.

- We also want to decide if we let the Aliens fly alone or in groups, that's quite an important decision.

- We need the rate of attack to increase as the level progress.

- We need the Levels to become more difficult with more triggers/flyers.

Starting with when they are going to fly, let's just use a random value as a timer? Well we could, it worked before but pure random systems, somewhat obviously, tend to produce values that are too random, it does depend on the range we seek, which now leads me in a potentially rather long and boring discussion about random numbers.

Random numbers are an interesting concept in games, because in truth there are no such things, CPUs actually find it very hard to produce true random numbers, but we can simply manipulate a start value, called a seed, and modify it using various means to produce a seemingly random sequence of numbers. This is the most common form of randomness computers use, which has an advantage sometimes in that the sequence derived from the same seed will produce the same results. That can be useful for ensuring a repeating pattern of events.

It also can be undesirable, if you truly want your triggered events to be unpredictable. But though the sequence that is generated is predictable, the frequency in which it is chosen and used, can be varied by truly unpredictable factors such as when a user presses a key, which is an example of a truly unpredictable and therefore random event, because no computer will know exactly when the user is going to hit a key. Setting a seed from unpredictable or changing values, like the time the app starts up, can also produce a sequence, which will be different from game to game.

So randomness can be partially controlled, or allowed to be seemingly unpredictable, like many things in programming what you need will depend on the needs of your project, it's up to you which you choose.

But that's enough about Random numbers for now; they have very significant uses in games, but be very careful about basic logic decisions on them.

How about a timer, well timers are by nature rhythmical, your player is going to very quickly sense the pulse of the game if some things happen in the same intervals. If you want that, then great, if not, it needs to be modified.

Usually a good solution as a mix of both, Random and Timer, using a base time to make sure we get at least some time between triggers and a modifier, that is, randomly generated, which extends that time to a less predictable event.

For our needs, this sounds like quite a reasonable thing, we'll set up a timer using a length we find reasonable, and once that timer counts down we'll reset the count to use a random value as a modification factor, then we can be pretty sure that a reasonable interval is going to happen but that it's not going to be so repetitive, we may still get a lot of 0.001 s values but our base value will let our player think that there's a beat happening until the random values do finally produce a noticeable change and it's also quite possible to reduce the size of that base value to increase the incidence of events. The Player will get a sense that the events will happen within given time frames, but not be able to accurately predict the exact moment.

But let's create a small timer to count down and set a flag to tell us it's time to do something. This little bit of code should be considered a housekeeping task in the Game loop, that ideally occurs before we move the Aliens

```
// do some housekeeping
Trigger = false;
TimeTillChoice--;
if (TimeTillChoice == 0)
{
 TimeTillChoice = BaseTime + Rand(30 * 5);
 Trigger == true;
}
```

I've defined BaseTime as a #define in my game.h, inside the class like so

```
#define BaseTime 3*30
```

Also inside the Game Class, add TimeTillChoice and Trigger

```
int  TimeTillChoice;
bool  Trigger;
```

Needless to say these need to be initialized, and in the first init I'd actually make them TimeTillChoice about four or five times longer than BaseTime. To allow the player to take view of what's going on before all hell breaks loose.

Now this is an example of a code-based timer, but it's not actually using time as such, it's just decrementing a value we set somewhere to 0, it's really more accurate to call it a counter, but we are using time, since we know that our game runs at 30 fps so 30 cycles is 1 s. We could however use real-time values if we wanted as there are in fact timers on board in your OS that can allow you to tell how long things have taken. Though most SBCs don't contain onboard real-time clocks (because of lack of batteries), once they are powered up and running they keep count of how long they have been awake, and once they have been allowed to get the time from the Internet or your input, they set that to the time in the time zone it thinks it's in. They keep quite impressive time as a running counter. We use this already with this line in our start up file Invader.cpp

```
gettimeofday(&t2, &tz);
```

We will discover cool things to do with this later, since it allows us to tell how long our game cycle takes, we call this delta time, the time that passed since last cycle, and we do keep track of it, because later as our projects become more complex it will have a very important use. We could for example subtract that delta time from our `TimeTillChoice` counter, for a really accurate value. But, this is a random value, actual proper time isn't that important to us, we simply want to create a variation in time. No need for microsecond accuracy here is there?

The time from the `gettimeofday` routine has many other uses, for example, it can be a truly Random seed because we have no way of knowing what time our game starts to the microsecond.

Back to our Alien selection, we keep getting distracted by geeky interesting things! Once we decide that we are going to fly, we also need to decide who is going to do it! That's pretty important, since we really want the two top guys to do their thing before the others get into a free for all, and we don't want them all doing it at once. So some rule is needed to decide, who gets priority.

We also would like them to fly in small groups, so when we trigger one, we should try to trigger some close companions.

So let's discuss what we're going to do. We're going to use the timer we just wrote, when the timer says we can go, we need to pick someone. Here random can help us as we'll set up probabilities, which we can use to stack the odds of a move.

We have three types of Alien, top is our Commanders, we want them to go first, in fact as long as there are Commanders in the line, we want them to always go first, things will only start to get more interesting when they are both dead.

Thereafter we'll let the Sergeants next in line have a go, then the privates.

I would like the Commanders to try to take two Sergeants with them when they fly, and also the Sergeants to take two privates.

Privates though can go off by themselves as long as the Commanders and Sergeants are dead.

Ok so that's the battle plan, let's try to code it up.

So, if we have three types of Aliens, let's have a small array that gives us a percentage chance which type we trigger and we can scan through, let's also keep a current running tally of how many of that type we currently have, which will be useful later. We didn't actually record the type of Alien when we created them, so we need to backtrack a little bit, and actually set that up. We can use an `enum` and `typedef` again to make that happen.

Inside the Alien Class after public: and before the #define put this code

```
typedef enum AlienType
{
 Commander = 0, Sergeant, Private
} AlienType;
```

Notice, I break my little rule about starting an enum at a different point from other enums, that's because in this case I am going to use these as an index rather than a simple compare.

When we originally set them up in our GroupManager init function we initially gave them hard numeric values in the table

```
int EnemyCoords[46 * 3] = // we could use a [46][3] but it's not so hard
to use a single
 {
   // top row ALIENS we use X,Y,Type
   (SCRWIDTH / 2) - 100,Row1, 0,
   (SCRWIDTH / 2) + 100 - 32,Row1, 0,
   //2nd row 6 aliens
   (SCRWIDTH / 2) - (3 * DIST), Row2, 1,
   (SCRWIDTH / 2) - (2 * DIST), Row2, 1,
etc.
```

We could leave them like that, but you know my feelings now about hard numbers…so time to do a bit of copy and replace, I don't recommend a full block copy and replace, just copy type the first `Alien::Commander`, copy it, then select the 1 in the next row and paste in the `Alien::Commander`. Then replace the first, two with `Alien::Sergeant`, copy it, then highlight the next two, and press CTRL to replace the two. Repeat till done then do the three and `Alien::Private`.

Why not a block replace? Well we're replacing the numbers 0, 1, and 2, which do appear a lot in the body of the chunk of code we're altering, so individual, select and replace is better if a bit tedious, it looks like this when done.

```
   // top row ALIENS we use X,Y,Type
   (SCRWIDTH / 2) - 100,Row1, Alien::Commander,
   (SCRWIDTH / 2) + 100 - 32,Row1, Alien::Commander,
   //2nd row 6 aliens
   (SCRWIDTH / 2) - (3 * DIST), Row2, Alien::Sergeant,
   (SCRWIDTH / 2) - (2 * DIST), Row2, Alien::Sergeant,
etc.
```

So that's done, for no other reason than we may choose to alter the values we know that we are looking at Commanders, Sergeants and Privates…If you compile that, you will not see any difference at all, the code in the setup routine is still using 0, 1, and 2, because that's what those enum values are set to.

This time though, when we get the `whatImages` value, we need to store it in the Type variable we make in the Alien.h Class.

```
AlienType Type;
```

And back to our Group setup, add this line

```
A->Type = (Alien::AlienType)whatImages;
```

Annoyingly we need the cast (`Alien::AlienType`) as a bit of a safety check, it quite rightly thinks our `Type` variable is an `AlienType`, but the array initializer allowed it to be stored as an `int`. It's a quirk of C++ that it will allow enums to be considered as `int`'s, but it won't consider it to be a typedef'ed enum without casting to make it clear that is what we want. So when we set up `whatImages`, it was an `int`, and we need to just tell C++ that it is really an `AlienType`.

While we're on the subject of casting, it's probably wise to note that (Alien::AlienType) is an example of a C style cast, C++ has different and more efficient types of cast, but we'll get to those later.

Ok, now that's done, we've now managed to store without too much effort the type value of the Aliens we create, which we can use in our logic, let's get back to the Game and Alien Classes.

We're almost ready, just need to make sure we set up our TimeTillChoice and ChanceOfHit tables like this, at the end of the Game initialization code

```
/Level variable initialising stuff
 TimeTillChoice = BaseTime * 3;
 ChanceOfHit[Alien::Commander] = 60;
 ChanceOfHit[Alien::Sergeant] = 5;
 ChanceOfHit[Alien::Private] = 0;
 HowManyOfThisType[Alien::Commander] = 2;
 HowManyOfThisType[Alien::Sergeant] = 6;
 HowManyOfThisType[Alien::Private] = 38;
```

Take special note of that comment, for later. Make sure you have ChanceOfHit[3] and HowManyOfThisType[3] as ints in your Game.h.

So we've set up the timer to be about 9 s that may be too long, but we can adjust later, and the Chance of a hit for Commanders is 60% and Sergeants 5% because we don't want to totally eliminate them from the first few dives. But we don't want the Privates to dive alone until the Commanders are dead, that btw, will need us to keep a bit more notice of what happens when things die, we'll check back to that in a minute.

Once our timer says we can go, we simply test our existing Aliens, and if the trigger is set we roll a Random chance, and compare it to the type % chance we gave. Don't go for 100% as the highest though; we need to add a little uncertainty, that's why we have a 60% chance that you will fly a Commander when the time is ready.

If we scan through the list and don't trigger one, it might need some code to reduce the timer value to try again, but for now let's see how it goes.

In our Moving step of the Alien update, let's test if we want to fly, replace the holding random routine with this:

```
if (TheGame->Trigger == true)
{
 // lets do some triggering folks
 if (Rand(100) < TheGame->ChanceOfHit[Type])
 {
  State = Arcing;
  ArcInit = false;
  TheGame->Trigger = false; /should we clear?
 }
}
```

Now run your code, we should see a nice delay after the game starts, then the commanders will fly to their glorious Kamikazi deaths but it seems ok so far. We've not added any formation code yet but that's ok, we will. Leave it even longer and you will eventually also get a sergeant or two taking the plunge. But with only a 5% chance every 3–5 s it's going to be a while before we clear the board of them, and the Privates are never going to go.

The key point is that when any enemy dies, we need to alter the probability. The best place to do that, is in the Dying step of the Alien, because that's the point when an Alien transitions to its dead state, and that's where we can review the variables and make some minor alterations.

Add this to the Dying step code after you set State to Dead;

```
State = Dead;
 TheGame->HowManyOfThisType[Type]--;
 TheGame->ChanceOfHit[Type] += 2; // every time we kill one of this type,
increase the chance of this type flying

 if (TheGame->HowManyOfThisType[Type] == 0 && Type != Alien::Private)
 {
  TheGame->ChanceOfHit[Type + 1] += 20; // increase the chance of the next
type flying
  if (Type == Alien::Commander)
  {
   // all the Commanders are dead so lets allow a few Privates to fly and
increase the Sergeants chances
    TheGame->ChanceOfHit[Alien::Private] += 10;
    TheGame->ChanceOfHit[Alien::Sergeant] += 10;
  }
 }
```

Ok, so we are doing a few small things, every time we kill a type, we increase the probability of that type flying. If we eliminate an entire type, we increase the probability of the next type, though we can't increase beyond a Private, so there's a safety check in there and also if we kill all the Commanders, we quite deliberately stack the odds for the Sergeant and Privates to fly.

All pretty good, so far, time to get them to attack in convoy now. We can fiddle about with the timing and also the increase we add to the chance of a hit to alter our gameplay but we're getting close to what we want. More kills = more dives, so the action should become a little more frenetic as the level progresses.

Breaker Breaker Rubber Duck

We're ready now to trigger some companions; we'll do this fairly simply by just scanning through the Aliens directly below the ones we trigger. Only the Commanders and Sergeants fly in convoy, so we only really want them to have any inclination of who's under them.

We will let the Commander fly with up two sergeants and the sergeants fly with three Privates, but that creates a problem for us, we have no idea what's under us, we'd have to scan through the vector list of objects for one that represents us, then get our coords and then compare all the other objects to see if they are of the right type and right range.

Well ok, that's one way, and it's a valid way, take our coords, and scan through the list to see who is in a certain radius. Actually not a bad approach. But I hate scanning for things that are likely to produce a lot of dead results. It's far better to do a bit of preplanning and let our Aliens know where to look. But to do that we need to backtrack a little again and make sure we know which Alien we are looking at, give them an ID that relates to their position in the Vector list.

I've a feeling this process might get complicated, and I don't want to mess up what is a very nice little movement step, so I'm going to add variable/member and a routine/method to my class, called;

```
void GetMyFriends(Game* G);
int   MyID;
```

And look, it passes a pointer to Game, and I will be able to know who I am from ID as the Alien I am currently updating, so that I can look up a list of Aliens I know are under me.

Go back to your GroupManager initialize routine, and in the loop where you create the Aliens after you actually new it, add this

```
A->MyID = i;
```

And that will give our Alien and ID number between 0 and 45 inclusive, perfect for looking up an array!

But we have a problem. Quite a big one; we have indexes we can use to look up an array, but we don't currently in our game have an Array of Aliens…what yes we do, we're updating them using Game::MyObjects, and that is true. But Game::MyObjects is *not* an array of Aliens, it's an array of GameObject's and the GameObject Class does not contain the MyID or State variables we need to change, they are in the Alien Class! We need another array, of Aliens, in the Game Class.

This can be a straight array because we know exactly how many we have, if you choose later to have more Aliens of an indeterminate number then make it a vector, for now though, add this to the Game Class in Game.h

```
Alien* TheAliens[46];
```

Annoyingly before we compile this, we'll need to add a small predefine for our Alien Class, so that Game Class knows about it. This is because of the fact our Alien Class includes the Game.h file to use Game* in its class define, but now Game wants to use Alien, so it kind confuses the compiler, as some things are attempting to be created before it knows about them and it is a bit of a cyclical mindbender.

Adding this line just before we define the Game Class, will tell it, that there is a class called Alien, and once it's all compiled the linker will fix things up for us. It's untidy coding at this point but trust me, it works.

```
class Alien;
```

Now in the init system for our GroupManager we need to populate this new Alien array with the address of each Alien as we make it, add this line after the push_back at the end of the routine.

```
ParentGame->TheAliens[i] = A;
```

Boom, we now have a trail of breadcrumbs our Aliens can use to find each other, which will let us write that GetMyFriends routine like this:

```
void Alien::GetMyFriends(Game* TheGame)
{
  if (MyID > 7) return; //Privates not allowed friends!! :(
```

```
int Count = 0;
for (int i = 0; i < 3; i++)
{
  if (TheGame->TheAliens[WhoAreMyFriends[MyID][i]]->State == Moving)
  {
   TheGame->TheAliens[WhoAreMyFriends[MyID][i]]->State = Arcing;
   Count++;
  }
  if (Type == Commander && Count == 2) break;
 }
}
```

This will make sure that Commander only takes two of his possible three friends, and sergeants can take all three if they are available. Privates, sadly have no friends, unless you want to add them?

You can see though that this routine needs a new array, called WhoAreMyFriends, so where is that? Well here of course!

```
int WhoAreMyFriends[8][3] =
{
 { 2, 3, 4 }, / 2nd 3rd Aliens for sure, and possible 4th Alien
 { 6, 7, 5 }, / move to the end of the sergeants
 { 8, 9, 10 }, / 8th 9th and 10th
 { 9, 10, 11 },
 { 10, 11, 12 },
 { 11, 12, 13 },
 { 12, 13, 14 },
 { 13, 14, 15 }
};
```

I put it just above the routine, and let it live in Global space, it makes it quicker and easier to access. Can you work out from the routine and the array what's going on? Run it now and fix any errors/typos that come up and see what happens.

That's pretty much it for the Aliens now, we can tweak some of those annoying hard numbers, though far better if we replace them with some nice easy to locate #defines at the top of the file, but overall we've achieved our goal, time to move on to our next problem.

Fred Reacts!

So what does Fred do when he's hit? Well he blows up, in fact he does pretty much the same things as the Aliens, we might show a little explosion graphic, then he dies, a life counter, which we don't currently have anywhere, will decrement, and then it's up to the game code to decide if he gets reborn or if the game is over.

And now we see we have a problem. We have no game management code at all in our Game loop, we're only doing the simple steps of updating and rendering objects with very little thought into how our game itself should flow.

So we need to put something on our to-do list, *write some game management code.

And first part of that needs to be to include some lives. So go back to Game.h, add a Lives variable as an int, and in the Game init code set it to a value, let's say three.

Now, our Fred/Shooter update code does not contain any concept of states like our Aliens do. Given that we now realize we need to have at least three states... Active, Dying, and Dead. We should add them as an enum, and a state variable in our Shooter Class.

Now be careful with this, we're maybe going to have states with the same name but relating to different actions. We don't want to use the Aliens enum, which we actually put in global space, naughty! We want to put the Shooters enum inside the class definition like this:

```
Shooter(char* filename, MyFiles* filehander)
 : GameObject(filename, filehander) {}; // creates an image from the
typedef enum Status
{
 Normal = 200, Dying, Dead
} Status;
Status State;
```

I put it just after the constructor to show you. Now we have a variable called State that the Shooter can check, and it's using a new type called Status, but it's enclosed totally in the Shooter Class, so when we come to set it up, after we create the Shooter (not before) we use this format:

```
Fred->Xpos = (SCRWIDTH / 2) - 16;
Fred->Ypos = (SCRHEIGHT) - 40;
Fred->State = Shooter::Normal;
```

As we might want to use Dying or Dead as a state, we can use that Shooter:: prefix to help us to make sure that we've got the Dying and Dead value we want for the Shooter, which is different from the Dying and Dead value the Alien has, just to be quadruple sure, I made sure the enum for the Shooters states started at 200 where the Aliens started at 100. This is a form of encapsulation. We're making sure that the variables we want to use for that class are only usable in that class we could enhance this even more by making the enum private inside the class, but I'm not a big fan of that, though real coders will disagree.

Ok, so let's make a few alterations to the Shooters update code, we currently only have the normal state, so let's put in a switch and use that as the normal case so we get this:

```
bool Shooter::Update(Game* g)
{
switch (State)
{
case Normal:
  if (g->InputHandle->TestKey(KEY_LEFT))
  {
     Xpos -= 5;
     if (Xpos < 0) Xpos = 0;
  }
  if (g->InputHandle->TestKey(KEY_RIGHT))
  {
     Xpos += 5;
     if (Xpos > SCRWIDTH - Image->GetWidth()) Xpos = SCRWIDTH
     - Image->GetWidth();
  }
  if (g->InputHandle->TestKey(KEY_SPACE) && TheBullet->ReadyToFire == true)
  {
     this->TheBullet->ReadyToFire = false;
  }
  break;
```

```
case Dying:
break;
case Dead:
break;
default:
 printf("The Shooter has a state that has no code assigned\n");
break;
}
}
```

Also if you've not already done so, I've taken out the redundant fire flag code from the old Invaders version.

Run this, and if you've set it up ok in the initialize this will work just perfectly with no apparent difference from the last attempts. But now we have the ability to do something cool when we get hit and all we have to do to trigger that, is tell Fred, he's Dying.

Let's put in some holding code, so we know that it gets to the right bit of code when we get hit.

```
case Dying:
 printf("Uggg he got me, farewell cruel world\n");
 State = Shooter::Dead;
break;
```

Now to actually make the bombs deadly, time to update and use that `DidWeHitFred` code we wrote way back in the bomb's update code, which now looks like this:

```
bool Bomb::Update(Game* g)
{
 Vector2D Step = BombMotion*10;
 Xpos += Step.x;
 Ypos += Step.y;
 if (Ypos > SCRHEIGHT + 10) this->MarkForRemoval = true;
 if (g->Fred->State == Shooter::Normal)
 {
  if (DidWeHitFred(g->Fred) == true)
   g->Fred->State = Shooter::Dying;
 }
}
```

Compile and run, and let Fred get hit by a bomb, and we should see that he will report his condition in the console window and then freeze up.

Remember also, we have Diving and bombing Aliens who can kill Fred, and they have a specific test that checks that, but are only removing themselves when they hit, now we can add this to the bottom of that code in Alien.cpp in `Alien::DidWeGetHit(Shooter* Fred)`

```
float Dist = sqrtf((diffx*diffx) + (diffy*diffy));
 if (Dist < (R1 + R2))
 {// we did dive into Fred so Fred can be killed
  Fred->State = Shooter::Dying;
  return true;
 }
```

Great, I mean, how sad, he's dead. But it's all good we have more lives, maybe. Though, we should probably stop the Aliens from starting new dives now as they clearly have completed their task, and of course that's another simple condition check on routine, which triggers the Arc. At the moment, I have this random routine in the Aliens Moving step condition

```
if (Rand(1000000) < 1150 && TheGame->Fred->State == Shooter::Normal)
  {
   State = Arcing;
   ArcInit = false;
  }
```

Our ability to know that he's in a normal or dying state allows us to tailor several of our behaviors. We could even trigger a little celebration dance, if we had the graphics for it.

But the most important thing we need to do is to get the game to check for an end game condition or a restart condition, which incidentally is where stopping the arc is quite useful, as we don't want to respawn in a swarm of diving Aliens.

Ok so we know it all works, let's add some explosions and some logic code to control the game flow. Go back to Shooter.h and replace the eloquent bit of text with some relevant code:

```
case Dying:
 if (g->Lives > 0) g->Lives = g->Lives - 1;
 State = Shooter::Dead;
 break;
```

I'm checking that Lives is not already 0 because there's the possibility of more than one bullet hitting, though in truth only the first one is ever going to set this, it's a good sanity check to make sure.

I'm also going to add a timer to the Game Class in Game.h called the respawn timer.

```
int RespawnTimer;
```

Its purpose hopefully is obvious, but do make sure at game init time you set it to 0.

To make it work in the Game Class, add this code before you update Fred.

```
if (RespawnTimer != 0)
 {
  Fred->onscreen = false;
  RespawnTimer--;
  printf("Get Ready for a respawn in %i \n", RespawnTimer);
  if (RespawnTimer == 0)
  { // time to bring him back
   Fred->State = Shooter::Normal;
   Fred->onscreen = true;
  }
 }
```

This will prevent Fred from being drawn and decrement the timer to reset him back. This should give you a clue to when we want to set that RespawnTime to have a value?

```
case Dying:
 if (g->Lives > 0) g->Lives = g->Lives - 1;
 State = Shooter::Dead;
 g->RespawnTimer = 30 * 3;
 break;
```

Although, if we want to put in an animation for an explosion, we could probably use an exploding state before this. I'll let you worry about that. Notice in the final code, I commented out the printf, rather than delete it, it's a personal choice, but it acts as a perfectly sensible comment, and who knows I may have a problem with this code and want to restore the print to check that the state is being called.

The dead state for our shooter can be simply an empty state:

```
case Dead:
  break;
```

Its only purpose is to signal to the game code that he's not currently able to have any influence until Fred is set back into normal state.

If you compile this now, you should actually have the first real gaming experience with lethal force and the chance of your shooter being killed, or clearing up all your Aliens. But then it does kind of stop, there's no way to continue, which is not a good thing.

Tidy Up the Logic

So, we've got Fred Dying, very sad, the Aliens testing his state and going into a holding pattern until he's ready to be reborn, and the Game loop itself, processing a respawn loop and keeping him offscreen when not needed, btw did you notice his bullet was still visible…you can fix that now.

Twiddles and Tweaks

Now it's done, our second fully functioning game. It's actually not too bad, but there are a lot of little things we could do to make it better. For example, how about sending the bullets down to where they expect Fred to be rather than where he is? It's not too hard to work out that if he's moving left he will be a few dozen pixels left of his current position in 20 cycles or so? Why are we only doing the arc in one direction? Could we do both if we had a flag to indicate which side we're on? Or, maybe get the divers to start to bomb a little earlier in a spread pattern of a random number of bombs. So that you cover where he is, and where he might be. These things are all pretty simple and you should be able to work them out now from the things we've done so far. Don't be afraid to experiment with it, it's your game, make it play the way you want it to play.

Btw I have a question for you, in our Game.h file we defined our vector lists as static, now aside from giving you some experience of using static variables, do you think that was a good idea? After all we only ever have one instance of Game. Think about it, consider why we have static variables in a class, and then consider if it was a good choice in this single instance?

For now though we've made a game, it's a nice little shoot-em-up. I hope you enjoyed writing it, but I hope you will enjoy making it better, even more.

Postmortem

Now this time we really didn't find it too hard to get access to the info we needed, by ensuring our Base Class contained the main data structures that connected all the other classes to that Base Class it was possible for one object to interact with another and also to generate bombs, put them in lists and do tests with the shooter, who likewise could make the bullet fly on command and the Aliens could test for collisions. There wasn't really much twisting around to get what we wanted.

We also had a bit of fun with 2D vectors, which really do make smooth motion and steady speed a lot easier. We're going to use them a lot more until we are fully comfortable.

There are few things I'm not happy with; for example, I wasn't totally happy with the fact we set a hard number in the list for the number of active Aliens and Fred, which meant we could never really delete them, as it would confuse the list indexing on the second part when we process the stars and bombs. That was bad planning, don't you agree? So we should avoid that in future, hard numbers are bad, mkaay?

Also why did I make the Aliens enum global and the Shooters encased in the Shooter code? I really should have encased both in their respective classes. But though some people allow all their enums to start at 0, I defend the choice of ensuring they had different base starts, it can be a useful fail safe in case you forget to add the correct prefix.

If I'm honest I really hate the scaled descent on the dives, it should upset you too, have you noticed how fast the aliens are if they are a long way from Fred when they start, how do you think we can level out that speed? You should know the answer, so I won't tell you!

For the most part though, the Game Class was clean and tidy and did its three main functions, initialize, update all objects, and control when to end or reset the levels. The individual classes themselves did the rest. That's tidier and allowed us to make simpler changes to behavior in the files of the objects that actually exhibited that behavior.

This was structurally a much sounder bit of code. It's still not the best way; purists might not like it too much, because real OOP architecture avoids too much interaction between classes in this direct way, but for a small game this works quite well. So now we can build on this until we expose other weaknesses we have to tackle.

Jumping around a Bit Though?

One thing you should also notice, was that, though I had a pretty fair idea of what the different classes and files were going to do when I started, as the project developed, I was not afraid to go back and make changes or additions. As the game grew we went back and forward into different classes, adding a bit here, altering a bit there; you may have got the idea that I didn't know what I was doing but really I did.

This is a *normal* development flow, which is hard to capture in a book tutorial but I hope you got it. Every beginners programming book I've read, shows you finished little masterpieces that do exactly what the author said it would do at the start. But what they didn't show you was the week or so of writing, rewriting, and then a bit more rewriting to find ways to serialize that finished bit of code in the book. This is not how game development happens!

This is important, a lot of beginners think they have to plan their projects to the smallest detail before coding and try very hard not to go back and alter things once coded. But this is how madness and bad code occurs. Never be afraid to go back, never be afraid to change things, and never be afraid to make a start before you've fully thought it out. So long as you have the basic structure set in your mind you can get things up and running, play with ideas, try things out, see what happens, and allow things to evolve!

There are no coders out there who know exactly what they are going to code before they type the first line. You need to be flexible, some ideas will sound fantastic when you think of them, and explain them to your coding buddies, but when you actually implement them; they suck. Or as you are writing you might come up with a small improvement, but it needs you to step back into your code to make some changes. We did that here a few times in Kamikazi.

There's a really important rule. *Don't be too precious about what you write.* Even a really great method can be improved as your code starts to grow and you can see how it behaves under real running conditions. Like that scaled dive!! It really is wrong, I just wanted to you to see that a bad idea might seem to work, but it really doesn't, you should fix it!

Don't be afraid to modify, alter, update, and improve, at any point in your project. Also, don't get too obsessed with having fully working systems in place before you try them out. Be willing to place holding systems or partial systems to make sure they get called at the right times, and allow you to observe the results. printf's are a great way of making sure your code is getting to where you think it's going, but don't leave them in the final builds.

Crawling Over, Time for Baby Steps

Pretty good stuff so far, even though these are really quite simple games, they presented us with some challenges on how to think about how we were going to do things, also we learned that we could get things to happen at the right times and we discovered how to use some basics of maths, Vector maths in particular is a very important concept that will come to be indispensable when we move to 3D. We also introduced a new type of very important array, vectors, not to be confused with the maths type 2D and 3Dvectors, Vectors are a form of dynamic array that can change its size and delete/replace objects inside it, as needed. This extra ability does have a few drawbacks with performance but the flexibility of an array type structure you can modify as the game is running is invaluable. These are going to become even more important in the next chapters.

And on top of all that, you gained some experience of creating classes, processing a game loop, and made use of a fundamental C++ feature of inheritance and the powerful but sometimes dangerous concept of overriding.

Object-Oriented Programming Is Not an Error

Let's not confuse oops with OOP, which stands for OOP. C++ is at its heart an OOP language, which means it is designed to allow certain concepts in programming, which we are just starting to make use of. Of course, the name is a giveaway in that we consider the things we create to be *objects*, and I've hinted at that so far. But *objects* can mean more than just our little graphic workhorse class. An *object* is anything we can describe as a self-contained unit. You'll find I use the word object a lot in this book, because we are going to be using a lot of self-contained units. And if we can define such a thing we can add functionality to it, that's where the OOP part comes in. We generally (though not exclusively) use classes to define our concepts of objects, which then allows C++ to come into its own as an OOP language. Up till now we've been quite lazy with our design of our code, which has resulted in my usual messy C with classes style, but we're going to make more effort now to move you toward better OOP principles. There are four major principles of OOP, which C++ embraces, here's some very simple explanations, which we're going to expand on as we go.

Encapsulation

Which essentially ensures that all the data and variables that an object needs to have access to for fulfilling its requirements are contained within itself? Ideally then an objects methods or functions will only act on its own data. This is probably the big thing with C++, the more you can avoid global concepts and nasty externs the better, an object/class should be totally self-contained.

Abstraction

Is harder to explain in simple terms, I like to think of it as moving away from the technical details of an object and looking at it from a higher level, for example, our Kamikazi Enemies, they are just enemies to me, I don't want to spend too much time thinking about the underlying variables and subclass that make them work, I just want to make the enemies move around. The fact that Enemies and Fred, are essentially the same workhorse Object Class, allows me to consider them as abstracted concepts.

Inheritance

Allows us to build on previous concepts and objects to create new things, thus creating a hierarchy of object concepts but able to refer to them as their base types. Again our Enemies in Kamikazi are a great example, all the Enemies inherit their data from Objects, but are controlled by their final class types.

Polymorphism

Which despite sounding like a nasty virus, simply means an ability to have multiple methods of the same name but having different functionality. This is usually denoted by passing or returning a different set of arguments. There's a bit more to it than that, but that's a decent one sentence explanation.

Real hard-core C++ programmers will adhere to these four principles as if their life depends on it, and if you really want to do proper C++ then so will you. But it can take quite some time to bend your brain around the concepts while you are still struggling to get to grips with, "what happens if I do this." So we are going to be slowly developing our OOP concepts and moving away from the very basic C and C++ with classes we've done so far. I'm just warning you ahead of time that our coding style needs to develop away from this fugly beginning, to something a bit more elegant. But as far as humanly possible, I'm going to keep the code readable, which will break some of the main OOP rules from time to time. Working a lot with beginners, I suggest readability and understanding will always be better than correct but confusing.

Start the Music

It's obvious that we need sound in our games; if not actually music we at least need some way to play some sound fx. So it's time to get some sound in, but how?

Well it's perfectly possible to access the targets sound chip, if it has one, write a tone generator, replay sounds, and ohhh all sorts of things, which we stopped caring about years ago, it is a lot of effort, and this is a case where keeping our rule of no external libs makes no sense at all. The amount of work involved in writing a sound system is vastly disproportionate to our desire to get a working game.

A word of caution though, in my experiments with different types of target, its become clear that not all SBC systems do their sound the same way or even have the sound systems activated when you boot up. Make sure that your system is capable of playing sound before we try to do anything. There is nothing more frustrating that trying to get something working and seemingly failing, only to discover in the final moments, you forgot to turn the volume up.

It's up to you to make sure you system currently has its sound working and the volume turned up.

The Raspberry range, come with a really effective sound and media system that lets it playback sound in all sorts of media, called OpenMax. This is available on a lot of systems but it isn't really designed with games in mind, so I decided to try a different and more conventional approach and not use OpenMax, we really want something that gives more than just playback, OpenMax won't allow us to provide user variable surround sound, which is very useful later when we do 3D worlds with objects in them, so cool as it is, it's not for us!

Time to go locate a free, easy to use and popular sound lib, and add it to our builds.

Welcome to OpenAL

As its name suggests this is or rather was, an open access Audio API, but it's actually named because it was designed in a similar way to the concept of the original OpenGL. It started out as a royalty free cross-platform system, but it is now proprietary, so you need to pay for the very latest version. However, it's not all bad, there is still a fully functional very stable and widely used version available called OpenAL Soft, which we can use royalty free, which more importantly, we can easily install on our target, and will do pretty much all we need to do with a modest amount of effort.

There ARE many other sound APIs available, FMOD, OpenSL, and as mentioned OpenMAX, for example, from the Khronos group would seem to be ideal, as we are looking for royalty free cross-platform systems. But though you can get some SBCs supporting them, not all do, audio on a SBC is often part of the main chips system, so it's up to the makers to decide on compatibility with audio APIs and that support is very variable. I can't locate it for most of my SBCs, including the very well-supported Raspberry range.

I also, for the purpose of learning, need a very general system that should work on all the available SBCs we are targeting in this book. You are, of course, absolutely free to use another sound API, if you accept you might limit your number of user targets. So for now, OpenAL it is! And the experience of using it will stand you in good stead when you want to upgrade to a better, more modern, or more target specific API.

Installing OpenAL

We have to break the no external library rule one more time for a good cause. This time though unlike our header-based graphics loader we're going to install a prebuilt library from the net, the process is a tiny bit different.

Open up a terminal or if you are in a console mode, enter,

```
sudo apt-get install libopenal-devl
```

In your console line, while (of course) connected to the Internet. That should be all we need to do as the apt-get app will go ask the servers it knows of, for the latest version of libopenal-dev, which is suitable for our target, it will install the libs on your machine, usually in the usr/libs/arm-linux-gnueabihf and usr/include/AL folders but different Linux flavors may go somewhere else.

To be sure, enter this command after the install has done its job

```
dpkg -L libopenal-dev
```

It will display the location of all the files in the package, including docs. No, I don't know what dpgk is supposed to mean, Linux is an absolute mystery to me, I don't know why it is so popular, let's hope that's the extent of the Linux we have to use...though I suspect not!

Hopefully you'll get something like this:

which lets us know our include files are as we hoped in the /usr/include and usr/include/al directories

We need to pass this info to the VisualGDB properties like so:

Preprocessor macros:	DEBUG RASPBERRY
Include directories:	/opt/vc/include /opt/vc/include/interface/vcos/pthreads /opt/vc/include/interface /opt/vc/include/interface/vmcs_host/linux /usr/include/AL
Library directories:	/opt/vc/lib /usr/lib/arm-linux-gnueabihf
Library names:	GLESv2 EGL bcm_host pthread openal
Additional linker inputs:	
	Read more about libraries and other linker inputs

You can see I added the include directory, to the Include directories, with a space after the last one. And the Library directories, notice we got the name of the *.so from our dpkg app and the name is openal. Library names are usually, the name of the *.so file with the lib prefix removed, so the libopenal.so file is named openal. Be careful as this is all case sensitive.

VisualGDB should take those values, and when you click apply do a test to make sure they are all valid, if you've entered them all correctly the libs are now installed and ready for you to use. There may be a short pause while it creates copies on your dev system.

Now that's done we are able to include the header files we need using <style> includes. The <> indicates known paths, and as we've set the path for these files up in the properties, Visual Studio will locate them for us, if you get a red line when you enter `#include <al.h>` double check you typed it all in correctly.

Getting OpenAL Working

We're only going to do some basic sound control, full 3D binaural sound is a little beyond our needs at the moment, even though OpenAL is fully capable of doing that. But we do want to have some sound fx that can be played and perhaps a simple background tune.

Now having it installed is one thing, using it and knowing how to set it up is another. There is, of course, a strong support network, and the first place you need to go is http://www.openal.org.

Where you may find updates, though as it's been unsupported for some time that might be unlikely, but you certainly can find documentation.

One very important point to know is that OpenAL just like OpenGL knows nothing about file formats, or indeed even about your target audio system, it can only work on data that has been placed in a buffer and is ready to be played and it then sends it to a device that is responsible for playing it. OpenAL simply does all the maths and timing things needed to make the sound play in stereo.

So now we also need to add something that can load sounds, and we need to be certain we have some kind of proper playback device.

Oh no, more libs?

Yes, I'm afraid so, but this is an easy one, we're going to install Alut, a utility toolkit designed to go with OpenAL. There is a tiny problem with this, it's horribly outdated, I mean horribly, you are probably going to be the first people to download it in decades, its outdated even to the point of being officially considered deprecated, but I'm going to use it now, just so we don't over complicate our life. As, and this is for your benefit, it is by far the simplest solution when using simple wav files. Once we get things up and running and you know what you are doing, you can replace it with a much more flexible system that can handle more stuff and deal with streaming of other formats. It's important to remember we're trying to write games, not get tied up in the minutiae of technical aspects. So Alut, is going to do the job for us.

Like OpenAL we are going to install the binaries from the linux servers so once again our friend apt-get comes into play

```
sudo apt-get install libalut-dev
```

Once installed we again need to ask for info on where it is with

```
dpkg -L libalut-dev
```

Only this time, we don't need to worry about installing all the include and lib directories as it will install itself in the OpenAL directories, we only need to add the lib name as Alut.

You *may* find that you get a red line under #include <alut.h> if you add it, and there's a reason for that, the VisualGDB's intellisense system, which takes care of our cross-referencing for functions, labels and file locations, only caches the libraries listed in the included directories, and we've not changed them, so they won't have been updated because we included the OpenAL directories. So our intellisense system does not actually know much about this new lib we've added because we only added the name, the files that it uses are not in the cache.

Your code will compile but that red line will cause us issues when we want to use/find functions, so go into your VisualGDB properties and select the reload all directories option.

Once it's done, select ok and you should find your red lines all gone. The intellisense works on the files cached in your dev machine, so now it will work again. If you ever add a lib and find you are getting red lines, even when you are sure the directory you put in properties is correct, this should fix it.

And now at last, we should be able to get our sound to work, we'll get that going shortly. If you don't hear anything it may just be that your volume is turned down, go to the audio preferences, make sure you select controls and activate the Pulse Code Modulation (PCM) control, which gives you volume.

If you are using a target other than a Raspberry Pi, it's going to be a total crap shoot if you have sound activated on your system, half of the target boards I have do not have working sound systems built into their OS as standard, which is a frustration to be sure. However, there may be some help at hand, in the form of another library we can add to provide sound play on most systems. If you don't already have it installed try installing pulseaudio on your target.

```
sudo apt-get install pulseaudio
```

5. Finally Our First Games

There's no need to alter our VisualGDB properties files, this is a system library we are installing into our OS, and this basically ensures your target has pulse audio functionality, if it does not already have it. I wish I could say that will work on all systems, but it won't if you don't have audio enabled on your board, then you need to chase the board or OS makers to activate it.

So we've actually covered three types of library we will use, one we compile ourselves, one we will download and use, and one we will expand our OS with. Painless eh?

You will have to make sure that you remember to provide the .so files associated with these libraries if you distribute your games, or make sure that the user also installs them, which is usually a safer bet.

Ok…now we're ready, though I am going to only focus on Wavs for now, we will recognize our need for a compressed longer format and use them later.

We need to make sure, we have some sound fx that are suitable and like most things there are a plethora of royalty free sound fx you can find on line, as well as royalty free music. For our purposes we really want to use music and fx which are quite short, because our machines don't have a lot of onboard RAM.

Music as one might imagine tends to be longer than a spot effect, it's not impossible to have 3 or 4 min of sound looping in a game. If you look at that as raw uncompressed data that can be many megabytes of data. We have to always be mindful of that. So compressed formats are generally best for such large samples. Of course, there is a trade-off, compressed sound needs to be uncompressed eating up some CPU cycles and stored somewhere once uncompressed; again perhaps eating our memory. Methods exist to prevent that, such as streaming where the sound is stored on our storage systems and pulled into working buffers as needed. But again, there's an overhead, loading data is not a fast process.

Since OpenAL does not actually care about file formats and works only on raw data, it can handle MP3, OGG, and FLAC and any other compressed format, it just can't actually load them or decompress them, that's a job for a support library, so we'll try to use those for background music later when we have a suitable loader.

For now we'll not worry too much about these technical details, let's just get some sounds loaded and give our game a bit of life. On the support site, you can find some simple sound fx and a background tune for Kamikazi, in the Sounds folder under Kamikazi.

As usual we need to create a folder, to store these new assets, and it's also wise to put a filter on your solution view, so that you can remind yourself of the filenames. Also don't forget to add *.wav to your VisualGDB properties so that the fx sounds are sent from your machines directories to the target.

In our solution, we can add a filter but filters do not map directly to our directory structures, so when adding resources like this that are not actually part of the build process, it's a good idea to create a single directory for our sounds in our assets folder.

In a large game, we may have many sounds to play at different times. But generally we need music and a sequence of so-called spot fx, shots, pings, booms, and bangs…the list is as endless as the types of graphics.

If like me you are not very good at making your own sounds, there are many different free sound sources available and I don't want to endorse any one in particular but I did find some nice sounds here at https://www.freesound.org/, which had everything I need for this, even if I used them in a slightly different way from their description, I used a nice arcade sound pack by contributor Cabeeno Rossley. You can, of course, use any sounds you want and maybe even make a few of your own. Take note though, I didn't have much luck getting 24 and 32 bit sound samples to work, so try to stick to 16 bit samples, they are smaller anyway.

So I wanted the following unimaginative sounds:

- Fire for bullets.

- Fire and whistle for missiles.

- Whistle for diving.

- Explode for ship.

- Two or three different explosions for enemy deaths.

- Also some music for the background, but that's tricky, so leave that till later.

- A fanfare for clearing the level.

- A death knell for losing a life.

- A bigger death knell for losing all lives and the game over.

Ok, that's enough, there's a temptation to add more and more, but, that's unwise. I'll explain in the next section why.

Dealing with Sound as Data

Sound is a funny stuff, when we break it down we are basically looking at samples, normally one for each type of sound you want to play, resulting in large quantities of data. To increase quality of a given sound, higher sample rates are used, and larger bit counts. Both of which creates larger sample sizes. Sound therefore has a range of quality available and it's important to know what quality the data is before it is replayed, most formats store that info in their file headers.

Raw samples, usually come in something called PCM format, and can take up very large amounts of memory, but there are several compressed and uncompressed systems available, which make up a range of different file formats. Many of these are available to use and OpenAL can play them when turned into raw data.

Generally, as with all things to do with coding, a compromise needs to be made. Larger samples such as music are best stored and loaded as compressed files, shorter more frequent sounds, as uncompressed WAV or even PCM.

So now that the sounds are in place on our system, we need to be able to play them, but like we discovered with our graphics, we can't really load them each time we want to play them. Imagine if we have a rapid fire shooting sound, and we are constantly pressing the fire button. Such constant loading would really slow things down, and eat up a lot of memory.

So we need to be clear what sounds we need in our game, and during our initialization phase, or a level set up, we can load all the sounds we think we will need ready to be triggered.

Remember though two things,

1. Sound is memory hungry; I keep saying this because it's important, only load what you need so that it's ready to be triggered. If you need to load a new set of sounds arrange them in an order that you can load at nongame critical times.

2. As sound data are generally quite big, loading from our storage system is going to be slow. Try to avoid loading in the game loop, it will cripple performance, this is why we use buffers.

Let's keep the sounds simple for the moment, adding it only to our Kamikazi project. We'll add a couple of explosions and a shooting effect, with some nice spot effects for different game events. That'll be enough for this game to let us get everything working and stand us in good stead for a project with more complexity.

To use our sounds we need a simple sound class, and a way call the fx. So let's start by giving the sound fx some easy to use names in an enum.

How Does OpenAL Work?

When dealing with OpenAL we need to think of three things, the so-called fundamental objects:

- *Buffers*: This is where our raw sound data live, this is not the same as the data we load from our storage systems, this is converted from wav or other formats into PCM data.

- *Sources*: Where in 3D space, is the object that is making sound.

- A Listener. You.

The reasons these are separate is to do with the way OpenAL *renders* sound. It does actually take into account the direction and distance of a sound as well as the speed the object emitting the sounds is travelling, so it can even simulate the Doppler effect of sound. Those are fairly complex equations, not unlike the concepts of OpenGL when it comes to working out what pixels are actually seen in a given direction, OpenAL works out the sound you should hear.

Buffers are the easiest of our concepts, it's simply a location in memory where a raw sound sample exists and then identified with a handle once it's set up. We should load up all the sounds we need and keep track of the locations.

Understanding sources as simply the objects in a game world which emit the sound is the easiest way to think of a Source. In time we will allow every object that emits sound, to be a source. But for a simple 2D game, the only real source we need is going to be fixed at a position that represents the screen we are looking at which hopefully has speakers to the side of it. In a 3D game though, we might have two ships, with engines humming, moving toward our location at different speeds. OpenAL allows us to think of each ship as a source, playing the same engine sound from a buffer, but we as the listener viewing the game world at a fixed point, will be able to determine that they are coming from two different locations in our stereo soundscape.

Unlike OpenGL though we don't need to set up massive amounts of values to get our sound to work, just let it know where our buffers are, where our sources are and where the Listener is.

The device we plan to play our sound on is difficult to know, some systems will have sound chips on board, and some will be using other means. But usually there is at least one device on your machine that is designed to play sound, it's rare for any SBC to not have a sound system, though it may not be automatically enabled. You should check that you have sound playback enabled.

We could give our users a choice of playback devices if there are multiple devices, but really all we want is a default player. So our first real task of our sound system is to find out the device.

Then we need to load up our sounds and have them assigned to buffers. We don't want to load them at the playback point, so preloading them is preferred.

On a 2D game we only really need one source and of course one listener, so it should be fairly clear now what our order of business should be?

How Does Alut Work?

OpenGL used to have a nice helper toolkit called GLut, it's still out there and popular with some people, but its outdated now, Alut was OpenAL's equivalent helper toolkit and like Glut it's outdated. But it does provide us with the simplest method to load and convert wavs so that OpenAL can use them. And they are pretty universal on all types of system. We're only going to use it to load and unload basic wav files, so it's a convenient system despite is age and limits. We'll use something a bit better when we need 3D sound.

It's important to initialize OpenAL and also ALUT. The sound class itself can be initialized from a constructor, but ALUT needs a specific call to its initialization system, this is probably best done in your Project start up, or in your Game initialization. But certainly somewhere before you start your actual game code.

```
ALboolean initAL = alutInit(NULL,NULL);
TheSound = new Sound();
```

We don't need to pass any parameters to alutInit, though it is designed to take parameters should it be called from a main function, you can give it command line parameters. In our case passing NULL, NULL is fine.

Ok a simple sound class header should look like this:

```
#pragma once
#include <al.h>
#include <alc.h>
#include <alut.h>
#include <stdio.h>
#include <sys/types.h>
#include <sys/stat.h>
#include <unistd.h>
#include <stdlib.h>

#define NUM_BUFFERS 8
#define BUFFER_SIZE 4096 /* 4K should be fine */
```

```
class Sound
 {
public:
 Sound();
 ~Sound();

ALCdevice *device;
ALCcontext *context;

 ALuint source, buffers[NUM_BUFFERS];
 ALuint frequency;
 ALenum format;
  void LoadSound();
  void PlaySound(ALint);
 };
```

For the moment, all we are defining are some data concepts and the very simple idea of loading and playing sounds. At this stage we don't really need much more, and we should not try to do much more. Let's just get it working.

So our Sound.cpp file only has to worry about our constructor/destructor pair, and the two simple concepts we asked for, Load and Play sound.

Our Constructor can set up all the main things, and we'll let LoadSound do the loading, I am going to add a few functions though to allow us to report errors and get access to some information that OpenAL can give us.

It should look a little like this:

```
#include "Sound.h"
#include <AL/alut.h> // we need this to load Wav
#include <string.h>

static void list_audio_devices(const ALCchar *devices)
{
 const ALCchar *device = devices, *next = devices + 1;
 size_t len = 0;
 fprintf(stdout, "\n Devices list:\n");
 fprintf(stdout, "----------\n");
 while (device && *device != '\0' && next && *next != '\0') {
  fprintf(stdout, "%s\n", device);
  len = strlen(device);
  device += (len + 1);
  next += (len + 2);
 }
 fprintf(stdout, "----------\n");
}

// unlike some other constructors this can do some things
Sound::Sound()
{
 // 1st check if we have multiple devices (quite possible)
 ALboolean testEnum = alcIsExtensionPresent(NULL, "ALC_ENUMERATION_EXT");
 if (testEnum == AL_FALSE)
 {
  printf("enumerations are NOT possible");
  // enumeration not supported
 }
```

```cpp
  else
  {
   printf("enumerations are possible");
   // enumeration supported
  }

  list_audio_devices(alcGetString(NULL, ALC_DEVICE_SPECIFIER));
  defaultDeviceName = alcGetString(NULL, ALC_DEFAULT_DEVICE_SPECIFIER);
  device = alcOpenDevice(defaultDeviceName);
  if (!device) {
   fprintf(stderr, "default device not available\n");
   return ;
  }
// tell us the device
  fprintf(stdout, "Device: %s\n", alcGetString(device,
ALC_DEVICE_SPECIFIER));
// clear the errors
  alGetError();
// create the context
  context = alcCreateContext(device, NULL);
  if (!alcMakeContextCurrent(context))
  {
   fprintf(stderr, "failed to make default context\n");
   return ;
  }

  ALfloat listenerOri[] = { 0.0f, 0.0f, 1.0f, 0.0f, 1.0f, 0.0f };
   /* set orientation */
  alListener3f(AL_POSITION, 0, 0, 1.0f);
  alListener3f(AL_VELOCITY, 0, 0, 0);
  alListenerfv(AL_ORIENTATION, listenerOri);
  alGenSources((ALuint)1, &source).
  alSourcef(source, AL_PITCH, 1);
  alSourcef(source, AL_GAIN, 1);
  alSource3f(source, AL_POSITION, 0, 0, 0);
  alSource3f(source, AL_VELOCITY, 0, 0, 0);
  alSourcei(source, AL_LOOPING, AL_FALSE);
  alGenBuffers(1, &buffer);
}

bool Sound::LoadSound(char* fileName)
{
 ALvoid *data;
 ALsizei size;
 ALfloat freq;
 ALenum format;
 ALboolean loop = AL_FALSE;
 data = alutLoadMemoryFromFile("test.wav", &format, &size, &freq);
 if (data == NULL)
 {
  printf("sorry can't load sound file\n");
  return false;
 }
 return true;
}
Sound::~Sound()
{// destroy any buffers and close things down
 alDeleteBuffers(NUM_BUFFERS, buffer);
}
```

Feel free to type this in, we are going to make a few changes; however, I still want you to enter this, the changes won't need a total rewrite and you'll be simulating a normal refactoring process.

As it stands, we can load up a few general sounds, eight in fact as defined in NUM_ BUFFERS, and it's quite trivial to play them, but we should be aware that there is a difference between music and sound Fx. Music tends to loop, which is a concept we can only apply to the source, not the sound it plays, so we will have problems getting a music loop to, ermm loop, and not have an fx loop, a constant ping ping ping effect that does not switch off, is not appreciated by many users.

So even though all this will work, having only one source, now proves to be a little tricky. Each source can only play one thing at a time, and having the source play our background loop is fine, but every single time we also call an fx the background *loop* resets.

This is troubling, but not a major issue. As we can have multiple sources and each source can be set up a little different. So let's set up a source purely for the loop, and maybe a couple of sources for the fx. All the sources can be *located* at the same spot, we just specialize them to purpose. In fact, let's have one source for our music loop and seven sources for fx the aliens want to make. In other words, we'll have the same number of sources as buffers, it's not really by design, we can have more sources if we want, but NUM_BUFFERS can be any size we need it to be.

Adapting the above-mentioned code to work with multiple sizes is simply a matter of using an array for sources in the same way we use arrays for buffers.

We decided that source 0, is going to be our looping *music* loop, so we just need a way to allow the other sources to be set up in turn, so a small helper function to find the first free one is needed.

The header file now looks like this:

```
#pragma once
#include <al.h>
#include <alc.h>
#include <alut.h>
#include <stdio.h>
#include <sys/types.h>
#include <sys/stat.h>
#include <unistd.h>
#include <stdlib.h>
#define NUM_BUFFERS 8
#define BUFFER_SIZE 4096 /* 4K should be fine */
class Sound
  {
public:
  Sound();
  ~Sound();
  ALCdevice *device;
  ALCcontext *context;
  ALCenum error;
  ALuint source[NUM_BUFFERS], buffer[NUM_BUFFERS];
  ALuint frequency;
  ALenum format;
  const ALCchar *defaultDeviceName;
  bool LoadSound(char* fname, ALint index);
```

```
  bool PlaySound(ALint index);
  bool PlayMusic(ALint index);
  ALuint GetFreeSource();
};
```

Notice the addition of a PlayMusic method, to allow me to differentiate from a sound and a music loop. PlayMusic is always going to work with source 0, PlaySound will work with sources 1–7 inclusive.

And the code for this now looks like this, though I have removed the text output format to save a bit of paper here.

```
#include "Sound.h"
#include <AL/alut.h> // we need this to load Wav
#include <string.h>
>>>> I removed the list_audio_devices and TEST_ERROR, as they are the same
as before

// unlike some other constructors this can do some things
Sound::Sound()
{
 // 1st check if we have multiple devices (quite possible)
 ALboolean testEnum = alcIsExtensionPresent(NULL, "ALC_ENUMERATION_EXT");
 if (testEnum == AL_FALSE)
 {
  printf("enumerations are NOT possible");
  // enumeration not supported
 }
 else
 {
  printf("enumerations are possible");
  // enumeration supported
 }

 list_audio_devices(alcGetString(NULL, ALC_DEVICE_SPECIFIER));
 defaultDeviceName = alcGetString(NULL, ALC_DEFAULT_DEVICE_SPECIFIER);
 device = alcOpenDevice(defaultDeviceName);
 if (!device) {
  fprintf(stderr, "default device not available\n");
  return ;
 }
// tell us the device
 fprintf(stdout, "Device: %s\n", alcGetString(device,
ALC_DEVICE_SPECIFIER));
//clear the errors
 alGetError();
// create the context
 context = alcCreateContext(device, NULL);
 if (!alcMakeContextCurrent(context))
 {
  fprintf(stderr, "failed to make default context\n");
  return ;
 }
// lets talk about OpenAL
 printf(" OpenAL Version %s\n", alGetString(AL_VERSION));
 printf(" OpenAL Renderer %s\n", alGetString(AL_RENDERER));
 printf(" OpenAL Vendor %s\n", alGetString(AL_VENDOR));
 printf(" OpenAL Extension %s\n", alGetString(AL_EXTENSIONS));
```

```
 ALfloat listenerOri[] = { 0.0f, 0.0f, 1.0f, 0.0f, 1.0f, 0.0f };
 /* set orientation */
 alListener3f(AL_POSITION, 0, 0, 1.0f);
 alListener3f(AL_VELOCITY, 0, 0, 0);
 alListenerfv(AL_ORIENTATION, listenerOri);
// generate a range of sources all at the screen 0,0,0
 alGenSources(NUM_BUFFERS, source);
// set up all sources
 for (int i = 0; i < NUM_BUFFERS; i++)
 {
  alSourcef(source[i], AL_PITCH, 1) ;
  alSourcef(source[i], AL_GAIN, 1) ;
  alSource3f(source[i], AL_POSITION, 0, 0, 0) ;
  alSource3f(source[i], AL_VELOCITY, 0, 0, 0) ;
  alSourcei(source[i], AL_LOOPING, AL_FALSE) ;
  TEST_ERROR("oops") ;
 }
// set the music to be a little quieter or it will overpower fx
 alSourcei(source[0], AL_LOOPING, AL_TRUE);
 alSourcef(source[0], AL_GAIN, 0.2f);
//Generate buffers
 alGenBuffers(NUM_BUFFERS, buffer);
 TEST_ERROR("buffer generation");
 return;
}
Sound::~Sound()
{// destroy any buffers and close things down
 alDeleteBuffers(NUM_BUFFERS, buffer);
}

bool Sound::LoadSound(char* FileName,ALint index)
{
 ALvoid *data;
 ALsizei size;
 ALfloat freq;
 ALenum format;
 data = alutLoadMemoryFromFile(FileName, &format, &size, &freq);
 TEST_ERROR("sorry can't load sound file");
 alBufferData(buffer[index], format, data, size, freq); / we could print
these
 TEST_ERROR("buffer copy");
 return alGetError() == AL_NO_ERROR;
}
bool Sound::PlaySound(ALint number)
{
 ALint source_state;
 ALint FirstFree = GetFreeSource();
 alSourcei(source[FirstFree], AL_BUFFER, buffer[number]);
 TEST_ERROR("buffer binding");
 alSourcePlay(source[FirstFree]);
 TEST_ERROR("source playing");
 alGetSourcei(source[FirstFree], AL_SOURCE_STATE, &source_state);
 TEST_ERROR("source state get");
 return alGetError() == AL_NO_ERROR;
}
//music is always source 0
bool Sound::PlayMusic(ALint number)
{
```

```
ALint source_state;
alSourcei(source[0], AL_BUFFER, buffer[number]);
TEST_ERROR("buffer binding");
alSourcePlay(source[0]);
TEST_ERROR("source playing");
alGetSourcei(source[0], AL_SOURCE_STATE, &source_state);
TEST_ERROR("source state get");

return alGetError() == AL_NO_ERROR;
}
ALuint Sound::GetFreeSource()
{
ALuint RetVal = 1;
ALint source_state;
for (int i = 1; i < NUM_BUFFERS; i++)
{
  alGetSourcei(source[i], AL_SOURCE_STATE, &source_state);
  if (source_state != AL_PLAYING)
  {
   RetVal = i;
   return RetVal;
  }
}
// if nothing is free, then just return 1;
return RetVal;
}
```

So the only major difference is the scan through to find a free source, and the new PlayMusic method. We're ready to set off the music in our Game Init using

```
TheSound->PlayMusic(2);
```

Where 2 is buffer number 2 (or sound 3 since we count from 0). We should really use our enumeration system though.

Horrible Earworms

Our looping sound works well, and does what we want, but human ears are sensitive to repeating patterns, so in a pretty short timescale this short loop is going to start to irritate our sensitive programmer ears as we spend a week or two listening to this droning on and on and on. We could just turn the TV volume down, but that's more of an ICT problem and you can never get an Engineer out on a Sunday!

So even though a longer tune will still start to make us crazy after a few days, proper music for our background is clearly something we want, but we are faced with a few more technical issues, and even a legal one. We already see just how large, even modest wavs, are in terms of memory. OpenAL can only cope with uncompressed data so longer fx or short tunes start to eat memory even more. We can comfortably use 400 or 500 MB on a few minutes of uncompressed sound. Since some of our targets don't even have that much memory to play with, alternatives methods have to be found.

Ideally we would try to save our music in a common compressed format such as MP3 and decompress it as we play it. But, sadly MP3 is not free to use, and though the people who own it have been a little less litigious in recent years, there's no sense in poking a sleeping bear.

So despite its market dominance and effective compression ratios MP3 isn't something we want to get into. But there are fortunately other options, which provide pretty much the same features.

Of course the open source community is filled with different options, but a few stand out and have gained enough support to have propagated to mainstream use, and can be considered reliable and usable. So we're going to use the OGG format, which is supported by several open source sound and music applications.

Once again we must break our no libs rule, but as before this is for a good, that is, no choice, cause, let's install it the same way we did with OpenAL in a terminal window and enter the following.

```
sudo apt-get install libogg-dev
```

And of course add OGG to the list of libraries you include. And the library should be located at /usr/include/ogg so add that to your library list in your Makefile settings.

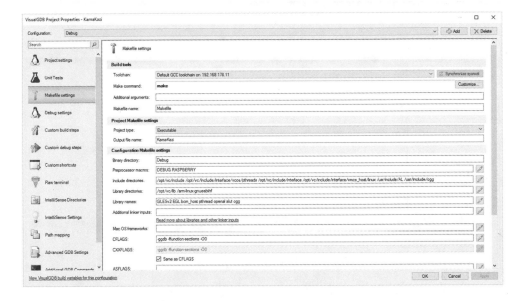

Using OGG files is as simple as loading graphics, it works in almost the same manner, we can load an OGG compressed file and let it occupy space ready for OpenAL to work with it.

Streaming

So we can load, decompress, and play sound, but you probably noticed we're still using staggeringly large amounts of memory, decompressing a small file into a big buffer does not eliminate our chronic shortage of memory on our systems.

We need some other way to deal with this, the process is known as streaming. What this involves is allocating a certain amount of space that we can afford to give, and having OpenAL work with that, but, keeping that space filled up with sound data coming from the process of decompression into that space.

There's a couple of technical challenges to this process; nothing overwhelming, but at this current stage of our development, we don't want to get too bogged down in this. So for now, we'll stick with our simple and annoying loop. I'll cover streaming in some samples on the support site, since we need to move forward now and we have a working system to be going on with.

This is all I'm going to do on fx/music from here on, simply to keep the book page count down a little. We can certainly assume all our games will need sound in them, but it's all done the same way and the final versions on the support site will have appropriate sound. I'll leave it up to you to add sound as you need it in the working examples from this point on, it will save repeating ourselves.

▮ The War against Sloppy Code Storage!

Up till now we've been happy to just add files into our Visual Studio Solution filter and our code looks fine. Here you see a nice tidy example of a base project, our usual Invaders start base, with source and header files neatly in their folders!

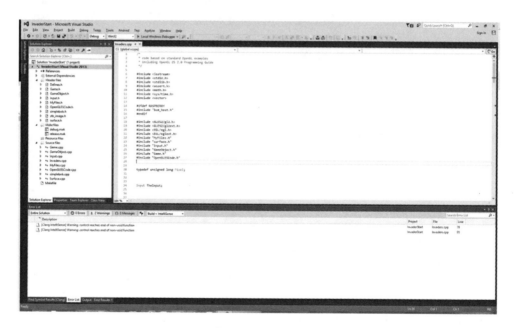

But the reality is different…take a look at our project directory and we see something horrible beyond words. A mish-mash of *.h, *.cpp's, make files, setting files, and so much more. It may all look neat and tidy in Visual Studio, but it's a mess in the folder itself. If we only had a couple of files it wouldn't really be an issue, so we've not worried about it so far. But we're going to start increasing the numbers of files with each project and while it has no impact at all on the compiling, Visual Studio knows where every file is and compiles it correctly, it will make it hard for us to locate files we may want to use in later projects. So it's time to grow up and clean up our bedroom a bit.

The simplest way to do that is to make sure for each filter you have in your solution, you also have a similarly named folder in your directory!

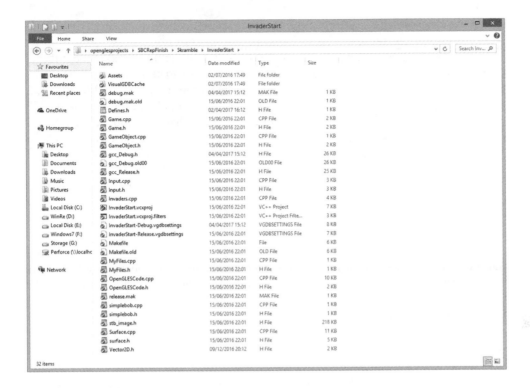

So it's time for a clean-up, it's a bit of a pain making new folders and moving files into them, since we'll have to delete and readd them in the Visual Studio solution, so next project we'll start with a cleaner template, and a more sensible name with Header, Source, and other directories as we need them, this all just serves to explain why.

Our Own Library

Another battle in the war against sloppy code is trying not to reinvent the wheel. Over just a few simple projects we've started to see that we are reusing the same basic code ideas over and over again, in some cases updating it, fixing a few bugs, but still basically the same. This has left us with different generations of the *same* files scattered in different projects.

Why do we care about this? Other than the waste of disk space, especially since most of these early projects are disposable learning tools, we don't have to be too concerned about this waste of effort.

We care, because already we're starting to get serious about how we keep code tidy in a solution, we need to also keep our repeatedly used code tidy and accessible. Time then, to develop another important tool in a programmers arsenal, a personal library, which is where we take the files, classes, code snippets, defines, and so on, which we see are becoming common in all our work, and where, aside from some additions to the existing features, the core features are not changing.

Some things are obvious, we clearly need input, file handling and sound in all future projects, the Surface Class in all our 2D projects looks good, that Vector2 Class will certainly be useful and might need expanding, later we'll probably add a few other workhorse classes.

What we are doing, is starting to rely on a core set of functions and features, which we reuse in our projects. These will be the basis our first library!

Since this library is expanding as we go, rather than actually making significant changes, we should try to keep it in one place, so we don't have to keep making copies of the files it contains. This will stop us having a copy of the files for project A, and B and .....Z, you get the idea. Making our library the go to code resource for all our future projects. It'll also avoid confusion over which version of which project did I have that cool define for Pi in?

By having it as its own project, we can dictate that instead of generating an executable file, it can be instead a standard linux static library, which any other projects just need to include the library and its header files to gain access to the functions.

This is considerably tidier and allows us a lot more flexibility. It also should impose a little discipline on us, because we must be careful not to actually destroy or change functionality that the library provides to older projects, which we may return to when we add new features. But adding new features we can, and will, and in turn future projects will benefit from it.

Let's set up a MyLibs project, which generates a static library, that is, one that is linked into our main project at link time, creating a combination of our new project and the MyLibs project. We will put all our workhorse classes in there, and create a simple header file to load all the workhorse header files in.

Setting up our own library is as easy as creating a new project, only instead of creating an executable we will create a static library. As before, create a new project and provide it with a location on your PC to live in. After setting up the name and directory, then select the type of application, a Static library, I also usually prefer a GNU make, but MSBuild is also good, though you will find some deviation in the format of the preferences panels compared to the book.

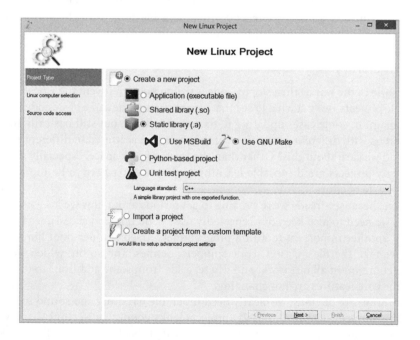

Pressing next takes you to the Build the project under Linux options, which we've already covered. Enter your Targets details and press NEXT... But, don't press finish on the next screen.

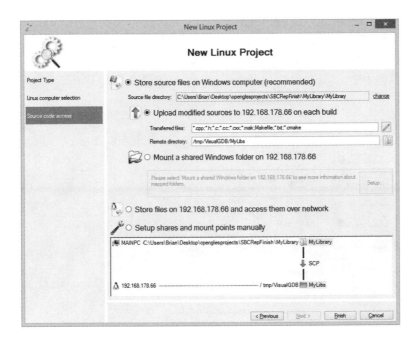

Take note of the Remote Directory option, by default it will use a copy of your PC's own directory structure, stored off the /tmp directory, and for the most part during development that will be fine, but this library is going to be used by many different projects now, so it really needs to live in one central place that won't change if you use a different PC or decide to relocate your projects on your PC. I've set it to use a MyLibs Directory just off the VisualGDB directory, that way I know it's my code and it is generated and maintained by my own VisualGDB projects. Now that isn't actually ideal, because the tmp directory is erased every time you power off your target, so it will not be there until you do a build. So it's important to make sure at the start of a code session, you build that library to replace it before your main program tries to build. You *could* and probably *should* put this in an actual permanent directory not associated with tmp. For now though as we are still learning and things are going to chop and change we can tolerate this need for a prebuild.

One Final thing to do, which I could have done when I named it, but I can still to do it here, is enter in the MyLibrary VisualGDB properties and rename the output file name, to libMyLibrary.a file.

The GNU Linker expects all libs to have a prefix of lib to their name, which it strips to get the library name. Our projects will therefore include this lib by naming it MyLibrary.

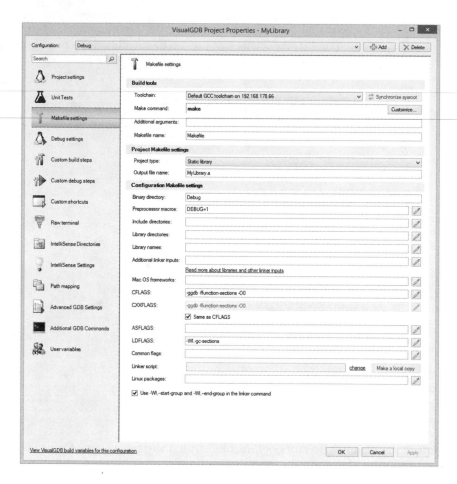

All that remains now is for us to add all the library's we need to use, they will get included in our main project when it links this library with the files the compiler generates.

Using This New Library

Now that the library project is set up; we need to tell our upcoming projects how to use it. That really is very simple. Initially, we know were going to be building the library so we can include it in our solution alongside our game. That means we just include it in each future solution we create. Visual Studio considers a solution to be any number of projects, so we can actually have one project dependant on another, and in this case, our new sets of game projects are dependent on our MyLibrary.a being compiled and up to date. By including the MyLibrary project in our solution, we can make changes to it, and allow it to compile before our new projects then link it into their executable. I'll detail that process in the next project.

Remember that this particular library is being set up just for our game projects, you can create any number of libraries that contain useful content/tools/functions you might want to keep handy in your projects. All you have to do is ensure that the header files are accessible and that the .a file can be linked in.

I should also explain the other kind of library in Linux, a Shared Object (SO) library. Shared Objects are libraries that are loaded into an application when it loads up, they are similar to the DLL concept in Windows. We use these kind of dynamic libraries a lot when creating interfaces to hardware or software systems that may get updated, the SO system allows for a new SO to be produced and made available when hardware updates or software interfaces change resulting in a need to change the software after it has been written, because the SO itself is variable and can be changed to reflect the new state of the interface, we can add new data to the same access points to give new updates or functions, whereas the old self-written application just calls a known access point in the .so library. OpenGLES2.0 and sound and most other types of libraries to systems are mostly provided as SOs, which allows different makers the chance to do slightly different things that relate to their particular systems.

Static libs are actually compiled into the executable when it is linked. Therefore they are a one time thing and not changeable after the link. The addresses of all routines are allocated at linker time.

One annoying issue I have discovered with having both projects in the solution is that it should be possible to let Visual Studio know that your main project is dependent on your library project, so that any changes to the library code will result in the library being rebuilt.

There is an option in Visual Studio called Build Dependency, which is supposed to allow you to assign a project dependency, that is, make sure Project Library A is up-to-date and compiled before I use it in Project B. But sadly I have found setting a Visual Studio dependency, results in a compile error, where the master project seems to try and is unable to build the Library, even though the Library has already been built. See the image below for details on the dependency setting and result.

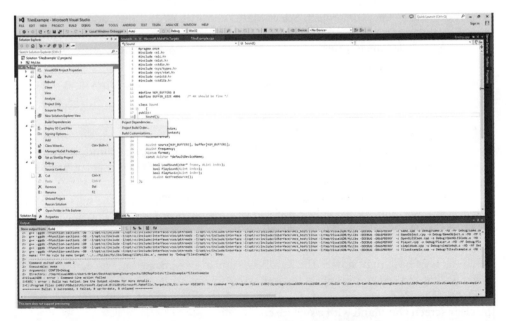

It may just be a minor niggle with the VisualGDB integration, I have reported it, so it may get fixed, but it's not the end of the world, just build (without dependency) and remember to make sure you have build MyLibs first, right click on the MyLibs project and build the library if you make a change to it. You can also make sure your library name is alphabetically before the project name, so it will always be built first.

It's not actually essential to include the library project itself in your solution, you can choose, perhaps wisely to only include the resulting libMyLibs.a file in the Makefile settings, and not actually touch the Library code when you work on your game. The wisdom there comes about because there's a horrible temptation in the middle of working on your game project, to just go change the library a bit to make this particular bit work! Rather than work within what the library provides you. Changes will be needed sometimes, but best to only really make them when you absolutely have to. Our early projects though are very much going to build that library, so for now let's include it in your projects, when you find you are no longer adding to it, we can stop including it and just use the static LibMyLibs.a file.

Another reason why it's wise to just load a libXXX.a file is because of the way VisualGDB maintains its remote cache for intellisense to work. If you make changes to the library project, and then recompile it, you also need to make sure you go to your main project and reload the cache for MyLibs. It's a minor irritation, which we will do away with later.

Lets Get a Bit More Compiler Speed

I've been a bit mean to you up till now, especially if you own a multicore SBC. As there is a way to get your compiler to work quite a bit faster. I wanted to wait till after you had compiled all the multiple classes, graphic and sound systems though since they presented the most obvious signs of compiler stress, which I wanted you to become aware of and which we can now try to alleviate with a very simple command. It won't do much at all for single-core systems but if you have a dual, quad, or even an octocore target, go into VisualGDB project properties for your project. Select MakeFile settings, and then add –j2 or –j4 or j8 to the Additional arguments field. This informs the compiler to run two, four, or eight tasks at a time, allowing it in effect to compile multiple files, one per core, at the same time.

Yes I'm sorry, it was mean, and you're welcome! We'll talk about even faster compilation methods a bit later on too, but for now this will ease the compile times quite a bit.

▋ 5.2   Tiles and Backgrounds

Despite our star field, Kamikazi was played on a pretty plain background, it would be nice if we could play a game where the background forms part of the gameplay. This is the principle behind a lot of platform games.

We could just dump a screen-sized image for a Surface Class into the m_screen surface in our game and use that to replace our clear screen, because there's no need to clear the screen if you are going to constantly dump a screen-sized image to erase the previous frame.

In fact, go back right now to the Kamikazi, find a nice image that you can scale with an art package to screen size, put it in your assets folder, create a surface with it, and use that to replace the clear screen and create your background, you can display it by replacing the clear screen command with a surface copy.

Go on…I'll wait.

Ok how did that look? Even though you probably got a really nice backdrop to your game clearly the backdrop was not something you could interact with, it's just an image.

The very best you could do is pick out what colors you have at certain points on the screen but that does not give you a lot of useful info.

But suppose we created a screen from tiles, a kind of mosaic of images, and some of those tiles were able to represent parts of the backdrop you want to interact with.

What Do We Mean by Tiles?

Now we've actually already used tiles, our simple font system is effectively a tile-based system, which is why I named it TileFont, we have been using ASCII values as our index into a group of *squares*, which represented alphanumeric images that we were able to control. This single-line index was calculated but it's quite possible that we could have had a single-dimensional array to provide that index, Possible, but a bit pointless, the calculation was trivial, so no point in wasting memory to create an array.

All we're doing now is extending that idea so that as well as text, we can have small images, which can produce larger images, like a big interactive variable jigsaw puzzle, or a mosaic, with the world's most boring patterns! We could still do a long single line of tile images but it starts to be a bit hard for us to visualize, so we need to change to a simple screen with rows and columns of tiles. The calculations are still trivial, but this time we will use an array, just for convenience, and as we will see later, speed.

Working with Tiles

The font system we used simply was a grouping of joined-up images and we indexed into it to get the right *tile*, we can continue to do that, or we can actually create individual tiles from that image. Hmmm choices…coders are often faced with choices; we need to learn how to make them based on the needs of our project. So let's consider this for a bit.

We're probably going to have rather a lot of tile images if we have any reasonable sized and detailed world, so we want to be as efficient as possible, which means keeping the graphics, in their uncompressed and usable form, as limited as possible, remember RAM limitation is a constraint we cannot overcome.

As with most things in game programming, there are pros and cons to every approach. I'm going to use a 2D indexing system to get access to my tile, which will be efficient so long as we don't have too much blank space added into it, because pointing at a blank space is pointless, and keeping multiple indexes to blank spaces is even more pointless. Actually we could be really clever and make sure our tiles are stored in a logical way, same as our ASCII systems were set up. The choice is always ours. Sometimes a little effort to calculate an index is worth the saving in memory that pointless padding of graphics and unused indexes cost us.

What a Wonderful World

We've been thinking of our screen coordinates as the actual physical locations where our objects live in their virtual 2D universe. That's perfectly fine when the screen is the absolute limit of the universe they exist in. However, if we want them to have a larger world, we'd have to increase the size of our screen to see it all (does not apply if you are using an EGL window). At the moment that's actually still possible, because we are displaying a 640 × 480 area on a monitor, which would have 1920 × 1080 (maybe more) pixels on show, but the physical real-world ability of our monitor display is not as important as that window into our game world, which we set to be a comfortable size for any monitor to display.

If 640 × 480 is the size of our window, then that's the limit of the screens we can view using only a screen-coordinate system. That's fine for now; we're only going to do a single-screen game.

Download the TilesExample example from the website and compile and run. You can see right away that it's a very simple program, but notice that instead of a clear screen routine each cycle it uses a draw map routine;

```
// this now has the job of scanning the map
void Game::DrawMap(float x, float y, Surface* a_Screen)
{
 for (int y = 0; y < SCRHEIGHT/16; y++)
 {
  for (int x = 0; x < SCRWIDTH / 16; x++)
  {
   Tiles[Map1[y][x]]->CopyTo(a_Screen, x * 16, y * 16);
  } // x loop
 } // y loop
}
```

This is nothing more than a loop that fills the screen with tiles going from the top to the bottom, one line at a tile.

These red and green tiles are being created in the Game Classes init routine

```
void Game::GameInit()
{
 this->InitDone = true; / ok we can set this to true so this won't be
called again
/* Tile example */
// make a red tile
 Surface* T = new Surface(16, 16);
 T->ClearBuffer(GREENMASK+ALPHAMASK);
 Game::Tiles.push_back(T);
// make a green tile
 T = new Surface(16, 16);
 T->ClearBuffer(REDMASK+ALPHAMASK);
 Game::Tiles.push_back(T);
```

And the resulting tiles are being pushed into a vector held in the Game.h file.

The Map itself is a big 2D array at the top of Game.cpp, actually held in what is known as global space, that is, not in any particular class. It's only there for now, so we can access it quickly, normally we would keep data in a class.

Aside from this new DrawMap and a few additions to Game, I hope you can see this is currently just a very simple template. But most of the content should be quite familiar to you. It's really not much different at all from the Invaders. But that map array is important as it contains the indexes of which tiles need to be displayed on screen.

This DrawMap system will effectively replace our clear screen system. It's a little slower of course but it is very effective.

Now when you compile and run that you will get a nice image of a map with a rough spelling of HELLO, which if you look in the Map1 array, you should be able to see it. Try adding a full stop to the hello in the map?

By now you should be able to visualize the concept of numbers in the maps relating to different tiles, but we humans also know that those tiles can also represent certain concepts in games, for example, floors, walls, ladders, and so on. The tiles that make up the floors, walls, and ladder are always going to be the same, so that means we can somehow tell what number is a wall, what number is a ladder, and so on. We're going to need a few more tiles though to represent anything more than just a floor or wall, we'll get to that soon.

Still with me? Good, let's expand things a bit more...If we have a screen made up of tiles, and that tile is held in those maps, you can make the connection that the map is, in fact, an encoded representation of the area we are playing on. And that map, is a simple 2D grid.....now that means they have X and Y coords. Are we making a connection yet?

The screen maps gives us two sets of information, what tile to draw, and what tiles are solid or have special features. We can build on that later.

Let's turn TileExample into a simple little game. In the assets folder you will find a few graphics. Four for a player, two for some family characters we have to save and an enemy hoverbot of some type.

Let's place 20 of the family on the screen not moving, and have 20 enemies randomly placed moving around in a simple way.

We will place our character in the center of the map, so we must ensure our enemy types don't spawn in the center.

The *game* will consist of us moving our character around with the keyboard, and *picking up* the family characters while avoiding the enemies, which should at least make some attempt to home toward our character?

Our task list for this:

- *Draw and display a map*: That's done for you as you can see.

- *Place our character in and interact with that map*: Still to be done.

- *Place the enemies*: Still to be done.

- *Set a win goal*: Still to be done.

We really need to work out what the win goal should be, do we just want to get to the top? Or perhaps we'll make it a bit more interesting and make it a collecting challenge. So let's arrange to collect a number of items while avoiding enemies, which are guarding those item.

First thing we need is a character to control, make a class called Player, and create the header like this:

```
#pragma once

#include "GameObject.h"
#include "Game.h"
class Player : public GameObject
{
public:
 Player();
 Player(char*, MyFiles*);
```

```
 ~Player();
 void Update(Game* G);
private:
 Surface* Images[4];
};
```

If you've been paying attention, you will remember in our Kamikazi and Invaders games, we defined a quite different update routine, which was deliberately designed to override this update routine in the GameObject;

```
virtual bool Update(Surface* s, Input* InputHandler);
```

This new form of update, passing the Game Class, is frowned on by C++ purists because I'm sending the calling class's address to the player code, and everything the calling routine has in it becomes exposed. That goes against every rule of C++'s encapsulation and protection of data.

But I really don't care, because I want to get access to quite a few of the Game Class' variables and I don't want to jump through hoops to do it. Not at the moment anyway. It's important we don't end up fighting with the language at this point; we just want to get things done. Once we are comfortable with the way things work, and we feel we understand how, then, and only then should we care about the perceived proper ways to use the language, remember it works for us, not us for it!

But to use this update system, I need the GameObject Class to have this same type of update. Why? I hope you are asking, well because my Game Class stores all the relevant objects it has to update and draw in this vector.

```
static std::vector<GameObject*> MyObjects; // this will hold all the game
objects we need in game?
```

And it's this vector we iterate through to do the updates, which is as you can see a Vector of GameObject pointers. So I can only call GameObject methods, not a specific Player Update. Though, of course, I could, there's only one player and calling one specific update is not a major problem for us, I just prefer to have them all in the same vector.

One solution is to add the same kind of update to the GameObject Class methods as a virtual and make it an Empty Class, like this, in GameObject.h:

```
virtual void Update(Game* g) {} ;
```

So we are both declaring and defining this in the header. We'll add to the concepts we might need later. For now, an update, a draw, and some coordinates are all we need.

The cpp file is also going to be a little different, we're used to doing empty constructors and destructors but this time we are going to do something a bit different. To begin with our player has four frames, one for each direction, and our header we made some space for that with an Images[4] array. So we should fill that, in the constructor let's load in the four frames that our character uses.

```
Player::Player(char* fname, MyFiles* fh) : GameObject(fname, fh)
{
 // we can create with this images but lets store the full set
 this->Images[0] = this->Image; // store the 1st one we loaded up with
(walk down)
```

```
this->Images[1] = new Surface((char*)"../Assets/walkUp.png",fh);
this->Images[2] = new Surface((char*)"../Assets/walkLeft.png", fh);
this->Images[3] = new Surface((char*)"../Assets/walkRight.png", fh);
}
```

Our constructor starts right away by calling its base constructor with a filename and file handle, this is fine because we know the image is the down image, and we're happy to let that get loaded into the GameObject Image pointer, and also now into our Images[0]. Let's load up the three other frames in to the array and that's done.

Now notice when we loaded the array, we used the new command three times. That means that memory was allocated for these instances, and done in this instance of the class. We must adhere to a golden rule, every new must have a delete.

So our Destructor is not going to be an empty one, it must be responsible for deleting these three objects when/if it is called. But what about the first image? Which will actually be the result of this call in the Game.cpp file

```
Player* GO = new Player((char*)"../Assets/walkDown.png",this->FileHander);
```

As this is called in the Game Class, we need to let the Gameclass itself handle its removal, so for now we're only going to worry about our three news, and make sure we have three deletes.

```
Player::~Player()
{ // because this class made 3 images we need to delete them
 delete this->Images[1];
 this->Images[1] = nullptr;
 delete this->Images[2];
 this->Images[2] = nullptr;
 delete this->Images[3];
 this->Images[3] = nullptr;
// but... we didn't create Images[0] here, it was created in the Game class
so let it remove it
}
```

There, that's done. We can create and when needed delete our player and store away his four images. The update routine can now be written:

```
void Player::Update(Game* G)
{
 Input* IH = G->InputHandle; // easier access;
 if (IH->TestKey(KEY_RIGHT))
  {
   this->Image = Images[3];
   this->Xpos += SPEED ;
  }
 if (IH->TestKey(KEY_LEFT))
  {
   this->Image = Images[2];
   this->Xpos -= SPEED;
  }

 if (IH->TestKey(KEY_UP))
 {
  this->Image = Images[1];
  this->Ypos -= SPEED;
 }
```

```
if (IH->TestKey(KEY_DOWN))
{
 this->Image = Images[0];
 this->Ypos += SPEED;
}
}
```

This will allow us to move our man around...once we have three things done in our GameClass, first in the init routine we need to create our player:

```
Player* GO = new Player((char*)"../Assets/walkDown.png",this->FileHander);
GO->Xpos = 400;
GO->Ypos = 200;
MyObjects.push_back(GO);
```

And we need our Game::Update routine to cycle through the MyObjects vector calling this new update system:

```
for (int i = 0; i < Game::MyObjects.size(); i++)
{
 Game::MyObjects[i]->Update(this);
}
```

Finally, we need a draw routine, just after the update loop:

```
for (int i = 0; i < Game::MyObjects.size(); i++)
{
 Game::MyObjects[i]->Image->CopyAlphaPlot(a_Screen, Game::MyObjects[i]->Xpos,
Game::MyObjects[i]->Ypos);
}
```

We could put it in the same loop as the update, but I prefer to keep logic and drawing separate. Reasons for this might become more obvious later when collision could result in the removal of an object already updated, and drawn.

Don't forget to add Player.h to the Game.cpp list of headers. Compile and run...it should look like this:

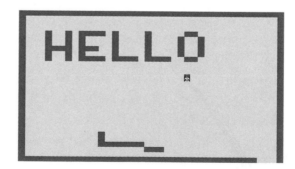

So this works pretty well, if we press left we go left, if right we go right, and our frame changes to suit the direction. But notice we use a speed value, defined in Player.cpp after the headers, with

```
#define SPEED 1.0f
```

We'll make more use of that later, but having our character move with such a value gives us so much more control over him. Here it's set as a #define but we could just as easily make it a variable, which gets altered depending on the situation we are in. Movement through water, for example. If you find the movement too slow, you can always increase the value.

So far so good, that wasn't much harder than moving our Kamikazi shooter, but now we have up and down. But move to the edges and we can see we have a problem, we don't want him to overlap our red tiles, they should be barriers/walls, so let's use our screen coordinates to test for red pixels. The solids are all red so that will indicate we have hit a barrier.

A little check at the players sprites position and we can indeed tell when we hit the wall and prevent the movement. But we need to allow for the fact that we reference the sprite by its top-left corner, so if moving right the whole sprite will actually overlap the barrier, which isn't desirable, so we need to add a small offset to the players x, for left and right movement, or y coordinate for up and down, to test just at the edge of the sprite and not at the center reference point. That's easy enough to add to the movement systems, just take into account the direction of travel and add an offset from the reference point we use.

We can get our reference point with this simple pointer into the buffer:

```
Pixel* Point = G->m_Screen->GetBuffer() + ((int)Ypos*SCRWIDTH + (int)Xpos);
```

If we want the Left we can just subtract 1 from that address, and Right adds the width of the sprite image to get to its top right corner. If we don't detect a red pixel we will allow the addition of the speed.

```
if (IH->TestKey(KEY_RIGHT))
  {
  this->Image = Images[3];
  if (*(Point + (this->Image->GetWidth())) != REDMASK + ALPHAMASK)
   this->Xpos += SPEED ;
  }
```

That awkward looking dereference symbol * is telling us that we want to actually test the pixel at Point + our calculated offset. There are other ways to address an area of buffer memory, but I thought it would be nice to see how we access memory like this, we'll be using a nicer system soon.

As we're looking directly at a memory address up and down need a slightly different approach, we need to know the width of the screens buffer, so we can multiply that by how far down we want to look, or just subtract the width of the buffer in pixels, to look.

Down would look like this:

```
if (IH->TestKey(KEY_DOWN))
{
  this->Image = Images[0];
  if (*(Point + (Offset * this->Image->GetHeight())) != REDMASK + ALPHAMASK)
  this->Ypos += SPEED;
}
```

See if you can write the tests for Left and Up yourself? All you need to know is that instead of adding the reference point they are subtracting.

Compile and run the code and try walking around, you can see that our player can indeed move until he hits a red pixel!

So that works, clearly we can detect the pixel at the point of interest, it's a very simple matter as we know which direction we are moving, to add an offset from a known point.

Not bad, we have movement, and we have interaction, Time to add a bit more functionality.

We need some enemies, which, of course, mean an Enemy Class, so create a CPP/H file pair called Enemy, and for now just create the con/destructors. We want them to be placed randomly within the edges, so they can be seen but we'll let an init system handle that.

Now one thing we do need to do is give them a sense of direction, the reasons for that are that they don't have keyboard controls, so they don't really know what direction they are going to use for the correct offset values to look for a collision with walls.

So as well as giving them a random placement, we will give them a random direction when we create them. A direction value seems to me to be quite an important concept for our enemies, so it might be better to add it to the GameObject Base Class rather than just into the Enemy Class, also an enum for directions would be a good idea. So let's add that to our GameObject.h:

```
typedef   enum Direction
{
   Up = 0,  Right, Down, Left
} Direction;
```

I made it a `typedef` so that it would allow me to do this for the variable type;

```
Direction Dir;
```

From now on we can load Dir with Up, Right, Down, or Left, rather than 0,1,2, or 3. It's just a nicer way to address things because hard numbers can be confusing sometimes if you forget what number relates to what value.

Ok, now I just remembered we said we were going to also include homing, so I will add that to the type of Direction controls we plan to have

```
typedef   enum Direction
{
 Up = 0,  Right, Down, Left, Homing
} Direction;
```

So our Enemy.h Class definition will look like this:

```
#pragma once
#include "GameObject.h"
#include "Game.h"
class Enemy : public GameObject
{
public:
 Enemy();
 Enemy(char*, MyFiles*);
 ~Enemy();
 void Update(Game* G);
};
```

And for now that's pretty much it, the code needs very little just now. The cpp file will look like this:

```
#include "Enemy.h"
#define SPEED 1.0f
Enemy::Enemy(){}
Enemy::Enemy(char* fname, MyFiles* fh) : GameObject(fname, fh){}
Enemy::~Enemy(){}
void Enemy::Update(Game* G)
{
 switch (Dir) //what direction are we moving in
 {
 case Up:
  break;
 case Left:
  break;
 case Down:
  break;
 case Right:
  break;
 default:
  break;
 } // end switch
}
```

We will fill in those case statements with proper movement and detection shortly, same way we did with the player. Let's try generating these chaps in the init of the Game Class, but before we do, we need to add a random function; ideally to our Game.h (it needs a proper home soon!)

```
inline float Rand(float a_Range) { return ((float)rand() / RAND_MAX) *
a_Range; }
```

We've used this before in our Kamikazi and Invader games. The Random placement will look like this, remember to add Enemy.h to the Game.cpp file and this is placed in our Game::Init routine after the player is generated.

```
for (int i = 0; i < 20; i++) // make 20 enemies randomly placed
 {
 Enemy* TempEnemy = new Enemy((char*)"../Assets/shooterEnemy.
png",this->FileHander);
 TempEnemy->Xpos = Rand(SCRWIDTH - 64) + 16;
 TempEnemy->Ypos = Rand(SCRHEIGHT - 64) + 16;
 TempEnemy->Dir = (GameObject::Direction) Rand(GameObject::Left);
 MyObjects.push_back(TempEnemy);
 }
```

Notice the cast to `GameObject::Direction`? Casting is generally bad, but because we explicitly decided to give, Up, Down, Left, and Right a typedef, so the Dir member wants that type, this ensures that we can use the values the Rand routine generates.

We can run that now and we should see a fair number of baddies. Though some may be on red squares, which we don't want, but we'll get to that after we move them, and you'll see why we don't want that.

Movement should be simply a case of doing the relevant add or subtract and the pixel test we used in Player. Think you can do that yourself? Try it.

Ok, now we're looking pretty cool except, of course, they are all going to go to the edges of the screen, so add one check to the test, if positive, change the direction to the opposite direction. Again I want you to try this on your own! If you get really stuck there is some info on the support site to help. But please do your very best to do this alone.

Let's place our 20 pickups randomly on the screen and then see if we can use a circle–circle collision system to detect if our character has collided.

We'll call this class Family. (Mom and Dad) and again it will inherit from GameObject.

They don't do anything except check for a collision with the player, because they only exist to be picked up, so that's all the update function is going to do. We can immediately tell we really need to know where the player is in the Game Class, which mean we have to go back to the Game Class where we first created the Player and create a variable that makes it easier for us to get hold of the Player. Add this to your public members in Game.h

```
Player* ThePlayer;
```

And in Game when we create him don't use and push a TP value use ThePlayer instead. Let's create these exactly the same way we did with the enemies.

Homing in

We've got enemies moving in nice predictable ways, reacting to the obstructions in the map, and we've got things to pick up. This is a pretty well-established game mechanic, but if we're honest it does not really do a lot. If we keep our wits about us we can avoid the enemies. So let's add that extra feature. Homing, where we said we would let the closest to the man switch to a homing system, not unlike our Kamikazi divers.

How can we determine the closest one? It's pretty simple for us to calculate range; our old friend Pythagoras did that for us. But do we really want to scan through 20 enemies every cycle to work out who's closest?

Well, yes, we actually have no choice, remember what we humans do is look and visually compute distances, but computers can't do that, they literally have to test every single relevant object and compare with the others.

But there is a logical way to do it. We already have a nice loop doing the updates in our Game loop, so if we can compare the range of each relevant object in turn we can compare with the last best, and if that is now better we will by the end of the loop know which is closest.

Notice I said relevant object. We have three types: (1) family, (2) player, and (3) enemy, we only want to test the enemy. There's at least two ways to do that, we could add a type value to the GameObjects, and in the constructor of each object set that up, it then becomes a simple test to see if it's an enemy or we could add a range value and allow all nonenemies to set that to a very large value meaning they'd never been chosen, and let the enemy put correct values in.

Range is actually quite a useful concept in a lot of games, so I'm going to jump for that, and add Range as a value in GameObject so that all types of game object have some value. But only the Enemies will actually calculate it each frame.

We can add a bit of code in the enemies update function to calculate and store that range, and the main loop can do a simple comparison test. The range calculation will look like this as a GameObject method.

```
float GameObject::DistanceFrom(GameObject* P)
{
 float XDist = P->Xpos - Xpos;
 float YDist = P->Ypos - Ypos;
 return (XDist*XDist) + (YDist*YDist);
}
```

Notice, even though this is a Pythagorean calculation I am not bothering to SQRT it, because I can work just as easily with the square of the value as I can with the square root, this used to be an important optimization, perhaps not so much now but SQRT is still a time-consuming function, so if you really don't need it, don't use it.

As we parse through objects in the vector, to update them, we now just need to add a call to this routine in the Game Class, which if it finds a closer object than we currently have it will keep his details in the CurrentClosest variable.

```
void Game::CheckClosest(GameObject* GO)
{
 static float Distance = 300000;
 static GameObject* CurrentClosest = NULL;

 if (CurrentClosest != NULL) // make sure we have a current closest
 {
  Distance = CurrentClosest->DistanceFrom(ThePlayer); // ok how close is he?
 }
 if (GO->DistanceFrom(ThePlayer) < Distance) // compare our current closest
distance with this players distance
 { // we found someone who was closer
  if (CurrentClosest != NULL) // make sure we have a current,
  {
   CurrentClosest->Dir = (GameObject::Direction) Rand(GameObject::Left + 1);
// he's no longer current so reset his directions
  }
  Distance = GO->DistanceFrom(ThePlayer); / our new enemy is the current
closest
  CurrentClosest = GO;
  CurrentClosest->Dir = GameObject::Homing; // make him a homing enemy
 }
}
```

Remember to add a descriptor for this function in the Game Class, we have one more step to do, which is to add to our game update to call this nice range checker like this:

```
for (int i = 0; i < Game::MyObjects.size(); i++)
{
 if (Game::MyObjects[i]->OBJType == GameObject::ENEMY)
 {
  CheckClosest(MyObjects[i]);
 }
 Game::MyObjects[i]->Update(this);
}
```

So much tidier, and that's what we need to always aim for, clean tidier code, is easier to debug, and usually easier to follow.

So having worked out who the new closest guy is, we can set his direction state to Homing, but we should also remember the old one and set him to a random standard move pattern. Though if you want a really hard game….let it stay at Homing.

We do need to first talk about how we are going to move, I am simply going to repeat the basic idea we used in Kamikazi, work out a vector direction to the target (the player) and then using a normalized version of that vector move toward the player at a speed of my choosing.

Ok well that's simple enough, but I also have to take the background into account, I'm not allowing my enemies to cross over a red barrier. And here we find ourselves in a dilemma, if we're homing we no long have any clear idea if we're moving Up, Down, Left, or Right, most likely with vector motion we could be moving in any one of 360° of direction and a few billion floating point fractions in-between. So clearly we need to use a maths solution to this issue and also use what resources we have.

We have the Xpos and Ypos, we also have a SPEED constant, we have the position of the Player, to calculate the vector, and we have the sizes of the image. AND we have the Vector2D Class we wrote for Kamikazi.

It might seem a bit MacGyverish, but that's enough. If we think of the square, or more correctly rectangle of our sprite as having a center point, the direction of travel viewed from the center of that sprite itself points to the outside edge of that sprite, sadly the vector for motion, being normalized, won't be quite big enough to reach the edge of our square. But we can use our old collision idea of drawing an encompassing circle around our square and get a radius for the circle to enlarge the vector. It won't be 100% accurate but it'll be close enough, so the code will look something like this:

```
case Homing:
  {
// calculate where we want to move to, then see if its safe
    float PX = G->ThePlayer->Xpos - Xpos; // vector toward the player
    float PY = G->ThePlayer->Ypos - Ypos;
    Vector2D MoveThisWay(PX, PY); // use these to make a vector
    MoveThisWay.normalise(); //normalise it so we can make better use

    float PossibleXpos = Xpos + MoveThisWay.x*SPEED; // keep a possible new
Xpos if test works
    float PossibleYpos = Ypos + MoveThisWay.y*SPEED; // same for ypos
// now we have to work it if the direction we are travelling to is allowed
// a reference point is needed. Work out the centre, since we know height
and width
    Vector2D sides(Image->GetWidth() / 2, Image->GetHeight() / 2);
    Vector2D CP(Xpos + sides.x, Ypos + sides.y); / Centre point is calculate
// getting the radius is easy too
    float Radius = sides.mag(); // we now have the radius
// we can use our radius to work out offsets fromour centre point that will
give us a test point
    MoveThisWay = MoveThisWay*Radius; // reuse the vector which now has an
offset
    CP = CP + MoveThisWay;
```

```
// re-caculate point with our new test position
  Point = G->m_Screen->GetBuffer() + ((int)CP.y*SCRWIDTH + (int)CP.x);
  if ((*(Point) != REDMASK + ALPHAMASK))
   { / we can allow this move
    Xpos = PossibleXpos;
    Ypos = PossibleYpos;
   }
  }
  break;
```

It's nice to see our old friend the Vector2D Class coming back in, we really should have used it for the whole game, hint hint. A nice small technical thing to note, I usually prefer to have my case statements in brackets, it's not always needed, and you've seen several instances so far where I didn't, but here I absolutely had to, because I was creating some local variables to hold temp values. If I had not put the case statement in brackets to contain the scope of the statement it would have thrown a confusing error when trying to compile. (Translation, I didn't put it in brackets and it threw up a confusing error! I suffer so you don't have to.)

A much more important point to make here, we did something we will do again and again in future, we worked out where were wanted to go, used that for testing but only updated the position of the sprite when we decided that it was a valid point. We will repeat that process a lot in future, movement in any game world often depends on knowing where you want to go to, rather than where you actually are.

Wrapping It Up

So now all we need to do is deal with some gameplay conditions. Clearly contact with enemies is a death, so we need to store the numbers of lives we give, and if we catch all the family, it's a win and then game over, with a nice little triumph message.

I'll let you do those, so that we can move on with this book, as you can tell from the very basic graphics and poor gameplay, this isn't a serious game, it's just a demo. But let's make it playable at least and add some scoring and end-game conditions. For later games though you should refer to the support site final versions source code, for game state info, as its going to be pretty much common code/methods for each game. You'll find a *finished* version on the support site to compare against your own efforts, but really how you want to tackle this is up to you.

Is This All We Need?

In terms of letting our characters move around a simple map with solid colors this idea actually works pretty well. Small offsets depending on our directions lets us to test what is in front of us in the direction we are moving and react accordingly. But it really only works as long as we are certain that our obstacles are on screen and have certain colors, it's not terribly flexible.

It is, however, an established principle and sometimes used for situations where a precise form of pixel collision or testing is needed, it's also good practice for working out how to get data from memory. But if we want to have multicolor tiles, and with more variety of tile this method totally fails to work. If we look at a map with more tiles such as this:

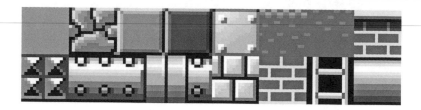

Clearly we have a lot more colors and more importantly these tiles can represent different types of things we might stand on, dipping into a pixel buffer no longer makes sense. But we do still have access to the tile or character map that can give us information.

We can see for example, that tile 0, appears to be a blank tile, tiles 1, 2, 3, and 4 are solid, tiles 5 and 6 are water, 7–13 are solid, though the pipes might be useful for other concepts, 14 very interestingly is a ladder and 15 is another pipe.

So we've got 12 of our 16 tiles seem to be some kind of ground, 1 is a ladder 2 are water and the 0 is blank, but might have a use.

Here's a simple play map set up with these graphics, nothing too fancy. I put this together in 10 mins using a lovely shareware package called Tiled, from Thorbjørn Lindeijer, it's available free from http://www.mapeditor.org/ but if you plan to use it please donate a few pennies to allow him to continue to support it. If you want to design your own maps this is a great app to own. Of course, you should put more care into your design than I have!

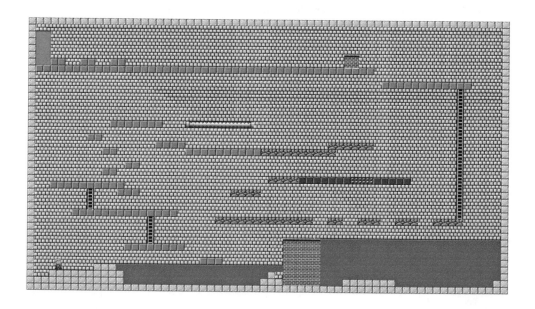

Let's look at this map in our game, download the BobsDay framework from the site. And get it up and running. You should see straight away its built the same way as the TileDemo, which we made into a little chase game.

If you look at the map code in Game.cpp you will see direct correlation between the numbers in the map and the tiles in the image.

Can you see a much more traditional and clear game style here, where the map is build up from different simple tiles? But as there's no logic or control in place yet, our pixel testing robot fiends are not going to be much use here, we need to check tiles not colors.

Now we have to think about this a bit more carefully. How can we actually tell what tile we are hitting? Color isn't going to help us, so the testing for pixel data has now become useless. But there are other things we can test, such as the map itself!

The principle is pretty simple, we move our objects around in unit coordinate that represent pixels. So they can move pretty freely around the screen. We also draw our tiles starting in unit coordinates. But our map array is being used to represent objects that represent 32, 64, or, in fact, any number of pixels square. So there is a common means of addressing the screen only the spacing between start points really changes.

As always we can only use the data we have to hand, in this case, the pixel-based positions of the objects we want to test. These are screen coordinates. If we know our tiles are 32 × 32 pixels, and the screen is full of such tiles. Then working out the grid position is simply a matter of taking the objects X/Y values and dividing them by 32, the width/height of the tile.

That then provides an offset into the map array, assuming the first tile in the array is drawing at position 0,0 on the pixel screen we do, in fact, have a direct relationship between the tiles position and their coordinates.

If the tile starts at a different point, for example, when a second area of screen is displayed in the same map, we only need to take account of the offset to find the tile.

I call this point to grid collision and it allows us to take any point on the screen and find out where the relevant tile is with a very simple method:

```
int GetTile(float PixelX, float PixelY)
{
  int Xindex = PixelX / TILE_X;
  int YIndex = PixelY / TILE_Y;
  return Map[YIndex][XIndex];
}
```

Where TILE_X and TILE_Y are values defined elsewhere that give the size of the tile (usually the same, but never assume!).

The fact we can check any point, means we can use our objects reference point, and/or any offsets from the reference point we want to use. That gives us great flexibility to test the middle, top, bottom, sides, and even corners of a rectangular sprite.

This allows us to have a pixel-movement system, which can comfortably read in the value in a character map at a given screen collision and gives us a quick simple way to tell if there is something there to hit.

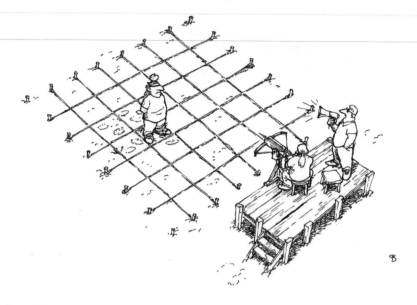

Ok, so that all works, we have a new collision system, as long as we know the type of tile we can assign different attributes to it and react accordingly when our characters detect they have come into contact with different tiles. Now let's work on a project that really makes use of these cool graphics and collision systems.

▋ 5.3   Single-Screen Platforms

A World with Gravity

Now let's start to use this information to create a new but very familiar type of game, time for us to do a platform game. And also we'll start to make use of our tidier file systems and MyLib.

I'm also going to make another couple of changes and move all that old C style graphic setup and swap code into a nice clean class of its own so that we can let the file containing the main function do only what it needs to do to set up the game. That's really what we should aim for, small self-contained files that contains code that does only what it is supposed to do. A main file is really only there to set up the system, call the game, and exit. That's all it does now. Also I changed the way I instantiate the Input and FileHandler routines, not just fixing the spelling.

We're finally starting to make a break from the old Hello Triangle code and make our code much cleaner, though we still have a few things to fix. You can download this much nicer template from the support site, it's called BobsDay. This will now form the base template for our projects until the next big improvement. As a bonus having the graphics as a separate class will make it far easier to slot in a different graphics file for different target systems.

Now let's get back to the game play, when you compile and run BobsDay it will look pretty much the same as the TileDemo, except when you move the much nicer looking character around, he is clearly presenting a side on view, he also has a much nicer four frame animation though as soon as you move him around the screen you will see we are not interacting with it at all yet.

You can see now that a top–down world is very easy for us to deal with, we are just basically taking account of the things we bump into and we are happy to think that our characters are always on the ground, but now that we take a side on view of our world things change. BobsDay is exactly the same display code as the TileDemo game, the same style of map and game structure but our concept of control and interaction are going to be quite different. The only significant difference is our perspective.

A different control system is achieved in the Player Class, which has a new constructor that loads up 12 images, 4 each for left, right, and climb. Then there is a change to the update code where you will see some slight changes to the movement, since we do actually have multiple frames of animation based on our direction. I have loaded the animation frames in this order.

Four Walk Rights, four Walk Lefts, and then four climbs. So I can be sure that the Walk rights go from index 0–3, Lefts 4–7, and Climbs 8–11.

Having multiples of 2, in this case 4 is quite useful, because it allows me to change the frame, using a simple increment system, which is then binary 'and'ed to be only in the range 0–3.

Adding that index to a base value lets me cycle through the four frames where each base starts.

```
BaseAnim = 0;
    this->Image = Images[BaseAnim+AnimIndex];
    (AnimIndex += 1) &= 3;
```

Each direction sets its own base, though climb up and down share, and I can make the choice of frame quite easily. Using base 0 for Right, 4 for Left, and 8 for Climb. Since this game is now looking side on, we have to consider how we're going to move. We've created a playfield where we recognize the concept of down being at the bottom of the screen, and presumably we adhere to some form of gravity, we want to walk on the floor, and any other platforms in our map and we should fall when we're not actually jumping up.

Let's start by introducing the basic idea of falling in our Player::Update code, add these two lines before the key reads

```
Ypos += SPEED;
if (Ypos > SCRHEIGHT - 48) Ypos = SCRHEIGHT - 48;
```

We can see we are simply adding speed to our Ypos, unless we're on the ground (allowing a slight offset for the fact our sprites reference is its top left corner).

Run this and you will see that we do indeed fall, while still retaining some ability to move left and right, and apparently stop when pressing up and falling faster when pressing down, can you understand why up and down are doing such odd things? They are effectively negating or compounding our fall system.

But clearly this isn't a very convincing fall, falling with gravity is an accelerating process. As anyone who's ever jumped out of a plane can tell you, you fall faster and faster until air resistance stops your acceleration and you then keep falling at that terminal velocity until you go splat on the ground, which is why parachutes are really important if you plan to test this in real life!

Our simple addition of a speed constant does not really work for us, we need to accelerate, and that means we need to actually increase the speed value up to a point we also consider our terminal velocity.

We can do this by adding to our currently dormant GameObjects YSpeed value, testing if it has reached terminal velocity and then adding that to our Ypos.

```
Yspeed += SPEED;
 if (Yspeed > 9.81f) Yspeed = 9.81f;
 Ypos += Yspeed;
 if (Ypos > SCRHEIGHT - 48)
 {
  Ypos = SCRHEIGHT - 48;
  Yspeed = 0;
 }
```

Adding the speed this way gives us a much more convincing fall, and also we must remember to still test if we hit ground and if so we either went splat or simply stopped falling, so we can reset the speed.

That's pretty neat, by always adding a gravity value each update we move but now we need a small test condition, giving us the power to stop gravity at a condition point we recognize as the ground. Let's try adding some jumping now and see how that works.

Jumping, requires you to exert a force to overcome gravity, I'm reliably informed by my much fitter nongame developer friends that to overcome gravity, you have to exert a force with your legs, which must be greater than the force of gravity, but it can only be applied once as an impulse at the point of the jump. Since in this case, we have a positive gravity force, to overcome it we need a negative jump force, add this line to your Up key get code before or after the animation

```
Yspeed = -SPEED*6;
```

It's nothing fancy, but that will mean when we press up, we are giving ourselves a negative force, which will propel our man up, but and this is the cool important part, gravity does its job every cycle, this happens only once (though for now we will trigger it as long as the key is pressed).

Try it and see, but don't hold the up key. So now we have jumping, our acceleration up is added to or position, but our acceleration up is constantly eroded and eventually overwhelmed by our gravity update, just like real life.

We need to stop the fact that we can continually apply the force if the key is pressed though, it should only be possible if we are currently on the ground.

There are two ways to do this, have an indicator flag to tell if we are in the current process of jumping, the flag gets set when the jump triggers and resets when the fall stops. This is quite a nice way, but another way is also possible and will aid our design. We can only allow the jump to trigger if we are on the ground to start with which at the moment would be done with this.

```
if (Ypos == SCRHEIGHT - 48)
    Yspeed = -SPEED*6;
```

But that's of limited use to us, we are not playing this game at only the floor level, there are platforms we want to walk on which are at different Y positions on screen, so it's time to start our testing of the map to find out if we are on a solid platform or if we let our falling system kick in.

Now, we know our screen is built up from a 2D map, which is basically an array, and we know our X and Y coords, we also know our tile sizes are 16 × 16 pixels.

So...if we wanted to know what tile we are standing on, we take our X and Y coordinates, divide them by the size of the tile, in this case 16 and we then get an index into the array that builds the screen.

Calculating the coordinate to test needs an adjustment, remember our sprites top-left point is the reference coordinate, but we need to test the bottom, so there is a offset to add, so long as I add the Height of the sprite to the Ypos, part of the reference coordinate I can get the bottom, Equally if I add width it to the X part, I can check the right point. This ability to test a point in our map, means we can extend it to look for objects to our left and right, letting us be stopped by walls and bumping our head when we go up. But we do need to be careful, because testing only one point is a little narrow, we should probably test two or even three points in the direction of our movement, representing the center point of our object, and the two corners of that direction. This will prevent us passing through a tile if we are physically larger than it or our contact point misses.

We also need to give our player some access to our Map, which currently is in our Game Class but not actually a member of the class. Add this line to our Game Class header in the public section

```
int* WhichMap;
```

This will provide us with a pointer to a location which is an int, and as our Maps are made of arrays, we can tell our Game Class to set the relevant map we want into this location and any object with access to the Game Class public members can get this.

Sadly, though we can pass the address of the base of an array quite easily, we can't pass the dimensions of a 2D array quite so easily as a pointer, so we will have to do a bit of gymnastics because I don't want to alter our Update entry parameters to make passing an array simpler.

In your Game init Class be sure to let the WhichMap variable know where the map we are using is with this command:

```
WhichMap = &Map2[0][0];
```

Now when our player is updating he can update gravity as before, but now is able to alter the test condition that stops or allows jumps, to take account of his position in the map like this:

```
int YMap = (Ypos + 33) / 16;
int XMap = (Xpos + Image->GetWidth()/2) /16;
int WhatsUnderOurFeet = G->WhichMap[YMap*64+XMap];
 if (WhatsUnderOurFeet == 4 && Yspeed >= 0)
 {
  Ypos = YMap*16 - 32;
  Yspeed = 0;
 }
```

The test condition now takes account of the X and Ypos of the player as a reference point 1 pixel below his feet in the center of his image, then dividing them down by the size of the tiles to find indexes into the map. WhichMap can still be accessed as an array, but only as a single dimension, so we need to multiply the YMap index by how many elements are in the X component of the original map. We already know this, so we can use a hard number. We then add an offset.

Our condition is now flexible enough to use, I've chosen 4 to be the main floor tile, but I'll show you how to expand that shortly.

Try it and see. We can now jump up onto another section, but no more midair jumps. Our jump trigger also used a condition to decide if a jump was allowed, so that also needs updating list so

```
if (WhatsUnderOurFeet == 4 && Yspeed >= 0)
    Yspeed = -SPEED*6;
```

Now we've got a lot more flexibility and a pretty convincing jump, but already you see the jump only really lands properly if we have that center bottom point on our map. We need to make some small changes now so that we can get this kind of control.

We want to fall in empty areas, land on solid, and be able to detect if a wall is going to stop our X-axis movement. What will that look like if we could see the tiles as tiles is depicted in the following image. Let's create a small list of attributes, which will relate directly to our 16 different types of tiles:

```
int Attributes[] =
{
 0, 1, 1, 1, 1, 0, 0, 1,
 1, 1, 1, 0, 0, 1, 2, 1
};
```

This very simple list tells us if something is solid, 1, or not 0, and there is the special case for the ladder, which is 2. We could also consider these as binary bit patterns for multiple attributes on each tile!

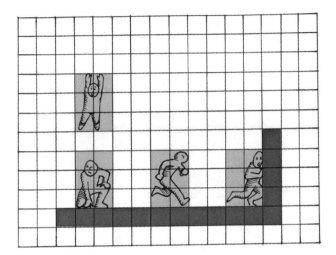

So now place that list in our Game Class under the map. Remember we will once again need to access this array in our player and later Enemy Classes, so have another pointer to the data called

```
int* WhichAttributes;
```

And in your game init routine set this up with

```
WhichAttributes = Attributes;
```

Notice we don't need the & address symbol or [][] because it's a single-dimensional array and C++ actually knows that such arrays are already treated as addresses. With the attributes for each tile now recorded, another small change to our ground test has it looking like this:

```
int WhatsUnderOurFeet = G->WhichMap[YMap*64+XMap];
int Attrib = G->WhichAttributes[WhatsUnderOurFeet];

if (Attrib != 0 && Yspeed >= 0)
{
 Ypos = YMap*16 - 32;
 Yspeed = 0;
}
```

We are now seeking out the attribute associated with a tile at the players feet, and if it's non-0 we will stop it, do the same for your jump condition:

```
if (Attrib != 0 && Yspeed >= 0)  Yspeed = -SPEED*6;
```

And compile and run. We now have many more platforms we can stand on, and though we're treating the ladder as a type of ground we are actually able to detect if it is, in fact, a ladder rather than a simple solid block, which will allow us to use a more suitable climbing animation. In fact, we can treat many of the blocks as having a different effect on our movement.

All this work gives us a totally flexible system; we can decide which tile is solid, or dangerous to stand on, or simply a part of the background with no interaction, no matter what our map position is. We are now ready to write some code that will work with many maps so long as the map tiles are the same.

One tileset, many many maps, is how a lot of 2D games are made, the maps can be any size and even have multiple tiles with the same graphics but different attributes, using a common access system and altering the base level.

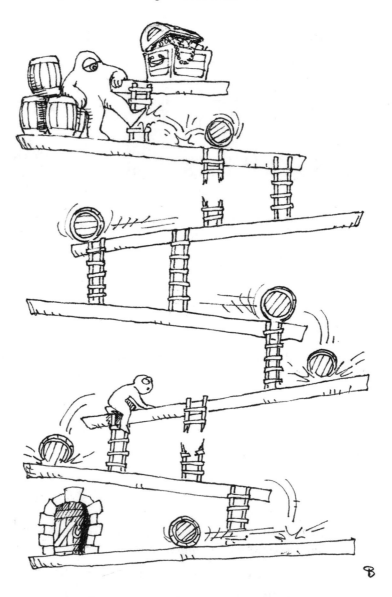

Routine Bad Guys

Our game does not really call for any significant intelligence in enemies, they just need to get in the way, and perhaps go for Bob, when he gets too close.

So let's have them do simple point to point motion for now, and decide if that's enough. We have an Enemy Class but it's designed for the top down tile demo, but we can still use this Enemy Class, since we know all enemies are going to have a few common features, such as their desire to obey the laws of physics, animate through some standard sequences and make some simple choices. We can create a couple of specific classes for a couple of enemies that do a specific task.

So let's start by stripping the top down logic from the Enemy Class and make our first enemy.

Point-to-Point

As you might imagine, point-to-point is simple a case of going from one place to another and back. And we actually already know how to go to a point, we did it in Kamikazi. The only real change then is that we have two points, and we need to detect if we have reached them before we change the point to focus on.

So as long as they are moving left<>right they are simply performing a straightforward action. We don't even really need to have them check if they are standing on a platform. We can comfortably place them at a point where there is no need to move up or down between point A or B. This bit of code will do just that.

We will of course need to define the two points somewhere, as this is essentially an enemy specific behavior, then we can put it in the Enemy Class, or perhaps more wisely create a new class that inherits enemy? If we plan to add multiple enemy types this makes sense, since we can isolate the update systems for each type of enemy and keep specific variables in the relevant class. The Enemy Class itself can now be restricted to handling animation, drawing, and testing for collision with player. So our Point2Point header can look like this.

```
#pragma once
#include "Enemy.h"
class Point2Point : public Enemy
{ public:
 Point2Point();
 Point2Point(MyFiles*);
 ~Point2Point();
 void Update(Game* G);
 Direction OurHeading;
 Int Xmin, Xmax;
 int Ymin, Ymax;
};
```

Update should by now be obvious, and then there are a few variables, which our update routine can make use of to do its moves.

In our Point2Point.cpp file, we just need to create the constructor, a simple default one and one which is going to load our images into the vector, so it needs the address of our file hander.

So now let's write those two constructors. The default isn't at all interesting at the moment, just creates an instance and leaves, the file based one loads the images, but that presents us with a problem, what if we create more than one set of images?

With our Player Class it's fine to have an array, because we only have one, but we might have five or six enemies on screen and it's best if they use the same set of graphics. We got over this with our previous invader code by being careful that we preloaded the graphics but in our war against sloppy code it's time for a better solution. I propose a way to check the graphics that we already loaded, and if we have it, use it, otherwise load it, we'll call it add or replace and it will look a little like this:

```
// check if a graphic already exists in the main map
Surface* Enemy::AddorReturn(char* fn, MyFiles* FH)
{
 char *cstr = &fn[0u]; // embarrasing side effect of the decision to use
char....

 if (graphics.find(fn) == graphics.end())
 {
  printf("New graphic to be added %s \n", cstr);
  // we never found it
  Surface* T = new Surface(fn,FH);
  graphics.insert(std::make_pair(fn, T));
  return T;
 }
 else
 {
  printf("Graphic previously loaded and now reused %s \n", cstr);
  return graphics[fn];
 }
}
```

I'm putting this in the Enemy Class because it's really only the enemies that I need to take care of. This system depends on something called a map, a very nice special form of array that instead of an index, looks up things based on other things, in this case a filename.

We will need to define our map in our enemy.h file, which I want to make static, as there should only be one map. Our new enemy.h header now looks like this:

```
#pragma once
#include "GameObject.h"
#include "Game.h"
#include <map>

class Enemy : public GameObject
{
public:
 Enemy();
 Enemy(char*, MyFiles*);
 ~Enemy();

 virtual void Update(Game* G);

 static std::map<char*, Surface*> graphics;
 Surface* Images[4];
```

```
// tests if we already loaded the graphic, if so return a surface it not
insert it, and return the surface
 Surface* AddorReturn(char*, MyFiles*);
};
```

As long as we also have a definition of this map in another file, ideally in the enemy class like this

```
std::map<char*, Surface*> Enemy::graphics; / created in the h file so
reference here
```

We are now able to use AddorReturn as a loading system, which will do exactly what it says. It does, however, create a very dangerous precedent. We will be creating new surfaces and storing them in this map, providing the calling function with the surface, but we are passing on the responsibility to delete those surfaces to whichever class creates the enemies and, in turn, destroys the map, normally if an object makes a *new* item it's up to that object to delete it, in a clean-up or destructor function. But since more than one enemy is going to be using these graphics, it's not practical for the first enemy to delete the surface potentially damaging the graphic integrity of any remaining enemy.

AddorReturn could just as easily be based in our GameObject Class too, it's up to you really, I would like to have a separate collection of images only for enemy graphics in this case, so there's no real reason to have it in the GameObject Class.

Let's get the constructors built, I'll just detail the ones with files, you can manage the others.

```
Point2Point::Point2Point(MyFiles* FH)
{ // we can test our map to see if the files already exist, if so use the
existing
 Images[0] = AddorReturn((char*)"../Assets/fungus_1.png", FH);
 Images[1] = AddorReturn((char*)"../Assets/fungus_2.png", FH);
 Images[2] = AddorReturn((char*)"../Assets/fungus_3.png", FH);
 Images[3] = AddorReturn((char*)"../Assets/fungus_4.png", FH);
}
```

Here we can see how to use the AddorReturn function, when we create the first Point2Point enemy, we will see that all four of them will load, but the second time, it will reuse the graphics. We will expand this a bit more as we find a need to initialize variables.

So a simple dumb left/right or up/down motion is fine and if we are careful to place them in the right part of the map, we will never have to worry about them appearing to walk off the edges or through walls. These systems are ideal for flying types of enemy, and the system is simple to expand with a counter into an array of points, and using normalized vectors to move to them.

But if we want them to do things a little more cleverly we need them to have much the same understanding of how to move around the map as Bob has. They should adhere to the concept of gravity unless flying and interaction with the map, meaning that they should fall when there is nothing to support them, they should stop if they encounter a wall, and they should try to make it look as if someone, or something is actually controlling them.

Dumb baddies in a game are fine, they make good obstacles, are easy to code and offer a simple fire, and forget kind of enemy. Smart baddies though, give a totally different feel to a game and allow you to interact with them in cool ways, it also paves the first steps of developing AI.

Patrolling Enemy

So let's have the first semi-smart baddie, we'll use the same graphics for him and his header file isn't a lot different, but this one has no need for min and max points. Create a new pair of file for a Patrol Class, this is the header:

```
#pragma once
#include "Enemy.h"

class Patrol : public Enemy
{
public:
 Patrol();
 Patrol(MyFiles*);
 ~Patrol();

 void Update(Game* G);
 Direction OurHeading;
};
```

Basically, nothing more than a stripped back Point2Point. Like before we won't actually use our Default constructor, but it's good to leave it in place.

Our Filehandle using constructor is going to perform the same duty of loading the files in for the images. Even though we only plan to use 2 again, there's no harm at all in loading them all if we find a way to make use of them another time they are there and ready for us, but if it worries you change things to use a two entry Images array.

```
Patrol::Patrol(MyFiles* FH)
{
// we can test our map to see if the files already exist, if so use the
existing
 Images[0] = this->AddorReturn((char*)"../Assets/fungus_1.png", FH);
 Images[1] = this->AddorReturn((char*)"../Assets/fungus_2.png", FH);
 Images[2] = this->AddorReturn((char*)"../Assets/fungus_3.png", FH);
 Images[3] = this->AddorReturn((char*)"../Assets/fungus_4.png", FH);
 BaseAnim = 2; // 0 is static frame 1 is s stand, 2 and 3 are the walk
frames
 Yspeed = Xspeed = 0;
 AnimIndex = 0;
 Image = Images[0]; // we need one to start
 Dir = Right;
}
```

So only a small difference here, mainly I am making sure I have an Image surface ready to be used before the update because I will need to gain access to my images sizes. The Update is where the main action is now going to occur. After working out the timing for animation, we again have a switch, this time for two directions as I won't make him go up and down.

The tests are now focused not on what's under our feet but what's along the edges of our fungus/mushroom guy, as he moves, right edge of the box when moving right and left edge when moving left. Rather than test only one point I test enough to cover his entire height, he's a 32 × 32 image, so I'm only going to actually test two points, one at his top and one at his center, but that will be ok for this.

As with the Point2Point if the test shows something in the way I can then change direction.

```cpp
void Patrol::Update(Game* G)
{
 float Speed = 1.2;
 Yspeed += 1.2f;
 AnimTime -= 1.0f / 60.0f;
 if (AnimTime < 0)
 {
  (AnimIndex += 1) &= 1;
  AnimTime = 0.2f; /0.2 seconds
 }

// lets move him
   switch (Dir)
   {
   case Left:
    {
     Xpos -= Speed;
// now we check for possible obstacles
     int YMap = Ypos / 16;
     int XMap = (Xpos-1 ) / 16;
     for (int i = 0 ;i < Image->GetHeight() / 16; i++,YMap++)
     {
      int WhatsAtTheEdge= G->WhichMap[YMap * 64 + XMap];
      int Attrib = G->WhichAttributes[WhatsAtTheEdge];
      if (Attrib & 1)
      {
       Dir = Right;
       break; // break the loop we are done
      }
     }
     break;
    }
   case Right:
    {
     {
      Xpos += Speed;
     // now we check for possible obstacles
      int YMap = Ypos / 16;
      int XMap = (Xpos + 1+Image->GetWidth()) / 16;
      for (int i = 0; i < Image->GetHeight() / 16; i++)
      {
       int WhatsAtTheEdge = G->WhichMap[YMap * 64 + XMap];
       int Attrib = G->WhichAttributes[WhatsAtTheEdge];

       if (Attrib & 1)
       {
        Dir = Left;
        break; // break the loop we are done
       }
```

```
      YMap++; // move downp to the next
    }
    break;
  }
  break; // break the case
}
default:
  {
    printf("default occured, setting direction to Rightt \n");
    Dir = Right;
  }
} // switch dir

  // check for gravity and get the frame
if (Yspeed > 9.81f / 4) Yspeed = 9.81f / 4;
Ypos += Yspeed;
int YMap = (Ypos + 33) / 16;
int XMap = (Xpos + Image->GetWidth()/2) /16;;
// we could also choose to not let him fall!
int WhatsUnderOurFeet = G->WhichMap[YMap * 64 + XMap];
int Attrib = G->WhichAttributes[WhatsUnderOurFeet];

if (Attrib != 0 && Yspeed >= 0)
{
 Ypos = YMap * 16 - 32;
 Yspeed = 0;
}

this->Image = Images[BaseAnim + AnimIndex];
// calculate a screen position for our object
this->SXpos = Xpos - G->ScreenX;
this->SYpos = Ypos - G->ScreenY;
}
```

You can create a Patrol fungus in your GameInit, in game.cpp, with this,

```
// make a standard patrol
 Patrol* Pat = new Patrol(FileHander);
 Pat->Xpos = 210;
 Pat->Ypos = 20;
 Pat->Dir = Enemy::Right;
 MyObjects.push_back(Pat);
```

Compile and run, and our smoother moving patrol fungus can now be seen going off to the right and when he hits the bricks, turning back.

It's not exactly cutting edge AI, but it's a good example of our enemies making decisions about their direction of travel based on the environment around them, just as we do.

Homing Enemy

Finally, one more type of Enemy can be added, a homer of sorts. We'll use what we know about calculating distances and have a fungus that sits quietly until Bob gets close then he tries to attack, hunt him down as far as the environment will let him. The movement parts are going to be the same as our Patrolling fungus, but to make them a bit more interesting let's introduce a sleeping mode, where they don't seem to do anything. Make a pair of Homer files and our Homer header looks like this:

```
#pragma once
#include "Enemy.h"
class Homer : public Enemy
{
public:
 Homer();
 Homer(MyFiles*);
 ~Homer();
 void Update(Game* G);
 float GetDistance(Game*);
 Direction OurHeading;
 float Distance;
 bool Moving;
};
```

Not really a massive difference, there's an additional variable for distance, and a bool, which we will need to initialize to a default false when we make the constructor. The default constructor again will be empty with a File handle constructor looking like this:

```
Homer::Homer(MyFiles* FH)
{
// we can test our map to see if the files already exist, if so use the
existing
 Images[0] = this->AddorReturn((char*)"../Assets/fungus_1.png", FH);
 Images[1] = this->AddorReturn((char*)"../Assets/fungus_2.png", FH);
 Images[2] = this->AddorReturn((char*)"../Assets/fungus_3.png", FH);
 Images[3] = this->AddorReturn((char*)"../Assets/fungus_4.png", FH);
 BaseAnim = 0; // 0 is static frame 1 is s stand, 2 and 3 are the walk
frames
 Yspeed = Xspeed = 0;
 AnimIndex = 0;
 Image = Images[0]; // we need one to start
 Dir = Left;
 Moving = false;
}
```

Aside from initializing the Moving flag it's not doing much more, the real meat in this class once again is evident in the Update functions, which are now being altered depending on the state of that Moving flag.

```
void Homer::Update(Game* G)
{
 float Speed = 1.2;
 Yspeed += 1.2f;
 if (Moving == false) // lets check if he's moving if not should we make him
 {
  BaseAnim = AnimIndex = 0;
  Distance = GetDistance(G);
  if (Distance < 16 * 6) AnimIndex = 1; // pop up and show interest
  if (Distance < 16 * 3)
```

```
    {
      Moving = true;
      Dir= (Xpos < G->ThePlayer->Xpos) ? Right : Left;
    }
  }
  else
  {
  if (GetDistance(G) > 16 * 6) Moving = false; // reset to wait if far away
    BaseAnim = 2; // we are walking
    AnimTime -= 1.0f / 60.0f;
    if (AnimTime < 0)
    {
      (AnimIndex += 1) &= 1;
      AnimTime = 0.2f; //0.2 seconds
    }
// we're moving so do the directional switches
    switch (Dir)
    {
    case Left:
>>>>From here on the code is identical to the Patrol movement, but notice
there is a close brace for the else to take into account options
    } // switch dir
  } // else
    // check for gravity and get the frame
>>>>From here on the code is identical to the Patrol movement
```

I don't need to paste in the full routine because it should be very obvious to you now what to do, the tests for the distance, are taken care of, and if we are not moving we do the old movement systems, but be careful to close your else brace before the gravity check because we want that to function even on a sleeping mushroom.

Create a new Homer in Game, but, of course, adding Homer.h, and then in the game init, add this:

```
// make a standard Homer
 Homer* H = new Homer(FileHander);
 H->Xpos = 310;
 H->Ypos = 20;
 H->Dir = Enemy::Right;
 MyObjects.push_back(H);
```

Compile and run, you should see that as you get close to the mushroom, he will pop his head up, if you get even closer he's going to charge at you, then move away and once out of range revert back to a sleeping mushroom.

As all three of our enemies have such similar code, some of it actually even repeats, it's tempting to have a single file with one Enemy Class and use a type variable to just choose different initialize and update routines. It might even be tempting to have each more advanced one inherit its primitive version.

But keeping the types separate allows us to make changes very easily without having an impact on the other types, it also lets us maintain small and focused files, which do specific things for specific types, which is an important mantra in C++'s OOP-coding concepts. There are small but subtle differences in our three fungus types, which might get lost if we have one large and confusing file or overdo the inheritance. But there is a valid argument for separating out the exact same movement code in the patrol and homing system. It could perhaps go into the Enemy code as a stand-alone function, saving a little bit of space and making the code more compact in those two classes.

I'll let you add collision systems to this, there's nothing different in the way you would do collisions here from how you do them in our space shooters. So add a collision with the Player test function in the Enemy Class, and perhaps set up a flag in the Game Class, which each enemy can get to with the G-> access. If you hit it, set the flag, and have the player detect if that flag is set and then has to die a horrible bloody death!

Ladders and Effects

I pointed out that in our attributes we set the ladder to 2, making it a special case, and indeed it is special because we need to make some subtle changes to our player's up routine if it detects a ladder, so that we can change our animations from walk to climb.

What makes the ladder special, is that if can trigger a transition from simple walk to climb on a key motion currently assigned to a jump. When we detect the need for a jump, we can now also check if there is a ladder object under us, and if so, switch to a climb.

Climbing is in some respects a different state of control, whereas on the ladder we don't really want to jump or be able to walk off until we get to the top. We don't really have too many states of play in this particular game, so climbing and walking/jumping are really the only things we should worry about. So this code here needs to change:

```
if (IH->TestKey(KEY_UP) )
 {
  BaseAnim = 8;
  this->Image = Images[BaseAnim + AnimIndex];
  (AnimIndex += 1) &= 3;
  if (Attrib != 0 && Yspeed >= 0)
   Yspeed = -SPEED*6;
 }
```

As it stands it is blindly allowing a jump but using the climb animations, let's alter things so that we can take into account when he's in a climbing mode we can use climb animations. Also we need to test when he can transition to a climbing mode and when he needs to exit it.

Add a bool flag called Climbing to your player.h and be sure to set it to false when you init your game. Also make sure you add the final two frames for the jumps in the constructor

```
Images[12] = new Surface((char*)"../Assets/brianJumpR.png,fh",fh);
Images[13] = new Surface((char*)"../Assets/brianJumpR.png,fh", fh);
```

Simply wrapping the test code in an if/then/else condition will let us use the bool:

```
 if (IH->TestKey(KEY_UP) )
 {
// this is the climb
  if (Climbing)
  {
   BaseAnim = 8;
   this->Image = Images[BaseAnim + AnimIndex];
   (AnimIndex += 1) &= 3;
  }
```

```
      else
      {

   if (Attrib != 0 && Yspeed >= 0)
     Yspeed = -SPEED * 6;
   }
}
```

We can compile and run this and see what happens, if we press up, we jump without a frame change but the ladder itself is treated as a platform and allows us to jump up, so let's add a little more tests for that climb, so it now looks like this:

```
 if (IH->TestKey(KEY_UP) )
 { // this is the climb
  if (Climbing)
  {
   Yspeed = -SPEED * 6; //<<<<<<<<climb speed
   BaseAnim = 8;
   this->Image = Images[BaseAnim + AnimIndex];
   (AnimIndex += 1) &= 3;
// we need to test if the climb is over?
   if (Attrib != 2)
   {
    Climbing = false;
   }
  }
  else
  { // now we check if we are on a ladder
   if (Attrib == 2)
   {
    Climbing = true;
   }
   if (Attrib != 0 && Yspeed >= 0)
    Yspeed = -SPEED * 6;
  }
 }
```

This looks good, we are changing the animation at the right time, the only issue now is that we are still basically jumping up the ladder, so reduce the amount of speed we add when we are climbing, to give a more step-like value, 2* Speed seems to work well.

This method allows us to clear the final top part of the ladder by allowing it to revert to a jump at the final step, is that something we want? Ideally we could have a little clambering up animation but sadly we don't have the graphics. So we have to leave it like this.

Now try to move down! We have a problem, don't we? Our attribute test is looking at our feet and right at our feet there's no actual ladder it's a row below our feet, so we need to do a second test and rewrite the down routine like this:

```
if (IH->TestKey(KEY_DOWN))
{
 int WhatsUnderOurFeetplus = G->WhichMap[(YMap+1) * 64 + XMap];
 int Attrib2 = G->WhichAttributes[WhatsUnderOurFeetplus];
 if (Attrib2 == 2) Climbing = true;
 if (Climbing)
 {
  BaseAnim = 8;
```

```
   this->Image = Images[BaseAnim + AnimIndex];
   (AnimIndex -= 1) &= 3;
   this->Ypos += SPEED;
   if (Attrib2 != 2 && Attrib != 2)
   {
    Climbing = false;
    Yspeed = SPEED * 2;
   }
  }
 else
 {
  // maybe add a toe test graphic?
 }

 }
```

It's a little different from the up routine, especially as you now have two attributes to test: the one directly under our feet and the one a tile down, this will allow it to travel to the bottom of the ladder before the Climbing flag is cleared. Compile and run....and it's not quite right, is it?

As we have gravity acting on our player at all times, we need to deal with the fact that gravity should not work while we are in climbing mode. This is why, Down is making a direct change to the Ypos, because the gravity should not allow us to drop while we're on the ladder.

We need a small change to the gravity section of the Game::Update function, to take account of this *one off* condition:

```
if (Climbing == false)
  {
   Yspeed += SPEED;
   if (Yspeed > 9.81f) Yspeed = 9.81f;
   Ypos += Yspeed;
  }
 else
  {
   Ypos += Yspeed;
   Yspeed = 0;
  }
```

So gravity works the same if we're not climbing, otherwise we add the speed, which Up climb will use, and make a point to immediately clear the speed so that the down will not fall.

But what happens if we do something we have not anticipated, try climbing the ladder, and then walk off.

Hmmmm not quite right is it? Our walk systems do not have tests for climbing, so if we are in climbing mode, and we walk off the ladder, we are still technically in climbing mode and gravity will not work. What's the best solution? Do we lock out/left right motion while in climb mode, or do we automatically clear the Climbing flag when we move left or right? Both are valid, try them out.

Animation might also need a little helping hand, we should probably return the player to one of his walk frames, or when jumping to one of his jump frames. But which one? Left or right? We don't keep any note of his direction of travel, we should keep a note in our players direction when moving, remember we have that nice Direction Dir; value in our GameObject Class. If we keep that up-to-date when we move Left or Right, we will always have a record of what direction he was moving before the decision to climb. Try adding that and make the jump animation take account of it as well as when you reset the Climbing flag.

One final thing we need to address for this before we wrap it up, relates to the precision of the testing. We are currently only using one single point, really we need a few more, and like the down-ladder check, the purpose of two tests is to make sure that we are completely in the area of the tile where the climb should be, so we can avoid things like this:

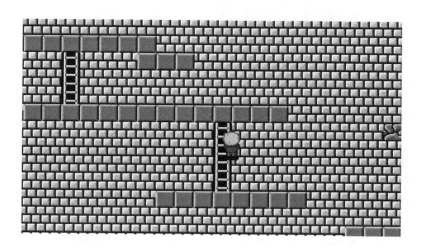

By testing two points, less than a tile width apart around the center point we already test we can make sure that the climb will be central, try adding these new methods for the player:

```
bool Player::TestClimb(Game* G)
{
 int YMap = (Ypos + 33) / 16;
 int XMap = (Xpos + (Image->GetWidth() / 2) - 6) / 16;
 int WhatsUnderOurFeet = G->WhichMap[YMap * 64 + XMap];
 int Attrib = G->WhichAttributes[WhatsUnderOurFeet];

 if (Attrib != 2) return false; // test for ladder
 YMap = (Ypos + 33) / 16;
 XMap = (Xpos + (Image->GetWidth() / 2) + 6) / 16;
 WhatsUnderOurFeet = G->WhichMap[YMap * 64 + XMap];
 Attrib = G->WhichAttributes[WhatsUnderOurFeet];
 return (Attrib == 2);
}
bool Player::TestClimbDown(Game* G)
{
 int YMap = (Ypos + 33 + 16) / 16;
 int XMap = (Xpos + (Image->GetWidth() / 2) - 6) / 16;
 int WhatsUnderOurFeet = G->WhichMap[YMap * 64 + XMap];
 int Attrib = G->WhichAttributes[WhatsUnderOurFeet];
 if (Attrib != 2) return false; // test for ladder
 YMap = (Ypos + 33 + 16 ) / 16;
```

```
XMap = (Xpos + (Image->GetWidth() / 2) + 6) / 16;
WhatsUnderOurFeet = G->WhichMap[YMap * 64 + XMap];
Attrib = G->WhichAttributes[WhatsUnderOurFeet];
return (Attrib == 2);
}
```

Don't forget to add the prototypes for these in your Player.h file. It's hopefully pretty clear that they are looking for two points within a tile width from the center and returning true if both of them are true. We can now use these routines to trigger up and down climbs, and the simple center tests to continue. Also be aware that the down test routine will cause a crash if you try to use it on the bottom.

Yeah, this works pretty well, we can only drop down the ladder when we are pretty central to it, we can adjust the tolerance a little to make those ±6 values bigger or smaller as we need so long as the distance between the two points is not more than the width of a tile.

Are we done yet? Nope, sadly there is still a small issue, try going UP when we're not quite central. What do you think is happening here? He's not climbing, because our new tests will not set the Climbing flag, and he's also not animating. Basically, he's jumping, and at the top of his jump he's recognizing a solid thing to land on. Hmmm, this is a problem and most of it stems from the fact our test for gravity is based on our attribute being 0 or not solid. But ladders are two. And, in principle, therefore solid. Arrghh what??

Here we've got a great example of a few simple changes to the basic rules of our movement causing knock on effects to other rules and cause us to make new functions to accommodate. This is a continuing issue with most interactive programming, you have to try to anticipate and correct for things you allow your player to do.

Having a tile being only one attribute at any one time is a pain, and means we need to write exceptions all over the place when we do our condition tests. But attributes can allow us some flexibility, rather than define the Ladder tile as a nonzero and solid tile, let's have multiple attributes for each tile and encode them in bits. So a Ladder can therefore be defined as nonsolid but climbable.

In Game.h add these lines:

```
#define SOLID    0b1
#define LADDER   0b10
#define WATER    0b100
#define METAL    0b1000
#define EARTH    0b10000
```

This gives us a series of binary values or masks, which we can encode into our attributes like this:

```
int Attributes[] =
{
 0, //0
 SOLID, //1
 SOLID, //2
 SOLID, //3
 METAL+SOLID, //4
 WATER, //5
 WATER, //6
 SOLID, //7
 SOLID, //8
 SOLID, //9
```

```
SOLID, //0
SOLID, //11
0, //12
SOLID, //13
LADDER, //14 / ladder
SOLID //15
};
```

For now, they are still mostly single values, though metal has two attributes that might allow us to play a tip–tap sound when our player walks on metal, but the ladder now has a LADDER attribute, and not solid, and it can have other attributes associated with it if I so choose, so if my test for landing on a solid now looks like this.

```
if ((Attrib & SOLID ) && Yspeed >= 0 && Climbing == false)
  {
  Ypos = YMap*16 - 32;
  Yspeed = 0;
  }
```

I can be a lot more confident that the gravity is going to ignore the ladder, and the ladder tests now using & LADDER are able to function much better. For example:

```
bool Player::TestClimb(Game* G)
{
 int YMap = (Ypos + 33) / 16;
 int XMap = (Xpos + (Image->GetWidth() / 2) - 5) / 16;
 int WhatsUnderOurFeet = G->WhichMap[YMap * 64 + XMap];
 int Attrib = G->WhichAttributes[WhatsUnderOurFeet];

 if ((Attrib & LADDER) == 0) return false; // test for ladder
 YMap = (Ypos + 33) / 16;
 XMap = (Xpos + (Image->GetWidth() / 2) + 5) / 16;
 WhatsUnderOurFeet = G->WhichMap[YMap * 64 + XMap];
 Attrib = G->WhichAttributes[WhatsUnderOurFeet];
 return (Attrib & LADDER) == LADDER;
}
```

You'll need to go through the code now and make changes to any attribute check, to use this mask system rather than the ugly hard-number system, and in future you should always use this kind of method. A 32 bit int will allow 32 possible attributes in a tile. More than enough to cover a wide range of possible properties or combinations of them.

Data, Our Flexible Friend

That's about it for a single-screen platformer, we're using the coordinates of our man to interrogate the map, and with that, find out both the graphic to draw, and the particular attribute it has that will impact on Bob's movement.

The baddies, do pretty much the same thing, and that allows us to put them in place with a little less precision, which can actually look quite nice as they fall to the nearest floor space.

It's not really much of a game though, but you can get from the bottom to the top, and if you feel like it, adding extra levels with a different map and a different pattern will give you some game play. Oh and scoring, don't forget scoring.

Feel free to enhance this any way you want, there were a lot of classic games done this way, and their simplicity of code makes them a good learning experience. We can spice it up with different baddies, alter the control we have over Bob, maybe even add some gun toting baddies, set traps, avoid traps, alter the map in play, and so on. All of these concepts will work with this same basic game-coding concept. But it takes good design and level building skills to make a great game. Remember that!

Loading Our Maps (and Other Resources)

Now, we're already comfortable with the idea of loading our graphics in, they then exist in our memory and are used by our projects. But there are other types of data we really should consider for loading. Most obvious at this point is our maps.

Keeping our maps in 2D arrays is fantastically easy, and simple to compile, but once compiled, that's it, the only way to change the map is to edit the array, or sequence of arrays then recompile. This places all the responsibility for the map layout on you as the coder, which for a quick test map is fine, but really it's much easier if we can load up the maps from a resource file. That allows a level designer or modder to create new maps without having access to the code.

Unlike graphics, there are no *standard* formats for data like this, the format of your maps, is pretty much up to you, it might be simple integers, it might be pointers to structures, the options really are unlimited. But what is fairly constant is that the data is going to be saved as either a chunk of binary that you can load in and sort out yourself. Or, it's going to be a text file and then converted into binary when you load it.

Binary files have the advantage of speed, for loading and installing in a suitable place, and compactness. A binary file is also usually much smaller than a text file.

But one overwhelming advantage of text tiles is that they can be edited in any editor, in fact you already have been editing them. Binary images, will need to be loaded in to some kind of specific editor program, before they can be edited.

The choice is always yours. For now, we'll discuss simple comma separated values (CSV) text files as they are easier to visualize and for us to edit to see different effects.

It's also the preferred format for most of the freeware tile editors out there and it is simple to edit in an editor or a spreadsheet program such as Excel.

Loading a file, either text or binary is a standard STL function, so we don't need to worry about including new libs to read them. But we do need to run through a process we call parsing.

Parsing is what we do when we read text, especially speed reading. We go through the text we are looking at and pick out the interesting stuff that we want. Usually looking for a keyword to focus our attention.

When we load a text file, we are indeed loading text, so if we have a line that says.
"0,1,2,3,4"

We are not actually loading the numbers 0,1,2,3, or 4, we're actually loading the ascii value of those numbers because that's what was typed into the file when it was created in a text editor.

So, if we want the actual numbers, we need to convert the ASCII('0'), which is actually numeric value 48 into the actual number 0, we also need to discard comments and commas, and some of the normally unseen function codes in a text file, such as a newline and EOF (End of File) marker.

We may use some keywords to indicate different sections of map, so we have to scan for those words to indicate what kind of data we are parsing. Finally (well for this explanation), we also have to look for lines of text which are not relevant, comments perhaps, and discount them.

So text is a little bit of effort. But it can be worth it.

Once we strip out commas, command codes, and unwanted text, we can load our numeric values into a holding area, or array. This can mean that instead of having 20 different arrays for your maps, you only need 1, and load the relevant map into it.

Now, words of warning, if your maps are all the same size, overwriting data into a container array is fine. But if you have various sizes of map, you have to make a decision.

1: Create a holding array that represents the biggest possible array, we can contain all the smaller arrays in it.

or

2: Dynamically allocate memory each time you load a map, and remember to deallocate it when you're done with it.

Both are viable, but Dynamic is probably better. Though it does mean we have to do a bit of trickery to get access to 2D arrays, which are very much a benefit of compiled arrays.

We can use <vectors>, the STL's standard dynamic list system, or more correctly vectors of vectors, it can be a rather clumsy and ungainly data structure when you examine it in memory and it is slow to create, but once set up it does give you the benefit of continuing your concept of accessing an array by Array[y][x].

Since we're keeping things simple as far as access is concerned, we will stick with this, and I'll let you explore cool ways to create multidimensional arrays dynamically when you are more confident.

In keeping with OOP principles of C++, it is best if we try to keep all this map stuff, loading, parsing, and storing in a class of its own, so we'll make a start by creating a MapManager Class.

Normally, any file handling we might do would, probably be put into the MyFiles Class, but as this is a very specific type of file for a very specific data system, we won't be using MyFiles, we'll write the code straight into the MapManager Class.

Our MapManager header is pretty straightforward, though there's a lot of header stuff in here because we're using a few C++ string features, as much as I like to use char* this is one time where strings are that bit easier.

```
#pragma once
#include <stdio.h>
#include <stdlib.h>
#include <vector>
#include <string>
#include <fstream>
#include <streambuf>
#include <sstream>
class MapManager
{
public:
 MapManager();
 ~MapManager();
```

```
 std::vector< std::vector<int>> TheMap; // a vector of unknown size, of
vectors of unknown size, (take care to write it >> not >> compiler
sometiles complains!)
 bool LoadMap(char*, int x, int y); // you must know the size
};
```

It really does not have a lot to do, just provide that vector of vectors and I'm giving myself a function to load and set the size of the map. I've assumed (I keep breaking that no assumption rule so let's say, I insist that) I will be using text-based maps, rather than binary, but you can just as easily add a binary reader to this. We might want to add a few different load functions, for example, if we discover that our map editor outputs some scripts, but the simple maps I'm using only contain raw tile data, so the load function is a very simple CSV parser pushing tile numbers into TheMap.

Unlike some of our other simple classes, this class has a few responsibilities, which is why I called it a MapManager rather than just a map. If we load things, we need to be careful that when we are done with them we release the memory. In this case, our memory is going to be gobbled up by TheMap vector. I will make sure the load routines and the destructor take care to clear or reset it when I kill this class or load a new map.

So in the cpp files our constructor and destructor will look a little like this:

```
#include "../Headers/MapManager.h"
MapManager::MapManager()
{
}

MapManager::~MapManager()
{
 //delete the map
 if (TheMap.size() != 0)
 {
  printf("A map still exists and is now being erased\n");

  for (int y = 0; y = TheMap.size(); y++)
   TheMap[y].clear(); // clear each of the elements

  TheMap.clear(); // now clear the main body

 }

}
```

As is often the case, our default constructor does nothing, we need to pass information, so we do most of the work in the load/init. But you can see the Destructor is being a good little function and checking to see if there is a map in place when it gets called, and carefully removes it.

Now, our load routine needs to actually load or more accurately stream the file, and then create the vectors as it parses through the file, so it might end up looking a bit complex, but the basic idea of setting up vectors inside vectors looks just like this:

```
for (int y = 0; y < ys; y++)
{
 std::vector<int> T; // a temp
```

```
  TheMap.push_back(T);
  for (int x = 0; x < xs; x++)
  {
    TheMap[y].push_back(x); // replace this
  }
}
```

This will fill an array full of 0,1,2,3,4.... on each row, not very practical but it helps to visualize things.

All we really need to do is insert some code to grab a line from our text tile in the outer for loop, and convert data to ints, in that inner for loop, so that instead of pushing back the x value we push back a converted ASCII value and loop through until we are done.

This is why knowing the size of at least the number of rows in the vector is useful, though we can be ignorant of it as long as we are confident in the formatting of the file we are loading. If it's from a map editor or other package we can be sure that we will have X number of values before the CR (Carriage Return) and the end of the line, and if it has a proper EOF marker we can scan down the lines to determine if we have finished, or continue with the amount of lines we want. So our formatting of the file itself will set up the size of the data, or we set hard values.

So, let's add some file handling, and as a safety measure, some checks before we try to build it to ensure that we have a valid file and valid sizes. I'm also being fussy and printing out the data in a visible format, just so I can see what's happening during debug. We should, of course, come up with a better way to report things, because at some point we have to go through all our code and comment out the masses of printf's that are happening. Also we will allow for the possibility that size errors might occur and we'll make sure that the loader can't make a map bigger than the data in the file. That can be handy if we are guessing the maps size, as long as the map has lines ending in \n, asking it to load a massive map will only have the effect of loading the map in the size it was saved as.

```
bool MapManager::LoadMap(char* fn, int xs , int ys)
{
  // does our vector of vectors already have data, if so we need to clear
  it
  if (TheMap.size() != 0)
  {
    printf("A map already exists and is now being erased\n");
    for(int y = 0 ; y < TheMap.size() ; y++)
      TheMap[y].clear(); // clear each of the elements

    TheMap.clear(); // now clear the main body
  }
  printf("Mapsize is set to %i\n", TheMap.size());

  if (xs == 0 || ys == 0)
  {
    printf("Map has a 0 value which is not allowed\n");
    return false;
  }
  std::ifstream t(fn); // open an input stream for our file
  // now load each value in turn store them into our vector make our vectors;
  for (int y = 0; y < ys; y++)
  {
    std::vector<int> T; // a vector for the columns
```

```cpp
    std::string Line; // a temp string for the line
    std::getline(t, Line); // ask t fora whole line, put it in Line

    if (Line.empty()) break; // check if its done, in case we misjudged it
    std::stringstream Ln(Line); ake this into a stream

    TheMap.push_back(T); // save our currently emptry vector

    for (int x = 0; x < xs; x++) // pull the columns along
    {
     std::string val;
     std::getline(Ln, val,',');
     if (val.empty()) break; // if not enough values break the inner loop
     int view = stoi(val); // only do this in debug
     printf("%2i,", view);  // only do this in debug
     / store the int of the string
     TheMap[y].push_back(stoi(val)); //<<<<THE MEATY BIT!
    }
    printf("<\n");// only do this in debug
  }
 printf("Mapsize is Y-%i : X-%i \n\n", TheMap.size(), TheMap[0].size());
 t.close(); // close the stream its done
 return true;
}
```

Nice, it's gained a few kilos in safety checks, outputs and pulling and then converting data from the input streams, but you can see still the core of this is a simple pushback of a number into the vector. All we need do from this point is load the map, provide real, or fake sizes for it to function and at the end of it we'll have an easy to access 2D vector of TheMap. As long as we don't mess with the data our tile editor spews out, this will be enough to work with for now. There are still a few minor issues, you may or may not come across them, but we should, of course, also add a check that the file name is valid and abort the load if not, you can add that yourself, hint, the object *t* has things you can test! There's also a slight flaw in this logic, if using TileEd to save your CSV you will find it has one blank line at the end. We will load that, and even though we won't put a final column vector in there, we will put in a final Row vector. Any idea how to fix this? It can be done here and should be, just test when you get a CR, that you do, in fact, have a column vector with some values. Or at the end of the routine test that final Row and see if its column vector has values.

Ok, so now that we know how to do this, we can create similar parsers, which load data for many other resources we are likely to use. Simple CSV, text parsers like this are very useful, but you will probably get more complex as you need more data in your managers, but as long as you use a "," to separate things you can pull tokens instead of strings of numbers and set up switch/case conditions to handle them.

As this is also a nice compact routine, which is likely to be used for at least the next couple of projects we should store it in our MyLibs library.

▌ 5.4 Lets Scroll This

We've done pretty well with our single-screen world, our x and y coords of our man directly relate to screen positions, which in turn directly relate to tile positions. Our world was limited to the size of the screen.

But what if we have a world that is much bigger than our screen, we can't always just increase the screen resolution, there are upper limits to that, and beside the higher the res the smaller our characters will look, which might not be so cool. In fact, let's make our screen resolution a bit smaller and try to see the impact having a window into our map will have on our game.

Change the screen resolution in the BobsDay header to a very retro-sized 320 × 200 and then compile and run the project. We now get a very cool retro-style screen, but only showing the top-left corner of the map. But where is Bob, and the enemies? Well, in fact, they are doing exactly what they were doing before, at start up Bob appeared on the map and promptly fell to the ground. He's still doing that, in fact, the entire game is still busily working away because it is doing all of its logic and tests based on the map data, not the screen. The visualization of our game is totally independent of the actual control so now we have to alter our visual systems to allow us to see Bob and his surroundings.

This will be our first attempt to scroll our world and use our screen simply as a viewport into that world. There are, as always, many ways to do this, but I rather like the idea of giving our screen itself coordinates that relate to their position on the map, these, in turn, are calculated as a point from the place where our main character is.

FRAMING

Look at the position of the character in the previous image, he's what we will call the controlling influence. It's clear that the screen only shows a part of the map, and that he's part of the map, but Bob here is the one who we are interested in and who is controlling everything. He will pull the screen around the map for us allowing us to see the different parts of the map that he moves around relative to his position.

The screens top corner is (nearly) always a fixed distance from where our friend Bob is. And it therefore has a position in the map. We can make small adjustments later to cope with edges of the world, but simply put, our ScreenX coord is always going to be our Bob mapX-half the screens width, and our ScreenY coord is always going to be Bob's mapY—half the screens height. So he will stay more or less in the middle and the screen will have its own map coordinates. To avoid trying to draw outside the map area, we can check for <0 and > Maximum Mapsize. Let's give our Game Class some variables, which will allow it to keep track of the screen. In the public members section add this:

```
float ScreenX, ScreenY;
```

We will need to make adjustments to our draw map function, but for now let's explain how we can load these important screen values.

We need now to remind ourselves that our Xpos value relates purely to our position in the map, and we will need to draw our sprites as a relative view from the screens location in the map, our draw systems then need to be given a new improved screen coordinate, which we will call SXpos and SYpos for Screen Xpos and Screen Ypos, add this to your GameObject Class because from now on all our game objects will need to have this to allow them to draw:

```
float SXpos, SYpos;
```

Our player Bob is the only one who pulls the screen along, so he is the controlling influence and as such it becomes his responsibility to work out the screens position every time his own position changes.

Add this code to the end of your player update code after all the other moves are done and a new Xpos and Ypos are calculated.

```
 G->ScreenX = Xpos - (SCRWIDTH / 2); // get the trial version of the screen
 G->ScreenY = Ypos - (SCRHEIGHT / 2);
// keep in boundries if it is outside limit it
 if (G->ScreenX < 0) G->ScreenX = 0;
 if (G->ScreenY < 0) G->ScreenY = 0;
 if (G->ScreenX > 64 * 16 - SCRWIDTH) G->ScreenX = 64 * 16 - SCRWIDTH; //
we know the map size
 if (G->ScreenY > 40 * 16 - SCRHEIGHT)  G->ScreenY= 40 * 16 - SCRHEIGHT;
// calculate a screen position for our player
 this->SXpos = Xpos - G->ScreenX;
 this->SYpos = Ypos - G->ScreenY;
```

This should all be fairly easy to follow, we are basically making sure our screen coordinates are a certain distance away from our player sprites reference point and a few tests to make sure we don't go outside the map area. Then simply work out a new screen coordinate as the players position minus the screens newly formulated map position!

Ok, so we know what part of the map our screen starts to draw, now our map draw system also needs a slight overhaul, we're no longer content with drawing at 0,0, and we want to draw at the point we just calculated.

We do need to make sure that our draw is done AFTER the player has updated, otherwise the data will be inaccurate and we also need to be clear that the player, our controlling influence, must update the ScreenX/Y before any other drawn object so that they too can work out a relative screen position.

Going back to the Game.cpp file, change the call to DrawMap function in your Update loop to now use the new coordinates

```
DrawMap(ScreenX, ScreenY, a_Screen);
```

Almost there, we still have to make a small change to the draw system so it can use the new values:

```
void Game::DrawMap(float mapx, float mapy, Surface* a_Screen)
{
 int Tmapx = mapx / 16 ;
 int Tmapy = mapy / 16;
 for (int y = 0; y < SCRHEIGHT / 16; y++)
 {
  for (int x = 0; x < SCRWIDTH / 16 ; x++)
  {
   Tiles[Map2[Tmapy+y][Tmapx+x]]->CopyTo(a_Screen, x * 16, y * 16);
  } // x loop
 } // y loop
}
```

We create a couple of temp values, which we use for the index into the map and add the offset given to us by the for loops, which also acts as the position on the screen to draw. Right, let's get this compiled and running, and see what happens. Now we can see our Bob is nicely on screen, and if we move to the right, the screen is scrolling, but it's not very smooth at all. We are not taking into account that Bob is moving in pixel values, and our Drawmap is only drawing in Tile values so we only scroll when Bob has moved 16 or more pixels, we need to take into account the 0–15 pixels that a tile is made of and account for them in the draw.

First step is to actually work them out and convert them to easy to use ints. At the entry of Drawmap before we calculate Tmapx add these lines:

```
int offsetX = fmod(mapx, 16);
int offsetY = fmod(mapy, 16);
```

The fmod function returns the remainder of a division on a float number, in this case by 16, so that will provide us the offset into a tile.

Now we have only to factor this into the actual draw with this line:

```
Tiles[Map2[Tmapy + y][Tmapx + x]]->CopyTo(a_Screen, (x * 16) - offsetX,
(y * 16) - offsetY);
```

We could drop the () around the *16 because the compiler will always do a multiply before it does the subtract, but for clarity it's always good to wrap steps of a calculation in a bracket, it does little to the compiling of our code but helps us and others visualize our intent better.

And now run that, if all goes well you will now have a very pleasant surprise. Smooth and clean scrolling, a little fast maybe but that's because of our change in resolution making the update a lot faster. There's also a niggle, what are those black edges?

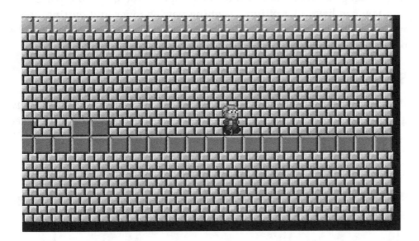

Clearly they are connected to our scrolling as they grow as we move, and it's really pretty simple, we are drawing 20 tiles, but because of the offset we actually are displaying 21, the tiles that are about to come on screen need to also be drawn. We can fix this by simply adding a +1 to our for loops so our finished draw maps now looks like this:

```
void Game::DrawMap(float mapx, float mapy, Surface* a_Screen)
{
 int offsetX = fmod(mapx, 16);
 int offsetY = fmod(mapy, 16);
 int Tmapx = mapx / 16;
 int Tmapy = mapy / 16;
 for (int y = 0; y < (SCRHEIGHT / 16)+1 ; y++)
 {
  for (int x = 0; x < (SCRWIDTH / 16)+1 ; x++)
  {
   Tiles[Map2[Tmapy + y][Tmapx + x]]->CopyTo(a_Screen, (x * 16) - offsetX,
(y * 16) - offsetY);
  } // x loop
 } // y loop
}
```

And that, basically is that, run this and we will now have a very nice smooth pixel scroll which allows us to explore our map with ease. We now only have to add a small GetScreenPos method to our GameObject so that the enemies and other drawn, nontile, objects in the world can calculate their relative screen position and be drawn correctly. I'll let you work it out for yourself, hint. Only Bob is allowed to create the ScreenX/Y values but everyone creates their SXpos/SYPos the same way.

Conversion of our single-screen game to a multidirection scroller turned out to be a pretty simple task, adding a few variables, introducing the concept of map, or world coordinates, and detaching our screen draw systems from the logic. It is very important from now on that we remove the notion that our screen coordinates are our map/world coordinates. We've taken our first steps to thinking of the render of our world as being very different from the update.

If you want to make more scrolling platform games, this template will serve you well. Gameplay on such games is more down to the design of the maps and placement of the baddies. But you can have a lot of fun designing new enemies and putting switches and puzzles into the level. But for now we will return to our shooting style games and see how they adapt to the scrolling methods we've just mastered.

Simple Scrolling Shooter

The scrolling methods used in the platform game can be adapted to almost any genre, including shooters. There's a long tradition of *on rails* gameplay where the screen constantly scrolls, so that our ship appears to be flying over a vast terrain that appears beneath us bringing new baddies in to play and testing our reaction skills to kill them before they kill us. Let's try to visualize what we are going to see both as a gamer and as a programmer.

The gamer in you can see that ship/plane flying along and the terrain underneath having highs and lows that we can easily use to hide rockets and other things to attack us. The programmer in you should be seeing the nice tidy tiles that make up that image. Later, we might use better quality tiles to make the tiles less obvious and allow the appearance of a more seamless large play field. Let's look at the map:

It's a classic, right to left scroll traveling through a tunnel, avoiding waves of enemies, with missile silos to add to our pain. The tunnel we travel through also is filled with zero tiles, we'll come back to that soon as it's got a second useful value.

We're still using the TileExample framework, but I've cleaned it up a bit and put it on the site as Skramble. Please download it and get it all compiling. I've set it up to load the ship, maps, support graphics, and all the baddie types and few other things, but at the moment it has no scroll system and generates no enemies. I won't ask you to type in all the classes this time, they are all there, you just have to add them, and take a bit of time to read the comments on the code to get a sense of what they are doing. I'll underline any important things you need to take note of, when it comes to adding new code to the files supplied.

The game itself does not trigger any enemies, so I'll walk you through how to add them soon.

Like before we are defining a base Enemy Class, and its main duty is to keep a track of all the textures we load. But we will expand a little bit on that too.

So, let's get started by scrolling, the scroll is constant, and the screen moves from right to left at a constant pace. In this case, the player/ship is not the controlling influence on the scroll, in fact the Game Class is, it now has a little code segment, which changes the screen's Map position and provides new start points for the draw. That is all we need.

Our ScrollScreen routine looks like this:

```
// scroll
 if (ScreenX < OurMapManager->TheMap[0].size() * 16 -SCRWIDTH)
 {
  ScreenX += 1;
  MyObjects[0]->Xpos += 1; // his Xpos needs to change
 }
 else
  ScreenX = OurMapManager->TheMap[0].size() * 16 -SCRWIDTH;

// keep in boundries if it is outside limit it
 if (ScreenX < 0) ScreenX = 0;
 if (ScreenY < 0) ScreenY = 0;
```

The big difference is that this code is now located in the Game *update loop* before the objects are updated. As horizontal scrolling is now an automatic process only the ship MyObject[0] needs to be influenced by it. The Ship still has some control over the Y scroll, so we can leave that up there. But now we are making it clear that our scroll will move the screen and our ship has to go along with it.

Of course, we need to do something with the control of our player, it still needs to test that it's been asked to move as before, but take into account it is tracking the scroll, and we will allow it to move up to ¾ of the screen to the right but not allow him to drop-off the screen. We can also create limits of tolerance in its Y movement, but really I don't think we need to in this case so we'll let the collision tests stop it going outside the tunnel. So his movement routines in the Player.cpp file now look like this:

```
// calculate a screen position for our player
 this->SXpos = Xpos - G->ScreenX;
 this->SYpos = Ypos - G->ScreenY;

 if (SXpos < 10) // check his SXpos
 {
  SXpos = 10; // if we override his SX we need a new Xpos
  Xpos = G->ScreenX + SXpos;
 }
```

```
if (SXpos > (SCRWIDTH / 4) * 3) // make sure he's over at his limit
{
 SXpos = (SCRWIDTH / 4) * 3; // if we override his SX we need a new Xpos
 Xpos = G->ScreenX + (SCRWIDTH / 4) * 3;
}
```

He can now travel with the scroll, get a little ahead of himself but be brought back if he goes too far. Get this all up and running and you should now have something like this:

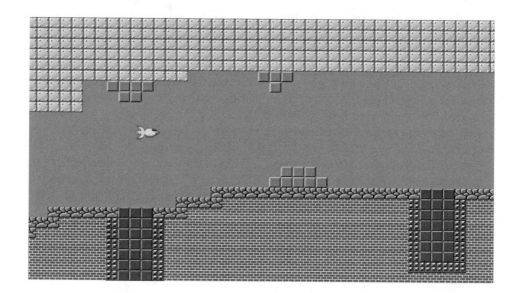

The net effect is that our Xpos is always increasing but we are testing that it's not going too far and if we do accidently go past the ¾ line we bring him back.

One final touch, I mentioned those zero tiles, they look a bit off, don't they? So let's not draw them, change the DrawMap routine to this:

```
void Game::DrawMap(float mapx, float mapy, Surface* a_Screen)
{
 int offsetX = fmod(mapx, 16);
 int offsetY = fmod(mapy, 16);
 int Tmapx = mapx / 16;
 int Tmapy = mapy / 16;
 for (int y = 0; y < (SCRHEIGHT / 16)+1 ; y++)
 {
  for (int x = 0; x < (SCRWIDTH / 16)+1 ; x++)
  {
   if (OurMapManager->TheMap[Tmapy + y][Tmapx + x] != 0)
     Tiles[OurMapManager->TheMap[Tmapy + y][Tmapx + x]]->CopyTo(a_Screen,
(x * 16) - offsetX, (y * 16) - offsetY);
  } // x loop
 } // y loop
}
```

You can see I've added a test, if the tile is zero, I won't print it, but how does that help, it just gives me a black tunnel area and it leaves artifacts of undrawn tiles (we have no clear screen remember)? Well let's add another routine to draw a background, and use our tile concept again. Remember to *add a prototype* to the header file and *add this function* to the Game.cpp file:

```
void Game::DrawBackground(float mapx, float mapy, Surface* a_Screen)
{
 return;
 int offsetX = fmod(mapx/32, 16);
 int offsetY = fmod(mapy/32, 16);
 int Tmapx = mapx / 16;
 int Tmapy = mapy / 16;
 for (int y = 0; y < (SCRHEIGHT / 16) + 1; y++)
 {
   for (int x = 0; x < (SCRWIDTH / 16) + 1; x++)
   {
     Tiles[12]->CopyTo(a_Screen, (x * 16) - offsetX, (y * 16) - offsetY);
   } // x loop
 } // y loop
}
```

Now it does not look quite the same as our DrawMap but you can see that it's not widely different, we could indeed display another map entirely with a little modification, but for now I'm making it draw one tile and doing a bit of messing with the position values. Run it and have a look.

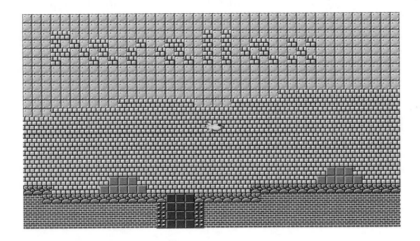

Cool, isn't it? This is a concept called parallaxing, where the background scrolls at a different, usually slower rate than the foreground. We could put any kind of background in there, a nice static screen, a noninteractive background map, or in this case, a single easy to access and easy to loop tile.

This particular version isn't that great because of our lack of Alpha values in the tiles, our CPU-based 2D system can't really cope with having tiles with see through areas, but we can always have our undrawn zero tiles to act as a window to the background. We *could* add alpha blending to the Surface Class copies but in due course we are going to move to a better more technically advanced framework, so I'd rather leave things as they are for now. But if you feel the need to have better alpha values, please go right ahead.

The scrolling work is now pretty much all done for you, but there's more to this game than that, we need enemies and we need collision with the map, which will give us some form of gameplay.

Let Them Eat Lead

If we're doing a shooter, then we really need things to shoot. In this case, bullets and bombs. Bullets to kill the charging enemies, and bombs to take out the missile silos I've just decided will be the prime goal of this game, it'll be like bulls eying womp rats from a T-16!

Bullets first. Clearly we need to add the Bullet Class, so *add existing files to the header and source file filters.*

Looking at the header there's nothing much here as you might imagine, I only have one graphic to hand for a bullet, and to be honest it's a bit small and hard to see against my brick background, so I'm going to accent it a bit by drawing a few at the same time, and very slightly deviating from the usual straight line, but that's for later.

Notice, I am using the Enemy Classes AddorReturn function to load or return the address of any texture. This in theory means the Enemy Class is in charge of the destruction of any graphics but because many will share the same graphics we will actually let the Game Class do that, so none of the Enemies will do anything to that graphics map.

Checking out the Bullet Class constructor I have set it so that the player will be the normal user and generator of the bullets, but bullets are such a common thing, we should try to reuse this routine, but players bullets can't be allowed to kill the player, whereas enemy bullets can. No problem we'll allow whatever generates the bullets to overwrite the type of bullet it is allowing for us to test later if the bullets need to hit the player or enemies.

So we have bullets, now we need to trigger them, which is done, of course, in the Player Class. Time to add a new case to the switch, we'll use the space as a fire button. We also need to make sure that we don't fire a bullet every single update, unless we decide later we want to. We really need a small delay or debounce between shots. So *adding a fireDebounce float* to our Players Class definition lets us *add this to the player Update*

```
if (this->fireDebounce > 0)
{
 fireDebounce -= 1.0f;
 if (fireDebounce < 0) fireDebounce = 0;
}

if (IH->TestKey(KEY_SPACE) && fireDebounce <= 0)
{
// make a small sequence of bullets, as these are a bit small we'll do
several
 int howmany = Rand(5) + 1;
 for (int i = 0; i < howmany; i++)
 {
  Bullet* b = new Bullet();
  b->Xpos = Xpos + 18+Rand(i);
  b->Ypos = Ypos + 12+Rand(i);
  b->Yspeed = 0.1f - Rand(0.2); // and spread them a bit
  Game::MyObjects.push_back(b);
 }
 fireDebounce = 12;
}
```

I chose to do a random little burst with slight alterations of direction in the Y to give more of a shotgun approach. You can increase the numbers of how many and the spread to suit, but these work pretty well.

Now that we have bullets, we'll worry about their collision shortly but for now have a play around with this and enjoy some simple shooting pleasure. Perhaps add some sound?

Bring on the Bad Guys!

Time to introduce some baddies and while we're doing that, let's introduce a slight difference in the way we load our images. We are always going to have situations where we need to load a sequence of frames individually, that's not a terribly bad thing, but loading from SD cards is pretty slow. It's usually faster for us to load one image, which contains many frames, and then chop it up into the individual frames we need. This mimics something we're going to use later when hardware comes into play, but for now, I really want to reduce the time it takes to load things and store them in our static stores.

I'll create four basic baddies in this demo, by all means you can add more and at the end a kinda boss baddie.

My four basic types will be

- Missiles which launched from the underground bunkers by launchers are our main targets

- Gun Towers which will shoot mines at us, and increase their rate of fire the closer we are to them

- Baddie1, for lack of a better name, is a green tractor-like dumb baddie, who just flies through the scene launching bullets at us. And as you can see his images are in one file

- Baddie 2, is a little more interesting, it's an animated eye character, so let's have him circle around a spot, also launching bullets at us

Our big baddie, is a bit of a semi-smart baddie who will duck and dive at the end of the tunnel launching bullets and mines at us, he'll also need several hits to kill.

One other feature we will introduce is fuel, we'll scatter a few fuel tanks around the map, and perhaps when we kill a number of baddies, and if we pick them up, we will top-up a fuel bar that allows us to progress. So another condition of play, so far we have, don't die, kill the enemies, then kill the baddie at the end, and don't run out of fuel. Sounds like fun!

I don't think I need to explain the classes to you again, though unlike our platform game we have many more types to use. I'm also going to experiment with a different form of shared resources system, so the Enemy Map Class isn't quite as useful for me this time because each class type will keep track of its own set of graphics.

Add the following headers and cpp files to your project, they are all there in your source and header folders, so there's no typing for you to do.

Bomb, Explosion, Fuel, GunTower, Launcher, Mine, Eye, Squid, and Missile.

Also *make sure you add* #include *thenameoftheseheaders.h* to game.h so that all classes that need to know can be aware of the new types.

These are all our basic types of enemy we are going to have and each is contained in its own class and will take care of its shared frames and logic. Read the comments to see the behavior and you may change it if you want.

But still at this point we're not actually causing any of these baddies to be created, so that's next.

Our Game Class is responsible for this, though really it should be a level manager that does it, because having only one level isn't much of a game, once we get this all working that should be your next personal assignment, get multiple levels in.

Looking in the Game Class we need to add some info that will tell us where to place our baddies on the map. There are two valid schools of thought on this, we could have a special tile, tiles or marker in the map, which we can detect when we are drawing, and use it to generate baddies at that point, or we could keep a simple list of the positions we want to place things.

I prefer the former, if the editor used to make the map, allows that, and many do, but we will do the latter just in case you are not able to generate those markers.

So let's start with the Missiles. We want the missiles to repeatedly fire when their silo is on the screen, so we need to place launchers there, which in turn generate missiles.

The Launcher Class is there for you now so here are the coordinates to place them, put this somewhere in your Game.cpp file, you can if you really want make it part of your Game Class, but it's ok to just put them in free space or in the GameInit Function as local variables, for now (more good data for a level manager though).

```
int MissileStartPoints[][2] =
{
 { 16, 25 }, // these are the locations for a silo
 { 49, 23 },
 { 75, 21 },
 { 171, 23 },
 { 182, 23 },
 { 186, 24 },
 { 190, 24 }
};
```

Now this is clearly a 2D array, but I don't need to enter the size of the row(y) component, since the actual initialization of it will fill that in, however if I end up typing a lot of them, or editing this array I may lose track of the number of entries. It's not possible to use sizeof() to get the row component of a 2D array, it will only return the total size of the array... But we can get the size of the column component even though we know it's 2, in this case, by using `sizeof(MissileStartPoints[0])`.

It's no great mathematical surprise that you can get the row size by dividing the total by the column, like this:

```
int total = sizeof(MissileStartPoints);
int column = sizeof(MissileStartPoints[0]);
int row = total / column;
```

Now let's create some missile launchers, like this;

```
for (int i = 0; i < row; i++)
{
 Launcher* l = new Launcher();
 l->Xpos = MissileStartPoints[i][0]*16;
 l->Ypos = MissileStartPoints[i][1]*16;
 MyObjects.push_back(l);
}
```

These, of course, go *in the GameInit* function (which is a good prototype for a level manager). Once you have this in, compile and run, you should see some nice deadly nukes flying and blowing up on the roofs as they hit them.

So you've got the idea, *repeat this process for these* arrays:

```
int GunTowerPlacement[][2]  =
{
 {  10, 18 },
 {  33, 17 },
 {  63, 13 },
 {  93, 15 },
 {  113,19 },
 {  127,21 },
 {  145,18 },
};
```

Not bad eh? Feel free to add more entries to the arrays, put more things on screen, or alter the behavior of things as you wish in the classes. Why not put your own FuelPickup placement array in there and generate some fuel cells. Now that all the components are all in place, let's get the collisions and gameplay features sorted.

Process Everything?

Our previous games had modest-sized maps, and in turn had enemies that were in it, which tended to stay in a particular area, so even if they were offscreen they didn't really interact with the player if they went through their simple logic regardless of their visibility.

Here though we have potentially hundreds of bullet hurling aliens all coming right at you and, in turn, hundreds of bullets coming at you from the dark reaches of the end of the level, which is a kind of the idea, but bullets travel pretty fast and if every enemy is shooting at you it won't be long before we have a screen full of bullets. So we want to limit ourselves and make sure that only enemies who are inside a reasonable range are going to actually do anything. The rest of the time we are going to leave them dormant.

The key issue here is when to trigger the enemies logic. In this game it's fairly easy, we've only got about 10 screens worth of world, we can keep them in memory and update them all, but only actually do the logic and drawing when they are within a certain range of the main ship...that works ok, and we've done that with some of the enemies using a distance concept, but, it's not efficient, and I can give you a few reasons why?

1. We're processing objects that for the bulk of their existence do nothing.

2. We're creating objects which even with careful use of their graphics are taking up memory.

3. We're doing range tests on every active, but dormant object.

4. We're not using the GPU properly, more on that later.

Now, we probably have the horsepower to processes several hundred enemies, so it's not all that apparent, but at some point we may hit a wall and start to see the update rate drop, especially if you are using a slow target. There are several indisputable facts in game programming, one of them is you can never have enough horsepower, the more content we add, the more horsepower we use and then we are going to run out of that horsepower. We are beginning to see the wall, even if we've not hit it yet.

So we have to reduce the amount of processing we do. There are a couple of hints in the Skramble code that should give us some ideas. The Missile Launcher. Eye's and Squids. generate or spawn more enemies, and do so only when its practical do to this. This concept means that we can place a single enemy or triggering object on screen, and simply test for an appropriate point for it to go into its emitter mode. That way instead of testing a few hundred enemies all waiting for our ship to get into range, we only need test a few dozen launching systems. They don't even need to be visible on screen (though out current system does insist on having something to draw). It's always faster to not do anything, than to do something and even a simple range test repeated a few hundred times is processing we'd like to avoid.

Equally valid, we could place enemy emitter tiles within the map data, or as a special class of object, which is designed to generate multiple enemies once the player comes into range. This also reduces our Game Init quite a bit, we can focus on things that have to be at specific points, such as our gun towers and generate our enemy waves with a simple generator object. Spawning objects in this way takes the responsibility away from the initialization routines and lets you dictate a more variable range of values, perhaps to increase difficulty or intensity of generation, rather than having multiple arrays in your level manager.

No More Mr Nice Guy

With our baddies and pickups in place, and working a treat it's time to face up to the reality of the situation. These enemies are here to do us harm and we live in a cruel merciless universe where bullets actually hurt, we just have to detect when that hurt occurs, and make things go boom.

Collision here is divided into four basic ideas, objects hitting the walls, which we may or may not allow for some of our more aerobatic aliens. Bullets hitting the enemies and enemy bullets, or mines. As I've named them, hitting us and the forth, objects hitting objects because we have pickups, there needs to be a distinction between head on smashes with bad guys and collection of fuel. Of course, which is why I've got a Type identifier in the Enemy Class.

Start with the easy things first, from which most others derive, Objects hitting objects. There is a simple box check in the GameObject Class that can be used for any enemy to test with other enemies. There's no real need for an enemy to test if they hit each other, so it's quite straightforward to ask them to just test if they hit the player. So add that test to the Enemy code. Also make sure that you add some kind of reaction to the collision in each enemy.

Next, let's consider objects hitting the environment, I quite like the spread/circle formation baddies and they generally work best if not interacting with the environment, but even so, we blowup the missiles if they hit something, so we should do something with the others. Detection is simple, though a little clumsy, just scan through the tile-size chunks of space the sprite inhabits and test if we hit something. Now's a really good time to go back to an attribute system like we did for Bobs World.

Making the mines and enemy bullets deadly, is really just an extension of the Objects hitting Objects, again with the mines being more interested in the Player than any other objects. So go right ahead and add that.

Finally, the players bullets, and here we have our first slight hitch. When we had only one bullet it wasn't a major issue for an enemy to test for the bullet and decide if it had met an honorable death in combat. We have a spread of bullets now, which do we test for and how?

Well all of them, of course, which means some form of scanning though the Object list is going to be needed. But that is troubling, since we might have a few dozen bullets, a few dozen enemy bullets, few dozen mines, a few...you get the idea. There are many more nonlethal things to enemies than there are lethal things, so if we scan through them all we are going to be doing that thing we fear most, testing several things for a mostly negative result.

Again, on a game like this, this probably isn't an issue, but we should always seek to optimize when we can. In this case, a simple option is to keep a separate vector list of bullets in the Game Class, and have each potential target test against that vector, rather than the main object vector.

Sure it means keeping two lists, and maintaining them, but it is going to save us CPU time and that's not a bad thing. Just make sure when you mark a bullet for removal, you also remove it from the second list. That can be done with a Player function like this:

```
void Player::RemoveBullet(GameObject* b)
{
 // remove the bullet from the set of collidable bullets
 MyBullets.erase(std::remove(MyBullets.begin(), MyBullets.end(), b),
MyBullets.end());
}
```

Not exactly simple is it, and you need to add #include <algorithm> to your headers in Player.cpp. But that is one reasonable way to remove a thing from a vector.

I should say when I say reasonable, I mean in fact entirely unreasonable, as it's a slow and nasty scan and remove system, but until we use a better method this will work.

For this to work, I also had to make sure I had a Player* APlayer in the Game Class, because I keep the bullets in a static list in the Player and only the Player gets to access them, this is a complication, because although I am using different types of Object quite often, I am normally treating them all as their Base Class GameObject and letting override functions take control.

To allow a different object to access something that is specific to a type rather than their common GameObject or Enemy members, I need to have an instance of that type. I overcome this in the Game::GameInit() function making sure that APlayer is indeed a pointer to the Player part of my object and storing that in ThePlayer, which is defined as a GameObject*, this allows access to the more general GameObject methods and members.

Once collision is established it then falls to the individual objects to decide how to react. Bullets or mines will just vanish, but we do need to make sure that their targets are aware they were hit. So I added an AmIHit add a flag to our Enemy Class to indicate that. Since any object is in theory capable of being hit, it's probably best added to the GameObject Class.

Now each object can test that flag and decide how it will react, which will depend on the type, the DidIHitThis routine I put in GameObject is also virtual, so that will allow me to provide a different type of test for each type if I decide to do that, though in this case, I don't see any need.

At the end of every enemy update be sure to add a test like this, which will use the Enemy TestBullets() function, which in turn will use the GameObjects DidIHitThis().

```
if (this->TestBullets())
{
 MarkForRemoval = true;
 Explosion* e = new Explosion();
 e->Xpos = Xpos - 32 + 8;
 e->Ypos = Ypos - 16;
 e->Xspeed = 0;
 e->Yspeed = 0;
 Game::MyObjects.push_back(e);
}
```

If you are totally sure you plan to do exactly the same thing with every enemy type, there's no reason why this can't fit in your currently empty Enemy Update(), and use this:

```
Enemy::Update(G);
```

At the end of each type update. Or even have a general Enemy::CheckForDead() method, it's all up to you. For cleaner code this makes sense, for simplicity and allowing for experimentation use the end of update test.

What Will Make It Better?

Now as a game, this is a great foundation, you can add any number of baddies, give them some kind of logic, increase the bullet counts, number of instances, add fancier explosions, and just keep them coming, but is that codie sense tingling yet? We must try to do things better! That's a mantra, you should always try to keep at the front of you mind when you get something working. Must make it better!

One thing that will make quite a difference is introducing some of the better understood concepts of games, Intro screens, menus, and of course levels.

We call these concepts Game states, they are all part of a game but the processing of each part will result in different things. But often they will use the same functions and rendering systems.

A simple start-up screen is easy to consider as a simple class. Put up your best piece of game artwork, start playing your music, and wait for a suitable key to press before moving to a menu, which then allows you to set options.

The main issue of Game states is that they are independent and yet they can cause other states to change because they will set up or change values.

Setting Games States is not a major issue, we'll demonstrate that in the next game demo, but it's important to make sure that a game state is properly set up and properly closed down, so that the next state can operate with a fresh slate, but using any value the previous state needed to set up.

First, we have a much more important improvement we have to tackle.

There's No Wrong Way...But There Are Always Better Ways

The tile idea is functional, it does give us massive flexibility, but it's not very speedy, and not using the system to its best, there are several ways we can optimize this. We are currently so focused on our use of surfaces we simply have not used our GPU at all. This is a massive error for us, our GPU is waaaaaay better at manipulating graphics than our CPU, and we can't even do proper transparency on our surface. Never mind flipping, rotation, scaling, or Shader effects as automatic processes. Everything needs CPU cycles and we only have so many millions of those to waste.

Let's do a demo that will really push our CPU, and let us get some ideas of its limits, so far all our games are working pretty well, and we're not doing too much to actually stress the limits, by which I mean, we're able to get all our logic running, get our limited numbers of graphics drawn, and our screen updated in one frame, so we don't encounter the horrors of frame drop (unless you have a whole load of background tasks running, rather than using a nice clean machine). So, let's see what I can do to impress on you just how limited CPU drawing is.

For a FireWork, Life Is Short But Sweet!

Let's create a simple particle system. A particle is a very basic object; it has very limited logic, and ideally should do nothing more than move, draw, and in time die, perhaps transitioning to a different type, color, state, or whatever. They are usually, very small, though can be any size, we can draw them as images or simple pixels, typically making use of Alpha effects and other things, although our 2D surface system isn't terribly good with Alpha effects, so we can't really do some of the cooler effects like smoke; however, there are ways if you use a bit of imagination. The principles of particles are the same in 2D or 3D, so what we learn here we can use later and take advantage of 3D image processing's much better abilities.

Particles' most obvious use in games includes, smoke, fire, dust, blood splatters, fireworks, and so on, also they can be used to simulate a range of other things that have dynamic properties.

First download the Fireworks demo from the support site, it does not currently do too much, it's just an empty demo project, we're going to add the features to make it work, don't worry, this isn't going to be a lot of typing these things are very simple.

One thing we are going to need for this demo though, is a mouse, moving a cursor, or other pointer around on screen with keyboard controls is a bit of a pain, so it's time for the long dormant mouse routines to do their thing.

There's not a lot we have to do here really, our input routine already has a mouse event handler in place, and it's actually been there working all along, it operates in exactly the same way as the key readers we used already except it returns its data in this structure.

```
public:
 typedef struct // A very simple structure to hold the mouse info
 {
  int PositionX; // contains the relative position from the start point
(take care to not confuse it with the GUI mouse position)
  int PositionY;
  unsigned char LeftButton; // TRUE when pressed FALSE otherwise
  unsigned char MidButton;
  unsigned char RightButton;
 } MouseData;
```

This is the basic info return of most standard mouses...mice, meeces? Hmm I don't really know the plural of a desktop mouse, I'll assume it's the same as the rodents! As far as we are concerned we're only looking for the standard buttons and, most important, the positional information. What we have to be very careful of though, is that the mouse does not return an actual fixed position to the handling routine; we simply get the amount it moved, which is added to the last position, so our position value is only accurate if we know the original start value. And the only way to know the original start value is to set it up before we use it. So during our initializations, we have to make sure we do that, ideally in the center of the screen. Also remember input needs to be initialized, so do the pointer position init just after the instance init. Like this:

```
TheInput.Init(); / kick it off
TheInput.TheMouse.PositionX = SCRWIDTH / 2;
TheInput.TheMouse.PositionY = SCRHEIGHT / 2;
```

Mice also need an indicator on screen, so we need to be sure that we create a nice pointer object that can then be used to draw a pointer. Be sure to create a pointer to a Surface called MousePointer then you can add this to your mouse initialization lines:

```
MousePointer = new Surface("../Assets/MousePointer.png", FileHandler);
```

Now, we do have to be careful of one thing, our mouse is being tested on a process called a thread (we'll go into these later), which means that no matter what our program is doing, as soon as the mouse moves or a mouse button is clicked, the CPU is probably going to go and deal with the mouse code. I say probably, because it will also depend on the refresh rate of the mouse. But that usually is a prompt response by the CPU to deal with the mouse, which means if we move our mouse around a lot and keep moving it, as you would do in most games, it's entirely possible that our Mouse variables are going to change at different points in our game-loop processing, if we use them in one section and then in another it may cause odd things to happen. It may even have a tiny impact on performance.

We'll allow this for now, so we can see what the effect is, but afterward we need to be a little bit smarter, so we will make that change when it becomes clear we need it. I just want you to be aware of this niggly point.

That's pretty much it for the mouse, so long as the draw for the mouse pointer itself is the first or probably better, the last thing our system tries to draw, we will have a cool pointer that will react to our movements. You could put this in a draw list if you want it to be the first thing drawn, but potentially obscured by the other objects you're going to add. But if you want it to be the last thing, draw it after your main update loop.

```
MousePointer->CopyTo(m_Screen, TheInput.TheMouse.PositionX, TheInput.
TheMouse.PositionY);
```

Try it now. You should have a blank screen with a mouse pointer.

Let's start with a simple firework particle system, which on a click will place a number of particles on screen ready for updating a main loop.

The particles themselves will fly out randomly in all directions, losing some speed as they do and falling because the effects of gravity on their y motion, and also changing color from white hot to dark red before dying off, perhaps turning into ash and fading away?

So clearly we need a Particle Class, create a new header file called Particle.h making sure to store it in your Headers folder and filter locations, and enter this:

```
/ a particle is an object usually with small surface
#pragma once
#include "Objects.h"
#include "MyFiles.h"
class Particle : public Objects
{
public:
 Particle(); // normal is 1 x 1 surface
 Particle(char* fname, MyFiles* FileHandler); // allow us to make particles
from (small) images
 ~Particle();
 void Update(Surface* s); // of course we need our update
 Pixel Colour = 0xffffffff;
 float Time;
};
```

It's very simple as you can see, like all our simple 2D games it's going to use an Objects Class, which contains the info for position and speed.

Now to write the class itself. Add a new item to your Source folder and make sure that you navigate to the source directory when you create Particle.cpp

```
// Our particles are basically surfaces, but most of the time they will be
empty or 1 x 1 buffers,
#include "Particle.h"
Particle::Particle()
{
 Xpos = Ypos = Xspeed = Yspeed = 0; // clear these
 this->MarkForRemoval = false;
 this->Image = new Surface(Rand(2)+1, Rand(2)+1); // make a small surface
 this->Image->ClearBuffer(Colour);// using a fixed colour(hmm ok for now)
 Time = 4.0f ;
```

```
 Xspeed = 3.0f-Rand(6.0f);
 Yspeed = 3.0f-Rand(6.0f);
}
Particle::Particle(char* Fname, MyFiles* FH) : Objects(Fname, FH)
{} // add a file loading system if you need it
Particle::~Particle()
{} // Nothing much to do here at the moment.
void Particle::Update(Surface* mScreen)
{
 Objects::Update(mScreen); // our base class does this already so let it
do the work
 Time -= (1.0 / 30.0f); // assume (possibly wrongly) a 30fps frame rate
 if (Time < 0) this->MarkForRemoval = true;
// colour is a bit tricky
  unsigned int r = (Colour & REDMASK);
  unsigned int g = (Colour & GREENMASK) >> 8;
  unsigned int b = (Colour & BLUEMASK) >> 16;
  r -= 2;
  if (r > 255) r = 0;
  g -= 5;
  if (g > 255) g = 0;
  b -= 5;
  if (b > 255) b = 0;

  Colour = r + (g<<8) + (b<<16) + ALPHAMASK; // give it some alpha
  if (Colour == ALPHAMASK) this->MarkForRemoval = true; // it's dead so
kill it
  Image->ClearBuffer(Colour);
  Image->CopyTo(mScreen, (int)Xpos, (int)Ypos);
// finally assume they are affected by gravity and reduce the Speed
 Yspeed += 9.81f / 100; // use a real world value but scale to suit.
// give it a terminal vel
 if (Yspeed > 10.0f) Yspeed = 10.0f;
// and dampen the xspeed
 Xspeed *= 0.99f; // reduces it slowly
}
```

Again very simple, the constructor sets things up, I've left an empty file-based constructor you can add code to handle that if you want, and I allowed the size of the empty surface it creates to vary a little for variety. The meat is in the update, where I am using the fact I derive this class from the Objects Class, and because Objects Update, has functionality to move an object and bounce it off the edges I'm going to reuse that routine. Even though I am overriding that routine, the base routine is still accessible; that can be very useful. Then I do a bit of a tricky bit of color manipulation. This is a bit messy on this 2D buffer system, but it will work. I am splitting the RGB values into unsigned ints and shifting them to the lower 8 bits, to make it easier to decrement them. I am checking for >255 because an unsigned int cannot test for <0.

I don't reduce the red component by as much, so I get that white hot to dull red appearance I wanted and I do a test to see if all the RGB parts are reduced to 0, in which case I will kill the object regardless of how much time it has left.

Then the speed damping, when you multiply a positive or a negative number by a fraction, it reduces the scale of that number making it a neat way to reduce a value to almost 0.

If I am using arbitrary colors and want them to fade to black, it would make more sense to use a similar damping method and multiply each color component by a fraction. Later, though we'll discover much better ways to do that.

So now all we need to do is get the Game Class update to handle the mouse and make some nice particles for us.

That is also a simple bit of code we can add after we draw our objects:

```
if (TheInput.TheMouse.LeftButton == true)
{
 for (int i = 0; i < 40; i++)
 {
  Particle* p = new Particle();
  p->Xpos = (float) TheInput.TheMouse.PositionX;
  p->Ypos = (float) TheInput.TheMouse.PositionY;
  TheObjects.push_back(p);
 }
}
```

I've set it to create 40 new particles, which generate at random speeds in their constructor. This is not an elegant way of doing things though, so we won't be keeping it, but for now it will serve its purpose.

Fire it up and press your left mouse button and we should get some nice pixels appearing white and then fading to red.

Quite pretty, we can essentially create lovely, though slightly square, starbursts on the screen and keep doing it. But the particles only appear at the point we press, because of that inelegant game loop I added, I'd like something a bit neater, that allows us to choose where we generate the particles and allow us to track to another point on screen, so let's create an Emitter instead.

An emitter's job is basically to generate a small number of particles each update for as long as they are told to. We can also decide on how the particles are generated, in a burst or as a plume from behind a rocket; for example, maybe even different types of particle. We'll stick with a burst for now and if you want to add more types that's fine.

Our emitter should be able to create different types of particle though, so we need it to know what those are, and because each type of particle has different actions it would make sense for us to create new classes for the different types. Why not then also have different types of Emitter? Well why not indeed; we could have a plume emitter, a starburst emitter, a random spark emitter, and all sorts. But because their basic functionality is simply to produce particles I'm not sure there's quite enough variation in behavior to create different classes for the different emitters, so this is for me at least, one occasion where I'm going to simply create a list of enums, and have one Emitter Class, but creating different styles of particle. The choice is yours, if you find your emitters start to become complex then breaking them down to different classes for each type makes sense.

Like a Particle Class, and anything we want to update in our list, our Emitter is a type that can use the base class *Objects*, so we will derive it from that. Unlike most of our Objects though, we actually don't plan to render it, but we still need a dummy surface in the Image Class, which we should probably avoid, we can do that later. Create an Emitter header file in the usual way and add this:

```
// Emitters
#pragma once
#include "Objects.h"
#include "MyFiles.h"
#include "Particle.h"
#include "Game.h"
class Emmitter: public Objects
{
public:
 Emitter();
 Emitter(char* fname, MyFiles* FileHandler); // allow us to make particles
from (small) images
 ~Emitter();
 void Update(Surface* s); // of course we need our update
// to add to the vector/list we need to know where Game is;
 void Init(Game* G);
 float Time; // how long do I emit for?
 int HowManyPerUpdate; // how many should I update
 Game* WhereIsGame;
};
```

Surprisingly small, isn't it? It will get a bit bigger when we add different types, for now we're just going to focus on making that squareburst system. Time to make a new Emitter.cpp file and that looks like this:

```
#include "Emitter.h"
// constructors and destructors
Emitter::Emitter()
{
 this->Image = new Surface(1, 1); // we need a dummy surface
};
Emitter::Emitter(char* fname, MyFiles* FileHandler) {}; // allow us to make
particles from (small) images
Emitter::~Emitter() {};

void Emitter::Update(Surface* s)
{
 Time -= (1.0 / 30.0f);

 if (Time < 0) this->MarkForRemoval = true;
 for (int i = 0; i < HowManyPerUpdate; i++)
 {
  Particle* p = new Particle();
  p->Xpos = this->Xpos;
  p->Ypos = this->Ypos;
  WhereIsGame->TheObjects.push_back(p);
 }
} // of course we need our update

// to add to the vector/list we need to know where Game is;
void Emitter::Init(Game* G)
{
 MarkForRemoval = false;
 Time = 1.0f;
```

```
HowManyPerUpdate = 4;
WhereIsGame = G;
Xpos = (float) G->TheInput.TheMouse.PositionX;
Ypos = (float) G->TheInput.TheMouse.PositionY;
};
```

Again surprisingly simple, though I've allowed for expansion with a constructor using a file name, I've not used it yet, but I know some particle systems might want to use an image. Notice that Init function? It needs to be called to set up the Emitter, and we can do that by altering the generation code in Game.cpp to now look like this:

```
if (TheInput.TheMouse.LeftButton == true)
{
 Emitter* Emit = new Emitter();
 Emit->Init(this);
 TheObjects.push_back(Emit);
}
```

Remember to add Emitter.h to your cpp of Game.h list of includes. We could make the constructor do all this setting up, but remember we're planning to add different types, so let's keep the constructor as simple as possible and we can expand the init or even add a different init or inits for different types.

Now compile and run, to try this code for size and notice that when you press and release you get nice individual squarebursts. Try not to keep your finger on the mouse key though, as you'll end up generating an awful lot of particles, and that will strain our systems, something I'll discuss shortly.

Why exactly are we getting squarebursts though? Why not nice round blooms? It's because of the way we are using clamped random values on the X and Y, they will produce vector directions going out from the point of origin and since they have an effective clamp not based on a radius, it can't do the nice round effect we want, so it looks unnaturally square, even if it is kinda cool it's not really what we want. So let's expand the system now to create different types of emitter so that we can have a bloom, and also different types of particles to get us going.

A New Dawn for Particle Kind!

Our current *Particle* is really a hot decaying Particle and we shouldn't really have its speeds for motion set up in the constructor, that's more the emitters job, but the key function of time and knowing when to die are what makes it useful, in fact that's kinda the only logic we care about here that makes it a particle. The individual behavior of the particle will vary so we should create new classes that process the behavior and then let the Particle Class update function, process the decay, and doom of our short but beautiful life.

Create a new header called HotDecay.h and maybe put it in a new filter on your solution, because you might make a lot of these, I've made a filter called Particles. The files themselves can still live in the Header and Source directories, but once these simple things are made we might want to fold away the filter and forget about these files later. HotDecay.h should contain this:

```
// a simple hot particle that is affected by gravity
#pragma once
#include "Objects.h"
```

```
#include "MyFiles.h"
#include "Particle.h"

class HotDecay : public Particle
{
public:
 HotDecay(); // normal is 1 x 1 surface
 ~HotDecay();

 void Update(Surface* s); // of course we need our update

};
```

As you can see, just a simple constructor/destructor pair and an update system, since I am inheriting from Particle, it will have the Time value, and since Particle inherits from Objects, all the other useful data are in there. This time I have not left a constructor for a file in here, since I'm quite sure that on this occasion I'm not going to use it.

Make a new HotDecay.cpp file, again perhaps by adding a filter in your solution, and add this code:

```
#include "HotDecay.h"

HotDecay::HotDecay()
{
// we can set these up here a defaults but the emmiter should change them
 Xpos = Ypos = Xspeed = Yspeed = 0; // clear these
 this->MarkForRemoval = false;
 this->Image = new Surface(Rand(2) + 1, Rand(2) + 1); // make a small
surface slightly different sizes
 this->Image->ClearBuffer(Colour);   // create a blue dot
 Time = 4.0f;
 Xspeed = 3.0f - Rand(6.0f);
 Yspeed = 3.0f - Rand(6.0f);
}
HotDecay::~HotDecay(){}

void HotDecay::Update(Surface* mScreen)
{
 Particle::Update(mScreen);
// colour is a bit tricky
 unsigned int r = (this->Colour & REDMASK);
 unsigned int g = (Colour & GREENMASK) >> 8;
 unsigned int b = (Colour & BLUEMASK) >> 16;
 r -= 2;
 if (r > 256) r = 0;
 g -= 5;
 if (g > 256) g = 0;
 b -= 5;
 if (b > 256) b = 0;

 Colour = r + (g << 8) + (b << 16) + 0xff000000;
 if (Colour == ALPHAMASK) this->MarkForRemoval = true; // it's dead so kill it

 Image->ClearBuffer(Colour);
 Image->CopyTo(mScreen, (int)Xpos, (int)Ypos);

// finally assume they are affected by gravity and reduce the Ypeed
 Yspeed += 9.81f / 100; // use a real world value but scale to suit.
```

```
// give it a terminal vel
 if (Yspeed > 10.0f) Yspeed = 10.0f;

// and dampen the xseed
 Xspeed *= 0.99f; / reduces it slowly
}
```

It should be pretty clear that this is the old Particle code itself, now with the logic separated into this class. The Particle.cpp update routine has had this code removed, and now looks like this:

```
void Particle::Update(Surface* mScreen)
{
 Objects::Update(mScreen); // our base class does this already so let it
do the work
 Time -= (1.0 / 30.0f); // assume (possibly wrongly) a 30fps frame rate

 if (Time < 0) this->MarkForRemoval = true;
}
```

Finally, our Emiter.cpp file needs to change a little, instead of creating particles it now creates HotDecay objects.

```
void Emitter::Update(Surface* s)
{
 Time -= (1.0 / 30.0f);

 if (Time < 0) this->MarkForRemoval = true;
 for (int i = 0; i < HowManyPerUpdate; i++)
 {
  HotDecay* HD = new HotDecay();
  HD->Xpos = this->Xpos;
  HD->Ypos = this->Ypos;
  WhereIsGame->TheObjects.push_back(HD);
 }
} // of course we need our update
```

Ok, let's try that, compile and we should get basically the same result as before, we've not added new types yet, so that's our next step. Remember to backup your work now.

Time to add different types of particle, let's do another simple firework-style particle, we'll call them ColourFades, the particle itself will be much the same as the HotDecay but let's not have gravity interact with it, and allow for a range of colors which will fade to black and die.

As before add ColourFades.h and ColourFades.cpp, ColourFades.h is basically unchanged from HotDecay but we still need to define the values so copy and paste it and change all the HotDecay to ColourFades. But add three new values to the ColourFade Class members.

```
float r, g, b;
```

Now, return to your Emitter.h file, we need to allow the emitter a means to understand what the different types are and to generate them accordingly, most of that we can do with a simple switch/case system, but we need to provide that, so alter the header by adding a new typedef set of enums and a variable called p_type.

```cpp
class Emitter: public Objects
{
public:
 typedef enum ParticleType
 {
  T_HotDecay = 1,
  T_ColourFade
 } ParticleType;

 Emitter();
 Emitter(char* fname, MyFiles* FileHandler); // allow us to make particles
from (small) images
 ~Emitter();

 void Update(Surface* s); // of course we need our update

// to add to the vector/list we need to know where Game is;
 void Init(Game* G);
 float Time; // how long do I emit for?
 int HowManyPerUpdate; // how many should I update
 Game* WhereIsGame;
 ParticleType PType;

};
```

I have prefixed the enum names with T_ just to avoid confusion with the class names, also I made the enum start at 1, because 0 can be a useful means to force a default error.

That should be all we need to do to the Emitter header for now, let's return to the Emitter.cpp and make a change to allow use of these different types.

Aside from making sure we add the relevant header files each time we create a new particle type, the action is going to take place in the init and Update functions, let's start with Update.

Which looks like this:

```cpp
void Emitter::Update(Surface* s)
{
 Time -= (1.0 / 30.0f);
 if (Time < 0) this->MarkForRemoval = true;

 switch (PType)
 {
 case T_HotDecay:
  { // I like to keep my case in brackets
   for (int i = 0; i < HowManyPerUpdate; i++)
   {
    HotDecay* HD = new HotDecay();
    HD->Xpos = this->Xpos;
    HD->Ypos = this->Ypos;
    WhereIsGame->TheObjects.push_back(HD);
   }
   break;
  }
 case T_ColourFade:
```

```
   { // I like to keep my case in brackets
     break;
   }
  default:
    {
      printf("We seem to be attempting an undefined Particle type");
      break;
    }
  } // end Switch
} // of course we need our update
```

I only have the HotDecay code at the moment but that's fine. Since we've added a concept of a type to the Emitter, we will need to provide that when we set it up, so in the Game.cpp file, change the trigger system to this:

```
if (TheInput.TheMouse.LeftButton == true)
  {
    Emitter* Emit = new Emitter();
    Emit->Init(this);
    Emit->PType = Emitter::ParticleType::T_HotDecay;
    TheObjects.push_back(Emit);
  }
```

And that's that, our system is set up so that when we Press a Left mouse button we will produce a hotdecay squareburst. Time to add a more subtle ColourFade to the RightButton, You can guess the code you need to add to the Game Class just after this, can't you? Do one for the Right button that generates ColourFades.

The ColourFade particle needs to have a color value to fade with, and the standard default particle sets a hard value as a default, and it's of a Pixel type, which is an integer value. Integers don't work terribly well for smooth scaling but it is what we are forced to work with. But there is nothing stopping us from keeping float copies of our values, which is why we added float r, g, b to our ColourFade header file. We should also add a new constructor definition to that header file, to turn our int color values into floats, so in there add this after the default constructor:

```
ColourFade(Pixel Col); // set up the colours
```

In the ColourFade.cpp file, that new constructor looks like this:

```
ColourFade::ColourFade(Pixel Col)
{
  // we can set these up here a defaults but the emmiter could change them
  Xpos = Ypos = 0; / clear these
  this->MarkForRemoval = false;
  this->Image = new Surface(Rand(2) + 1, Rand(2) + 1); // make a small
surface slightly different sizes
  Time = 4.0f; // set a reasonable lifetime
  Xspeed = 3.0f - Rand(6.0f);
  Yspeed = 3.0f - Rand(6.0f);
  Colour = Col;
  this->Image->ClearBuffer(Colour);
  r = (float) (Col & REDMASK);
  g = (float) ( (Col & GREENMASK) >> 8 );
  b = (float) ( (Col & BLUEMASK) >> 16 );
}
```

The default constructor is cleared out and is now empty as this now is the main constructor we will use, so it sets up the values it needs.

We still need to tell the emitter how to do things with this new constructor, so replace the empty code in your emmiter for the T_ColourFade case with this:

```
case T_ColourFade:
  { // I like to keep my case in brackets
    for (int i = 0; i < HowManyPerUpdate; i++)
    {
      int Colour = 0xffe0e0e0; / reddy yellow
      ColourFade* FD = new ColourFade(Colour);
      FD->Xpos = this->Xpos;
      FD->Ypos = this->Ypos;
      WhereIsGame->TheObjects.push_back(FD);
    }
    break;
  }
```

So we've got color the new constructor breaks it down into floats and it's time for the Update in ColourFade to now use those floats and covert them back to int, so it will look like this:

```
void ColourFade::Update(Surface* mScreen)
{
  Particle::Update(mScreen); // add the velocity
// colour is a bit tricky
  r *= 0.98f;
  if (r < 0.05f) r = 0.0f;
  g *= 0.96f;
  if (g < 0.05f) g = 0.0f;
  b *= 0.96f;
  if (b < 0.05f) b = 0.0f;
  Colour = ((unsigned int) r + (( (unsigned int) g ) << 8) + (( (unsigned
int) b ) << 16) ) + 0xff000000; / <<<<< ugggh

  if (Colour == ALPHAMASK) this->MarkForRemoval = true; // it's dead so kill it
  Image->ClearBuffer(Colour);
  Image->CopyTo(mScreen, (int)Xpos, (int)Ypos);

// and dampen the speed
  Xspeed *= 0.99f; // reduces it slowly
  Yspeed *= 0.99f;
}
```

Yeah that casting of floats back to ints is pretty horrible, but we can rest easy that we won't be using such horrible methods when we have some proper maths systems to play with, for now it's a side effect of our Pixel system encoding its colors as bytes.

And there you have it, you should be able to press the left button to get a gravity-affected squareburst with white to red particles, and right button for a nongravity-affected erm squareburst. Time to change that.

Our Emitter is using the Particle default random values for speed, but we can alter those, we want to create a bloom, which basically is a circular pattern, so let's randomly pick a certain number between 0 and 2PI as our angle (remember 2PI is 360° represented as Radians), don't forget to add #include <math> to our list of headers in this file because we're going to use some standard maths functions.

Our new ColourFade emmiter looks like this:

```
case T_ColourFade:
{
for (int i = 0; i < HowManyPerUpdate; i++)
  {
   int Colour = 0xffe0e0e0; // chose
   ColourFade* FD = new ColourFade(Colour);
   float deg = Rand(2*PI); // somewhere on the circle
   float radius = 10.0f; //any value will do
   Xspeed = cos(deg)*radius; // store them in our unused speed values
   Yspeed = sin(deg)*radius;
   // normalise the range
   float Mag = sqrt(Xspeed*Xspeed + Yspeed * Yspeed);
FD->Xspeed = ((Xspeed / Mag)*Time)* (3 + Rand(1.0f)); // add a bit of
randomness
   FD->Yspeed = ((Yspeed / Mag)*Time) * (3 + Rand(1.0f));
   FD->Xpos = this->Xpos;
   FD->Ypos = this->Ypos;
   WhereIsGame->TheObjects.push_back(FD);
  }
 break;
}
```

Just a bit of maths to ensure that the values are normalized to less than one and then multiplied by a scale factor. I added a tiny bit of randomness to the speed to avoid too much regularity creating interference bands.

Ok add this, run it, and hopefully be happy with the result, but when we stop the demo, we may start to curse the fact we cannot redirect the mouse clicks away from the GUI and find we have multiple windows open on our GUI, which opened up when we pressed the right mouse. This is indeed annoying and something I am chasing Sysprogs about, but never fear, the simplest thing to do on a Raspberry is ctrl/alt/F1 all at the same time, and now we're in the terminal mode, where the mouse does not give us any hassle. Though you may find yourself with a long list of terminal gobbledegook if using key controls, it's not likely to be anything more than a syntax error. Our mouse, however, can do real damage because we have no idea what we are opening/closing/saving/sending our pin code. If you want to go back into GUI mode (not wise at the moment), type start and enter.

We can now add any Particle Classes we want, just extend the enum in Emitters.h, write the particles behavior in a class, and provide the correct emitter for it. We'll do more of these later, but it's time to take stock of what we can do with our Double Buffer style architecture.

I'll give you one more simple type and you can work out how to add it yourself now. It's called a plume and probably best used for engine exhausts or things that need a constant stream of particles that never ends. I won't give you a walk through on this one, you know enough now to add this yourself, use the middle button to place it though consider that it could be attached to another object? Here's the h file:

```
// a simple directed direction colour fading to red, no gravity
#pragma once
#include "Objects.h"
#include "MyFiles.h"
#include "Particle.h"
#include "stdio.h"
```

```
class Plume: public Particle
{
public:
 Plume(); // normal is 1 × 1 surface
 Plume(Pixel Col, float lifetime); // set up the colours and life
 ~Plume();

 void Update(Surface* s); // of course we need our update
 float r, g, b; // we need float versions
 float ThreeQuarters;
};
```

Note, I've added another variable specific to this type, ThreeQuarters, since I want to allow for some time to pass before I modify the red component of the color, as you can see in this cpp file:

```
#include "Plume.h"
Plume::Plume() {}
Plume::~Plume() {}
Plume::Plume(Pixel Col, float LifeTime)
{
 Xpos = Ypos = Xspeed = Yspeed = 0; // clear these the emitter will set
them
 this->MarkForRemoval = false;
 this->Image = new Surface(Rand(2) + 2, Rand(2) + 2); // make a small
surface slightly different sizes
 this->Image->ClearBuffer(Colour);  // create a dot

 Colour = Col;

 this->Image->ClearBuffer(Colour);
 r = (float)(Col & REDMASK);
 g = (float)((Col & GREENMASK) >> 8);
 b = (float)((Col & BLUEMASK) >> 16); // its going to be 0 but allow for
other options
 Time = LifeTime;
 ThreeQuarters = Time * 0.75f;

}
void Plume::Update(Surface* mScreen)
{
 Particle::Update(mScreen); // add the velocity
// colour is variable, we don't need blue, and we want red to only decay at
1st, so that the tail becomes more red use time to increase the red content
 if (Time > ThreeQuarters)
 {
  r *= 0.98f;
  if (r < 0.05f) r = 0.0f;
 }
 g *= 0.98f;
 if (g < 0.05f) g = 0.0f;

 Colour = ((unsigned int) r + (((unsigned int) g) << 8) ) + 0xff000000;
 if (Colour == ALPHAMASK) this->MarkForRemoval = true; // its dead so kill it

 Image->ClearBuffer(Colour);
 Image->CopyTo(mScreen, (int)Xpos, (int)Ypos);
// and dampen the speed
```

```
 Xspeed *= 0.98f; / reduces it slowly
 Yspeed *= 0.98f;
}
```

Finally, the Emitter trigger looks like this:

```
case T_Plume:
{
 for (int i = 0; i < HowManyPerUpdate; i++)
 {
  int Colour = 0xff00ffff; // choose start yellow
  Plume* Pl = new Plume(Colour, 1.5f); // create

  float randRange = Range - (Rand(Range * 2)); // add a + or -1 rand to
the direction to create a cone
  float deg = DEG2RAD((this->Direction+randRange));
  float radius = 10.0f; //any value will do
  Xspeed = cos(deg)*radius; // store them in our unused speed values
  Yspeed = sin(deg)*radius;
   // normalise the range
  float Mag = sqrt(Xspeed*Xspeed + Yspeed * Yspeed);
  Pl->Xspeed = ((Xspeed / Mag)*Time)* (3 + Rand(1.0f)); // add a bit of
randomness
  Pl->Yspeed = ((Yspeed / Mag)*Time) * (3 + Rand(1.0f));
  Pl->Xpos = this->Xpos;
  Pl->Ypos = this->Ypos;
  WhereIsGame->TheObjects.push_back(Pl);
 }
   break;
}
```

Take care to notice, there are two new variables added to the Emitter Class not shown here: (1) Direction and (2) Range. Direction is naturally enough the direction in which the particles flow toward, expressed as a degree value in a float, and range is a ± amount we can deviate around that direction to create a cone. I'll let you work out how to add them in your header.

All three systems working together on one spot do create rather a nice image, hence why it's called Fireworks.

Plume is probably best not to be continually activated on a mouse button, better to activate it once with a very long lifetime, or have it activated every second or so, behind a ship for an exhaust effect? That might mean having an Emitter attached to your ship so that the ship's position is reflected in points of emission.

You can tinker with these values to get nice effects, and, of course, it would be much better if you could pass the controlling variables as parameters to your system.

As the level of complexity increases you will find that you may need to add a few more *standard* variables to the Emitter so that it can create the right kinds of particles. You may also prefer to send more variables to the particle types constructors, themselves rather than use an init system. It's up to you how you manage it.

All three of these simple particle systems could be plugged into our existing games quite simply for explosions, engine plumes, and so on, and ideally make proper use of our vec2 Class, which I omitted here. I've written them to be stand-alone and just add the headers you create. The particles can actually work as stand-alone concepts, but are best used with Emitters.

Now, I don't really want to spend too much more time on these, because without transparency, scaling, rotation, and other nice effects we don't have with this 2D system, these particles are rather lacklustre, limited, and a bit dull, but the principles for creating and using them are consistent in 2D and 3D, so we will come back to particles when we have a bit more technical knowledge to give us these missing features.

There's Always a Price to Pay

Hopefully, you will have noticed something as we've done this demo. Did you keep your finger pressed on the buttons so that it continually produced emitters which in turn produced particles? And did you notice how it become more and more sluggish, though having them die-off allowed it to keep going. Perhaps you have the FPS counter displaying on your debugger, did you notice the FPS drop? I hope so or this particular exercise will be in vain! But let's really push the boat out, in the Emitters init routine, change,

```
HowManyPerUpdate = 4;
```

From 4 to 40, make sure you can see your debug output on your debugger and try again. Press and hold the button and move around.

Wow…now…that's what I call a slow down, and look how quickly it happened. We finally can clearly see we have very distinct limits on how many things we can process and update, and as we increase the numbers of things being drawn, our game gets slower and slower, which is sad as it's only really drawing a few thousand pixels, we'd expect to do so much more, but the processing needed to make those few thousand things work is immense! We're starting to get the idea, that no matter how powerful our CPU is, there are limits that can quickly be reached just by repeating a few functions often enough. It's not the end for this system, we can still use it for simple games and even for moderate use of particles, but clearly its time we took a step up, and try to maximize our use of our targets power not just its CPU.

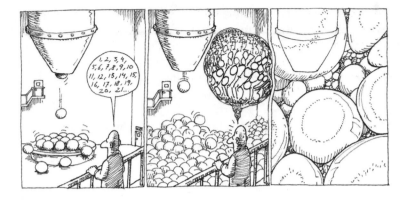

Handling Large Numbers of Objects

The heavy use of particles easily maxed out our drawing abilities after trying to draw a few thousand pixels it became noticeably chuggy, even doubling the CPU clock speed is only going to give us a few thousand more pixels before the frame rate drops, the actual number will depend largely on your CPU's clock speed. So the limit is finite and aside from a little optimization of code, and cheats using delta time to create the illusion of timed movement, it is pretty much an unbreakable upper limit of how many clock cycles we get to use. No matter how fast our CPU is, no matter how many cores, threads, or other tricks it has to improve performance, we can only do so many instructions in 1/60th of a second. This is one of the most annoying constraints you will have when you work on a target machine. Be it a Raspberry Pi, or a 10th-Gen console they are always designed to run at a certain speed and no more! PCs can update their CPU every so often and still have their projects able to run faster, new GPUs also can give a boost. But a Raspberry Pi Model2B, is always going to be a Raspberry Pi Model2B. You have no means to boost its hardware, you just have to buy a Model3B and start again.

We could make a lot of improvements by using the GPU properly and setting up some code to use the GPU to render 2D, but that's a bit of a waste of our time just now and ironically it involves us actually knowing how to do 3D on the GPU, so for now it's time for us to leave 2D behind. I hope you had fun with it, you can come back to it anytime but I suggest you wait until you have a better grasp of how to use OpenGLES2.0 properly and can use it to write a proper 2D render system.

Locking the Frame Rate

Just before we finish this section, let's talk very briefly about the frame rate. Our rather slow choice of update method has effectively meant our games have updated at a more or less consistant 30 fps on a Raspberry Pi3B. And there are logical reasons for this. Most SBCs and even PCs have their update rate locked to the frame rate of their monitors, which is usually 60 fps. But because we were using a system, which required us to write a massive amount of data to a texture buffer before the screen was swapped, we effectively took one frame to process and write that texture, and then our system waited for what's known as a vblank, a signal from the monitor to inform the display system that the screen is not currently updating and it is safe to update without causing a tear pattern on the screen. Its always best to update during this vblank point, because we don't really want to see part of the previous display and a part of the new display, this shearing effect is unpleasant on the eye.

A smaller texture size might have allowed us to get the process/update and display done before the vblank, but it would be a bit small.

Now 30 fps is actually quite an acceptable frame rate for most things, but 60 is better, but what about 100 or 200?

Well the actual frame rate you can update, can be pretty much anything, it will depend entirely on how much work you do in your main loops, but we're always going to be stuck with the frame rate of the monitor. You can release the lock by adding this line to your graphics init system;

```
eglSwapInterval(state->display,0); / set to 1 for frame lock
```

With this in place your game will now run totally free and you can ask the GPU to update the instant you have sent the last values to it, though you should also recall that GPU instructions can take a little time to process, so you might also look into adding this at the end of each game update after you swap the screens.

```
glFinish();
```

Which will hold the system until the GPU is done allowing you to proceed. Though it will work fine, if you are running without a lock, you have no real idea where or when the draw is going to start, and as a result you will almost certainly get sheering, but, it will be faster, and sometimes slower, and then faster again, inconsistency can be quite annoying, we'll discuss that soon.

These lock functions make more sense in 2D games than 3D, simply because in 2D, things tend to be a little more consistent, but as we'll see in 3D, a lot more data flying around deciding what gets drawn and not drawn can make the speed of your processing and graphic loop so much more variable and then it's time to make a choice to lock your frame rate down, to something you know can handle a worst case situation, 15 or 30 fps, or unlock your frame rate and aim for a desired rate, while keeping accurate time of how long things have taken and use compensation systems to allow for the fact some frames run slower than others. We've touched on delta timing before, but we'll soon start to use it more seriously.

▉ Recapping the 2D Experience

So we've written a bunch of games, mostly based on classic titles from the past, which have taken our understanding of manipulating of objects to new levels, we've seen how improvements to our data and resource management can vastly improve performance and memory usage.

We've got a nice little utility library, we have collision, culling, basics of AI, or more accurately enemy logic, even some basic understanding of physics in the form of gravity and motion in place. We've learned how to organize our project files and introduced some structure into our game organization, progressing from very messy C style code to something approaching organized C++ architecture.

We can scroll, we can give characters logic, and we can automate processes. We know how to read keys (and mouse but that's better in 3D). We understand how our memory is organized and we can create massive numbers of objects and maintain them without leaking memory. We have established working systems for displaying maps, screens, text, sprites, particles, emitters, and quite *importantly* we've recognized that there are better ways to do some things that make better use of our hardware.

We did a lot, I sneaked in some things when you weren't looking too, and you are using the same kind of logic and maths systems the pros use.

But we can do more. YOU can do more. Now's the time for you to make a game of your own, you have all the tools you need to create pretty much any classic arcade game, or something totally new of your own design.

Take a look at some of the classic 1980s and 1990s arcade games before 3D really became a force. Pick one that you feel you can do. There are thousands, and I want you to try one. Find something that has its graphics and audio available online and get cracking. You can start from scratch or adapt one of our games here to make your game.

Don't be afraid to copy a game, there's no harm in writing your own homage of a classic game for learning purposes, so long as you don't distribute it or seek to make money out of it.

I would LOVE to see some screenshots of your game, you'll find a contact e-mail on the support site, show me your efforts, and let me know how you found your first attempt to work alone on a full game.

6 A New Third Dimension

The world of 3D may seem a radical change from 2D, though it seems to be simply a case of an extra direction, the whole means of display and interaction totally changes in 3D. Our code needs to be able to handle that extra dimension and our graphics systems change considerably. BUT, the concepts of the games themselves don't really change that much. You still have objects that you manipulate in normal code, you still have an environment to interact with, and you still have the basic game loops. 3D certainly adds a new direction, but, in general, the gameplay code isn't going to change so much that you can't adapt.

Its ultimately up to you how much you want to involve yourself in the technical side of 3D rendering and other technical skills, by now you should feel a bit more comfortable in your coding, getting some games up, and running in our simple 2D system should have removed a lot of fears. We're passed our baby steps and it's time to take some long strides in our walking.

That said, there is no escaping the fact we're about to venture into a pretty heavy and scary chunk of technical stuff, we need to make direct use of our hardware through OpenGLES2.0 and gain a greater understanding of how 3D works, to get it working the way we want.

This will be a BIG leap for a beginner and even taking it slow we've got to absorb a lot. (Translated… I'm going to waffle about tech for a hundred pages or so, this is a BIG chapter). It would be so much easier for us to proceed by simply ignoring the rendering as much as possible; I could just give you the framework and we could then move into the games. But I think we're here to learn how to push ourselves and our targets; so I'm going to spend this chapter exploring the development of our 3D framework.

So get ready, make a fresh pot of caffeine-based beverage and order some pizza. The next chunk of heavy text is going to go into that, but take heart, once we have a *functional* rather than excellent rendering system, we're going to move into gameplay mechanics and not worry too much about the technical stuff, which we'll add in smaller easier to digest bites.

Are you ready? Let's get started!

▮ A Short Explanation of 3D

Now so far we've focused on controlling a character/avatar, which we move around the flat world it inhabits either side on or top–down, and we simply show what's around it to create some form of interactive environment. Movement of all objects is done in X and Y planes and we have ignored the concept of depth, which in 3D is represented by the Z-axis. But even though we ignored it, it was always there, set to 0.

Three-dimensional games do exactly the same kinds of logic and interaction as 2D, BUT, that pesky third dimension now comes into play. However…consider we are still moving an avatar left and right, up and down, inside of some kind of world space, as we have done already in map-based games. It's not really a massive leap to consider moving our character in and out. In fact, that's pretty much all we need to do, add Z concepts to our code and let the characters move in three dimensions.

There's a bit of trickiness insofar that we need to figure out some way to add a control for that in and out movement, we also need to change some of the interaction system, and we no longer have simple tiles we can check. The biggest technical problems actually come from being able to represent or render what is going on in our play world on a screen. We do understand the concept of direction, we did it in our top–down chase game, but suppose instead of eight directions, we have full 360° of direction in three axes, that is, point it to that third star on the left and up a bit, and keep going till morning.

So if it's that easy why is it so hard to write 3D games? Well, movement is easy, we know how to use vectors now, and 3D vectors are simply the addition of a third Z element, but visualization of our objects on a 2D screen, is rather more difficult and requires us to think differently about how we draw or *render* our world. We also need to consider things such as orientation and distance from our viewpoint, giving us rotation and scaling issues, and working out what to draw on screen and what to cull, and dealing with things going in front of other things.

That third dimension really adds a tonne of new visual features but also a tonne of problems to overcome.

Now it's important, very important that you think about this, because this will keep you grounded. You need to be confident that though visualization is complex; manipulation of objects in your world space is not. We know that we can detach drawing from our object manipulation, so even if you find the technical side of rendering hard, all we need to do is just get the basics up and running and then we can focus on movement.

Movement is a case of taking the 2D code we have, adding a third dimension, and reworking some of the motion maths to cope with 3D coordinates and terrains. Manipulation of our characters when kept separate from the rendering is quite a trivial task, but until we have our display code working we can't properly see it, and a text-based 3D shooting game is a genre that's not done at all well in sales charts.

Try to think about how you look at something, this page for example…your head is probably tilted slightly forward, the book will be in front of you, and you're comfortably reading this at a distance you find most suitable for your eyes to focus. If you have it flat on the table, pick it up for a moment and hold it in front of you while we do a small demonstration.

Holding the book open with both hands, turn the book about 45° to the right keep your head upright.

Clearly relative to your head the book is now 45°, now tilt your head 45° or so to the left, try to keep your eyes looking forward relative to your head… I know it'll make reading this a bit hard but keep glancing back.

Both your head containing your eyes, which is your camera to the world around you, and the book have essentially created a 90° angle. Each moved relative to the other….45° left and 45° right.

Now suppose you tilt your head back….say 45° again. Your camera (eyes) are now pointing well away from where that book is…your camera and your book, are twisted and turned relative to each other and in their own right.

But your head is still on top of your shoulders, and the book is still in your hands, both things are still in the same place in the universe…only your relative view has changed.

Ok, return to your normal reading position, and let's talk a little about what that all means, that tiny example, of things moving and rotating relative to each other, moving in space, and rotating in their position, is an example of the kind of things we have to calculate, it's actually quite intensive, and even worse we have to do this for every point that defines a part of an image. These points, called vertices, (singular vertex) can number in the 100's of thousands on an average game! So doing calculations on all of them becomes a massive amount of computation. We've already seen how poorly our CPU handles a few thousand particle pixels. So can our GPU cope with so much more?

Well yes, is the simple answer, because our GPU is specifically designed to calculate the positions of vertices relative to a camera viewpoint, but it relies on two things.

- Vertices, which are points in 3D space, representing x, y, and z coordinates, give the basic position of a dot in space.

- Matrices, which are fancy mathematical arrays that contain information that relates to position, rotation, translation and scale, or size of the object.

These two concepts are key to the way we can move things around.

So, there's no way to escape the fact the visualization is hard, very hard, but again it's pretty much a very well understood series of mathematical processes that work out how to represent the 3D we want to view onto a 2D screen. We don't need to reinvent the wheel, we just need to make sure it's round and has enough tread on it to do the job.

As with our 2D games we'll start with some simple systems to allow our framework to grow and handle the new problems we're about to incur when we write our first game.

Our 3D systems will be basic but functional and we'll add features as we go.

The first and most important thing to think about is that we are placing objects into a 3D space, which we call a world or a scene. When doing our 2D games we were also employing a scene, but it was a scene with one flat object on it with a texture we altered to give the appearance of a screen. Basically imagine yourself in the middle of the front row of a cinema watching a movie; all you can see when you are that close, is the screen right in front of you. So all we did was show that screen with an image updating every 30–60 fps or so.

The scene we want to create can have many hundreds or even thousands of objects in it. If you look out your window you can see a whole range of things visible from your viewpoint… But suppose you look at it from the viewpoint of someone across the street from you? Their view is quite different, but has all the same objects in the world that you can see.

The viewpoint concept is very important to us, because when we build a world, we effectively populate a world with all kinds of objects, but we only view it from one point. A place where we position our viewpoint in 3D space. We refer to that point as the view or camera position.

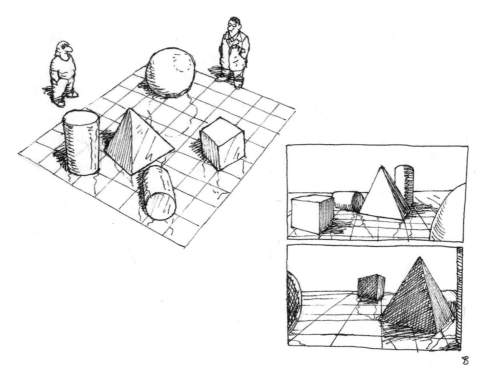

What you actually see depends on where you are, what you are looking at, and also the angle of your field of view.

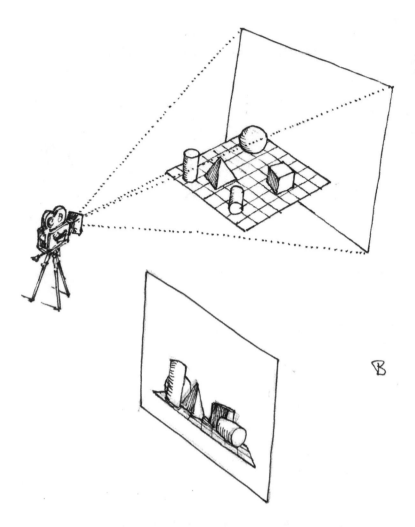

Cameras can point up and down, left and right, whereas their central core position never moves, so we have to take that into account when we are calculating all the things the camera can see, we'll explain that further when we explain what a LookAtMatrix is.

We must give a lot of thought about which of the objects in our scene we are actually going to render. First off, we can immediately discount anything behind our camera, and to replicate a field of view we will probably discount anything in what could be considered outside our peripheral vision, or so far away, beyond what we all the far plane, that it would not register as more than a few dots. What's left is what we call a view field.

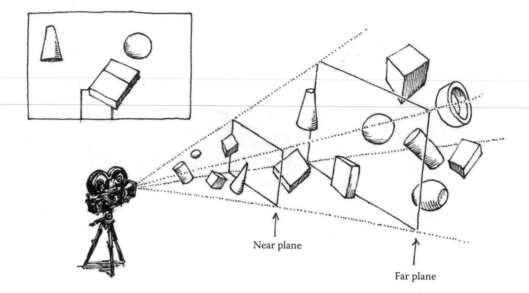

Near plane

Far plane

Notice also we also have a near plane, because we really don't want to have things right in our face even if we could see them, they would engulf our screen, so we take a small liberty and produce a cutoff point.

Now we can cheat a little bit and have two types of view fields, a square one, also called an orthogonal view, which is basically what have had in our 2D, or a more realistic pyramid, which gives a sense of distance, making objects smaller the further they are from our view point. This is called a perspective projection view. Whatever shape it is, it's called a frustum and it represents a defined area that we are going to consider as being the part of the scene we can actually see and should draw onto our monitors.

So our Camera is going to look at a point and what it sees at that point and around it, is what we have to draw to the screen using some 3D to 2D maths we're going to have to learn now.

Ok so far, now take a short break, relax, put on some peril sensitive sunglasses, and get ready.

▓ MATHS!! Don't Be Scared (Much)

I hate maths, I am rubbish at maths, it's no secret in my programming department at my University I am THE worst person with maths on staff and am constantly teased about it, but it's not important to be good at maths to be a good programmer, though many will tell you otherwise, they are wrong! To be a good programmer you only need to know that that you always have access to Maths, and that you learn how to *use* maths. As far as I'm concerned most of this stuff is *magic* (Do Jazz Hands when you say it). I've given you some very simple maths so far, just enough to do the jobs we needed to do, but now things are going to get a bit more complex, at least in one sense.

But though this magic can be confusing, in this case it's magic that everyone has done before. The maths libraries, functions, and standard systems that everyone uses are available to us, so let's use them, learn how the magic works if you must, and trust me, if you are capable it's a good idea. But don't be scared of it. If you learn to use the right maths magic at the right place, that's all you really need.

You can do an incredible amount with very limited understanding of maths; you can code pretty much any maths function if someone explains what it does and you can break it down into code steps…if it then produces the correct result, it's happy dance time. Even with little maths, look what we've managed to do so far?

If you feel that you do want to learn some maths, there are a plethora of books on the subject, but try to focus on finding one or two, which are specially designed to teach you maths used in game programming; specifically, things that relate to 3D graphics, motion, and collision detection. These three are the main fields where we need the type of maths we use in game programming, there are, of course, many others, but these three are specialized and exciting…if you like maths! And if you don't… code it!

How Does This Witchcraft Work?

The funny thing with 3D is much of what we do in 3D; we can and have been doing in 2D.

- We can move around in our world. That is called Translation.

- We can rotate our object, that is called, ermm rotation, though sometimes also Orientation depending on how you use it.

- And finally we can Scale, make things grow or shrink as we need them to.

In 2D that's all pretty simple stuff, and it's not usually needed to do anything more complex than keep a single rotation value, which lets our sprite spin, a vector 2D for position, and a value for scale.

But 3D is different and yet the same, mainly the difference is down to the extra dimension we have to take account of. Instead of moving along X and Y coords, we have X, Y, and Z. Also orientation can change, we don't just rotate around our Y-axis, which gives the impression of spinning, but we can also do X and Z Rotations.

Finally scaling, like orientation we can scale by different values in all three directions, though we usually do all three at once with the same value.

And then there's another issue, I don't know how far in the future this is going to be read, but at the moment, we don't have 3D displays, which means we need some kind of system that will allow us to represent a view of a 3D world on a 2D screen, that lets us maintain the idea that we are looking at 3D. This is called projection and that needs another whole load of calculations.

But not to worry, the grand wizards of maths long ago discovered a form of witchcraft that we can make use of: Behold, the Matrix!

No not that kind of matrix, though who can say for sure eh? No, a matrix is rather less interesting, it's a group of numbers that look like this:

X-ROTATION in 3D

$$\begin{bmatrix} 1 & 0 & 0 & 0 \\ 0 & \cos\phi & -\sin\phi & 0 \\ 0 & \sin\phi & \cos\phi & 0 \\ 0 & 0 & 0 & 1 \end{bmatrix}$$

Z-ROTATION in 3D

$$\begin{bmatrix} \cos\phi & -\sin\phi & 0 & 0 \\ \sin\phi & \cos\phi & 0 & 0 \\ 0 & 0 & 1 & 0 \\ 0 & 0 & 0 & 1 \end{bmatrix}$$

SCALE in 3D

$$\begin{bmatrix} S_x & 0 & 0 & 0 \\ 0 & S_y & 0 & 0 \\ 0 & 0 & S_z & 0 \\ 0 & 0 & 0 & 1 \end{bmatrix}$$

$$(4 \times 4) * (4 \times 1) = (4 \times 1)$$

Y-ROTATION in 3D

$$\begin{bmatrix} \cos\phi & 0 & \sin\phi & 0 \\ 0 & 1 & 0 & 0 \\ -\sin\phi & 0 & \cos\phi & 0 \\ 0 & 0 & 0 & 1 \end{bmatrix}$$

TRANSLATION in 3D

$$\begin{bmatrix} 1 & 0 & 0 & T_x \\ 0 & 1 & 0 & T_y \\ 0 & 0 & 1 & T_z \\ 0 & 0 & 0 & 1 \end{bmatrix}$$

MATRIX MULTIPLICATION

$$\begin{bmatrix} a & b & c & d \\ e & f & g & h \\ i & j & k & l \\ m & n & o & P \end{bmatrix} \begin{bmatrix} x \\ Y \\ z \\ 1 \end{bmatrix} = \begin{bmatrix} x' \\ Y' \\ z' \\ q \end{bmatrix}$$

Hmmm not the most imaginative thing ever is it, but you know, mathematicians are not known for their imagination, but that group of numbers is able to do quite amazing things if you create a function that allows you to manipulate a point in space so that it can be moved to another. It can also let you scale multiple points and change their orientation.

The nice thing about matrices is that they are the key to making changes to vertices, those points in space we've been using to great effect so far by moving sprites from point to point as position vectors. We can produce different kinds of matrices, and then use them to mess up a vertex or series of vertices to do very cool things. Try not to worry about how to make a matrix yet, just focus on the fact that once made, it is used to modify all the vertices in an object that we will draw to screen.

There are multiple sizes of matrix, 3×3 and 4×4 being the most common in games, but for third model movement we use 4×4 as that allows us to fit the rather pesky Translation calculations into the fourth Column.

You may also have noticed a sequence of ones in a diagonal, especially in the Translation Matrix where they don't actually get altered.

A Matrix containing only those 1s in a diagonal is called the Identity Matrix, represented usually by the unimaginative letter I. It's essentially the base for any initialization we have with matrices and it's important that when we create a new matrix we start with I.

The only real difference in each matrix is where in the matrix the correct data live.

A rotation matrix for the X axis looks like this in isolation from the others, the others are in the previous figure.

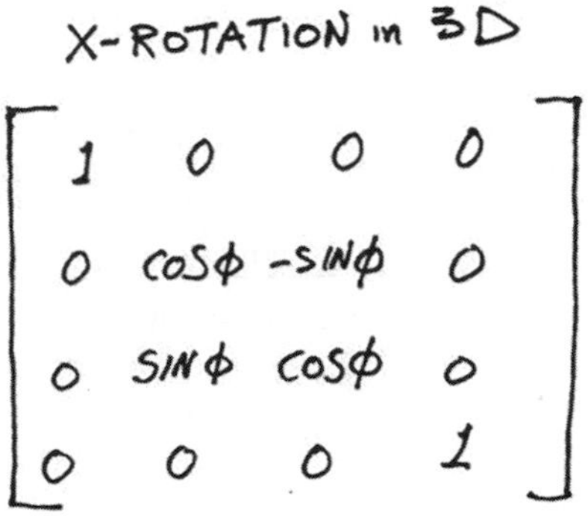

X-ROTATION in 3D

$$\begin{bmatrix} 1 & 0 & 0 & 0 \\ 0 & \cos\phi & -\sin\phi & 0 \\ 0 & \sin\phi & \cos\phi & 0 \\ 0 & 0 & 0 & 1 \end{bmatrix}$$

How these matrices are used though, is pretty cool, this is the real witchcraft! It is possible to multiply a vector with a matrix and create a new vector whose data represent the transformation action on the numbers in the vector, that's any of the transformations! So if we want to rotate around the X-axis, we plug-in the cos, –sin, sin, and cos of the angle into the matrix and do a Matrix*vector multiply.

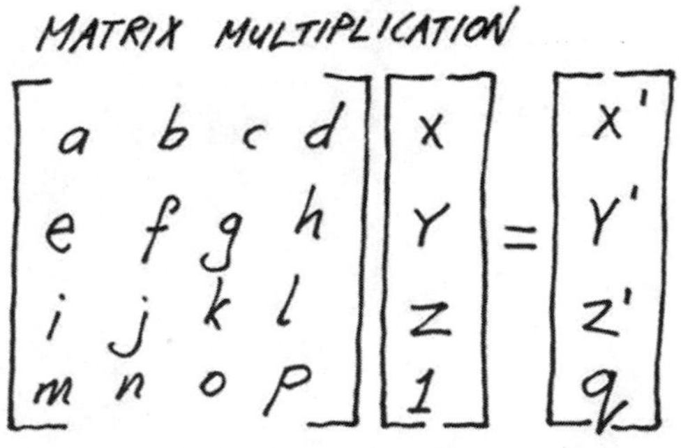

MATRIX MULTIPLICATION

$$\begin{bmatrix} a & b & c & d \\ e & f & g & h \\ i & j & k & l \\ m & n & o & p \end{bmatrix} \begin{bmatrix} x \\ y \\ z \\ 1 \end{bmatrix} = \begin{bmatrix} x' \\ y' \\ z' \\ q \end{bmatrix}$$

There is no actual arithmetic function in the C++ compiler that allows you to do this, we usually overload the * operand so that if the compiler sees we are trying to multiply a matrix by a vector to produce a new vector, it instead performs a fairly simple, but extensive, set of multiplies and divides. The actual way this works looks a bit like this: 16 multiplies and 12 additions.

$$\begin{bmatrix} a & b & c & d \\ e & f & g & h \\ i & j & k & l \\ m & n & o & p \end{bmatrix} \times \begin{bmatrix} x \\ y \\ z \\ w \end{bmatrix} = \begin{bmatrix} ax + by + cz + dw \\ ex + fy + gz + hw \\ ix + jy + kz + lw \\ mx + ny + oz + pw \end{bmatrix}$$

We then get the result in a new vector, we can also set up Translation and Scaling matrices and then multiply the resulting vector, which each one in turn to get a final position for our point in space after its been scaled, translated, and rotated…OR…wait for it! We can actually combine the three different operations into one *master* transform matrix, which can then operate on a vector. This ability to combine matrices is frankly staggeringly useful, and it makes what would otherwise be a pretty lengthy repeated sequence of multiple calculations, much shorter. When all the different matrix types are combined, we then have a master transformation matrix, which we can then use on every single vector we have to manipulate.

Let's look at the different operations in isolation first, and then try combining them.

So if we want to rotate a series of points around an origin point, we can use an orientation matrix, …but wait, what's this Origin you just mentioned….Well we need to think about a center point, our models, are generally stored or created as objects that simply exist in an up/front orientation like this:

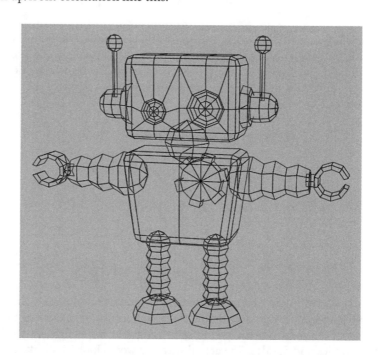

This friendly looking chap is on the support site for you to play with, but for now he's doing his best DaVinci Vitruvian man pose facing front (almost) and standing vertical, he has no rotations on any axis, except for the very slight Y-axis twist, and is located at an origin of 0, 0, and 0 in world space. He's basically boring…and yet quite lovely.

Clearly he needs to be able to rotate around any of his 3D, which is done at his own center point, but if we use a matrix to rotate him at a point in space rather than his center point we get this:

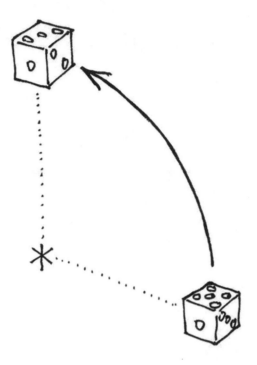

The Object rotated, but because it wasn't at the Origin, the distance of each vertex, was used to work out new positions… We really want this.

Where the center of the cube is the Origin.

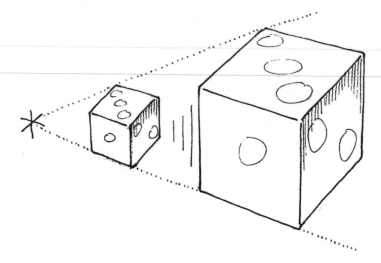

Exactly the same issues happen with Scaling, if the object is not at the origin, then scaling actually also causes a move and a scale. We want something more like this.

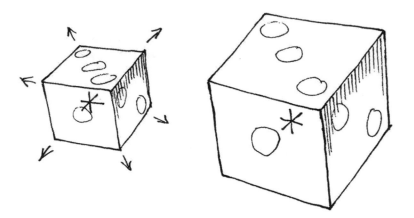

Now it does depend how you think about this, we are either moving our models center to the middle point of his universe or we're moving the middle point of the universe to his center…but either way we think of it, our model has to be at the 0, 0, 0 origin and then moved back to his world position. Since we rotate around the origin, trying to rotate him at his world position will actually move him around that origin, so move, or translation is needed. Once his own center point is at 0, 0, and 0 though, we can spin him in any of the three axes and then slide him back.

One good thing is that we generally always have our models based at a 0, 0, 0 location, the translation systems we use simply move them after the scales have been done.

So there's a two-stage process, rotating/the object as if at 0, 0, 0 (default) location then translating to the point in space where he lives.

Two stages…and if we want to do scaling, which also needs to be at the origin, before the translation, that's three…stages, hmm that's a lot of calculations.

Ok, so how is this a good thing?

Well it's not, lots of calculation is never good, but there's no way around them, we have to do them, so the trick is to reduce the number of calculations we can get away with.

And that's where this Matrix stuff is very cool, because it allows us to combine, the three different types of transform into one super-duper all-purpose *transform* matrix.

This is done by combining the matrices together, in a specific order. The order is vital, because if you do them in the wrong order they simply don't work as we expect them.

Most C++ maths libs have their own way of combining matrices (plural of matrix), a process called concatenation, using operator overloads or new functions to provide the methods we need, it's not strictly a standard C++ concept, and sometimes the methods to concatenate matrices will vary, but the principles are pretty standard. We have a baseline 3D project on the support site. Called…3Dbase, not surprisingly. Go download and make sure it builds. It won't do much yet. It contains only basic 3D maths at this point and not much in the way of any useful code yet. We'll write more functions as we need them.

Ok, so that's the theory of using matrices to orientate our models, but that's only half the story.

Once oriented according to the needs of the game world…we still have to display them, and having them all at 0, 0, 0 in our virtual universe isn't realistic.

3Dbase as it stands is a model viewer, it's very simple and should provide some insight, the key to it really is that our mouse and key controls are moving a camera that changes the whole dynamic of how we can view the things we place in our world or scene.

Now, how do we get models to have a real-world position and get them to appear in some kind of relative position based on our viewpoint?

This is where it all starts to get very strange, we have a camera, which itself can rotate, and we have any number of objects, which have their own coordinates and an orientation relative to the camera, which has its own orientation. It's no wonder this stuff baffles me.

It's now getting a bit mind-blowing, but this is where witchcraft, I mean maths comes to our help, because it always works, as long as it's been set up right.

If we maintain the record of orientation of our objects with a matrix, and we maintain the orientation of our camera with a matrix, it's a relatively simple bit of processing to work through all the different models we have in our scene and work out the final display coordinates of the vertices, which make up our object.

Try to think of the world we are viewing as being in a box…and there is a hole at the end of the box that you are looking at… Now move that box around but keep your eye at the hole. Relatively speaking, nothing seems to be moving. But in the real world your box and all its contents are, perhaps letting light into a window in the box, which alters some of the colors and shadows you might see. You can also keep the box still and tilt your head while still looking in, things seem to tilt, but in fact the objects in the box are not moving at all...they do so relative to your tilting eye, or camera.

This is the essence of 3D computer graphics... Moving the objects around in that box, keeps them in a safe secure 3D environment.

We can do quite a lot without actually knowing what is going on under the hood. That is the way most game engines work, but we are trying to be programmers, so there are a number of functions we need to know, and be able to code. We clearly need to be able to multiply vectors and Matrices together, and have addition, subtraction, comparison, and a few other functions so that we can do the things we want to do, like move, rotate and scale our models.

The code for these Maths functions has been supplied in a basic form in the 3Dbase projects Vector.h and Math.h files; there are a few others that are more useful, and I really think it's a good idea to later use a more comprehensive library with even more useful features. But for our first steps, these basic functions will do, and I'll explain how to use them as we go.

This Is All a Bit Much?

Well yes, it is, we have introduced and explained the concepts of Vectors and Matrices, and how they all work but we have only a tiny fraction of the functionality we are going to need to make a decent 3D game. We don't have the means to manipulate them at all, so we need to use a maths library. Our humble and much loved Vector2D Class is not up to the job in our 3D world.

It's a valid argument to write our own, we can learn a lot, but to be honest, we'd only build a library that did just the things we need at the moment; it's a great idea for us to write a full maths library and use that for all our projects from now.

This is something I really want you to do, at some point in your development, when you fully understand what you need your maths library to do. But as that process could take weeks, even months, perhaps even years, it's best we dip back into the public domain and find a good reliable system.

▐ Installing a Maths Library

There are dozens, I do mean dozens, of free Maths libs, and probably all of them are very good, because a Maths lib that does not do what it's supposed to do, tends to get removed, or repaired, pretty quick.

But the *library* I have chosen is GLM, which stands for (Open) GL Mathematics. It's a fully featured maths system, which consists of a series of header files, which then generates the code to handle the maths. It's already in place in the new framework because this is a header-based library, and only needs *.h files to install.

It's available for download from: http://www.glm.g-truc.net or just Google for GLM downloads.

Now, GLM uses *.hpp to indicate it is a header file, so we need to add *.hpp to the types of file VisualGDB should send down, it's also making use of a file type called .inl, so we'll add these two types to the type of files to transfer, and in doing so it will transfer all the files we currently need on the next build.

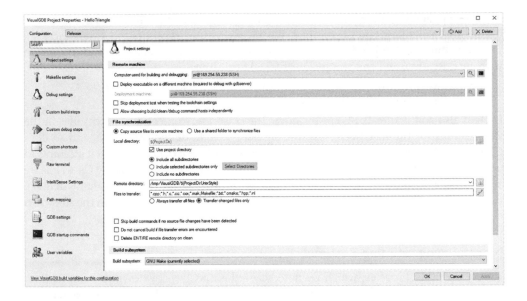

To use it in our project now we can add the following headers where needed:

```
// Include GLM
#include "glm/glm/glm.hpp"
using namespace glm;
```

Which will include the main core GLM features or you can choose to only include the features your files actually need like this:

```
// Include spefici GLM features
#include <glm/vec3.hpp> // glm::vec3
#include <glm/vec4.hpp> // glm::vec4
#include <glm/mat4x4.hpp> // glm::mat4
#include <glm/gtc/matrix_transform.hpp> // glm::translate, glm::rotate,
glm::scale, glm::perspective
```

Danger, Will Robinson!

I'm doing something I promised myself I would not do, and am time traveling back to an early part of this book to give you a warning from the future. Toward the end of this book, I noticed that I was using a slightly older version of GLM, and so I updated. There's an old coder saying about never update in the middle of a project, and it's a wise precaution, because updating my version of GLM totally broke all my code from this point on.

Knowing that the version of GLM you would download will also be a later version I had to prevent you from having the same issues.

The reasons for the problems are actually quite strange and took quite some finding, but in the end it was traced to a problem in the later version of GLM clashing with some system files on my Pi. It would throw up a mass of compiler errors, which had nothing to do with the code that was actually compiled. There was, as it turns out, no easy fix for it, and though it has been reported to the GLM team and the makers of the gnu compiler just in case that's at fault, there is no immediate fix! There is, however, a hack. It's not ideal, but it's one that will allow you to continue. We have my students Viktor Zoutman and Rick van Miltenburg to thank for their vast understanding of compiler behavior and coming up with a fix. Before using any glm include files add this line:

```
#undef countof
```

I might also add it after the GLM includes. The reason is, some of our system files in the video setups for the Raspberry, when using bcm_host.h, define this value, and so does GLM, which can result in a compiler confusion creating a lot of errors when it attempts to use one define rather than the other. It's basically a fault in GLM when using C++11 as we are doing, one of those arrghh moments in game dev we just have to deal with. I will make sure all files on the support site using GLM have this fix and let you know on the site when it is properly fixed by the GLM team.

Normal Programming Resumes

Unlike the SOIL libraries, which we noted caused a massive slowdown in compile time and required wrapping to make compile time a little easier, GLM is quite compact, and is easy enough to include in any file that needs maths without wrapping. But you can if you want! We will be using GLM from now on, and in much more detail when we move to 3D, so it may be quite a good idea to add it to your library of useful functions.

The main reason for choosing GLM, is the sheer volume of features it has, and the massive following it has in the open source community, so if you run into issues, you should be able to ask for help on a whole range of forums, and get help quickly. Ok, now we have a full set of maths functions and features, which we can get when we need, including Vector2D, Vector3D, Matrix 3×3, Matrix 4×4, Quaternions, and all the math's functions we need to manipulate them, and many more, which will make our life a lot easier.

So now we can create and manipulate matrices, we do need to be aware that there are a couple of rules when it comes to using matrices. We have to be very aware that a matrix cannot be empty. Filled with 0s, multiplying a vector by an empty matrix would produce 0, which makes sense in standard scalar arithmetic but not in Matrix maths, a Matrix is designed to alter vector values not clear them. So the way to initialize a Matrix is to load it with I, the Identity Matrix. That way you can be sure that a vector, V * I is going to be the original vector. Same way as 1 * 20 = 20; I * V will equal V.

Second and most important is that when you combine or concatenate matrices in order to do your scales, rotations, and translations in one operator, the ORDER of the combination is vitally important.

In everyday scalar maths, 7 * 8 will equal 63, and 8 * 7 will also equal 63. It's known as a commutative property.

But matrix maths is not commutative, while M1 * M2 results in T1, with T1 being a transform matrix you can use for some function. M2 * M1 will most certainly not equal T1, it will be totally different T2, sometimes if you mix them up, that can result in values that are odd in a fun new strange way, but more often than not, in a not so fun, pull out hair and throw computer out the window, way.

The correct order for Matrix combines as far as 3D graphics are concerned is Scaling, Rotation, and then Translation. If you get the order wrong, it will probably be very obvious, but to make our life more complex, the code will look like this:

```
glm::mat4 mModelMatrix = mTranslationMatrix * mRotationMatrix *
mScaleMatrix;
```

Backward??? It's because compilers work backward when they see a line of equal priority operands. Yeah I know, confusing isn't it...but I'm here to stop you making the same mistakes I made, and avoid losing both hair and computers, just be aware that there's a slim chance if you are using a new or nonstandard compiler, it might, just might, work the other way around. So always test your matrices as soon as you can to assure yourself the correct order is being done.

Three Types of Matrix

Yeah, I'm sorry we're not quite done with Matrices yet, so you might be getting a sense of how important they are, but it's ok, now that we know what a matrix is and what it does, it's time to explain how we use them in our projects.

There are three basic types of matrix used in 3D games for rendering, each is distinct, and does slightly different things, but all need to be fully understood.

The three types are the Model, View, and Projection matrices; I'll talk about each in turn.

Model Matrix

This is the easiest one to explain. The model Matrix represents the combined value of the Translation, 3xRotation, and Scale matrices for an object that we are going to mess with. In the same way, sprites have a central point, and the corners are defined as offsets from that point. A 3D object, will have a Model matrix, which can act on a center point 0, 0, 0 and the entire set of vertices that make its image are described as relative to that point. When each of these vertices are multiplied by this matrix they will find themselves at the world position they should be at!

The model matrix needs to be recalculated when any of the other matrices that control Translation, Scale, or Rotation are altered, but once created, the model matrix can be used over and over again.

So basically, our Model matrix is the container of the rotation and scale and position of our model in the world and can be used to move it around the world and represent its scale and orientation in one fairly simple Matrix, all worked out and ready to use.

View Matrix

The View matrix is even more fun, it relates to the camera and harks back to a concept I talked about in our 2D scrollers. Does the screen move or does the map? I chose to think that the map moves around the viewpoint, and here we have a similar idea. Like a Model, our camera itself exists at a 0, 0, 0 point in space. Now we can place it around but mathematically it's actually a lot easier to consider the point where the camera is to be 0, 0, 0, that means if the camera moves, the whole world has to move, or more accurately the things in it have to move.

This is straight out of the moving without moving idea in Dune, if your camera is a spiced-up ship; it stays where it is, whereas the universe moves around it. That's not to say the camera does not actually move, it does, of course it does, it has world coordinates that allow us to move around, it's just that to bring things into view, we need to use a view matrix to relate them to the camera, to work out their relative positions to the camera!

To make it even more of a mind bender, cameras can rotate, I suppose they can even scale but I've never seen that, not sure it would actually have any effect, but certainly you can rotate a camera and thereby change the area/volume of space your camera is looking at.

See, this; this is why I hate maths, even explaining this to you is making my head hurt, but it does explain why we tend to use nice shortcuts such as overloading operands and adding little helper functions to simplify things.

This is one of the most helpful helper functions GLM gives us, the lookAt function

```
glm::mat4 camMatrix = glm::lookAt(
  camPosition, // the world position of your camera!
  camTarget,   // what are we looking at
  upVector        // which way is up! (or down if you prefer)
);
```

Now that takes care of all the nasty rotation stuff for us, at least for now it gives us a much simpler idea that we can relate to, in terms we can understand.

Projection Matrix

Now this one is trickier still to explain, but effectively what we are trying to take the view of what the camera can see, to mimic a human eye or camera's field of view, and inside, which there are going to be a lot of vertices relating to modes/objects. Think back to that box we are peering into, the box has physical size and depth that define its edges; this is a way to try to define those edges and use different shaped boxes in a mathematical way.

Once we have that *box* defined, then, somehow, we turn that in to a view that we can then use to turn 3D vertices in that box into 2D screen coordinates.

Things that are closer to the camera need to appear bigger than things that are far away, making things appear like a pyramid view and because we've turned a cubic area of a *real-world* sample, into that pyramid view, we also have to deform/scale the objects a little to make them appear correct….I said this was tricky! Let's try to visualize it!

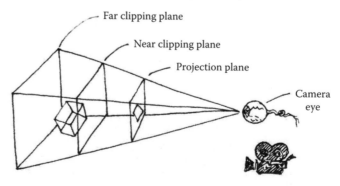

Our Eye starts at the beginning of sort of pyramid on its side, and at some point along that pyramid, is our screen, the Pyramid is correctly called a Frustum, and because it's

essentially a known mathematical shape, we are able to translate the coordinates of the vertices that are visible to the Projection plane we want to represent on our screen. The Near and Far clipping planes are essentially cutoff points, beyond or inside of which we don't want to actually bother with things or we'd be drawing to infinity.

There are three common types of Projection, but we usually only focus on two. The old 2.5D style has not been used in an age, if you need to use it, it'll be long after this book is finished and you'll know what to do. The one we want, seen in the previous figure, is Perspective Projection. But we can also use another type for 2D style games called Parallel Projection, but we won't use that just yet (it's great for GUI, HUDs, front of screen text and 2D sprites, etc.).

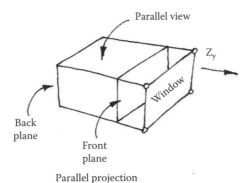

Parallel projection

Instead of our eye we have a window, or screen, onto which we draw the pixels, which related to the positions of the vertices after the transformations are all down. Everything that was in that original pyramid field of view gets squished or stretched to look right on a screen. It's really very hard to visualize but we're in luck GLM gives us another of those lovely helper functions to create a projection matrix

```
glm::mat4 projectionMatrix = glm::perspective(
  FoV,            // The Field of View
  4.0f / 3.0f,    // Aspect Ratio.
  0.1f,           // Near clipping plane.
  100.0f          // Far clipping plane.
  )
```

A couple of these things need explanation, FoV, for example, is a new term. It stands for Field of View. It basically describes the size of the horizontal angle you see when you look straight ahead. Humans eyes can *see* about 180° in front of them, though in reality, we only perceive movement at the extremes and not detail, our stereo view is limited to around 130°, though still mostly related to motion and color, and our sharpest view is really quite a narrow range in front of us, which varies from person to person. This is why we as visual animals, look directly at things we want to examine, so we use our sharpest most detailed view.

But the point is we can relate the range we want to see as a value in degrees typically we want to look at a narrower field than our own stereo range as we tend to focus our gaze on our central point, so anything from a quite tight 30°–90° of view is a comfortable human-like focus when we look at a screen, but you can create nice fish eye effect with larger values if you want to play with them.

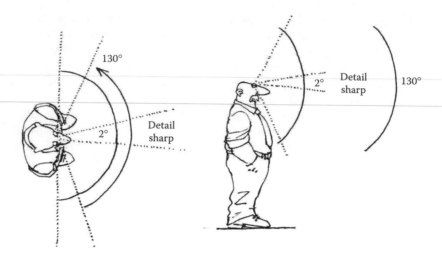

We tend to ignore the vertical field of view, though there are ways to incorporate it, I've never seen much use, I'm sure that will change with Virtual Reality (VR) headsets though.

Aspect Ratio is something you can set depending on your screen, but it's typically going to be a 4:3 square TV style view for a window view, or a 16:9 wide screen view for a full screen view. You can even make it the Width:Height of your screen. That will usually equate to 16:9, it's your call, we're normally quite comfortable with 4:3 and 16:9 because we see them all the time on screens, small variations because of odd resolutions tend to be forgiven by the human eye.

The Clipping planes decide the points where we see things and don't see them. If you put your hand right up to your face, it's going to obscure your view of things beyond that. Our camera does not have any kind of physical limits on where it can move, so it is more than likely it is going to move right in front of an object, which will then obscure the view. Being able to remove things allows us to take away that odd going into something and seeing in the middle of objects sensation. Though you can keep it if you want.

Likewise the far plane dictates the limit of our cameras view. As objects get further and further away the ability to make out what they are is reduced and it's more effective then to ignore them. Infinity vision isn't ideal for games, but who knows you may find you want to make that number massively large for an effect.

The Relationship of These Three Matrices

So why do we have three different matrices? It's because of the fact we have to alter all the vertices and somehow get them to make sense on a 2D screen. We may have 10's even 100's of thousands of vertices, and every single one of them needs to be transformed in some way to work out the relative position on screen. Taking into account the fact that the object can scale, rotate, and translate in its local space and world space, and the camera being able to translate and rotate. The actual amount of maths calculations needed is extraordinary.

Yet amazingly it's also fairly simple, and we have produced hardware, in the form of our GPUs that is exceptionally good at coping with this...if we send it the right data! What it needs is, the Model View Projection (MVP) Matrix, which I'm about to explain, and then the list of these 10's of thousands of vertices and it goes off and does it stuff.

So there's a three-stage process to produce our final result:

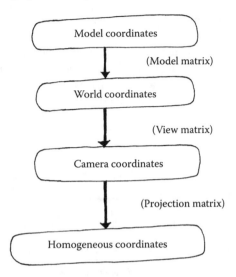

First we take our model coords, and then we can turn it into world coords, using whatever transforms are needed, such as translation, scale, and rotate.

Those world coords are then transformed by our View or camera matrix.

And then, our Projection matrix turns them into nice 2D coords.

Of course, we can then combine these different matrices into one super-duper, does everything transform MVP matrix like this:

```
glm::mat4 MVPmatrix = projection * camera * model;
```

(Remember it's written backwards as each has equal arithmetic priority)

So, we've got the MVP transform matrix, if we use that on an object's vertices we can work out where on the screen (or indeed off) it will draw a point, or in our case a collection of points filled with a texture.

Other Matrix Functions

There are several other functions that matrices provide, which can allow us to do even more fun things, such as

- Transposition, to swap between Row and Column major formats.

- Scalar manipulation, to essentially multiply a matrix by a scale value.

- Addition and subtraction of matrices.

- Determinant, used among other things to find the inverse of a Matrix.

- Inverse, is used to allow for the fact division is not possible.

- Voodoo, black magic, and sorcery, which basically cover all the other matrix functions I may have used once or twice in my entire career, but do exist and are present in almost all maths Libraries.

I'll explain these as and when we need them, as overloading ourselves with lots of complex maths we're not quite ready to use might overwhelm anyone with a genuine aversion to maths.

We can't really escape the need for such maths, but we can try to introduce it as it becomes relevant to our needs, and as such learning it becomes a little easier when we see it in action.

Moving Around

There's one more thing we have to think about, motion! So far, Up, Down, Left, and Right are pretty simple concepts and we've been happy to slide up and down the X- and Y-axis. Increment the Y to go up, increment the X to go Left, decrement X to go right (that seems counter intuitive but using a camera, we are looking backward toward the 0, 0, 0 point in OpenGL 3D).

We can now also add to that, In and Out, using the Z-axis. Six degrees of motion you might say moving along an axis, but what if we're not moving along an axis?

There are two more concepts of motion we need to consider: Forward and Back where we want to be moving in the direction we are pointing, which can be any of $360° \times 360° \times 360°$. This is where orientation comes in and it gets complex. Though really all we ever want is a vector to add to the current position so that we move in the direction we are pointing. We'll cover that as we need it as there are different ways to get this vector.

Forward and Back also lead us to relative Left, Right and Up and Down, or even thataway, that is, depending on the direction we are facing, a relative Left might in fact be an absolute up if you are rotated 90° on the Z-axis.

This...is why 3D gets confusing, but we'll introduce these things slowly.

Ok, that's the Maths lesson done...for now! We've earned a break, I'm going to let you think about that for a while, since it's a load of stuff to absorb, let's do a little bit of simple stuff before we bring this mathematical wizardry into effect. We really need a simple base project where we can then experiment with these magical matrices.

▮ Revisiting Hello Triangle

Now way back when we did the first Hello Triangle project it was a very simple project, mainly designed to help you enter code and test you can get your OpenGLES 2.0 to work. But I noted then it really was a very long way from being a usable project.

But if we add some matrices to this, we might find we can actually get a bit more out of this.

Let's first consider what this program does.

It starts off naturally enough setting up a window, which is used simply to provide a place for our render to be visible, then initializing our OpenGL, during which it did something very important indeed. It loaded and compiled a vertex Shader, which in our code looked like this:

```
GLbyte vShaderStr[] =
  "attribute vec4 a_position;\n"
  "attribute vec2 a_texCoord;\n"
  "varying vec2 v_texCoord;\n"
  "void main()\n"
  "{gl_Position=a_position;\n"
  " v_texCoord=a_texCoord;}\n";
```

We're going to go into a lot more detail on Shaders later, but we do need to try to understand how a Shader works, so that we can make use of matrices.

This particular Shader really does not do a huge amount. If defines a few values as attributes, which are values that are input into the Shader. This one also does something with textures, but for our simple triangle it's not actually relevant so we'll ignore it.

The output of a vertex Shader is `gl_Position` the code here is not actually performing any kind of manipulation if you look at it cleared up from the ""

```
void main()
  {gl_Position-a_position;
   v_texCoord=a_texCoord;};
```

All we are doing is loading the attribute that goes in, into the value that goes out. What we want to do is use the MVP matrix we talked about so that we alter what we see depending on where the camera is placed.

Copy your Hello Triangle project into a new folder called HelloMatrix, fire it up from this new directory and make sure it's all working ok.

Remember to add *.hpp and *.inl to the file types for the VisualGDB project properties.

All good, now to our HelloTriangle.cpp file you can add these headers:

```
// Include GLM
#include "glm/glm/glm.hpp"
#include "glm/glm/gtc/matrix_transform.hpp"
using namespace glm;
```

Compile and run, it's not going to do anything yet, just make sure you can find all the files, and you still get your normal triangle?

Ok, so far so good.

Now this part is messy and we're only doing this to demonstrate the concept, but let's rework the draw routine a tiny bit.

Like this:

```
void Draw(Target_State *p_state)
{
 UserData *userData = p_state->user_data;
 // Projection matrix : 45° Field of View, 4:3 ratio, display range : 0.1
unit <-> 100 units
 glm::mat4 Projection = glm::perspective(45.0f, 4.0f / 3.0f, 0.1f, 100.0f);
 glm::mat4 View = glm::lookAt(
  glm::vec3(17, 23, 3), // Camera is at (17,23,3), in World Space
  glm::vec3(0, 0, 0), // look at the origin
  glm::vec3(0, 1, 0) // pointing up( 0,-1,0 will be upside-down))
  );
// hard code a model matrix here as empty (I)
 glm::mat4 Model = glm::mat4(1.0f);
// make the MVP
```

```
glm::mat4 MVP = Projection * View * Model; // Remember order seems
backwards
GLuint MatrixID = glGetUniformLocation(userData->programObject, "MVP");
//LOOK!!!!
GLfloat TriVertices[] =
{ 0.0f , 0.5f , 0.0f,
 -0.5f, -0.5f, 0.0f,
  0.5f, -0.5f, 0.0f };
// Setup the viewport
glViewport(0, 0, p_state->width, p_state->height);
// Clear the color buffer
glClear(GL_COLOR_BUFFER_BIT);
// Use the program object
glUseProgram(userData->programObject);
  // Send our transformation to the currently bound Shader,
  // in the "MVP" uniform
glUniformMatrix4fv(MatrixID, 1, GL_FALSE, &MVP[0][0]);/LOOK!!!!
// Load the vertex data
glVertexAttribPointer(0, 3, GL_FLOAT, GL_FALSE, 0, TriVertices);
glEnableVertexAttribArray(0);
glDrawArrays(GL_TRIANGLES, 0, 3);
if (glGetError() != GL_NO_ERROR) printf("Oh bugger");
}
```

There are not too many changes here, but at the start you can see I created some Model, View, and Projection matrices, using some hard numbers, which we would not normally do.

Also very important, notice where I commented LOOK!!!! Twice. This is a reference to the fact that we are actually getting a handle from the Shader to the location of a uniform called MVP, and in the second instance, we're sending that MVP to the Shader.

But at the moment the Shader has not been written.

You can run this…it will compile, but it will not actually work correctly you'll get a blank screen, or perhaps even a Shader error.

So we need to write a new Shader, in the init code, replace the vertex Shader with this:

```
GLbyte vShaderStr[] =
  "attribute vec3 vertexModelPosition ;\n"
  "uniform mat4 MVP;\n"
  "void main(){\n"
  " gl_Position = MVP * vec4(vertexModelPosition,1);\n"
  "}\n";
```

The quotes and \n values are a necessary evil at the moment, one we will dispose of soon as we have our Shader manager in place. Removing those quotes though we get something simple to read:

```
attribute vec3 vertexModelPosition ;
uniform mat4 MVP;
void main()
  {
  gl_Position = MVP * vec4(vertexModelPosition,1);
  };
```

Now we can clearly see that gl_Position isn't just the input data fed right back out again, this time the input vec3, the vertexModelPosition, is being transformed by the MVP, which we calculated in the draw and sent to the Shader.

Run this now and you will see something wonderful.

No really, that is wonderful, that is our old friend the triangle, but now viewed from a camera that is positioned some glm::vec3(17, 23, 3) Units away. Change the position value in the lookAt function to glm::vec3(7, 3, 3), which is a bit closer and compile again, cool eh?

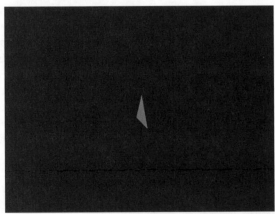

Now try glm::vec3(0, 3, 3).

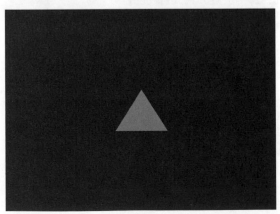

Is it starting to make sense? Your triangle has been placed at 0, 0, 0 thanks to our setting of the model matrix to I. And our LookAt matrix positions our Camera some distance from it, then the projection matrix, or more accurately the combination of all three, put into the Shader code, turn it into a view of how it would look if your eye were looking at this point.

Of course, this is horribly clumsy and useless with hard coded values but it serves a useful purpose of allowing us to create a simple vertex Shader, which should we find a more effective way to alter the model and camera matrices will give us a means to move around. We are not likely to alter the Projection matrix though, unless we plan to use a different Projection from other models, say for a GUI.

What we need to do is create objects that have their own independent Model matrices, which most importantly can be moved around, rotated, or scaled as we want them to. A camera (or if you really want it, multiple cameras) with its/their own camera/view matrix, and maintain a fairly consistent Projection matrix for objects, which exist in free space, and a different type of projection, which we might play with later. For now, let's keep our Projection matrix fairly constant.

Let's Try a Cube

Drawing a cube is fairly simple, it's just more vertices to define and draw, and actually it's close to the limits we want to set for hand-crafted data, because the more data we enter by hand the more likely it is we will input an error, but entering the cubes vertex list isn't the only thing we need! We're still a little bit hampered by the fact our draw system is hard coded to only do single triangles, let's alter that so we have a much more flexible draw system, and create a base 3D Object Class called ObjectModel, that can handle some more general shapes, which can derive from the base in fact that class should be responsible for the draw calls of its own model and hold the data for them. I'll change the draw system to run through all active objects and create their own MVP matrices and their vertex lists.

I won't make you type this, it's available on the support site, download HelloMatrix2 and unzip to a folder called HelloMatrix2.

The main difference here is instead of TriVertices we now have CubeVertice that look like this:

```
GLfloat CubeVertices[] = {
       -0.5f, -0.5f, -0.5f,  0.0f, 0.0f,
        0.5f, -0.5f, -0.5f,  1.0f, 0.0f,
        0.5f,  0.5f, -0.5f,  1.0f, 1.0f,
        0.5f,  0.5f, -0.5f,  1.0f, 1.0f,
       -0.5f,  0.5f, -0.5f,  0.0f, 1.0f,
       -0.5f, -0.5f, -0.5f,  0.0f, 0.0f,

       -0.5f, -0.5f,  0.5f,  0.0f, 0.0f,
        0.5f, -0.5f,  0.5f,  1.0f, 0.0f,
        0.5f,  0.5f,  0.5f,  1.0f, 1.0f,
        0.5f,  0.5f,  0.5f,  1.0f, 1.0f,
       -0.5f,  0.5f,  0.5f,  0.0f, 1.0f,
       -0.5f, -0.5f,  0.5f,  0.0f, 0.0f,
```

```
    -0.5f,   0.5f,   0.5f,   1.0f, 0.0f,
    -0.5f,   0.5f,  -0.5f,   1.0f, 1.0f,
    -0.5f,  -0.5f,  -0.5f,   0.0f, 1.0f,
    -0.5f,  -0.5f,  -0.5f,   0.0f, 1.0f,
    -0.5f,  -0.5f,   0.5f,   0.0f, 0.0f,
    -0.5f,   0.5f,   0.5f,   1.0f, 0.0f,

     0.5f,   0.5f,   0.5f,   1.0f, 0.0f,
     0.5f,   0.5f,  -0.5f,   1.0f, 1.0f,
     0.5f,  -0.5f,  -0.5f,   0.0f, 1.0f,
     0.5f,  -0.5f,  -0.5f,   0.0f, 1.0f,
     0.5f,  -0.5f,   0.5f,   0.0f, 0.0f,
     0.5f,   0.5f,   0.5f,   1.0f, 0.0f,

    -0.5f,  -0.5f,  -0.5f,   0.0f, 1.0f,
     0.5f,  -0.5f,  -0.5f,   1.0f, 1.0f,
     0.5f,  -0.5f,   0.5f,   1.0f, 0.0f,
     0.5f,  -0.5f,   0.5f,   1.0f, 0.0f,
    -0.5f,  -0.5f,   0.5f,   0.0f, 0.0f,
    -0.5f,  -0.5f,  -0.5f,   0.0f, 1.0f,

    -0.5f,   0.5f,  -0.5f,   0.0f, 1.0f,
     0.5f,   0.5f,  -0.5f,   1.0f, 1.0f,
     0.5f,   0.5f,   0.5f,   1.0f, 0.0f,
     0.5f,   0.5f,   0.5f,   1.0f, 0.0f,
    -0.5f,   0.5f,   0.5f,   0.0f, 0.0f,
    -0.5f,   0.5f,  -0.5f,   0.0f, 1.0f
};
```

I hope you are asking yourself why there so many more vertices, and why five in each line? Well a cube needs a lot more vertices to make it up, 36 in fact, 6 per face, and 6 faces. So are now 36 vertices here, each line of these vertices represents the relative point from the center where the vertex is. But a vertex is only three values, the final two numbers actually refer to a texture that we're going to add soon, for now, ignore them, they're here to save bit of typing time later and demonstrate the skipping options when setting up the Attribute Pointers.

Notice also in the Draw function where we send the attribute pointers and actually draw the Triangles the values are different to reflect the larger amount of data we are sending and interestingly that we are skipping some of the data (the last two entries per vertex)

```
glVertexAttribPointer(0, 3, GL_FLOAT, GL_FALSE, 5 * sizeof(GLfloat),
CubeVertices); // use 3 values, but add 5 each time to get to the next
glEnableVertexAttribArray(0);
glDrawArrays(GL_TRIANGLES, 0, 36);
```

But, aside from a different vertex list and a slightly more careful setup of the attrib pointers where I am using the sizeof operator to check the internal size of a float to allow the skip over the two final values stored in the CubeVertices, the drawing system is pretty much the same for a Cube as it is for a Triangle! Try it out and you get this:

Now we are starting to get somewhere, we can actually draw a solid object that is clearly 3D and visible to us. It's a little monochrome and static though, but we'll tackle that soon.

First though we need to make this draw routine a lot more flexible, so let's examine what it actually does.

It sets up a view…it then sets up the array(s) it wants to send to the GPU, and then it sends the data. Nothing actually happens though until the `glDrawArrays(GL_TRIANGLES, 0, 36)` is executed, and then nothing is actually seen until the `eglSwapBuffers(esContext->display, esContext->surface)` Command is called, which lets us see what we have drawn. This means we can set up and draw any number (within reason) of these arrays, send them to the GPU, call `glDrawArrays`, and repeat until we are ready to show the screen.

We did a similar thing with our 2D games, we had a draw routine in our basic gameobject system, which drew the images/sprites, related to an object, then we moved on to the next object, processed it, then drew it. Repeating until done.

So not much here is really that different. At the moment we don't have any Object Classes, which is why this increasingly clunky Draw function is starting to look weak. If we add a draw system, to a class, which represents our 3D objects, and that class itself contains its data, or pointers to common data. We should then be able to process our objects, draw them and then finally display with a SwapBuffer command, in exactly the same way our 2D games did.

Here's more evidence of the fact that 3D games are really not that much different from 2D games. Just a bit more complex.

Mistakes Waiting to Happen

One thing I need to warn you about is the order of the matrices we are using with GLM and OpenGLES2.0. When you manually load them with values! I've visually represented them as if they are similar to 2D arrays. And they are, but the way you access them is quite different.

In a 2D array, you use a [Row] [Column] order (Row Major) to set or get data in that array. But matrices in OpenGL and the default GLM libs use a [Column][Row] order (Column Major). This can be a bit of a mind twister for you, but generally as long as you remember to view it as a Row Major System, and use it as Column Major, things will be fine.

$$\text{TRANSLATION in 3D}$$

$$\begin{bmatrix} 1 & 0 & 0 & T_x \\ 0 & 1 & 0 & T_y \\ 0 & 0 & 1 & T_z \\ 0 & 0 & 0 & 1 \end{bmatrix}$$

Tx here is visually at Mat[0 row][3 col].

But really it's at Mat[3 (col)] [0 row] when using [][] to index into the Matrix use Column Major order, to set the Tx, Ty, and Tz values, that is, Mat[3][0], Mat[3][1], and Mat[3][2].

DirectX coders will of course complain that this is just wrong....but it's just different. DirectX uses Row Major, so if you are transitioning from that it will probably catch you out a few times.

Later, you will use faster ways to set up your matrices, less likely to twist your mind, but for now as you are doing them by hand so you get used to them, this is an important point to remember. If you see strange behavior/shearing in your models, most likely you have mixed up the Major/Minor order.

▌ A Quick Word about Using Quaternions

Don't.

That's pretty quick!

Don't. For now! More experienced coders and math geeks will at this point be spitting feathers that we are using Euler systems to do our rotations. As they will be aware that Euler (Degree based) angles, have a few massive flaws, which we might encounter from time to time. One being the dreaded Gimbal Lock!

It's hard to describe this, but it's obvious when you see it, sometimes when rotating multiple directions, two or three axes will line up, and one or more axis will then turn in the direction of a different axis, and effectively mess up your visualizations. It's a frustrating flaw, in an otherwise elegant way to do our rotations. You can hack it, by testing if your axis line up...and tipping an affected one over by 0.01 of a degree from the calculation, but it's a nasty hack and rarely used now.

Lucky though there is an answer, in a numerical concept called Quaternions! But, they are complex concepts to explain, even if I were a good mathematician. I could easy spend a chapter or two doing it, and probably get it wrong as I've seen multiple conflicting explanations in different maths books and from different experts. This book is aimed at beginners, so for now, I want you to bear with me and continue to use Euler rotations despite the Gimbal lock issue. I want you to use something that we can get our heads around that lets us progress, rather than get tied up in complex and advanced mathematical issues.

Later, when we really need to, and you have a better understanding of special concepts, I'm going to try to explain them in a page or two, and show you how use them in specific instances. They form an important part of a physics system we will use later, but we're just not doing enough at the moment to justify their introduction even though they will solve the Gimbal lock issue we will come across.

▐█ HelloCubes

I don't want to us continue with this rather poor extension of Hello Triangle, we've moved away from that old school C style coding, and should try to build our new 3D framework. So download and unzip HelloCubes from the support site and get it up and running.

Take some time to look at the code, it has pretty much everything the later 2D projects had, independent graphic set up, a controlling Game Class, some shader management and the ability to use base objects only this time I'm introducing a new kind of base object called a ObjectModel. I could have extended our old 2D GameObjects but really these are a little different and will work quite differently, so I prefer to keep the two base types separate. When you run this you should now be able to see two cubes in space, and look, they are rotating. If we choose to use some GameObjects we just make sure we update and draw them separately.

Look a little closer at the ObjectModel Class, which now takes responsibility for moving the object, creating, and maintaining the model for each instance of ObjectModel, and then having a draw routine, which sends the correct vertex or attribute list to the GPU. The Draw and Update routines, however, are pure virtual, that is, they are defined as = 0, having no content, meaning that any class that derives from this, must supply its own Update and Draw functions. This provides flexibility, we know we are going to need matrices, but we don't really know what kind of object we are going to update or draw, so let the objects that use ObjectModel as their base do that work. Let's look at what it contains.

```
#pragma once
#include "glm/glm.hpp"
#include "glm/gtc/matrix_transform.hpp"
#include "MyFiles.h"
```

```cpp
#include "ShaderManager.h"
#include <GLES2/gl2.h>

using namespace glm;
class Graphics;
class ObjectModel
{
public:
 ObjectModel();
 ObjectModel(char* filename, MyFiles* FH);
 ~ObjectModel();
 virtual bool Update() = 0; // we need to have an Update to move and create
the ModelView
 virtual bool Draw() = 0; // and we need to draw from the vertices
// used by simple attribyte array systems
 GLvoid*  Vertices; // a pointer to our attribute array, which should
contain vertices and texture coords
// a few basic utility functions
 glm::vec3 GetPositon();
 void        SetPosition(glm::vec3*);
 void        SetPosition(glm::vec3);
 glm::vec3 GetRotations();
 void        SetRotations(glm::vec3*);
 void        SetRotations(glm::vec3);
 void        SetXRotation(float); // if you need to set indivdual rotations
 void        SetYRotation(float);
 void        SetZRotation(float);
 void        SetModelMatrix(); // initialises and resets
 void        MakeModelMatrix(); // makes and returns the model matrix
 void        MakeRotations();
 void        MakeTranslationMatrix();
 void        StoreGraphicClass(Graphics* Graphics);
 GLuint      texture1; // a handle
 bool        LoadModel(GLvoid* vertices);
 glm::vec4   Colour;
 glm::vec3   WorldPosition; // where am I in the world?
 glm::vcc3   Rotations;  // what are my rotations? Stored as Radians!
 glm::vec3   DegreeRotations;
 glm::vec3   Scales;
 glm::mat4 mTranslationMatrix;
 glm::mat4 mRotationMatrix;
 glm::mat4 mScaleMatrix;

 glm::mat4 RotationMatrixX;
 glm::mat4 RotationMatrixY;
 glm::mat4 RotationMatrixZ;
 void MakeRotationMatrix(); // since these get altered alot
 GLuint programObject, vertexShader, fragmentShader; // programObject used
for draw. vertex and fragment used to create programObject
 glm::mat4 Model; // the model matrix will effectivly hold all the rotation
and positional data for the object
 GLint positionLoc; // index handles to important concepts in texture
 GLint texCoordLoc;
 GLint samplerLoc;
 Graphics* TheGraphics; // anything that uses a shader will need access to
the graphic class set up in the game app. Make sure this is supplied
 GLuint vbo;
};
```

One or two things won't be obvious but we'll cover them soon; however, already you can see there's quite a bit of matrix work, and seven different matrices, three of them just to deal with rotations. But it's still a very light and fairly easy to understand class. There are familiar concepts of Setting and Getting position, a couple of easy for humans to understand concepts such as WorldPosition and DegreeRotations, some MakeMatrix functions, which our update methods will be expected to handle as needed, and.....that's pretty much it.

A couple of new things that won't be too familiar yet are these handles:

```
GLuint programObject, vertexShader, fragmentShader;
```

These relate to the Shader code we are going to play with a lot more later, but their use will become clear before we delve into Shaders properly.

So as a header file, we can see we have two pure virtual functions, meaning any Shape Class, which inherits ObjectModel MUST includes its own version of draw and update.

In our project, I create a vector or a list of this base type, and essentially all I want to do is loop through that list and call the update and draw functions, which will then go to the Shape Class versions of those functions.

Previously most of our 3D code has been set up in the main cpp file (the file containing the entry point main()), this is an homage to the original hello triangle project everyone starts with and to keep things familiar. But now we know better than to expand on old C style projects, so we are branching out, and reducing the overhead on the main file. Its role is now correctly reduced to starting up our project, creating an instance of a *Game* Class, letting that run, and on return, exiting the project.

The main draw and initializing functions, which were in the old C style demos are now removed to a Graphics Class, which has the job of setting up OpenGLES2.0, so we can use it and of course process the draw calls. Later, we'll expand on this a bit more.

We can now pretty much leave that file with its main Draw function and initializations alone, we make our modifications now in the Draw routines of our model classes; we can also plug in a different Graphic Class if we are using a non-Raspberry device, so that from now on, the main bulk of the code, as we did with 2D projects is unconcerned with the target, so long as we stick to the constraints that OpenGLES2.0 puts us under.

I Thought We Could Move 100's of Thousands of Them?

Well, in an ideal world we might, but the actual numbers of triangles/vertices/faces/whatever you want to measure, that can be drawn per second on the GPU is very hard to quantify, since we have Shaders doing a lot of our work for us! How complex those Shaders are will impact our performance quite a bit. But at the moment our Shaders are about as simple as you can get so we really should be able to get thousands of triangles with ease.

We all know that what someone advertises isn't usually what we're going to get delivered. Yes, the Pi and other SBCs can easily throw 100,000s of triangles around in a standard test condition, but how big are those triangles? Are they textured, scaled, lit? What screen size and other factors will impact on our *real world* use of the GPU. We're not going to make too many games with just simple triangles; we need to produce more complex shapes with texture and colors, which drop the numbers down.

Let's examine our current performance. If you check the HelloCube.cpp file, I am creating the first two random placed cubes using a for/next loop. Try changing the number from 2 to 30 and compile and run it.

Ok, that seems fine. Now try 60, on a Raspberry Pi Model 3B or faster machine with proper graphic drivers, it's probably still going to show a stable 60–80 fps frame rate…on a lesser machine though you're going to notice a drop in the FPS. Try 150 and you will see a distinct slow down no matter what speed your target?

Why is this happening, we know a GPU can handle 10's even 100's of thousands of vertices, and our cube has 36 vertices, times 150 cubes, that is only 5400?

Well, that's because its capable of handling 100's of 1000's all right, but we're not in those test lab conditions, and here we can see a classic problem that it's not capable of reading the data from the CPU's area of RAM fast enough to set them up. For us to get maximum performance we need those vertices to be sent once to the GPU and reused over and over again without a reload. Right now that 150 writes each frame is a lot of dead time and the more we have the more time we kill, the more frames we drop.

This is exactly the same principle when we were loading a sprite every time we created it or animated it in 2D. The time it takes to set up the GPU is something we have to avoid; it will utterly cripple our frame rates.

If we assume a modest game has 10,000 vertices, that can be represented by changing the for/next loop to 277. On my system I get around 14 fps, and we're not even doing textures. That's just not acceptable. And it's so unacceptable that I want to resolve it now before we move any further. We don't want to be limited to 3000 vertices, or even 6000, we want those 100,000+ the GPU promises to give us!

How the GPU Gets Data

So far we've been sending our graphical data from our CPU memory to our GPU, calling a draw function then a swap for it all to magically appear. And appear it does. But we've probably noticed that as our 2D screen size gets bigger, or we try to draw more than a few 3D objects on screen our frame rate is falling, sometimes quite markedly.

Our Frames per Second update (FPS), is very important to the smooth running of our games, ideally we want at least 60 fps, but if they don't run at least 30 fps we end up with noticeable jagged movement and our games start to run slower, no matter what impact some CPU manipulation of movement using a delta time does, to make it appear to move smoother. Our eyes can see the update rate is slowing down.

Why then is this happening? Well the key point is in that first sentence "… we've been sending our graphical data from our CPU memory to our GPU…," we need to think about exactly what is happening.

On all current SBCs, our CPU and GPU share memory, but in fact internally, the two units have fenced off their memory from each other, and claimed it as their own. The two memory pools may even operate at different speeds and have different access methods and address widths, so that when one unit, wants to talk to the other units memory, there has to be some kind of way to jump over that fence.

Depending on your machine, this fence will take several forms, but bottom line is, there's a lot of inter chip negotiation that goes on when one unit wants to access memory from the others pool, that negotiation takes time, and during that time, the data we want to move have to sit on an area called a bus, which will take that data where it want to go to, though like real-life buses it's not going to do that at Ferrari speeds and it can only take so many bytes at a time.

The size of our bus will vary depending on our systems, we may have 8, 16, 32, 64, 128 or more bit buses, but however wide it is, we have to put our data on the bus, let the chips negotiate the transfer then move the bits to their new home.

All of this is incredibly slow, in fact many orders of magnitude slower than shifting 32/64 bits from CPU memory to CPU memory.

So when we are sending our attribute array data from our CPU to our GPU, it's just painfully slow. There are often Direct Memory Access (DMA) methods that can be used that are a little faster, but for real speed we need the GPU to access its own memory, because when the GPU accesses its own memory, it is incredibly fast. Clearly we need to think a bit about this. We've just got to avoid bus transfers at all costs. How then can we send graphic or geometry data to our GPU? What does OpenGLES2.0 give us that will prevent us writing the same attribute lists from the CPU to the GPU over and over again?

Buffers, Buffers Everywhere

Preloaded buffers are one of the main keys to faster FPS. Chucking vertices and textures at the GPU each frame in a draw call clearly works, and if we are only talking about a few dozen simple models or a few hundred 2D sprites we can get away with it, but the true power of our GPU should allow us to have 100,000+ triangles on screen, so we need to know how to do that. Our programming mantra of must make thing better, should never allow us to make do with, just because we've been getting away with it so far.

Our GPU needs to access data directly on its own address space in its own memory, anytime we pass data from one system to another through a bus, or other internal transfer system, we are losing massive amounts of time and time lost means low frame rates.

We must do all we can to not have our GPU constantly getting data from CPU RAM and repeatedly doing exactly the same set of processes on exactly the same set of vertex/texture/normal/whatever data. If we can locate data inside the GPU RAM, in areas called buffers, they are now always on tap to the GPU and we should see a massive kick in the pants for performance.

OpenGLES calls them Object Attribute Buffers (OAB), and we can usually have a few of them in our projects or one massive one, the choice is ours. I tend to refer to them as Vertex Buffers, quite incorrectly, but it's a throwback to my use of full fat OpenGL, so you will see me use a VB or VBO rather than OAB abbreviation in code. It's a habit I will try to break.

OpenGLES2.0 only offers a few different kinds of buffers, and for passing information to the Shaders it actually only offers us one, unlike full fat OpenGL, which has several. But OpenGLES2.0's one buffer is a little more flexible. Full fat gives us different buffers for many different kinds of attribute, and uses them accordingly, but the flexibility of our OAB mean we can store all the different things we want to use in one buffer and simply address the different attribute using, base values, counts, and spread values to let our GPU know where in the buffer the attribute starts, how many bytes it needs and where to get the next set.

Though there is only one type of object attribute buffer, there are other types of buffer in OpenGLES2.0. Frame Buffers, Render Buffers, and Texture Buffers, also Texture and Frame Buffers can be tweaked to hold data other than graphics! But which ones are needed for which things and how do we set them up?

For now I'm only going to focus on the buffers we need at the moment, which are something which can work with our Texture and Vertex data, let's focus on Vertex Buffers, and as I noted I tend to refer to them as VBOs or VBs (though still really an OAB).

Vertex Buffers

So, it should be obvious that a vertex buffer is there to keep vertices in one place, more specifically in one place somewhere in our GPU memory, where it can be very quickly accessed and its contents sent to our Shader for use.

Actually a VB, in keeping with the whole concept of an OAB, is a very versatile form of buffer and it can actually hold pretty much any kind of sequence of data that the GPU needs to use when it turns the values in the buffer into *attributes* for the Shader. It does not even need to specifically work with vertices, it can just as easily work with pairs of texture coords, or even floats, but its main function is to work with vertices. There are some performance issues with odd sized data but we'll deal with those later, for now nothing we're doing is going to create major speed issues.

I'll explain a little later exactly what an attribute is, when we come to use our Shaders in anger.

In very simple terms, we want to store our cube vertices, and the texture coordinates that we use to draw it, inside the GPU memory and not have the GPU load and reload them form CPU memory every time a draw call is triggered.

If we can store it there, then once we've set it up its there for our GPU to use over and over again, no more loading the vertex list to the GPU, let's try that.

We can set up a Vertex Buffer with a very simple command.

```
GLvoid glGenBuffers (GLsizei n, GLuint* bufferhandles);
```

Used like this:

```
glGenBuffers (1, &vb);
```

But, all this does is allocate the concept of a buffer or buffers in the GPU, and return handle(s), which we can now refer to, to access it. The buffer does not yet actually exist in any real sense, as nothing has been put into it, so it's a buffer or buffers with 0 bytes of content. But now that we have created it we can send stuff to it.

We write data with a simple gl draw command, which will initialize that buffer and give it a size equivalent to whatever we write to it.

Now the data is there in GPU memory and it's ready for us to use, we don't need the data in CPU memory anymore, so if we loaded it we can release it, from now one we're going to use the buffer.

We're not quite done, if we have another chunk of model data we want to store in GPU memory, we could potentially insert our data into this buffer, but we do need to first make sure the buffer itself is big enough to take the subsequent values. We can only set the size of the buffer once at the initialization. So it's possible to insert new data after the first batch, but not possible to append data to it.

Once we insert the new data, we have to just remember that the second model's data is going be at the end of the first set of data and the third after that and so on. For now though I'm going to use a different buffer for each, just so we can get things going.

Next question is what exactly is this data? Well that is going to depend; if you look at our current simple vertex Shader you will see it lists a couple of things as attributes.

And that's the connection. These Shader attributes are data that is loaded each time the Shader is called, from our buffer stored in the GPU.

We can have different buffers, for example, right now we have vertex data in one and texture data in another, but it's also possible and often desirable to interleave the data, so that you have a chunk of vertex data, then a chunk of texture data. As long as the chunk sizes are the same, you basically are skipping through the data sending the parts you want when you need them.

All we have to do to parse through the different chunks of data that have to be loaded into those attribute variables, is let the GPU know, how much data we are going to send it, where it starts, and what kind of data its getting.

So suppose we have an interleaved set of data, three values for the vertices and two for the texture coordinates. We know they are all floats.

Next question is where to set up the buffers? I hope you think of this as a kind of initialization process, so setting up the buffers needs to be done when the model is created, not at the point it is drawn (which we've already seen is very slow). So we will add some code to our model constructor, and set up a VB. Setting up a buffer will look like this:

```
glGenBuffers(1, vb); // generate a buffer and put handle in vb
glBindBuffer(GL_ARRAY_BUFFER, vb); // bind the buffer stored at vb
glBufferData(GL_ARRAY_BUFFER, sizeof(GLfloat) * size, vertices, GL_STATIC_
DRAW); // write the data to it
glBindBuffer(GL_ARRAY_BUFFER, 0); // unbind to make sure
```

That's pretty much it, our vertices which were in CPU memory at the location called vertices. Are now happy and cosy and warm sitting in GPU memory. We don't know exactly where, the GPU does though, and it gave us a handle we stored in vb.

To draw that buffer we need only to bind it, set up the step values, enable the transfer by indicating which attribute the Shader is going to use it, and draw our triangles from the array with a glDrawArrays command, like this.

```
glBindBuffer (GL_ARRAY_BUFFER, vb); // we're going to use this buffer
// Set up the attributes
```

```
glVertexAttribPointer(positionAttribute, 3, GL_FLOAT, GL_FALSE, stride,
(void*)0);
glEnableVertexAttribArray(positionAttribute);
glDrawArrays(GL_TRIANGLES, 0, NumberOfTriangles);
```

There's a small issue of an ugly (void*)0 cast, because this routine is dual purpose and uses a CPU address when there is no bound buffer, and an offset when there is. So we have to turn our offset into an address to make it work. It's a small price to pay for 10+ times the speed.

Let's put this into action by modifying our cubes program to use a buffer.

Compile and run....try changing the 150 squares to 1500, or 15,000....we really are seeing a massive boost in performance. I bet that makes you feel like a coding god! Just a few simple changes and you see a hundred times increase in the performance.

We could have done this when doing 2D, but you really would not have seen the benefit. Drawing tiles is a pretty easy thing; drawing vertices, however, needs a bit more care and that care is rewarded with the programmer's favorite reward, speed!

Attribute Pointers

We briefly skipped over the attribute pointer command but it is very important and is the reason our single VBO is so flexible because it allows us to feed our Shaders with data. We can feed several Shader attributes at one time, and interleave those data in the *vertex* data we send.

Consider that attributes are variables in the Shader that are loaded with data from a buffer each time the Shader operates. This suggests that the data are being transferred and moved along to the next section of data ready for the next cycle.

The attribute pointer command is how we explain what to transfer, and where to transfer it to, and how much to move along.

It also has a dual function where it can describe an offset in a VBO, or a direct memory location. We have to be careful not to get those mixed up.

Look at the command we just used:

```
glVertexAttribPointer(positionAttribute, 3, GL_FLOAT, GL_FALSE, stride,
(void*)0);
```

This is telling us that the attribute we associate with position, should be loaded with 3 floats, which are not normalized, then we need to jump *stride* amount of entries from our current base point, and finally, the data start at a position 0 index in a VBO, or less likely at the data at address 0. We need to cast it to (void*) due to this dual nature of the command where it can take an address or an offset.

So if we have a sequence of values like this:

```
GLfloat TheCubeVertices[] = {
 -0.5f,-0.5f,-0.5f, // 1st set
 0.0f,0.0f,
 0.5f,-0.5f, -0.5f, //2nd set
 1.0f,0.0f,
 0.5f,0.5f,-0.5f, // 3rd set
 1.0f,1.0f,
 0.5f,0.5f,-0.5f,
 1.0f,1.0f, >>>>continue
```

We can see how these values relate to the command. Three vertices, then two tex coords, five entries per vertex. We don't just have to pass vertices, we also pass texture coordinates, and we can pass other attributes as our Shader might require, perhaps adding three floats for normals after the texture coordinates, increasing the stride to account for the new size of the data.

We can have any number of different attributes in the buffer. The only concession is that every *set*, will need the same quantity of data laid out in the same format.

Texture Buffer

We've used a texture buffer before, of course, but I glossed over the fact it was a buffer until we were ready to discuss it. Now we can talk about it a bit more.

How texture buffers are used is really quite complex, as internally there's a massive amount of work going on which really makes our GPU come into its own we'll touch on that complexity very soon.

But basically, we want to store as many of our textures as possible in the GPU memory, there are some limits, of course, not just in terms of sizes. Memory usage is never going to go away, I touched on the power of two (POT), and the fact things need to be flipped, also we can actually only have a certain number active at any given time, which might vary depending on the GPU. But the nice thing about texture buffers is that we can store a decent number of them, and use them with different Shaders and even on a wide range of vertices. Though usually we'll have a set of textures associated with a particular set of vertices.

We used one big texture image on our 2D sprites, which gave us the ability to display each tile of the texture with two triangles, and we can still do that with 3D, the limitation on the numbers of textures we can store, does not really limit the number of tiles we can access. We're not using proper textures just yet, but we will be soon!

Frame Buffer

This one is easy because we have been using it since our very first project, though the system provided Frame Buffer is not quite the same as an application provided Frame Buffer.

The simplest way to explain a frame buffer is; it's the place where the image gets produced, just before the swap sends it to the screen. When we have done all our different kinds of renders and Shader work, the Frame Buffer is what will contain the final product.

When in a Frame Buffer, we can choose to save that data for later, grab and save it as a raw data file or as we normally do, send it to the screen. We could add a few extra effects, stencils, or other things, though it would need to go back to the CPU first, but essentially it's a temporary area set up after the rendering is done ready to be sent to somewhere for storage or view.

We can have many instances of a Frame Buffer, and choose to send them in different sequences, which is basically what we did with our 2D projects.

We can create application Frame Buffers using this command, which you have seen before:

```
GLvoid glGenFramebuffers(GLsizei n, GLuint* framebuffers)
```

where:

- *n* equals the number of Frame Buffer's you want to be generated.

- *Framebuffers* is a pointer to a variable to store the generated IDs/handles. It's set up so that if you want more than one to be generated, the pointer will point to the start of an integer array.

Deleting a framebuffer is, of course, also possible using;

```
GLvoid DeleteFramebuffers(GLsizei n, GLuint *framebuffers);
```

Which, of course, is basically the reverse of the create function with the same arguments. There are a few advanced functions relating to framebuffers we'll look at later. For the moment though, the only other command that really is needed for a Frame Buffer is

```
GLvoid glBindFramebuffer (GLenum target, GLuint framebuffer)
```

Binding as we noted in the past puts this particular Frame Buffer into the GPU's focus, OpenGLES2.0 can only ever focus on one Frame Buffer at a time, so no matter how many you create, the last one you bind is the one OpenGLES2.0 will work with and send data to or from.

Strangely the variable `target` will always be GL_FRAMEBUFFER, though maybe in a later implementation of OpenGLES, it may change to allow for something else. The variable `framebuffer`, of course, will be the ID/handle that is associated with that buffer.

Unless you are planning some post processing or have a reason to implement a triple/quad buffer, you only really ever need the system Frame Buffer.

Render Buffer

Ah, now these are a bit complex, because in one sense they don't actually exist in OpenGLES2.0 but are such a mainstay of normal OpenGL that we find ways to emulate them. We're not actually going to use them for a while, so we're going to gloss over this for now. It is, however, as the name suggests a buffer where things can be rendered into, which is essentially what the Frame Buffers offer. A true Render Buffer can be sent to the screen, but OpenGLES2.0 only allows for one Render Target, the one we swap to view, so we use a combination of Frame Buffers and textures to give us a fair approximation of a Render Buffer. This can and will be useful if we want to render things in different ways and combine them later. Rendering allows us to create buffers with different output types; these are the types OpenGLES2.0 supports:

```
DEPTH_COMPONENT16, RGBA4, RGB5_A1, RGB565, STENCIL_INDEX8
```

We will use this later but for now just know that they exist and we will play with them soon.

Buffers Are Not Free

Now, it's become very clear if we intend to do any decent amount of poly shifting we have to use buffers, but buffers by definition need to use up some RAM space. And on SBCs, we really don't have a lot of space, our GPU memory needs to hold some RAM for its own needs. So adding massive numbers of buffers, tempting as it is, isn't always possible but it is very desirable.

Sure, we can expand the size of our GPU memory, manually when needed, or allow the dynamic GPU allocation on some SBCs to do it, but that then eats up into your CPU RAM… You have to find a balance, which is going to directly depend on the needs of your game.

Sixty-four megabytes is a lot of memory, it really is, but it can vanish in no time if you don't think carefully about how much data you load into it.

Another thing we have to be very clear about, and best to say this now, the GPUs in most SBCs are….well, not to put it too politely, rubbish! They really are painfully bad. Most are only two cores running at less than half the CPU speed, and most often use shared slow RAM with the CPU. There is just no way to expect an SBC's GPU to be as powerful as even the lowest power PC graphics card. In fact they are less powerful than an average current android phone.

So we're faced with an interesting dilemma, OpenGLES2.0 more or less allows us to do anything that the big boys can do, but that basic lack of processing power means it's slow to do anything beyond basic tasks. This is when game development starts to become painful, because we are soon going to get to a point where we want to do something really cool, but doing it will make our games suck. That's the challenge! Work with our limits, embrace them, push them, but respect them and amend your approach to your game design to deal with the lack of power. But let's not be too down about this, even though right now asking our GPU to do more than a few things will choke it, it does not mean those few things can't be fun to learn and we can find ways to make them happen.

▮ Let's Get Back to It

Now we're on the move. We can load up the attribute buffers with a vertex list, and the draw call has been modified to use a buffered list if it exists or set one up if it doesn't as long as we don't bring in massive numbers of new models in a cycle that should be fine. Though we can add a preload option to our code later.

As we did with GameObjects in 2D, we can add any number of instances of an ObjectModel or its inheritors to the processing list, in fact, why not try and do a triangle or pyramid object using the CubeModel Class as a template, all you need do is create a class, write an update routine similar to what is there, a Draw method, which accounts for the number of vertices and steps, point to a valid set of vertices for your object and you should be able to draw your own objects at positions of your choice (stay within a −11 to +11 range on X and Y though, so we keep our models in our immediate view)!

What we'll try to do now is move our camera around a bit to make viewing a bit more interactive. Take note of the Camera Class, and the fact I am moving it around, normally you'd move a character/ship/object around and the camera will be somehow attached to that object, but for now we just want to get a feel for moving around in the space, so our camera itself is the prime object.

Neat huh? Our camera is moving around, we have multiple axis of control and our cubes just keep on spinning. We have a real sense of freedom and movement.

As an exercise, try to make the cubes move in a circle around the origin, while spinning. It's not a massive leap from when you did the KamaKazi invader arcs.

As you are writing this though, don't move your camera around too much, set it so you can view the motion from a reasonable distance and ensure that it's doing what you think it is doing. Movement of the camera can sometimes alter your perception of motion, so stay static until you're sure it works.

Time to Texture Our Cube

So, now we've got fast rendering sorted, it's time to turn our attention to the other major concept of a model. Textures.

At least we're familiar with the concept, having used them in our 2D sprites, but now we have to apply them to vertices, which may or may not be as regular a shape as a quad or cube. It's not quite as complex as it might seem, but in truth, it gets a lot more complex as we add vertices, and each vertex needs to pin a starting UV to itself so much so that UV mapping, layout out a texture over a set of vertices, is not a task you really want to do manually. It's one of those tasks the artist needs to take care of with their own tools.

Also we have to take into account that every single object, might have its own set of textures, and possibly may require its own Shaders. Our current system of setting up a single Shader system during our project initialization no longer seems valid.

Every renderable object, when it's created, now needs to take some responsibility for loading graphics and turning them into textures, or using an existing texture. Also our Shader manager is now going to need a lot more Shaders.

Technically, we're starting to get a lot more complex. But, in principle, it's all exactly the same.

Let's just start out and put a nice image on our cube faces. First though we need to address the fact our simple 3D Shaders currently have no capacity to handle textures. The current particular pair of Shaders is only interested in transforming vertices and drawing cubes as colors. But no worries we've used a texture Shader before when we did our Frame Buffer, what we have to do now is combine the way we transform and draw our 2D buffer texture with our 3D MVP system.

What could go wrong?

It's time to introduce a couple of new Shaders, ones which not only allow us to see a cube but also to use the MVP and also give textures. This is our Vertex Shader.

```
precision mediump float;
attribute vec3 a_position;
attribute vec2 a_texCoord;
uniform mat4 MVP;
varying vec2 v_texCoord;

void main()
{
  gl_Position = MVP * vec4(a_position, 1);
  v_texCoord = a_texCoord;
}
```

And our Fragment Shader.

```
precision mediump float;
varying vec2 v_texCoord;
uniform sampler2D s_texture;
void main()
{
  gl_FragColor = texture2D(s_texture, v_texCoord);
}
```

Not doing much, though now we are using texture 2D, which in simple terms is taking the pixel from the point given to it by the vertex Shader.

In the resources folder you'll find my favorite pic of my grandson taken by my son in law and daughter, she'll hate me for using it, but let's make Harvey the most famous cube texture in this book, and put his image on our cubes.

Add this code to your cube instantiations, remember to add a prototype:

```
// Load, create texture
CubeModel::CubeModel(MyFiles* FH) : CubeModel()
{
 int width, height;
 char* image =FH->Load((char*)"../Resources/Textures/Harvey2.jpg", &width,
&height);
 glGenTextures(1, &texture1); // create our 1st texture and store the
handle in texture
 glBindTexture(GL_TEXTURE_2D, texture1); // bind it, so it now is what we
are looking at
// Set our texture parameters
 glTexParameteri(GL_TEXTURE_2D, GL_TEXTURE_WRAP_S, GL_REPEAT); // Set
texture wrapping to GL_REPEAT
 glTexParameteri(GL_TEXTURE_2D, GL_TEXTURE_WRAP_T, GL_REPEAT);
 // Set texture filtering
 glTexParameteri(GL_TEXTURE_2D, GL_TEXTURE_MIN_FILTER, GL_LINEAR);
 glTexParameteri(GL_TEXTURE_2D, GL_TEXTURE_MAG_FILTER, GL_LINEAR);
 // now put the image in there...might be tricky
 glTexImage2D(GL_TEXTURE_2D, 0, GL_RGBA, width, height, 0, GL_RGBA, GL_
UNSIGNED_BYTE, image);
 glBindTexture(GL_TEXTURE_2D, 0); // Unbind texture when done, so we won't
accidently mess up our texture.
}
```

This will load in the image and make a nice texture active and its handle available in the variable texture1. What the code now has to do is set up the system to send two values to the Shader each time the Shader needs them, one for the actual location of the three vertex points we used before, and now there are the two texture coordinates. This data is supplied to the Shader by using the handles for positionLoc and texCoordLoc. The set up looks like this:

```
//load the vertex data
glVertexAttribPointer(this->positionLoc,
```

```
3, // write 3 values
GL_FLOAT, // they are floats
GL_FALSE, // not normals
5 * sizeof(GLfloat),//now many bytes till the next(stride)
TheCubeVertices // where does it start
);
```

And a similar set up for the texture info, but the texture coords start after the three vertex coords so we need to be +3 from the base, but the offset needs byte values so we multiply 3* the sizeof a float (usually 4 bytes) to get a value that indicates where in the buffer memory the texture coords start. I say usually 4 bytes, because the size of a float can vary depending on what machine it is running on, its best never to assume and so we use the sizeof function to make sure when we compile we get the right size.

```
// Load the texture coordinate
glVertexAttribPointer(this->texCoordLoc,
 2, // write 2 values
 GL_FLOAT,
 GL_FALSE,
 5 * sizeof(GLfloat), // stride does not change
 TheCubeVertices +(3 * sizeof(GLfloat))
      );
```

The next step is to enable these values so that each time the Shader operates it will pull in this data in chunks of threes for vertices and twos for texture (UV) coords, as we defined them.

```
glEnableVertexAttribArray(this->positionLoc);
glEnableVertexAttribArray(this->texCoordLoc);
```

Ok, so the buffer is set up to feed the Shader with vertex and texture data, now fix the correct texture to the process by binding it, making it the current active texture:

```
glBindTexture(GL_TEXTURE_2D, this->texture1);
```

and finally, reset the sampler 2D value in the Shader to 0.

```
glUniform1i(this->samplerLoc, 0);
```

Make these small changes to the draw code then run, we should see this.

Ok, so that's looking pretty good, isn't he cute? He gets his good looks from me you know! But wait something isn't quite right...look carefully at the textures, things seem to be cutting out?

And if you think about it, it's exactly what should happen, as a face tumbles toward you it's going to be closer in the Z-axis that one that is tumbling away, creating a kind of clash, and because of the default nature of the culling on OpenGLES the face, or triangle that's further away, clips out...it looks very odd, and clearly not what we want to happen. So how do we fix it?

The Fixed Pipeline Isn't Quite Dead

Yes there are still some throwbacks to the old fixed pipeline on OpenGLES2.0. Certain state flags need to be set in order to allow certain things to happen. One of these relates to Depth Buffers. For us to stop our clipping triangles, we need to give OpenGLES2.0 some sense of where in the Z coord a vertex is to avoid it over-ruling another vertex, which is clashing with it and trying to draw 2 pixels at the same point, this will allow the face/pixel closest to the view to be the one drawn.

It does this by keeping a depth buffer, a buffer than relates to the Z coord of the vertices and pixels it is drawing, and allowing decisions to be made based on another fixed function value. To use a Depth Buffer, two important things need to be done.

During your set up, your EGL context needs to be told you want one, and it has to respond with an enthusiastic ok...I've never known it say no, though its enthusiasm might depend on the space available.

Also you need to enable the depth Buffer in OpenGLES2.0 itself, usually at your Set up with this:

```
glEnable(GL_DEPTH_TEST);
```

Simple enough, you also need a condition test for the Depth buffer and there are a number of options, which should be apparent from the GL2.h header.

```
#define GL_NEVER          0x0200
#define GL_LESS           0x0201
#define GL_EQUAL          0x0202
#define GL_LEQUAL         0x0203
#define GL_GREATER        0x0204
#define GL_NOTEQUAL       0x0205
#define GL_GEQUAL         0x0206
#define GL_ALWAYS         0x0207
```

Quite a collection and these provide some interesting options. For what we want though all we need is

```
glDepthFunc(GL_LEQUAL);
```

Once the Context is set up with a depth buffer AND we have enabled the GL_DEPTH_TEST AND correct depth function, we are good to go. There are several other values you can set to influence your Depth Buffer, but for now, default values work fine, so let's not get too deep into this.

Mapping a Texture to Our Faces

If you only want to have one texture on each face, we can use UVs of 0.0f and 1.0f. We've had that in our attribute list for some time, with no problem, as the start and end points, but what if we want each face to be different which is, of course, is the more usual situation for a real-world item or something like a die.

You may have noticed that my lovely picture of grandson Harvey worked perfectly even though it was not a POT image. Any idea why? Any thoughts on the implications of using an odd size?

A cube is thankfully pretty easy to deal with, and a texture for six sides might look a bit like this.

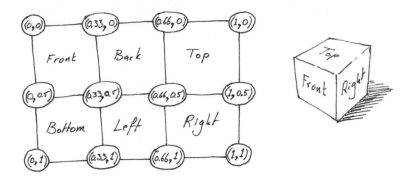

Clearly we can see (because we put text there for you) where the top, bottom, and sides are, and I also have highlighted the UV coordinates, for each start point, I am not personally too happy using one-thirds for a UV, as it's a repeating fraction we'll discuss this soon, but for now this will work. This is our new texture; it has POT sizes of 128×64.

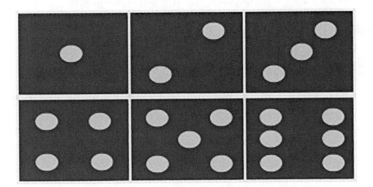

We already have a cube table with UVs tacked to it, but now we need to change those values so that we can get the right UV to pin itself to the right vertex. Load the Die texture this time instead of Harvey, and change the cube table textures according to the texture layout in the figure above, and you should now get this:

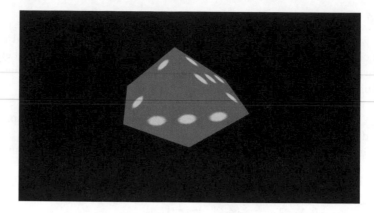

All that really is changing in the code is the UV coord we give to each vertex, and, of course, we load up a texture, which contains the six different faces we want to display.

Now one small thing I want you to play with, our die is not actually correct, the opposite faces of a normal die should add up to seven; you should be able to work out how to do a correct die, try altering the UV coords in the cube list array.

We probably won't ever have to manually enter such information, there are a great many art packages, which provide UV mapping systems for shapes that are far more complex, and we should certainly use them rather than typing things in. But knowing how your textures map onto your vertices is important should you need to locate some pesky off point image that is throwing up an occasional graphic glitch.

Choose the Size to Suit

Another consideration with textures is scaling, the smaller your texture, the less convincing it looks if scaled up. Though GPUs have amazing internal algorithms to deal with scaling a texture, you can't stretch a couple of pixels to a large size without seeing some form of pixilation. So we need to consider what size we are going to view our image. As a general rule, if your image is going to be predominantly 128 pixels in size on screen, use a 128 pixel texture, if you use a 16 pixel texture, as an extreme example, you'll get horrible artifacts.

Generally, we can expect a texture to appear wrong if it's scaled too much, either up or down in scale, but within a range it's usually fine and the eye can forgive a bit of pixilation on a well-drawn texture, also we can blur things a little using some antialiasing systems.

However, we can easily display an item with different sized textures, to create Level of Detail (LOD) effects to reduce the impact on our eyes. And also there's a technique called mipmapping to make this a semiautomatic process at the expense of a more texture memory.

We'll get to all that later though, for now we can be happy we have a firmer grasp of what a texture is, how to place it over vertices (wrapping), and how to avoid some easy traps that create glitches.

Limited Numbers of Textures?

Textures are funny things though, depending on your target, you can actually only work on a certain number of different texture images at a time. Though you can store almost any number, it of course also relates to how much memory you have allocated to the GPU.

Shaders too have some limits on how many textures they can address at once. The Raspberry Pi and most other SBCs I've checked, has a limit of eight, meaning the Shaders can only work with eight at any given time.

You can find out how many textures your fragment Shaders can handle with this pair of lines.

```
GLint MaxTextureUnits;
glGetIntegerv(GL_MAX_TEXTURE_IMAGE_UNITS, &MaxTextureUnits);
```

This will load the number of texture units/images the GPU can handle into the variable MaxTextureUnits and on my Pi it gives eight.

You can also ask how many the vertex Shader can handle with;

```
GLint MaxVertexTextureUnits;
glGetIntegerv(GL_MAX_VERTEX_TEXTURE_IMAGE_UNITS, &MaxVertexTextureUnits);
```

Again on a Raspberry Pi Model3B it's eight. Now, eight textures per Shader does not sound like a lot, but remember we have UV mapping, so we can actually put a lot of individual parts of a models texture in one or more big texture units/images. So, in fact, eight is quite a lot and in most cases you'll only ever really need to use two or three for some effects.

It's not especially wise (though possible with a bit of gymnastics, and a spare image unit) to have a model using more than one texture for its graphics, so try to keep the texture images in a tidy order and manage them well, so you have the right textures in GPU memory when you need them.

Another thing to test is the actual max size of your textures, which you can find with another simple enquiry:

```
GLint MaxTextureSizes;
glGetIntegerv(GL_MAX_TEXTURE_SIZE, &MaxTextureSizes);
```

On the Raspberry Pi Model3B it's 2048, so you could set your video memory to 192 MB, have 128 MB of texture space and the rest can be buffers. That is more or less the max size you'd need your GPU memory to be. Some higher spec machines can give you more Texture units in your Shaders and have more GPU memory, but 2048 is pretty much the current max for size. And as far as I know the OpenGLES2.0 spec has a maximum possible of 32 texture units. Of course, there are many good reasons why even 192 MB isn't going to be enough; all will become painfully clear as we start to stress our hardware.

From the CPU side, we can only really operate on one texture at a time too, the bound one, (the Shader, however, can operate on several (GL_MAX_TEXTURE_IMAGE_UNITS) at once) it's true we can unbind one and bind another but that's the gymnastics I was talking about, we don't really like to do this.

This limit on textures means it's actually a pretty good idea to keep your textures managed separately from your models vertices. If your model loads up textures itself, it may not have access to info on whether that texture is already loaded or bound.

Having info beforehand on what texture goes with what model is important, and keeping track of what textures are loaded at the moment, so that the model can then be informed if its texture is in place, is a good way to work, especially when we have a lot of models.

Anyway…as I said, textures are complex, and we'll increase our understanding as we go.

Everyone Loves a Triangle But!

In our 2D game, we created sprites from two triangles, to represent our characters on screen, and in OpenGLES2.0 we make them up from two triangles laid flat and joined up to create a square shape.

In our HelloCubes example, we still made our cubes out of triangles, so it might seem that triangles are the only game in town...well speaking personally they should be but...

Triangles are great; in fact, triangles to a programmer are the epitome of perfection... A triangle is the building block of so many things in any 3D game, but OpenGLES very kindly offers us a few other basic types of primitive

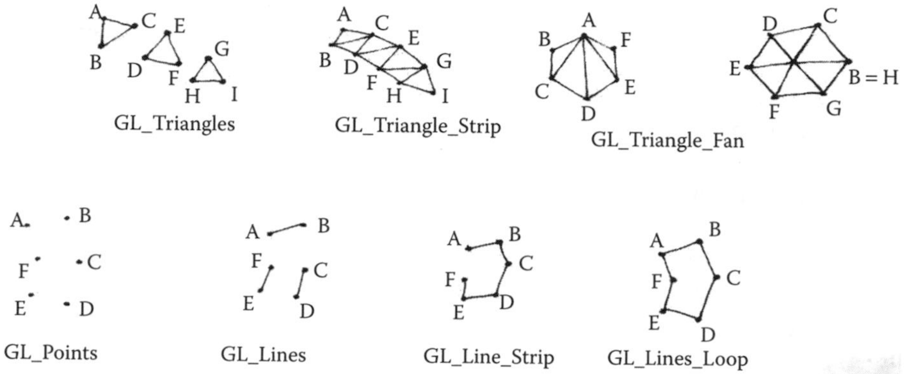

| GL_Triangles | GL_Triangle_Strip | GL_Triangle_Fan |

| GL_Points | GL_Lines | GL_Line_Strip | GL_Lines_Loop |

So we will see a lot of things done with triangles, fans and strips, but never ever give up on the triangle, it's still the most important basic shape we have! You may have noticed our draw system currently only uses Triangles using this command to inform the OpenGLES system of its intent.

```
glDrawArrays(GL_TRIANGLES, 0, 3);
```

As programmers we will mostly use Triangles, some Lines, and a few Points and they work fine as you'll see, but the other types are less common from a programmer's usage and tend to be decided by a model's design needs. So long as we set up the data before doing the glDrawArray, or other draw command, which sets up the GPU to do its thing all will be fine.

A large collection of these triangles and the other basic shape types all joined together creates what's called a mesh...when you see a mesh with no texture you can understand the name.

The following image shows a robot model, which contains around 830 vertices, roughly 200 faces. A face being either a triangle or other closed polygon. In this case, we're also seeing most of the faces represented as quads. This is because the drawing package used provides quads as a base type, even though we almost certainly will output them as triangles or one of our other supported primitive types. Artists though, like to use quads as the fewer lines they have, the easier it is to see where there might be a poly overload (errors or inefficiencies in their model).

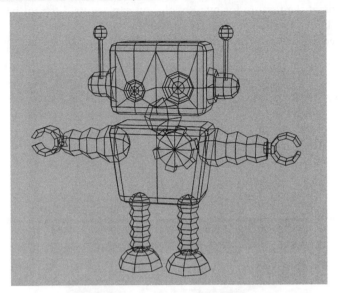

We used textures on our sprites to spread over the faces and create a nice regular looking square or pair of triangles as needed, but we can spread a texture over a massive number of triangles or quads, which *fills in* the holes in our mesh, this basically creates our basic concept of a model.

Unlike our flat 2D image of two triangles, which made up a sprite, our model contains hundreds of triangles, and has a new Z-dimension that gives it shape and depth. Each of these triangles though has a face…our sprite *square* had two faces and we covered them with a texture, now we have several hundred faces to cover. How do we do that?

Take a look at the texture for our Robot. You can see its different parts laid out in what is hopefully the smallest surface area possible to lay them out. This is the exact same method we used to place our sprite textures into a larger draw texture.

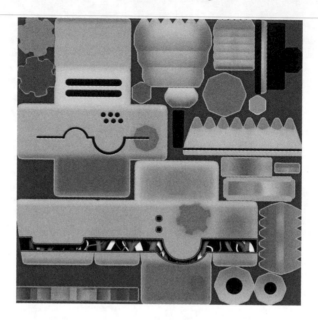

You can see all the individual textures are combined into one big texture, which has a size that can be anything from 32 × 32 to 2048 × 2048, it actually depends on the GPU you are using and the amount of memory it has allocated. But whatever size we settle on for our texture, we use a normalized coordinate so that we have values of 0 to 1. Each triangle in the wire mesh then covers itself with a part of this big texture referenced by a normalized coordinate, called a UV coordinate. Given we have a quite limited amount of texture RAM on an SBC, we really want to use as small as texture as possible and make it as efficient as possible. The Robot texture has a lot of gaps in it, that's something we should try to avoid as much as possible.

Now if you're just trying to texture up a cube, it's probably not a massive chore to work out coordinates, type them in, and so on, but our little 800+ vertex model is already waaaaay beyond the limits of any normal human programmer to input without error.

Which is why models of any complexity are not input by hand? This is a job for an artist, or a modeler to be more specific.

We could do an interesting exercise in texture mapping on our HelloCubes code, but really the chances of you actually needing to hand texture a model are tiny, though should you ever need to, by the time we've finished this section you'll be more than able to.

3D Lets Get into the Heart of Our GPU

At the center of our Raspberry Pi and pretty much any other target machine, beats the combined beating heart of a CPU and a GPU. CPUs are pretty well understood but GPUs are something else, something else entirely. So far all we know is it does graphics and eats up some of our RAM to do its magic but in fact it is potentially the most powerful piece of hardware we have at our fingertips.

GPUs are in effect, incredibly specialized processing units, which, like a CPU, accept programming and manipulate data, but spit out results far faster than any CPU. This is because they are dealing with data that is designed to be displayed. Unlike the general nature of a CPU, a GPU's whole design is based on knowing exactly what kind of data it has and what it has to do.

For the most part that revolves around the fastest way to draw triangles, and render them as pixels, using colors and light to influence the final output.

If an average screen has 1920 × 1200 resolution these days…that's 1920 × 1200 pixels or 2,304,000 pixels… each one of which has potentially had its color, intensity, transparency measured tested against others, and displayed. That's a lot of pixels!

So a GPU is continually processing massive amounts of screen memory to present an image for you. AND in 3D it's also dealing with the conversion of 3D space into 2D space to display on a flat screen!

It is a mind numbing thing to actually consider, just how much work a GPU does to present an image every 60th of a second (or less) for you to see a yellow Pizza man eating dots.

With each pixel probably containing a byte for Red, Green, Blue colors and a byte for an Alpha (transparency) that's over 8 MB of data to display a screen….8 MB!!! And yes you can even have two, four, and even more bytes for the RBGA…each doubles the amount of memory being addressed.

When I started coding Spectrums, in the 1980s, last century! Screens took up to 6 K and we bitched at the fact they used up a big chunk of our available 48 K? I feel old, but also excited at the way computers have become capable of such advances in processing power and graphic manipulation.

So our GPU does an immense amount of work, it's a beast of a chip, and it has to be, but what it does at heart is inherently simple, it just does it better than anything our CPU could possibly do, so long as we tell it exactly what we want it to do, in the way it can understand.

What Else You Got?

Triangles, marvelous as they are though, do have some limits; there are many occasions when we might need our other types of primitive or just want to do Points, or Lines.

The basic types give us immense flexibility when it comes to choosing the right kind of primitive to draw our objects, and we can visualize these pretty easily to do a massive range of simple procedurally generated objects.

There are a lot of mathematical shapes we can create, as easy as triangles are, cubes and pyramids are just a little bit more complex, spheres, tori, and other regular shapes are also possible. But aside from messing with them in demos, they are very seldom if ever used in games. It's great to be able to use them for holding images or to experiment with

Shaders, but since we're about to actually get into loading models, we don't need to spend any real time on them, but feel free to experiment yourself and perhaps make up a few stock shape objects, like our cube, or perhaps a torus. You'll find the vertex code is easy to locate and I've posted a few standard shapes on the support site.

Having these stock shapes available is helpful, they are compact and effective, feel free to use them when you need to. But really we need things in our games that look like they are part of the environment they belong to. A pulsing sphere isn't really a good representation for a hammer throwing Thunder god, in your Asgard set fighting game! For that we need;

An Artist.

Yes, sadly there are limits to a programmer's art skills whenever we try to actually produce something that we want to look like a character or an environment. So in those circumstances we need to feed some fish heads to the semi tame artist every pro programmer keeps in their basement.

But artists know nothing of the joy of procedurally generating a character, they instead shun the sensible logic of a programmer and use an art package and express their creativity with imagination and skill, with a pen, sometimes on a tablet so that they can actually create realistic or cartoony looking characters. Which probably is a better idea than typing in 2000 vertices into a text file, fun though you may find that!

Artists generally produce models and that's what we want to get our hands on rather than spend 20 more pages on creating elegant torus shapes.

But whenever you have one member of the development team doing something different to another, you need some form of transfer of information. The art packages used by Artists are frankly mind numbingly complex, and they output the results of their work in a vast range of formats. But ultimately it's all data, and data is something we can use, as long as we know the format of that data.

We don't really need to know how the artist produces the work, but we do know how make use of that work in our games. It's time to explore rendering and display of models.

Loading Models (OBJ)

Now loading a model, like loading a graphic image file, is a bit of a kerfuffle. Models are several orders of magnitude more complex than the simple hand coded shapes we've done already and they will usually also have complex texture mapping to take care of.

OpenGLES2.0 or any graphic API for that matter, does not provide any means to handle such files, it really only knows how to draw the primitive triangles and simple types that make it up, it will be up to us to feed the details of the mesh to our GPU and that is usually done by routines in our SDK.

That is both a limitation and a freedom that OpenGLES2.0 gives us, if all we actually have to worry about is sending the primitives to the render system, the way the data itself is arranged, stored, and distributed, is basically up to us, or ideally up to smarter people than us.

Whatever format we use, the end result is that we need the raw data that makes up the model, at a minimum, that will be the vertex data, but we may also need UV information for the texture, and other technical pieces of data relating to lighting and other forms of texture mapping. There's a lot of information we can push into a file format, some of which will become clearer later.

So, there's a range of different model formats, which will give us more or less of the data we need, but there are a couple of standards. They don't always provide the best means of storing graphics but since we are a bit short of options that are both free and easily available for Linux-based machines, we need to use what we can find!

Locate and Install an OBJ Model Loader

Yes it's library time again and as usual with open source there are many available. I had a good look around at the options, measured their features against what we need in our projects, and came to a choice detailed later.

The simplest possible common format is .OBJ, this is a fairly universal format first adopted by Wavefront and made open source by them, meaning pretty much any other 3D graphics package can save in this format, or you can find a converter that does. For example, there is a nice online free converter available here http://www.greentoken.de/onlineconv/.

I say simple, but in fact OBJ has several rather complex features that allow for a lot of flexibility and detail in their models and it continues to be added to but generally most low/midsize poly models convert quite well.

There is a downside though, the .OBJ file format, is not compressed, it is a text-based system, which can be useful, but also means it occupies a lot of storage space on your SD/EMMC and when it is loaded. It also contains only 3D geometry of a model. Textures are not included by default, though UV position data are. It is, however, usually accompanied by a material file (.MTL), which can define textures and several other relevant details about how the surfaces of the model should be rendered.

This means we need to load the file, parse it, create buffers and then generate the raw binary data we have to send to the GPU along with the textures, if not already loaded.

Like image processing this is something many programmers will happily spend their working days doing, but we don't really have the time! So we're going to locate a tool that can take .OBJ files, and allow us to take advantage of some decent graphic tools we might have access to. But the more formats we have, the more complex the library and the more internal memory it will take when our project is up and running, here's a new Golden Rule to remember, if you don't need it, don't waste the memory with it.

So the choice; well I went for…TinyObjLoader

Here's an example image (above) from the Github download site for TinyLoaderObj. This is actually the Rungholt scene,* a well-known test scene. Don't be fooled by all the pretty images, we actually have to do a lot of work to get an image like this on an SBC, but it can be done! Though not in real time, this image has 6.7M triangles in it and as much as I like and have faith our tiny machines, this would be a step too far. We could build it up and create a static image, but viewing all the triangles like this is pretty much impossible for our tiny machines. But the point that TinyObjLoader is capable of loading such a large scene is impressive.

I chose TinyObjLoader, simply because it's compact, effective and very well supported. There will be other model loaders available, and almost certainly some will be better for the models you plan to put in your game, but for now, this will work for us, so we'll use it. You can access it from:

```
https://github.com/syoyo/tinyobjloader
```

I won't include it in the support site; since it will probably get updated periodically and it's best you download it, or another with similar features, yourself.

In actual use, it breaks down into a single header file, so just like our file/image handling system; we need a small cpp file to take care of compiling it and allowing us to access it. Unlike our file/image systems though we don't create a new class, just a simple cpp file, which includes it with a #define, creating a namespace wrapper around some global functions.

---

* Rungholt is available from McGuire, Computer Graphics Archive, accessed on June 28, 2016. http://graphics. cs.williams.edu/data

But as always with libs, you are free to put your own system in place, and even try writing your own if you find that kind of work appeals to you. An Obj Loader isn't the most complex of things to parse, but it does take some time, and that particular wheel has already been invented.

One important point though, it's a loader; there's a clue in the name, TinyObjLoader. It's NOT a display system; we will get to that later, because that's a whole other kettle of fish. But it's not a kettle of fish we're entirely unfamiliar with!

If you have access to a tame artist who can output their models and textures in a more compact and usable format, please do use them, if you can locate an open source library for Linux that can load them, you will find that a lot more effective than constantly using .OBJ, but fall-backs are designed to always be there, so let's consider .OBJ as our fall-back.

Installing and Using TinyObjLoader

Installing TinyObjLoader is a little bit like installing the required part of the SOIL library we did already. But with a twist, this time we're not going to wrap a big slow to compile system, the header actually contains all the code and we just need a simple means of letting it compile and be forgotten about. The cpp file we need for this is painfully simple:

```
#define TINYOBJLOADER_IMPLEMENTATION
#include "tiny_obj_loader.h"
```

Yup, that's all, just make sure now that you include the tiny_ob_loader.h file in your Headers directory, and we are then good to go. But don't use the #define in any other file it may result in two sets of TinyObjLoader functions. The header compiles and creates a group of global (not contained in a class) functions wrapped in a `tinyobj` namespace, which won't please C++ purists but if it gets the job done, I'm not too interested in rewriting it.

Any other cpp file, which wants to make use of the loader needs only to include the header and access the functions by entering `tinyobj:: Function_name(args)`.

Considering that TinyObjLoader's main purpose in life is to load Obj files, there is really only one function we care about `LoadObj()`, it does come in two flavors, passing different arguments to overload the function, but basically it's there to load our Objs. There's also a load with callbacks and a `LoadMtl()` function, but we don't really need those to do what we need to do.

The LoadObj code in the header gives us this information:

```
// Loads .obj from a file.
// 'attrib', 'shapes' and 'materials' will be filled with parsed shape data
// 'shapes' will be filled with parsed shape data
// Returns true when loading .obj become success.
// Returns warning and error message into `err`
// 'mtl_basepath' is optional, and used for base path for .mtl file.
// 'triangulate' is optional, and used whether triangulate polygon face in .obj
// or not.
bool LoadObj(attrib_t *attrib, std::vector<shape_t> *shapes,
             std::vector<material_t> *materials, std::string *err,
             const char *filename, const char *mtl_basepath = NULL,
             bool triangulate = true);
```

We should by now, be getting used to reading headers and understanding what they do, this one is a bit long but it's pretty straightforward.

Loading most OBJs is usually a two-stage process, it's started by loading the vertices, but we also, in the case of textured objects need the graphic file or files that make up the texture. So, first stage is to load the Obj and the corresponding material (MTL) file, and allow it work out all the attribute data for the model. We are actually providing it with empty vectors for the shape_t and material_t structures, which it will fill, for our later use.

TinyObjLoader will not, however, load and convert our textures, that's the second stage, it will simply put info about them into the material_t struct and we need to check that later. So after the shapes are built we then have to parse the data files for any graphic files that might also need to be loaded and converted into textures.

I've done all the typing for you again and adapted the example code on the TinyObjLoader git hub, which needed converting from OpenGL to GLES2.0.

The result is we can now load a properly formatted OBJ file, and its associated MTL and texture files. Though sometimes things will go wrong. So I'm going to make one or two alterations and not use TinyObjLoader directly but wrap it in a function that will do some of the donkey work of loading textures as well, and report any errors for us. We need to talk a little bit about how we get hold of those textures and later how to use them properly.

Do We Care about the Data?

While TinyObjLoader will make our life easier there are a few other factors we have to think about. Loading the data is one thing, but using it is another, like most data, it's just a lot of seemingly random numbers and attributes. Also some of the data that was loaded needs to be used in specific ways by our renderer, which we've not fully written yet.

The entire format of the OBJ model can be rather complex, so some of that is handed off to another file called the material file and represented with a .mtl file extension.

Our OBJ file in its simplest form will focus mainly on three types of info,

Vertices using an identifier *v* like this:
v 38.268581 66.621857 -19.958624

Texture coords using an identifier *vt*
vt 0.657997 0.129749

And faces or surfaces of our polygons using *f*
f 382/532/507 409/586/5098 406/545/454

Faces, in this instance, are actually indexes into the list of vertex triplets we have identified beforehand. OBJ is smart enough to not list the same vertex twice, making the indexing the correct way to build the triangle.

There are a few other things you might see like *g* for grouping *s* for smoothing, and so on, but for the most basic of models, v, vt, and f are all we need as far as vertex info is concerned.

Take special care to notice the use of mtllib, a command that tells the Loader and the render to make use of a material file, which will contain info on how the surface should be rendered, and with what textures and texture/lighting effects. So if you see this in your OBJ file

```
mtllib walk-frm1.mtl
```

It indicates we need to use a material file called walk-frm1.mtl, which looks like this:

```
newmtl RobotBuddy_meshSG
illum 4
```

```
Kd 0.49 0.49 0.49
Ka 0.00 0.00 0.00
Tf 1.00 1.00 1.00
Ni 1.00
Ks 0.00 0.00 0.00
Ns 0.00
```

Newmtl RobotBuddy_meshSG is just indicating a name for this list of odd and obscure references to things called Kd, Ka, Tf, and so on…we don't really want to get too far into this just now, but when you get into your rendering you will find these numbers and the order they are sent will relate to your methods of rendering, things such as color and radiosity and…erm other stuff we've not done yet.

But none of this is really too important to us just yet, TinyObjLoader very thoughtfully puts them into a data structure called a material_t, which gives logical and easy to access names to the values and you may recall from reading the header, it stores material_t info in a vector. An OBJ file may use more than one MTL file, hence why we need to store them in a vector.

Even so there's a lot of info here that we don't really know how to use yet, and all we initially want to do is get a few models on screen, so we will push forward and ignore the niceties of clearcoat_thickness and sheen among others. Developing renderers that can handle all that is something for another time when we're a lot more comfortable with how rendering works.

First things first, we have OBJ models and we've got to learn to use them before we can really make massive changes, but we do sometimes needs to edit the OBJ or MTL files because of small inconsistencies between graphic packages, especially if you download models, and TinyObjLoader can't actually handle every single type of OBJ, only the most common ones, also the OBJ format, is sometimes extended from time to time. You might also find that our graphic file handling system can cope with some type of graphic formats and not others, so if you convert images to more accessible formats, you will need to let the MTL files know the new filename or extension.

This is a lot to take in though, as I said before models are many times more complex than simple images. So we need to try to make things a bit easier for ourselves. Fortunately, there's a wonderful example routine in the TinyObjLoader examples, which loads and processes our OBJ and MTL files and stores our data in as GPU VB buffers, with all the info we need.

As it was written for an older version of full fat OpenGL, the render parts of the example code are not as useful and it needs porting to work on our OpenGLES2.0.

I've taken that code, and ported it to our new framework, it is located in the ModelManager Class, which is the class we're going to use, to load, save, and take care of our models. As it stands, it only creates a simple vertex array buffer, we could actually gain a quite bit more performance with an index buffer as well, but I want to keep things simple at the moment, we can work on enhancing our parsing and rendering systems later. First, we need to have a render system that can at least put the basic meshes on screen in a simple way for us to use.

Let's load a simple model and display.

On the support site, I have included several nice models supplied by my colleague and occasional excessive drinking buddy bestest mate ever, Colin Morrison, his work is available on the Unity Store, if you want to find more. There are also 10's of thousands of freely available or very low-cost models available online (hint: don't search for catwalk or photo models. They cost a lot more and waste so much programming time).

For now, he's given us a few useful models to use in our project, which will allow us to produce our first demos. TinyObjLoader's download also has a couple of nice but untextured test models you can play with.

Let's load them and have a look at them in what is for now only a visualization project, we'll start work on an actual project where we control the view in the next section. Oh by the way, a very nice feature of Visual Studio is that it can actually display the models contained in an Obj/Mtl pair of files, try loading from the menu, or dragging one into the screen. We can't do a lot of editing on it, but one thing we can do that's very useful, when our artists supply us with a quad-based model, we can triangulate it using the tools triangulate option.

If you want to delve into the artist's world and produce your own models, there are many amazing modeling packages out there, which range in complexity. I personally can't get my head around most of the pro packages, they are by their very nature designed to produce anything an artist can imagine and provide tools and methods that make that possible.

For us lesser, can't really draw a stick man, type of nonartists, there are packages such as Blender, which are almost easy to use and something I discovered recently called 3D Builder, which is a nice free Microsoft product designed mainly to produce 3D printer models, but has the benefit of outputting in the simpler standard formats. Though only the Windows 10 version seems to save Obj files, it also comes with a load of nice bundle of simple models you can use. Sadly, it can't add textures to your stick men (at least not yet). Careful though, the sample models are copyright owned by Microsoft, so don't include them in any final games, but for personal testing, they are ideal.

It also has some quite decent tutorials on the Win10 version, which can get your stick men up and running in no time. Until you get yourself a tame artist who can produce mega art. Use simpler packages like this to create simple holding assets that you can work with and allow you to progress with code. It's usually a lot easier to create or load simple generic shapes than just using cubes. Just please remember never leave holding graphics or assets, that are owned by massive corporations with unlimited resources and expensive, eager legal departments, in projects you release to the public. Ok?

▌ Lights Camera Action

This is the point where the Maths Magic(*jazzhands*) we are all a bit scared of turns into something approaching Witchcraft (run away!!), because we're about to start using maths in ways we've not even attempted so far, but no matter whether you ultimately understand how this Witchcraft works, you can be reassured by one overwhelming point!

It does work!

And, it works the same way in every 3D game you've ever played, so there is a ton of information, tutorials and easy to follow....well, kinda, easy to follow, tutorials on the web. But for some of us, Maths will always be something to fear, but never to avoid!

So take heart from knowing that I have no clue how the Maths in this book works, I just know that it does, if I do this, to this, and make this do this to this, I get...THAT!! And that puts things on screen.

But...we do need to have a bit of a short primer on what is going on...so take a few deep breaths and prepare yourself for the second most terrifying section in this book...you can skip it, if you really are worried about it, but it's best to get some vague idea of what it is we're trying to do. Even if we don't totally understand how it actually gets done.

So how can I explain how Maths works when I don't know it? Stick around and ask me later, I might actually understand it better when I write this all down.

Truth is, my own fear of Maths prevents me fully knowing why it produces the results, but I have no problem understanding the steps, using the Maths structures and functions and sending them or their results to a GPU. So if I can explain that much to you, you can work with that, but I sincerely hope that use it to jump off and develop a genuine interest in the Maths behind 3D gaming.

We need to ask a very important question. How do we see the world?

Well it's not as simple a question as you think, if you consider how the eye works, (ignore stereo for now) you are effectively looking at the world by creating an image in your mind. It's done by processing a load of information that is made up of thousands of multicolored light beams, focused through a lens, and then striking onto your retina, where, certain nerve cells are stimulated and send info to the brain about color, intensity, and hue, to provide a nice clear image. Ermmm no! In reality, science has shown that much of that image is very blurry upside down and poorly resolved, also that our eyes/brain focus, varies from point to point as our brain thinks we need to check different things that are of interest or danger to us, this means our brain fills in a lot of details our eye simply does not provide. Also even more remarkable, it seems to us to be a seamless analog process, which is smooth and unbroken.

Blurry or not though, for us to make some sense of it the brain needs to do some amazing amount of calculations in real time far faster than any known computer, it image processes the blurry bits, pays special attention to bits that are moving, and puts most of its attention to the very small clear bit in the middle, once it's filled in the hole that the optic nerves placed on the retina uses up! It does this remarkably fast, I don't know exactly how, and I'm also pretty sure it varies from person to person, but unless we have had some damage to our visual processing systems, our view of the world is remarkable.

And...easy to fool.

Which is important because it's how games work, also films, TV, animation, and so on, we quite deliberately take advantage of our brain not being aware of how often it samples and processes the images the eye takes in. There is a concept known as image retention, where if you flash an image in front of your eyes, the brain holds on to that image long after the image itself has gone. Flash another image immediately after, and your brain tries to connect the two. Animation and movies actually flash images 24 frames per second, TV's 60 times, HD 100+ times per second, and your brain connects what are in effect static images to create motion.

When we are working in 3D we somehow have to resolve all the information that the world we create has, and then magically throw pixels on to a flat screen every update frame, in such a way that we, looking at the screen, see images one after another, that somehow appear to be correctly represented and then flow as if in motion. Just like a movie, or more accurately an animation.

Not only do we display objects on our screen in a relative position to how they should appear if we look at a flat screen, we also, allow light in that world to alter the look and color of any object in that world that is lit up by that light source, and we can have many light sources.

If you think about space...with no stars...it's very dark, even in your own room, you are seeing things only because light from a light source somewhere, is bouncing off that thing and into your eye. If there is no light source, you can't see anything. Three-dimensional graphics are generally the same, without a light source of some kind, our images cannot be seen.

We also have to determine how we see color... Your old physics teachers might have told you that we only ever see the light that is reflected off an object, and that's perfectly true, Green leaves are not actually green they are every color but green. The Sun's white light is actually absorbed by the surface of a leaf, except for the green, which is reflected back into our eyes and translated by your brain as GREEN! It would be too much effort for us to say, the actual color of the leaf is shades of Red, Orange, Blue, Indigo, and Violet, we just say what we see. It works like this:

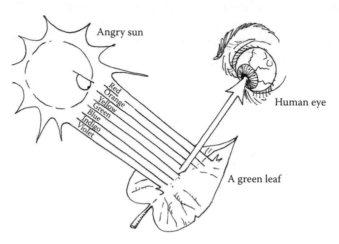

Now the fact that colors are absorbed makes it really easy for us to give color to objects.

If we assume our light source is white light and our object is an orange color we can get this:

```
vec3 SunlightColor(1.0f, 1.0f, 1.0f); // white is all 3 RGB colours
vec3 ObjectColor(1.0f, 0.72f, 0.11f); // a slightly orange colour
vec3 FinalColour = SunlightColor * ObjectColor; // = (1.0f, 0.72f, 0.11f) a
slightly orange colour
```

So white light will produce exactly the color we expect...

But what if we want to use a blue light?

```
vec3 SunlightColor(0.0f, 0.0f, 1.0f); / Blue is only the Blue part of RGB
vec3 ObjectColor(1.0f, 0.72f, 0.11f); / a slightly orange colour
vec3 FinalColour = SunlightColor * ObjectColor; / = (0.0f, 0.0f, 0.11f)
pastel blue
```

Our orange object is going to lose its R and G components and its Blue component alone will be left.

Calculating the resulting color you should expect when you shine a light on a colored object really isn't hard, what is hard is working out how much of that color is shining on your object, so we have to discuss what a normal is, and how it's calculated.

This color concept is key to understanding of light, what we are basically describing here is the concept of diffuse light, the idea that anything with color will radiate that color, though it needs a bit of stimulation in the form of a light source. We've been doing this kind of lighting already just by using textures to provide pixels that display our variations of RGB.

To get more info on other types of light though we have to start using a bit more maths, and learn a few new maths functions.

The Return of the Vector

Well it never really went away, we've been using it really well so far to create motion and represent directions or speed as well as using the data type itself as a position. But, now you're starting to see that there may be more uses for vectors especially now we're in 3D. Light is represented in directions and light bounces off things, at angles. We will probably need to calculate things like that. Vectors as a direction concept become far more important to us in 3D because how we see things is very relevant to the direction things are facing. So a few new ideas for our old flexible friend need to be explained.

We've done a lot of work just adding and subtracting vectors, maybe multiplying them with scalars to change them, but we need to look at what happens when you multiply vectors with other vectors, which actually allow us to do two different types of multiply, one which returns a scalar value or product, and one which returns a vector value or product.

Dot Product

This is extremely handy, if slightly confusing function, which basically returns the cosine of the angle between the two vectors. Its proper name is the Scalar Product, but because we traditionally use a · symbol to indicate the operation it's known as the dot product.

When you look at the actual mathematical explanation of it:

$$a \cdot b = |a| \times |b| \times \cos(\theta)$$

It's actually a bit scary so I don't really think we need to go into the actual maths… (Yes I am a coward) all we need to really know is that a · b returns the angle between the two vectors. GLM of course has a dot product function (That's my get out clause right there!). But my fears are largely unfounded, despite the new name and funny symbols this is actually just a case of using the length of a vector (easily calculated with high-school Pythagoras theorem), and then doing a multiply of the component parts of the vector to return the cosine of an angle.

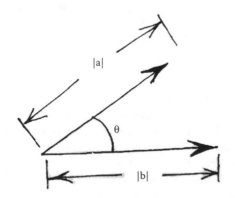

Another Fun Vector Fact-Cross Product

Another very useful vector function we only really need in 3D, mainly because it does not actually exist in 2D is this, the Cross Product..ta daaaah:

$$\mathbf{a} \times \mathbf{b} = |\mathbf{a}| \, |\mathbf{b}| \sin(\theta)n$$

Keep calm, keep breathing, it's just a formula, it won't hurt you. It's just telling us the vector multiplication of, a and b ($\mathbf{a} \times \mathbf{b}$) is equal to the magnitude of a ($|\mathbf{a}|$) * the magni.....yeah but no but... I've lost the will to live too; I wish I'd stayed awake in maths classes. But it's ok, don't worry, our friendly maths library, GLM gives us this, so we don't really need to code it up, but we do need to know what it is and what it can give us. This is the Cross Product, sometimes also called the Vector Product, because unlike the Dot Product, it returns a Vector. A slightly confused Vector as far as its direction is concerned, it has no idea if it's up or down, but we can fix that with a little bit more information that will become available when we need it. Visually it becomes a bit clearer when you see it like this.

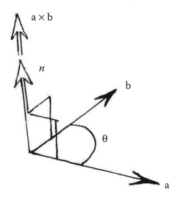

It's called the Cross Product because the maths symbol for vector multiplication that returns a vector is × rather than the usual *, some things are more obvious than you realize!

The Cross Product is fantastically useful thing but it's a bit hard to get our heads around the calculations going on, so don't try, just be assured that the Cross Product returns a vector, which is at right angles to two other vectors. This is the key principle of calculating a normal, which you can see by the n symbol, is part of the process, we'll talk about next.

Oh, if you are really interested in the maths behind these things, and how to code them from scratch, buy a maths book, or find a nice online maths site. I prefer not to reinvent the wheel.

Who's to Say Whats Normal?

So after we hoped we'd been done with maths we find we have to talk about another interesting type of vector, which we've been using already, though we've pretended it's always one value, Up. And for most flat things Up is the most normal, normal we can think of!

So what is a normal and what's it got to do with things: The correct definition of a normal is, it's a vector, which is perpendicular (at right angles) to a face, and a face being any collection of vertices, that when connected, form a flat surface. It's usually represented as going out from the model that contains the face, but sometimes it can be going in.

Think of an Arrow stuck through a target board. Hold the board flat, and the arrow is pointing straight up in the air. Wobble the board around and the arrows go with it, still perpendicular to the board. Now it does not matter if the arrow is pointing up through the center, slightly off center or right at the edge, as long as it's somewhere on the face, it's still going to point the same way. So we can work out the normal of the individual vertices that made up the face. They will all have the same normal.

Assuming all the arrows went in at perfect right angles, when we turn the board over.

We can see that despite the board being a simple flat face, all the arrows point in the same direction. Normals are used for all sorts of reasons, but especially for lighting. The normal can be used to tell us how much light from a point (or points) in space, is falling onto the surface of the face and by extension how bright it is, or how much color of the light it will absorb, or how much it will reflect toward our view, or, well, lots of things as we'll see.

Types of Light

For lights to have an impact in our world, they have to exist there, and that means we need to define some of the types of light we might have. Light is a complex concept in physics and real world light is insanely complex to replicate, but in a digital world we can simplify and conceptualize light in easy to use ways that provide us quite realistic representations of light.

The most obvious form of light that is all around you, from the Sun or your home light bulbs, is Ambient light. As light from a very bright source can scatter around bouncing and reflecting off everything in a room seemingly at once, everything in your world is lit, even if it's not actually in your immediate line of sight.

Generally, the only thing we are ever likely to do with ambient light is define its intensity, color or strength. Like a dimmer switch on your light bulbs, or even the Sun. When we've put colors into our models so far, we've simply dialed in 100% intensity, which certainly makes them pop out; it's just not very realistic. But we're free to adjust it as we'll see soon.

Next up on the light wall of fame is Diffuse lighting. Diffuse lighting is similar to Ambient but it comes from a directed source and does not have the intensity of ambient light so it does not flood the entire scene with its photons to create ambient light, and as such it only actually lights up the faces of things that have the light in front of it, but not behind it. We refer to our textures, which contain the colors we want to display as our diffuse textures, because the color of the pixels themselves comes from that texture but the intensity is dependent on the way the light shines on and off it.

We're going to start coding with diffuse and ambient lighting as these are the easiest to implement, and we pretty much have that in hand already, but a little later, once we have some better data to work with we'll try a couple of other types of light.

Specular lighting is next and are interesting effects that create the shine or highlight on a shiny object. They also vary depending on where the light hits them making for a more dynamic lighting effect. These are a bit harder to explain so I'll explain by doing shortly.

Finally, the nicest in my view, Emissive lights. These are actual objects, which glow and themselves become a light source. So you can make a model of a neon light and give it emissive properties that will make it and the surrounding area glow.

There are quite a few other forms of light and light effects, but they generally are computationally expensive and best left to the next generation of GPUs. You can slowly introduce them into your Shaders as you get more confident, but I'm pretty sure you'll hit a point where our little GPUs won't cope and frame rates will tumble. So I'm not going to cover advanced topics such as reflections, physically based rendering, scattering effects, and so on, in this book. But, we can try to dabble with them on the support site and I'd love to see how far you manage to push these systems to produce cool effects and still maintain playability in your games.

Light Sources

As well as types of light, there's also a certain number of sources of light. Ambient light is generally considered to be the result of powerful directional light, which comes from a very intense source and lights up the entire scene with the same brightness. The Sun is our best example though in fact it's actually a very very powerful but far away point light.

Point lighting is our light bulbs, in our scene, they serve to produce emissive and diffuse lighting in all directions, which decreases the further from the source of the light, but still radiates light in all directions. It's basically an ambient light with intensity issues, their ability to light up an object is directly related to the objects distance from the light and what surfaces face that light source.

Spot Lights are, as you might imagine, highly directional versions of Point Lights. They have a central intensity that reduces as it goes to the edges, in a cone shape, they possess a property called attenuation, which defines the intensity of the cone and its impact as it gets away from the light. We'll leave these for another time, probably on the support site; they are the most fun to see in action but are a little expensive to produce.

Shadows, a Place Where Danger Hides

No discussion about light can really be done without discussing shadows.....but, shadows are hard, really hard! As a shadow isn't actually part of our model, it's outside its boundary, it needs to be procedurally generated, worked out on the fly.

When we have an object, even a simple one like a cube, that has directional light coming at it, the area where that light is blocked and not going to show is, of course, not going to be lit, hence a shadow and we have to work out the shape direction and intensity/sharpness of that shadow, which can vary incredibly depending on the angle, and intensity of that light.

And what if the model moves, or is animated, that makes them dynamic, potentially changing every frame, worse still what if the light moves, what if both move? What if, coding gods forbid, we have many lights at different points with different colors and intensity, creating lots of shadows! Or, how about surfaces that have reflections, showing shadows in them...hmmm, complexity does not really ever end when we start to think about the way light and its absence works.

Things like transparency and reflective and refractive surfaces can also make for amazing scenes, all are possible at least on a coding level, but I'm not going to go into that in this book. It's pushing our luck a bit too much and I'm going to end up writing a technical book on graphics rather than learning to code games. Another reason, we don't really have the GPU power to really get them to work well enough for our games to use.

So there are going to be limitations, not just because of our hardware power, but because a true real time representation of lighting effects does not really exist. We simulate as many things as is mathematically possible with the processing power we have to hand, over time we've discovered a lot of cool ways to create incredibly intricate ways to produce (near) realism in our scenes and the push for ever more realism will continue for quite some time.

Shadows were for a long time a very difficult thing to do in 3D environments, and even now they are a problem that requires a fair chunk of processing power to really do well. We don't have a lot of processing power!

But we've let the cat have a peek out of the bag by mentioning them so we have to at least accept we need to make some effort to do some, but don't set your expectations too high. We can do shadows, but their computational expense means we need to do them with care, and only if the game you want to write really needs them. The next example project does not really need them, so we're going to look at this properly when we create an environment that will benefit from shadows. Shadows need one very important concept though, Shaders, which we are about to get into. For now this cat needs to stay in its bag.

Shaders

Now having talked about light and shadow, and all the nice little maths functions we use to get lighting to work, we have to now turn to a rather complex issue, there's just no avoiding this question. How do we actually do all that maths in our code?

We can do it on our CPU, and some small parts will still be done there but the fact is it's time to tackle the powerhouse system in our target and what makes it possible to get our graphics looking good. The GPU and the API that lets us control it.

OpenGLES1.1 was quite a nice API, which could do some really nice things, but it used what was called a fixed pipeline, which basically meant you could set some flags and variables, tell it where your lights were, send your data to it for rendering and *BOOM*, you've got a display. That was fine, but it meant it was usually one type of rendering for all types of object sent, stopping and starting rendering to set different flags for different effects.

OpenGLES2.0 however changed that idea, and instead of the fixed pipeline where everything had to behave according to the way the flags were set. A programmable pipeline was introduced, where we now pushed our data through a choice of Shaders allowing much more variation and graphic effects than was ever possible. Though our machines almost certainly still support OpenGL's original fixed pipeline concepts using OpenGLES 1.1, it is only for legacy reasons so that old titles still work, there is really little reason to try learning it, as it is so far removed from OpenGLES2.0 that it will only confuse a beginner.

As we have rightly taken the option of using OpenGLES2.0, which is similar to later versions of desktop OpenGL, we have Shaders. I've added a few standard Shaders in our projects and we've seen what they can do, but I've avoided explaining too much about them simply because it really is a sub set of specialized graphic coding, which I didn't want to distract you with until you had gained more confidence in your game coding.

But now we have a lot of nice demos, it's time to jazz them up a bit by getting our GPU to really do its thing and that means understanding in more detail what Shaders do and getting you to write a few of your own. This is where the real power of a GPU comes into play and allows us to do amazing things to every pixel or vertex that our CPU would choke on. Shaders represent the most power we can apply to our games. Some people; crazy, mad, delusional, amazing people, even write games in Shaders…they are astounding things that make the visuals of modern games come alive.

That said, they are so powerful and offer so much that there are some massive books out there that explain what you can do with them, there are almost no limits, but they are technical enhancements rather than fundamentals of game programming, so fully explaining how to use them is (again) out of the scope of this book, the best we can do here is briefly explain what they can do, how to do it, and show a few simple samples to expand our games, that should be enough to let you start a journey into technical graphic programming if you find that path exciting.

So What Is a Shader?

Shaders are at the same time, very cool and very confusing for beginners. Before Shaders, 3D was pretty dull and lifeless, and we relied on a lot of basic concepts of light and texture mapping to do anything that looked even remotely cool. It took a lot of imagination and considerable effort to create really cool effects. They were all possible of course, but usually needed a lot of intensive CPU processing before the GPU, which then used a fixed pipeline to do its thing. Flags were set up to do certain things. Data went in…things came out. It was a pretty simple system.

But the introduction of Shaders as an extension in OpenGL1.4 and then as a full feature in OpenGL2.0 opened up a whole new range of dynamic possibilities in the way pixels could be drawn, interacting with CPU sent values or mathematical light sources or textures as we wanted them to. Flags and states can still be set up, but now: Things go in, get mashed around any way we want, get mixed with other things, get checked and tested, and things come out.

It was, and still is a fantastic breakthrough in graphics. The flexibility this Shader concept adds is immense, but it did introduce a level of complexity that some new coders find confusing. So let's try to explain it simply.

There are basically two types of Shader in OpenGLES2.0; Vertex and Fragment Shaders. They both do different things but are compiled and run in similar ways and most importantly allow interaction with each other. The fact they are compiled gives our biggest clue to why they are so cool. We write them, and they do what we want them to do…mostly.

The Vertex Shaders job is to provide the values that result from transforming the 3D coordinates given to it by the CPU into 2D screen coordinates; this is where most of the matrix and frustum maths we talked about in the 3D code really comes into play. It outputs a calculated value called `gl_Position`, and optionally can send the next Shader values it might find useful, in fact the fragment Shader has no real way to get access to certain data types, so the vertex Shader has to pass them on.

We can send data to the Shader from the CPU or client RAM, via special variable types called Attributes, which provide access to a sequence of data structures, we set up as we see fit. We can also send some constant values, known as Uniforms to both Shaders, which represent possible important constant values calculated and passed by the CPU. The Shader can also hold some simple variables of its own that can be manipulated for calculation storage, and then discarded or sent to the next Shader using Varying types of values. One thing the Shaders in OpenGLES2.0 cannot do sadly is send information back to the CPU.

Vertex Shaders are the first stop in our programmable rendering system, barring any precalculation we might have done with the CPU before handing over to the Shaders.

Vertex Shaders know only about the data sent to it via the CPU and any const values it holds or has been supplied with, generally as you might expect that data will be vertices, but it can in fact take any data we want, so long as it eventually outputs the gl_Position value for GPU to continue its processing of the pixel it wants to draw. Other data that might get sent to the Vertex shader might include the MVP matrix and location of light sources, as well as values that can be passed onto the next Shader using a varying variable type.

As we supply the code that the Shader uses, we can make variations of the kind of transforms we want, on a model by model or even on a vertex by vertex basis. This ability to plug in our own code to do that computation makes for a very broad range of methods that can be used. But the key point is they essentially turn the points in the 3D world into a 2D view according to rules we set. For the most part, we're probably always going to do the normal standard things like frustum culls and matrix transforms, but there are many options we can use.

The other type of Shader is the Fragment Shader, this is potentially the most interesting and hardest to use, but at its very simplest level, as we've been using, it takes the color of our texture at the point where it is supposed to be drawn, and manipulates it in any way we want before placing it in the draw buffer.

We can have that pixel influenced by other pixels, variables from the CPU, light(s), we can generate its own light variables to influence other pixels, control the individual colors of the pixel on variable that can alter as we want and so on! There's very few limits, it really is a whole new bag of goodies that we can use to make interesting things happen to our graphics, away from the CPU and *generally* incredibly fast, at least faster than the CPU!

As data from the CPU has to go to the Vertex Shader first, the second most important job for the Vertex Shader, after whatever we are asking it to do to get `gl_Position`, is to pass on the values that the Fragment Shader will need, so if you want to pass the Fragment Shader details of a texture coordinate, you first pass it to the Vertex Shader, which then passes it in a *varying** variable to the Fragment Shader.

Shader code is a little different to the kind of code we used so far, it's also a bit mysterious in that it's usually compiled by some hidden systems we don't really get access to. Also even worse it's shockingly bad at reporting errors other than compile errors. But hey we've got used, that with C++'s error reporting haven't we?

If we look at our standard very boring Shader code in our first demos we have this.

```
GLbyte fShaderStr[] =
 "precision mediump float;                             \n"
 "varying vec2 v_texCoord;                             \n"
 "uniform sampler2D s_texture;                         \n"
 "void main()                                          \n"
 "{                                                    \n"
 "  gl_FragColor = texture2D(s_texture, v_texCoord);\n"
 "}                                                    \n";
```

All this is, is a small text segment, which could just as easily be written in another file and saved as standard text and loaded. Take away the array it's being loaded into as well as the \n and "'s, and you get this

```
precision mediump float;
varying vec2 v_texCoord;
uniform sampler2D s_texture;
void main()
  {
  gl_FragColor = texture2D( s_texture, v_texCoord );
  };
```

Which looks suspiciously like code?

From these files/snippets, we can see something that should be recognizable to you as code, though the terms `varying` and `uniform` may be unfamiliar to you, the idea of

---

* A *varying* variable, is a special kind of shader variable, I'm just about to explain.

what they are isn't. A `varying` value is, quite simply a value that varies, yup a variable, we're well used to those, though in this case it's a variable that is coming from another Shader, on OpenGLES2.0 that's only going to be the Vertex Shader, as OpenGLES2.0 only has two types of Shader.

A `uniform` is something which is not really designed to change and remains `const`, again a recognizable concept. It most often is a calculated value sent from the CPU that the Shader can then work on in this case though it's the ID of a texture held in GPU memory but the address was supplied by the CPU using its attribute buffer systems which fills the uniform each time the Shader is activated, resulting in a progression through the attribute buffer until there are no more values to process.

It's important to remember that in OpenGLES2.0 Shaders work in pairs.* A Vertex Shader is always paired with a Fragment Shader, the resulting pair being called a ProgramObject, which then allows them use the same `varying` variables. As long as the Shaders are passing and expecting the same values, you can mix Shader pairs to make a whole range of ProgramObjects.

Reading the small main function again;

```
void main() {
            gl_FragColor = texture2D(s_texture, v_texCoord);
            };
```

It's telling us that a value gl_FragColour which is the required output of this fragment Shader is taken from the texture `s_texture` at the coordinates held in `v_texCoord`.

There's no sign of any actual manipulation here, because we are not doing any, yet! But we are passing `v_texCoord` from our vertex Shader to this Fragment Shader!

There are only five Storage qualifiers in GLSL 1.0

- None

- Const

- Attribute

- Uniform

- Varying

And it's also possible to qualify the type of parameters they are so that you know if data are coming in, going out, or do both but some Shader compilers don't like this in GLSL 1.0

- None/in

- Out

- Inout

---

* It is actually possible to have more than two Shaders but you still need a Vertex and Fragment shader *pair* at least, usually extra Shaders are there as functions but it's hard to give a good reason to create shader functions and then attach them, but if there's a thing that can be done, someone will do it, probably better than me.

Their use becomes clearer with practice, but should be clear from what we've done so far. We can also alter the precision of our calculations, which is often useful, but there's normally a time penalty for higher precision. The Qualifiers are:

- Highp

- Mediump

- Lowp

It's possible to set any variable in the Shader to a particular precision but try to use the same precision types in your calculations, also once you set a precision, all following variables are set to that precision unless otherwise set to a different one.

Keeping Track of Them

In most games we are going to use a few Shaders, things can get a bit dull if everything looks exactly the same. So we are going to have to create different shader combinations. This presents us with a decision over how we store all these Shaders.

The Shader compiler always assumes it's working on a text *file*, which is why our normal in code default Shaders have been stored in an array of characters with the "" and newline /n symbols. This simulates the memory pattern you would get when you load a text file in. But while that works fine, it's a real pain to edit and near impossible to format cleanly. If you have a whole range of Shaders it can be a bit of a nightmare to keep track of them. So I've given you access to a simple Shader manger that will load Shaders from text files. The Graphics Class Init routines automatically produce a standard default Shader pair, using the array method, but you can override that later in your object's instantiation or update methods. Or if you want you can scrap that default altogether.

Introducing the Shader Language

Shaders use their own language, called OpenGL Shader Language, and like OpenGL and OpenGLES it's an evolving standard. At the time of writing, it's currently at version 3.2. But for us using OpenGLES2.0, we're still using version 1.0. It's usually abbreviated to GLSL across all formats of OpenGL. Make sure you find a reference system that is appropriate to the version of the language you are using, like the Khronos OpenGLES2.0 reference card. They also provide an excellent reference PDF located at:

https:/www.khronos.org/files/opengles_shading_language.pdf.

As always you can check what your GPU supports with these four handy lines you will find in most of the sample projects;

```
printf("This GPU supplied by :%s \n", glGetString(GL_VENDOR));
printf("This GPU supports :%s \n", glGetString(GL_VERSION));
printf("This GPU Renders with :%s \n", glGetString(GL_RENDERER));
printf("This GPU supports :%s \n", glGetString(GL_SHADING_LANGUAGE_
VERSION));
```

The strings can of course be sent to a buffer instead of the console, if you need to parse for specific information to tailor your project (i.e., if your system supports GLSL 300es as some do, you can load in more advanced Shaders or use the base level 100 versions.)

These will output the two main things you need to know, The OpenGLES version and the Shader Language, but you may also need to know who the vendor is and what renderer is being used. Especially if you have any crazy plans to produce a game that will work across a range of different machines and you want to allow for the slight differences between them.

At the time of writing, I haven't spent much time on OpenGLES3.x to play with newer versions of the GLSL. I've been too busy writing this book! I'm looking forward to finishing it and getting my teeth into some of my OpenGLES3.x compatible SBCs to see what they can really do.

The 1.0 version of the language itself is pretty straight forward, it contains only a few concepts and as you might expect most relate to maths and conditions. There are no pointers in GLSL but everything else is pretty much as you would expect from a simplified C/C++ style language.

The language consists of very familiar style keywords

```
attribute const uniform varying break continue do for while if else in out
inout float int void bool true false lowp mediump highp precision invariant
discard return mat2 mat3 mat4 vec2 vec3 vec4 ivec2 ivec3 ivec4 bvec2 bvec3
bvec4 sampler2D samplerCube struct
```

Most of these are pretty familiar to us, a mixture of data types and flow control concepts and used in pretty much the same way. We also have the ability to call functions and pass arguments. So even though our control with if and else, is limited we have enough to make decisions, and change flow.

There's also quite a big list of keywords, which are designated for future use, I'm not going to list them here, you can find them in any GLSL reference, but if you get an error about reserved keywords...you're using a reserved keyword.

You're also not allowed to use variables or function names starting with gl_, which is pretty obviously reserved for gl_typethings!!!

As Shaders are designed to do a specific job, there are a number of built in variables for both vertex and fragment Shaders, which relate to that specific job, that is, putting pixels on screen

```
gl_Position, gl_FrontFacing gl_PointSize
```

Relate to the Vertex Shader the most important being gl_Position, which is the final output value of a Vertex Shader.

For Fragments these are the built in variables;

```
gl_FragColor, gl_FrontFacing, gl_FragCoord, gl_PointCoord
```

In this case gl_FragColor, is the final output value of a Fragment Shader.

We've used this of course in our very simple Shaders so far.

The compile process is kinda vague and mysterious, because Shaders are actually compiled as your program is running, unlike your C++ code, which is compiled before it is run. Every graphic driver needs to contain a small compiler to compile Shaders. These are supplied by makers of the video cards and therefore your Shader will be compiled into code that the GPU can use, it may therefore vary from GPU to GPU, this makes having the correct maker supplied drivers for your particular GPU very important.

Once compiled, the code for the Shader lives in GPU memory and stays there until you remove it, you can usually have several Shaders in place at once, though.

A full explanation of what Shaders can do for you is hopelessly outside the scope of a general coding book like this. They are almost limitless in their potential, but can be quite hard to master. Persevere though, as Shader coding as a discipline is a very hot topic in game coding.

Games are now becoming more reliant on greater Shader effects for their visual display, but even though Shaders can do incredibly complex things very fast, they have to do those incredibly complex things a lot of times. So try to keep Shaders as simple and efficient as you can, avoid calculations that bring the same result, which a CPU could have provided, especially on low power systems like SBCs. Some complex lighting systems or effects use a lot of code and that can't be avoided, but always consider that the Shader has to run as fast as possible to keep your frame rate up.

There are some amazing books on the market dealing with the subject, which is changing rapidly as more and more GPU makers have realized that:

Better hardware + Imaginative programers = All Kinds of AWESOME!

Let's Light It Up!

Now that we have the tools; Shaders, matrices, vectors, and a tiny bit of understanding of how light works it's time to implement it in our games.

Light makes by far the biggest differences to how our display will look. Without light we see nothing, up till now we've assumed a very simple basic kind of assumed ambient light to allow us to see or tint our 3D objects, but now we can alter them and maybe even give them their own lights which, in turn, will dictate what is being seen by our camera. But lights bouncing off moving surfaces, or surfaces that are static while the camera moves need a bit more work.

At the simplest level, we only need to do a little bit of maths in our Shaders to brighten or darken our fragments depending on the angle of the light coming in and the angle of the light bouncing toward our eye. That angle needs a normal to be used.

The normals we stored and never used in our VB now start to make sense; these give us a fast access to each vertex normal to allow us to work out where the light is going to bounce off. We could calculate the normal in real time but, the values never change, so recalculating hundreds maybe thousands of them each cycle is a shocking waste we need to avoid. So we nearly always store them in the model data and it's far faster to access such data while it's in the VB.

We're ready to really start messing with Shaders now, let's review a simple Shader using a light source. Most of the work is going to be done in the Vertex Shader, so we need to be sure we give it access to the Vertices as before, the new Normals and the usual texture coordinates.

```
uniform mat4 MVP; // A constant representing the combined model/view/
projection matrix.
uniform mat4 MV; // A constant representing the combined model/view matrix.
vec3 u_LightPos = vec3(1.0,2.0,3.0); // The position of the light in eye
space.
uniform vec4 Ambient; // we will discard this
attribute vec2 a_texCoord;
```

```
    attribute vec4 a_Position; // Per-vertex position information we will
pass in.
    attribute vec3 a_Normal;   // Per-vertex normal information we will pass in.

    varying vec2 v_texCoord;
    varying float v_Colour;    // This will be passed into the fragment
shader.

    void main()
    {
      vec3 modelViewVertex = vec3(MV * a_Position);   // Transform the vertex
into eye space.
      vec3 modelViewNormal = vec3(MV * a_Normal);     // Transform the
normal's orientation into eye space.
      // Get a lighting direction vector from the light to the vertex.
      vec3 lightVector = normalize(u_LightPos - modelViewVertex);

      // pass the output values to the fragment
      v_Colour = max(dot(modelViewNormal, lightVector), 0.1);  // dont allow
totally black
      v_texCoord = a_texCoord;
      gl_Position = MVP * a_Position; // usual position calc
    }
```

The actual calculations are reasonably short, so it's not too hard to work out and we're still doing the usual things vertex Shaders do, like passing the texture coordinate to the fragment Shader and setting gl_position. But notice the two new lines, which are there to calculate the very important varying v_Colour value. That's the one the fragment Shader really needs to make light cool. The v_Colour value provides an intensity value for the fragment Shader to use so the pixels on or near that vertex will be suitably lit by the light.

All we've really changed in our fragment Shader is to add a slightly different calculation to get gl_FragColor. I didn't bother to use the ambient value though I still passed it to the Vertex. But I could still use it if I wanted to.

```
uniform sampler2D s_texture;
varying vec2 v_texCoord;
varying float v_Colour;

void main()
{
  gl_FragColor = texture2D( s_texture, v_texCoord )*v_Colour;
  gl_FragColor.a = 1.0;
}
```

By using the calculated v_Colour value we can alter the final gl_FragColor by more than the simple value returned in the texture, making it darker or brighter, which is what light or its absence does.

Of course we need to adapt our set up of our render a little in order to pass the attribute info for normals in our VB, and also send extra uniform and attribute values, but once added our new visuals become quite impressive.

So for now we'll use this, it will work fine with our upcoming space ships, and assume that the Sun, strongly located at a fixed point and out of our view point is our light source.

You can see on the screen shot (above), two instances of the same model, but on the left, no lighting, and on the right, lighting. It creates a much more subtle and realistic image. Especially when you can see the shaded areas in this next shot, the light is above and to the right of the ships, which means their underbelly has no light directly on it. We will add light to the Left ship as we are below it and can see its belly.

Not too shabby is it! This is an example of vertex lighting, where the vertex Shader is deciding the intensity of the light for the entire face (or at least a third of it), by distributing the intensity across the face's vertices, it's the fastest way to do light and it is indeed very effective for soft lighting, as long as our faces are fairly small and we don't have a lot of contrast in the color values. *But, be warned*, it does have an impact on our frame rate, this is one of those constraints we have with our relatively low powered systems. We can do light, but the increased complexity of the Shaders needed to achieve it, takes more time to process.

For our lower power machines vertex lighting is really the preferred system where we must have light, but it is also possible to do a more detailed form of lighting called per fragment or per pixel lighting, which as you might imagine is going to calculate the color of every pixel in the polygon not just relative to the vertex. That's a bit more intense work, but does give a much nicer image especially if you are viewing an object up close.

There is an example of per pixel Shader on the site, feel free to try out LightFrag.fsh and LightVertex.vsh to replace the LightObjectFrag.fsh and LightObjectVert.vsh files.

Like before our Vertex Shader does some of the base work, but now we let the Fragment Shader earn its keep as well, and get it to do a lot more, but whereas a Vertex Shader is going to work on only three vertices (assuming triangles), a Pixel Shader is going to work on every pixel contained in that triangle, this could be anything from one to a few dozen to several hundred pixels. All doing those complex maths equations. Repetition of a task can take up a lot of processing time, and even our fast GPUs don't like to spend too much time doing calculations repeatedly. You will find the drop in performance on this Shader to be quite noticeable. True you get even prettier light effects, if you look closely, but that performance drop is now so noticeable at times that it has to make you question if you should use it.

The choice is always up to you, in a game with multiple lit objects, you probably won't be able to render a very detailed involved scene with per pixel lighting, and still maintain a steady fast frame rate, but you can mix and match the methods you use, on a per model/mesh basis. As always, the balance of performance against quality of graphics is never ending and you need to make technically based design choices in your game that give the best results for you.

You may also find that you can use different Shaders at different points in a game, to use different levels of shading. Given that a more complex light Shader will take a little more time to process than a standard ambient Shader, the option to choose different Shaders for different situations on the same model becomes a viable concept as it will impact on your update rates. How we decide that, is dependent on the game, or your hardware speed or both; but at this stage it would be wise to have your update routines make some decisions on the choice of Shader, a fast ambient, moderate vertex, or a slow but detailed pixel Shader, depending on distance from the light source or view point, for example. For now though we'll press ahead with one type of Shader in the demos to allow you the chance to make the decisions that will optimize your own versions of the code.

Notice though I did tie myself in a bit of a knot by having to make tests for which Shader I was using to set up new attribute handles and make choices to pass or not pass the normal attributes. We'll need to make a mental note about that and clean that up, since tying ourselves in knots suggests complexity and we don't want that.

Oh, it might be interesting to note, we can also have multiple lights in a Shader, we just need to loop through them in sequence, either passing from the CPU or hard coding them in a value or a uniform as an array, and combining the values to acquire our final intensity value. But we have to be cautious. Too many lights in a scene, will overload the Shaders ability to calculate a final result quickly.

For low end machines, we should really try to stay at 1–2 lights, but feel free to add more if frame rate is not an issue. A multi light demo is on the Support Site to view.

That's as much as I want to do with lighting at this point, I'm going to stick with the vertex lighting from now on as it gives me the performance/quality balance I think most dual core GPUs can cope with, using a modest amount of lit models. If you have a quad or higher core GPU, you should be able to extract a bit more quality out of it with a per pixel Shader. But try to remember your target audience; the more generic you can make your system the better it is for market penetration. That usually means targeting the lowest common denominator, or at least the lowest viable one.

Sadly there's no hardware call we can use to ask a GPU how many cores it has to decide on the level of lighting you use. You can keep a record of known GPU hardware, which you can get from the `glGetString(GL_RENDERER);` interrogation, and store a table of how many cores known makes have, as long as you keep an up-to-date list! But you also can't easily find out things like the speed of that GPU, which of course has an impact on performance. You can try to ask the user, and accept that they might not be totally honest or sure but give it your best effort based on the response. It's even possible to run some small internal timing tests on a set number of draws to test the frame rate that will probably be the most accurate way to determine if your system is capable of running your most intensive Shaders. But the user might not like having to wait for these tests to complete. This is one of those fun market fragmentation issues, there are no standards in terms of the hardware design of our GPUs only the software interfaces remain consistent.

The Camera Never Lies

Well actually, it does, every pic I ever see of me, has me looking like a fat, aged, worn out wreck of a man, when in my reality I'm a healthy 24 years old Adonis. But enough of my issues. Cameras can be made to lie, if we want them to, we can alter the depth of view, the scaling of the ratios, and a range of other things, but apart from using such things for a few fx, we generally need a camera to represent an accurate view of our scene.

So far we've made do with a *hard* camera, set up before we draw things and made use of fixed view/projection matrices to create the MVP but really these important matrices need to be located in a class and be allowed to modify and be consistent for all classes to use, so that for example, our camera can move in space with our moving vehicle or avatar to give a viewpoint from that objects location.

There are multiple forms of camera, in so far as what we expect to visualize; we can have first person, where we place the camera firmly in the head/viewing of the avatar/ship that we control so, we see what they see and the camera moves with them as they travel through the scene.

Fixed camera, as we have already had, is useful for 2D or God view games where we want to see the overall playfield, with or without scrolling.

Second person is similar to fixed camera is so far as from that view you can see yourself, so a fixed camera can be second person, it could also be a view from another avatar's perspective,

Third person is where you control the camera but the camera itself is outside of your avatars eye/view space, usually above and behind, though rotating around you is considered quite normal if the camera gets obstructed.

First and third person views are the most common, so when we write a Camera Class these will be the main things we focus on, but second and fixed cameras are quite trivial to include later.

Cameras can twist and turn in space the same as any other object but generally we like to keep them under a degree of control as detaching them too much from their world has a similar effect to you shaking your head side to side while on a roller coaster, best not to have lunch just beforehand.

There is also a problem with cameras that twist and turn and it's a big problem indeed. Our concepts of using degrees of rotation, or Euler angles have a major issue when it comes to calculating those twists and turns in space, such as Gimbal lock. We can't actually escape it if we are using degrees. The solution requires us to use Quaternions (Quats), which I already said I don't want to talk about yet but here we are in an odd situation where we are going to need a full axis camera to get a dog fight game working. But I still don't want to get into Quats yet. So I give you a method for doing 3D with Euler angles in the full understanding that under certain situations you will get gimbal lock and things will go wrong... It's ok, it's not really as bad as it sounds and it's something you should really experience, even though when we do cover Quats this particular annoyance will fade away.

We'll create an abstract Camera Class, which our Game and objects can use to access the View and Projection matrices we need to create our MVPs, and try a couple of different types of camera on top of that Base Class, which will make our lives a bit easier.

But What Does It All Do?

The principle purpose of a camera is naturally enough to allow you to see, but on a more technical level it sets the point in space where you begin your View Space. That then means all the other objects in that Word Space, spinning and flying around, will be seen from a new variable point in space. The View Space, that cone of space we see from the point of the camera and in the direction it is pointing.

Assuming a fixed camera at 0, 0, 0 is where we see everything simply won't work if we are attaching our *eye* to a ship, or axe wielding dwarf's head. As soon as the carrier moves, the View Space becomes variable and that's what makes it a factor in the Matrix calculations we have to work with. As we need to twist the world coordinates around to fit in with the View coords.

With a single screen display, we tend to have just one View Space, that is, your viewpoint of the world from the position we are. Generally all the objects that actually exist in that world need to be rendered based on that View Space. There are a couple of other possible view spaces that may relate to HUD and other effects such as a rear view mirror.

For convenience in this demo, I've created a small variation on a first person Camera Class, which overrides the base Camera Class we will use from now on. This allows us to *attach* a camera to a Player object, which will be a ship; I'll call it a 3DCamera. I've limited the players' axis rotations to Yaw and Pitch, which along with forward movement will give us the ability to move around in space. Roll is possible but our camera really won't like it, so let's keep it to two axes of rotation, even then we might have issues.

One point about using Euler angles in rotation calculations is that some values can produce the same results, −180° is the same as +180° for example, so we should make a bit of effort to ensure our Degree values increase and decrease from 0 to 360 and avoid <0 and >360. This is also why we're not using the Roll at this point, our source data is Euler angles and they have issues, if we were to add Roll to the calculation it would at times cause Gimbal lock, even though we could convert the angles to Quats, our source data is always flawed.

Our simple Camera Class is going to take players ship position and with that, rotation data, which can let us generate and access a new View Matrix. We *could* also generate a new Projection matrix but it's probably going to remain pretty constant, unless we want to play with some effects so for now we will leave Projection as a default and simply access it. Up to now we've allowed Projection matrices to be recalculated with each model, it's not a big calculation but since they are all working within the same camera it's now the camera's job to maintain it.

Objects that need to be rendered will need to create their MVP matrices so of course the Camera will need to provide the V and P parts, so we'll provide access to those. Let's take a look at the header for base Camera Class, which all other cameras will inherit.

```
#pragma once

#include <GLES2/gl2.h>
#include "../Headers/ObjectModel.h"
#include "Frustum.h"

class Camera
{
public:
 Camera();
 ~Camera();

 glm::mat4* GetView();
 glm::mat4* GetProjection();

 virtual void Update(ObjectModel* ControllingObject);//updates using model
data
 virtual void Update(); //updates using its own position and matrix values

 glm::mat4 View; // used by MVP calculations
 glm::mat4 Projection;
 glm::vec3 CameraPos;

 float Roll; // when we move independant of an object
 float Pitch;
 float Yaw;

 Frustum* MyFrustum; // will be used when we do culling
 float Ratio;
 float FOV;
 float NearPlane;
 float FarPlane;
 glm::vec3 Target;
 glm::vec3 UpVector;
};
```

The only thing not obvious to us at this point is the Frustum, but we'll get to that later, it's not needed yet and will not be set up until I explain it. I've also added the variables to create the Projection and View values here. They can become much more important later, for now just make sure you set them up in the Camera Class you want, you could also provide get/set systems for them.

As you can see its really pretty similar to a 3D model, it has position that allows us to place it in space, and some rotation values to deal with its orientation, we could maintain a Model type matrix for it too, but at the moment it's not needed, our aim is to create the new view matrix with each update to pass that on to our objects.

As the base Camera Class itself is designed to be overridden, the code supplied in the cpp file is incredibly basic and provides almost no functionality. You could just leave the Camera Class methods blank or make them pure virtual if you desire. But the GetView and GetProjection methods do work and are important, returning pointers to the relevant matrices, (it's faster to return pointers).

The Base Class is a static view from a fixed point camera looking down from a point on high to the point at 0, 0, 0. That means I have provided a choice of four different types of camera, three which inherit it and override the update routines.

- A 3DCamera, which is attached to a player as used in this demo, with an offset. Really it's a basic first person camera.

- A ChaseCamera, which is actually the same but with a larger offset and allows for the player to be drawn just in front of you to which you might want to add a bit of sway logic.

- An FPSCamera for First Person games, which we'll talk about later and of course the base…

- A FixedCamera or God mode, which as you can imagine views our game scene from a fixed point.

We could create different instances if we wanted and switch between them. For now we are going to use the 3DCamera, which is an example of an almost free camera allowing 360° rotation in two axes. Feel free to add more types, smart cameras for example, which home to a point can be made to feel like drone views.

All our model types so far have code to use the camera supplied View and Projection matrix, just comment out the hard coded versions in your chosen model type (mostly ShipModel) and uncomment the *get from Camera* methods.

Now compile and run…you should now be able to see our world as you did before, but this time our camera is able to be moved around. All we need to do is give our Ship the Yaw and Pitch values we expect.

▌ In Space, No One Can Hear You Smashing Your Keyboard As You Scream Why "Don't You Work!!!"

Ok so now we know quite a bit about 3D and Shaders, it's time to actually produce a proper 3D game example. As we did with 2D, we'll start with something simple, building on what we did with our models and adding a few other primitives

As before when tackling something new, let's consider what we plan to do, We'll create a simple 3D game framework, which can load OBJ models, as part of a game objects data, and like our textures we will take care not to load multiple versions of the same OBJ.

- Our player will be in control of a ship in space, rather selfishly trying to harass and rob other ships of their cargo. So we need control and visualization that allows that.

- Control should consist of thrust, braking (is so far as braking in space is possible), and some type of left/right/up/down methods.

- We want to create a Space environment, not just a blank and empty space.

- We want multiple *enemies* on screen at once.

- We want it look good.

None of this sounds too complex, does it?

7 Space the Final Frontier

Space games are easy, all you really need to do is enclose your player in a massive space-themed skybox/sphere* and populate a few space stations/planets in there... There's not a lot of rendering you have to do, just make sure that any object in your line of sight is drawn in a proper orientation and scale and boom we have a classic Space game and even worse, after all our playing with animation of models, ships don't really animate. But no worries, we'll get to animation soon! But we can certainly put our model-loading skills to use now; we've got a pretty decent framework of features in place to put anything we need in.

We can rework the HelloCubes project to make our space game; it is after all basically nothing more than a game loop displaying graphics. But it's also rather limited because of some oversimplification of the code. I knew we were only going to draw a few shapes of models, so I didn't make a very good job of allowing the different objects to communicate with each other.

Let's rebuild things, we still will use the basic idea of an ObjectModel Base Class because we know it works well, but we'll add a bit more control over our assets, textures, Shaders, and more importantly create a few management classes to look after our objects and not leave them in global space.

Encapsulating our models in a Manager Class will allow us to get a game object to talk to or interact with other game objects; we'll need that for collision tests and other interactive points.

---

* We're going to discuss this soon.

So it is time to download the slightly improved Flying Cubes project called SpaceCadet from the support site and familiarize yourself with the layout.

The main thing you will notice this time is the full incorporation of the TinyObjLoader files and a brand new constructor in the ObjectModel Class, which takes, not surprisingly an OBJ file, which it then loads.

The project also does not allow the main entrance routine to control the workings of the code, that was a very lazy hack, and I hope it made you uncomfortable. No? You've not been paying attention then, that was one of those now infamous bad design choices…try to keep up!

Instead, it now creates and calls a Game Class, which among other things is the new home for the vector containing all our objects and the support classes we need for the game to work. The entrance code of a project should never be responsible for any game functions; its role is to start-up the game, not to run the game. Let's never do that again.

I've added a little bit of extra code to our Model loader to load and manage material files, which describe the surfaces of the faces, and, of course, any associated textures.

The code is heavily based on the examples provided by TinyObjLoader, modified to suit our loading systems and OpenGLES2.0s slightly different way of handling textures.

So we're good to go, we can load any OBJ file, though please make sure they live in the Resources\Models\ folder along with their associated .mtl and texture images.

—ELITE—

Our space game is going to be fairly simple for the brevity of this book if nothing else, but let's establish the concept. You control a ship with some degree of pitch and yaw control, using the most basics of momentum/impulse physics, and you have to attack other ships in your area, which, in turn, will attack you.

Sounds simple? Well it is if we can come up with some logic that will allow the enemy ships to dogfight reasonably well. Though in space it's perfectly possible to spin/roll to face your enemy, it's much harder to alter your direction because of momentum. So we need to either take that into account or ignore the laws of physics and have our ships behave in a more conventional aircraft flying style. This isn't as mad as it sounds, because it's a familiar concept for anyone who's ever ridden a bike or flown an aircraft, banking, and rolling being the means to change the direction of these vehicles. Sadly though we've discounted rolling, so we'll use yaw or rudder control instead.

But first, our list of tasks. We have a framework, but we need to load some models. We should try doing that in levels. I've given you three lovely low poly models one of my students designed for me, thanks Mohsen Behvar, they worked really well. Let's set up three rounds with different ships each time, and give the ships slightly different behavior and attributes. We'll set up a fourth round where we will bring them all in, in waves, similar to a scrolling mega shooter.

- Create classes for our ship types

- Load and Display our ships

- Set up a level manager

- Create some kind of flight control for the ships

- Do collision tests for contact with ships

- Do collision tests for lasers/bullets

- Manage game states

Ok, that should do it, let's start with creating classes. We've got three ship types, let's not use the traditional reptile names, everyone does them, how about something less loved? Amphibians! Those cute slimy little things? Here are our ships:

We can have a Newt Class, a sleek-looking Salamander Class, and one of our ships looks similar to a big heavy class, so let's make that a Toad Class.

We have to think about how much our ships have in common. We could give them some special attributes, but for the most part they are all going to fly the same way, only at different speeds because of differences in mass, thrust, and so on. Or in their weaponry.

So let's create an Amphibian Class, that inherits from our Object Base Class, but, in turn, we can also write three specific classes that set up the variables that control behavior, but also allow us to add some special features they in turn can inherit from the Amphibian Class.

Let's start by establishing a few ideas. First space is big, I think Douglas Adams explains best exactly how big it is, and it's really too big for us to visualize, so we're going to set a few limits on how big our space could be. A pretty decent size should be 100,000 units cubed.

But what is a unit? Well that's up to us, our all models use numbers, usually −1.0 to 1.0 to represent their relative positon to their origin, and scale factors allow us to increase that size as it suits us, but it's best if we think that a unit should represent some real world standard unit of measurement. Most common are millimeters, centimeters, and meters. Larger values can, of course, be used, but tend to be less useful for us because we don't refer to everyday objects as fractions of a kilometer. For the most part, we'll consider a unit to be a meter and if we want centimeters our scale will be 0.01 to divide it by 100.

We shall populate our space with a few baddies, though first we need to create some. The template has three types of ships available to you: (1) FastShip, (2) BigShip, and (3) Carrier Ship. They only have some very simple directional movement logic and constructors to allow us to access their vertex list and textures.

We're going to add more content as we go, so let's do what we've done before and place a few dozen of each type in our universe randomly spaced around and randomly scaled for now.

Quite an armada?

Ok, we still have our simple look around controls on our Camera Class, which we're going to get rid of soon, but hopefully if you look around, you will see a few of your generated ships? If not don't worry, they are there somewhere.

It's time we created a ship of our own and gave ourselves some reasonable means of flying around. As our view of the game is going to be from the ship's viewpoint facing forward, our own controlled ship itself is effectively the camera, so we are going to make sure our ship actually has access to a Camera Class, which it can set to the ship's positions to give us a sense of flying in space.

For us to have a camera attached to a ship it stands to reason we need to use the ships positional data to place the camera, that's pretty simple. But we do need to be sure our Camera ship is, in fact, our own ship, so we should differentiate that in some way from all the other riff raff flying around in space. I'm going to create a Player Class, it is using the ShipModel Class, but this one is a bit different, it will also provide input data and be referenced in the Game Class with a Player* MyPlayer value to allow access from other instances of ships and cameras. Add Player.h and cpp to the projects and include a

```
Player* ThePlayer;
```

In the Game.h Class define. Then a small modification our init to create our player as the first object, make sure this is the first thing we create, the Player is important to us, we will reference him by his name, like we did with Fred and Bob, but the ship is still part of the collective group of objects.

```
ThePlayer = new Player(&this->Handler, (char*)"../Resources/Models/
brian_03.obj", &this->MainModelManager);
glm::vec3 Pos = glm::vec3(0.0f, 0.0f, 0.0f);
float MScale = 0.95f;
ThePlayer->Scales = glm::vec3(MScale, MScale, MScale);
ThePlayer->SetPosition(Pos);
MyObjects.push_back(ThePlayer); // he's on the system for possible updates/
draws
ThePlayer->StoreGraphicClass(MyGraphics);
MyGraphics->Init(ThePlayer);
glUseProgram(0); // free the program
ThePlayer->TheGame = this;
```

And then a small change to our game loop.

```
ThePlayer->Update(TheInput);
TheCamera->Update(ThePlayer);
    for (int i = 1; i < MyObjects.size(); i++)
    {
     MyObjects[i]->Update();
     MyObjects[i]->Draw();
    } // for
```

You can see that I update the player and then the camera outside of the main loop, which starts from 1, not 0, so the player is never going to be updated or drawn by this loop, so long as he's the first one created. There are certain advantages to making your character the first in any list, this is a good example.

There's a couple of small issues, with the 3Dcamera, which you might not notice, mainly without an offset, we have essentially put the camera in the middle of our ship, and if we leave our ship in there it might render itself around it if we decide to render the ship (you should conditionally decide to render ships, more later), fun in one way but it's a bit of a hindrance in gameplay to have a blindfold around us, we have two simple options. Provide the Cameraoffset value in the camera to be just on the outside the ship, or make sure we don't render the player ever.

We could also choose to use the chase camera, which at first glance is identical to the 3D-attached camera as it is dependent on the players' position and offsets. However, a chase camera should have a little more functionality, for example, having it on an extendable selfie stick behind you, or being able to alter it a bit from side to side, or even better to have it on a slightly springy selfie stick, so as you go around corners the camera lags a little before going back to its correct view point. I'm not going to get too into this in this book, it's another of those big topics, but the Chase Camera is there for you to play with those ideas rather than strip the 3D camera down.

■ Space, Why All the Asteroids?

Let's keep the population of our space fairly simple, and create a small asteroid belt around the centre point of our view, and have some simple convoys of ships traveling from point A to B to C and back to A, with a couple of them doing attack runs. Does any of this sound familiar?

I'm going to do about 30 asteroids, randomly scattered around the 0,0,0 point, and also have two convoys going from point to point. I can make this totally 3D and have a spherical field, but for convenience I'm going to keep it fairly flat so that even Star Trek's Kahn's 2D thinking can get around it.

I've included some nice simple geometric asteroids in the assets folder, named GeosphereXX.obj, which go from 8 to 80 faces, courtesy of my colleague Bojan Endrovski, who uses them in a small asteroids game he created, call Blasteroroids. There's also a class called Asteroid to process them, because they don't have textures, it's not really ideal to use any of the textured Object Class types to update and render them. But I have made the lighting conditional on them to demonstrate how to do that. This is also a useful class for any future untextured but potentially lit models you may want to play with. So perhaps naming it something more neutral would be a good idea. UnTexturedOptionalLitSimpleModel.... for example.

We could use more asteroid types, or even higher res version, but there are also going to be some performance issues, if we try to create too many asteroids at the moment, this will soon become clear. These models have no texture, so we also need to make sure we use a Shader that accounts for that. So, when we create them use the NoTextureLit Shader pair.

We're still moving in 3D but it's easier for us to find things looking around rather than spinning up and down too, even though that is available to us.

Asteroids are mainly there to give visual points of reference and a boundary to your play area because a blank space gives no sense of motion or direction.

Try creating a ring of asteroids using the Asteroid Class available (but not currently added) to your project.

And create a nice ring of them using something like this in your init code.

```
float angle = Rand(360);
float dist = 20 + Rand(30);
float Xpos = cos(glm::radians(angle)) * dist;
float Zpos = sin(glm::radians(angle)) * dist;
 sprintf(Buffer,"../Resources/Assets/Models/%s",AsteroidFiles[x]);
 printf("string out is %s\n", Buffer);
 Asteroid* A = new Asteroid(&this->Handler, Buffer,
&this->MainModelManager);
 Pos = glm::vec3(Xpos, 15.0f - Rand(30.0f), Zpos);
 float aScale = (Rand(1.2f) + 0.15)/2;
```

I will let you work out how to put this in a loop and complete the required info needed. Note we've done this kind of thing before! When we wanted to make our KamaKazi sprites arc. It's the same principle, place them in a ring around our center point (Y is up this time, so we use X and Z) and put in a few random scale values to alter the size. A small array somewhere in your Game Class can give you the different model file names, which the sprintf function is demonstrating and printf outputting for you to see.

```
char* AsteroidFiles[] =
{
 (char*)"GeoSphere8.obj",
 (char*)"GeoSphere16.obj",
 (char*)"GeoSphere20.obj",
 (char*)"GeoSphere32.obj",
 (char*)"GeoSphere64.obj",
 (char*)"GeoSphere80.obj",
};
```

The Asteroid Class provided is expecting to use the SimpleTri Shaders, which works fine but really are a bit dull; you might, however, want to use the UntexturedLit Shader pair, I'll let you work out how to change the class to cope with the extra needs of those Shaders.

▌ Skyboxes

After all that complex stuff, let's discuss something simple but very cool you've already seen me using on screenshots for the light Shaders (e.g., in the previous image). A Skybox can make a massive change to your game graphics and sense of being in an environment. It's also rather a clever trick, which relies on the end of a rainbow effect where you can see the rainbow, but you can never ever get to it. So how is it done?

So far we've considered models to be textured on the outside and we view them that way, with no regard to anything inside them. But a Skybox has an interesting variation on that, it's designed to be seen from the inside and it's also as you might imagine nothing more than a simple box or cube, possibly without a bottom, because we often won't see that. There are other variations too, Sky Domes and Sky Spheres are sometimes used but they increase the complexity a little, so I won't cover them here.

One thing about a Skybox is that it's usually quite large. Large enough for our game world or at least a large section of it to be enclosed within it. In fact, what we are doing is *boxing up* our world and then looking up from it, to see the inside of the box in any direction we are looking at. As the box's faces can never be reached it's always going to be like a rainbows end, unreachable.

Of course, we don't always have to encase our entire scene/world in a box, only the viewing object, that is our camera, needs to be in a box, which as long as it moves with the camera (but not rotating), the edges will never be reached. If the box was too big it would understandably cause a lot of texture stretching. So we make a box big enough to seem far away, along with a few perspective tricks. And we texture it with nice blue sky and clouds, for a world base scene or star clusters and distant planets, for a space scene. Things we are never going to reach stay just out of reach but we no longer have to care about the blank space that exists where we are not drawing models.

It can be tricky if we have a small box, and we get terrain or buildings that exist outside the box boundary, and then suddenly pop in to existence when you take one step forward, but that's a problem we can hide with larger boxes, or a distance fog system that will allow far objects to fade into view as they cross into the box's range.

The best way to see this is to do it, so let's create a simple *space* box in our code. As always, if we are creating a new thing, we should create a new class for it. Lucky for you I already supply it, in the project it's just not added to the solution.

Add the Skybox.h/cpp files to your solution in the source and header filters, and then in the initialization of the Skybox.cpp file, make sure you load the textures in this order, again I supplied the textures for you, and will explain where they were sourced shortly.

```
faces.push_back("../Resources/Textures/vr_rt.tga");
faces.push_back("../Resources/Textures/vr_lf.tga");
faces.push_back("../Resources/Textures/vr_up.tga");
faces.push_back("../Resources/Textures/vr_dn.tga");
faces.push_back("../Resources/Textures/vr_bk.tga");
faces.push_back("../Resources/Textures/vr_ft.tga");
```

This class is pretty much totally self-contained, but you will need to load your own different Skybox textures for different games, so in theory that's the only edit you ever need to worry about. It is also possible to load a single cube texture, where the single texture has all six faces laid out in a cross. But I think that may also introduce some wasted space in the texture space, I'm not 100% sure about that but I prefer to avoid it. However, if you wish to alter the cube map generation, there are some very fine free examples of single cubemap textures available here:

http://www.humus.name/index.php?page=Textures

We also need some Shaders and once more I've provided SkyBox Shaders for you in the..Resources/Shaders/ folder. They are already set up in the Skybox init. But it's a good idea to have a look at them, because they are a little unusual because we use cubetextures, and don't ever send texture coordinates to them. Any thoughts why?

Interestingly, the SkyBox is one of the exceptions to the idea of the camera having a constant projection matrix, that's simply because it's not actually part of the world; it's not trying to represent any object within the world space. So its projection matrix is quite different from a normal model and uses a different set of projection values.

```
glm::mat4 Projection = glm::perspective(85.0f, 16.0f / 9.0f, 0.1f, 1000.0f);
```

With distance set at 1000 units or higher, this gives a good depth. We will still be using the View matrix of the camera though, which will let us look up, down, and around in our enclosed gameworld giving us a sense of motion.

Now with a SkyBox in place, even if you have no enemy ships visible, you have a sense of depth and position now, so as you move around you can get a sense of where you are in space. You should be getting a pretty decent idea that you are moving around, and have some sense of flying.

I also mentioned Sky Domes and Sky Sphere's, which as you can imagine are a similar principle but a little more processor heavy, encapsulating our world in a full, or semi-sphere over the top. As semi or full spheres are geometrically a bit more intense, they can take a bit more processing, but they are going to be living full time in our GPU buffers, so they are not really going to make a massive impact once it's set up. A Sky Dome is not normally going to have anything but the most simple of Shaders. They also tend to be able to use a single texture, unlike the box that needs six, which can be a win. The decision on which method to use is up to you, I find a well-defined SkyBox to be just as effective and as fast to render as a Sky Dome in nearly every case.

The main trick with either system is that the highlights in the box can never actually be reached, they are always set equidistant from our position, so it only works with detail, that is, consistent with far distant things such as clouds, the sun, mountain tops, and in our case stars, planets, and so on…and as long as we maintain the concept of movement under or around us, our eyes won't care that the horizon, such as a rainbow, can't ever actually be reached.

One small pain about Skyboxes though is that to work really well you need a large detailed texture, to avoid scaling artifacts, and because there are six needed, they can be an immense GPU memory hog. As with all things you need to find a balance.

A second small pain is that to get the best out of them, the edges of the six faces should match to avoid seams, and that tends to require the careful and steady eye of an artist. If you don't have a tame artist locked up in your cellar, you can find a lot of cool ready to use and free skyboxes at http://www.custommapmakers.org/skyboxes.php.

I'm using the mp_vr skybox from that site for our space game coming up now. It's supplied under the GNU License, so do remember if you use it or any other from that site, and distributing it you must include the license text.

It's not perfect, the 512 × 512 size on each face, projected onto a full 1920 × 1080 screen creates a lot of obvious stretching of the textures and the planets and things are a little too close to us really, but it highlights the concepts fantastically and does not eat up too much of our GPU memory. In an ideal world, I'd use 2048 × 2048 skyboxes, but that's 100 Mb of RAM gone, on an SBC it's probably too big a chunk to lose.

But even at 512 × 512 and with obvious stretching we get a nice effect and we're going to add more improvements soon. I'll leave it up to you if you feel you should leave this as it is or try to reduce the stretch (Two clear options, reduce the display buffer size, or find higher texture images). Is it making your skin crawl?

▮ The Game's Afoot Which Way to Turn?

With all this set up we're doing, it's easy to think we've missed out on the actual game itself but, in fact, there's really not much more to do. Simple space games don't need a huge amount of effort once the render systems are up and working. We do have to have a bit of a think about collision in 3D, which we'll tackle soon, but for now we need to consider how we control both our ship and the enemy ships in this new 3D expanse.

Now creating a space game is pretty easy, we don't need to worry too much about the physics, though physics does not actually disappear in space, we just have a certain expectation from decades of watching Sci-Fi, that physics isn't a problem in space. You're going to sit nice and safe in your seat, you can fly faster than light, and not worry about the g-forces going from 0 to 186,282 m/s in 1 s, you can also turn on a dime without squashing yourself into your boots; micrometeors, traveling at near light speed are never going to smash through your windscreen and explode in a molten mass as it enters your brain. No, physics does not happen in space....games! All we really need to do is move around in straight lines with a reasonable means of turning and braking.

Simply moving them from point A to point B is fine, it will work, but we must take more account of our new important concept of orientation, which is not exactly the same as direction of travel especially in zero gravity space. For a ship or any 3D object to move logically, it needs to relate its movement to the direction of facing or in some exceptions such as side thrusters, the opposite to where the propulsion system is located.

This was easy in 2D, and honestly it's not that much harder in 3D, except in 2D we could represent direction with simple cardinal points, of up, down, left, and right, or even consider a vector motion giving 360° of travel. But we now have 360° in 3 axis! Orientation becomes a slightly more complex factor. But we can still relate it to some familiar ideas and code those.

No matter what your orientation, you can relate to the concept of forward, back, and left and right, relative to your facing. Forward is as you might expect simply taking a step in the direction you are facing. Back the reverse. Left and right might seem tricky but remember we have that interesting Cross-product function, which can give us right angles to pairs of vectors.

So forward and back movements are going to be pretty easy, but turning can present a few issues for things in motion, if we want to obey some of the laws of inertia.

And here we hit an issue.....inertia is a concept in physics; we don't have a physics engine. Yet! We are going to have one soon, so it might seem a bit pointless to add physics concepts to a demo at this stage only for it to be totally replaced by a proper engine later.

But as the intent is to learn a bit of the concepts of motion, this will have value. But yeah, I don't want to spend days on something we're going to ditch in the next chapter. So my inertia motion concepts are basically very simple and quite inaccurate. We'll simulate inertia and motion, by keeping a current direction of travel, and a desired direction of travel. We will apply our directional force (another physics concept) depending on our requested direction to create movement, changing our direction so that it matches our orientation.

It's not perfect, especially because friction in space is a negligible concept and I'm not applying any negating force to our forward motion but it will look and feel ok.

You can see how this is done in the Source code giving us a reasonably good-looking game.

We're Going to Need Some Game Mechanics

HUD and Cockpits

Now a space game viewed solely from the players' eyes is very hard to orientate. You can add a small image in the middle to act as a sight, this is called a reticule. And then you suddenly have some concept of what you are looking at. Very important when there are no enemies on-screen though is to have something that the reticule can relate to; stars though, even if they are only dots in the distance are superb at giving a sense of movement.

But while a reticule will give you a sense of direction/location, it does not give you any real sense of interaction with a space game. After all, pretty much every space game you can think of has you sitting in a ship.

So we should really generate some sense of being in a cockpit. In a 3D scene, we could make it up from textures, and make it part of the world, but it's not, it's part of *us*. It gives our view point at some sense of centre. And it needs to feel like it's part of us and not part of the world.

This can be produced with a 3D system, but it's far better done as a 2D system using the orthogonal projection system. So yes, we still need 2D drawing in 3D games.

GUI

GUI, stands for Graphic User Interface, essentially it's the part of the screen that passes information to us, and may also have buttons or boxes that we can click or swipe that allows us to interact with our program. In games we also have HUDs, a lovely old military term for Head-Up Display.

If you don't have interaction with your game then you have a HUD, which gives you all the information your game needs to pass to you. If you do have interaction you have a GUI. But more often than not lazy programmers use the terms interchangeably, mostly to annoy designers.

In one very useful way, we've pretty much done a HUD, without actually realizing it. Our Single screen texture, 2D screen, double buffer idea, is effectively a HUD, we can continue to use that as much as we like to put what would normally be static information in 2D, such as scores and other useful icons, this gives our old dynamically modified texture a new lease of life.

Screen or Render

A GUI can also be rendered, using an orthogonal projection matrix that was the basic principle of our double buffer, though the projection matrix wasn't actually defined. But if we're going to use orthogonal projection in a 3D game, drawing a GUI is the most usual place to use one. GUIs can be pretty big though, perhaps even screen size, but we've got our graphics in GPU memory, unlike our double buffer. Dynamic allocation, where we created new textures every frame, is to be avoided; we should try as much as possible to not alter the texture, which will cause FPS drop. There will always be situations where parts of a texture need modification, for example, updating power meters, or score counters, and so on. So we have to give some thought to how much of the screen is going to update and if there are ways to reduce the making of new textures, perhaps by breaking the screen into multiple smaller textures, where most are not in fact updated.

The easiest thing to do is to keep the variable parts of the GUI separate from the static parts. Take a look at the GUI3D demo on the site, it has a simple ship screen overlay we are going to use, most of the texture is indeed screen size, but there are *holes* in the texture, where status bars are updated and radar is displayed. The dynamic parts will be updated differently from the static parts.

3Dfont

3D games also need us to display text, and we could continue to use the old simple 2D tile font on a surface and draw the surface exactly as we did in 2D, but CPU writing to pixels buffers is so last week now. We really need something a bit more flexible, but still fairly simple. Essentially, we're going to do the same basic idea of keeping the font as a set of tiles in a texture, but this time allow the Shader to get to the correct point in the texture to draw the relevant tiles to create text. All we need to do is create a small quad of six vertices per tile, map the texture UV for the required letter (making sure to not bother with space), and build up a small buffer of these vertices that then get drawn with a single draw call.

I've included a Font3D system on the support site. It's really quite basic but it will allow us to print using our 2D font images and we can also change font images to get different text styles and sizes. Just be sure to set the background color to an alpha of 0, or we will draw the whole tile rather than just the pixels that we want to see.

Notice when using it though it is not actually drawing *in space* but to the screen or clip space so that it will always appear a little detached from the scene, perfect for debug, and direct user info-like scores.

Feel free to experiment with the Shaders to give some nice effects and maybe add some MVP functionality to put text in the game itself, hint! (This is how you can do 2D sprites with hardware)!

Hit Em Where It Shows

We have ships, we have a sense of direction and orientation from our GUI, the enemies follow a path, and will try to intercept us using theirs, "I want to be where you are," basic logic to chase us. Now it's time to unleash the full fury of a pixelated proton propelled particle p. I can't think of another good P word. We need a firing system and we need to know if we hit a barn door size ship.

Being able to detect the hits on a ship from our bullets/lasers/phasers or whatever we want to call our death rays is one thing. Showing the player that they've hit something is another; we need some nice effects to really get across the impact of a hit.

We could, of course, just make the target lurch a bit, but that won't work terribly well with directed energy weapons, lurching really only works with mass-based projectiles. If we hit something we can though probably assume the area hit will deform and break up.

What better way to show that the particles being emitted from the point of impact?

But the one thing we need to do is actually decide if, whatever kind of weapon we fire, has it hit our enemy ship? That's where we need to take the Death Ray idea a little more seriously because we are in a sense going to use a Ray to decide on the success or failure of a hit. Sadly not a Death Ray, but a more elegant and plain old-fashioned maths Ray.

A Ray is simply a line starting at a point of our choosing and heading off into infinity in a certain fixed direction. Think of an ultra powerful laser pointer that can reach the moon and beyond. It's not a physical real line, though we can draw it if we want.

It's actually a mathematical concept, and because it has both a start and a direction represented by a vector3, there are lots of interesting calculations that are possible. Most of which revolve working out if a mathematical shape intersects with that line somewhere in the space it is heading off to. That makes them especially useful for collision calculations. In fact, a lot of collision systems depend on the concept of a Ray, often using the normal of a face, plane or triangle, as a direction for a Ray to do tests. So if I wanted to know what was under my feet, presuming gravity is pulling straight down, a ray cast straight down could test for triangles in the triangle mesh that makes up my environment. Also casting a ray in front of me, I could ask if I am hitting any triangles that make up a wall!

There are a number of basic intersection calculations that Rays are especially good for; intersecting with a plane, or cubes, polygons, spheres, and a couple of others. The most useful to us though, are plane and sphere. But the others crop up from time to time.

Why is this useful? Well imagine you do indeed have a Death Ray in the nose of your ship, and you hit fire…That ray is instantly going to fire off into space, and all we need to know is did we hit the ship we were aiming at? If the ship itself is encased in a simple sphere, then there is a test for a ray to sphere interaction, which will tell us, not only that we hit it, but also the distance between the start of the ray and the contact point. The distance is especially useful if I detect a wall in front of me, but if it's 2 light years away, I don't need to take evasive action until it gets a lot closer.

These 2 bits of information taken from relatively simple and pretty much standard functions allow us to not only decide to damage the enemy ship, also by how much depending on the distance.

This is our first really useful 3D collision system. Let's add the Ray.h/cpp files you have in your working folder to gain access to them, and add a fire system to your Player Class. But we need to talk about some more collision systems before we can actually use it. We don't currently have the right understanding of the things we are testing against.

3D Collision

Here's another can of worms, whole careers have been formed out of attempts to perfect collision systems for 3D, and in many cases these careers have been well founded. But 3D collision with objects made of meshes, which can have almost any shape or size, inevitably means some form of compromise when it comes to maths trying to mimic the responses we see in real life.

3D collision, probably represents the ultimate expression of maths in coding, as such it can involve levels of complexity that are capable of making old fat Scottish programmers weep.

But when all said and done, there is no perfect system that works for everything. Even the very best systems present some degree of compromise or set conditions on the form of the data used. So it's no surprise that we're going to simplify things as much as we can for now, but we'll introduce a few standard methods that are easy to understand.

One key point of 3D collision is that, as I say, it's complex, and complexity is the natural enemy of a low-powered CPU. Complex tasks take longer to evaluate and that, in turn, can cause our games to run slower, especially if we do a lot of these tasks with mostly negative results.

To reduce the amount of complex tasks we do, we tend to use a combination of primitive collision types and culling systems that prevent us doing tests that are simply not needed, as we did in 2D games we probably don't need to process objects that are out of our field of view, that are nowhere near certain other objects, or that are well above the playfield we use as a ground. Being able to focus our complex and expensive efforts on things that are more likely to produce a result is always valuable.

Primitive Collision Types

Testing a complex geometry model against another complex model is seldom needed in most games; the greater the precision, the more complex and slower the process to decide if collision has occurred. That all takes a lot of CPU time and needs to be avoided.

To avoid this strain pretty much all current game and physics engines abandon complex collision at least for the most part, and rely instead on simplified shape structures that are quick and easy to define and can provide a usable level of detail on collision that we can choose to best suit our game needs.

The most common are Spheres and Boxes, which are nothing more than 3D extensions of the 2D circle and square tests. Also popular are cylinders, ellipses, and capsules, the choice is quite broad, but basically it's a means to encase our model in a simpler to work with shape. Then the level of complexity can be set by us, using simpler meshes enclosing a more complex mesh. Collision does not need graphic detail, it simply needs spatial accuracy, and that is more flexible.

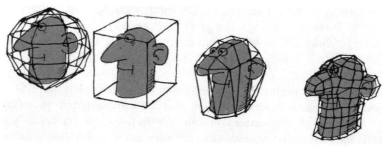

Several of these simple meshes are mathematical concepts in themselves, boxes and spheres, in particular. Maths systems for normal geometry already exist to make these tests fairly easy, and we'll use them in code, without too much explaining.

There are also a couple of abstract concepts we can use such as rays and planes, which allow more complex collision concepts to be used.

Different primitives are able to react well with each other to different degrees and this allows us to determine broad-phase collision quite simply, which allows you as a coder to decide if a more precise collision is needed.

Culling Concepts

But no matter how simple our collision primitive is, we may still need to test a lot of things, and for the most part the test will return negative. A world with 30 characters in it means each character has to test the other 29 to see if it hit it, regardless of it being on the other side of the game world. That's a high degree of negative results; in fact, most of the time your tests are going to return no useful interactions.

It's very much in our interest to reduce the number of pointless negative tests and try to isolate the most likely to collide. This is the basic principle of a collision cull. There are a lot of methods that allow us to isolate objects of interest in nodes or cells. Grids and Quad Trees are fairly simple well-documented systems to keep track of an object based on its world location. Using that we can get every object (they still all need some kind of test) to only test objects in its own immediate space. They work by using a cell of data representing a small subspace of the world, in the structure that keeps track of only the objects in the immediate area, so each cell has maybe two or three objects in it, those objects, in turn, only need to test other objects in the same shared cell.

What we are essentially doing is using a data structure to direct our tests, that structure has to be built, typically at the start, and occasionally updated, so some processing is needed, but usually, less than the wasted processing on mostly negative collision tests.

Having a Quad Tree or similar space partition system, will reduce the number of complex collision tests, though Quad Trees have some issues when you have a lot of objects moving around, rebuilding the Quad Tree is a little time-consuming. However, even one or two complex collision tests could take as long to do as building the Quad Tree that would prevent those one or two tests. It's simply a question of balance, as much as possible we want to avoid doing the expensive collision tests and an equally expensive but one-time calculation to prevent multiple pointless tests is highly desirable.

Working out which objects to test, is a good way to decide if we want to do collisions, but we can also do a very simple, and very quick broad-phase test to decide further.

Let's talk about these partition systems in a bit more detail.

Grids, Quad Trees, and OctTrees

Let's start with grids as it's the simplest thing to describe and use, I don't even need a diagram for it. All models in a game exist in a space, and as such can be represented as a point in space, if you consider a map on a desk with little flags on it, each one represents an object. That map is usually subdivided with letters down the side and numbers across, making it quite possible for you to look at Grid position F23, and see that there is no flag in the grid area, there's no object there. In other different cells of the map, there are 100 different objects scattered around randomly.

Now put four flags in that grid cell at F23, you now have four objects in the immediate area, all of whom might interact with each other, they may collide. But any object in cell F23, is not going to collide with an object in H14. They are clearly not in the same cell? We might have a few issues with F22, F24, E22, and G22, but that's still only a few things to check.

In a 2D map this is so easy to see, our map is a 2D array, and we can parse through our objects, work out the grid, and do tests only on the objects in the same cell. The other 96 don't need to be tested. 4×3 collision tests, as opposed to 100×99 tests. Quite a difference? All we have to do is make sure when we move our object we update our grid.

That's the principle of a grid, it's simple, straightforward, easy to visualize in 2D and in 3D. All we need is an array 2D or 3D if dealing with 3D space containing a simple data structure that keeps track of the objects.

A Quad Tree is a variation on the grid concept, but a Quad Tree is excellent at dealing with areas with large variation of data, allowing you to totally discount sections where no viable data exists.

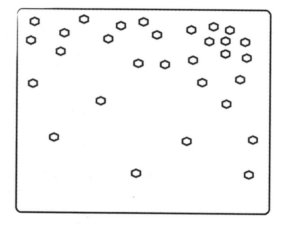

If we examine the image above, assume that the whole square represents the entire world we want to render. We can see a load of model objects (30 hexagons).

Now cut it into four equal square sections, we will call them nodes. Some nodes contain more objects than the others. Now take the bottom-left square and divide that into four equal nodes.

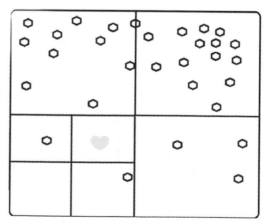

We now start to see that some of the squares are empty. We'd repeat that in the other sections until our nodes contained a maximum number of objects. If my character represented by the heart were located in a map area where the square was empty, I would be able to look in the Quad Tree and work out that at that point there are no objects for me to interact with, either for collision or render. If I were to move into the immediate left, I'd only need to check 1. So with a simple check, I can completely avoid testing all the 30 other objects. This is especially useful if I have many hundreds or thousands of objects.

I can take this much further, and subdivide the nodes again and again, perhaps setting a max number of objects limit per node. But, however, deep I take it, it's only a couple of simple recursive checks that will get me to the node I am in, and that will tell me how many things I need to interact with.

Here's an example of a Quad Tree where I stop dividing if I have four or less in the node. (I cheated on the bottom left and could have left it as one level but wanted to demonstrate the concept)

You can see that for the most part I only need to go two nodes down to get a situation where there are four or fewer objects in each node, but the top corner has six (Seven, if you choose to consider overlapping objects), so it needs another subdivision. And if my heart were in that area, I'd need to go down three levels to find the objects. So, at most I have to test four objects whereever I am in the world...often less or none.

Incidentally, notice in that last diagram that even though the top corner had a quad in it, the rest of the world was subdivided in equally sized spaces. That's a simple grid! But back to quads.

This is a very common concept for collision, especially in 3D where collisions with the environment can be tricky. But it can also be used for rendering. We can keep info on models, or individual triangles, once we know which area we are in, we can select the vertices in our area of interest.

OctTrees work exactly the same way as quads, but represent 3D space, and as you might image use cubes with eight smaller cubes in each node. These are much more useful if you have an environment that has a lot of relevant data in the y dimension, buildings with stairs and balconies and multiple levels, for example.

We can use such systems for keeping track of objects, even allowing them to move around a little, or for much larger data structures such as the individual triangles that make up a terrain. This is one of the key principles of collision using Ray casts and allows us access to the triangles making up a mesh so that we can walk on the mesh triangles by doing specific tests on specific triangles in a specific area. The structures give us a way to drill down into data, potentially consisting of thousands of testable things and isolating the minimum number to test. That speeds up our collision tests considerably and improves accuracy.

These concepts are designed to make our life simpler, be that for collision systems, or rendering decisions, we should be able to take any point in our world, which is covered by the Quad/OctTree and then work out what the relevant areas are by simply working out the nodes we want to look at by performing a few collision tests to see if we hit something. So despite the complexity of the scene and increased numbers, we've reduced the test to a simple "What is in this section I am testing?" And, "Have I hit anything in this section?"

That is a massive saving in the processing time. This simplicity of access is crucial to the success of a tree structure.

Trees like this do have some failings though, they, of course, take up space, though given the massive boost you get in speed and avoiding wasted cycles, that's acceptable, and they take time to build, you have to parse through your mixed-up soup of data a few times to get the nodes set up. So, ideally, we really only want to build it once. Maintaining it dynamically presents us with a problem if we keep movable objects in our world, and put them in the tree the scene is effectively changing and the tree needs to be rebuilt. Fine for one or two things, but a nightmare for a very dynamic and large group of things to test.

We can create and use reasonably effective remove and replace functions, but there is a diminishing return on that. So as far as possible, keep the tree for static objects and maybe a small number of important moving ones. But generally an object moving around is an object moving around, treat it as an object and use object to object methods to determine if it's relevant to your current interest.

For most simple terrains OctTrees are overkill, as are Quad Trees, because a terrain for the most part is going to have the same number of triangles in every square meter represented, you can just as easily use a simpler 2D grid system to keep track of the vertices in any particular area, just define a grid with a structure containing a list or vector of your faces, and you can use the tile method of looking into an array to find the most relevant faces that relate to your position.

But these store methods are flexible enough for you to use what works best for your particular environment.

The support site contains a few examples of other partitioning systems you can try, the complexity of the data and method of encoding increases, and the space taken with it, but the access to the data remains simple and fast, allowing our compromise of trading RAM for speed, to be valid, as long as we don't fill the RAM with a BSP, OctTree, or Bounding Volume Hierarchy (BVH), a current trend in tree systems.

We're going to come back to these kinds of data structures later, because they can be much more useful than just keeping track of world positioning and density of areas.

Possible Collision Systems

Having now established a means to access the smallest possible number of tests, we still have to do the tests themselves, and what test we do will very much depend on what we are testing against.

The two most common forms of broad-phase test are variations on the concepts we learned in 2D Box and Circle checks. Only in 3D they turn into Axis-Aligned Bounding Boxes and Sphere tests. We can consider a Ray to ObjectType as a broadphase too, it really depends what we want to use it to detect, because it potentially goes to infinity, it can actually spear more than one object, but we tend to put a range on it.

Spheres should be easy to grasp, it's just the circles with another dimension added, and are probably the fastest when used with other Spheres.

The Axis-Aligned Bounding Box though needs a bit more explanation. Our previous Bounding box systems, are still the core, but they automatically assumed that the X and Y axis of our objects naturally aligned, had we rotated them in some way, the Bounding box we used to make the tests also gets rebound, and things start to get confusing and inaccurate. That's mainly why I stuck with circle-to-circle checks in our shooters.

But an Axis-Aligned Box has benefits and is commonly used, it just requires that we consider the position of our boxes' corners and extend the *bounding box* when it rotates, which allows for a simple calculation.

Objects testing against other objects have a whole range of cool established systems we can use and code up easily. Objects testing against terrains need some different approaches.

Let's look at a few of the most popular methods all of which basically rely on you having either very simple meshes or encapsulating primitive systems to make the best use. We'll start with the very cool, very easy, and flexible Sphere-to-Sphere.

Sphere-to-Sphere

We've used the circle-to-circle collision system in our 2D games and for the most part they gave a pretty decent resolution that didn't really need much refinement. We can easily expand that 2D system to produce an encapsulation system to see if a sphere that wraps our object as best it can, intersects in any way with another object of interest in our immediate area. This kind of test is marvelously fast, but not really very accurate, unless we are actually using spherical objects.

But as a first-pass test to see if we should dedicate the time, it really is super, and for many games where high-resolution collision is not needed it can be more than enough.

Remember this?

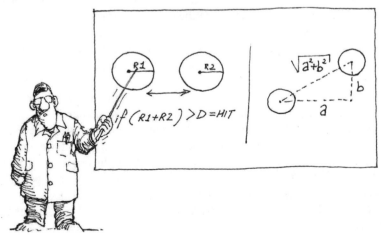

If you look at the two spheres from any point in space, they are still basically circles. And the radius for a circle is exactly the same as the radius for a sphere. What's slightly different is the means to calculate the distance. But as long as we know the *x, y, z* point in space of both spheres' centers, we can treat the points as positions in space subtract from the other to get a new vector and use a glm::length(v) to get the distance, allowing much the same test to be used. For me, this makes encapsulating spheres the simplest to use, so this will be the method I use for now. To use them in anger we only have to create a sphere around our ships, now we can do tests on other ships to see if we collide and take appropriate action, we can also make that Death Ray work, by using the RayToSphere in the Rays Class to test in our players' fire systems. Watch out though because you should be letting our Enemy ships shoot back, and rays are hard to avoid.

Bullets are also possible, using Ray to Sphere, in exactly the same way, let your bullets fly for a reasonable distance at a reasonable speed, so you can avoid them, and have each of them do the RayToSphere test, just make sure the distance of the ray from the bullet to the ship is very small before you record a collision hit.

▌ 3D Particles

When we did particles in 2D it was actually pretty simple to create emitters and build a vector of the particles as they emerged and do the simple bit of code to move them around, decay them, and kill them off when done.

There's really no reason at all why we can't do the same things in 3D, except...there kinda is.

We've seen how much faster things are when we use data in our GPU buffers; the speed difference is simply immense. Those speeds rely on the fact that the vertex data being supplied is essentially static in the GPU; we can't in effect change it once it's there. Instead, we rely on a set of CPU side computed, model, and view and projection matrices to reposition our objects, so that we can see them where we expect them. Three matrix writes is not so hard for our system to work with and from that, thousands of calculations are done in the GPU.

But particles are far more active than our models, and we will have many more of them, several thousand at least to get good effects. Their positional data are more dynamic and totally nonstatic unlike a model's vertices, so we can't keep them in the VBO. To draw them, we need to send positional data from the CPU to the GPU every frame...and yeah, that's not desirable. But if we can't escape the fact we need to shift a lot of data to the GPU, let's at least make sure that the GPU takes some of the calculation load off the CPU by doing as much of the maths as possible, so that we will arrange for the data we send to be relevant to the particle.

Information such as age, time, position, and velocity all need to be used to work out the final position of the particle. So, we will pass them to the Shader.

Just like our 2D software particles though, there's no getting away from the fact that the more particles we have the more work both our processing units have to do. There are ways of working with *unlimited* numbers but this is one of those discretion, is the better part of valor situations where we put a sensible limit on the number of particles we can have, and use them sparingly for the best effects.

The support site contains a 3D particle system you can play with, using similar plumes and cascades, sending both particle info and emitter info to produce different results. Download and include the Particle3D files into your project, and simply follow the instructions to trigger the particle types you want in your game.

Particles are also often generated using GL_POINTS, or point sprites, a nice and very quick way OpenGLES2.0 has to draw simple quads with a texture, very similar to old school sprites, but they have the disadvantage of only ever facing the camera and lack rotation in any axis, though it can be scaled. As such, they are great for 2D games, but not so useful in a full 3D geometry world. I've included a Particle2D Class for you using this method if you want to work on a 2D game.

The Wrap Up

That's pretty much all I want to do with this particular space game. There is one or two rather obvious things wrong with it, such as the lack of full 360° motion in the Z axis. For now, it simply represents a limitation on using traditional Euler-based angles. It's not impossible to overcome but really we want to get to a point quite soon where we no longer rely on them for our calculations. But looking back on this and the previous foundation chapter, we've again learned a number of notable concepts

Not least of which is 3D rendering but also

- Camera control (with limits)

- Shaders

- Light calculations

- GPU optimization

- Simple 3D collision

- Ray Casts

- 3D particles

- GUI rendering

- 3D vector motion

- Skyboxes

- Matrix maths

These are all basic tools to add to your arsenal and will crop up again and again in every 3D game you do. In addition, quite importantly we've discovered that we have a major limit in our understanding of maths when it comes to camera control; we are going to cover that soon.

Some of the basic features of all 3D games developed in here are going to be common to all our new 3D games, so from now on our 3D framework is going to keep hold of some of these features as standard. I will rename and tidy up the ShipModel Class, because really it's a standard OBJModel style class, and not just a ship. To make it a little more flexible, I've also added a new pair of Shaders called CondOBJLight.vsh/fsh. Though conditions should be avoided as much as possible, especially in our low power Shaders, the flexibility they give us makes up for a slight drop in performance. If you decide, however, to always use the lit or unlit systems, you can adapt the OBJModel Class yourself to provide the Shader you need (Ultimately that's a better solution for performance).

We will need Cameras too; at least the base class should be a common construct and finally Skyboxes. These will all be put into a basic VisualGDB/Visual Studio template; I will call Standard3D you can download from the support site. Giving you a starting system that you can add to as we go when you create a new project, it will let you create a project from a custom template in the New Linux Project Dialog, and then navigate to the template file.

We've still lots to learn though, but so far, so good. Let's press on!

8 Recognizable Environments

Space as I said is easy, flying through the air is also not too hard so long as you avoid the crashing into hard things and blowing-up in flames part, but moving around landscapes that look similar to landscapes and are then expected to behave like a landscape, is somewhat harder, because we need to keep track of a lot more collidable things.

A lot of our 2D thinking can be used for games that keep a gravity bound character moving around a play area. But realism means we need to try to make sure everything in our environment behaves as much as possible as it should be in life. Trees should have leaves, grass should wave majestically in the wind, and water should ripple. These things all take effort from the CPU and GPU and we will face brick walls if we try to do too much.

Perhaps more importantly, if we are creating environments we are essentially attempting to create some form of realism, in which case, our rather static OBJ models are not going to work as well for us. It's time we looked into model animation, which in 3D is not quite as straightforward as it was in 2D.

With a 2D game, there are only the frames given to us by the artists, we display them, in turn, in the correct sequences, perhaps even having the benefit of a few intermediate frames to allow for transition from one sequence to another. But animated 3D models are harder to work with, because they are not direct representations of our artists intentions, that are produced, but rather mathematical representations of it, we are now faced with other challenges and opportunities. Our frames are not just static images, they are more dynamic and are visible from any angle and distance, and are generally less able to fool our eyes the way 2D images do. We need to take more care of not only what we draw, but how we draw it. That can be quite a challenge. Animation, in particular, gives us a lot of interesting options.

We're going to spend quite a few pages now discussing some of the technical challenges we need to deal with to introduce this sense of realism and bring in more usable models and playfields, there's no way to sugar coat this, we're going to be going through this stuff for a few days before we can get back to writing a proper game again. Don't skip it, tech stuff can be dull but the benefit of understanding it will allow us to make the games run faster and smoother and squeeze more content in.

▌ Let's Talk about Time!

It's been a long time since we did, but we're probably getting to a point where we need to start taking more notice of it, we're about to add animation to our arsenal of skills, which depend on timing, and also getting to the point of lots of different types of things going on, on-screen, at different depths. Our triangle counts are going to start rising and our systems are going to get pushed. Even using our GPU well, we are going to find that we start to hit limits, and that means we need to bring the concept of time back into focus, and use it in the games.

We are incredibly lucky to have a frame-lock system on our EGL display, which as long as we manage to get everything we want to be done in 1/60 of a second, ensures that our games are running in sync, locked to a vblank, making it smooth and effective. Our 2D buffers took a little longer than 1/60 of a second to prepare and send to the GPU, so that meant our 2D games usually took 1/30 of a second. But it was consistent, so we were comfortable enough to just move twice as fast as it probably should have. Consistency is the key to smoothness. If we are certain we're moving at 1/60, 1/30, even 1/15 of a second, we can simply scale-up the movement unit factor and our games will more or less feel smooth, though 1/15 is pushing our luck.

But what if we are using a much faster GPU, or even a much slower GPU? What if we have a 100 or 200 Hz display and our GPU can sync to it, it might sound like a great thing, faster smoother movement, but that's actually giving us less time to draw our images. Some cycles will always take longer than others to produce and display.

Consistency isn't always that easy to guarantee; in fact, on a true 3D game it's utterly impossible. As an object with 1000 triangles can take a long time to draw close-up to you, filling the screen with scaled textures or a very short time, far away from you, the number of actual pixels rendered is going to vary even for the same model, that's going to take the GPU different amounts of time to draw. We have a glFinish(); function at the end of our update loops, so we really have no idea if the update of one model is going to take 1/100,000th of a second, or 1/100th. But as long as it takes less than 1/60th, are we ok? What happens when we do hundreds of those models, some close, some far, and most in the middle? Timing becomes utterly impossible to fix to a desired amount, though we can measure it.

Our frame lock is going to help us tremendously when we are certain that we're never going to push the limit of our particular GPU. But we don't live in a world where that is certain and we need to realize that we are misnaming the game cycle, the amount of processing we do to get an image on screen, as frame! This really relates to the fixed and constant display rate of our display. Game cycle is not consistent, frames are! I don't really know why we use that terminology, we should probably stop, I'll send a memo to the game developers' community and see what happens. In the meantime, I'll continue to use frame and sometimes cycle, context should keep it clear?

It's time…time to go back to the concept of Delta Time! The fractions of a second we calculate in our program loop and pass to our game loop, so far without much interest.

What we need to do is think of movement not in terms of number of pixels per cycle, or in 3D, number of units we move each cycle, but as distance per second! We must think of movement as a function of time and speed, which, of course, it is, ($d = st$ in your first school physics classes). Since each frame we do is effectively a part of a second, we should be able to get our objects to move to that desired amount, or very close to it, when one entire second has past, if during each 1/60th or 1/30th, we moved an appropriate amount for the time it took.

It adds a small extra level of complexity to our movement but it also means that when our FPS rate is inconsistent we are able to compensate for it, albeit retroactively, we have no means to tell how long a game cycle is going to take, only how long the last game cycle took. But over the course of the number of cycles we take to get to that 1 second, we can be pretty certain that we moved the required amount of movement units expected.

Similarly for animation, we normally talk in terms of FPS, say, 5 FPS for frame 1 of a walk sequence, but if some cycles take twice as long as 1/60th of a second, then an animation frame may end up being visible on screen for as much as 10 frames of display, a very obvious visible cue that the human eye will be able to see and you get stutter.

We still want to use our frame-lock functions because syncing our draw systems to the vblank is great for avoiding screen tearing. Our goal must now be for most of the time, to try very hard to have an update ready in 1/60th of a second, but there will be the occasional 1/30, maybe a 1/15, and using Delta time will help on any function where time is a factor to maintain its *displayed* FPS, rather than tie it to *game cycles* per second, which if it has not confused you utterly, brings us nicely to animation.

Animating Models

There are several ways to animate models; the simplest, like we do with 2D, is to just hold many versions of the model in different poses, though usually using the same materials and textures. If your models are not too massive then this can be quite an effective system.

If you do, however, have 10,000s of vertices in your model, then repeating that number for each frame can be quite a memory eater, particularly using OBJs, which are uncompressed. Though, it actually is considered a quite reasonable amount when you consider how many kilobytes of texture memory you would need to animate a large 2D sprite. A 128 × 128 pixel 2D sprite takes up 64K of memory per frame…imagine 30 frames of that? Whereas a 10,000 vertex model, ignoring textures for now, could have six times as many animation frames. In 3D we'd probably only have 2000–3000 vertices per model, often much less, that's a lot less GPU memory being wasted.

Animation alternatives abound, but also increase in their code complexity and mostly focus on what's known as a rig where a *skeleton* of vertices is laid out in the model, and attached at key points to the mesh that can be generated or supplied. Moving the Rig moves the mesh and moving the Rig from one point to another can be interpolated in many ways.

This all works in pretty much the same way as your body moves when your skeleton is moved. Actions on a joint cause movement, sometimes having an effect on other joints, which, in turn, changes the position of your body.

What about all these talk of rigs and joints and key frames and texture stretching and other wonderful things that you see on high-end games, why am I teasing you with such delights and not demonstrating them?

Oh! That would be nice…but really it's an incredibly complex subject, and it starts to become far more technical than I want to get into in this book. If you feel up to it, the current best thing to look into is FBX format files, which would allow us to load in models with all those wonderful animation systems to build it and be able to replay sequences of animations that the animators/modelers created when they made the model.

But to get the most out of those systems, we need to have a lot more understanding of 3D concepts than we currently have, so a discussion here is just going to get us bogged down in tech info. I really want us to move forward. So for now, this book is going to focus on very simple methods, which you can replace with slightly more complex systems as you improve your skills.

Limitations of OBJ

Now because it is a simple and easy to use format, OBJ does have a number of limitations, one of the biggest drawbacks is that it has no actual support for multiple animation frames in the format. It does not contain information that other formats have that allow us to process rig movement or cycle through frames, often allowing common vertices to be unchanged and further adding to compression. So the simplicity of OBJ will eventually prove to be a problem when we want to do a lot of models or have a model with a massive number of frames.

An OBJ isn't always composed of a single mesh though, one good thing in its favor is the fact that an OBJ can have multiple component meshes stored, which makeup the whole. If you look at our render systems' code, we do actually render multiple shapes inside a loop. These shapes are named, therefore there are ways to isolate individual shape components and run them through a different MVP, creating some degree of motion inside an OBJ, such as rotation of or bouncing of wheels, which you might want to play with later. But actual animation in the sense of moving from one pose to another isn't in the OBJ bag of tricks.

We can fake animation though, in the same way we did with our 2D images, where we replaced one graphic image for another, to create an apparent stop frame movement. If we have eight slightly different model meshes, representing eight frames of a walk, we can do a walk animation by simply replacing one model for another. Unlike sprite animations where we show a different graphic, all we need for model animations is a different set of vertices pointing to the same textures.

But such a load and play animation is really quite clunky and it also needs us to load multiple OBJ files to keep track of the frames, and make sure we have enough frames to make the animation smooth. It's all possible, but really it would be very clunky and actually looks quite bad. I have a small demo on the support site, called OBJAnimation for you to see just how bad it is. But I am going to say this is a developmental dead end and leave it as a curiosity to review.

OBJs then are really best suited to items that don't animate, require some additional detail or content, and are preferably only loaded once. They are ideal for, but not restricted to, fixed terrains, unanimated detail objects, and basically anything that is nondynamic in a game.

So what can we use for animation? We clearly need to have animated models, if OBJs are not really up to it, what other options are there?

We could, of course, write our own proprietary model format, if you think you're ready for that then feel free. But I'm not a massive fan of reinventing the wheel. There are a plethora of model formats around which are used mostly for animation, and indeed for our level of processing power I think I have the perfect system to start us off.

The MD(x) Systems

One easy format for animation of 3D models can be found in ID's Quake series of games, which used a pretty reasonable key frame/vertex-based animation system. The levels of complexity have risen over the years as ID, the makers have altered and expanded it as their needs expanded. They started out with MDL format, and currently it's now MD5, which is a fun but challenging task to implement on your systems when you are more confident, but the simpler MD2 version is pretty well suited to the basic level of animation we want to achieve and, let's hear a round of applause for ID; the format is open source, meaning we can use it free of charge. And because it was the system used in several Quake games, there are countless people out there who modified the game, called Modders, who made their models available to use free of charge.

It is fair to say though that at this point in time (2017), MD2 is basically obsolete, and you might baulk at being asked to use it, but it does provide a good starting point to the understanding of vertex-based animation and how to code it giving us a bit of practice using some nice maths. I am using it here mainly because it's viable on even the most basics of our target systems. We could try to code up complex, skeletal animation-based systems, which are preferred on modern games, but I think we should all learn to crawl first before attempting to run the 100 m. If you can get this working well, you will be able to learn for yourself at another time, how to do better systems.

As mentioned, MD5 is a fun but relatively complex challenge, and one you may feel confident to take on when you have completed this book. With help from my friend and former colleague Jamie Stewart and current colleague Abhishek Biswas, we managed to prove that MD5 was perfectly possible on a Raspberry Pi3B, though it is pretty heavy on the CPU and GPU, so it is best for games that only need a couple of main animated characters. In a couple of years as SBC power increases, it might even be possible to do FBX that would be a cool system! I'll leave my MD5 demo for you on the support site to look at another time.

But enough wishful thinking, let's start with something we know can work and build up. The concept of MD2 really isn't that far from a multiloaded OBJ store and play system, the only real difference is that they are all prepacked, and even better, in a binary chunk, so no text parsing is needed. But how do we know where the different and specific data we need to use are?

The secret is the header, which is the first chunk of data that makes up our binary MD2 file. Here's what it looks like.

```
struct md2_header_t /* MD2 header */
{
  int ident;              /* ID number encoded: "IDP2" */
  int version;            /* version*/
  int skinwidth;          /* texture width */
  int skinheight;         /* texture height */
  int framesize;          /* size in bytes of a frame */
  int num_skins;          /* number of skins */
  int num_vertices;       /* number of vertices per frame */
  int num_st;             /* number of texture coordinates */
  int num_tris;           /* number of triangles */
  int num_glcmds;         /* number of opengl commands */
  int num_frames;         /* number of frames */
  int offset_skins;       /* offset skin data */
  int offset_st;          /* offset texture coordinate data */
  int offset_tris;        /* offset triangle data */
  int offset_frames;      /* offset frame data */
  int offset_glcmds;      /* offset OpenGL command data */
  int offset_end;         /* offset end of file */
};
```

That's it, the file format is simply a guideline to the way the data in the first part of our binary image, the header, are laid out. Once we load that binary image, we can overlay these values onto the first section of the data and consider that to be the header; from that, we know that the header gives information that allows us to make sense of the main body of data.

MD2 is really a very simple format, essentially it works in the same way as OBJ with a list of vertices, some indexes to them, and its own reference to materials and textures, but where OBJ stores only one frame in a file, MD2 can store multiple frames and we can index through those frames to get to the relevant data. It also contains some other cool bits of data that we'll try to get to as we go through it.

MD2 is outdated, of course, and exporters needed in our graphic tools for this format are also old, but they are available for most free and commercial 3D packages, especially with a bit of hunting, Blender, which is very popular with the Linux community and is free.

There is still wealth of models out there and building our own MD2 loader and rendering systems will give us a good grounding in how to implement MD3/4 and maybe even MD5 systems if you choose to use those.

I would not be too concerned with things being outdated, remember that we need to keep our expectations realistic. Our SBCs are not current generation PCs or Consoles, or even previous generation. They have limits, that we have to work within, and basing our systems on older formats such as this that provide much of what we need, will allow us to expand a little until we reach the limits or our machines. It's much easier to push a limit that's imposed on us than it is to cut back on what we want to do, to meet that limit.

Be aware, with each version of MD(x), the complexity levels rises, but because our aim is to eventually reach something close to modern standard, you can build them up one step at a time. MD3 isn't a massive leap from MD2, so I encourage you to try writing a loader and renderer to cope as you expand your knowledge.

As I don't have any skills with Blender or other art packages, I located some MD2 files online, and found this to be a good resource:

http://www.md2.sitters-electronics.nl/models.html.

The models here are all available under GNU and CC_attribution/by license, which means that you can use and modify them so long as you give credit to the original creators. Quake mod communities also regularly still share their work and you can find lots of different model types in the MD2 format with a bit of searching.

https://www.quaddicted.com/ is an absolute treasure trove of models, maps, skyboxes, and other things Quake related, but I'm less sure that the licenses are properly defined and it's more a case of collecting all online content in one place in the hope it falls into Public Domain. But for education purposes, there's nothing to stop you using these, just verify ownership before you try to distribute them.

I am going to use a pretty standard and easily available Quake model, the (in)famous knight.md2 model by James Green. It's a good simple starter model to work with as it has a lot of different animation sequences and only uses one texture, so it's easy to set up and get going. I am not 100% sure that this is in the public domain, though it is used by so many engine and demo coders, and Green seems to be uncontactable. So I will err on the side of caution, acknowledge there is evidence of a copyright in 1998 in his name, and not supply the actual model files on my site; you will have to locate them yourself. So my use of it in screenshots is subject to a fair use for education policy, and in no way I do claim any ownership of the design. (Legal stuff is there to protect us all even if it can be a bit of a pain)

You can get an idea of what it should do by looking at the nice MD2 demo viewer I found at http://www.glge.org/demos/md2demo/.

So let's push on and add a model loader for MD2, the code is on the website and is annotated, it will load the images, parse the data to work out the number of vertices per frame, how many frames there actually are, and also the names of the animations and their start/end points, and most important, create the mesh of vertices and normals for use with lighting, if you want lighting. I have kept them in both CPU vertex buffers, and in GPU vbs to allow you to choose your own render methods.

Download the MD2Demo files from the site and add your knight or other suitable MD2 model. As usual we are not going to do much beyond set up and add files but you will see you can now create an MD2base Class. The ModelManager file has always had an MD2 loader called LoadMD2. Now we get to use it! The loader is very simple and loads the binary block extracting each frame in turn, using its indexing system to create vertex meshes, which it stores in a vb for later. Quite a lot in fact...perhaps I should look at that?

It should be noted that though a lot of these old models used PCX format for their textures and our stbi_image loader currently does not support PCX, but don't worry, even though the texture file names are encoded into the data and not editable, I have tweaked the loader so that if it finds a PCX format file it will attempt to load a TGA or a PNG file in turn. If you find you have downloaded a model pack with PCX skin

(MD2's name for a texture) files, just convert them to TGA or PNG,* in any decent art package before you put them in your Resources/Textures directory. You can also make edits to the `LoadMD2` in ModelManager to try other formats that stbi_image can handle. Also have fun editing the skin but don't alter the size of the image.

Oh and one more point! It's also possible for an MD2 model to not have any internal reference to skins at all, that is, num_skins = 0, in which case, it's your responsibility to ensure that a skin texture is correctly loaded. In that situation, the draw function will use the old OBJ texture1 handle as its one and only texture for render, the Knight is a good example of this.

Once the mesh vbs are created we need to consider what approach we want to take for moving from one frame to another. The MD2Demo as downloaded only allows us to draw individual frames, so animation is our next point of interest, and I've arranged it so that to draw an MD2 model is a simple case of drawing with the right frame number, pretty much the same way we do with sprites.

Download MD2Demo and can see the project has all the loaders and renders systems in place. It is also currently animating through all available frames of the model, just using a simple increment in the update function.

Switching frames like this clearly works but it does seem a little bit jagged and abrupt not at all like the smooth motion the online viewer gives us. There are two reasons for this, if we set the update rate at 5/60 s, that basically means for 5 frames he or she will draw the same image before abruptly going to the next one, for another 5 frames. The abruptness is because an MD2 animation sequence is generally saved with the minimum number of frames needed. We know though that the faster the update rate of an animation the smoother it seems to us. But only 6 frames of run sequence is played every frame in 6/60s of a second. That will look faster than a Keystone cop! So our timing is actually needed, but we can introduce an element of *inbetweening* where we can calculate the frame between two frames and produce an inbetween frame; in fact, if we want to get very smart we can produce an extreme number of inbetween frames, but a set number of frames between a first and the second frame, spread over the time, will smooth out animation, without us having to install another costly memory sequence of vertices. At each cycle, the display

---

* PNG format tends to be the most reliable format.

will show a slightly different frame making the animation smoother. So, even a 2 frame animation can produce dozens of step sequences if we tell it to take its time. This is one of the joys of working with numbers rather than drawn art. Maths makes such tasks simple.

The process is known as linear interpolation or Lerping. Basically, if you think of a journey from point A to point B taking x seconds, you can actually work out where you would be in half x seconds, creating a point C right in the middle.

Taking that idea to data, if we are drawing a frame, we are able to look ahead to the next frame, which we can, then the vertices from one frame to another move a certain distance. If we want to create an intermediate point, we simply find the midpoint C (50%) between the points and we've created an inbetween frame, which can now be used to smooth out the frames. We can also create a lot more points between the two frames; it all depends on how much smoothing we need.

Lerping can be done in either the CPU or in the GPU, it's really up to you to decide, but given the fact it's a vector-based system, the GPU will make more sense. Unfortunately, if the GPU is overloaded with complex Shaders, it might not be possible to use it.

When MD2 first came out, Shaders were still in their infancy if not actually still a glint in OpenGL's eye. So there are very few online examples of MD2s using Shaders, but we live in enlightened times and OpenGLES2.0 lives on the strength of its Shaders. MD2 Demo has a Lerping Shader in place, press L to see the full effect. Impressive? We've gone from jerky to super smooth. Just by making sure we get the Shader to do all the calculations, and our render routine simply gives it access to the first and second frames with a time value that represents the percentage of lifetime for the animation. We can now smoothly interpolate between frames at any speed we deem suitable.

As I say, you can do this on the CPU, and if you are heavily using your GPU for effects, it might be useful, but do remember that you will have to keep hold of the original vertices the loader extracts, AND keep a suitable-sized buffer, that you will have to calculate in each update to provide the draw systems with a client-based buffer to draw. That can amount to several hundred kilobytes of data for a complete model such as a knight. Pure Shader systems can release that memory as soon as it's shifted to the GPU. In addition, it is indeed slower to CPU parse and lerp a few hundred vertices each cycle, but if you have the CPU time available rather than the GPU time, you should consider this. I've allowed the MD2 loader to keep the RAM-based vertex buffers, if you choose to remove them, just do so after they are sent to the GPU.

Lerping is only possible on MD2s because every frame has the same number of vertices, so when you are working out the lerp ratio for the 472nd vertex, you know that in each frame of the loaded model, that vertex is always going to represent the same point in the model.

This is both a virtue and a failing of MD2s, it enforces a maximum size that all frames have to adhere to, but we're not talking massive amounts of data, so we can live with it, for now.

▮▮ Controlling the Animation of Our MD2 Model

MD2 is at its heart an animating system, we can see all the frames available to us in our current demo system, but clearly he's not going to be of much use to us in game, running through all his frames in turn. We have to control the sequence of animation we want at a given time, and the speed of it and make decisions on whether it cycles, stops, or needs a trigger. Basically, the same issues we would have with a 2D sprite system.

MD2 does provide us with the names of our animation sequences, and for each sequence the number of frames used. The actual names are nonstandard and depend entirely on the modeler who made them. So what animations you use and how you reference them will depend on you and your game needs. You can even just ignore the names and use simply indexes if you like, your call!

I've given you a simple animation system, which assumes only a few states. Though this is pretty heavily tied to MD2s and could, in principle, live in the MD2Model.h/cpp files but I decided to create a new class, MD2Anim, and add an instance of that to our MD2Model.h

```
#pragma once
class MD2Model;
class MD2Anim
{
    typedef enum
    {   HOLD = 12313,
        TRIGGER, // increment as a cycle each call
        TRAVEL, // go from start to finish then stop
        BOUNCE, // bounce from start to finish to start and repeat
        CYCLE, // loop from start to fish then back to start
      DONOTHING
    } AnimType;
public:
    MD2Anim();
    ~MD2Anim();
    bool Update(float dt); // do what you need to do
    bool SetSequence(char* Animname, MD2Model* Model, AnimType How = CYCLE,
float Step = 5.0/60);
    bool SetSequence(int start, int stop, AnimType How);
    bool QueueSeqence(char*name);
    bool QueueSequence(int start, int stop, AnimType How);
    AnimType WhatType;
    int CurrentFrame; // what to draw
    int NextFrame; // used by interpolaiton
    int BaseFrame; // start of sequence
    int FinalFrame; // end of sequence
    int Direction; // forward or back travel for the

    float Time;
    float TimeStep;

private: /
    int QNextBase;
    int QNextFinal;
    AnimType NextType;
};
```

Nothing too complicated here is there? The basic types of animation are the key; the comments explain what they do pretty well. I'll give you the update function, but am sure you can work out what the other functions are for yourself (don't look at the final versions until you've had a try).

```
bool MD2Anim::Update(float dt) {

    if (WhatType != TRIGGER) // trigger will always set the next one in
    {
        this->Time -= dt;
        if (Time > 0) return false; // no animation took palce
```

```
            Time = TimeStep;
    }
// watch out for single frames
    if ( (FinalFrame - BaseFrame) <= 1)
    {
        CurrentFrame = NextFrame = BaseFrame;
        return true;
    }
// handle the different cycles
    switch (WhatType)
    {

    case HOLD:
        {
            NextFrame = CurrentFrame;
            break;
        }
    case TRIGGER: // trigger is basically a cycle but without timestep
    case CYCLE:
        {
            CurrentFrame += Direction;
            if (CurrentFrame > FinalFrame) CurrentFrame = BaseFrame;

            NextFrame = CurrentFrame + Direction;
            if (NextFrame > FinalFrame) NextFrame = BaseFrame;
            if (NextFrame < BaseFrame) NextFrame = FinalFrame;
            break;
        }

    case TRAVEL: // go to the end and stop
        {
            CurrentFrame += Direction;
            if ( (CurrentFrame > FinalFrame) || (CurrentFrame <
BaseFrame) )
            {
                NextFrame = CurrentFrame = (Direction <0) ?
BaseFrame:FinalFrame ;
                return true; // we're done
            }
            NextFrame = CurrentFrame + Direction;
            if (NextFrame > FinalFrame) NextFrame = FinalFrame;
            if (NextFrame < BaseFrame) NextFrame = BaseFrame;
            break;
        }
  case BOUNCE:
        {
            CurrentFrame += Direction;
            if (Direction > 0)
            {
                if (CurrentFrame > FinalFrame)
                {
                    CurrentFrame = FinalFrame-1;
                    Direction = -Direction;
                }
            }
            else
            {
                if (CurrentFrame < BaseFrame)
```

```
                        {
                                CurrentFrame = BaseFrame+1;
                                Direction = -Direction;
                        }
                }
                break;
        }

        default: { }  // choose to report here?

        }
        return true; // no issues reported
};
```

You can see that as well as the current frame, it calculates the next frame so that we can lerp. So with these in place all we need to do to trigger an animation is

```
Animation.SetSequence((char*)"run", this ); // update using default speed
and CYCLE
```

Of course, this assumed you to know what the name of the animation is, but that's easy enough to find, by asking the MD2Mode->animations map for the name of the animations that are stored there. BTW, MD2 models don't usually have their weapons included, so they are normally a second model, but use the same animation names, which will allow you to sync a sword/gun/broomstick movement in a model's hand. But you will also have to remember to provide the weapon with the same MVP data as the holder, so that it can be rendered in the models hand; however, it is oriented. It is a little wasteful, which is why in MD3, the weapons were an extension of the main model. Something to do later when you are tired of MD2.

The Demo program starts up by creating a knight as an MD2Model, we already we know that is not a good form, but it helps with the testing, it's time to create a proper Knight Class derived from MD2Model, and a Player Class that can be derived from Knight so that we can control it. That way we can have a player Knight, and an enemy Knight.

```
#pragma once
#include "MD2Model.h"
class Knight: public MD2Model
{
public:
    Knight() {};
    Knight(MyFiles* FH, char* FN, ModelManager* MM);
    ~Knight() {};
    bool Update(); // we only need to supply the update, Draw is part of
    MD2Model
};
```

So all I really want to create are a constructor, and an update like this

```
#include "Knight.h"

Knight::Knight(MyFiles* FH, char* FN, ModelManager* MM)
    : MD2Model( FH, FN, MM)
{
    Animation.SetSequence((char*)"stand", this);
}
bool Knight::Update()
```

```
{
    // do what ever logic needs doing
    MD2Model::Update(); // then do the update for matrices and anim
}
```

All my constructor is doing is using its base class constructor with the same signature, then setting the sequence to animate, just so it has something to present at the first update.

All we need to do now with our Knights is move them around; this will vary depending on our game, but clearly stand, run, attack, jump, should be pretty simple, and be used when we make decisions on our actions.

The Player code is, of course, exactly the same, just substitute the Player for Knight, but I can choose to make him a knight, or a Princess or an Italian plumber, when I create them. Instead of AI, we'll use key controls to move him/her around triggering animations as we need them.

The players' animations are equally straightforward and directly tied to key controls. Less obvious might be taunt, wave, and point? These would be more likely to occur at specific game points. In this case when standing idle for too long. Keep a timer and if the user does not input a key value, select one of these sequences to get their attention.

Try to do your own animation selections, and take note of the concept of queuing, some of these animations especially the taunts, should return to another sequence when done rather than stop or loop. That has not been added to the supplied animation class. Also, take care of some of the sequences, which can have multiple subsequences, just to make life extra interesting. You just need to take note of where they start and end.

Having our models animating and moving under control is a big step, but without some form of ground to walk on it is little more than a sprite floating around in an empty universe. If we plan to have a character animating and doing things in a world, we have to take another big step and talk about environments.

▐ Explaining Environments

Although not all games need a big world, there does need to be some virtual space concept where the objects you control/avoid/interact with, can exist and your camera can view.

The type of environment you choose will vary according to your game. Most 3D free-moving games will require a world of some kind and, in turn, that world will probably have a data structure behind it, depending on its size, it might use an optimization system such as a partition tree to access it for logic and sometimes rendering.

I'm once again going to have to explain a few things before we can leap into our next 3D game. Sorry, I know these long explanations can get a bit boring but they might help you to understand the route we are taking despite you having possible knowledge of better routes. The road to coding enlightenment is often paved with some really dumb ideas we thought were clever at the time and experience eventually shows us how stupid we can be.

3D space was easy because our expectations of what happens in space are not fixed in our brains, not too many of us have actually been in space! But environments that we allow things to interact with, in more or less real-world style, require a whole host of considerations that we must try to work out and make as realistic as possible. So let's try first to outline some of the technical things we have to incorporate.

The Ground, the Place Where You Will Fall to!

In 2D games it's very easy to think of the ground as just being a solid tile or area that our sprite falls down to and cannot fall through, gravity acted as we expected until we hit something that we considered solid and stopped gravity. But in 3D we have to think of the ground a little differently. For our basic purposes, we can consider any flat plane to be ground and have it be level with the up/down Y axis at 0, so if our object wants to move around on this plane we just make sure his Y coordinate is 0, or returns to 0 if he jumps or gets blown off his feet.

That will be a perfectly acceptable way to do things, if the world was made up with perfectly flat play fields. True, we can arrange to have arenas or playing fields that are flat, but it's a very dull view. So, we need to consider how to take into account the undulations and changes in height of a typical terrain. Whether it's a grassy field, or a city with roads and kerbs, and steps to buildings we have a considerable challenge to know what we are stepping on and how it will change our height above that base 0 level.

There are also matters of visualization, to work well a ground plane will need to extend some distance ahead of us, we will need to see where we are going and it needs to look good.

We'll examine the issues, in turn, to see what we can do to overcome them. But let's first have a play around with a very simple single quad ground plane and get a character walking around on it. Download the GroundPlaneDemo from the site, and get it running.

You will see a simple character on a very large single quad groundplane. But one quad, on its side stretching one texture to such extremes isn't giving us much sense of ground; it's also stretching the individual pixels of the texture so much that it ends up looking like a horrible mosaic when close up.

We could try a higher res texture but our texture limit is around 2048 × 2048 pixels, and our plane width is far in excess of that, so stretching is inevitable, but we will still get the same issue over time if we have a large ground plane.

Though strictly speaking good texture design, usage and placement in a mesh are the job of an artist, we at least need to be aware of how to make the best use of our textures to make the artist's job a bit easier. Also we can make use of some cool concepts of maths to improve the visuals.

▌ A Simple Ground Plane

The type of ground you use will, of course, make a lot of difference to your type of game. But if we plan to have a flat point to jump, run, drive, and takeoff from and splat into from a height, a ground plane of some kind is needed! We can visualize and create a flat ground pretty easily as a simple quad, or very large pair of triangles, and if we display it in monochrome with a basic Shader, that will be fine. That's not uncommon for debugging.

But for all but the simplest games, a ground plane should be made up of a number of triangles; it's easier for the GPU to cull the unwanted parts allowing you to create quite a complex ground plane. The extra resolution of more triangles per unit square also has the extra welcome effect of allowing us to manipulate the component triangles of the ground plane, especially the Y component of the vertices to give height and undulation to our plane. The more detail you have in your plane the smoother these height effects can be. Mapping your terrain to another data source to provide texture data and object placement, can also then allow a lot more variation for not much data. Unlike a very large OBJ with multiple added OBJs or subshapes to provide detail such as trees, grass, rocks, and so on. This is the beginning of procedural generation of terrains, and is quite an exciting subject.

For now, I've included a very simple GroundPlane Class in your GroundPlaneDemo. It works by generating two initial triangles to represent the outer corners of a square terrain, then recursively splitting that into two and generating as many triangles as you need by setting a maximum level of recursion.

So you start with two base triangles, it works out the midpoint of each triangle, splits it into two, and then splits those two into two, and so on. The result is as many or as few triangles making up your ground plane you need. Don't set the MAX_TRIS level too high though, recursion like this is based on powers of 2 doubled, so you very quickly go from 2 triangles to 8192 in only 11 steps. As with all these things you must find a balance, more triangles gives greater detail but increased GPU usage, it's a variable rate though, and you can add other variables to alter the detail later.

Simply add GroundPlane files cpp/h to your future projects, create an instance of a GroundPlane in your game initialization, set your MAX_TRIS value, and then call Init() to load and create textures, and Generate() to create a vector of the vertices, which you can decide should go into a vb, or remain in the client RAM to test against. Update will place it flat, but rendering is then up to you depending on how you store it. I'll use a vb for now and my render system is based on that.

Sadly after teasing you with a bit of procedural generation, we're not going to go any further, but we can tinker with it a little bit. There are a few extra options added to the GroundPlaneDemo to alter the height of parts of the mesh making up the plane (when set to a MAX_TRIS level above eight) both randomly and using a heightmap. These are useful concepts to keep hold of, but not of much use to us currently. Study the code to see how they work, because we are not going to use them in our main demos. I won't write them up, we still have a lot to cover before we can get back to coding something fun.

Level of Detail

The GroundPlane Class touches on the idea of altering the level of detail, with its MAX_TRIS value, but what exactly does that mean? LOD methods basically take into account the fact that the further something is from our viewpoint the harder it is to make out detail, so a low-detail object far away is not going to look much different from a high-detail object equally far away. This can be apparent if we have a high poly model in our extreme view, it may have a few thousand triangles but it's probably only going to look like a few dozen that are rendered. Our GPU is obligated to try to draw the thousand triangles even if it ends up looking like a blob because of the distance. If, however, we had a selection of models of lower level of detail, we could ask the GPU to render an appropriate model depending on the distance from our view point

If done well with a good selection of LOD models, we would not really notice the change in mesh. But there is, of course, a downside to these LOD models, they will take up space. The compromise between performance and memory always comes into play. But performance nearly always wins the debate if memory is available, and we should try to make it so. Look at this example in the next screenshot. Here, we see 30 cars in a row. But the further cars are using a small 168 triangle mesh, the middle ones use 1338, and the ones at the front use 2146. If you look very close you might see a few small differences, but really how close do you look at a model moving quickly on the screen? The large reduction in mesh size has a very direct impact on the amount of processing that your GPU has to do, so making sure you add an LOD option to your draw options can be a big performance boost.

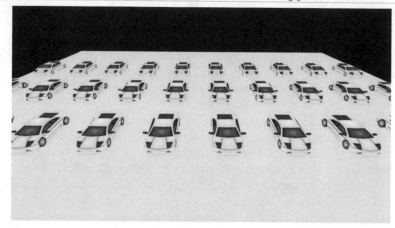

This might clearer to see if we render these models as GL_LINE_STRIPS rather than GL_TRIANGLES, which is a quick, cheap, but not very accurate way to replicate wireframe on GLES2.0.

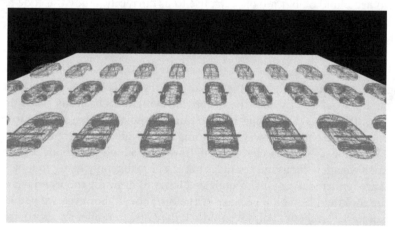

But we're not talking models yet, we're talking about our ground, and our ground is currently one single variable-sized mesh, so there's no (simple) efficient way of operating a LOD system at least on an environment we design and is mappable, though procedural generation using systems such as ROAM* can be very effective. It would be fairly trivial

---

* ROAM-Real-time Optimally Adapting Mesh is a level of detailed algorithm that does, in fact, allow us to create variable detail in a terrain around the area that is visible from a camera. It works best with procedurally generated terrains and is not easily implemented in a user-mapped environment. But can be a great method of creating endless wilderness-based terrains that can render in real time. Look it up, it's very easy to code, but not quite suitable for the games we are trying to produce.

8. Recognizable Environments

to turn the GroundPlane Class into a basic working ROAM system, calling the generate function of each frame in the update with a few variable detail, but that won't really suit our current needs.

So, if we can't easily reduce the mesh info, what else is open to us? Well, stick around, there are a few things we can do that are fairly simple and effective, and a few things that are very complex and perhaps not so effective on our targets. We should deal with some of the cheap easy things first.

Some free tools also allow you to procedurally produce environments in different levels of detail as you need. This avoids the problem of our limited resources being asked to do more than they can cope with, and instead makes things available for loading. L3DT from Bundysoft, is especially useful for creating large terrains and splitting them into usable sections; try it out, there is a free and low-cost pro version, how to use it will become more apparent with experimentation.

Mipmapping

This brings us to a concept called Mipmapping. Mipmapping is a means of taking a basic texture, halving its resolution by simple but precise scaling that reduces its level of detail, storing that in a way our GPU can easily access, then taking that and making a quarter-sized version, then an eighth, and so on.

This image has been taken from Wikipedia, used under the GNU-Free Documentation License.

The effective result is that you have one main texture and four or five progressively half sized slightly reduced quality versions. The scaled versions clearly are lower res, but represent a better texture to use if you are viewing the texture from a distance or using an LOD model, where the main image no longer needs to be scaled by so much.

This can dramatically improve the overall quality of the texture sampling at different view points, but does come at the relatively high cost of around 50% more texture memory needed for the mipmaps. However, we also get a speed boost, because the GPU is not scaling things so much to fit in smaller spaces. How much of a boost will vary but it's more than worth the effort.

Implementing mipmaps is especially easy as GPUs are very much in favor of using them and OpenGLES2.0 has the ability to automatically generate and use mipmap textures if it's told about them. Even better it can automatically make them using the `glGenerateMipmap(GL_TEXTURE_2D)` function already in place in OpenGLES2.0. You do need to ensure that you have applied the appropriate filters when you create the Texture and load in its image. The ModelManager Class has appropriate filters in place around line 150ish, uncomment these lines and also a few lines down, look for these commands:

```
glGenerateMipmap(GL_TEXTURE_2D);
```

and:

```
glTexParameteri(GL_TEXTURE_2D, GL_TEXTURE_MIN_FILTER,
GL_LINEAR_MIPMAP_LINEAR);
glTexParameteri(GL_TEXTURE_2D, GL_TEXTURE_MAG_FILTER,
GL_NEAREST_MIPMAP_NEAREST);
```

And you will now be automatically using MipMaps every time you load an OBJ with TinyObjLoader. Notice the speed increase? Any increase in speed is well worth a bit of effort, but take care, not to fill all your GPU Ram. You should also consider making the Mipmapping optional on models you are not likely to scale or show moving away from the camera.

Mipmaping also highlights the fact that the GPU really prefers to use smaller textures when it's rendering the pixels, ideally as close to a one to one relationship is possible. Even without Mipmaps, using the smallest possible texture can give a big speed improvement. It's again down to balance, the more we can fit in a texture, the easier it is to add detail to a model, but the bigger the texture is, the more work the GPU has to do to scale the texture to fit the resolution of the pixels it's trying to draw.

Filtering

We can't talk about Mipmapping though without talking about filtering, which relies on us understanding, that when in GPU memory, our texture pixels as we see them, are not actually pixels as the GPU sees them, in GPU memory they are called texels, and they essentially act as the data we are going to store in the pixels of our framebuffer, which will be displayed.

Normally, in an ideal one to one scale situation, 1 texel will equal 1 pixel, but if you operate any kind of scaling you have to use more or less texels to make your pixel?

If you scale by four, for example, then your 1 pixel now has to occupy 16 pixels (4 × 4) but there is only 1 texel in the GPU that corresponds to the pixel so that texel gets repeated in all 16 pixels, that's an example of magnification.

At the other extreme is when you scale down, called minification, where you have a situation where you may have more texels going into 1 pixel, and something has to be done to merge the different texels into the 1 pixel.

Both magnification and minification have downsides, they can create sharp blocky graphics on magnify, and, of course, you lose detail in minification.

The blockiness is caused by the simple repetition of texels to fill the space, known as Nearest-Neighbor interpolation. It's a perfectly viable system and you may want to have blocky scaling, but most of the time we want to smooth it out. To reduce the blockiness, you can use other interpolation methods built into the GPU, often referred to as antialiasing, though technically it's known as bilinear interpolation. Instead of throwing 1 texel into all 16 possible pixels, it looks at the color of adjacent texels and smooths or blends the colors outward, creating a much smoother image, which is more pleasing to the eye.

Though best results are seen in magnification, minification can also benefit from bilinear interpolation but the loss of detail is a fact of life. The smoothing effect of the interpolation can make that less harsh on the eye if the image is static, but movement at a distance will create a lot of noise in the image as it will use a different set of texels each update to create the pixels, so how do we overcome this? Our mipmaps will contain scaled texture samples, which allow us or rather the GPU to use a texture that is a more appropriate size for the scale that is being minified, this will greatly reduce the noise as there won't be a massive difference in the texels used to produce the pixels.

Finally, there is Trilinear Filtering that helps us to avoid a jump effect when the GPU switches from one mipmap to another. It does this from taking samples from the next and previous textures in the scale providing a kind of inbetween set of values from one texture image to another.

I could put in a lot of diagrams to explain this, but really it's quite a simple thing to see on-screen. On the support site, you will find a short demo called FilterDemo, fire it up, and have a look.

Our demo is pretty simple; we start with a simple quad, clearly overstretched. Pressing 1 will introduce Mipmapping for an immediate improvement in visuals and maybe even a bit more speed.

Pressing 2 gives us Bilinear filtering, and we can now see a lot less blockiness and a smoother though perhaps slightly blurry image. The blurriness is really down to the crazy choice of spreading 1 texture so thin. Press 3 to use a repeating system.

Pressing 4 will demonstrate the Trilinear filters. Not bad eh?

There is a computational expense to doing filtering, but at most it will only cost a few FPS and most GPUs are highly optimized to cope with at least a 4×1 texel filter (set in the EGL attributes in Graphics.h), though it is sometimes possible to increase the range until performance drop becomes marked and not many SBCs are actually capable of doing more. Filtering and using Mipmapping can make the combination of the two an effective way to handle graphics and reduce noise or scaling issues.

We Don't All Live in the Netherlands

So, visually, we have made our simple ground plane appear nicer, but really all we have is a massive flat stamp, it may be mathematically a ground plane but it's just dull to look at and will be quite dull to play. Unless you enclose it in walls and make it into an arena, it's a very limited playfield.

We can use various procedural techniques to alter the height of our triangles, which make up the meshes, and in so doing, create variation in the maps. We can overlay different textures, again based on height, or some other data structure that maps to our mesh. But, in general, all this comes into the realm of procedural methods for making gamefields look moderately interesting, and as with so many other things it is easier to get someone else to do it. That's not to say that procedural generation isn't a great option, it is indeed a pinnacle of coding skill, but like many things our little SBCs are going to struggle to do justice to the modern methods of creating detailed landscapes, and simply don't have the space/power/graphic capacity to do it well, so for now I'm going to abandon attempts at procedural worlds. The older methods our systems can handle, don't really cut it, so let's not waste our time. Our artists and terrain creators can do a better job, so let them have the glory, we'll use their results. But if you want to try it out, do some research on procedural terrains, especially heightmaps.

Using an OBJ File—The Simple Solution

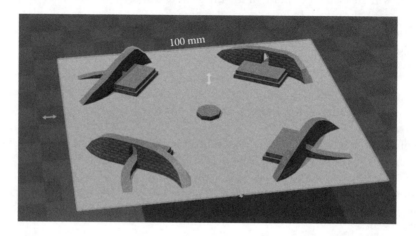

We can, of course, make use of a simple OBJ as our terrain, so long as it's not too big and does not contain billions of triangles, this can be very effective for games with small playfields and like 2D tiles, it's possible to stitch lots of them together to make larger worlds.

How Far above Sea Level Are We?

There is one obvious thing about a terrain, at least a good one that we need to address; it's bumpy, it has little highs and lows. If we want our characters to walk ON that ground, as it rises and falls they need some sense of height for them to make full and logical contact with the ground our gravity is pulling them onto.

This is totally simple; if we have a totally flat plane, we just test for a known value, but our procedural generated or loaded OBJ terrains are totally variable, almost every point in the mesh is going to have a different height value.

A height map if used, can give us some sense of height a section has but it's going to be an average of a few different sample faces, we're not likely to have a height map that has a 1–1 pixel resolution. It was always an approximation of the height of an area with some smoothing to make it look smooth.

So it's time to think about our ground as part of our collision systems, at least as a special part. For any object/character we put in the world, if it's going to have gravity, it needs to know where the ground is directly under it and that requires us to test a lot of polys in a mesh.

Now the principle of this is pretty straightforward, the practice, however, is a bit more complex, there is some magic maths that will allow us to look directly below our feet/talon/pogo springs as the character needs and gets the height. But that maths is actually pretty simple and breaks down into a series of code sections to test for interactions between a *ray* and different types of mathematical object, planes, cubes, spheres, and so on.

What is this ray concept? It is for all intents and purposes a simple vector, starting at a point in space, for example, the middle of your model and heading out into space in any given direction, for example, straight down!

We know our terrain is made up of triangles, and I just told you that we can test for ray intersecting with triangles, so we should now be able to make a pretty cool leap to realize that triangles can be used for more than just rendering.

▌▌ Interacting with Our World

Collision Maps

If we look at any terrain geometry we plan to use as our ground, strip away its textures we see it clearly made up of polys, usually a mix of triangles. These tend to be optimized for drawing, but they can also be used as noted, as possible collision systems. A collision map or mesh is a stored reference map of all the triangles we use to draw, in essence and using meshes to render those, which can be used to detect collision.

One thing we know about the ground is that it's below us; we stand on it, gravity drags us down to its level and forces us to rest at the highest point under our feet.

As gravity is uniform in its straight-down nature, we can simulate the concept of gravity using a ray, or a line pointing straight down, defined from the central reference point of our model, and a direction going straight down.

A Ray to triangle calculation is actually pretty simple, even though it has a horrible messy big maths formula. It is a basic concept that will be used a lot, so it really is something we are going to need to understand, but explaining how it works in maths terms is, as usual a bit beyond me but I'll try with a bit of code I wrote what seems like 50 years or so ago when I was able to understand these things, and which I still use.

```
//Ray equation
// Q = P + t*Dir
//
// Plane equation
// Ax + By + Cz + D = 0
//
// normal.Q + D = 0
// normal.(P + t*Dir) + D = 0
// normal.P + t*normal.Dir + D = 0
//
// t = -(D + normal.P)
//     ---------------
//        normal.Dir
//
// For any plane, D is the distance from the origin to the plane.
// By definition, D can be computed by calculating the negative
// of the normal dotted with any vertex on the plane.
// D = -normal.vertex0
//
```

Ok, it made sense to me at the time, when broken down into code it's pretty straightforward and can be coded in less than 25 lines of moderately sane code, which you can find in the RayIntersectTriangle method, which I put in the GroundPlane Class. It's functional but I'm unlikely to use it as we will have better methods coming along, but it is an interesting example of how to take a maths formula you don't understand and break it down into code that might be easier to understand.

If the collision mesh itself is kept in some kind of reasonable data structure such as a quad/oct tree, finding out if we hit a particular triangle, is a pretty simple case of running a Ray to Triangle intersection system on a subset of the mesh to check for a hit.

The upshot of this maths stuff is that we have a means to test if there is something under us, and as a bonus there's also a means to return the actual coordinate of where we hit that triangle. This is wonderfully useful so long as we've made reasonable efforts to not have to test for every single triangle in the mesh. In fact, that's a very important point, any decent mesh for a terrain is going to consist of 1000s of triangles, and we are probably only standing on 1 or 2. We need to do something to avoid doing hundreds of pointless tests, which requires us to be a little smart about how we keep track of the data and use a collision map.

Our collision map can be anything from a simple grid-based system, where we keep an array containing vectors, or a Quad Tree where we delve into the quad until we have a small number of objects to test.

As long as our terrain has only one level of play area, both these methods are perfectly acceptable. If, however, we have different levels, for example, in a building with floors where you allow travel freely up and down stairs, you will need to use something more complex.

A collision map can be precalculated and loaded, or just as easily you can parse relevant meshes to make your map. Depending on the size they are not massively complex to set up but, of course, should only be done at an init. I've provided a means to pull the mesh data from OBJ files, which I'll talk about a bit later.

Render Culling!

It's a pain that two different concepts share the same name but in one sense they are doing pretty much the same thing only for different reasons. You've already seen the massive benefits of sending all the data to the GPU and letting it do the drawing, It's so much faster than CPU style drawing, but now that we have environments, you must have noticed we're sending EVERYTHING to the GPU and letting the view systems decide what does and does not get drawn, but internally you should realize that every single vertex and associated fragments are being tested to see if they need to be drawn.

But sending everything is really rather wasteful, we may be filling our GPU memory with hundreds, maybe even thousands of vertices that we'll never see. We know our targets have quite limited GPU power and memory, they are not going to be able to keep up as our environments get bigger and bigger with more and more models and more and more vertices being sent to the limited memory we have, even the biggest PC video cards have limits, we have much stricter limits, so so much stricter!

So we need to bring our CPU back into play again, and allow it to make some general decisions about what it does and does not send to the GPU for processing.

The concept of render culling is simple and rather obvious; we've done it already with our 2D systems and with our collision systems. Just as collision culling prevents us doing collision checks we don't need, render culling prevents us trying to render models that we can't see.

There's just no point sending a model with 800+ faces to the GPU if you know it's never going to actually draw them. We also know those 800+ faces are contained in an object/model that occupies a certain amount of volume in our scene. It's therefore quite easy for us to do a basic check on whether an object that contains those 800+ faces is going to be visible. It's worth wasting a little bit of CPU time to avoid wasting a lot more GPU time sending and processing those vertices when they are not going to be seen.

There are really two types of culling test, similar to the way we do collisions in 3D; we can do a broad-phase and a narrow-phase cull. Essentially, this breaks down into deciding on which models are sent to the GPU and for narrow phase, on which actual vertices get sent. Though on games the scale we are doing at the moment,* narrow phase really isn't worth the effort, and we ironically need a lot more GPU power to carry that off. So we'll stick to broad-phase systems.

We don't need to do anything too fancy, broad phase by definition is a rough check, unlike an internal GPU frustum cull, which goes down to the triangle/vertex/pixel level, we can just make a rough check if our models/meshes are indeed inside or outside the area our frustum is looking at. Even something as simple as testing if it's behind us or not, can eliminate a good number of our unseen models. A more effective but quick scan though a few hundred models in a simple game scene will probably reveal that as much as 80% of the models are not going to be drawn. That saving in time both for the CPU sending the vertices or the draw call and the GPU's own saving of time in not drawing unseen models will make a marked difference to the performance.

If we again consider what our models represent to us, we can reimagine this image as a guide to deciding what to draw and not draw.

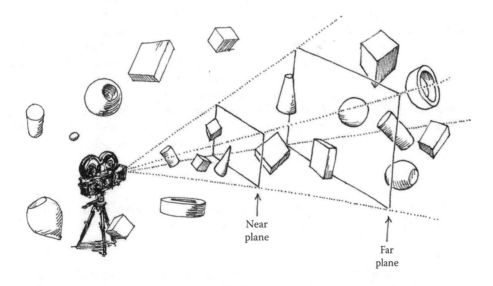

Near
plane

Far
plane

---

* I'm really hoping by the end of this book you will start to push your boundaries and find ways to really optimize your rendering, but the scale of the projects here just won't challenge you to do that.

We will look at our model's position, and a rough encapsulation system like we did with collision, either a box or a sphere, and check to see if that capsule is totally outside the view frustum. If it is outside, there's no need for us to send it to the GPU.

If it's partially or wholly inside the view frustum, then we can send it! We can let the GPU handle the straddling models. This simple concept is slightly confused by the fact that our frustum is an odd shape, but it's only an odd shape because of the projection matrix we used to create it, we can also use a matrix to twist our calculations back again.

Adding the Functionality

Add the Frustum.h and .cpp files to your project, and add an instance to your Camera Class. Ensure that when you update your camera you update the frustum as it needs to use the camera's matrices to get some of its data.

You could also incorporate most of these functions into your Camera Class itself, the choice is yours, and I am only keeping it separate for clarity.

The Frustum Class works by calculating the six different faces or planes of the frustum and keeping a record of them.

After which if a model wants to test if it's in the frustum's view and needs to be drawn, it can test with a simple position point of its center and radius of its encapsulation sphere, well I say simple, it's maths again, but reasonably simple maths using the concept of an intersection with a line and a plane. Yeah…I know <jazz hands> Maths, there's an equation $N \cdot P(r) + D = 0$; but I'm none the wiser, the code itself is easier to work out though, and revolves around the basic idea that we can define the six planes that make up the sides of our frustum and with that we decide if a ray, starting at the center point of the model, and pointing in the direction of the plane, has intersected with that plane, and if so, it is the distance from the model's center to the point of intersection less than the radius of a sphere or other test parameters.

I've given you a Sphere test as it's the simplest but feel free to add Rectangles, Points, or Convex Hulls if you think there is a need. When you add this to your model draw systems, you can check each model to see if it returns false on this test, if so, do not try to draw it!

That's a lot of processing saved. You may even have a valid reason to not update it at all, depending on the games' needs. Setting up and testing a frustum cull is not without some CPU cost, but if it stops you sending even a few dozen vertices to the GPU you will make a net saving on time, helping to keep your frame rate up.

Of course, no amount of culling can compensate for situations where your game design has every model in its camera view, in such situations frustum culling will provide no benefit, and indeed even in a free roaming environment it can be hard to ensure that you don't overload your view frustum. That is something your AI may need to give some thought to, making the frustum test potentially part of your AI to prevent spawning in, or traveling into the frustum view when stressed.

To test all this out, add the Asteroid.h and Asteroid.cpp files to your Space Cadet project, and in the game init, create a good number of randomly placed asteroids.

```
for (int i = 0 ;i < 20; i++)
{
    Pos = glm::vec3(100-Rand(200) , 10 - Rand(20) , 100-Rand(200) );
    Asteroid* T = new Asteroid(&this->Handler, (char*)"../Resources/
Models/A2.obj", &this->MainModelManager);
    T->Scales = glm::vec3(MScale, MScale, MScale);
    T->SetPosition(Pos);
```

```
        MyObjects.push_back(T);
        T->StoreGraphicClass(MyGraphics);
        MyGraphics->Init(T);
        T->programObject = lightsh;
        T->MyLightShader = T->programObject;
        T->TheGame = this;
}
```

Build and run. You should now be able to see a few of these new Asteroids not too far from your start point. Our space game was running at a reasonable number of frames depending on your target, because there were only four or five ships that are active at any one time. My Pi 3 was doing 50+FPS quite happily. But the addition of these rather large asteroids has caused the frame rate to plummet. Assuming you have added the Frustum Class and correctly updated in the Camera Class, uncommenting the test at the start of the Asteroids Draw function and building again will see that frame rate go up again.

Our 20 asteroids are still there spinning around doing nothing but looking pretty, but we're just not drawing the ones we can't see. This is a principle we can now add to any model we plan to draw, with the exception of the SkyBox, or a single mesh terrain, because they are (nearly always) going to be in our view, so testing them is worthless.

Why not try to add a bit more gameplay to your Space Cadet game by shooting the Asteroids and giving them some collision properties, so that they can bounce off each other?

Physics, More Scary Maths Stuff?

Subtitle…More Long Winded Explanations!

All these talks about motion and collision means we are actually engaging in the world of physics programming. So far we've avoided using much clear physics in our demos, or have we? We have gravity, motion, collision, and collision response, which as it just so happens, are staple parts of creating some form of physical realism in our games and are the foundation of most physics libraries. But we've really only scratched the surface and provided the most basic of motion and testing with only a small degree of response. Sadly like many of the big topics here, physics is just too big and yes, a bit scary, to go into in a chapter or two, so I'll point you to some of the basic things you need to consider if you want to have your games behave like the real thing.

Our main concern for things that are basically moving around in a world we create is to somehow emulate Newton's three laws of motion, which are as follows:

1. Newton's first law sometimes called the law of inertia; an object at rest will remain at rest unless acted on by an unbalanced force. An object in motion continues in motion with the same speed and in the same direction unless acted on by an unbalanced force.

2. Newton's second law sometimes called the law of acceleration; acceleration of an object is proportional to the force acting on the mass of that object.

3. Newton's third law is the one everyone knows; *<translated from Latin>* to every action there's always opposed an equal reaction: or the mutual actions of two bodies on each other are always equal, and directed to contrary parts.

Or as most of us know it, every action has an opposite and equal reaction.

On a small level, emulating these laws is pretty simple, as long as we are not too picky about realism, we did this with our 2D gravity and 3D motion, but as the complexity of our world builds, the interactions between objects in that world starts to grow and we know how dangerous that can be to our frame rates.

If you're good at maths and physics you may well want to build up your own physics library or include basic systems in game, but if like me, you suck at maths, or just want to save yourself a LOT of effort, there are many alternatives. One of the simplest for SBCs, being, to use an off the shelf physics library. Yes, time for another dip into the public domain to avoid doing the hard work ourselves.

Introducing Bullet Physics

There are quite a few different physics systems out there, and like maths libs, they are all pretty well established and do what is expected of them, but unlike maths libs, they involve much more complex concepts and as such, coders have taken different approaches to the challenges that representing a Newtonian world presents. These different approaches sometimes need extra hardware to function, or individual reserved cores, even special types of instructions. They nearly all use some common approaches, but may alter precision, use slightly different methods, and in some genuine cases use random values to decide in cases where values are too close to call. This means that there is a lot of variation in the results different physics engines can return. Claims of improved accuracy from different engine supporters are pretty irrelevant, because almost all physics engines are approximating a lot of things according to algorithms or heuristics that give a best fit for a test case, you are not writing test cases! For the most part though, they will all provide a result, which on the surface at least appears to be realistic enough for us. So long as that apple falls down from the tree, we should be ok.

Given that physics is always going to require a heavy amount of processing, we need to limit our search to a light but effective physics system, and one that is available off the shelf for free. I chose the Bullet Physics Library as it gives a good balance of performance over result and it's 100% free. It's installed on your target using.

```
sudo apt-get install libbullet-dev
```

That will take a few minutes, but once done you will have installed the header files and library files you need to include and run Bullet. You then need to add the four-core libraries to our list of library names, (1) `BulletCollision`, (2) `BulletSoftBody`, (3) `BulletDynamics`, and (4) `LinearMath` in our VisualGDB library list! These are "*.so" libraries, so you will have to be careful if you distribute your project to ensure that the user installs this also, or that you also supply them in your distribution. Also remember to add to your list of include directories.

```
/usr/include/bullet
```

At the time of writing, this gives us version 2.82. There is a 2.86 version available, but you may have to build it from source and I'm not sure if we really need to worry about that, the later 2.xx versions don't contain any significant differences, and we're not going that deep into them. So stick with the current installable version for now and update when you feel a bit more confident. Bullet is due to make a transition to GPU-based calculations when it becomes version 3. That will make it much less likely to be usable for us, as the vast majority of our GLES2.0 GPUs are not capable of the kind of manipulation needed. But in time when GLES3.1+ becomes normal, they will. Until then, version 2.82 is perfect for our needs. Don't try to use other versions without a great deal of understanding on what they are doing.

You may also consider downloading the PC version 2.82 or later from the http://www.bulletphysics.org website and running its demos on your computer to aid your understanding. It's supplied as a zip file. After setting up Visual Studio builds by clicking on the build_visual_studio or versus 2010. Bat file in the main folder it will produce usable solution and project files, in the build folder, albeit in Visual Studio 2010 format. But later versions of Visual Studio will update them for you when you try to load. Almost all the demos in there will run, but a few are not so friendly. It's still a confusing mess the first time you try to use it, but once you load and retarget your solution to your current SDK, set App_BulletExampleBrowser as your start-up project and run that, you can see what it does. It isn't the most intuitive of systems, but it does help to visualize what each aspect of the demos are doing and can provide you a lightbulb moment as it has for me on a few occasions. http://www.bulletphysics.org also has a forum for noobs like us to ask silly questions, which mostly get ignored, but it's been active for so long the answers to most questions are usually buried in there somewhere.

Now I'm also very new to Bullet, I dabbled with it a few years ago to see what it could do on a phone and my tests showed that it worked but probably wasn't good enough for the job in hand, my client at the time paid for something a bit more detailed and I left it. It has moved on quite a bit since then, but I am still much more used to quite large and fairly robust but heavy physics engines, so I'm going to focus only on the basics of what I need to get my games to work.

Despite differences in methods and terminology though, most of the principles of physics engines are pretty much standard, so we should be able to dip our toe in the water and get the things we want to work. Even if not always the best way, as with our coding, we can examine those better ways once we have something up and running and ready to optimize.

How It Works, and Finally Quaternions

Bullet works by creating a physics-based world, populated with objects that represent your objects and providing a set of base classes, which you can attach to your own objects and keep track of their position and orientation so that you can render them. And in doing so, it provides physical property concepts of velocity, mass, orientation, shape, and other real-world properties and you can expect a 300 m long spacecraft to have, and a 5′ 2″ overweight but surprisingly athletic plumber. Once these representative physical objects are set up, Bullet then updates their motion and forces acting on or against them and keeps track of all the positional and orientation information in its own class members, allowing you to use them in your own position and rendering systems.

In the simplest terms, Bullet has all these objects in this unseen physics world, and then works out what happens to them when they all get thrown up into the air bouncing off each other and then landing and bouncing on the ground. Rotational effects, friction, material properties, momentum retention, and absorption and many other things are taken care of for us.

For this magic to work we must allow Bullet to create and maintain this world, which will mainly contain mathematical concepts of our terrain and of any moving or static objects we deem important enough to be part of that dynamic world. The objects are added to the world, given some physical properties, and a suitable *solver* function is then called, which then does the work to move them around. With a few optimizations added to the mix for efficiency and speed, such as a choice of method for a broad-phase collision to reduce unwanted tests.

We can have quite some variety of basic object shapes, which are based on our previous ideas of Primitive collision types, and of course, every object can have its own physical properties and different solvers can be used for different kinds of motion and interaction.

By using Bullet methods to implement motion, we effectively can let it take care of all the movement, collision, response, and reactions we should expect our objects to have. That lets us focus more on logic and decision-making. Bullet will create those events which we can detect and objects that we can test, when something important happens, such as a collision, allowing us to make the right kind of sound, or destruction of a relevant object, and then Bullet can be asked to continue to work on the motion of the interacting objects according to standard rules of how we think the universe should work.

We should bear in mind that though it's not exact, physics in the real universe works on a quantum level, everything is checked and tested at all times. Computers work on a sequential level, one at a time and at a given point in time. But it does work quite effectively, at the cost of quite a lot of processing!

We'll include Bullet into most of our projects from now, to demonstrate the use, but going into a lot of detail about what it can do, how to set it up, and so on, will eat up pages, and there are some reasonable tutorials and a knowledgeable, if slow to respond, online community available at the Bullet website, http://www.bulletphysics.org/wordpress/. I'll let the source code of the demos explain things in more detail, what and how things are being set up and why. But to get started we need to be aware of a few concepts, which will be the basic systems that we will use to create the Bullet world, set it up, define how it handles things, which solver to use, and so on; these should be descriptive enough to not need much explanation.

Let's Get to It, at Last

Now one thing I've avoided up to this point is quaternions, and I'd really still like to, but we're about to start using them in anger, because Bullet uses them internally and for a lot of its setting up, so it's time to dip a toe in those murky waters and start off by explaining what they are.

They are essentially a mathematical way to represent rotations using a vector4 type of number consisting of x, y, z, w components. Now that's not to suggest they are directions or positions, just rotations, only rotations, try not to think of them as anything but rotations, if at any point you consider them directions or positions you are lost.

The xyzw values represent these values:

$$X = RotationAxis.x * \sin(RotationAngle/2)$$

$$Y = RotationAxis.y * \sin(RotationAngle/2)$$

$$Z = RotationAxis.z * \sin(RotationAngle/2)$$

$$W = \cos(RotationAngle/2)$$

The Rotation Axis itself is any actual direction that you are pointing at, which itself can spin. Point a pencil at the top-left corner of your room right now and look at the pencil, that's the axis, represented, of course, by xyz values in 3D space. Spin the pencil in your fingers while still pointing at the corner, count how much you spin, and you have the rotation angle around that axis.

When lined up like that it doesn't look quite so scary, does it? What this then does is give a neat way to combine rotations and create new values without the problems of gimbal lock. But how they actually work is so incredibly unclear that it is pointless to even try to explain until you've got yourself masters in arcane magic, I mean mathematics.

But they do work, it's possible to combine Quats representing different rotations around different axis, and return a new Quat that represents the result.

We use Yaw, Pitch, and Roll to represent movement around an axis, because the familiar XYZ axis is only relevant if we are pointing directly along the Z axis, whereas flat on the X axis pointing up to the Y axis.

Our new concept of a Rotation Axis removes those fixed axes and means for example, the left/right Yaw motion, is no longer fixed on the Y axis, but relative to our current direction.

Using Quats we don't really set directions or rotations we move to them. Any change in the orientation from one direction to another is done by applying a new Quat. So if we are looking at a $-45°$ turn on the y axis, left $-45°$ (yaw) we want him to be at $-35°$, we multiply it by a Quat representing $10°$ yaw and we then get $-35°$. Multiplying Quats in this simple instance gives additions to the angles? Yeah ok but….well it works, and it does have the advantage of being fairly simple.

These amounts to be applied are controlled by your input systems, left provides $5°$ of yaw, for example, up, gives $5°$ of pitch. Make a Quat to represent a value and you simply multiply the current Quat direction by the additional one, to get a result, which can then have another Quat applied, till all your maneuvers are done.

This totally eliminates the issues with Euler angles, no more Gimbal lock, no more vagueness of negative and positive angles, and it sounds like a wonder drug to cure all things.

Sadly, the problems start when we want to make use of them in our other calculations; we can't actually use Quats in any of our Shaders directly. Quats are not a standard numerical type, so Quats are traditionally turned back into rotation matrices after they have done all their maths, and those matrices are then used to make your usual model matrix, you might even consider doing a converter in your Shader, but on our low-powered systems I doubt there's much benefit.

Quats can still produce gimbal lock though, if you still are using Euler maths as your primary means of positioning and orientation on your controls, then Quats won't help you, converting to Quats, allows maths to work, but you are still effectively working in Euler degrees and still subject to the problems of gimbal lock and unclear angle values.

If you need full 3D orientation, only set up a Quat in your init systems, from then on only use Quat maths and you'll be fine. You can extract Eulers from it to allow you to visualize and display but don't convert them back.

And that's quaternions, I don't know why I was so afraid of them, well wait, yes I do, they are confusing. Trying to read a Quat in a debugger is almost impossible and totally unintuitive to human eyes. You are not looking at a representation of direction or position, despite using xyzw, you are looking at the result of a computation, which is not simple to visualize. You have to actually know what the acos of numbers are, to be able to read them. But I guess 90% of the time you don't need to read them, and it's not too hard to use conversion systems to turn them back to degrees for output and display.

Also there's no standard usage of them, C++'s standard maths libs do not have them, so you need to rely in your maths libs. Some libs want you to set up with degrees, some with radians, some provide easy matrix conversions, some don't. Because of the lack of standard, you may be forced to write different systems for different libs, you might even end up writing your own Quat functions, but that's troublesome, as they might not match up with your chosen physics libs. Oh the horror!

Both glm and Bullet have quaternions, and use them in different ways, for example, the conversion to rotation matrices is confused because Bullet allows creation of Matrix 3 × 3 using a Quat as its constructor parameter, glm has a function glm::toMat3 (or toMat4), which does the same job.

So Quats, amazing things, confusing as hell until you get used to them, so keep your interaction with them as simple as you can. There are several other functions that Quats can give us access to, especially Lerping, but I'll leave that to your own exploration. At some point, go back to the Space Cadet game and move your ship using Quats, because the camera is related to your position and orientation, you will be able to get full 3D motion, and soar among the stars as you should do.

Let's get back to using Bullet.

Setting Things Up

Adding #include <btBulletDynamicsCommon.h> to our Game.h file allows us to create these members in the Game Class, public or private, it's up to you.

```
btBroadphaseInterface* BroadPhase;
btDefaultCollisionConfiguration* CollisionConfiguration;
btCollisionDispatcher* Dispatcher;
btSequentialImpulseConstraintSolver* ConstraintSolver;
btDiscreteDynamicsWorld* DynamicPhysicsWorld;
```

In the Game Class itself at initialize, we'll create these things using some basic functional concepts, other options are available though as we will discover.

```
// create the main physics systems
    BroadPhase = new btDbvtBroadphase();
    CollisionConfiguration = new btDefaultCollisionConfiguration();
    Dispatcher = new btCollisionDispatcher(CollisionConfiguration);
    ConstraintSolver = new btSequentialImpulseConstraintSolver;
    DynamicPhysicsWorld = new btDiscreteDynamicsWorld(Dispatcher,
BroadPhase, ConstraintSolver, CollisionConfiguration);
// set a "normal" gravity level
    DynamicPhysicsWorld->setGravity(btVector3(0, -9.81f, 0));
```

That, in essence, is all we need to set things up and get started, we'll cover updating in a moment, from here on we have to add some collision shapes and give some means of handling our reaction to collisions, but that's best explained in the code as it will depend very much on what we load and the size and shape it best represents. To create new physical objects I have added a small helper function to the Game Class.

```
PhysicsObj* Game::CreatePhysicsObj(btCollisionShape* pShape,
    const float &mass,
    const btVector3 &aPosition,
    const btQuaternion &aRotation)
{
    // create a new game object
    PhysicsObj* pPhysicsObject = new PhysicsObj(pShape, mass,aPosition,
    aRotation);
    if (DynamicPhysicsWorld)
    { DynamicPhysicsWorld->addRigidBody(pPhysicsObject->GetRigidBody());}
        else {printf("Dynamic world does not exist\n");}
    return pPhysicsObject; // return to place in an objects data or
    another list
    }
```

This will simplify the process of creating new objects, we just supply the shape, of which there are few types, and occasionally more are added, then Mass, Position, and Rotation, but Rotation as a quaternion.

I've provided default values of 0,0,0 Position and no Rotation (0,0,0,1), so you don't have to get your hands dirty too much.

Stepping Through

Once our world is created and populated, updating Bullet and most other physics engines involves a process called stepping. All the movement in Physics is based on the idea of how far things will move in a given time, and it deals with any collisions, which might occur in that period, so if we want to see them move at 60FPS, we must step the physics at 1/60th of a second if we have a fixed time step and we are maintaining that, then a simple

```
DynamicPhysicsWorld->stepSimulation(1 / 60.0f);
```

is all we need, but we usually need a bit more precision, especially if we have fast movement, so we can allow what are called substeps, or how many times in that 1/60th we will step, to increase the precision, say by a factor of 10, like this:

```
DynamicPhysicsWorld->stepSimulation(1 / 60.0f, 10);
```

In effect, the step system will then iterate though 10 tests at 1/600 of a second, giving much better precision. The actual number of steps is something you should experiment with, but generally the more steps, the better the result, but more processing! The actual frame rate is going to be very dependent on your game, usually it's better to use delta time but so far we've got away with the fixed rate. Though we will uncouple ourselves from the fixed rate when we start to have large numbers of objects moving around that occasionally takes us over the frame lock.

Visualizing Things

One very nice thing Bullet allows you to do is to visualize the abstract mathematical things that you create, which really does make debugging and placement of important objects/parts a lot easier. This debug rendering will allow you to *overlay* the basic primitive shapes of your physics objects by extending an Onboard Class called btDebugDraw.

This contains a list of virtual functions, which you can then supply. It's really designed for full OpenGL or DirectX though, as it works best using a sequence of line primitives sent to the GPU as required, which GLES2.0 isn't terribly good at because it prefers to use buffers, but we can produce a Shader that works for it. And because we produce our own versions of drawLine and drawContactPoint, we can produce render functions that work with our system. Here's an example of using a drawLine function that does not in itself draw the lines, but stacks them into a vector, for a later final draw all at once.

```
void PhysicsDraw::drawLine(const btVector3 &from,
    const btVector3 &to,
    const btVector3 &color)
{  // draws a simple line of pixels between points but stores them for
    later draw
    LineValues Line;
    btVector3 scolor = btVector3(1, 0, 1);
    Line.p1 = from;
    Line.Colour1 = color;
    Line.p2 = to;
    Line.Colour2 = color;
    TheLines.push_back(Line);
}
```

Since this does not do any actual draws as the older Line draw system was designed to, we now have the responsibility to call an additional render function like this to produce our lines:

```
void PhysicsDraw::DoDebugDraw()
{// set up the line shader and then draw the buffer
            //load the vertex data info
    glVertexAttribPointer(this->positionLoc,
    3, // there are 3 values xyz
    GL_FLOAT, // they are float
    GL_FALSE, // don't need to be normalised
    4*sizeof(float),  // (be aware btVector3 uses 4 floats)
    (GLfloat*)&this->TheLines[0]  // where do they start
);
glEnableVertexAttribArray(this->positionLoc);
glDrawArrays(GL_LINES, 0, TheLines.size()*2);
            TheLines.clear();
}
```

A very simple Shader with a Matrix 4 × 4 uniform and a a_position attribute can then draw the relevant lines as the last part of the render section of our game update loop. We just supply it with the combined View and Projection matrices, they are points in space, so no need for a Model matrix, though we'll reuse the full MVP matrix pointer in the Shader, and ensure we have a handle in positionLoc for the a_Position attrib. Here's a code snippet from the end of the Game Update, after normal objects have been updated and rendered, we should wrap this in a #ifdef...DEBUG because it will only be needed in debug.

```
    DynamicPhysicsWorld->debugDrawWorld();
glm::mat4* Projection = TheCamera->GetProjection();
glm::mat4* View = TheCamera->GetView();
    glUseProgram(PhysicsDraw::ProgramObject);
```

```
GLint MatrixID = glGetUniformLocation(PhysicsDraw::ProgramObject, "MVP");
// use the MVP in the simple shader
    // make the View and  Projection matrix
glm::mat4 VP       = *Projection * *View;  // Remember order seems
backwards
    glUniformMatrix4fv(MatrixID, 1, GL_FALSE, &VP[0][0]);
    this->m_pPhysicsDrawer->DoDebugDraw();
    // after our draw we need to swap buffers to display
    eglSwapBuffers(MyGraphics->p_state->display,
    MyGraphics->p_state->surface);
```

I've given you a PhysicsDraw Class, in combination with a PhysicsObj Class. The PhysicsObj Class should be added to our most basic model type, ObjectModel like so.

```
// bounding box info when we need it, model manager provides for OBJ types.
    float bmin[3];
    float bmax[3];
    PhysicsObj* MyPhysObj;
```

Even if we choose not to give an object type its own physics object and leave this blank, it's not going to use up much space, better to have it as an option and use `CreatePhysicsObh` when we need to.

`CreatePhysicsObj` It is best suited in the Game Class or wherever you create the objects. Once created, a physics object is placed in the Dynamic world and we can interrogate it as it gets updated by the physics update functions. This is especially useful if we include a pointer back to our object's base or derived class instance, so that we can ask the physics system, which PhysicsObject is associated with which game ObjectModel, using some pointer systems that the Bullet provides. This provides two-way links, so our game ObjectModels and our Bullet PhysicsObjects will be able to know about each other.

We still need to register our new draw systems with the inbuilt but currently passive DebugDraw, which is simply done by creating an instance of our PhysicsDraw method and telling the physics world where it is.

```
m_pPhysicsDrawer = new PhysicsDraw();
m_pPhysicsDrawer->setDebugMode(1+2);
this->DynamicPhysicsWorld->setDebugDrawer(m_pPhysicsDrawer);
```

The physics-based demos on the support site all have debug rendering enabled by pressing the W or F key to provide a wire frame. I only really do the contact point and line functions though, but you can fill in the others if you need them. You can have a look at the BulletDebugDraw Class to see how that works, it's not very complex at all.

Debug rendering does slow your frame rate down a bit though, as you are effectively adding another draw cycle, albeit a short one, so best not to keep it active all the time! Debug functions are usually written for functionality, and not for performance.

This might seem like a lot of trouble to go to, but being able to visualize how the physics world sees and manages your objects is very important, you will be able to spot errors of structure and position much faster and ensure that your model visualization matches the physical world that controls its movement and orientation.

Force, Torque, and Impulse

We can't really have a physics discussion without explaining what these things are. Although it's perfectly possible and indeed valid to just set the speed and direction of an object using some form of set linear motion function, we know the universe does not work like that! We expect things to accelerate, have inertia, and be prone to little deviations of direction because of friction and air resistance among other things. In fact, we're so used to this that we mentally reject things that don't do that. Our Amphibian Class ships took this into account by not allowing them to go from 0 to full speed in one step; we had to allow an acceleration to occur. It was still a bit on/off though.

How can we make our physics seem more realistic then? The first step is to explain a bit about concepts of motion and forces, starting with what Linear Motion is, and then its equally important cousin, Angular Motion.

Linear motion or velocity is easy, it's when things move through space, moving along a line of trajectory that is usually defined by the propulsive force that pushes it forward or pulls it along. We can move in all possible directions radiating from any relative 0,0,0 point in space. In a line. Hence linear.

Angular relates to the rotation of an object, which though it might spin in any direction, its center point, or center of mass, which defines its point in space does not change.

Both Linear and Angular velocity need some kind of force applied to trigger the motion of the object. And on the reasonable notion that things we move have mass, they will also have some inertia or resistance to moving, which needs to be overcome.

An Angular force applied to a body causes it to twist around its center, making it spin! This should be pretty obvious to anyone who has spent any time in a children's playground. A roundabout pushed directly forward in a line from the center will not move, unless you're unbelievably strong, or the installers did a shocking job! But pushing from off center causes it to spin.

Spinning is cool, we can do that a lot in games; however, if a body has a linear force being applied, then the application of an angular force will also alter the direction of that linear force, causing the body, not to spin, but to alter its direction. The degree of twist/spin/change is all dependent on where the forces are being applied in relation to the center of mass of the object.

Now I'm using the word force, in the general common way we all use force as something that pulls/pushes against something else, and that holds true in physics too, but force needs to be defined a little better than a value, which is applied for as long as we ask, may the force be with us.

Angular and linear force acting on a body, of course, result in angular and linear velocity, which is our ultimate aim to get things moving. How we apply that force has a couple of options that will let us make things realistic and we have to remember that we don't have the luxury of, always on, real world, real-time physics, we take samples at different times, so we need to make our time steps be as accurate as possible.

So now let's differentiate between Force, which we think we know about, Impulse which we used without much detail in the past, and Torque which I thought was something to do with high-performance sports cars?

These are our main ways of applying forces in different ways to create our motion.

Force is applied to an object over time, and as such, how much time the force is applied will result in a different final velocity after a given passage of time. If we are working on systems that have different update rates, it could mean that one machine naturally takes longer to accelerate its objects up to speed, despite both machines applying the same force. That can be tricky but it's possible to be technically accurate, as long as we find a way to incorporate the correct passage of time.

Impulses, however, do not depend on the time passed; they are still a force but a force that is applied immediately to the object resulting in the object being given an immediate velocity. In simpler terms, Force results in an acceleration factor, which is applied to the velocity to create a new velocity, Impulse results in a final velocity!

Torque isn't actually just about how powerful your car is, it's to do with rotational force on your object, because it has mass, it has inertia even if not moving in a linear way, so some degree of force is needed to get it up to spin speeds or an impulse to set its spin speed.

Bullet allows us to apply forces using

```
applyForce();
applyTorque();
applyImpulse();
```

which are methods in the btRigidBody Class. Each method requires a btVector3 value and also a local point on the object where the force is actually applied to that allows us to replicate movement around the center of mass.

There are couple of other methods, which can be very useful too, and indeed we tend to use them more:

```
applyCentralForce();
applyCentralImpulse();
applyTorqueImpulse();
```

The applyCentralxxx methods allow us to push against the center of mass of an object, so we don't need the local offsets, so you just provide the btVector3 value, the center and the whole thing will move. There is logically no way to replicate a Central torque as such a concept does not exist in physics, so why try eh? That's enough info for now to get started; we'll pick up the detail in the code as we go along.

Collisions

Bullet actually handles all our collisions for us, at least in the sense that it detects them, and causes things to bounce off each other as though they were unbreakable statues. That's fine for the most part, but we generally want to do more with a collision than just bounce! We may want to trigger some game-based response, for example, a simple sound effect or a more complex response such as setting up an explosion, or a simple case of reducing a life counter. The actual response is, of course, totally dependent on the game you write, and the actual types of objects that collide. So Bullet does not even try to do anything like that. It just provides a mechanism for you through its collision dispatcher, using a concept called manifolds.

Bullet maintains a set of these manifolds, which give information on pairs of objects, which during a broad-phase test have become of interest to Bullet. That does not always mean they are touching, yet, but that their bounding volumes have interacted and that they are at least on the verge of colliding, or perhaps just collided and moving away but still close.

These Manifolds exist in our collision dispatcher, from the point that they are discovered as interacting in the broad phase until the point when they no longer interact, the so-called separation phase. We can keep track of how many manifolds there are with a simple interrogation of the dispatcher, which lives in our Game Class

```
int numberOfManifolds = Dispatcher->getNumManifolds();
```

We can also more usefully, when we know we have a manifold, gain access to it.

```
btPersistentManifold* Manifold =
Dispatcher->getManifoldByIndexInternal(index);
```

Depending on the complexity of our world and numbers of objects in there, the list can grow, and we will have to go through each, in turn, so being able to get them by index is very useful.

With a Manifold available to us, we can get some very useful information, such as info on which two rigid bodies are colliding, and how many contact points there are. Contact points are very important, because it's possible that there are 0 contact points, in which case, the objects are simply close to each other, not actually touching. But more than 0 means that there is a clear collision occurring and they are in contact and we can do something about that.

But we do need to be very clear about the concept of interact, contact, and separate. Three different points in the life of the two objects. We have to decide which of these are important to us and when we should do our own event that will trigger our response.

Most times, we want to trigger our events at the exact point of collision, but that can be a little tricky to work out, we would need to know two things: first, are our pair currently touching, and if yes, were they touching before? If no to the second part, then we can be certain that this is the first point of contact.

Equally for the separation point, we need to know that at the moment they are not touching, and that they were touching in the last sequence. We could take note of the interaction event, really it's more of a proximity alert, which might have a value to your game, but for now, of the three possible events we're going to focus on the CollisionEvent, and the SeparationEvent.

Clearly, all we need is a time machine to go back to the last 60th of a second and compare... ah wait! there's a flaw in that concept. Time machines weren't invented when I wrote this! That's inconvenient. We need to come up with another plan.

What we can do, is keep a record of all the current manifolds, and in the next frame, compare our new set of manifolds with that old list, which once we're done, we set them as the last record for the next frame.

It sounds complex, and yes there might be a few dozen/hundred objects, but we can manage that. Keeping vectors and maps has been fairly standard for us so far, and we could do it again, but in the interests of simplicity, there's another couple of quite nice STL functions that we can use, one especially designed for pairs, called...std::pair. It's a simple data structure, which we can define as our Pair of collision objects

```
typedef std::pair<const btRigidBody*, const btRigidBody*> CollisionObjects;
```

We do need to be careful though, because the order of a pair will make them a distinct std:pair, so body0:body1 is considered a different pair from body1:body0. I have a neat way to deal with that as you will see.

We could create a map of these CollisionObjects but there's another factor to consider, any individual object may, in fact, collide with more than one object. That makes a map a little hard to use, because a map needs one of the index values to be unique and we can't be sure of that. A std::vector or std::list could be used, but we'd have to scan through it and to add some qualification code for situations where we have more than one collision on a body.

The solution is std:set, a new-fangled C++11 structure,[*] which allows us to compare a set with another set, and extract the differences. It's not especially fast, but it is especially clean and effective, so in that vein we will create a set of CollisionObjects called ManifoldPairs.

```
typedef std::set<CollisionObjects> ManifoldPairs;
```

We also need to add three new functions to the Game Class, a Collision Checker, of course, and handlers for the types of collision events. They are nearly always called the CollisionEvent and the SeparationEvent, so let's not break with tradition. Finally, we will need to keep a record of our last set of pairs. In Game.h you can add these:

```
typedef std::pair<const btRigidBody*, const btRigidBody*>
CollisionObjects;
typedef std::set<CollisionObjects> ManifoldPairs;

ManifoldPairs pairsLastFrame; // the pairs from last frame need to be
storeed
void CheckForCollision();
void CollisionEvent(btRigidBody* RB0, btRigidBody* RB1);
void SeparationEvent(btRigidBody* RB0, btRigidBody* RB1);
```

All we need to do now is add the code for the Collision Check which looks like this.

```
void Game::CheckForCollision() {
        // keep a list of the collision pairs we find during the
        current update
        ManifoldPairs pairsOThisFrame;

        // go through all the manifolds in the Dispatchers list
        for (int i = 0; i < Dispatcher->getNumManifolds(); i++)
        {
```

---

[*] See, even I use C++11 sometimes when I need to, this is too useful a function not to use it!

```cpp
        btPersistentManifold* Manifold =
Dispatcher->getManifoldByIndexInternal(i);

    if (Manifold->getNumContacts() > 0)// we only care if they have
contact points
        {
//getBodyx actually returns btCollisionObject, and we really need to get
btRigidBody instead for compares
//so we have to use the C++ styly static cast. (or plant an idvalue in the
rigid body if they are unique)
        const btRigidBody* Body0 = static_cast<const
btRigidBody*>(Manifold->getBody0());
        const btRigidBody* Body1 = static_cast<const
btRigidBody*>(Manifold->getBody1());

//they are pointers & have numerical value, use that to store them lowest
value first

        const btRigidBody* FirstRB = (Body0 > Body1) ? Body1 : Body0;
        const btRigidBody* SecondRB = (Body0 > Body1) ? Body0 : Body1;

        // create the pair
        CollisionObjects NewPair = std::make_pair(FirstRB, SecondRB);

        // insert the pair into the current list
        pairsThisFrame.insert(NewPair);

//this pair definitely are colliding, if they are brand new we can safely
say it's a collision event
            if (pairsLastFrame.find(NewPair) == pairsLastFrame.end()) //
        search the old list for this new pair
            {
            CollisionEvent((btRigidBody*)Body0, (btRigidBody*)Body1); // got
            through to the end...it wasn't there so this is a new hit
            }
        } // if
} // for i
// another list for pairs that were removed this update, they will be
separated events
        ManifoldPairs removedPairs;
// compare the set from last frame with the set this frame and put the
removed ones in the removed Pairs
std::set_difference( pairsLastFrame.begin(),      pairsLastFrame.end(),
                    pairsThisFrame.begin(),      pairsThisFrame.end(),
                    std::inserter(removedPairs, removedPairs.begin())
                    );

// iterate through all of the removed pairs sending separation events for
them, can't use an index for this so this is a C++11 iterater
    for (ManifoldPairs::const_iterator iter = removedPairs.begin(); iter
        != removedPairs.end(); ++iter)
            {
            SeparationEvent((btRigidBody*)iter->first, (btRigidBody*)
        iter->second);
            }
// because the names for sets are pointers, we can simply tell the Last
pair it is now the current pair
        pairsLastFrame = pairsThisFrame;

}
```

Of course, make sure that you call this routine; I just spent 5 min trying to work out why I had no collisions, before realizing I hadn't actually called the test. It's probably best after the Physics Step. The Collision and Separation event code is very trivial, because we're not going to actually do the response, just acknowledge it, what happens should be up to the objects themselves, at which point it might be helpful if we used Bullets rather than handy pointers I mentioned before to get back to our game ObjectsModel base or derived class, using

`RB0->setUserPointer(&SomeThingRelated);` to help us get access to the instance of the game objects we just hit.

```
void Game::CollisionEvent(btRigidBody* RB0, btRigidBody* RB1)
{
    ObjectModel* First = (ObjectModel*)RB0->getUserPointer(); // assumes
we set up the user pointer with an ObjectModel* and setUserPointer
    ObjectModel* Second= (ObjectModel*)RB1->getUserPointer(); //and there
are handling routines in ObjectModel or overrides in derived classes
    First->HandleCollision(Second);
    Second->HandleCollision(First);
}
```

Repeat this for the SeparationEvent system and decide if you want to have a different collision handler for that event.

Since ObjectModel is our base class, no matter what type of object we created, if we stored its address in its RigidBody's user pointer, we can cast that back to an ObjectModel, and provide HandleCollision routines, at least in the ObjectModel Class. If that routine is marked as virtual, then derived classes can be given their own proper handler, and now you can have a specific type of handling routine to do whatever you need to do when hit by the other object.

The one flaw in this nice idea is that we can only pass an ObjectModel pointer, so you are limited to the base values in that class, but you could include a Type enum or an ID value, to check if you got hit by a bullet type, or a soft bouncy ball type. I'm told that one of those is bad for your health.

As different games will need to use collision in different ways it can be hard to generalize your collision system. But certainly the idea of collision response is pretty universal and using a virtual base function allows you to create specific class functions for derived classes.

I've added and moved all this code from my Game Class into a CollisionProcess Class in my 3D game template, and extended it a little bit to keep track of contact events. This might be useful when we want to know if contact between objects is constant, on a floor, for example, though it's a bit more wasteful than testing for simple collision and separation events. What is important is to make sure that Bullet provides access to the base class you use, and that there is some simple form of ID available there to tell what you are hitting, or is hitting you.

That pretty much covers collision, what we do with it is up to us and our game logic, we can let it bounce around as it does by default or we can set off sound effects, making an object die, blow up, get mad, and hit back. It's open to lots of options. You can see this in operation in all the Physics-based Demos that follow from now.

The Downside

Now it's a word of warning time. I already said there is a cost of a lot of processing using Bullet. Bullet and other physics engines you might find will work on our limited targets pretty well if used wisely, but there are always going to be functions that try to do a lot of *stuff* to emulate reality. A LOT of *STUFF*! Not all that *stuff* is actually going to make a massive difference to the majority of games you write. Some things we can switch off or reduce precision or frequency of tests, at the cost of some accuracy, and some things will just become bogged down by large numbers of units and recursion. Even on the latest hardware for PC and Consoles, a physics engine represents a large commitment of processing resources and more than a few games have seen their FPS drop in an effort to have the most realistic physics possible. But we must remember we are writing games, reality is an optional feature, you may or may not need.

Unless you actually need spot-on physics, you should try to restrict your use of physics to only the main things that need it! We can use our own rudimentary systems for anything not in focus of the dynamic world, so what we learned to do ourselves is not wasted. We've done pretty well so far without *proper* physics, and we've not really got to the point where keeping things simple starts to not work for us, so let's just keep things simple when we can.

If your game has a lot of physical-based objects, you will need to make some tests to see how many of your system can cope with comfortably. There's no hard and fast rule for this, the shape and size/complexity of your objects are all factors that impact on the speed. A Raspberry Pi 2 or 3 can cope with around 100–150 Sphere/Cube-shaped rigid body objects on a single core quite well, more than that it starts to struggle.

The other downside is that the control of your objects can become quite a bit more complex. We no longer place things, rotate them, or add direction vectors to their position. Bullet does all that for us, so it can be hard to get our head around the fact that we have actually very little control on an object aside from setting or applying forces or velocities but as long as we are able to extract motion state data from Bullets useful. btDefaultMotionState we can keep track of where we are, and occasionally nudge things back with a SetPosition or SetOrientation helper function but for the most part we're observing and reporting the physics world and influencing some of the events. It's a different way of looking at things.

All that said though, physics is really good fun to play within your games, even for mathphobes like me. We're only going to scratch the surface of it here, so make sure to spend some time with Bullet, or another library with good samples and resources and have fun learning how the real world actually works, even if you're not in the woods to hear the tree fall on the dead cat living in the box that wasn't there till someone saw it 5 light years away at the same time!

Yeah physics is fun!

Basic Racing Game

Finally, after all that explanation and bluster and scary boring stuff, we can get to a game again. Our basic concept of a racing game needs only two things: (1) a track to race on and (2) a car to do the racing. In some ways, our 2D games use the same concept as a race game, the only real differences are where the camera is and the use of larger terrain tiles rather than character-sized tiles...in fact, we will see we are still using quite some number of tile concepts despite this being an entirely 3D game.

Once we have these basics in place we'll talk about adding something to race against and how to actually make the race obey some of the rules of racing, such as going around the track.

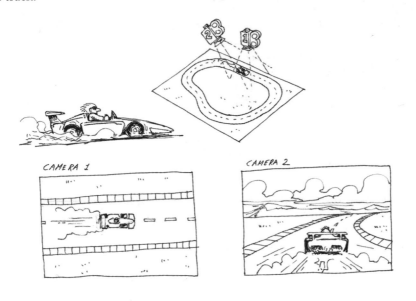

Getting and Making the Car Controllable

Before we start to create the track, we really need to get the car working, and as we're going to use Bullet in this game it gives us a chance to test out some of the basics needed, using a very simple idea of a ground plane and a simple box-shape collider shape for a car. I won't get into anything more complex at this stage; let's just focus on displaying a nice model, and controlling it with keys.

I found quite a few models for cars available online, and some very nice ones I wanted to use, but after struggling a little with higher than I can handle poly counts I eventually settled on a low poly simple Italian sport car model, which is available from TurboSquid here: https://www.turbosquid.com/FullPreview/Index.cfm/ID/458545. I won't name it here in case of trademark issues, but it's one of those cars you don't let loose in China shops…ermm…ok, well, that's enough of being cryptic. It does need converting from its DirectX format to OBJ, but I used http://www.greentoken.de/onlineconv/ to convert it. It's a great online resource, if you use it often then send them $5, they earned it, and you will save a lot of time, especially if you are not familiar with graphic packages. I also included a low poly cartoon car model from Turbo Squid, which didn't need conversion and went in with little effort.

For fun, I also added a very simple model done by one of my students Layl Bongers in 10 min, called simply Car, it's about the lowest poly car you can get and it works fine. In some ways, we are not too bothered about the quality of the model, we need to focus more on the code to display it, but you can clearly see that the art time spent on a model will make your game's visuals worth the effort you put in to create it, so keep your artists happy and well fed and they will reward you.

If you don't have your own artists, then downloading models from the web is usually pretty safe and secure, but there can be frustrations, sometimes the textures are too big, we can only handle 2048 × 2048, but resizing textures can be done with any art tool, and it's rare that our small games need much more than 1024 × 1024. Sometimes the texture format isn't quite compatible with our file handling. Sometimes the mtl files accidently reference the creators' actual drive mapping, or worse, a different texture, sometimes there are spaces in the file names and they need to be edited. You'll experience all these frustrations in good time, you just need to be adaptable enough to accept and fix the issues, or have cool friends and students who'll do it for you. A bit of both is probably the best.

I Like to Move It, Move It

The most important thing about using physics to propel the motion of an object is that we don't use positional motion as we did before, adding speed to point A to get point B, we apply forces to move, which themselves can be altered by other forces, which, in turn, determine our speed to provide a final placement for the next segment of time.

So a car moves forward as a result of the engine supplying force to the back wheels, which turn and propel it forward. Now there are a lot of other forces at work! Friction of the track, air resistance, even downforce, a degree of power loss through the drive train, and a whole mess of other things, which you would expect to see properly implemented in a real driving game. But we will just make a range of massive assumptions that we can move forward and back, and implement some turns, with a bit of skidding allowed to take account of the inertia of a 2 ton race car. We can build up the other things as we need them.

So our first and *simplest* task is to apply the forward or reverse motion. To do that we need some concept of orientation, that is, which way are we pointing. Bullet does gives us an orientation but only as a btQuaternion and I am never too happy using them, because they are only useful for rotations and not direction, but not to worry, it can be used, because multiplying a Qauat by an Axis aligned forward vector, in our case +Z is forward. We can get a direction vector. Unfortunately, Bullet Physics does not seem to have a way to multiply a Quat by a vector3, to return a vector3. But it has the next best thing, a quatRotate function, which does exactly the multiplication we want, like so.

```
Forward = btVector3(0, 0, 1);
Forward = quatRotate(orient, Forward);
```

Clearly, we can also return Left, Right, Up, and Down directions from this concept if we need them, using relevant direction vectors to multiply the Quat. I added btVector3 Forward; to the ObjectModel Class because it's going to be important. Take note that Bullet clearly has its own version of a Vector3, compared to GLM, it's an irritation that the two are not directly transferrable without having to do some form of wasteful casting, but because we are not doing much with glm::matrices and glm::vectors while using Physics we should just use what is available to us.

Another method to extract the forward vector is this:

```
btMatrix3x3 rotationMatrix(orient);
Forward = btVector3(rotationMatrix.getColumn(2)); // we will keep this its
useful for all sorts
```

Right can be obtained from column 0 and Up from column 1. Here, we are creating a small 3 × 3 matrix and extracting the forward direction from it. I think the first version might be slightly slower because of the internal multiplication that goes on, but both versions provide what we need and the first makes getting cardinal points much simpler.

Once we have that vector, we can normalize it and it can then be used to push us forward, or the negative of it to push us back, as a force, a simple scalar can be used to provide the acceleration value needed, and we can increment that scalar up to a maximum value.

I set up a small test case in my game loop to move the first car:

```
MyObjects[0]->MyPhysObj->GetRigidBody()->setActivationState(DISABLE_
DEACTIVATION); // DON'T LET OUR PLAYER GO TO SLEEP, or we can't move it.
if (this->TheInput->TestKey(KEY_SPACE))
 {
 MyObjects[0]->Forward.normalize();
 MyObjects[0]->MyPhysObj->GetRigidBody()->applyCentralImpulse
(MyObjects[0]->Forward * 10); // forward vector
 }
```

As it's a normalized value, it's quite a small impulse so multiplied by 10 or an acceleration factor, just for this example. Ok so that was nice, a reasonable degree of acceleration topping off at the max we set for the impulse added.

You should have noticed that "don't let our player go to sleep" comment? This is a feature of Bullet physics, which can sometimes work against us. When it has an object moving very slowly or not at all, it makes a decision not to move it any more. It's still part of the physical world, and responds and reacts to collision, but at a certain point when it's clearly not moving, it puts it to sleep and stops calculating its motion. This saves a lot of processing, as a static object not moving, but having movement calculated is a terrible waste of effort.

Once it's asleep it can only be activated again by a collision causing motion or by changing its activation state. Strictly speaking, we only need to do it once to inform Bullet that this object is always alive even when motionless. If we leave that out, as soon as the object stops moving, it becomes immovable.

Now it's time to add steering, this isn't going to be totally accurate visually, because steering is a result of a change in the mechanical position of wheels, which our OBJ model can't represent, but the code will work even if the graphics don't. We effectively are going to alter the direction of our car while still allowing it to move forward, this concept of forward is key to its motion, actual direction is no longer that interesting to us.

To steer we need to set an angular velocity, which will alter our orientation and, in turn, the direction of our forward motion. The amount of angular velocity would normally be reflected in the amount you turn a steering wheel, but as we don't have a steering wheel, we will use the A and D keys to apply an increasing force the longer they are pressed to a max, and when not pressed allow them to reduce to 0, in the same way a steering wheel returns to a center point naturally.

We could use Impulses and Torque, but that's best left for a proper vehicle class with wheels, so I've implemented a cheap and dirty system that will give us a sense of control, yet punish us if we go too fast. This code should be in your Player Class because you are now effectively in charge of the car as the player.

```
if (this->TheGame->TheInput->TestKey(KEY_UP))
{
    motion++;
    if (motion >20) motion = 20;

} else if (motion > 0) motion--;


if (this->TheGame->TheInput->TestKey(KEY_DOWN))
{
    motion--;
    if (motion <-20) motion = -20;

} else if (motion < 0) motion++;

if (motion <= 0.0001f) LRDIR = 0.0f;
LRDIR = 0;

// some basic steering
    if (this->TheGame->TheInput->TestKey(KEY_A))  LRDIR = -0.2f;
    if (this->TheGame->TheInput->TestKey(KEY_D))  LRDIR = 0.2f;


// set modest damping to decelerate
    MyPhysObj->GetRigidBody()->setDamping(0.2f, 0.15f);
// if we are turning, increase the damping on the linear(forward) motion,
if not tunring set the steer to 0.
    if ((TheGame->TheInput->TestKey(KEY_A) == 0) && (TheGame->TheInput-
>TestKey(KEY_D) == 0))
            LRDIR = 0.0f;
            else MyPhysObj->GetRigidBody()->setDamping(0.6f, 0.115f);
// slightly reduce damping on angular

// apply an impulse for forward motion and a simple Vel for steering.
    MyPhysObj->GetRigidBody()->applyCentralImpulse(Forward*motion * 30);
    MyPhysObj->GetRigidBody()->setAngularVelocity(btVector3(0,-1.0,0)
*LRDIR*6);
```

Once entered, this compiles and now we have steering, braking, and turning. We have a car! It can drive around pretty convincingly on a currently plain flat ground, and it basically works, apart from being able to spin on the spot. How could we stop that? Of course, because we have no actual terrain, only the model itself gives us a sense of motion and turning. But Bullet really comes into its own when we add more than one object and allow them to interact.

This is a good foundation for us to move to the next step of putting a realistic terrain or track to race around. However, the basic use of simple forces like this isn't actually the best way to make a vehicle work, its acting more like a hovercraft than a car, there's simply no sense of it trundling along the ground and having its suspension create the bumps and bounces we normally associate with the movement of a four-wheeled vehicle. We need a slightly better system to increase the realism, and improve the experience. Bullet does provide a means to do more realistic vehicle movement by providing our collision box with wheels, which, in turn, drive it forward and use a suspension system to throw things off a bit...

Even if the wheels themselves are not displayed we can still keep a pretty good eye on the collision box itself, which is influenced by our invisible wheels and get a more accurate representation of cars.

The system is called btRaycastVehicle and provides a fairly accurate means of creating a decent movement. I say fairly accurate because trying to create a single system to encompass every form of two- or four-wheeled vehicle is simply not viable, so a lot of compromise and tweaking is usually needed to get exactly the responses you expect for a particular car shape.

The support site has a demo called TrackRacer2, which shows how to make use of this and gives a much better representation of car motion, at the cost of a bit more processing, but codewise it has the same basic systems. It also took quite some man-hours to tweak and fiddle till I was happy with the motion, so if you decide to change the car or add different types, shapes, weights, and power, be prepared to invest some serious time to get things moving as you want them. Implementing it here in this book is overkill for what we want to do, so we'll stick with the basic systems we have and get our game up and running. It's up to you if you want to add the enhancements to make the game more realistic, I'm just aiming for a fun arcade style game, so realism isn't on the agenda today.

Staying on Track

Time to make our track visible and we have quite a number of different ways of creating a realistic track. We can hold a pretty decent-sized world/track for our game as one very large, or at least scaled OBJ file, but really there is a finite limit, and remember we only really want to display the bits we see, if we have a large complex OBJ there's going to be a lot of vertices in that OBJ that at any given time are going to be processed but never rendered. Quite a waste. So, we can take a bit of time to use some ingenuity in creating our world so that it can be much larger than the area we want to display and prevent ourselves from trying to display things that are not there.

If, rather than having one large playfield, we have a selection of smaller playfields, we can use them in the same way as tiles, and have a simple array that represents which tile we draw.

Yes it's exactly the same process we used in the 2D games! Make our *map* out of sections of OBJ, which are also allowed to repeat, and chop the playfield; in this case, a terrain down into smaller chunks. This allows us to cull/not draw, some of those tiles before rendering to reduce the amount of calls to the GPU. The size of tiles is up to us, but certainly we know that we can create a nice selection of worlds from even a few basic tiles properly arranged in an array.

As this is a racing game, we need a set of tiles based on that theme; I've supplied the very simplest options, four corners and two straights. That's enough for us to make a small oval or a range of simple maps. There are quite some number of commercial or free for personal use construction kits that use similar tiling principles, so feel free to use these ones so that you have a firm grasp of how this all works.

Putting together a simple track is very easy, and again I've provided a nice bit of code for you in a TrackManager Class, it's in the source and header directories, but I didn't add it to the solution, so you can do that now and create an instance of it is in Game.h then call Init to generate the track.

Take note of the track init, which also adds the terrain to the physics world, even though it's still pretty flat and we could comfortably continue to use the ground-plane concept but at the moment the track is just window dressing. We need some way to interact with it, deal with going off the track, and also know which is the right way around. That's what we will cover next. But to demonstrate that fact our track is made up of single tiles, the next image shows our car and two tiles joined together.

As with most simple things, this isn't actually ideal, at the joint of the two tiles there's a high risk of interference showing the join as the camera moves around. Though I've only seen it myself a few times, so maybe we got lucky. But there is a massive benefit in being able to create our maps our way, and allow our code, and the GPU's internal clipping to dismiss tiles not visible to our camera view.

The TileManager Class in the race demo is responsible for creating the track, first it loads and creates the six different tiles I have available, and creates and stores triangle meshes for the collision maps we're going to use shortly. It then discards the track models in turn, because its main purpose is to set up the vb and texture systems and generate a collision mesh. The ModelOBJ does not clean up its vb or Texture's on destruction, that's a task for the Model Manager when it closes down, so the OBJ shapes, along with the vb's and texture images loaded are safe and sound and usable.

As with our old 2D tiles graphics, we can then reuse the vb's shapes, materials and collision map in different models, but like the 2D Tiles we do need to create new instances of individual physicsObjects to use them at different points. From a simple grid like this

```
int TileMap[6][6] =
{
    { 0, 5, 5, 5, 5, 3 },
    { 4, 9, 9, 9, 9, 4 },
    { 4, 9, 9, 9, 0, 2 },
    { 4, 9, 9, 9, 4, 9 },
    { 4, 9, 9, 9, 4, 9 },
    { 1, 5, 5, 5, 2, 9 }
};
```

we can do our old 2D trick of parsing through a tile map, and placing tiles in space, like so.

Those old 2D skills don't die easy, do they? Sadly, I don't have a plain grass tile to put in a bit more detail, but you get the idea. I used the tile number nine to indicate a simple blank space.

Using a high god camera like this is quite inefficient as we're pushing a lot of tiles to the render system, and this does drop frames, but for sure we can consider setting some of the tiles to a "not seen, don't render" state, which will get our frame rate back.

But a better camera, better culling, and some more effective rendering will get this running at a nice 60FPS, even with a few other cars on the track. Try adding some, you have a choice of camera available to you, just create the type you want, and add a culling system into the currently inactive tile draw routines, to avoid sending unseen tiles to the GPU.

Using Bullet to Collide with the Terrain

We discussed collision maps and ray casts, a little earlier as a concept for terrain interaction, so now it's time to try using them because it's the main method Bullet uses to interact with terrains… Our racetrack tiles are still quite flat but we do have some undulation and gradients in there, which we can use to give some level of bumpiness. Especially at the red and white rumble strips around the edges of the tarmac.

I explained already how a collision map is essentially made up from a mesh of the triangles that make up a shape, ideally a simplified version of it, these can come from our art department, or we can extract them from our OBJ or other preloaded format files. Bullet Physics has some inbuilt methods of using a terrain mesh to create different internal formats of collision map, but notice I said it uses a terrain mesh, not the OBJ itself. There's too much data in an OBJ, we need to strip out quite a lot of it, all we actually need are the triangles, and that presents us with a bit of a quandary.

We use TinyObjLoader at the moment as our main OBJ file loader, and it has a pretty neat converter system, which parses through it and pulls out all the vertices, normal, colors, texture coords and shapes, which it then sends to the GPU and discards everything as it's no longer needed.

Is there some way we can keep the mesh, which is the groups of three vertices that make up the triangles, so that we can provide that to Bullet to make a terrain collision map with its btBvhTriangleMeshShape system, which is Bullet's nice way of saying we're going to make a Bullet(bt) Bounding Volume Hierarchy(BVH) Triangle...something.

Well duh, yes of course, but it will involve a bit of work, we've got two options: (1) add some extra conditional storage to the Convert functions in LoadandConvert, or (2) write a totally new extraction system. We still need to use TinyObjLoader to actually load and create the lists of vertices; we just want to avoid the nasty throwing good data away part.

Or the second option, write a new routine that only extracts the mesh and stores it in an accessible format for later use. This might be a valid option, especially if we plan at a later time to extract meshes from other formats and have different types of mesh storage.

I'll do the first, because basically its quick, and I don't really want to load the file twice if I can avoid it, even though this will all be done during initializations, loading files, especially fairly big text files is not a quick process.

I also want to use the existing LoadOBJModel system, but don't want to have to go through all my old load systems adding an extra condition parameter. So I won't, instead if you look at the ModelManager.h and cpp files, I added a pointer to an extra Collision mesh vector parameter with a default value of 0. And in the LoadAndConvert I also added that default parameter again with a value of 0.

By providing a default, it means that all the old LoadOBJModel calls passing only three parameters, still work, but are given an additional fourth parameter of null, or 0. Allowing them to continue as they always did and ignore the new parameter.

```
bool    LoadOBJModel(ObjectModel* MyModel,
                     MyFiles* FH,
                     const char* filename,
                     std::vector<btVector3>* CollisionMesh = 0); //note
                     default null
// the workhorse loader for obj
bool  LoadandConvert(std::vector<ObjectModel::DrawObject>* drawObjects,
                     std::vector<tinyobj::material_t>& materials,
                     std::map<std::string,GLuint>& textures,
                        const char* filename,
                        MyFiles* FH,
                     std::vector<btVector3>* CollisionMesh = 0);
```

Thereafter, it's a simple matter in the parsing code to locate the section where the vertices are pulled out to be stored in our vb vector, and additionally if it exists, add them to our passed Mesh vector (around line 330 in the ModelManager.cpp file.)

```
if (Mesh != 0) // if we are storing to a mesh, lets collect the vertex and
send to the supplied mesh vector.
    {
    btVector3 vert = btVector3( v[k][0], v[k][1], v[k][2]);
    Mesh->push_back(vert); /remember it's a pointer.
    }
```

This Code is already in place for you, it's just been dormant as we've not added any Object types that need to create any form of collision mesh. I stored it as btVector3 because it's eventually going to be used by the Bullet, so best to provide its format.

Adding null or harmless default parameters like this is an effective way to build on older code, when you have a lot of systems already calling these functions, but you need to add conditional extra functionality, it can save a lot of rewriting. Any new object type can now load its vbs as before but also keep a Mesh vector to use as it wants, the old objects can just load their vbs and let the mesh vanish.

Now that we have access to a mesh, we can send it to Bullet and ask it very nicely to make a btBvhTriangleMeshShape or other shape and add it to the physics world. Our TrackTile Class can now use this enhanced system and once created and added, switching on the wireframe will show you that the track itself is now also part of the physics world. Our ride is considerably bumpier and overall we are getting a sense of being in a proper physical environment.

The Code to make a terrain tile physical is not exactly direct, though we can extract the mesh now, it's not in a format that Bullet understands, so a bit of translation to its format allows it to be used, like so.

```
// make a tracktile (in the init sections) TrackTilemakes a collision mesh
    TrackTile* Tile = new TrackTile(&this->Handler, (char*)"../Resources/
Models/track_90_01.obj", &this->MainModelManager);
    scale = glm::vec3(0.012f); / it's a big tile
    Tile->TheModelManager->GetBoundingBoxes(Tile);
    Pos = glm::vec3(-6 + (0 * sizeofXTile), 0, -0.0f);
    Tile->SetPosition(Pos);

>>>> These are the interesting physics parts that turn our mesh into a
bullet mesh.

    btTriangleMesh* triangleMeshTerrain = new btTriangleMesh(); // fresh
and new
    for(int i = 0 ; i < Tile->CollisionMesh.size() ; i+=3)
    { // load it up with the vertices from our load systems
        triangleMeshTerrain->addTriangle(Tile->CollisionMesh[i], Tile-
    >CollisionMesh[i + 1], Tile->CollisionMesh[i + 2]);
    }
>>>>This is the cool bit we can now use that mesh.
Tile->MyPhysObj = CreatePhysicsObj(
        new btBvhTriangleMeshShape(triangleMeshTerrain, false), // send
that bad boy to Bullet
        0, // mass
        btVector3(Pos.x, Pos.y, Pos.z) / position}
        );
// don't forget to deal with the scale
        Tile->MyPhysObj->GetRigidBody()->getCollisionShape()->setLocalSc
aling(btVector3(scale.x, scale.y, scale.z));
        Tile->CollisionMesh.clear(); // were done with this now so kill it.
```

In the image, we can see that the tile now has a wire frame collision map associated with it, it's now part of the physics world, and those little gradients and undulations become part of the physics process. It will get much more useful with meshes with clearer undulations but this is a good start.

The TileManager creates our six dummy tiles to generate the vbs and shapes, but it also creates six collision meshes, we are allowed to reuse the mesh in multiple instances of a PhysObj because each PhysObj has its own coord and orientation systems to it that can translate a mesh to reposition it. The same tile graphic, but a different instance with its own position and other data, can therefore use the same collision mesh, saving quite a bit of memory, here is a part with its wireframe for the collision map, you can see repeated tiles on the straights sharing the same mesh, but at different positions.

Can't Find My Way Home?

Let's talk about moving around, and how to work out if we're on the road or on the grass, it's not as easy as the old attribute system for 2D tiles, but it's not so different. Let's introduce a flow field! A flow field is a really nice and simple idea, quite similar to the idea of tiles that create images that we can see as distinct patterns, but rather than images, the tiles indicate the direction of travel. They are especially useful for a game that has a lot of objects moving along a known track. Tower defense games and race tracks are prime contenders because your AI is going to go in a known direction without any real need to change direction, so no sense in using up CPU time with expensive pathfinding.

Look at the next image, it's quite close to the track we have, it's pretty clear this is a race track, it's pretty clear that we can create graphics that will represent the different sections of straight and curved graphics that will make it up! It's also clear that we have a lot of tiles that represent movement in one direction, but what about those blank squares in the middle?

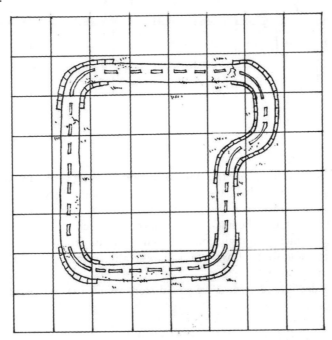

If we divide the space that our tiles occupy up into a grid, we can see that some squares have track and some don't. Now we've used this principle to have tiles represent graphics, and can do this here, both in 2D and in 3D...but suppose we now use the tiles to indicate arrows of direction. If we had a lot of graphics that indicated direction, rather than the track display it might look a little bit like this.

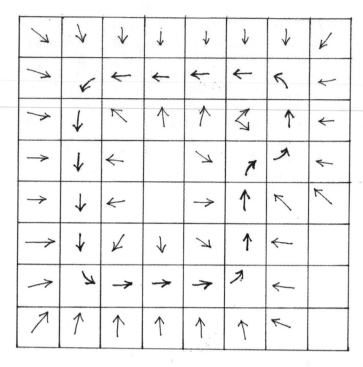

Here, we can see quite clearly that the track direction is going around and around in circles. And the squares that didn't have a piece of track are pointing to the track itself, so that if a car was on that track area, and we cross-reference this direction grid, we could tell which way to go to get onto the track. We can have any direction we want, we can even have a couple of attributes that might indicate a choice of direction as indicated by the double-headed arrow, and we can leave some squares blank, which might indicate a desire to stop or create a no-go area.

Of course, we don't store arrows; we would store values that represent the arrows like this:

```
enum { Up, Upleft, Left, Downleft, Down, DownRight, Right, UpRight, Line };
```

That gives us eight possible direction and a means to tell if we crossed the line, and our direction map is simply going to be a 2D array with these, and maybe some other values that give us indicators where to move. I say indicators, because we also have to take into account that fact our cars are moving, and will have inertia, so the directions in the grid are telling us where to move to, not giving absolute values.

Our track is effectively telling us the direction we need to move to stay on the track and the direction we need to go to if we come off the track. It's a neat system.

Flow fields are one of my personal favorite methods for autonomously moving things around, because they are usually preproduced or sometimes precalculated during initialization, and provide a very simple and easy to understand method for getting from one place to another.

Essentially, a flow field is a series of signposts, where directions, in the form of hints or absolutes are giving to point a character in the direction it's supposed to head.

That way if circumstances push an object off its path, it will have a pretty sure way of finding a way back onto the track/path it was supposed to be on.

It's ideal for track racing, because you really don't race your cars in the space between the track, but also has uses in games with large numbers of characters in motion where a traditional path finder might take too much time, all a character has to do is look under its feet and a direction of travel is clear and direct.

You can begin to see the concept visually. The car in this case, needs to keep traveling in one direction, if it veers off because of skids or bumps, it can easily find its way back by looking at the flow-field map at its current position, which will immediately tell it in what direction it has to turn to get back on track.

It's not especially hard for us to pinpoint which cell in a grid we are looking at and find the correct motion to head back, we know the tile size, in units at least, and there is a direct-scaled correlation between the flow map and the track tile map. So, we can get hold of a lot of good directional info very easily. For AI, this can provide a steering force, for a player we could put up an arrow to indicate the direction to get back to the track, or a barrier to prevent us going off the track, though usually the installation of actual barriers that are given physical properties would be a better way to stop our wandering and give something a bit more exciting to crash into.

The final step in the Racetrack demo only needs some very simple logic to make use of our flow field and also to try not to get too ahead of our player if leading, to give him a chance to catch up. This can be refined quite some amount by adding skill levels to the AI player to prevent skidding and losing speed, or by simply adding speed limits, which are a little below what we allow the player, but expecting the player to abuse and misuse all this horsepower and not drive a clean line around the track, so the AI will benefit from the players' errors.

Overall, the use of physics for motion and collision, a flow map for control and some very simple response-based AI will give us a very simple and manageable race game. Additional features such as a nice spectator stand and other track furniture would make this really pop out. Such things are available on most of the race construction kits out there. In addition, better animated models with separate components to allow you to spin wheels, and visualize steering that would bring a sense of realism to the whole thing. Try to find some nice models that will let you do this. Finally, sound of course, a race game without sound just isn't going to cut it, see what you can find in terms of engine samples and try to alter the frequency values to get your heart racing as you rev up.

The support site has a BasicRaceLogic to give you access to the Flowmap, and an AICar Class, you can use, all this will do is allow to create CPU-controlled players to take note of their current flow-map information and steer accordingly. It has little forward checks, to see if there are also corners ahead, and uses that information to adjust its braking. Suggestions for features are also commented on, and you can add them or other options to produce a more fun experience when you play. Ideally, you would want to use a tile-based concept for your flow tiles as well, matching them to the equivalent graphic tiles. But in this case, I've just given you a separate set of flow maps to avoid the confusing fact that up/down and left/right graphic tiles are the same tile. Just add some AICars to your init and watch them go.

▍ Other Optimizations

This has been a fun little game, and starting to look like a semiprofessional product, but it already throws up a lot of issues, frame rates dropped at times, and though Bullet's version of delta time compensated there were times when the game might have been a little jerky. All is not lost though, because from the start I've mentioned that our systems are functional, but far from optimal. We need to start being much more careful about how we do things, and also which things we do at any given time.

Now having recognized that our systems usually can't do everything we need, all the time we need them to. There are quite some number of directly usable things we can do to increase our overall performance, we can cull a lot of things in our CPU side, preventing us doing excessive collisions, or sending pointless draws or logic systems, but we could also improve some techniques for our use of our GPU, and it might be worth investing some time in explaining them. But we are really getting into the realms of tech coding if we do that.

Some are obvious and have been covered, such as reducing the resolution of our display or frame buffer, choosing when to use vertex lighting rather than per pixel lighting (maybe even no lighting). Making good use of LOD systems for both the vertex buffer and texture sizes can also make a lot of difference, Mipmapping, and so on. How much these will impact your performance will very much depend on the game you are doing. LOD will only work, for example, if you have objects you know will travel in and out of your depth view, if they largely stay in the front of your screen, there is no benefit and your depth base LOD calculations are wasted.

Our current GPU rendering is also something that needs review, I stated way back when we started using TinyObjLoader, that we were only using simple vertex arrays. There is also quite some performance to be gained by using index-based buffers, but there is a slight increase in the level of complexity needed to create them.

I will cover a few of these optimizations, but not in massive detail, and only when we really need to use them or highlight them, when we start to stress our hardware. For now, we will focus on functional rather than optimal rendering, and deal with performance issues only if they impact on the actual projects. We will start to consider adding optimizations as our next demo has increased complexity and will really benefit from more optimal systems.

Other Performance Options

Being able to dismiss things with a frustum cull is clearly a big win, but depending on the game, we may still have problems with a large number of unused/unseen but still processed triangles going to our GPU. So we need to give a bit of thought how to stop that.

Our tile concept allowed us to comfortably not draw large areas of a scene if it wasn't visible. But what if we have is an untiled terrain representing a play area as far as the far plane can see. Or an interior environment when the whole spooky mansion we are exploring is represented by a massive 500 K+ polygon mesh but we only see 4K or 5 K or polygons in front of us, and realistically we're not going to be able to push that many poly's anyway.

We've got some issues, and the reasons are simple. Our model formats are designed to allow us to easily load and create meshes, then to dump them to the GPU. They define an object or thing in our world, but as formats they are not really designed to render chosen parts of the model beyond the subshape concept. We just can't pick and choose the vertices. They give us all or nothing options and it's our GPU that decides if the vertexes we send it, are in the view space, to draw or not. Our average 45° angle of visibility has to contend with the fact that the other 315° we are not looking at are still being sent, quite some number are being processed, and clearly that's a huge waste. We don't like waste.

So we need to move away from standard formats when it comes to finding highly optimized rendering systems, which is where data structures such as BSP, Quad Tree's, BVH, and so on come back into our view; we saw how we were able to allow our collision systems to focus on the relevant objects in a given area. Partition tree systems like this can also be used to allow us to keep track of more render-friendly items, such as polygons.

There are a lot of options, which can provide different levels of detail and come at different costs in terms of memory or performance, but they basically are ways to keep the data we want to render in a format that makes it easier for us to decide what to send to the GPU, dramatically reducing the number of unseen waste when a large static mesh is being visualized.

We've already been happy to make a Quad Tree structure and use it to reduce collision tests, so what about using similar tree systems directly as the source of our rendering?

Well, hold on, first things first, do we currently need a complex rendering system? For the race and space games, and even for a bit of outdoor wandering around pillaging and plundering, the basic system is working pretty well for us. We need to give consideration to how much we actually need a partition tree and with good reason. There is a downside to them that is a direct issue for us, they generate or use very large data structures eating up a lot of memory, we have a problem with high memory usage, which will itself impose limits on how far we could go with these ideas.

As we move away from the book projects you will start to encounter situations where we do, in fact, need to take note of what they render, not just simple object-based frustum culling, but triangle/shape frustum culling, also occlusion culling...why try to render what's behind that wall right in front of us, and field of view culling?

Now sadly, going into a full discussion on this is going beyond the fundamentals of game coding and moving into more advanced concepts of data structures and rendering techniques.

I could easily spend two or three chapters discussing that, but my publisher is already sweating over the page count. So, this has to go to the support site, and maybe a later book. You are at least now aware of this issue, and can start to think about it. A good place to start is the Quake/Doom BSP rendering system. For now, focus on good design of your environments, the tile system, or even better a section system (basically, 3D tiles or chunks of playfield), improve your rendering with indexes where possible, and using your frustum culls effectively.

Our next project is going to be using a slightly more complicated environment, which will give us some issues, but we should still be able to use our standard systems to get a good result. It will, however, be very useful for you to research better options on your own.

9 Let's Go Indoors

▮ The Beginnings, Doom, and Beyond

The first 3D game I can remember playing was Wolfenstein 3D, which isn't given nearly enough credit for its role in popularizing 3D, though even it wasn't the first. But the big one, the one that finally made 3D mainstream was Doom! What a game this was and indeed still is. If you've never played it, go take a moment to locate and download it. Ignore its low-res graphics and just enjoy the majesty of being able to explore a world you can go into rather than look down on.

But what is interesting about these early games is that they were not actually 3D, they only appeared to be; in fact, these games were played totally in a 2D environment, which was made to look like 3D. A few tricks were employed to create some up and down levels but it was still all done on a 2D map, but viewed from a first person players' perspective.

They used a technique called ray casting to look ahead of the player and see what walls were in his/her field of view, by casting a ray in each of the sectional degrees of the field of view, then draw lines that made up those walls, scaled to create an illusion of depth.

My first ever attempts at 3D centered on this concept, and indeed I even managed to get it working on a fantastically underpowered original Nintendo Gameboy, albeit you had to hold it on its side, as that allowed for a consecutive memory access. I've seen this actually running on calculators and watches.

But as fun as this method was, there's really no point in detailing it here, its horribly outdated and would mean returning to our double buffer system we left behind in a 2D land.

If we are going to do indoor 3D, we need to do proper 3D, which owes its gaming DNA to the work of John Cormack and the role he played in coding the Quake series of games, which popularized the concept of using polygons in engines, developing, and enhancing the then largely unused techniques and systems to improve the basic position and display systems.

▮ Occlusion, a Discussion to Have for a Problem to Solve Later

There are a lot of issues with indoor (and sometimes outdoor) games, some of which we need to be aware of but it's going to be too tricky with our current systems to deal with but I want you to consider them.

If we are indoors and look up at the ceiling, do we ever see the Skybox? Generally no, so we could avoid wasting GPU time and not draw the skybox, but what if there's a window in the ceiling?

If we're walking through a level with doors, and the doors are closed, do we still draw the polys that make up the room behind the door? Well yes, we probably do, our GPU is sorting the polys, drawing the furthest ones first and then drawing over them with closer ones, the so-called Painters algorithm. What about the shuffling zombie hordes we can so clearly hear behind that door. Do we draw them? You know we do, if we're looking directly at them regardless of the door and its surrounding wall.

In fact, with our current render systems, we are probably going to be drawing masses of triangles that we can't see. Frustum culling can only go so far in eliminating models, groups, or component shapes in its area. But if we are indoors and using an entire model to represent our world, we indeed are going to send every single polygon to our GPU and let it ignore the ones outside the view, but draw the ones we can't see which are obscured by the ones we can see.

Our very simple render systems rely on buffer-based drawing, using an, "it's in a visual range, draw it, let it be overdrawn by something closer," mentality. We don't really have any way to prevent a buffer in a VB from doing its all or nothing draws, but we can make some decisions on data we build CPU buffers for. It is possible for us to calculate only the foreground polys and send those selected polygons to the GPU by building buffers, which only keep the polys directly in our view.

Occlusion culling, basically, relies on us making important decisions about drawing things we know we cannot see, in the same way as frustum culling, but this time using line of sight-based system, rather than the outside of our box methods.

There are multiple methods of occlusion culling, and different levels of complexity we can work with and a whole range of problems that real-world situations give us. How do we deal with a transparent polygon? What if we have a half height wall and can see over it, or maybe wooden oak beams where we can see over and under but not through?

Render systems can be optimized by quite massive margins by working out only the polygons you want to draw and avoiding sending things behind things. We've touched on that with our partition-tree storage methods, but when using standard models and meshes, we need a more viable real-time method. But, and it's a big but, there's a cost to that, in a scene with many 10s of 1000s of polygons but only 100 or so to draw, we still have to check all of them to work out which 100 we want. Balance as always, between the time it takes against the gain we make is vital.

The simplest solution is to use data systems such as partition trees, if that's not possible try to maintain manageable-sized meshes, which are not going to have endless numbers of unseen polys. Accept that there is a certain percentage of them will be unseen, even quite a high percentage, and do your best to ensure that unseen dynamic objects are not draw if not seen. Frustum culls will remove the majority of your dynamic objects, those still in *view* can be tested with simple ray casts from their edges to your view point should allow you to tell if you have a wall or other obscuring object in the way.

Keep the sections of your world modular, and switch between them, as we did with the race tiles. Remember that all culling is about doing a small test to get a big gain, try to do that at all times.

Sadly, I just don't have a big enough environment model to really get you to work on improved rendering systems using occlusion-based rendering, and if I did, I probably would make it into a BSP or similar system. So you're really not likely to get to a point where there is such fun but technical things as occlusion-based rendering are needed. Perhaps that's wise because you should not really have such large scenes in a machine with this level of power. However, we'll do our best to test and occlude our dynamic objects and keep our FPS up to the standard needed.

Let's get on to using a map where we can practice a little of our occlusion concepts on a model rather than per poly basis.

▮ Exploring the Maze

Ok, it's not the most exciting game concept ever, but I have limited resources and I just want to show you stuff that you can go away and do better. We're going to move into the first person view point now, with occasional third and god modes, and explore an environment that has a lot of walls. I could also have ceilings but I wanted to keep a god view to let you change your camera view to visualize the play area. This will help us to see how our characters are moving around and making good or bad choices.

Download and compile the demo, 3DMazehunt. It's more complete than our other projects because we really don't need too much handholding now. We will add some extra features though. Our primary interest here is discussing what we can do to make our render and movement systems better and for our AI, such as it is, to be more aware of how to behave when there are obstacles in the way. Clearly the model works, we can move around, and our frame rate is fine, even with god camera mode forcing our GPU to draw all the triangles of the OBJ, we can do it pretty well. It's really quite a low poly maze.

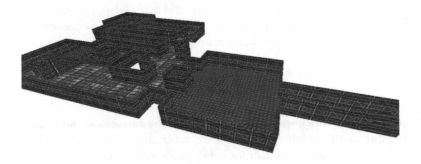

Thanks to my student Channing Eggers for this, he knocked it up as part of his first year Raspberry assignment, and I asked if I could use it for this demo. In parts of his map, there are a lot of walls, and when we are in the enclosed spaces we know we are going to draw characters behind the walls in front of us, so it's a good example to use for attempting some first-generation sneaking around using rays to detect walls and practicing occlusion with frustum and line of sight occlusion ideas.

Take a moment to notice the way I move the Player and by extension other objects around. I am not using forces or impulses and indeed I'm overriding most of the main motion systems by resetting angular velocities to 0. Why would I do that?

It's to do with the nature and expectation of the game, and also some convenience. It's quite viable to move players and objects around in this 3D maze by supplying a force-based movement, and if we balance everything well it will work nicely and feel very realistic, but we're not trying to emulate a real-world environment, there's nothing remotely real world about a first person shooter, and that balancing can take quite some time to get right.

We need more direct control of our motion, so rather than applying torque or direction impulses, I am actually adding ± angles to a models' orientation to change it. I'm also applying forward linear speed, not force, to move him forward and back. That gives me a more immediate sense of movement and control in a game like this while still allowing friction to stop me and collision detection to prevent me moving through walls, though not, because of the override, providing any nice bounce off the walls. It's a small price to pay, or I could even create my own bounce off using a collision-response system.

Bullet still provides us with Gravity, because that's pretty useful for controlling jumps and falls, the collision, of course, is still very useful, and even without force-based movement it gives us speed/movement and orientation control. Other benefits include the rather useful btRay cast systems we can use for shooting detection and line of sight tests. These features really do help us and keep the use of an expensive physics engine relevant and useful to us. We can still have normal physics-based crates and things in the game if we find a need. But players and enemies need simpler motion systems.

Set up the FPS camera, which will replace the god camera and create a Game init loop to instantiate all the objects you will find in the Enemies.h file. It's a simple array structure, so you should be able to follow it ok.

There are two very simple Enemy Classes, for (1) a PatrolBaddie and (2) a StaticBaddie, they do very little at the moment beyond animate and acknowledge when you are in their sphere of interest. You can add more content, or better yet create new classes derived from these two basic types. Feel free to make them do some patrolling, there's some coordinates available for you in the Enemies.h file.

Why not add a SkyBox? After all there's no ceiling, and then maybe a McGuffin of some kind you have to pick up and run back to a base point with? No? Oh well, I'll do that on the support site.

Ok good, so this works, we can wander around, we can attack and be attacked. It's all working fine. But we might be finding that our frame rate is dropping quite alarmingly because of the number of baddies being processed. In fact, it's not the processing that's causing us hassle but the drawing, even with a frustum cull, we have quite some number of reasonably detailed characters to draw that we don't always see, a good example of occlusion issues, but we'll talk about that soon, first let's get these characters doing their things.

Moving the Baddies Around, Things!

In some ways, moving isn't so different from the 2D versions we had already mastered. In a level-based game where you are on a open ground, you simply need to work out where the X and Z points you want to go to are, and home in on them the same way we did with the 2D sprites. Using normalized vectors to step to it, or to provide a direction of force or velocity to apply. Getting from A to B across a terrain is pretty simple, just ignore the extra dimension!

Sadly, an indoor area isn't so easy to get from A to B; there are walls and corners, maybe stairs. These are not easy things to negotiate; in fact, they can be a pain to even detect. Fortunately, Bullet takes care of detection for us, and in doing so gives us an easy way to determine that we have line of sight on the point we want to get to with its ray systems.

Our ability to move around, especially using AI, has become a little more complex, sure we can let the physics control our collision with these walls and stairs, but that's not exactly going to impress our player when he sees the baddies pummeling themselves off the closest wall over and over again as they try to get to the spot on the other side.

What's needed is a means to either limit their travel, the simple solution, by giving them predefined bounding areas. Or if we do want them to move away from points, give them the logic to hunt you, or to move to another place.

Flow maps won't work here because flow maps assume a fixed direction and purpose of travel. It we want to set up patrols going around our area, they will work fine, but if we want to go from an arbitrary point A to arbitrary point B, because of a condition that gets triggered in the game (for example, you trip an alarm), the best the flow map will do is similar to a travelator, get on and wait till your stop comes up. Too bad if you got on one stop after the point you want to go to and you're going to go the long way around.

This is a complex problem, but we've done lots of simple solutions before, with good reason, so let's try to also find simple solutions here. Basically, we need some kind of pathfinding. If an enemy decides to go and hunt you, or travel, he needs to be able to move from point A to point B, regardless of walls, then maybe C, D, and infinity and beyond.

So pathfinding…that's a fun topic, one of the stalwarts of AI, and it's a kind of catching all term for several methods of finding your way around. Whenever I ask my Dutch University students about pathfinding they usually respond. "A*", maybe a few will know Dykstra, because he was Dutch. But while these are well-established and useful systems, there's more to it than that.

The basic idea of a pathfinder is interesting, essentially what you want to do is find the shortest way from A to B, negotiating around any walls, swamps, fire pits, dog poo, and deep impassable trenches that are in the way. For most of us in the real world, that's pretty easy, we use our primary sense of sight, we look around, take stock of the area, map it out in our brain, and its turn to the general direction we want to move to and head for it, cleverly and nimbly avoiding the fire pits and going around the swaps, leaping over the trenches, though sometimes forgetting about the dog poo!

Easy right? Ok now do it blindfolded after being kidnapped, drugged, driven through the night, and dropped into a strange house without even being offered a cup of tea to welcome you! Suddenly it's not so easy, is it?

This is the problem our computer has to deal with, it has no vision, our code can only deduce it wants to go… thataway…in a direction suggested by the some other factor in the code, and head thataway, through mountains of dog poop, swamps, and fire pits before mercifully lurching into a bottomless pit!

Well, if we can't *see* our way around, what else is open to us? We have other senses and so does our computer, kinda!

The way our brain maps out a possible route from our start position is the key to making a pathfinder work. Whatever happens we'll have a start point, and with sight we have the ability to see points ahead of us that should lead to where we want to go, but without it, we need to feel our way around, I'm deeply regretting the dog poo idea now.

But feeling around is as good a method as any for a computer. It just needs to know what to *feel* for. The method of building our brain map is far less important than the fact we actually are producing a brain map. It really does not matter if we see, feel, smell, touch, or taste…yeah! let's take the dog poo out; our way around, so long as we can build up some kind of mental map of our surroundings, and with that work out how to get to where we want to go.

The points we are looking for represent different things, maybe restart points, a safe point from the start point to *here*, where we know we can feel ahead and not bump into anything. Every point that gets us closer to our goal becomes a new safe point to be remembered.

What these points are is debatable and dependant on the game, but essentially it's a signpost. It can tell you either the location of the next safe signpost, or more usefully, the direction of the next signpost on the way to where you want to go to?

But, of course, there's no way for the signpost to know where you want to go to…unless you have cleverly placed on in your map somehow, maybe before you started the game, or when the game fired up, part of its initialization was to work out all the paths from one signpost to another and loaded the signposts with info on where the next one to go to was.

We use signposts all the time, go to any city center and you will see signposts directing you to where you want to go to, but consider that whoever put those signposts there had to know which way the signposts had to point.

The more proper term for these signposts is nodes. A node is an odd concept but it's basically a data structure that maintains a link with other data structures, allowing you to traverse from one to the next. Nodes are a common feature in a lot of coding tools but especially for AI and pathfinding.

Once we have a signpost telling where we have to go in *thataway* direction to get the next signpost, we can move thataway and when we do get to the next signpost, it will then tell us to head ThatNewWay, to take us the path we want to go to! We most likely will use a vector 3 to indicate the points to travel to, but we probably are going to ignore the y component, even if our target is upstairs, all you need to have is a sign at the top and bottom of the stairs, pointing to each other, the movement systems will take care of the rest.

It's a simple system, mainly because it relies on us to fill in the directions manually, using our good old Mark1 eyeball and brain. It would, however, be very cool if you could get the computer to fill it in on Game init, try doing a bit of research on pathfinding methods to work out how to do this, or indeed put in a better system?

Our signposts, though usually invisible, are really nothing more than a list of pointers to other nodes. They have a little bit of logic, which looks around the currently active objects to see who's there. If it finds an enemy, it implants its address in the enemies' closest signpost stored value. And the enemy is then able to move to that signpost knowing that moving in that direction, once there it's free to head to its target node. I've made the signposts in the 3DMazehunt visible, so you can see the connection to them. But they have no physical properties, so it can't be collided with. When you have a place to go to from here to the signpost, you have a standard A to B system just like we had in 2D.

Standard A to B systems might not be effective though if, for example, there is a wall in the way, the signpost concept might well allow us to put a signpost at every possible junction but really its better if we try to put them at key points and allow our AI to have a little bit of simple logic.

That's where our ray cast concepts come in useful, if we know we want to get from point A to point B, we can have a look to see if there is a clear path by simply casting a ray toward our target. If the path is clear, we move directly to it in a straight line, if not, if a wall is in the way, for example, we can make decisions to move in the general direction and use ray's ahead and to the side of us, to find corridors that will allow the player to move closer to a point where a free path is available. A scattering of sign posts will provide ways to update our target direction and that should allow us to move around reasonably well.

That will deal with the general direction of our motion, but we still need to try to avoid bumping into things. Lots of enemies rushing from point to point mean lots of characters getting in our way and sometime walls that need a swift change of direction. Of course, we need to be careful where we place the signs. They ideally need to create a clear line of sight matrix, so that you can be sure of moving along a free space from one to another, but as I said, we don't want to drown the map in signposts.

Avoiding bumping into other enemies is best done with other systems, I quite like using proximity boxes or antenna rays (see the next image), which test the areas immediately in front of us, and if it finds another moving character, both obey aviation law and move to the left, to avoid collisions. Or is it right? Actually, as long as they both do the same, it's fine. Equally, such systems can be used to *see* how close we are to a wall by checking to the relevant left and right, if they find a wall or other obstacle, they either stop or deflect us away. All of which mimics how a fairly well-ordered colony of ants might negotiate around a maze.

The screenshot in the above image shows the antenna ray in front looking for an object to avoid and the ray to the right test finding a wall to avoid. We could add any number of such antennas searching ahead and around to make decisions based on contact with things about to hit us but generally ahead and to the side will give us enough info on what our character can *see*.

Of course, it's not a perfect system, but actually that's part of its joy, if enemies are running too fast, their change in direction is not going to be smooth/quick enough sometimes, and they will bump into walls and each other, just like you see in every blooper show on TV show with that Storm Trooper hitting his head!

Review the MoveToPoint(x, y, z) code in the provided EnemyLogic Class, you can now add to the project. This will give you methods to move your enemy characters around to move around and also detect your presence and respond to alerts in a simple way. As always, feel free to add new behaviors.

You'll find a *finished* but unoptimized version of 3DMazeHunt on the support site, where I have made everything work for you, don't cut and paste! Try to write your own versions, and then compare it with mine. If you must cut and paste, try to find some better ways to achieve what I did, there are several.

What Do We Draw?

Accepting for now, that we have to draw the entire maze, because we don't have a decent render method that would make it better (you can research a few though). We need to focus our efforts on the enemies and other details that we've placed in the world.

This is where we get to our model occlusion. Using Bullet every model has an AABB bounding volume we can access, using Bullets inbuilt function.

```
MyPhysObj->GetRigidBody()->getAabb(aabbMin, aabbMax);
```

which gives us two possible corner points, which we can extrapolate to a full eight for the cube, we can use these to cast a btRay to each corner from our camera view, if any of these rays goes from the eye point to the corner without hitting a wall we can see it, or at least be very close to seeing it, as the AABB is often larger than the model. But if all eight are obscured by a wall, we can't. Eight (though we could actually reduce that to four) simple tests could save us from sending a model to the GPU and the associated time is gained.

It is sometimes valid to allow a model to hide another model behind it, but usually our models do have a lot of empty space, which we can be seen through. Basic occlusion systems work on bounding volumes, which regard that empty space as a valid area of occlusion, so it's probably best to focus only on avoiding a draw on an object obscured by an environmental feature.

I've added an unoptimized occlusion test method to the ObjectModel Class, it returns a simple bool for true, it's visible, or false, it's behind a wall, for you to try it out, it's totally self-contained, all you need to do is add it to your draw systems, and if the draw is not needed abort the draw.

Your fun task now is to optimize that method and get it even faster and, of course, if you don't want to use Bullet you need to use a different ray cast and have a different way to access the bounding volume.

One small point I should make you aware of as is, it caught me out when I was writing it. In an FPS the camera is located at the models head, and because our player character is himself a physical object, even if not rendered, he is also detectable by a ray-cast system, and it is therefore entirely possible that the ray test can return him as the resultant hit of a ray cast. This makes sense when you think about it, we are encased in a collision shell, and firing a ray from inside that shell we will always hit the inside of it. But because all collision tests are done as pairs, and dynamically sorted with some small elements of unpredictability, it may be that sometimes you get the wall and sometimes you get the player, such random returns can play havoc with your logic. So take care when using ray casts from objects not to start the ray from inside the collision container. I add an offset slightly larger than the radius of the character multiplied by a normalized direction to avoid that. If your camera is not a physical object, you won't need that normally or you must take care to ignore any ray-cast result that returns your player.

Whats the Point?

Oh yeah! we don't really have a game here, do we? Just a couple of things to demonstrate some points. Well add a game! That's what you're reading this book for, isn't it?

I've made the baddies shoot at you if they see you, and you can kill them, if you installed the signposts correctly then they can move around pretty independently to whichever position you are, and you can change your camera views to allow you to get an idea of what the enemies are doing. That's a pretty decent set of basic abilities, and, of course, you can add more.

Try making a stealth game where instead of shooting them automatically, you need to avoid being seen by patrolling guards. If you are spotted, the guard radios in and surrounding guards will stream to that location. If you can destroy the reporting guards before the reinforcements arrive, you have a chance to remain stealthy again, and the guards will return to their patrol paths.

Your ultimate aim is a simple capture a flag at the end of the level, and makes it out alive. You might even want to add an option of a hunt and destroy if you do manage to get the flag, forcing you to fight your way out.

You've got all the means you need to do this, I'll post my version on the site, and you can compare. Do yours first though, no peeking!

Ray Cast and Picking

From time to time in a game we will need to use our mouse as a controller for our viewpoint or as a controller to access objects in our game, also perhaps to access icons on a 2D GUI.

How and when we switch the method of control is entirely up to the design of the game, but we will need to know how to use it in its different modes. Selecting 3D objects in our 3D world using a 2D pointer presents some fun problems.

Our mouse obviously works on a 2D screen, it only has X and Y coordinates, and the Z is probably going to remain at 0 or near that. But our objects are living in a 3D world, and only appear to be 2D on our screen. To pick a 3D object we need somehow to get our mouse to go inside the world and *pick* the object/item we are interested in.

Obviously, we can't put our mouse into the screen, so we need somehow to work out what is we are looking at with our eye, and pointing at with our mouse. Which gives us a clue!

If we draw a line from our eye viewpoint to the pointer on screen, we are effectively creating a line, or as we more accurately now call it, a ray. A ray is a vector...and we know a few things about vectors. For one, they can be of any length but still point in the same direction. Normally, we've shrunk vectors to make them unit size. But what happens if we extend the line from our viewpoint, to the mouse pointer, into the screen...we get something like this.

We get a line going from our eye to the mouse pointer into the screen. But how does that help us? Well the screen is effectively our near plane of our camera, and our eye, for all intents and purposes is the start of the view frustum, so we can trace our point of visual origin back to get a line from our eye, to the xy point and then using the projection of our camera send a ray off in that direction in space. Yes its maths again…hold on, it's not too bumpy! Once we have the ray we know there are nice equations that we can use, to test if an object that we have been surrounded with a sphere for collision purposes has been intersected by that ray.

So if we do a quick scan through all our known objects in the scene, nonvisible ones culled preferably. Do a picking ray test, we can tell which objects the ray is interacting way. I say objects plural, of course, because it's a ray and will keep going forever but we can use the far plane as a limit. It may intersect a couple of objects, so we'll just focus on the closet to us on the valid assumption that we're clicking on the one with the highest draw priority. Using one of the rather nice Ray->Shapetype systems available to us, we can tell if we have a hit. If we're using Bullet-based objects they are already encased in their collision shapes, if not we should at least enclose them in spheres.

Lucky for us, we are using Bullet physics, which we know has its own ray-cast code, though it does not have a specific pick method, we have to supply our own.

You should decide from the start if you are going to use a Bullet-based ray cast or write your own. As I plan to use Bullet in all 3D demos in some form it's probably best to demonstrate a Bullet version. We've already used a simple glm ray cast for our Death Rays; the process is exactly the same.

The process is simple though there are two clear steps:

Step 1: Create the directional Picking ray, this uses <jazz hands> Maths, but basically takes the x and y coordinates of our mouse, jiggles it about a bit with the camera view and projection and produces a ray as a vector3. This is where having access to the camera's variable data finally becomes useful; I hope you added access systems? For now, I will just grab them from the camera itself.

Step 2: Cast the ray, using the internal Bullet systems, which returns the RigidBody and other info IF there's a hit.

I won't detail the maths; the code is in the Rays Class in the next RayPick demo for you to look at. All we need to know is we now have a very nice Pick function, which if we have a mouse in use will tell us what we are clicking on and allow our code to take whatever action is needed for that.

Are We Going to Do Any AI?

Oh Heyaall No!! AI is another of those massive topics where I'd have to write another 20-chapter book on this subject. But I have given you a lot of basics in practical use, such as point to point, homing, state management system, steering systems, linked nodes, stealth, triggered and determined responses, and randomness as triggers and seeds, and a few other things that were specific to the games we produced.

AI is such a big subject because it tries very hard to be generic, which is probably impossible. Every game has its own little needs, and while we can recognize some of the similarities, we need to tweak things to suit the situation we are in. All the games we've done actually feature some elements of *AI* and you are free to expand or replace those elements.

A great many AI concepts are also available in various forms as libs or as simple cut and paste solutions to issues, A* Pathfinding is a great example of a heuristic solution, which people have produced multiple very impressive versions, which will work better in some circumstances than in others, but there are significant issues over how you define the nodes it needs to operate.

The final versions of the demos on the support site will include a few concepts that can be considered as AI, and I'll try to post some articles and create discussion groups on-site, on methods to demonstrate different AI concepts in the games that need them.

If you really want to get into AI, and I suggest you do, my old friend Mat Buckland wrote a couple of the best introductions to AI you can find, and he needed 500 pages or so to do it. Check out his website, http://www.ai-junkie.com/ and find links to his books and where to buy them and links to some very useful and relevant tutorials and discussions.

10 Graphics Need a Boost

■ That Cat's Been in the Bag Long Enough

We've pretty much got basic concepts of different types of game up and running, but our graphics are still a little on the lighter side; ideally, we want to delve deeper in the technical side of graphics programming, but that's a lot of maths to get your head around, and again a 20 chapter book, most of which isn't really going to be a lot of use on our itty bitty dual core GPUs. But one big graphic boost you can add and probably get away with is shadows. I hope you remember we put them in a bag for later, well now it's time!

I mentioned before about shadows and their reliance on Shaders, which we were just beginning with, so it was a bit of a complex topic to get our heads around at the start of our Shader journey. We should now be comfortable enough with Shaders to start doing some complex stuff. We now have suitable models and terrains, which will be able to demonstrate them properly, so now is the right time for shadows, this topic is a bit technical though, despite being a fairly simple premise, shadows are hard on OpenGLES2.0. I used to use a variation on an approach I used in a full fat OpenGL, but since playing with SBCs and OpenGLES2.0, I found I was jumping through hoops a bit too much and had to simplify things, I've since found some easier methods that seem to work pretty well. There are a couple of other methods and more being discovered but let's stick to something we know works and which there are plenty of examples of use in games.

Before we start though, you need to know why I've left it this long to discuss, it's simple, shadows will kill your frame rate, because we're going to have to run two passes of our graphics through the GPU, there's just no getting away from that, it's a computationally expensive process on even the best GPUs, our little twin and quad cores GPUs might be able to run the code, but you have to consider this feature only when you really need it and not in a game with dozens of shadow-casting objects. You can develop tricks and methods to improve performance, and that's definitely something you need to do, but any form of shadow other than a prebaked built-in model shadow, is going to kill performance.

All that said, let's try out the most useful system and get it working, the Raspberry 3B might struggle with this, but perhaps by the time you read this the Raspberry 7 will be more than capable.

■ Shadow Mapping

I think I'm right in saying that Shadow mapping is one of the best of the current methods used for creating dynamic shadows. They have been around a few years now and work pretty well. But like all shadow systems, they do come at a bit of a cost, as they are a result of a multiple passes through our GPU to set up buffers, which will *render* a scene from the light's point of view rather than the camera. Rather than render pixels, it will store depths from the point where the light is placed to the point of the pixel being lit. The resulting framebuffer will contain depth information on the pixels the *light-positioned camera* draws, but only as a distance from the light source.

Think of it as a light directly overhead a model of a character holding an umbrella we want to render, the light is shining down on the umbrella, which clearly gets lit but stops the light at that point, everything under the umbrella will be in shade and lit only by the ambient light in the scene. So that means we have a concept of height, where the umbrella is! Anything we draw under that level is darker. Changing the angle of the light does not make a massive difference, remember matrices allow us to twist and turn points and directions in space, which is all a light is from our viewpoint, the distance the light travels until it hits an obstacle, can be comfortably worked out and then used to decide if pixels on the same line of light are in front of or behind the shape absorbing the light. Rain and umbrellas work the same way really.

That, in effect, means we have access to a concept of things that the light hits and how deep into the draw plane it was hit…which we can twist around into a value of above and below things that light is going to hit. Things above the barrier can be drawn as lit normally, things below can be in shade or totally dark as we decide.

Okay, that, kinda sounds simple doing the calculations might be fairly trivial but there's a lot of them and they need to be easy to access.

This is where we need the power of our GPU and its Shaders. OpenGLES2.0 has so far been perfectly happy calculating and drawing our RGBA pixels into a big render target buffer, which then becomes the screen.

It also can create other types of buffer not directly related to color info, especially… drum roll please. A depth buffer! Which not surprisingly can hold info on how far from a point of interest in our 3D space is…something interesting such as a light, for example.

Yup, OpenGLES2.0 already has all the main tools we need to do shadows, but we still need to get the Shaders up and running and we do have to do two draw calls to our GPU: one to create the depth buffer, and one to create the actual image, which uses that depth buffer.

Unfortunately, OpenGLES2.0s means of accessing depth buffers during the pixel render is a little tricky. Unlike full-fat OpenGL where we can have multiple render targets, one to contain depth values, one to contain pixels, and so on, on OpenGLES2.0 we can only have one. So, the render target buffer we would put the depth values into is the same render target buffer we would write our pixels to, and they'd get kinda lost as one overwrites the other. Tricky.

But where there's a will there's a way. Since we can't write to our render targets, we have to work out what we can write to. Of course, it's a type of buffer, and we have options to use.

Depth textures would be my preference because there are some cool and cheap ways to draw to a texture and use extensions to produce depth values, and in an ideal world I'd be happy to use those, but extensions are not guaranteed on all machines, so if you are planning to release your projects to the community, you have to allow for the fact not all GPU's support the same extensions, so we'd need a fall back, so I'll do this first using a fall back position and later you can try to use the GL_OES_depth32 or GL_OES_depth24 extensions, though I must say I think all the units I tested had this, it's still a good practice not to assume. But you do get a bit of a speed boost if you define your texture type that way.

The fall-back position is to use normal textures generated from a Frame Buffer object, this will be universal in all implementations of OpenGLES2.0. But first let's explain the basic technique.

The process involves doing a pass through the scene to calculate the distance between the source of the light rays and the points where they hit objects in the scene, if you have more than one light, you have to do a pass for every light, and so multiple lights will cause a slowdown. However, these Light Passes are computationally quite simple, so tend to be much faster than a standard Render pass.

Once all the depth data has been collected, it's time to do the normal render call, which tests if the pixels being drawn are in shadow or not, if they are, then some calculations need to be done to work out the amount of shade the pixel has to represent. As you can imagine, this gets a bit more complex if there are more lights in the scene as some shadows will be canceled by some lights. I don't even want to think about that just yet, but we can play with that later.

Since each pass is doing different things, collecting data, and then finally drawing images, clearly we need two sets of Shaders designed to produce the results we want.

Framebuffer Objects are things we can make textures out of, we can't sadly transfer them directly to the screen, but having a texture at least gives us access to it in the Shaders. Shaders love using textures.

First, we have to make the concept of an actual texture, the usual way, but careful to define it in full just in case previous values from other textures are still active.

```
glGenTextures(1, &Texture);
glActiveTexture(GL_TEXTURE0);
glBindTexture(GL_TEXTURE_2D,Texture);
glTexImage2D(GL_TEXTURE_2D, 0, GL_RGBA, Width, Height, 0, GL_RGBA,
GL_UNSIGNED_BYTE, NULL);
glTexParameteri(GL_TEXTURE_2D, GL_TEXTURE_WRAP_S, GL_CLAMP_TO_EDGE);
glTexParameteri(GL_TEXTURE_2D, GL_TEXTURE_WRAP_T, GL_CLAMP_TO_EDGE);
glTexParameteri(GL_TEXTURE_2D, GL_TEXTURE_MIN_FILTER, GL_LINEAR);
glTexParameteri(GL_TEXTURE_2D, GL_TEXTURE_MAG_FILTER, GL_LINEAR);
```

Width and height being the size of the screen (resolution, not display), but everything else is pretty much the normal system, what happens next is cool though, we now create a framebuffer:

```
glGenFramebuffers(1, &FBO); / allocate a Framebuffer
glGenRenderbuffers(1, &RenderBuffer); / allocate a render buffer
glBindRenderbuffer(GL_RENDERBUFFER, RenderBuffer); / bind it
glRenderbufferStorage(GL_RENDERBUFFER, GL_DEPTH_COMPONENT16, theWidth,
theHeight); /give some parameters for it
glBindTexture(GL_TEXTURE_2D, NameTexture); / bind the texture
glBindFramebuffer(GL_FRAMEBUFFER, FBO); / and the frame buffer

glFramebufferRenderbuffer(GL_FRAMEBUFFER,GL_DEPTH_ATTACHMENT,GL_
RENDERBUFFER,RenderBuffer); / they are now attached

glFramebufferTexture2D(GL_FRAMEBUFFER, GL_COLOR_ATTACHMENT0, GL_
TEXTURE_2D, Texture, 0);/ and so is the texture that will be created
```

You might want to add a test to make sure that the FBO is properly set up, too, but it's unlikely to fail. You can use `glCheckFramebufferStatus(GL _ FRAMEBUFFER) != GL _ FRAMEBUFFER _ COMPLETE;`

Now we're set up, we have initialized a Frame Buffer and it's there for us when we need to use simply by binding it

```
glBindFramebuffer(GL_FRAMEBUFFER, FBO);
```

Our subsequent draw and renders will go to that frame buffer, which is a texture. Just remember to unbind the frame buffer after we have done with the light passes.

So, we now have to look at the Shaders we need to make those textures something more interesting than just color. The Light Pass is very simple:

```
attribute vec4 a_Position;
uniform mat4 LightMVP;
varying vec4 v_TexCoord;
    void main()
    {
        v_TexCoord = LightMVP * a_Position;
        gl_Position = LightMVP * a_Position;
    }
```

In fact, you've seen most of this simple Shader before a few times, it's only calculating the position of interest and passing on the texture for the Fragment Shader to use. But this time, it's using the Light source as the point of view, not the camera. The texture coordinate though is very interesting and used later. The real work is done in the fragment Shader; instead of loading RGB values into the texture we are going to put a scaled value:

```
precision mediump float; / only need medium precision, no need to choke the GPU
varying vec4 v_TexCoord;
float value;
float val2;
float vn;
float f;

void main()
{
value = 10.0 - v_TexCoord.z; // force the range to be -15 to +15 (alter if
needed)
val2 = floor(value); // remove the decimals
f = value - val2; // get them back
vn = v * 0.1; // reduce to fit
gl_FragColor = vec4(vn, f, 0.0, 1.0); // this would normally be RGBA, but R
and G have depth values, B is unused. A needs to be 1 or the colour might
get ignored
}
```

Ok, so our texture depth buffer will be ready after the first draw call, all we have to do is pass it an MVP matrix for the light source and it's going to do its things.

Of course, you need to run a render loop through all your objects to generate this *depth* texture, so the number of objects you have on-screen will have an impact on this process as it does with any render pass.

If you plan to use shadows in game, then clearly you need to create a simplified render system, which will allow you to pass the light MVP and attributes, nothing else is needed. The current individual render of each object is not the most efficient system, but it is useful for allowing us to experiment with different types of model. But the downside is that you will need to write a specific shadow render method, to conditionally call the shadow Shaders.

Most of our different model types have their own special versions of drawing, and use different attributes, so it might actually be a bit of a pain to put conditional code in there. I find the simplest thing to do is to have a second draw system, which when I run my game update loop, pulls the light values. Since all we really need is a Model matrix, light, and vertex attributes, it would be a much simpler call to run. It's also quite acceptable not to lerp the MD2 version, the slightly different but almost right nature of the resulting shadows is not unpleasant But that's your call.

That's not the end of it either; any Shaders we currently have and plan to use with shadows now have to be altered to use shadows. This can be done conditionally in the Shader, but really the less work a Shader has to do the better, so it's better to keep different Shaders for different conditions and use the glUseProgram() to set up the correct Program Object for your selected conditions.

Load and compile the MD2Shadow demo, and press F1 to cycle through different Shader methods. The Shaders used are all available to you but do take note that the Game Loop itself has been altered to account for a Shadow pass being done to gather the depth map, and an additional ShadowDraw virtual function has been added to the ObjectModel Base Class.

Shadows like this are not perfect though, the most obvious failing is just how sharp and jagged our shadows are. Real-world shadows don't really have such well-defined edges except in the very brightest light, and like most things we see in the real world when they are not correctly produced in a game, they tend to jar our senses. The shadows would be much more convincing if they had softer edges.

There are several ways to do this, but all of them come at a cost, you are just going to have to deal with the fact that quality costs and on a dual/Quad/Penta core GPU, quality probably costs more than the hardware can deliver. But in time we will have more power, so practice and be ready.

Most of the methods currently used involve some form of antialiasing filter, where you take a sample of the area around a pixel and smooth it down.

If I get the time, I might include an example of how this can be done on the support site, but honestly I think that the cost is too high, really too high, as even some of my more high powered SBCs systems tend to choke on this. It's better to just have an antialias filter on the EGL context than to use a Shader-filtering method that costs so much.

▌ Recap the Processes

A lot of good stuff has now been covered; we can roam around in free space. We can fly and crash under the influence of forces and ram our enemies. We can drive cars, and let them spin off and roll depending on their mass and how bad our driving is, hitting mountains of cardboard boxes with abandon.

We also can roam around a plane, which we can generate ourselves, and for good measure we can take shelter and explore in any nearby buildings we happen to find in our worlds.

We can let our objects that we've given some intelligence, find their way from point A to B and then C, and provide simple signposting systems for path or track-based motion.

We can view almost any real-world environment we are able to model, and properly avoid drawing things we don't need to draw allowing our GPU to focus on its task of putting our nice visuals on-screen.

As with our 2D recap, we have come a long way, but we're not Jedi's yet.

All we have done so far is making that scratch on the surface of what is possible a tiny bit deeper, there's a 100 different ways to do most of these things, and more than one flame war has been started on, which is the correct way. But hopefully by now you are also starting to see some ways to make things work better.

How effective a method is, is going to depend a great deal on what kind of project you are writing. Some methods will work brilliantly in some games, much more than others. Always remember the lesson we learned with the 2D double buffer. Yes, it worked and worked well, but it was slow, it was ungainly, it had limits when drawing transparency, and it was CPU heavy. You need to consider what the best option is every time you write a code.

But one thing I really hope you have learned, it's that in 2D or 3D the basic concepts are all the same, Space Invaders to Halo and everything in between pretty much all operate on the same principles, move something around under human control, avoiding things that can cause it harm, while getting the CPU to control something that is obstructing you in some way.

Games really are not massively different project to project. The main differences come from technical needs. Do we need 1000 models on-screen with physics, or do we need our GPU to do part of the physics for us, are we going to use a detailed path-tracing system for photo-realistic graphics? Technical content can be a money pit in terms of your learning, and in some ways it will never end, because tech always changes, and eventually it will slip away from even the most die-hard tech nerd. We've had to do some tech stuff, because well, we needed to have at least the basics in place to allow us to see things moving around. But game programming is a multifaceted skill set, and tech is only one part of it, which you are more than welcome to dive into and find even more pleasure in some of the more modern hardware. Unless you are working directly for a console or GPU maker, you'll always be slightly behind the curve.

But focus on gameplay, understand the principles of gameplay, and how games are put together and you can stay ahead of the curve, because gameplay really does not change as rapidly as tech.

We'll move into the home straight by working with a few of the technical things we need to know, mainly because if we ignore them our resources will vanish. Taking what we know so far and refining it will allow us to make the games a bit faster, smoother, or just a bit more shiny.

Hopefully, your confidence levels are high enough now for us to tackle pretty much anything, and even if you don't quite understand something you're ability to research and learn online will be improving.

11 Populating the World

▌ Keeping Track of the Assets

We've come a long way and in doing so we've started to notice that the size and complexity of our content has increased dramatically. We can create a lot of different playfields to put our game into and we've discussed some of the standard physics and AI systems used in the majority of games.

But all these things come at a cost…memory. Our target has a limited amount of on-board memory, and if we plan to target all possible variants we must therefore work with the lowest spec system. In our case, a 512MB Raspberry Pi Model B. Though who knows, we may want to use the Model A with 256MB. (Programmers, traditionally, count a high percentage of masochists in their number).

Hmmm suddenly our use of libraries and loading of assets starts to become a problem, our code gets bigger and bigger, our data areas get larger every time we load a file, and it really isn't long before we get to the point where we simply run out of memory. We can't add more…even if we change our base model to a more realistic Raspberry Pi 3 Model B with 1024MB our actual usable memory is finite and must be managed.

So let's consider when and why we load things into our project?

By far, the most obvious things we load in are our graphics and our data structures. On SBC systems, we need to accept that loading is a slow process, so we therefore have to make sure it is done only when the game is not running in a main loop. This is why level design and check points are important. Compression systems and chunk-based loading mean we can reduce the load times quite well, but we do have to be careful about the memory overhead we use. Our slightly self-imposed minimum machine level has 512MB of Ram, but in that, our code has to live, along with the OS. And, of course, our GPU that shares the memory, steals at least 64MB, most likely 128MB, so in reality we may find we only have less than 200MB of data to play with. The old school Spectrum programmer in me is somewhat stunned by that amount of memory, but the more cynical modern Console coder knows that just one model can take that much memory.

We need to always make sure we are realistic in our asset size. Streaming from our SD/eMMC memory IS possible, but it's really rather slow, so at best we can only do one thing that way, usually music!

Other memory eaters are the graphics; the sooner they are loaded into the GPU memory and treated as a fixed immovable asset the better. Always ensure that you keep only what you need in any given level or checkpoint area. Most games have a certain number of assets that every level has, and many more variable ones. Keep careful records and work on your design to ensure that you don't fill all your graphic memory with 500MB of different models of grass!

Keep your loads in one place, loading in a game loop isn't an option, we demonstrated that way back in the 2D shooting games, so careful note of what you need and when you need it is a key to success. Once you have model or texture data locked in the GPU make sure that you free that CPU memory for reuse.

Keep data you want to save together. It's far easier to write out a chunk of memory with all the info you need, than it is to create a buffer and load things in. Consider the way the MD2 file format is laid out, if your own memory mimics that header layout you don't have to do much work to save a header, and then save the memory chunk that follows. Likewise, reloading it allows you to point straight to a prepped area.

Compression systems are incredibly useful, loading a compressed graphic will be fast and allow you to keep more data on the storage medium. But with few exceptions (compressed textures, for example), compressed data cannot be used directly, it must be uncompressed into a workspace. So, in practice, you have the memory you load the compressed data into, and the memory you decompress the data into. That clearly means that you actually will use more memory than loading raw data directly into a prepped buffer.

Loading scripts can be a godsend here. Even the simple act of creating one can help you to visualize what you are using and where. If your level system works by loading a script, where all assets are listed and loaded. You can see clearly how much memory you are using, both in GPU and CPU.

▌ Scene Management

When we have a big world, we tend to have a big problem. Storing every single object in a scene as individual lumps of data means an absolute massive amount of data to be wrangled.

Games that let you to travel around massive environments going from place to place grinding points and experience as you go need to place key points of a game play at key points in game. Also consider that something you kill or destroy in that environment, needs to stay in that environment, unless you can provide a good logical reason within your games' narrative why they can be removed. Hundreds of dead pigs might not need much logic to play dead, but they do still need to be processed and then displayed. Ever wondered why so many characters in games disintegrate or turn into spirits and fade off? The sooner they are out of the scene and off the processing list the better. The code can focus on active objects and not waste GPU time drawing a corpse from 30 min ago.

There's also the fact that not all objects need to be in your world all the time. Putting 100 enemies in a map might seem like a good idea, but really how many are you going to need to process at any one time? Keeping them dormant and inactive if out of range will work ok, but you still need to deal with your processing list handling 100 mostly inactive enemies.

It's sometimes a better plan to create a spawning system, which can be a simple Manager Class, whose job is to test for certain conditions, time, proximity of player, and so on. And then generate the object(s) needed, putting them in the process list, and then removing itself, or staying around to create more baddies when you slaughter its offspring!

Spawning objects is far more effective than manually placing and sometime replacing, because the spawner can be responsible for deciding when the good time to actually spawn is. If you're too close, for example, it can prevent camping (the cheaters way to rack up kills, by waiting near a spawn site with gun ready, killing new baddies as they are created) by not spawning if you are too close, or spawning in another location (behind the camper is always good).

I tend to use two types of spawner. A global spawner, which is a class that is always processed (never rendered it has no need), which compares the player's position with a map of spawn sites, and depending on conditions sets up a new enemy. This can be quite involved and will essentially drive the flow of your gameplay as one class is going to do all the, if you have this, then do this, type of decisions on what to spawn and where.

There's also the simpler, range-based specific spawner. This is basically a baddie, who is never drawn and only exists to process logic, so it is in the processing list and will be processed each cycle, (booo), but is great for automatically producing a control system for a few baddies in a given area. One specific spawner can take responsibility for generating multiple types of baddie when you go into a room, and also for removing them when you exit the room. It's a kind of team manager.

However, keeping track of objects dead or alive status in game is not a massive issue, you will quickly work out how many objects you should aim to keep active in a game, and your code will largely deal with them correctly.

A more worrying issue is getting them all in the scene in the first place. Like most issues, this is best tackled by creating a data structure to hold your world. We've done this a few times in small ways like having a list of enemies to draw, with their position data. But mostly we are hard coding our instantiation of objects in our Game init systems. There's nothing wrong with that on a small scale, but it's clearly a very rigid and fixed way of doing things.

If, for example, we want to have a game with multiple levels, in our Init systems, we need to have switch or condition tests to set up different baddies and environments depending on the level, with their different locations, orientations, and so on.

Fine for two or three, maybe four levels but throughout this book I've noted the need to keep things simple. The smaller a file is, the easier it is to keep track of what the class it contains is doing, and filling our game.cpp file with masses of set ups is just not clever.

This is where we should use some form of package or script system. They both do the same basic thing. A package is usually a binary file, where a header gives you info on all the data. We saw how to use that in the MD2 Loader.

Each level we simply load the package for that level, parse through it creating the environments, enemies, skyboxes, and so on, and then fall through in to the game to process things.

This has the distinct advantage that our entire level initialization system can be reduced to a single command LoadLevel(NameOfLevelPacket). Great examples of this are Doom's WAD files and Quakes PAK files, which typically contain, among other things, Textures, LevelMaps, Models, Sound data, or names of sound files, and most important placement lists for characters and objects, all in a easy to access formats specific to the loader's needs.

Of course, there is a down side, binary packets need to be generated, and for that you will need a particular tool specific to your needs, probably on the PC that knows what kind of objects you have in your game, and saves out the data. The other problem with them is that once the data structure is set up, it's rigid, it cannot change, and only one loader on your system can load one type of package.

It's a bit of work, but it has the advantage of keeping your data relatively secure, if you don't make the header public, and compact, both on disc and memory.

A more flexible approach, especially during development, is to use text script systems. Text scripts have the advantage of being easily edited.

You can reduce level creation to the simple process of load a script file, and then have some code to parses lines like

LOADMODEL "Environment1.obj",0,0,0;

LOADPLAYER "Knight.md2",0,0,0;

LOADENEMYTYPE BadKight,10,10,10;

It's relatively easy to read, and in your code, you can simply scan for keywords, LOADMODEL, LOADPLAYER, LOADENEMYTYPE, and in a switch/case system, parse out the filename to load, the position to place, and on finding the ; line terminator, move through to the next one.

Each keyword will have an associated set of minimum, values it need, LOADMODEL, only wants the obj filename, and position to place it, we could also add scale and orientation if we wanted though?

A simple Parsing Level system is available for you on the support site, LevelLoadDemo. You can expand on this system as much as you want and use it to create levels.

▌ Wrangling All That Data

We saw with our scene management that there are times when things need to be loaded and times when they need to be removed…there are equally times when things should be in memory and not. This presents us with two distinct but equally important concepts of data storage.

Asset Management

The biggest key to asset management is to make sure you have good folder structure. It may indeed be a bit of a pain typing in full directory names, but the simple fact is, that having your textures in a texture directory, and your materials in a material directory makes it easier to keep track of them. Many times in the early projects I had files in *shared* directories and hard coded the load systems to look in those directories. Only later did I split them out. It's quite true that having all our assets in 1 super folder is viable, for a small project with under 10 files is probably quite desirable, but as games get more complex it really is important to separate them into relevant locations.

In game, keeping track of what assets you have in place in the memory at any given time is also very important. We used C++'s MAP structures to allow us to keep the names of assets live in our system and compare them, so that in itself suggests we need to ensure our naming conventions are clear and ideally descriptive. A file called *RobotHead.png* is simple to read and find, unlike *L1ARH1.png* Even if Level 1 Asset, Robot head 1, might seem obvious, it's not! As with variables, keep filenames clear, a proper name avoids confusion and lets you keep track.

But having them on the SD or eMMC memory in nice tidy formats, is only half the battle, we need to also think carefully about how we load (and occasionally save) data.

Loading data from any kind of storage media is always slow, but with systems that have limited memory it's often the only way we can keep data available. We just can't load 1GB of art into a 512 MB memory. So our games need to think about what must be loaded, what can be streamed, and what can be loaded in anticipation of its use.

All these factors are hugely dependant on the type of game you are writing but some obvious and common things come to mind.

Sound effects need to be in memory, and knowing what effect a particular level might need will allow you to create lists of the right sounds to load at the level initialization (remembering, of course, to remove the data at a level's end).

Music, however, will most likely be too big to store in a memory, but you can pull in chunks of it to a buffer every so often on a thread system to keep a player such as OpenAL fully stocked with data.

This concept can be used for many other forms of data, so long as it's linear. Randomly accessed data requires our storage system to seek new loading locations, and even SD and eMMC memory needs a bit of time to adjust itself.

Some types of map, models, and textures, for example, racetracks or endless runner style game can be pulled from an open file system so long as the game play is adjusted to never exceed the pull rate of the stream. This will, of course, require you to write a tool that creates those files.

With limited memory, we will usually design our games to work within the memory limits we have, but using streaming systems can make a considerable improvement in the size of data you can process at any given time. I do need to caution you that streaming from an SD is incredibly variable, even a fast access card might be hamstrung by a poor OS loading system.

Fragmentation, a Problem That's Hard to Solve

One problem we tend to have on machines with limited memory is an issue called fragmentation. This occurs when we ask for a block of memory, use it, and then release it back to the system. However, since other areas of memory will also have been used up, there are now holes in the contiguous block of our memory where chunks of memory are currently in use of having been freed up and are empty.

To explain this simply is tricky but I'll try; that original block of memory can only be reallocated to another memory request that is equal or less than the original size that was allocated. An equal allocation is great because the memory manager in our system will provide the pointer to the block that was just released.

But a smaller amount will result in the pointer to the block being given and the unused area of RAM at the end being written off. If the new smaller block is itself released…it's only going to return to the new size to the pool, that old chunk at the end that wasn't used is effectively lost and remains as a hole in our memory map.

Over time we will have a lot of memory allocated and deallocated, and memory managers struggle to find spaces in memory that are big enough to meet our needs, if it can't find a chunk big enough, the manager will start to report that there is no memory big enough for your current needs available, because as far as it knows, all the chunks of memory are going to be too small.

So even though your system knows all these chunks of memory are there and free and can total a large amount, the system just does not see an area of continuous memory to allocate the amount you ask for, and you get out of memory errors.

This can be a major issue, there are no simple one-stop solutions, but there are a few following logical things that can be done:

- Try not to create and destroy things too often.

- Try to ensure that you create the same size objects.

- Avoid unnecessary dynamic allocation of objects, if your game needs 100 things in it, creates them and leaves them active, using a reset/sleep method rather than delete.

- Memory is usually allocated on a first come first serve basis from the base of the memory block up, so make sure you create the big objects first, so that small objects do not try to use a previously large block cutting it back into a smaller block.

- Finally…you could create your own memory manager to allow for more logical allocation of memory and some defragmentation ideas. That's quite a lot of fun, but outside the scope of this book.

▌ Expanding to an SDK?

Now at this point, we have a whole load of useful functions, which allow us to access our graphics, our files, our models, our textures, our memory, and our input devices, play sound handle animations, and so on.

We haven't really had to go to our API layers for quite some time; we've quite deliberately added functions that we find easier to understand, which then does all the hard works. Our 3D Object loader, for example, does not ask for us to all the nitty gritty communication with that hardware we first had to do. We have combined all the different steps needed into one simple function.

This is the start of an SDK; we can collect all our helper functions into libraries, create header files, and include them in our precompiled build process, allowing for faster compilation times.

It's pretty light as an SDK though, there are traditionally a lot more helper functions in an SDK, and they tend to break themselves down into different sections, such as memory management, input device management, graphic management both low and higher level, Audio, GUI, and many things as the SDK designers need to add. We could also develop a few tools to make things a bit easier for us to use or configure our data to formats that we find easier to handle and make a point of using that format all the time, perhaps creating our own data structures.

The more helper functions or alternative means of creating and manipulating objects we can have the easier the SDK becomes for our possible new target users.

When we have an SDK that we are happy with, we would expect users to use the high-level calls knowing that they will do a particular thing, and return to a particular result, what's important is that our users should not be particularly concerned with how that is done.

This allows a hardware maker, or indeed an API developer to make changes to their systems, and the SDK can be altered to allow for those changes, but the user's access and return operations are not unduly affected.

We have a nice collection of projects now with lots of features, why don't you take our projects, locate all the really useful functions and create some library subprojects, and create your very own simple SDK. As you discover new ideas and ways to do things to expand it, and over time it will become your own faithful SDK for all your game development.

▌ The Last Project

We have a sort of SDK, it's (very) light but it does work, we have skills that we didn't have at the start of this book and most important we have confidence that we *sort of* know what we're doing.

It's time to take a few steps on your own, you are now capable of programming just about any kind of game you can think of, and you should now not only be able to use your current skills but be able to enhance and expand those skills with much less trepidation.

Before we start to talk about enhancements to our new skills, we're going to end our game code journey essentially where we started. By producing a game where the object is to move around, avoiding fire from a rampaging wave of aliens, while shooting them and taking cover as we do it.

But this time in a full 3D!

Let's write an environment-based shoot em up with waves of enemies, buildings to hide in populated by those enemies who come at you or exhibit some kind of logic, essentially a cut-down Halo!

You can download 3DHalo from the support site. It has almost everything you need except the logic of the Enemy Classes and indeed only a few basic enemies. The environment is there, the GUI, your character, and your pickups and weapons are all ready for you to add your legions of enemies. The physics and AI systems are in place, I just want you to turn it into your own game. There's a load of free MD2 models supplied and loading and rendering code is all there, and, of course, you can add your own models, environments, and anything else you feel. The whole project is designed to be added to, so long as you maintain the basic concept of the ObjectModel for things that you want to update and render it should be simple to expand on. Just create the enemies, make them do what you want them to do, and make a great game.

See, when I said a long time ago, every shooting game is basically Invaders from Space. I wasn't kidding…only the complexity changes.

For now, we're done with basic gameplay concepts, we should be very comfortable from this point in setting up a project, defining some form of entity/object we want to control and using game loops and events to handle it. We didn't tackle things such as puzzle games, but if we remember that the key to games is to separate the visualization from the logic. We should be able to visualize almost anything as a form of object, and let the code that handles the game rules to do its thing quite separately, so though we've focused on arcade style games, more thoughtful games are just as simple to do.

The remainder of this book is about the niggly bits we need to also master to ensure that what we write looks good, uses its resources well, and functions at an optimal level.

▌ Ready-Made or Roll Your Own

Obviously, we went out of our way in this book to avoid libraries unless we absolutely needed them for a specific task. But even with that rule we still had to import, file handling, sound handling, physics, and model loaders…lucky we found the free versions and they did what we needed to do. But we could have rolled our own, hand-written systems that were just a bit faster, just a bit more compact or just a bit more focused on our needs. That though would have taken time, maybe manpower if you needed to ask for help, and almost certainly would have needed debugging.

But, aside from the genuinely glorious satisfaction of proving that you are a god-like coding machine, this approach is generally not the best idea in the world if you want to get a project up and running in a fixed amount of time.

In the real world of professional game dev, we need to use whatever is available to get our project done as fast and effectively as possible. Time is money and time spent coding is time not letting people buy our game and play, we have to face the reality that however much we are enjoying what we do, we need to aim for a final goal of a complete project ready to present to a hopefully eager public.

Now that you have started to develop your skills as a programmer, you have now come to a point where you can start to review the options that are available to you. There are countless libraries, and APIs to libraries and engines that are all designed to make your life easier.

They generally have a cost, however, not just in financial terms, though these days even the most advanced AAA engines are available free, but in terms of how much control of your machine you sacrifice to your chosen library. This choice becomes more important when engines force you to produce your game the way the engine itself was originally designed.

Engines are great, Unity, CryEngine, Unreal4, and so on, all represent the current pinnacle of game tech. They are very well supported, continue to improve, and can make producing even very complex games a simple task.

But you do lose control, you no longer have total access over how you want the internal memory management to work, how you want the order of processing to occur, and a host of seemingly pointless things that only a programmer would consider important. Yes, you have scripting, and yes you can modify the variables you expose in run time, but it's not really the same.

Engines make games easy, so long as the type of game you have in mind was considered when the engine was written. No engine is 100% efficient, they try to be all things to all men, and there will always be some things they do better than others, and some things you can do better.

The rise of engines in game dev has been staggering, and it's made for much faster prototyping and development of concepts, which can be quickly and effectively *knocked out* in a fraction of the time to take even a crack team of developers working from scratch.

Now the SBC market isn't exactly busting at the seams with game engines. There are a few hobby projects on the open-source sites, but it's not exactly in demand, and also it's very hard to do. Engines, by the nature of trying to support all game formats and types, have very high overheads and demand much from your available resources. If we know one thing from our games so far, is that memory and processing cycles are finite, and we can't really afford to eat them up with an all-purpose GUI/animation/multiformat display/insert feature of your choice, system. We are forced to stay as lean and mean as possible.

But for me, that's the fun!

Limitations of Hardware

So far, we've done a lot of cool things and not even come close to the full potential of what we can do, but we must remember our target machine has limits. Even a PlayStation 4 has limits, they just happen to be hundreds of times more powerful than our Raspberry Pi.

We have limited amount of on-chip memory we can use, there's no way to add memory directly, we can add storage in the form of USB drives but our onboard memory is fixed, and as mentioned if we want to target the largest possible market we need to set the base level at the lowest viable machine.

I say viable, because even though the 256MB machines are capable of running our projects so far, they are barely working, this limitation of such a small amount of memory is just too much to let us create effective games with large play areas or numbers of models, and so we really should focus on the 512MB machines as being our base.

Our GPUs can only handle so many gazillions of instructions per second, well actually more like a few bazillions...(Yeah I have no idea, it varies between systems). It's still monstrously faster than the many 16 and 32 bit games consoles of a few years ago, but it's a limit we have to respect. We saw how our FPS rate dropped when we pushed too hard on the GPU, so we need to take that into account. Detailed multitextured 10,000 poly models maybe are possible if we max out our video systems, but you can't realistically expect to have many of them on-screen and maintain a decent frame rate. Our poly budget needs to be worked out as a function of our GPU power and our desired frame rate.

These limitations are very real, and not always possible to overcome. Careful design of our game's technical features should take into account the limits we have and adjust or adapt the game to suit that target machine.

You must choose; target only the very highest machines with a limited uptake from users, or target the larger pool of viable machines.

That said, it is quite possible to make some detection on what hardware your game is running on and allow the game to ramp up details accordingly, it does, however, add considerably to the complexity of your code.

▌ Cross-Platform Compilation

I'm guessing you are wondering why I have left this so late...well quite simply, when I set out to write this book as an initial collection of notes, I didn't know exactly how to do it on a Raspberry Pi, and when I worked it out midway through the process, I felt I was already well into remote development and didn't want to break my train of thought. Or as this book took shape to give the reader more things to worry about.

But here we are now, our projects are getting bigger, our compile times are taking longer, and our poor old Raspberry Pi is starting to feel the strain of compiling lots of quite intensive files even with good make file and file structure, the linker itself is now taking quite a while to do its thing. And all those source files and assets sitting in working directories on the target are eating up the storage.

So you now have a choice, and I will leave it entirely up to you. We can stay with our perfectly functioning but a little slow remote building or switch our compiling/linking processes to our main PC, which is considerably more powerful and then send the executable and assets and only the executable and assets to our Raspberry Pi for running and debugging.

This is a very powerful thing, and as Spiderman fans will tell you, with great power comes great responsibility. In our case, the responsibility of maintaining the correct libraries on our PC for the build, which match those on our Raspberry Pi, and keeping the assets folders up-to-date on the Pi.

We can automate some of this, and that is always a good thing because humans are fallible and often forget things.

Setting up cross compiling is simply a matter of ticking a box at the set up of a new project, so try setting up a simple example of a cross-compile project and a simple batch system to send our assets across so that the project can access them when running on the target. The process is automated by the onboard wizards, so I don't need to document starting a new project up here.

If, however, you want to swap a project over from an on-target build to cross compile it is a little more complex, and if we're honest, why would you want to? Start all your projects in one format or the other. I still like target-based compiles despite the slowness. But it's up to you. There will be an outline on how to add a new cross-platform configuration on the support site. That's your clue…create a new configuration, set it up with all the info the wizard asks for and boom! You're ready to blast off on your PC to your target.

I will cover some of this on the website, as it seems to have altered in the last couple of versions of VisualGDB, so best I keep it somewhere I can update it.

12 Some Advanced Stuff

▌▌ Multicore Fun

For those of you with original Raspberry Model A's B's B+'s and the fun little Zero and other single-core SBCs…this chapter isn't going to work well for you. You don't have multiple cores to work with, so nothing in here will have any real impact. It won't actually crash your machine to try, because we use systems that work out the number of cores and divide the workload. So, if you have a single-core machine, the managing code will allocate work to one core and simply allocate some time to each process to try to give the sense of all tasks running at once.

Even with a single-core machine you should still work through this. If you keep up your programming after this book you are bound to eventually work on a multicore machine at some point and this will all be useful then.

So what is multicore programming? Basically, it's a concept that seems to give you multiple CPUs on the one chip.

That's the concept, the reality is a little bit different, it's called a core because what you actually have in your chip is multiple processing core units, each with their own register sets and memory caches, they also share a lot of internal bits and bobs, to allow access to specialist hardware; however, some things are protected, certain address lines, and so on, only one core can usually access these protected bits at a time.

Having two cores does not mean you can run a project twice as fast, but it does mean that you can run two applications or processes or even projects at once as long as they are not trying to access the same areas of memory or protected hardware at the same time. This ability to run two processes seemingly at once is called multitasking.

Multitasking is the key to understanding how multicores work. A modern CPU is designed to multitask, allowing you to move your cursor around on-screen while still testing your keyboard and playing music and several other tasks, all seemingly at the same time. A CPU with only one core will use a time-slicing concept for its many tasks, spending a little of its processing time on one task, then a bit on another. Sheer-processing power will allow that to appear like it is all happening at once and making the multitasking seem smooth and seamless, until you try to do more tasks than it can reasonably cope with, then things get a bit sluggish. This is why the older single-core machines really are quite sluggish when they display their Linux Desktops with even a few windows open.

But having more cores, means more tasks can be sent to a different core, which itself can slice up its tasks. More cores = more tasks.

◼ What Is Threading?

Threading is the basic method used to allocate tasks to cores or time slots, it's not to be confused with hyperthreading, which is a concept more valid to x86 style chips seen on most desktop and laptop machines, which have internal architecture that allows each core of the processer to make use of some unused clock cycles when the CPU is running to do other things. x86 chips have very complex instructions, which mean several of them need to use multiple-clock cycles to function, and often wait several clock cycles to complete that the threaded app gets to use. So, each core on a hyperthreading CPU can have multiple threads running on each core. But hyperthreads are only able to process in the background of the main CPU processes. Hence, they do not always complete their tasks in the same amount of time. But it is a fantastic boost to the CPU's ability to do twice as much work inside each core, using up clock cycles that would otherwise be wasted, when it's waiting for input/output from internal or external sources.

ARM chips, however, do not do this, the RISC-based design concept means that there are few if any wasted clock cycles, meaning something that relies on unused cycles would have to wait a long time till there were any before it could process. So rather than put hyperthreading capabilities onto the silicon die that makes the CPU, ARM's chip designers decided instead to squeeze-in new cores that had the ability to fully process their own internal data and only put it into waiting states if it was accessing the same external bus, which we can effectively avoid with careful coding. This is why ARM and other RISC chips talk of being multicore rather than having hyperthreading, though confusingly coders still speak of threads.

But these cores can be loaded up with info, have their own sets of internal registers and bits of cache memory, and are able to compute internally at the same time as other cores. It's only when you need to access the same main memory or have the address lines talking to hardware, such as the GPU that you can get clashes, that means one core has to wait for another to finish before it can do its thing. But a core that is not accessing the same memory or hardware as another core is able to run at full speed on the task(s) it has been given.

The key to maximizing multicore coding then is to make sure that each core is doing something unique and specific that does not need the same memory as other cores, does not clash, does not access the same hardware address lines, and is able to do a stand-alone job.

It does not mean that your quad-core computer is four times as fast all the time, every time, but with careful management of your code it potentially can be, especially at key points in your code where you are doing very intensive processing and each core is running code that is not trying to access the same memory/resources as the others you can indeed make it work nearly four times faster.

Think of it as four guys in the same hole, digging with four shovels, they can't dig the exact same spot, so they work on different parts of the hole to speed up the process. At times when they are working on the separate parts of the hole it is indeed four times faster hole digging than one man can do, but as they come closer together, they need to decide who is going to dig at the point they clash, fights ensue, and things come crashing to a halt and your men spend more time arguing than actually digging.

For me the simplest way to use threads/cores is to think about all the multiple jobs or sections of jobs I have to repeat over and over again on large instances of objects before I can then proceed to do something else. Anything that involves a particular set of calculations that take a certain degree of time to finish makes a good candidate for a thread.

Creating threads is painfully easy, and we have already done so with our keyboard and mouse systems, which are nice simple threads we know we need running at all times to test for keys and mouse, regardless of what our code is doing. But making more complex threads is also quite possible if, for example, we want to set up some tasks to run at the same time as our games. The kind of task needs a bit more discussion, as we'll soon see.

But threads are easily introduced, as they are part of the STL and part of our system, so no need for us to download any libs just yet. Threads are defined as the STL functions using the thread class, though to use them well we also need something call a mutex. So just add these to a program.

```
#include <thread>
#include <mutex>
```

We will need a function, which is the actual task we want to be done on the thread, let's do something simple like a printf, here's a little code snippet you can add into your main file on any project, put the code in before the main() function.

```
std::mutex m;
int count = 0;
void SayHelloGracie()
{
    m.lock(); / About to use a function or change data so stop other
    threads being able to access things
    printf("Hello Gracie %i\n", count);
    count++;/variable count is safe until m.unlock() is called
    m.unlock();/we now allow access to count
}
```

The only thing odd about that is the mutex variable, which means a mutually exclusive indicator, and is used to indicate to other threads that there is code or data that these threads need to have exclusive use for a bit, so please wait. printf may or may not be entirely thread safe (explained soon), so that little mutex variable now comes into play, by locking it, we tell any other threads using the same mutex variable as an indicator that they can't have access just now and effectively have to wait for a little while, and we will let them know when they can continue, they, in turn, will sit and wait for the mutex to be clear before they then try to lock it for their own use.

Now to get back to Gracie, to call that function we just need to create a new thread and pass the name of the function:

```
std::thread AnIdent(SayHelloGracie);
```

Since *Say Goodnight Gracie* was a catch phrase of the late great George Burns, let's make the Ident George. Now, we can make four Mr Burns' giving a little homage to the great man.

```
/ have 4 Mr Burn's speak
std::thread George1(SayHelloGracie);
std::thread George2(SayHelloGracie);
std::thread George3(SayHelloGracie);
std::thread George4(SayHelloGracie);
```

If we run this now, we will get four *Hello Gracie* outputs and then nothing, but we know that the thread ran because the output showed it, and also showed an increase in the counter value. But it's too short a process to really get any sense that its running along with our game, it might as well have just been a function call, so let's do something mad and ill advised, change the code inside SayHelloGracie to this:

```
void SayHelloGracie()
{
    while (1)
    {
        m.lock(); // About to use a function or change data so stop
        other threads being able to access things

        printf("Hello Gracie %i\n", count);
        count++;//variable count is save until m.unlock() is called

        m.unlock();//we now allow access to count
    }
}
```

The addition of the while loop means that this function will never stop. Run it again. And take care to look at your debug output window.

You can see now that you are outputting quite mad amounts of Hello Gracie's and yet your game is still running?

Those four George threads are running and never ending, spread across your available cores, whereas your main game loop is behaving in a normal sequential manner. If you can see your CPU core indicators somewhere, you should notice that assuming a quad core system, three of your cores are probably totally devoted to printing out Hello Gracie, whereas one is doing your game AND printing out Hello Gracie.

There are few situations where we would actually make a thread repeat a function like this but it certainly helps to understand how the threads are working.

Let's do one more equally crazy thing and comment out the lock and unlock on the mutex, run your project again in debug mode...take note of the output.

After allowing it to run for a few seconds hit the pause or stop button and look back on your output values. It won't be immediately obvious, but you should see in some places that the count has not increased sequentially? Why do you think this is? I'll comment on that a little later.

Threads and Pthreads

As we are using Linux-based systems we tend to use pthreads (Posix threads) rather than standard threads (std::thread), and yes there is a difference, though not much, they are both designed to do exactly the same thing, threads are sometimes considered the more correct way of doing things as they are now built into the STL, pthreads, however, are not part of the STL you need a library to use them. But pthreads are generally more reliable across more platforms, the code has been refined and used for longer and is more stable, they are better suited to cross-platform work so that code that works on one machine will usually work on others with no threading issues.

Threads and pthreads differ a little in their parameter passing, Threads are very easy to pass parameters to the thread application to work with, pthreads requires a bit of syntax hopscotch to get things passed, but it's not rocket science. There are arguments about speed and flexibility for one over the other that are probably valid but I think generally we can use whichever we find most comfortable to use.

The good news though is that on Linux and Windows, either approach is perfectly acceptable and you can even mix them up, I've used pthreads for my key/mouse handlers in the game demos, and will describe a job manager I've supplied, using threads next.

Job Managing, Also Kinda Simple

I say kinda because for me personally I've always found this harder to get my head around and again it needs you to be more careful about your architecture, so for the simplistic game systems we have here, there's a limited chance to do this, except perhaps for allocating each object's logic update as a job when separated from the rendering. You will find a small demo JobDemo on the support site.

At the core of a job manager is naturally enough; a manager keeps track of a certain number of available threads, and tasks you want it to handle, which are assigned to those threads. Threads are usually only set up when the job manager is instantiated but dormant until given a job. This reduces a lot of the overhead of creating and destroying threads. Once instantiated, you pass the manager the address of the job or task to perform, and if there is a thread free, the task will be assigned to it; otherwise, it will be stored for later. When the task on a thread is done, the manager will note that a thread has a space and assign another job, which it kept in a to-do list, into that now free space. Usually, there will be a thread/slot for each core, but there's also some advantage in having two or three task threads running on each core just to make sure that the core always has something to work on, if the manager itself is not ready to update the slots, though overdoing it will choke the process.

The advantage of this kind of system is that once working, you are keeping all your cores working almost all the time. If the job manager itself is on a thread, it's nearly always working, and keeping tabs on what jobs are finished and what slots are free to feed the next job in.

There are many upsides to this approach, a well-fed job manager can keep your cores fully loaded and working at 100% and a few downsides, the lack of knowing when a thread is actually fired being one. We also need to be much more aware of what the jobs are, what resources they use, whether they are allowed to run concurrently with other tasks, whether they need to be locked out when other tasks are working, and so forth.

So a great deal of understanding of what your jobs are doing is needed before you can comfortably assign your jobs. We also need to understand the concept of a mutex and locking and being clear what a resource is and what threads are using them.

Yes, it can be a little complex but like many things the level of complexity depends on how much you want to do, so I'll explain the basics and if you want to take it further you can find lots of good online resources and make a few small changes to some of our update managers, sound systems, and perhaps a few other things you can see in your games.

To get an idea of what a job manager does, there are three basic concepts that we must be aware of: (1) threads, (2) jobs, and (3) resources.

Threads we've covered, pretty well; our main program is running on a thread, we call it, unsurprisingly the main thread, and we can create new threads to run on other's core, or if all cores are full it will run on the same current core, but take up 50% or so of the processor's time, the more threads we add to a core, the more they will time slice. Once a thread is started, only its calling thread can stop it, though a thread can be asked to go to sleep for a while making it hibernate and stop working until some internal hardware (or a timer thread) wakes it up after the allotted time.

A thread once started generally is always running; our main project is considered a thread of the OS that launched it. Unlike a job, it never ends unless we make it end, also we have keyboard testing systems that are always working, and timers, and several other system threads going on.

Jobs are the tasks we want to perform, jobs should be able to reach a conclusion and end, and they are intended to be functions or processes that can be computed with a minimum of interaction with the main process.

Resources are simple, it's normally the data in memory we want to manipulate, but it can also be a hardware process or a class that accesses a hardware process. Only one core and by extension one thread can reliably access a given area of memory at any given moment in time. It's a hardware impossibility, but it won't actually damage your memory if all possible cores crash into an address looking to change data at the same time. But a crash is not impossible and can be confusing to locate because they are all attempting to read or change the same data it becomes unpredictable for any given thread. The actual result of uncontrolled threads is basically unknown. So keep threads under control at all times.

When a job is using its own personal areas of memory and not accessing any shared resource, it is considered thread safe. You are free to fire off as many thread safe jobs as you like.

You can also make a nonthread safe process, thread safe, by asking it to mutex lock when it wants to use data or functions that can be damaged by other threads, and releasing the mutex when done, to allow another thread to proceed. This is fine if you are only accessing a few things, but if you lock a thread and your job takes some time before it releases the memory to others, it might be thread safe but it's hogging the resource, and forcing other threads to wait, not a good practice.

In addition, keep in mind, few hardware processes allow multiple core access, so classes that use hardware are seldom themselves thread safe. If we think back to our four guys digging a hole, as long as they are all digging in separate parts of the hole, they have no conflict. But if they have to dig the same spot in the hole, or in your CPU memory, clashes will occur and three guys will have to wait until the fourth guy is done, which by the way assumes he will tell the others when he is done!

This is one reason encapsulation of our data within classes is a great thing, we can update objects on continuous jobs because we can be fairly certain that the update functions are going to simply update their AI, change some animation values, and create new positions and matrices for their movement all related to data inside the class instance itself. That is a nice thread safe function.

We can't, however, be so confident with the rendering of our objects as that needs access to a hardware resource only one thing at a time can use. All the four cores in a quad system can happily update the objects, but only one should access the GPU at any given time because we can't be sure when the cores will finish their updates, so all four might go knocking on the GPU's door at once. Even worse than the GPU hardware forcing a wait, which it will at the point of hardware access, we have to consider that as the threads all do their thing trying to set up their renders calls, certain values in OpenGLES2.0s state system will find themselves being set and then reset by one of the other three different threads. Finally, the actual hardware calls to the GPU will end up being queued as the first one to get there tries to get its data rendered with no idea if the data setup it wanted OpenGLES2.0 to have is still there. The net result is....unpredictably crazy rendering and possibly a horrible crash.

This is what happened in our SayHelloGracie example with no mutex locks, some threads tried to access the counter then have it printed when other threads had altered it as it was used, and it became unstable.

Imagine that instability magnified over dozens of important variables that are altered when you get ready to do a GLdraw?

▌ With Great Power Comes Great Heat

If you're running on a Raspberry, you might have noticed that with the mad looped SayHelloGracie, the demo job manager, or even a library system such as OpenMP (check it out, it's very cool), running lots of tasks, things changed! You maybe have seen an overheat warning in the top-left corner of the screen, and had you left it running it might have started to get very very slow. This isn't a case of overloading your system with work; it's a case of overusing your system with all your cores operating with tight loops you would be operating at or close to 100% of CPU capacity. Other non-Raspberry systems will most likely have just slowed down or even crashed and reset. This is sadly one of the only real hardware issues we have to be aware of. Running our multiple cores at full capacity causes the CPU to heat up to very high levels, and we risk potentially damaging the CPU, though in reality the internal safety systems will kick in and just throttle back the power usage, until they cool, causing the slow down.

How soon this throttle effect will kick in will depend on the conditions that are outside of our control. A CPU already overclocked will start to stress first, a CPU with no cooling system will heat up quicker than one with, a board in a closed box will get very hot pretty quick because of the lack of flowing air, and a fan-cooled system might not even heat up at all.

If we distribute our software to users to play we also have no idea what kind of cooling or containment the user will have, none of these factors are under our direct control.

But regardless of the environmental factors we do have control over how often we run our systems at full power and we need to carefully choose when we do it, and make sure we provide a little respite from time to time before the system decides to step in.

▌ The End Is Near!

Well that's it, we're pretty much done. If you started out as a total beginner then you've come a very long way very fast, some of the topics may not have sunk in fully and you need to keep working on them until that magical *click* moment happens when it will all make sense. So please go back over the projects again, try to update and expand them, fix the deliberate bad decisions in the early projects, and if you feel up to it, please write your own versions of the games and even a few new games.

For me also this has been a fascinating and at times frustrating journey, I wasn't lying when I said I'd never coded these devices before, nor had any experience with Linux, which I find a very acquired taste. So I made and documented a lot of mistakes along the way, which I hope you took notice of.

I avoided going back into this book to fix parts where I later discovered that I'd made bad choices so that I could mirror what you as a new coder were also going through. But sometimes where it was likely to impede your progress I did make an edit and noted it for you. It's important that you realize no matter how much experience you have, there are always new things to learn, and new mistakes to make, and a lot of old mistakes to repeat. Just remember, if you are starting to see errors, you are starting to think like a coder.

There were several things that were done quite deliberately badly to show you how impressive the better ways were. Some were also done badly because of my ignorance of the target system at the beginning.

Also the lack of and quality of GPU drivers on some target SBCs is something I have no control over, it's a shame that makers put these systems together but often never consider the needs of coders to actually interact with them at a low level. Welcome to the world of hardware, sometimes we just can't always get what we want. But, if we try really hard we can at least use a double buffer (groan). At least the Raspberry machines all work out the box.

As I've learned more about using SBCs, I've found lots of do's and don'ts on them that I hope you will also start to see. It's important not to get too upset that a machine does not do *x*, or is prone to *y*. For better or for worse the machine you target is the machine you have to get working. Live with its faults, and work around them where you can, and if it still crashes for no reason causing you endless frustrations and moments of green tinged rage…smash it into small pieces, use a big hammer, it was asking for it! You'll feel better after! But you won't have a target to play with anymore!

This book was never ever intended to teach you the C/C++ language, at least not directly, but I hope that in the process of working through it, you have increased both your knowledge and confidence in the language to continue to explore it and maybe some other languages. There are dozens of books on coding, and some amazing online references. What I have presented here is what I call a core set. It's by no means a full or efficient use of C/C++, but I really hope that you will realize you can write pretty much anything using this core set. Imagine then what you can achieve if you decided to stretch your C/C++ knowledge even more?

If what we've done together here makes you think that you might enjoy a career in games dev, I will have achieved one of the goals I had when planning this book. But please don't jump straight in, not yet. There's still a lot to learn, and I do mean A LOT!

I hope I've given you a foundation to build on, the fundamentals I was aiming for, and if I have that will take you forward.

Coding is like bodybuilding, you don't develop big muscles just by saying you are a bodybuilder, you get them by training, practicing, pumping iron, and pushing yourself ever more past your limits. Coding is a mental form of bodybuilding, to get better you must actually do it, you must actually code, and you must actually get past that last 5% of a project at the end that just pushes you past what you know now.

Games programming at a professional level is hard; you need to work with people who are always going to be better than you, and know the hardware and C/C++ language and all its tricks, and you need to keep up. So if you want to get better at C/C++, find some good resources online, find good comprehensive up-to-date books, C/C++ does update every few years, you need to too, and keep pumping the code!

If you were a slightly more advanced coder but a game novice, then I hope this book gave you an insight into some of the methods and techniques used in games' programming. I tried to give you a practical taste but it's a drop in the ocean of what is out there, because, of course, no one book is going to be able to cover the topics in enough detail to satisfy the different experts that thrive on disciplines such as AI, compression, data management, graphic programming, and many others.

Game programming has evolved so much in 40 years; people are now able to expand what were simple ideas into almost limitless subtopics. If any of the topics in this book left you feeling that you wanted more, then that is fantastic, go find more. There are so many resources available to you now that simply didn't exist when I was learning.

Books may seem an old-fashioned idea these days, but I don't really get the same sense of understanding when I cut and paste a piece of code from a website into my projects. Maybe that's why I've never fully understood Maths <jazz hands>. The best way to learn something is to do it, to comprehend what it is doing, and then to expand. Try typing something in, work out the progression of the code as you type each line, think like a CPU, what are you trying to get out of this bit of code, visualize the desired result, and compare with the code you are writing, always asking, is there a better way to write this? Cutting and pasting just won't give you that sense of understanding you need to fully understand the code you enter.

Books can go into a lot of detail, especially on specific topics. Detail which I hope now you can start to appreciate after processing what you've learned in here. This is just a first step in a journey that can take you to exciting new places and expand your understanding of virtual worlds and even a little into the real world. It won't, however, help you get a date! No one ever said "Computer games programming, that's sounds so sexy!" Ever! We just have to hope that the Ferrari parked in the garage you bought with your royalties will do instead!) (Yeahhh…that never happens either, I have a Kia!).

So go find yourself a few nice books, Maths, AI, Engine development, C/C++, and so on; build yourself a reference library, it will never go offline, it will always be there and most important it will let you gain an insight into the minds of the people who wrote it, who nearly always are going to be experts in their fields who are trying to help you get some nice big brain muscles developed.

And remember…you have learned much, but you are not a games coder…….yet!

Complete your training, practice!

Appendix I

▌ Where Files Live on Non-Raspberry Machines

Since I have written most of my projects here on the Raspberry Pi series of machines, there were a few things very specific to the Raspberry range. The most obvious being the OS, Rasbian, and less obviously, the use of Broadcom's graphic libraries, which enhance the standard EGL systems. If you are not using a Raspberry machine, there is no need for you to include any bcm_* libraries. I also used different set up routines to create our rendering windows, EGL for non-Raspberries, and Dispmanx for Raspberries. This initialization only impacts the way the display is represented.

Rasbian can often be run on other target SBCs but it's usually a badly ported and/or incomplete copy, it's normally far better to find a clean version of Debian or Ubuntu, which was specifically built for your target, it will tend to be a lot more stable. That then means the Rasbian/Raspberry specific bcm_* libraries are not needed, even if they are included, they probably won't work as you expect.

It also means that some of the key libraries we need to build our project are not going to be where I've described them in our Raspberry Pi-based tutorials. They may not even be part of the OS as it has supplied meaning that you have to install them yourself.

I've covered quite some number of the different SBCs available on the support site, so feel free to check out the other SBC's section. If your board or OS is not covered then leave a note on the forum and hopefully you will get a response, but once you know the basics of getting a target setup, the process isn't markedly different on other systems.

Appendix II

▮ Updating versus New SD

When you burn an SD with any maker's distro of an OS, you basically are creating a brand new clean formatted SD card with the very latest version of the OS and any drivers needed to make your particular board run. This is, of course, a good thing. But as you spend a few weeks creating projects and using your target board for any number of fun things, you will find that you add your own apps, libraries, and useful assets to your SD card. These are lost when you burn a new SD.

Losing them each time a new OS becomes available and is burned to your SD, is annoying! Yes, you can save them, or redownload them, but it's really quite a tedious process, time should be spent coding not reinstalling apps and data (Backups...remember to use backups for all personal data).

Unless the distro from the maker actually fixes a known issue with the core use of your target machine, try not to continually burn new SD cards. Rather, focus on an update and upgrade cycle every so often to make sure you have the latest version of your apps and libraries.

Linux systems keep track of the current version numbers of all your apps, and using the following will make sure that your system is updated with any latest apps and libs. You should also always do this immediately after you have burned and repartitioned a new SD

```
sudo apt-get update && sudo apt-get upgrade
```

This will keep your boards public drivers and all your onboard apps up-to-date and functioning. Do this every so often just to make sure you have the latest versions of things. I don't, however, recommend this in the middle of a project development session. Sometimes changes to libraries can be quite major causing new ways to access features, and your code itself might then need to be altered in ways that are not always obvious.

It's also a very good idea to keep a backup of your SD on your PC from time to time with all its current updates and the tools and libraries we install. It's not at all unknown for coders to damage their storage medium, especially when doing some form of media-access systems that forget to close files or accidently format things. Having a backup of your SD, available in that unhappy event, will save you a lot of time updating and reinstalling your working tools.

Appendix III

▌ A Word or Two about Source Control

I'm hoping that you have come here from early in this book, where I thought about putting this section, but was concerned with scaring you off or overloading a beginner's enthusiasm. So let's assume when you go through this, you're still at a finding your feet stage and this is something you want to find out about, but the choice of what and when to use, are still open to you.

Source control or revision control is a form of backup system that all professionals use, there are many different types, and the most popular currently are SVN, Git, and for professionals, Perforce.

Like most situations when there are two or more options. People tend to fall into one of the camps and defend it while putting down the others. It's not for me to suggest a choice, I tend to use all three in different development environments, though I have a soft spot for SVN, even though it's starting to be overtaken in popularity by Git.

Perforce is popular in commercial situations but it can be complex to use, for simple home coding I think it's overkill but feel free to seek out single-user free demo versions.

Whatever you choose you just need to remember one thing…use it!

How does it help us? Good question, I am glad you asked. As we go through this book, we are going to be building up a framework and creating many generations of buildable files, we're also going to make some almighty cock ups, typos, missed lines, attempts to do something different, and so on, which are going to create bugs that we may not be able to immediately solve and will create considerable annoyance as we are trying to learn new things. Earlier in this book I demonstrate how easy it is to make mistakes with our early memory management, and those were deliberate! More mistakes are sure to follow, programmers are human and make mistakes; it's going to be frustrating.

Frustration is the biggest drawback to learning I can think of, it's important to build your confidence and sense of ease in coding, and bug hunting for seemingly impossible bugs is never anything else but frustration.

A source/revision control system will provide us with a means to step back to the last stable build we had before we made the error, and start again. This is often the fastest way to deal with complex bugs, which are avoiding your bug squashing debug hammers.

This works best if you have regular backups of your code, in general if you write any small module of code, and it is running fine, back up, and commit it to your online repository. Do this as many times as you want in each session, don't leave it to the end of your session. EVERY time you write some decent-sized chunk of code that works…submit your code to your server…then if you screw something up, you are at worst only going to lose the time it took to enter the faulty code, and you can be more careful when trying again to add the code to the last working version you had from 30 min ago.

Whatever system you use, you're going to need a client side app. SVN and Git both have a very usable interface, you can download SVN from here https://www.tortoisesvn.net/ and Git from here https://www.tortoisegit.org/.

You will also need to locate an SVN or Git hosting server where your projects can be uploaded to. These range in price from free to very much not free. But I won't specifically recommend any. Simply Google for free SVN (or Git) hosting, and you'll find something.

If you are network minded and have your own server, you can even host your repository yourself.

Perforce is a different kind of system, and in my view much more complex, especially for simple projects, but if you already are using it, you may want to continue, it's available from https://www.perforce.com/. It also needs a host server and again there are commercial ones available, including some free ones.

Take some time to read the instructions on the sites and pick one. So long as you remember the golden rule of committing often, you will save yourself a lot of time and effort, especially when things go wrong.

If all this sounds confusing and scary at the moment, don't worry; it will become clearer, for now, just work through this book carefully and just don't create any bugs! No bugs at all, just, don't.

Appendix IV

■ Bits Bytes and Nibbles Make You Hungry!

I briefly touched on the topic of bits when we were discussing the colors we used to make the pixels. It's a bit of a false view these days that computers only work in binary, 1's and 0's. It's true they use binary a lot, but these days on modern computers not as much as they used to, except in one or two areas, such as Graphic and audio data.

I don't honestly know the reasons why the basic units of computers have some connection to snacks, but there are, the following basic units:

Bit, Nibble, Byte, and Word, which traditionally were 1 binary digits (8 to a byte), 4 binary digits (2 to a byte), 8 binary digits, and 16 binary digits (2 bytes combined). These were the limits when I started with 8 bit machines. Over time as the sizes of units got larger as CPUs were able to process more, new units, such as longwords, 32, Doubles, 64, and so on, came to be as memory size grew as did the sizes of registers, but the basic units still exist.

A bit is the smallest possible digit a computer can recognize, the traditional 1 or 0. But your target's memory is not laid out as a large number of 1's and 0's, which allows you to target any one at any time. It's laid out in various sizes of chunks that the CPU or GPU grabs in one mouthful. When we talk of a 32 bit or a 64 bit computer, what we are actually saying is, the CPU grabs 32 bits at a time, and holds those 32 bits as a number in its registers to manipulate any way it sees fit. 64 bit machines grab 64 bits. This wider address size has a side effect in that the code will grow in size; most variables will now be 64 bits long rather than 32, pointers need to be 64 bit and many of the machine's instructions are also now 64 bit increasing the actual size of our code. That's something we need to think about, we generally still have the same amount of RAM available, and our code will increase in size. It won't double, but it will be more. But 64 bit machines are usually much faster for various reasons and that is well worth the increased size. We also tend to consider that the term word now, as a 32 bit value, as the old 16 bit value has more or less been left behind as computers have grown in size and power.

Now most of the time we don't really need to worry too much about the bit patterns of our 32 bit words, but we do when it comes to graphics. Since a 32 bit word contains 4 bytes of data, with 1 byte each containing information on the red, green, blue, and alpha components of our pixels. It's also contained in a specific part of our word. A red pixel, for example, might look like this in binary

11111111000000000000000011111111b

Oh and to make it even more fun, it might be

11111111000000000000000011111111b

Yeah…the same, the difference here is that the Alpha value is at the start, it's a wonderful way to confuse a PC coder, make them look at ARM binary values. Oh and let's not forget that in C/C++ component colors and alpha values are floats between 0 and 1.0f.

All this depends on whether your CPU prefers to read data in a big or little endian format, ARM is actually capable of both for even more head exploding madness.

It can be hard to get our heads around the size of things, for example, is int 16, 32, or 64 bits. The answer is yes, to all 3, but it totally depends on what machine you are running on. C++ has a very useful sizeof(x) function that returns the byte (8 bit) size of any basic type and helps you to overcome some of the problems of how much space you need to allocate from time to time.

Appendix V

▮ OpenGLES3.0+

Obviously, this book has focused on OpenGLES2.0 because of its current total dominance of the marketplace, but even now there are a few systems capable of running OpenGLES3.0. So it might be interesting to outline a few of the things that it can give you. In fact, at the time of writing the current cutting edge version is OpenGLES3.2, SBC/SoCs that can use this are currently quite scarce, but give them a few years and we will see these versions come into play.

At least one board, the Asus Tinker Board, appears in theory to have a GPU that is capable of OpenGLES3.2, which adds other types of optional Shader to the mix. Geometry Shaders that can dramatically improve graphic effects and allow additional processing on primitives, and Tessellation Shaders to greatly increase the numbers of vertices you can work with from a basic set of data.

The board is too new for me to have had any chance to try it out, though having used Geometry and Tessellation Shaders on full fat OpenGL on a desktop being able to play with them on a credit card-sized machine is mind boggling.

But OpenGL3.0 is here and a lot of fun to work with and represents the next big step in SBC GPU coding.

First and most important, any machine that can run OpenGLES3.0 is using a more modern GPU and almost all are multicore rather than the limited cores we're used to and incorporate several internal improvements, which make rendering faster and more flexible. This usually makes them considerably faster in real FPS terms than their OpenGLES2.0 running predecessors running the same code. That single point has win all over it.

Apart from technical enhancements and speed, OpenGLES3.0 mostly provides an updated and more flexible version of GLSL, which does have a few more features and changes a few concepts but it's not a massive leap. It also offers significantly improved texture and compression systems handling, and it can cope with larger and more complex buffers and those buffers have more manipulation possibilities.

Though not always guaranteed, it seems most OpenGLES3.0 machines can also cope with OpenCL. At least so far, that has been the case. Making heterogeneous programming possible for significant speed increases for those who know how to make best use of all these compute features; this may be down to the hardware makers though, so it's not certain that all new boards will feature this. But it sort of makes sense with the way an OpenGLES3.0 chip works to provide at least OpenCL1.1 (OpenGLES3.1 even offers compute Shaders).

I hope that soon the leading brand makers will follow Hardkernal and Asus's trail blazing and bring out an OpenGLES3.0+ supporting machine, which will really explode OpenGLES3.0+, and who knows, I might update this book to make use of these extra features.

One mighty good thing also about OpenGLES3.0 is that its fully backward compatible with OpenGLES2.0, so even if a whole bunch of new systems come out the day after this book is released it will stay relevant for quite some time.

One bad thing about all this increased power though, and this may be a limiting factor for a lot of SBC designers and a reason why they are still focusing on OpenGLES2.0 for a while yet; that extra power of our chips requires more power to operate. We're seeing more systems needing 3 even 4 amps power draws and that kind of power usage generates more heat and heat needs to be dissipated making the units bigger with heatsinks added. There's probably a cut-off point where the heat produced and the ability to get rid of it will no longer make them suitable for the mobile devices they are intended to drive. Also batteries, which are often used to power most of these things drain pretty quickly as the ampage goes up.

So unless we see another significant breakthrough in low-power processing, the way ARM revolutionized the market with it first came out, we may see that SBCs will plateau at a certain performance level. So learning to work on their constraints will become an important industry skill.

If you want to play with OpenGLES3.0, for me the Hardkernal Odroid XU4 is the best option. At the time of writing the Asus Tinker board can run GLES3.1 but it does not have full working drivers. Scan the market, see what's out there and double and triple check the drivers offer full hardware access and get you on the OpenGLES3.0 learning curve. I'll maintain a list of boards I have on the support site that can handle OpenGLES3.0+ and provide some info on how to use the extra features.

Appendix VI

▮ The Libs We Used

Despite not wanting to, we did use a few different libraries, some of which needed to be installed on our systems to work for us. Should you find you need to format your storage system and reinstall your OS, these libs will be lost and need to be reinstalled. So here's a short run down, in one place, of the libs you need to reinstall if you do have a fresh OS.

Always do an update/upgrade whenever you make a fresh install

```
sudo apt-get update && sudo apt-get upgrade
```

Then the following libraries can be installed:

```
sudo apt-get install libopenal-dev
sudo apt-get install pulseaudio
sudo apt-get install libalut-dev
sudo apt-get install libbullet-dev
sudo apt-get install libogg-dev
```

If you cannot find graphic drivers on your system, these may allow you to create the projects, but at possible suboptimal frame rates, and only if your system has access to the GPU.

```
sudo apt-get install libgles2-mesa-dev
```

If you have a multicore CPU you might want to try using OpenMP to handle some of your multicore work. It should already have OpenMP's libs installed but you can check by trying to install anyway. All single-core system will still work and compile but you won't see any benefit and indeed you might see a slow down, as threads are being constantly set up and the CPU is time slicing rather than processing on idle cores.

```
sudo apt-get install libgomp1
```

▮ On the PC End

We also downloaded a couple of header style libraries, which we then compiled to be part of the finished executable, so they will not be affected by a new storage setup, but in case you change PCs and forget what you used you can reinstall these.

SOIL, or more correctly the STB file loading was downloaded from https://www.github.com/nothings/stb.

GLM The Maths Lib was downloaded from (but check for latest versions) http://www.glm.g-truc.net/0.9.8/index.html.

Tiny Object Loader for loading our basic OBJ files from https://www.github.com/syoyo/tinyobjloader.

Appendix VII

▮ Writing My Own Games?

Oh boy this is a biggie… I get asked so often by people, how do I write my own games, I've got a great idea? Well technically the answers are in here; everything you need to know is here and can be built on, except for that one crucial thing.

A vision!

There's no real way to get past this, but most programmers don't have that vision, we see the project as a series of logical and technical problems, which must be overcome to do….what?

Without vision, the clear and full picture of what the game is going to be, starting out on a technical path of superfast fancy wizardry, is going to be wasted and frustrating.

I've tried to simulate vision by using game genres that we should all be familiar with, so you can do even a basic bit of research to understand what the games are hoping to turn out like, but if I were to suggest to you we do a game about Doggies Piloting Atomic Power Balloons, In Space! You might quite rightly scratch your head in confusion.

This is why we have designers, those happy smiling people who want you to deliver the moon on a stick, and convince you that making it 30% more fun is somehow possible.

The days when we could take a cool programming effect and turn it into a game are largely gone, despite the occasional exception (I'm looking at you Flappy Bird)! Games need to have a clear outline of what they plan to be.

So if you have an idea for a game, the first thing you should be doing is writing it down on paper and planning it out. Identify the goals and aims of the game. What will the player be asked to achieve, how will that be done?

What are the aims of the AI? What obstacles will be put in the way? What will be the progression of the game? There are a great many design questions you need to answer before you touch a coding keyboard in anger. Be fully aware of what the tasks are that you need to tackle, the scale of them, and most important, the feasibility of them. Some things are just not possible on the hardware you choose, are there alternative means to do them?

Once you have planned your game, consider its core make up. I've put forward the notion that all games are basically variations on Space Invaders, but, of course, some games bend that notion to near-breaking point. At the core of the game, technically it will still have a main loop, taking input, processing, and rendering, so you can take some comfort in that. The issue is how do you create a play world, what will be in it, and how will they all interact.

Focus on those points! You should be clear about what it will look like, how the objects move or are moved, what influences the user will have in the game, and what random factors will it have.

Once you have that vision, get a designer to check it out for you...they'll tear it apart for sure, but that's good. You need to be sure that what you want is going to be fun, playable, and possible.

Appendix VIII

Visual Studio 2017

It had to happen; this book took so long to write that Microsoft came out with a new and improved version of Visual Studio, version 2017. Aside from all the usual improvements you might expect in optimization and changes of format that I might take a look at in 2 or 3 years. It has included a new development for Linux option.

This was available as an extension for VS2015 but I felt it was a little clunky then, so didn't spend much time on it. This new version is much less clunky and indeed provides a way of directly targeting Linux systems from your PC. It has a few issues, though.

It does not redirect console output to the development machine, making printf and cout less useful to us. And it only does an *on target* build, at least through that configuration manager, but cross compiling can be worked out with a bit of head scratching as can redirecting the output.

But it does indeed send files to the target, which then compiles them and sets up a debugger so that you can work through your code. So as a target-base compiler system it works just fine and with a bit of work you can get pretty much all the same features that VisualGDB provides, for free.

If you find that you are following all the VisualGDB concepts ok, you should be able to adapt them very simply to the new VS2017 properties it provides.

But for now I'm still going to continue with VS2015 and VisualGDB, its less effort to get things working. But maybe if there's a next edition of this book I might swap over.

I will put an update on the support site when I get round to using VS2017, sometime around the spring of 2023.

Index

<<, 12
<>, 179
2.5D style projection, 293
2D
   collision system, 102
   games, 51–52
   indexing system, 199
   shooting games, 456
3D
   camera, 353
   collision, 368
   particles, 374–376
   space, 389
3Dbase, 287
3Dfont, 366
3DMazehunt game, 437, 440–441
3D Object loader, 461

A

Abstraction, 176
AddorReturn function, 223, 248
AI, 224, 429, 444–445
Alpha effects, 255
Alpha value, 126

Alut, 179–180
   working, 184–190
Ambient light, 338
American Standard Code for Information
   Interchange (ASCII), 111–112
Amphibian Class ships, 358, 410
Android phones, xvii–xviii, xxii
Angular force, 410
Antialiasing filter, 452
A* Pathfinding, 445
APIs. *See* Application Programming
   Interface (APIs)
Apple devices, xvii–xviii
Application Programming Interface (APIs),
   xxii, 32–33, 461
applyCentralxxx methods, 411
Armbian, 14
ARM chips, 468
Arrays, 93
ASCII (American Standard Code for
   Information Interchange), 111–112
Aspect Ratio, 294
Asset, 54
   management, 459–460

Asteroid creation using Object Class, 360–361
Asus Tinker Board, 485–486
Attenuation, 339
Attribute(s), 341
  pointers, 311–312
  shader, 310
Axis-Aligned Bounding Box, 373

B

Back buffer. *See* Framebuffer
Backgrounds. *See* Tiles and backgrounds
Back motion, 296
Base Class, 88
bcm_host library, 41
BigShip, 358
Bilinear interpolation, 395
Binary files, 235
Biswas, Abhishek, 381
Bits, 483–484
BobsDay, 213–214
Bool flag, 229
Bounding Volume Hierarchy (BVH)
        Triangle, 424
Box check, collision detection, 101–102
Brain map, 439
Brian Beuken
    at NHTV in Breda, xxx
    at Ocean Software in Manchester, xxix
    Virtucraft, xxix
Broadcom libs, 51
Broad phase cull, 399
Broad-phase test forms, 373
btDebugDraw, 407
btRay cast systems, 438
btRaycastVehicle system, 421
Buffer(s), 308–309, 313–314
    depth, 318, 449
    double, 68, 75, 366
    OpenAL, 183
    pixel, 68, 119
    render, 313
    texture, 312
    types, 449
    vertex, 309–311
Buffer-based game design, 434
Build Dependency in Visual Studio, 197
Bullet, 402
    apply forces, 411
    -based objects, 444
    physics, 402
Bullet Class, 89, 248–249

Bus, 308
BVH (Bounding Volume Hierarchy)
        Triangle, 424
Bytes, 483–484

C

Camera, 350–353
    in 3D space, 278–280
    view matrix, 291–292
Camera Class, 358
Carrier Ship, 358
Cars in racing game, 417–418
Casting technique, 99, 166, 207, 433
Chase camera, 353
Cheap target system, uses, xvi
Chunk-based loading, 456
cin (), 12
Circle checks, 2D collision system, 102–103
CMake software, 19
Cockpits, 365
Code-based timer, 163
Coding, 475
Collision
    cull, 369
    detection, 101
    division of, 252–254
    map, 397
    system, 208, 372–373
CollisionEvent, 413
CollisionProcess Class, 415
Collision-response system, 437
ColourFade particle, 262–270
Comma separated values (CSV) text files,
        235, 239
Commutative property, 290
Compression systems, 456
Concatenation, 287
CondOBJLight.vsh/fsh, 376
Console window, 9
cout (), 10
C++ program, 10
    namespace, 11
CPU, 473
    -based 2D system, 247
    manipulated graphics, 70
CreateTexture2D routine, 64
Cross-platform compilation, 464–465
Cross product, 336
C++'s MAP structures, 459
CSV (comma separated values) text files,
        235, 239

Cube drawing, 300–302
CubeVertice, 300–301
Culling, 369
    test, 399

D

Data storage concept
    cross-platform compilation, 464–465
    expanding to SDK, 461–462
    hardware limitations, 463–464
    scene management, 456–459
    track of assets, 455–456
    wrangling, 459
        asset management, 459–460
        fragmentation, 460–461
DaVinci Vitruvian man pose, 284–285
Debugger, 28
Debug mode, Visual Studio, 8
Debug rendering, 409
Delta time, 164
Depth buffer, 318, 449
Depth textures, 449, 451
Dereferencing symbol (*), 86
Determinant, matrix functions, 295
Dev Kits, xvii
Diffuse lighting, 338
Direct Memory Access (DMA), 308
Direct X from Microsoft, 32
Doggies Piloting Atomic Power Balloons game,
    489–490
Doom's WAD files, 458
Dot product, 335
Double buffer, 68, 75, 366
DrawMap
    function, 241–242
    system, 200
Dynamic allocation, 86
Dynamic arrays, 93

E

EGL, 41
    system, 477
    window, 51, 76
Embedded systems (ES), 32–33
Emissive lights, 338
Emitter Class, 259–261
eMMC memory, 459–460
Encapsulation, 176, 473
End of File (EOF) marker, 235
Enemy Class, 206
Engines in game dev, 463

Enum command, 133–134, 170
Ermm rotation, 281
ES (embedded systems), 32–33
eth0, 15
Euler maths, 405

F

Faces, OBJ, 330
FastShip, 358
Field of View (FoV), 293
FileHandler, 86
File synchronization, 57
FilterDemo, 395
First Person Shooter (FPS), 122
Fixed camera, 350, 353
Fixed pipeline, 318, 340
Flow field, 429
Flying Cubes project, 356
Folder management, 58
Font system, 199
Force-based movement, 437
Forward motion, 296
FoV (Field of View), 293
FPS camera, 353, 438, 442
Fragmentation, 460–461
Fragment Shader, 342–344
Framebuffer, 68–74, 312–313, 448, 450
Frame-lock system, 378
Frame rate, 271–272
free() function, 67–68
Frustum, 280, 292–293, 400
    culling, 434–435
Frustum Class, 400
Full-fat OpenGL, 449

G

Game
    cycle, 379
    dev, 463, 474
    initialization, 391
    init systems, 458
    mechanics
        3D collision, 368
        3Dfont, 366
        cockpits, 365
        collision systems, 372–373
        culling concepts, 369
        Grids Tree, 369–370
        GUI, 365–366
        HUD, 365
        primitive collision types, 368–369

Game (*Continued*)
    Quad Tree, 369–370
    screen/render, 366
    Sphere-to-Sphere, 373–374
  program features, 50
  programming, 475
Game Class, 201–202, 250
GameInit Function, 250–251
GameObject Image pointer, 203
GameObject methods, 202, 209
GameObjects YSpeed value, 216
Game states, 255
Game::Update function, 231
GDB program, 28–29
Geometry Shaders, 485
GeosphereXX.obj, 360
Get functions, 73
GetScreenPos method, 243
Gimbal lock, 405
Git, 481–482
glDeleteTextures, 65
gl_FragColour, 61
GL Mathematics (GLM), 288, 290, 335
GLM The Maths Lib, 488
Global spawner, 457–458
glUseProgram(), 452
GLut, 184
GNU, OS, 19, 29
God mode, camera, 353
GPU. *See* Graphics Processing Unit (GPU)
Graphics, 32–33, 447–448
  APIs, 32
  process recap, 452–453
  program, 53
    frame buffer and switch system, 74–76
    loading, 53–57
    texture, creation/display, 59
  projects, 35–41
  shaders, 35
  shadow mapping, 448–452
Graphics Class Init routines, 344
Graphics Processing Unit (GPU), xxii, 32, 34
  chip, 32
  data, 307–308
  hardware, 473
  pixels memory, 3D, 325
  stock shape objects, 325–326
Graphic User Interface (GUI), 14–15, 365–366
Gravity, 397
Green, James, 383

Grids Tree, 369–370
GroundPlane Class, 391
GroundPlaneDemo, 390
GUI (Graphic User Interface), 14–15, 365–366

H

Hard-coded numbers, 51
Head-Up Display (HUD), 365
Heightmap, 391
HelloCubes in 3D, 304–306
  attribute pointers, 311–312
  buffer, 308–309
    frame, 312–313
    render, 313
    texture, 312
    vertex, 309–311
  GPU data, 307–308
Hello Triangle in 3D, 296–300
Heterogeneous programming, 486
Homing Class, 226–228
Homing system, 208–211
HotDecay, 261–265
HUD (Head-Up Display), 365
Hyperthreading CPU, 468

I

IDE (Integrated Development Environment), xviii, 31
Identity matrix, 283
Image
  array, 224
  retention, 333
Image Loader, 54
Impulse, 411
Indoor games, 433–434
  3D game, 434
  occlusion, 434–435
inet addr, 16
Inheritance, 88, 176
  Bullet Class, 89
  code of human, 88–89
Init_ogl routine, 51
Integrated Development Environment (IDE), xviii, 31
InvaderStart, 85
IP address, 16

J

Java, xviii
Job manager, 471–472

K

Kamikazi Invader, 123–128
  alien
    behavior, 132–135
    types, 164–165
  arcing state alien, 133, 137–141
  baddies in, 130–131
  Bomb Class, 154–161
  bomb state alien, 133, 144
  bullet to hit Fred and aliens, 153–156
  dead and dying state in, 158–159
  delta time, 164
  diving state alien, 133, 142–144
  enemies in, 176
  FlyBack stage alien, 145–146
  flying state alien, 136–137
  FlyOff stage alien, 145
  from Fred, 152–155
  Fred reaction, 169–173
  going offscreen alien, 133
  hitting Fred, 161
  moving state alien, 133–136
  pixel colour in, 126–127
  postmortem, 173–175
  Ship Class in, 128–129
  SimpleBob Class, 125
  sloppy code, 192–193
  sound, 182–183
    PlayMusic method, 188–190
    streaming, 191–192
  StarField Class, 124
  timer used in, 162–164
  UXB bomb in, 161–162
  vectors in, 146–150
Khronos group, 32, 35

L

Ladders, 229–234
  attribute, 234
  Bob's movement, impact on,
    234–235
  climb animations, 229–230
  CSV text files, 235, 239
  gravity, 231
  jump animation, 232
  maps, 235–239
Launcher Class, 250
Law of acceleration, 401
Law of inertia, 401

Lerping, 385
Level-based game, 438
Level of Detail (LOD),
    320, 391
Libs, 487–488
Light-positioned camera, 448
Lights
  camera action, 332–353
  sources, 339
  types, 338
Linear interpolation, 385
Linear motion, 410
Line draw system, 408
Linux, xxii, xxv
  project creation in, 37–41
  systems, 471, 479
Linux Project Wizard option,
    17–18
LoadMD2, 383
LOD (Level of Detail), 320, 391
LookAt function, 292

M

Magic numbers, 51
Maker boards, xxiv
malloc(), 67–68, 74–75
Manifoldpairs, 413
Manifolds, 412
Map(s), 235–239
  array, 200–201
  brain, 439
  collision, 397
  ladders, 235–239
MapManager Class, 236–237
Material file, 330
Maths, 280–288
Matrix, 277, 282
  concatenation, 287
  difficulty in, 276
  functions, 295–296
  identity, 283
  multiple sizes, 283
  translation, 283
  types, 3D games, 291
    model, 291
    projection, 292–294
    relationship of, 294–295
    view, 291–292
MD2Demo, 383–384
MD2Shadow demo, 452

MD2 system, 381
  animating system, heart, 385
  binary chunk, 382
  controlling animation of, 385–389
  lerping, 385
  loader, 383
  Quake model, 383
  shaders, 385
MD3/4 system, 382
MD5 system, 381–382
MDL format, 381
MD(x) systems, 381–385
Members in C++, 72
Memory, chunks of, 460
memset(), 75
Mesa 3D Graphics library, 34
Mesh, 322, 397
Minification, 394
Mipmapping, 320, 393–394
Modders, 381
Model
  animation, 379
  matrix, 291, 452
ModelManager Class, 394
Model View Projection (MVP) matrix, 294
Modern CPU, 468
MousePointer, 256
MSBuild tool, 19
Multicore programming, 467
Multitasking, 468
Mutex variable, 469
MVP (Model View Projection) matrix, 294
MyLib, 214

N

Native Development Kit (NDK), xviii
Near and far clipping planes, 293
Nearest-Neighbor interpolation, 395
Newton's laws of motion, 401
Nibbles, 483–484
Node, 440
Non-Disclosure Agreements (NDAs), xvii
Non-raspberry machines, 477
Nonthread safe process, 472

O

OBJAnimation, 381
Object Attribute Buffers (OAB), 309
ObjectModel Class, 415
Object-Oriented Programming (OOP), xx, 98,
  175–176

Objects Class, 88–89, 175
OBJ file format
  loading models, 327
  location and installation, 327–329
Occlusion culling, 435
OctTrees, 371–372
Onboard memory, 455
On-chip memory, 464
OOP (Object-Oriented Programming), xx, 98,
  175–176
OpenAL, 177
  buffers, 183
  installation, 177–179
  Soft, 177
  vs. OpenGL, 179
  working, 183–184
OpenGL, 32
  ES, 32–33
  eye, 385
  shader language, 344
  vs. OpenAL, 179
OpenGL1.1 coding template, 70
OpenGL3.0, 485
OpenGLES1.1, shaders, 340
OpenGLES2.0, 33–35, 42, 275, 309, 448–449,
  473, 485
OpenGLES 2.0 Programming Guide (book),
  35, 41
OpenGLES3.0, 486
OpenGLES3.0+, 485–486
OpenGLESProjects, 19
OpenMax, 177
OpenMP's libs, 488
Operating system (OS), 14
  GNU, 19
  for keys scanning, 78–85
Orthogonal projection matrix, 366
Orthogonal view, camera, 280
Overloading, 149

P

Painters algorithm, 434
Parallel projection, 293
Parsing, 115, 235
Particle system, 255–261
  ColourFade particle, 262–270
  heavy use of, 271
Partition trees, 435
Pathfinding methods, 439–440
Path-tracing system, 453
Patrol Class, 224–226

PCM (Pulse Code Modulation) control, 180
PCX format, 383
Perforce, 481–482
Per fragment/per pixel lighting, 348–349
Perspective projection, 293
    view, 280
PhotoFrame, 65
Physics programming, 401
Pixel buffer, 68, 119
Pixel-movement system, 211–214
Pointer, 67, 86
    attribute, 311–312
Point lighting, 339
Point-to-point, 221–224
Polymorphism, 176
Posix threads, 471
Postmortem, Kamikazi Invaders,
        173–175
Primitive collision types, 368–369
Projection matrix, 292–294
Pthreads, 471
Pulse Code Modulation (PCM) control, 180
Pure Shader systems, 385
Pyramid view, 292

Q

Quad system, cores in, 473
Quad Tree, 369–370, 398, 431
Quake games, 434
    maze exploring, 436–438
        applying torque/direction impulse, 437
        brain map, 439
        Bullets inbuilt function, 442
        direction of signpost, 439–440
        drawing, 441–442
        Enemy Classes, 438
        moving baddies, 438–441
        pathfinding, 439
        PatrolBaddie, 438
        StaticBaddie, 438
Qualifiers, 344
Quaternions, 303–304
Quats functions, 405

R

Racing game, 416
Radians, 139
RAM double buffer, 68
Random number, 162
Range-based specific spawner, 458
Rasbian OS, xxiii, 477

Raspberry Pi, 13–14, 28, 464
    GDB replacement in, 28
    installation, 2
    model, xix–xx, xxii–xxiii
        A+/B+/Zeroes, xxii
    via hardware cable, 17
    via wifi, 17
Raspberry Pi 2/3, 416
Raspberry Pi 2 Model B, xxii
Raspberry Pi 3 model, xix
Raspberry Pi 3 Model B, xxii, 455
Ray, 367, 397
    casting technique, 433, 440, 442
    to triangle, 397
Reference point, 205
Remote compiling, 57
Render buffer, 313
Render culling, 398–399
Render surface, 41
Render systems, 434–435
Resource, 54
Respawn timer, 172
Reticule, 365
Retina, 333
Revision control backup system,
        481–482
Rig, 380
RISC-based design concept, 468
Routing, 28

S

SBCs. *See* Single board computers (SBCs)
Scalar manipulation, matrix
        functions, 295
Scalar product, 335
Scene management, 456–459
Screen-coordinate system, 199–200
Screen displays, 32
Screen resolution
    in BobsDay header, 240–241
    Bullet Class, 248–249
    collision, division of, 252–254
    draw map function, 241–242
    Emitter Class, 259–261
    flexibility, 255
    frame rate, 271–272
    Game states, 254–255
    loading images, 249–251
    particle system, 255–261
    processing, 251–252
    scrolling methods, 243–248

SD card, xxiii
    updating *vs.* new, 479–480
SDK, 461–462
    game dev, 463
    game project in, 462
    helper functions in, 461
Secure Shell connections (SSH), xxv
Set functions, 73
Shader(s), 35, 340–344, 452
    code, 61
    compilers, GLSL 1.0, 343–344
    language, 344–346
    tracking, 344
Shadow mapping, 448–452
Shadows, 339–340
Shared Object (SO) library, 197
Sheer-processing power, 468
Signpost/nodes, direction of, 439–440
Simple OpenGL Image Library (SOIL), 54, 488
Simply SBCProjects, 19
Single board computers (SBCs), xvi, xxii, 14
    systems, 456
Single-line index, 199
Single-screen platforms
    BobsDay, 213–214
    coordinates, 217
    Enemy Class, 221
    gravity value, 215–216
    Homing Class, 226–228
    jumping process, 216–220
    ladders. *See* Ladders
    Patrol Class, 224–226
    point-to-point, 221–224
    test condition, 217–218
Sizeof(x) function, 484
Skeletal animation-based systems, 381
Skybox, 361–363
    indoor games, 434, 438
Sky Dome, 362
SoC (System on Chip) machine, xix
SOIL (Simple OpenGL Image Library), 54, 488
SO (Shared Object) library, 197
Source control backup system, 481–482
SpaceCadet, 356
Space games, 355–356
    Asteroid Class, 360–361
    chase camera, 359–360
Space Invaders, 77
    Aliens Class, 99
        constructor in, 121
    aliens creation using array, 93–95

animation in, 98–100
bullets hitting on enemies, 101–102
bullet test with shelters, 104–110
Enemy Class creation, 91–92
features, 87
font drawing system, 113–118
inheritance, 88–91
InvadersFin, 87
InvaderStart, 85, 87
loading graphics in, 119–122
moving direction, 96–98
MyBullet, 89
Shooter Class creation, 89–90
    creating bullets in, 101
text display in ASCII values, 111–112
TileFont Class, 114, 116
update function, 90–91, 95
Spawning system, 457
    objects, 457
    types, 457–458
Specular lighting, 338
Sphere test, 373, 400
Sphere-to-Sphere method, 373–374
Spot lights, 339
Sprites, 85
    2D games using, 101
    display, 85–86
SSH (Secure Shell connections), xxv
Standard Template Library (STL), 10
    function, 235–236, 469
stbi_load function, 66
std::, 11
Stepping process, 407
Stewart, Jamie, 381
STL. *See* Standard Template Library (STL)
Storage qualifiers, GLSL 1.0, 343
Streaming of sound, 191–192
String, 12
Surface Class, 70
SVN, 481–482
Switching frames, 384
Sysprogs, 28
System on Chip (SoC) machine, xix

T

Target-base compiler system, 491
Tessellation shaders, 485
Texels, 394
Texture(s), 320–321, 390
    buffer, 312
    coords, OBJ, 330

cube, 315–318
    faces, mapping, 319–320
    fixed pipeline, 318, 340
    shaders, 321
    size selection, 320
Third dimension (3D) games, 275–280
    HelloCubes, 304–314
    Hello Triangle, 296–303
    matrix, 291
        model, 291
        projection, 292–294
        relationship of, 294–295
        view, 291–292
    quaternions, 303–304
    self involvement and, 275
    Z concepts, 276
Thread(s), 256, 471
    job manager in, 471–472
    safe, 472
Threading, 468–471
Throttle effect, 473
Tidier file systems, 214
Tiled, 212
TileFont, 199
TileManager Class, 422
Tiles and backgrounds, 198–199
    casting, 207
    collision system, 208
    constructor and destructor, 202–203
    direction value, 206
    font system, 199
    Game Class, passing, 201–202
    homing system, 208–211
    map array, 200–201
    new update system, 204
    pixel-movement system, 211–214
    reference point, 205
    screen-coordinate system, 199–200
    speed value, 204–205
    TilesExample, 200–201
    wrapping, 211
Time-slicing concept, 468
TinyObjLoader, 329–332, 356, 424, 430
_tmain, 8
TrackRacer2, 421
Translation, 281
    matrix, 283
Transposition, matrix functions, 295
Triangle
    3D game, 322–324
    code, 44–49

Trilinear filtering, 395
TurboSquid, 417
Two-dimensional arrays, 131

U

uniform value, 343
Unit vector, 147
UV coordinate, 324

V

Vector(s), 93, 335
    erase function, 156
    maths, 175
    product, 336
Vector2D Class, 147–148
Velocity, 410
Vertex, 277
    buffer, 309–311
    OBJ, 330
    Shader, 296–297, 341–342
View matrix, 291–292
Viewpoint concept, 278
Virtual function, 91
Virtual Reality (VR), 294
Visual C++, 5
VisualGDB, xxiv–xxv, 16, 25, 28, 57,
        491–492
    console, 28
    installation, 2, 17
    intellisense system, 180
Visual Studio, xviii, xxiv, 8
    Build Dependency, 197
    console window, 9
    debug mode, 8
    executing stages, 8
    Hello World, 10–12
    installation, 2
    overview, 2–10
    templates group, 5
    Win32 Console Application, 6
Visual Studio 2017, 491–492

W

Wifi, 17
    dongle, xxiii
Win32 Console Application, 6
Wired network connection, xxiii, xxiv
Wolfenstein 3D game, 433

X

x86 chips, 468